ENGINEERING MECHANICS

ENGINEERING MECHANICS

Prof. (Dr.) K.S. Yadav
Professionally U.K. Trained Educationist and Writer
Director,
ABSS Institute of Technology
Meerut

Formerly: Professor and H.O.D., Mech. Engg.
Northern India Engineering College, New Delhi

VAYU EDUCATION OF INDIA
2/25, Ansari Road, Daryagagn, New Delhi-110002

ENGINEERING MECHANICS

ISBN : 978-81-906518-2-0

First edition: 2008

Reprint: 2013

Published by :
VAYU EDUCATION OF INDIA
2/25, Ansari Road, Darya Ganj, New Delhi-110 002
Ph.: 011-41564445, 65235268 Fax: 91-11-41564440
E-mail: vei@veiindia.com • Website: www.veiindia.com

Price : 240.00

Design & Layout by :
Limited Colors, Delhi-110092

Preface

Engineering Mechanics is a course taught in the first year of B.Tech.. curriculum and in this subject the students need to develop capability to view an actual problem into an engineering problem and find the solutions using laws of mechanics. An engineering mechanics problem involving forces, may be solved easily, if the free body diagram is drawn correctly. Hence emphasis has been given for drawing neat and clean free body diagrams.

With the emphasis on formulating practical problem and applying equations of mechanics, the attempts have been made to prepare the students to solve the problems of Engineering Mechanics. The object of this book is to present the subject matter in a most concise, compact, to the point and lucid manner. To make it more useful, the book has been written in an easy style. Care has been taken to arrange the subject-matter from simple to complex and known to unknown. A large number of solved examples have been given. At the end of each chapter, few exercises have been added for solving them independently by the learners.

The subject-matter has been developed from the point of view of Engineering students. Having had an overall view of the subject-matter together with the foundational concepts, in Chapter 1, the students should start thinking in terms of idealisations of bodies and applications of the laws to set up the equations governing their behaviour under different conditions. It is hoped that the students and the teachers will enjoy reading the book. Comments for further improvement of this book will be gratefully acknowledged.

DELHI
31.03.2008

PROF. (DR.) K.S. YADAV

Contents

SYLLABUS (LESSON PLAN)

G.G.S.I.P. University, Delhi

ENGINEERING MECHANICS

(Semester-I/II)

Class	:	1st Year
Subject Code	:	ETEM - 110
Total Teaching Weeks in Semester	:	15 weeks
Total Lecture Classes Available	:	45
Total Tutorial Classes Available	:	15

Topics to be Covered	**Total No. of Lecture / Tutorial**
1. Force System:	
Treatment of Coplanar force system, Types of supports, loads, reactions at support,	1 L
Free body diagram, Euqilibrium equations and applications,	1 L
Moment, Varignon's principle,	1 L
Equilibrium equations, System of concurrent, parallel, general forces	2L
2. Friction	
Static and Kinetic friction, laws of dry friction, coefficient of friction, angle of repose, cone of friction, friction lock (self locking).	2 L
Friction of flat, pivot, and collared thrust bearings.	1 L
Friction in Journal bearing, friction in screws, Belt Drives, Derivation of $T_1/T_2 = e^{\mu\theta}$ for belt and rope drive and its application	3 L
3. Structure	
Plane Truss, Perfect Truss and Imperfect Truss, Assumptions in the truss analysis, Analysis of perfect plane truss by Method of Joints, Method of Section and Graphical Method	3 L
4. Distributed Forces	
Determination of Centre of Gravity, Centre of Mass and Centroid by Direct integration and by the method of composite bodies	2 L
1st Terminal Examination	
5. Mass moment of Inertia and area moment of inertia by direct integration and composite bodies method, radius of gyration.	2 L

Parallel axis theorm, Pappus theorems, Polar moment of inertia 2 L

6. Kinematics of Particles

Rectilinear motion, uniform and variable acceleration 1 L

Problems in displacement, velocity and acceleration, Rectangular components, components of acceleration - normal and tangential 3 L

7. Kinetics of particles

Equation of Motion in rectangular components 1 L

Equation of motion – Tangential and normal components 1 L

Work energy equation, conservation of energy 1 L

Impulse and momentum, conservation of momentum 1 L

Impact of bodies, co-efficient of restitution, loss of energy during impact 1 L

8. Kinematics of Rigid Bodies

Concept of rigid body, types of rigid body motion, rectilinear and rotation, absolute motion 1 L

Relative velocity, relative acceleration (Coriolli's Component Excluded) 1 L

Instantaneous center, velocity and acceleration, polygons for four bar mechanism and single slider mechanism 2 L

2nd Terminal Examination

9. Kinetics of Rigid Bodies

Equation of motion, translatory motion and fixed axis rotation 1 L

Application of work and energy principles to rigid bodies, conservation of energy 2 L

10. Beams

Shear force and bending moment diagrams 3L

End Term Examination

SYLLABUS

[Effective from the Session : 2008-09]

U.P. TECHNICAL UNIVERSITY LUCKNOW
B.TECH. COURSES

[Common to all Branches of B.Tech. 1st Year except B.Tech. Agricultural Engg.]

EME-102 / 202 : ENGINEERING MECHANICS

UNIT I

Two Dimensional Force Systems: Basic concepts, Laws of motion, Principle of Transmissibility of forces, Transfer of a force to parallel position , Resultant of a force system, Simplest Resultant of Two dimensional concurrent and Non-concurrent Force systems, Distributed force system, Free body diagrams, Equilibrium and Equations of Equilibrium, Applications. 5

Friction: Introduction, Laws of Coulomb Friction, Equilibrium of Bodies involving Dry-friction, Belt friction, Application. 3

UNIT II

Beam: Introduction, Shear force and Bending Moment, Differential Equations for Equilibrium, Shear
force and Bending Moment Diagrams for Statically Determinate Beams. 5

Trusses: Introduction, Simple Truss and Solution of Simple truss, Method of Joints and Method of Sections. 3

UNIT III

Centroid and Moment of Inertia: Centroid of plane, curve, area, volume and composite bodies, Moment of inertia of plane area, Parallel Axes Theorem, Perpendicular axes theorems, Principal Moment of Inertia, Mass Moment of Inertia of Circular Ring, Disc, Cylinder, Sphere and Cone about their Axis of Symmetry. 6

UNIT IV

Kinematics of Rigid Body: Introduction, Plane Motion of Rigid Body, Velocity and Acceleration under Translation and Rotational Motion, Relative Velocity. 4

Kinetics of Rigid Body: Introduction, Force, Mass and Acceleration, Work and Energy, Impulse and Momentum, D'Alembert's Principles and Dynamic Equilibrium. 4

UNIT V

Simple Stress and Strain: Introduction, Normal and Shear stresses, Stress- Strain Diagrams for ductile and brittle material, Elastic Constants, One Dimensional Loading of members of varying cross-sections, Strain energy. 3

Pure Bending of Beams: Introduction, Simple Bending Theory, Stress in beams of different cross sections. 3

Torsion: Introduction, Torsion of shafts of circular section, torque and twist, shear stress due to torque. 3

CHAPTER 1

Force System

INTRODUCTION

ENGINEERING MECHANICS: It is that branch of Applied Science, which deals with the laws and principles of Mechanics alongwith their applications to engineering problems. The branch of science, which co-ordinates the research work for practical utility and services of the mankind, is known as APPLIED SCIENCE. The knowledge of Engineering mechanics is very essential for an engineer in planning, design and construction of various types of structures and machines. The subject of Engineering Mechanics may be sub-divided into the following two main groups.

STATICS: It is that branch of Engineering Mechanics, which deals with the forces and their effects, while acting upon the bodies at rest.

DYNAMICS: It is that branch of Engineering Mechanics, which deals with the forces and their effects while acting upon the bodies in motion. The subject of Dynamics may be further such-divided into the following two branches.

KINETICS: It is that branch of Dynamics, which deals with the bodies in motion due to the application of forces.

KINEMATICS: It is that branch of Dynamics which deals with the bodies in motion, without any reference to the forces which are responsible for the motion.

SCALAR QUANTITIES: Scalars are those quantities which have magnitude only, such as length, mass, time, distance, volume, density, temperature, and speed etc.

VECTOR QUANTITIES: Vectors are those quantities which have both magnitude and direction such as force, displacement, velocity and direction such as force, displacement, velocity, acceleration, moment, couple, and momentum etc.

FORCE: It is an agent which changes or tends to change the state of rest or motion of a body.

RESULTANT FORCE: If a number of forces, P, Q, R, ... etc. are acting simultaneously on a particle, it is possible to find out a single force which could replace them i.e. which would produce the same effect as produced by all the given forces. This single force is called Resultant Force, and the given forces, P, Q, R ..... etc. are called COMPONENT FORCES.

COMPOSITION OF FORCES: The process of finding out the resultant force of a number of given forces is called COMPOSITION OF FORCES or compounding of forces. The resultant force, of a given system of forces, may be found out analytically by the following methods:

1. PARALLELOGRAM LAW OF FORCES: It states, "If two forces, acting simultaneously on a particle, be represented in magnitude and direction by the two adjacent sides of a parallelogram;

their resultant may be represented in magnitude and direction by the diagonal of the parallelogram, which passes through their point of intersection". Mathematically, resultant force,

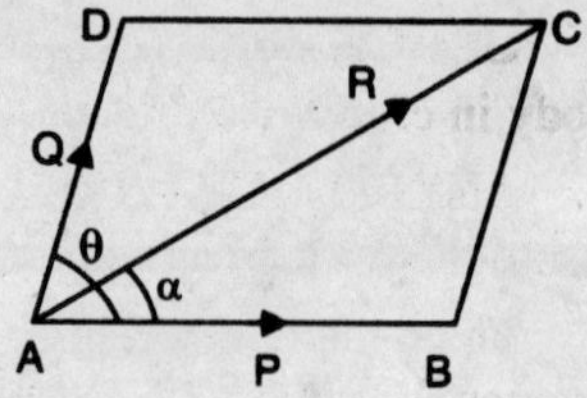

$$R = (P^2 + Q^2 + 2PQ\cos\theta)^{1/2}$$

and $\quad \tan\alpha = Q\sin\theta \,/\, (P + Q\cos\theta)$, where

P and Q = Forces whose resultant is required to be found out.

θ = Angle between the forces P and Q, and

α = Angle which the resultant force makes with one of the forces (say P)

COR.

1. If $\theta = 0$ i.e., when the forces act along the same line,

   then $\quad R = P + Q \qquad (\because \cos\theta° = 1)$

2. If $\theta = 90°$ i.e. when the forces act at right angle,

   then $\quad R = (P + Q)^{1/2} \qquad (\because \cos 90° = 0)$

3. If $\theta = 180°$ i.e. when the forces act along the same but in opposite direction,

   then $\quad R = P - Q$

In this case, the resultant force will act in the direction of the greater force.

2. RESOLUTION OF FORCES: The process of splitting up the given force into a number of components, without changing its effect on the body is called RESOLUTION OF A FORCE. A force is, generally, resolved along two mutually perpendicular directions. Resultant R of the given forces will be given by the equation: $R = \sqrt{(\Sigma V)^2 + (\Sigma H)^2}$ and the resultant force will be inclined at an angle θ, with the horizontal, such that $\tan\theta = \dfrac{\Sigma V}{\Sigma H}$.

TRIANGLE LAW OF FORCES: It states, "If two forces acting simultaneously on a particle, be represented in magnitude and direction by the two sides of a triangle, taken in order; their resultant may be represented in magnitude and direction by the third side of the triangle, taken in opposite order."

POLYGON LAW OF FORCES: It states "If a number of forces acting simultaneously on a particle be represented in magnitude and direction, by the sides of a polygon taken in order, then the resultant of all these forces may be represented in magnitude and direction, by the closing side of the polygon, taken in opposite order".

MOMENT OF A FORCE: It is the turning effect produced by a force, on the body, on which it acts. The moment of force is equal to the product of the force and the perpendicular distance of the point, about which the moment is required, and the line of action of the force. Mathematically, the moment, $M_A = F \times L$

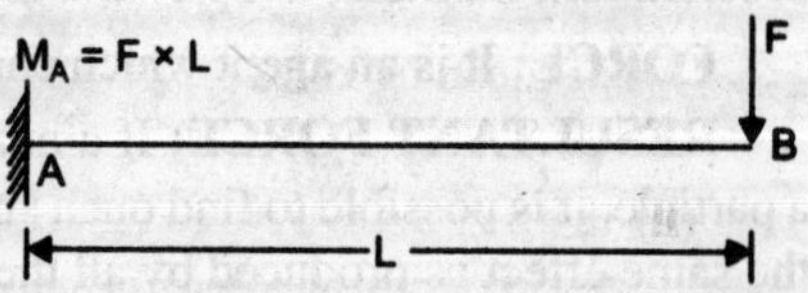

where,

F = Force acting on the body, and

L = Perpendicular distance between the point about which the moment is required and the line of action of the force.

CLOCKWISE MOMENT: It is the moment of a force, whose effect is to turn or rotate the body in clockwise direction.

ANTICLOCKWISE DIRECTION: It is the moment of a force, whose effect is to turn or rotate the body in anticlockwise

The general convention is to take clockwise moment as POSITIVE (+VE) and anticlockwise moment as NEGATIVE (– VE).

COUPLE: A set of two equal and opposite forces, whose lines of action are different, form a couple. A couple is unable to produce any translatory motion (i.e. motion in a straight line). But a couple produces rotation in the body on which it acts. The simple examples, of a couple, are the forces applied to the key of a clock, in winding it up, and the forces applied to the key of a lock, while locking and unlocking it.

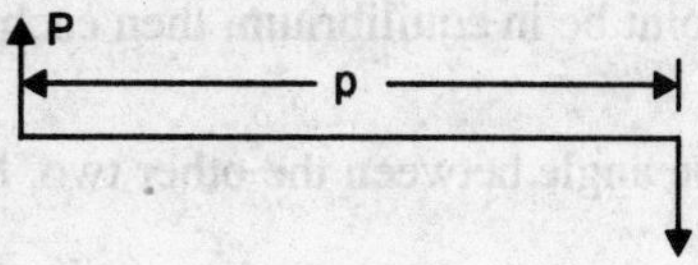

The perpendicular distance (p) between the lines of action of the two equal and opposite parallel forces, is known as arm of the couple.

MOMENT OF A COUPLE: It is the product of force (one of the forces) and the arm of the couple. Mathematically, moment of couple = Pp, where,

$$P = \text{Force},\ p = \text{Arm of couple}$$

CLOCKWISE COUPLE: A couple, whose tendency is to rotate the body, on which it acts, in a clockwise direction, is known as a clockwise couple. Such a couple is also called POSITIVE (+VE) COUPLE.

ANTICLOCKWISE COUPLE: A couple, whose tendency is to rotate the body, on which it acts, in an anticlockwise direction, is known as an ANTICLOCKWISE COUPLE. Such a couple is also called a NEGATIVE COUPLE.

PARALLEL FORCES: The forces, whose lines of action are parallel to each other, are known as parallel forces.

The forces, whose lines of action are parallel to each other, and all of them act in the same direction, are known as LIKE PARALLEL FORCES.

The forces, whose lines of action are parallel to each other and all of them do not act in the same direction, are known as UNLIKE PARALLEL FORCES.

Equilibrium of Forces: A particle will be in equilibrium if the resultant of the forces acting on it is ZERO.

PRINCIPLE OF EQUILIBRIUM

(i) **TWO FORCE SYSTEM:** If two forces are acting on a particle, it will be in equilibrium, if these two forces are equal in magnitude and opposite in direction along the same line of action.

(ii) **SYSTEM CONSISTING OF MORE THAN TWO FORCES:** If more than two forces are acting on a particle, the resultant of the force system may be found out either by using LAW OF POLYGON of FORCES or by RESOLUTION METHOD. In resolution method the resultant is given by $R = \sqrt{\Sigma X^2 + \Sigma Y^2}$. If the resultant is zero, it follows that $\Sigma X = 0$, and $\Sigma Y = 0$. Hence we may state this as follows:

"If a system of forces acting on a particle is to be in Equilibrium the sum of components of each forces in X and Y directions must be respectively ZERO.

(iii) **THREE FORCE SYSTEM:** If a body in equilibrium is acted upon by three forces then the resultant of any two forces must be equal, opposite and collinear (in the same straight line) with the third force. This is a special case and LAMI'S THEOREM can be applied.

EQUILIBRANT FORCE: The equilibriant of a force system is a single force having its magnitude equal to that of the resultant of the force system but opposite in direction, and along the same line of action, so that when it is applied to the body, it brings the system in Equilibrium.

If any body under the action of a number of forces is in equilibrium, any one force of the system is an equilibrant of the force system containing the remaining forces.

LAMI'S THEOREM (EQUILIBRIUM OF THREE FORCES ACTING ON A PARTICLE): If three coplanar forces acting at a point be in equilibrium, then each force is proportional to the sine of the angle between the other two. Mathematically, $\frac{P}{\sin\alpha} = \frac{Q}{\sin\beta} = \frac{R}{\sin\gamma}$ where *P*, *Q* and *R* are three forces and α, β and γ are the angles.

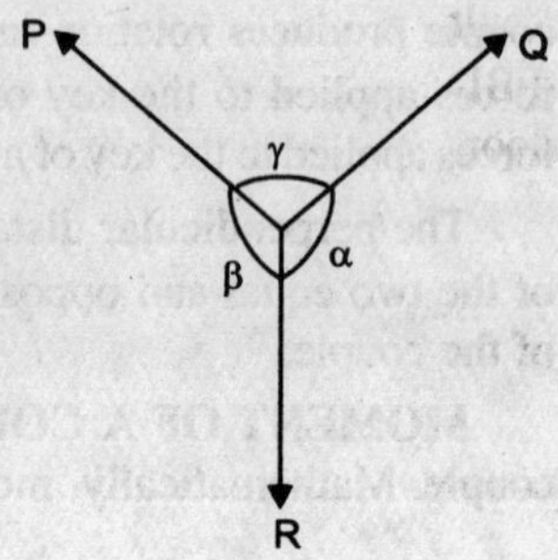

EQUILIBRIUM OF NON-COPLANAR FORCES: This can be easily done by resolving the non-coplanar forces, in one plane and studying the equilibrium of their components in that plane.

CONDITIONS OF EQUILIBRIUM: Consider a body acted upon by a number of coplanar non-concurrent forces. As a result of these forces, the body have one of the following states:

1. The body may move in any one direction.
2. The body may rotate about itself without moving.
3. The body may move in any one direction, and at the same time it may also rotate about itself.
4. The body may be completely at rest.

1. THE BODY MAY MOVE IN ANY ONE DIRECTION: If the body moves in any direction, it means that there is a RESULTANT FORCE acting on it. If the body is to be at rest or in equilibrium, the resultant force causing the movement must be zero. In other words, the horizontal component of all the forces (ΣH) and vertical component of all the forces (ΣV) must be zero. Mathematically, $\Sigma H = 0$ and $\Sigma V = 0$

2. THE BODY MAY ROTATE ABOUT ITSELF: If the body rotates about itself, without moving, it means that there is a single resultant couple acting on it with no resultant force. If the body is to be at rest or in equilibrium, the moment of the couple causing the rotation must be ZERO. In other words, resultant moment of all the forces (ΣM) must be zero. MATHEMATICALLY, $\Sigma M = 0$

3. BODY MOVES IN ANY ONE DIRECTION AND ALSO ROTATES ABOUT ITSELF: If the body moves in any direction and at the same time it rotates about itself, it means that there is a RESULTANT FORCE and also a RESULTANT COUPLE on it. But if the body is at rest or in equilibrium, the resultant force causing the movements and the resultant moment of the couple causing the rotation must be zero. In other words, horizontal component of all the forces (ΣH), vertical component of all the forces (ΣV) and resultant moment of all the forces (ΣM) must be zero. Mathematically, $\Sigma H = 0$, $\Sigma V = 0$, and $\Sigma M = 0$.

4. BODY COMPLETELY AT REST: If the body is completely at rest, it means that there is neither a resultant force nor a couple acting on it and in this case the following conditions are already satisfied.

$$\Sigma H = 0,\ \Sigma V = 0 \text{ and } \Sigma M = 0$$

The above mentioned three equations are known as the conditions of EQUILIBRIUM.

FREE BODY DIAGRAMS: The force analysis of a structure is made in a simplified way by considering the equilibrium of a portion of the structure. For that, the portion is drawn separately showing applied forces, self weight and reactions at the point of contact with other bodies. The resulting diagram is known as FREE BODY DIAGRAM (FBD). In free body diagrams, all the supports (like walls, floors, and hinges etc.) are removed and replaced by the reactions which these supports exert on the body.

(i) Consider a sphere of weight w resting on a friction less plane surface as shown in Fig. 1.1(a). The sphere exerts a downward force W on the surface and this weight acts through the centroid C of the sphere. The surface exerts a reaction R_a on the sphere at the point of contact A as shown in Fig. 1.1(b). Since the sphere is in equilibrium R_a and W are equal.

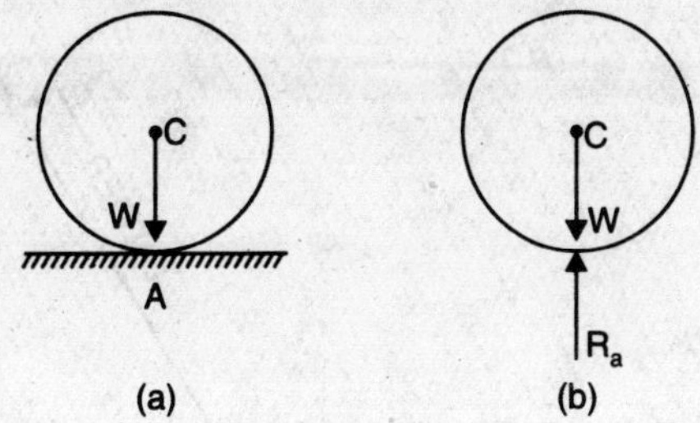

Fig. 1.1

(ii) A circular roller of weight W hangs by a TIE ROD (BC) and rests against a smooth vertical wall as shown in Fig. 1.2(a). The system is influenced by weight W of the roller, wall reaction R_a at the point of contact A and tension T in the tie rod BC. Free body diagram is shown in Fig. 1.2(b).

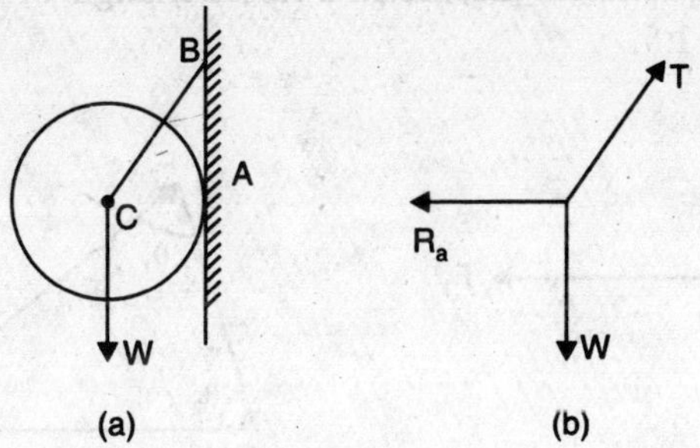

Fig. 1.2

(iii) A spherical ball of weight w rests in a V-shaped groove [Fig.1.3(a)]. R_A and R_B are reactions at the contact surfaces and the FREE BODY DIAGRAM for the ball will be as shown in Fig. 1.3(b).

Fig. 1.3

(iv) A uniform LADDER *AB* of weight *W* rests against a smooth wall (Fig. 1.4a). The forces acting in the system are:

(a) Reaction R_B of the wall.

(b) Weight *W* of the ladder

The Free Body Diagram for the ladder is shown in Fig. 1.4(b).

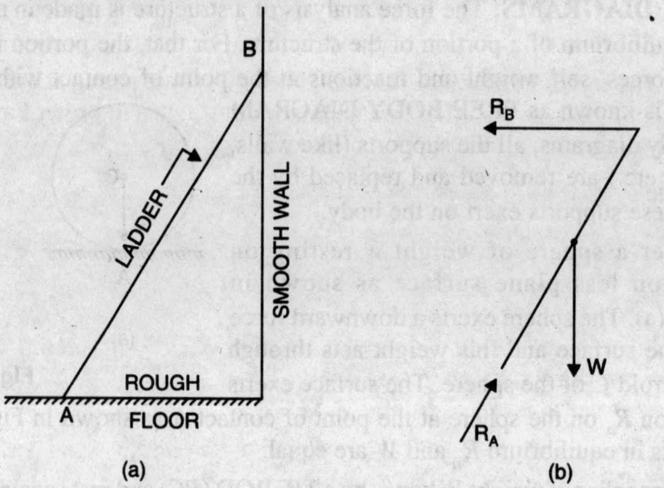

Fig. 1.4

THREE FORCE SYSTEM (EQUILIBRIUM):

Three concurrent forces in equilibrium must form a closed triangle of force when drawn in head to tail fashion as shown in Fig. 1.5.

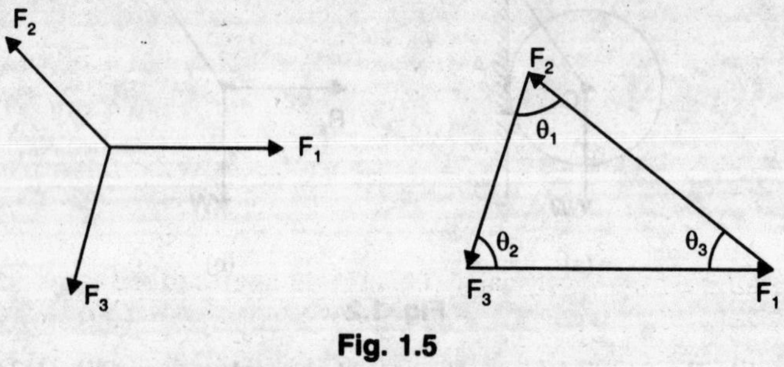

Fig. 1.5

Considering the law of forces, the law of sines $\frac{F_1}{\sin\theta_1} = \frac{F_2}{\sin\theta_2} = \frac{F_3}{\sin\theta_3}$ can be conveniently used to solve the problems.

EXAMPLE 1.1. Two forces of 100 N and 150 N are acting at a point. What is the resultant of these two forces if the angle between them is 45°?

SOLUTION: Given $P = 100$ N, $Q = 150$ N, and $\theta = 45°$

we know that the resultant of two forces

$$R^2 = P^2 + Q^2 + 2PQ\cos\theta$$

$$= (100)^2 + (150)^2 + 2 \times 100 \times 150 \times \cos 45°$$

$$= 10{,}000 + 22500 + 30{,}000 \times 0.707 \text{ N}$$

$$= 53713.2 \text{ N}$$

$$\therefore \quad R = \sqrt{53713.2}$$

$$= 231.76 \text{ N } \textbf{Ans.}$$

EXAMPLE 1.2. The forces 20 N, 30 N, 40 N, 50 N and 60 N are acting at one of the angular points of a regular hexagon, towards the other five angular points, taken in order. Find the magnitude and direction of the resultant force.

SOLUTION: The system of given forces is shown in Fig. 1.6.

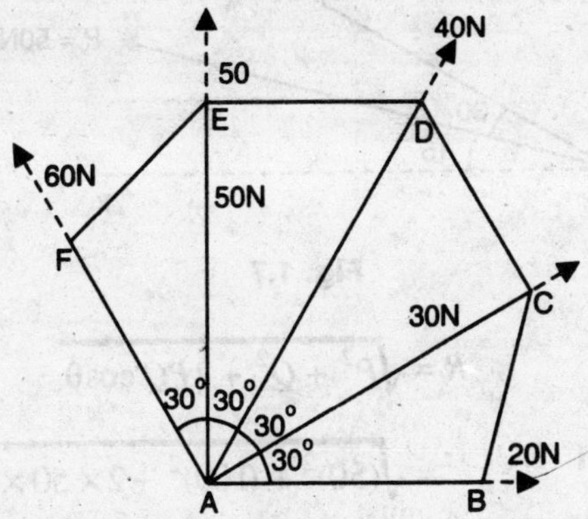

Fig. 1.6

Magnitude of the Resultant Force: Resolving all the forces horizontally (i.e., along AB)

$$\Sigma H = 20 \cos 0° + 30 \cos 30° + 40 \cos 60° + 50 \cos 90° + 60 \cos 120° \text{ N}$$

$$= (20 \times 1) + (30 \times 0.866) + (40 \times 0.50) + (50 \times 00) + 60(-0.50) \text{ N}$$

$$= 35.98 \text{N}$$

$$\therefore \quad \Sigma H = 36 \text{ N} \quad \text{...(i)}$$

And now resolving all the forces vertically (i.e. at right angles to AB),

$$\Sigma V = 20 \sin 0° + 30 \sin 30° + 40 \sin 60° + 50 \sin 90° + 60 \sin 120° \text{ N}$$

$$= (20 \times 0) + (30 \times 0.5) + (40 \times 0.866) + (50 \times 1) + (60 \times 0.866) \text{ N} = 151.6 \text{ N}$$

We know that magnitude of the resultant force,

$$R = \sqrt{(\Sigma H)^2 + (\Sigma V)^2}$$

$$= \sqrt{(36)^2 + (151.6)^2} \text{ N} = 155.81 \text{ N } \textbf{Ans.}$$

Direction of the resultant force:

Let θ = Angle, which the resultant force makes with the horizontal (i.e., AB)

$$\therefore \quad \tan\theta = \frac{\Sigma V}{\Sigma H} = \frac{151.6}{36.0} = 4.211$$

$$\therefore \quad \theta = \tan^{-1}(4.211) = 76°39' \textbf{ Ans.}$$

$$= 76.64° \textbf{ Ans.}$$

Note: Since both the values of ΣH and ΣV are positive, therefore the resultant force lies between 0° and 90°.

EXAMPLE 1.3. Two forces are acting at a point 0 as shown in Fig. 1.7. Determine the resultant in magnitude and direction.

SOLUTION: $P = 50$ N, $Q = 100$ N, $\theta = 30°$

The magnitude of the resultant R is given by the equation:

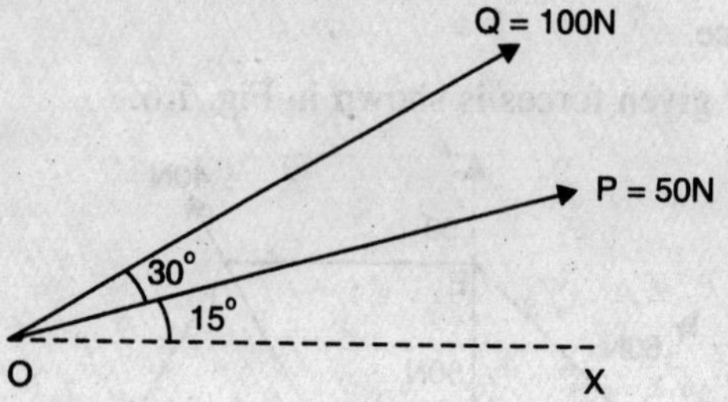

Fig. 1.7

$$R = \sqrt{P^2 + Q^2 + 2PQ\cos\theta}$$

$$= \sqrt{(50)^2 + (100)^2 + 2 \times 50 \times 100 \times \cos 30°}$$

$$= \sqrt{2500 + 10{,}000 + 8600}$$

$$= \sqrt{21160} = 145.46 \text{ N } \textbf{Ans.}$$

The angle mode by the resultant with the direction of force P is given by the equation,

$$\tan\alpha = \frac{Q\sin\theta}{P + Q\cos\theta}$$

$$= \frac{100 \times \sin 30°}{50 + 100\cos 30°}$$

$$= \frac{100 \times 0.50}{50 + 100 \times 0.866} = \frac{50}{50 + 86.60}$$

$$= \frac{50}{136.60} = 0.3660$$

$$\therefore \quad \alpha = \tan^{-1}(0.366) = 20.10°$$

$\therefore$ Angle made by the resultant with X-axis = 15 + 20.10 = 35.10° **Ans.**

EXAMPLE 1.4. The resultant of two concurrent forces is 1500 N and the angle between the forces is 90°. The resultant makes an angle of 36° with one of the forces as shown in Fig. 1.8. Find the magnitude of each force.

SOLUTION: Given, Resultant R = 1500 N

$$\theta = 90° \text{ and } \alpha = 36°$$

Let P and Q are two forces

Using the relation,

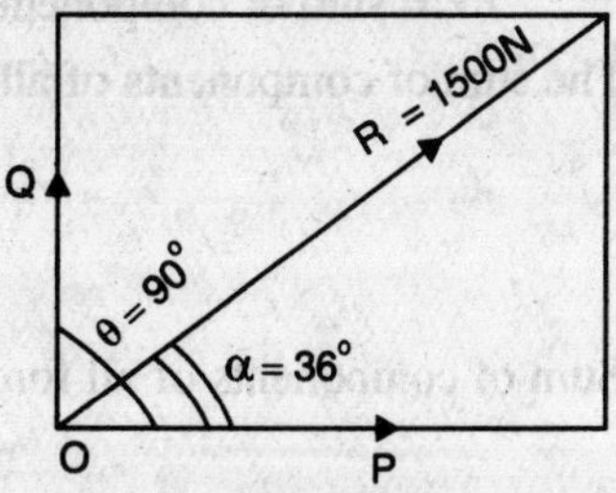

Fig. 1.8

$$\tan \alpha = \frac{Q\sin\theta}{P+Q\cos\theta}$$

$$\therefore \quad \tan 36° = \frac{Q \sin 90°}{P+Q\cos 90°}$$

$$= \frac{Q\times 1}{P+Q\times 0} = \frac{Q}{P}$$

$$\because \quad 0.7265 = \frac{Q}{P}$$

$$\therefore \quad Q = 0.7265\, P \quad \text{...(i)}$$

Now using equation,.

$$R^2 = P^2 + Q^2 + 2PQ\cos\theta$$

$$(1500)^2 = P^2 + (0.7265\,P)^2 + 2P(0.7265\,P) \times \cos 90° \quad (\because Q = 0.7265P)$$

$$(1500)^2 = P^2 + 0.52786\,P^2 + 0 = 1.52786\,P^2 \quad (\because \cos 90° = 0)$$

$$\therefore \quad P = \sqrt{\frac{1500\times 1500}{1.52786}} = \frac{1500}{1.236}$$

$$= 1213.59\, N$$

$$\therefore \quad Q = 0.726 \times 1213.59$$

$$= 881.06 \text{ N } \textbf{Ans.}$$

EXAMPLE 1.5. Two forces are acting at a point 0 as shown in Fig. 1.9. Determine the resultant in magnitude and direction.

SOLUTION: Let us first find the angles made by each force with X-axis

∴ Angle made by P with X-axis = 15°

Angle made by Q with X-axis = 15° + 30′ = 45°

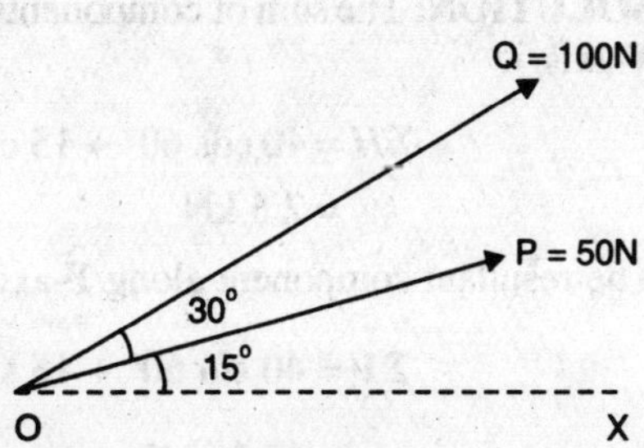

Fig. 1.9

Let

ΣH = Sum of components of all forces along X-axis

ΣV = sum of components of all forces along Y-axis

The sum of components of all forces along X-axis,

$$\Sigma H = P\cos 15° + Q\cos 45°$$

$$= 50\cos 15° + 100\cos 45° = 119 \text{ N} \quad \text{...(i)}$$

Sum of components of all forces along Y-axis,

$$\Sigma V = P\sin 15° + Q\sin 45°$$

$$= 50\cos 15° + 100\sin 45° = 83.65 \text{ N} \quad \text{...(ii)}$$

The magnitude of the resultant force is given by,

$$R = \sqrt{(\Sigma H)^2 + (\Sigma V)^2}$$

$$= \sqrt{(119)^2 + (83.65)^2}$$

$$= 145.46\ N \textbf{ Ans.}$$

The direction of the resultant force is given by the equation,

$$\tan\theta = \frac{\Sigma V}{\Sigma H}$$

$$= \frac{83.65}{119} = 0.7029$$

$\therefore$

$$\theta = \tan^{-1}(0.7029)$$

$$= 35.10° \textbf{ Ans.}$$

Here θ is the angle made by the resultant R with X-axis

EXAMPLE 1.6. Three forces of magnitude 40 kN, 15 kN and 20 kN are acting at a point 0 as shown in Fig. 1.10. The angles mode by 40 kN, 15 kN and 20 kN forces with X-axis are 60°, 120°, and 240° respectively. Determine the magnitude and direction of the resultant force.

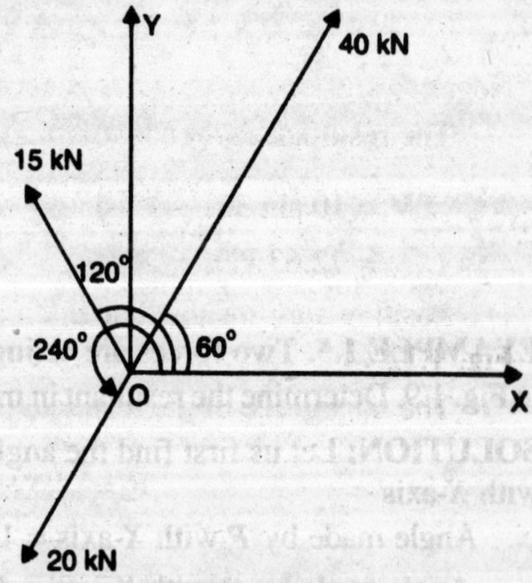

Fig. 1.10

SOLUTION: The sum of components of all the forces along X-axis.

$$\Sigma H = 40\cos 60° + 15\cos 120° + 20\cos 240°$$

$$= 2.5 \text{ kN} \quad \text{...(i)}$$

The resultant component along Y-axis is given by

$$\Sigma V = 40\sin 60° + 15\sin 120° + 20\sin 240°$$

$$= 30.31 \text{ kN} \quad \text{...(ii)}$$

$$R = \sqrt{(\Sigma H)^2 + (\Sigma V)^2}$$

$$= \sqrt{(2.5)^2 + (30.31)^2}$$

= 30.41 kN **Ans.**

$$\theta = \tan^{-1}\left(\frac{\Sigma V}{\Sigma H}\right) = \tan^{-1}\left(\frac{30.31}{2.5}\right)$$

= $\tan^{-1}$ (12.124) = 85.28° **Ans.**

EXAMPLE 1.7. Four forces of magnitude 10 kN, 15 kN, 20 kN and 40 kN are acting at a point 0 as shown in Fig. 1.11. The angles made by 10 kN, 15 kN, 20 kN, and 40 kN with *X*-axis are 30°, 60°, 90°, and 120° respectively. Find the magnitude and direction of the resultant force.

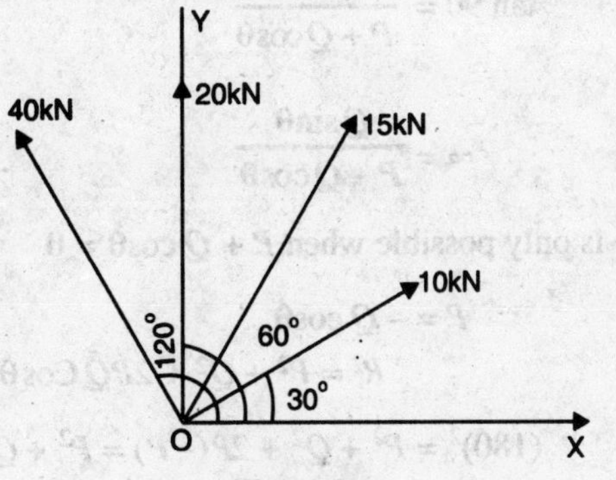

Fig. 1.11

SOLUTION: The resultant components along the *X*-axis is given by,

$$\Sigma H = 10 \cos 30° + 15 \cos 60° + 20 \cos 90° + 40 \cos 120°$$

$$= -3.84 \text{ kN} \quad \text{...(i)}$$

Negative sign means that ΣH is acting in reverse direction (along X') as shown in Fig. 1.12

The resultant component along *Y*-axis is given by the equation,

$$\Sigma V = 10 \sin 30° + 15 \sin 60° + 20 \sin 90° + 40 \sin 120°$$

$$= 72.63 \text{ kN}$$

Positive sign means that ΣV ia acting along *OY* as shown in Fig. 1.12.

The magnitude of the resultant force is given by the equation,

$$R = \sqrt{(\Sigma H)^2 + (\Sigma V)^2}$$

$$= \sqrt{(-3.84)^2 + (72.63)^2}$$

= 72.53 kN **Ans.**

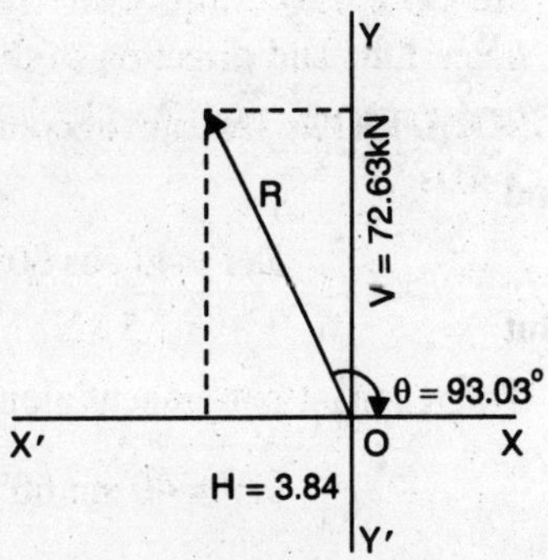

Fig. 1.12

The direction of the resultant force is given by,

$$\tan\theta = \frac{\Sigma V}{\Sigma H} = \frac{72.63}{-3.84} = -18.91$$

$$\theta = \tan^{-1}(-18.91) = -86.97°$$

$$\therefore \quad \theta = 180 - 86.97 = 93.03° \textbf{ Ans.}$$

EXAMPLE 1.8: The sum of two concurrent forces *P* and *Q* is 270*N* and their resultant is 180 *N*. The angle between the force *P* and resultant *R* is 90°. Find the magnitude of each force and angle between them.

SOLUTION: Using the equation,

$$\tan\alpha = \frac{Q\sin\theta}{P + Q\cos\theta}$$

or

$$\tan 90 = \frac{Q\sin\theta}{P + Q\cos\theta}$$

or

$$\infty = \frac{Q\sin\theta}{P + Q\cos\theta}$$

But the value of tan 90° = ∞ is only possible when $P + Q\cos\theta = 0$

Hence

$$P = -Q\cos\theta \quad \text{...(i)}$$

Now using the relation,

$$R^2 = P^2 + Q^2 + 2PQ\cos\theta$$

$$(180)^2 = P^2 + Q^2 + 2P(-P) = P^2 + Q^2 - 2P^2$$

$$= Q^2 - P^2 = (Q + P)(Q - P)$$

or

$$(180)^2 = 270(Q - P)$$

or

$$Q - P = \frac{180 \times 180}{270} = 120 \quad \text{...(ii)}$$

But

$$Q + P = 270 \text{ (Given)} \quad \text{...(iii)}$$

Hence from equations (ii) and (iii), we get

$$2Q = 390$$

$$\therefore \quad Q = 195 \text{ N } \textbf{Ans.}$$

and

$$P = 270 - Q = 270 - 195$$

$$= 75 \text{ N } \textbf{Ans.}$$

But

$$P = -Q\cos\theta \quad \text{or} \quad 75 = -195\cos\theta$$

$$\therefore \quad \cos\theta = \frac{-75}{195} = -0.3846$$

$$\theta = \cos^{-1}(-0.3846) = 112.619° \textbf{ Ans.}$$

EXAMPLE 1.9. A weight of 1000 N is supported by two chains as shown in Fig. 1.13. Determine the tension in each chain.

SOLUTION: Given

$\angle CAB = 30°$, $\angle CBA = 60°$, $\angle ACB = 90°$

In right angled triangle ADC,

$$\angle ACD = 90° - 30° = 60°$$

In right angled ΔBDG,

$$\angle BCD = 90° - 60° = 30°$$

$\therefore$

$$\angle ACE = 180° - 60° = 120°$$

$$\angle BCE = 180° - 30° = 150°$$

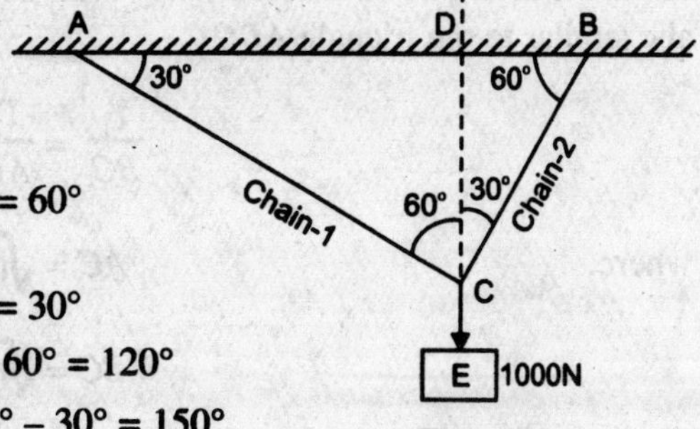

Fig. 1.13

Let,

T_1 = Tension in chain – 1

T_2 = Tension in chain – 2

Applying Lami's theorem at point C (Fig. 1.14)

$$\frac{T_1}{\sin 150} = \frac{T_2}{\sin 120} = \frac{1000}{\sin 90}$$

or

$$\frac{T_1}{0.50} = \frac{T_2}{0.866} = 1000$$

$\therefore$

$$T_1 = 0.50 \times 1000 = 500 \text{ N } \textbf{Ans.}$$

$$T_2 = 0.866 \times 1000 = 866 \text{ N } \textbf{Ans}$$

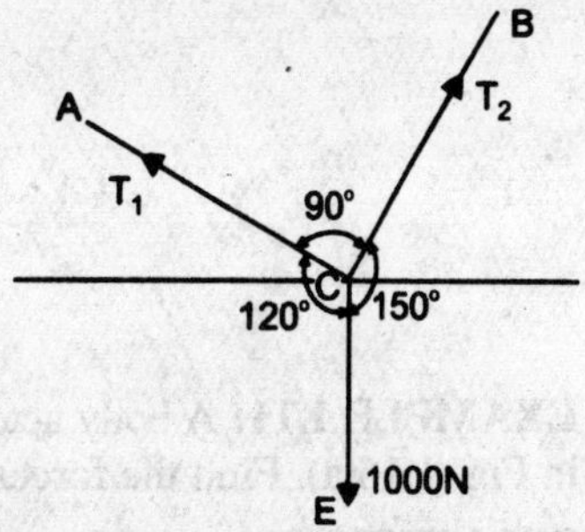

Fig. 1.14

EXAMPLE 1.10: Two bars AC and BC are hinged together at C. Their other ends are hinged to a vertical wall at A and B as shown in the Fig. 1.15(a). Find the axial force in the bar.

SOLUTION: Axial forces induced in the bars AC and BC are internal forces. But when we consider the FREE BODY diagram of point C these become the external forces acting at a point C. Let these be T_1 and T_2. Here each bar is acted upon by only two forces at its ends. One of these forces is the component of 1000N and the other is the reaction at the hinge. So each bar is a FORCE MEMBER.

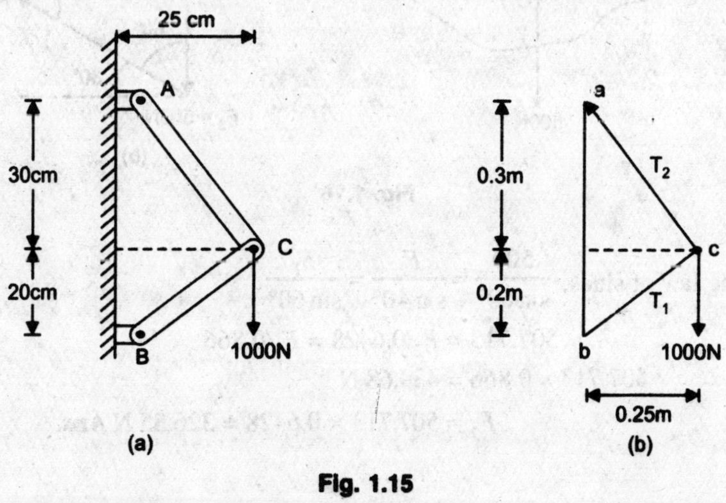

Fig. 1.15

FREE-BODY diagram of the point *c* is shown in Fig. 1.15(*b*). As the point *C* is in equilibrium under the action of three forces, they must be concurrent and should form a closed triangle of force abc similar to the triangle *ABC*

$$\frac{T_1}{BC} = \frac{T_2}{AC} = \frac{1000}{AB}$$

where, $$AC = \sqrt{(0.3)^2 + (0.25)^2} = 0.3905 \text{ m}$$

$$BC = \sqrt{(0.2)^2 + (0.25)^2} = 0.3206 \text{ m}$$

or $$\frac{T_1}{0.3206} = \frac{T_2}{0.3905} = \frac{1000}{0.50}$$

$\therefore$ $$T_1 = \frac{1000 \times 0.3206}{0.50} = 641.20 \text{ N}$$

$$T_2 = (1000 \times 0.3905) / 0.50$$
$$= 781 \text{ N}$$

EXAMPLE 1.11: A body acted upon by three forces F_1, F_2 and 500 N is in equilibrium as shown in Fig. 1.16(a). Find the forces F_1 and F_2.

SOLUTION: Since the three forces are Non-parallel and are in equilibrium they must intersect at a common point 0 and must form a closed triangle of force as shown in Fig. 1.16(b).

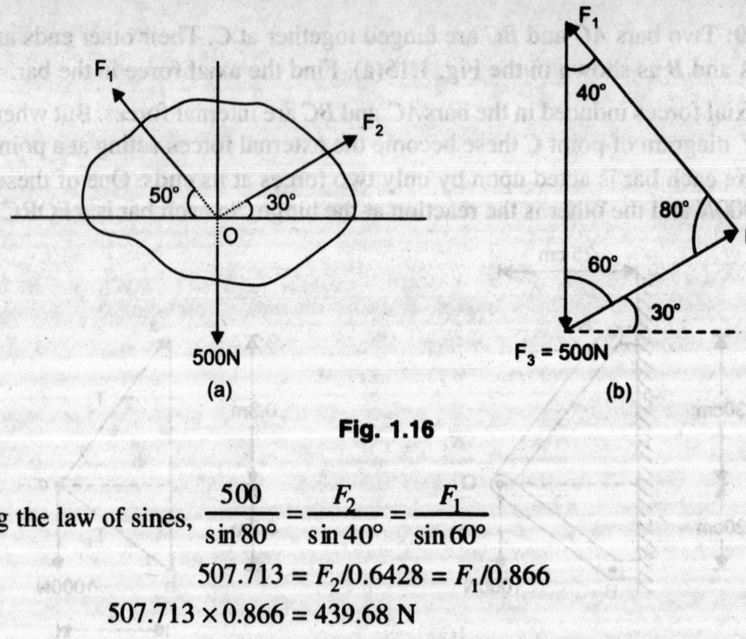

Fig. 1.16

Now applying the law of sines, $$\frac{500}{\sin 80°} = \frac{F_2}{\sin 40°} = \frac{F_1}{\sin 60°}$$

or $$507.713 = F_2/0.6428 = F_1/0.866$$

$\therefore$ $$507.713 \times 0.866 = 439.68 \text{ N}$$

$$F_2 = 507.713 \times 0.6428 = 326.35 \text{ N } \textbf{Ans.}$$

EXAMPLE 1.12: A corner plate ABC is hinged to a fixed support at A and rests on a roller at *C*. If a force *W* = 1000 N is acting as shown find the reactions at the support.

SOLUTION: Consider the FREE BODY DIAGRAM of the plate. The forces acting on the plate are:

1. Force *W* = 1000 N, acting vertical downward
2. Reactions R_c acting normal to the surface of contact, i.e., acting horizontally.
3. Reaction at the hinge R_A

As the plate is in equilibrium under the action of THREE FORCES, the forces must pass through a point *O* as shown in Fig. 1.17.

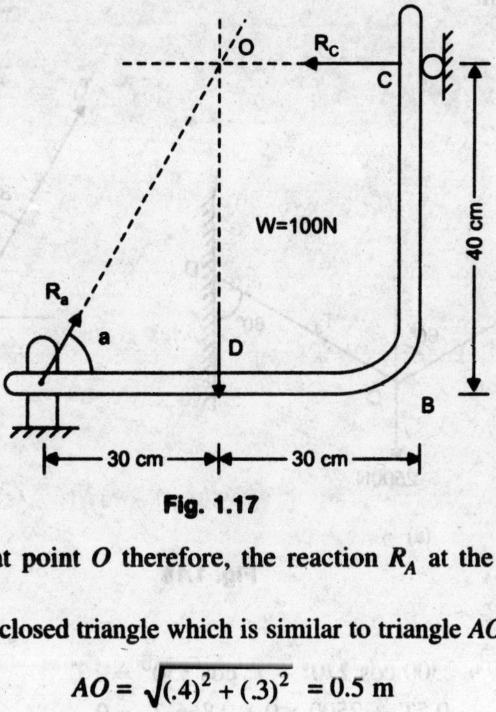

Fig. 1.17

Forces *W* and R_C intersect at point *O* therefore, the reaction R_A at the hinge must also pass through *O*.

The three forces must form a closed triangle which is similar to triangle *AOD*.

$$AO = \sqrt{(.4)^2 + (.3)^2} = 0.5 \text{ m}$$

$$\frac{W}{OD} = \frac{R_C}{AD} = \frac{R_A}{AO}$$

or
$$\frac{1000}{0.4} = \frac{R_C}{0.3} = \frac{R_A}{0.5} \qquad (\because AO = 0.5 \text{ m})$$

or
$$R_A = \frac{1000 \times 0.5}{0.4} = 12.50 \text{ N } \textbf{Ans.}$$

$$R_C = \frac{1000 \times 0.3}{0.4} = 750 \text{ N } \textbf{Ans.}$$

Now Angle α that R_C makes with horizontal is

$$\tan\alpha = \frac{\text{Perpendicular}}{\text{Base}} = \frac{0.4}{0.3} = 1.333$$

$\therefore$ $\alpha = \tan^{-1}(1.333) = 53.13°$ **Ans.**

EXAMPLE 1.13. Two equal loads of 2500 N are supported by a flexible string *ABCD* at points *B* and *C*. Find the Tensions in the portions *AB*, *BC* and *CD* of the string.

SOLUTION: Let the tensions in the portions *AB*, *BC* and *CD* be T_1, T_2 and T_3 respectively as shown in Fig. 1.18(a).

Consider the FREE BODY DIAGRAM of points B as shown in Fig. 1.18(b) and writing the equations of equilibrium.

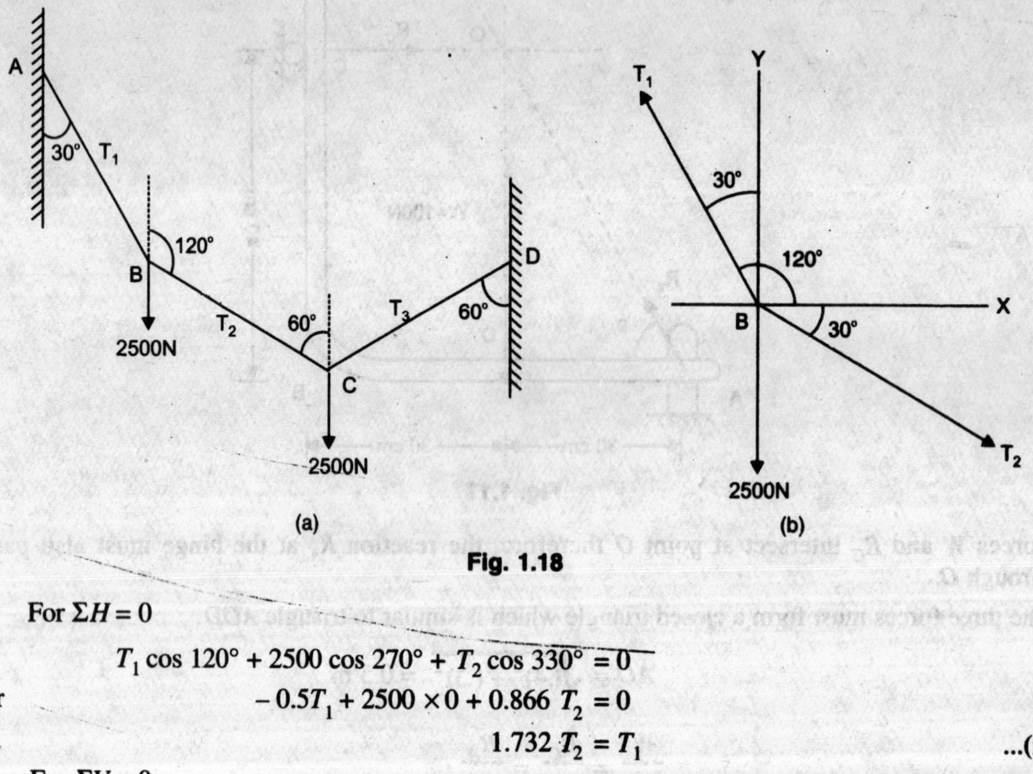

Fig. 1.18

For $\Sigma H = 0$

$$T_1\cos 120° + 2500\cos 270° + T_2\cos 330° = 0$$

or $$-0.5T_1 + 2500\times 0 + 0.866\,T_2 = 0$$

$\therefore$ $$1.732\,T_2 = T_1 \quad \text{...(i)}$$

For $\Sigma V = 0$

$$T_1\sin 120° + 2500\sin 270° + T_2\sin 330° = 0$$

or $$0.866T_1 - 2500\times 1 - 0.50T_2 = 0$$

or $$1.732\,T_1 - T_2 = 2500\times 2 \quad \text{...(ii)}$$

or $$1.732\,(1.732)\,T_2 - T_2 = 5000$$

or $$2.999824\,T_2 - T_2 = 5000$$

$\therefore$ $T_2 = 5000/1.999824 = 2500$ N **Ans.**

$\therefore$ $T_1 = 1.732\,(2500) = 4330$ N **Ans.**

Consider the free body diagram for point *C* as shown in Fig. 1.18(c).

For $\Sigma H = 0$

$$T_3 \cos 30° + T_2 \cos 150° + 2500 \cos 270° = 0$$

or $$0.866\, T_3 - 0.866025 \times 2500 - 2500 \times 0 = 0$$

or $$0.866\, T_3 - 2165.0625 = 0$$

$\therefore$ $$T_3 = 2165.0625/0.866 = 2500 \text{ N } \textbf{Ans.}$$

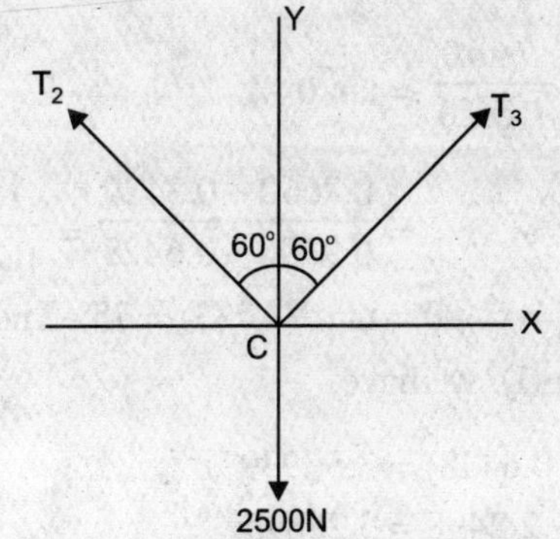

Fig. 1.18 (c)

ALTERNATE EASY METHOD:

Applying Lami's Theorem at Points B and C:

$$\frac{T_1}{\sin 60°} = \frac{T_2}{\sin 150°} = \frac{2500}{\sin 150°}$$

$\therefore$ $T_1 = 4330$ N **Ans.**

$T_2 = 2500$ N **Ans.**

$T_3 = 2500$ N **Ans.**

EXAMPLE 1.14. Two ropes are tied together at C as shown in Fig. 1.19. If the maximum permissible tension in each rope is 3.5 kN, what is the maximum force P that can be applied and in what direction?

SOLUTION: Consider the equilibrium of point C.

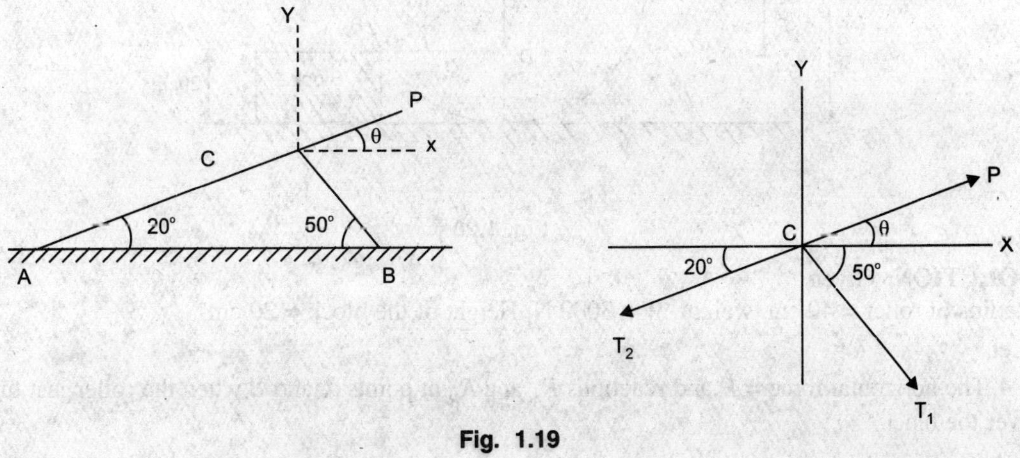

Fig. 1.19

From $\Sigma H = 0$

$$P\cos\theta + T_1\cos 310° + T_2\cos 200° = 0$$

or $P\cos\theta + 3.5(0.6428) - 3.5(0.9397) = 0$ ...(i)

From $\Sigma V = 0$,

$$P\sin\theta + T_1\sin 310° + T_2\sin 200° = 0$$

or $P\sin\theta - 3.5(0.7660) - 3.5(0.3420) = 0$ ...(ii)

$$\therefore \quad \frac{P\sin\theta}{P\cos\theta} = \tan\theta$$

$$= \frac{0.7660 + 0.3420}{0.9396 - 0.6428} = \frac{1.108}{0.2968}$$

$$\therefore \quad \theta = \tan^{-1}(3.733) = 75° \textbf{ Ans.}$$

Substituting $\theta = 75°$ in equation (I), we have,

$$P\cos 75° + 3.5\,(0.6428) = 3.5(.9397)$$

or $$P(0.2588) + 2.2498 = 3.28895$$

or $$0.2588\,P = 3.28895 - 2.2498$$

$$\therefore \quad P = 1.03915/0.2588 = 4 \text{ kN } \textbf{Ans.}$$

EXAMPLE 1.15. A roller of radius 40 cm, weighing 3000 N is to be pulled over a rectangular block of 20 cm height as shown in Fig. 1.20, by a horizontal force applied at the end of a string wound round the circumference of the roller. Find the magnitude of horizontal force which will just turn the roller over the corner of the rectangular block. Also determine the magnitude and direction of the reactions at A and B. All surfaces may be taken as smooth.

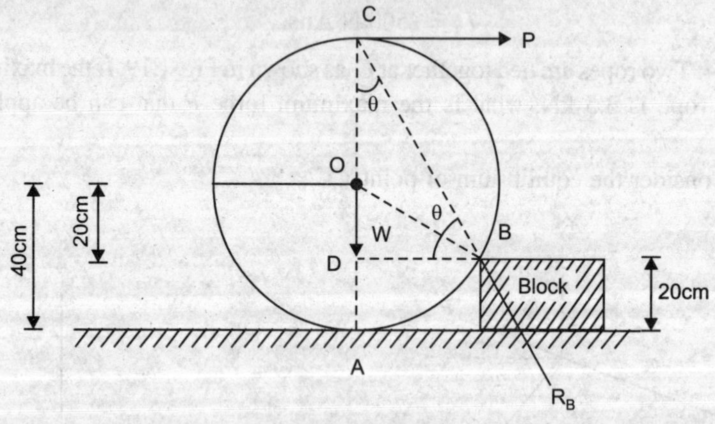

Fig. 1.20

SOLUTION: Given

Radius of roller = 40 cm, weight, $W = 3000$ N, Height of the block = 20 cm

Let,

The horizontal force = P and reactions R_A and R_B at points A and B when the roller just turns over the block.

When the roller is about to turn over the corner of the rectangular block, the roller lifts at point A and then there will be no contact between the roller and the point A. Hence reaction R_A at point A will become zero.

Now the roller will be in equilibrium under the action of the following three forces:

(i) Its weight W acting vertically downward

(ii) Horizontal force P.

(iii) Reaction R_B at point B. The directions of R_B is unknown.

In ΔBOD, BO = Radius = 40 cm, OD = OA – AD = 40 – 20 = 20 cm

$$\therefore \quad BD = \sqrt{BO^2 - OD^2} = \sqrt{40^2 - 20^2}$$

$$= 34.64 \text{ cm}$$

For the equilibrium, the above three forces should pass through a common point. As the force P and weight W is passing through point C, hence the reaction R_B must also pass through the point C. Hence, the line BC gives the direction of the reaction R_B

Now in ΔBCD,
$$\tan\theta = \frac{\text{Base}}{\text{Perpendicular}} = \frac{BD}{CD}$$

$$= \frac{34.64}{40+20} = 0.5773$$

$$\therefore \quad \theta = \tan^{-1}(0.5773) = 29.999° = 30°$$

Now taking moments of all the three forces about the point B (i.e., corner of the rectangular block)

$P \times CD = W \times BD$ or $P \times 60 = 3000 \times 34.64$

$$\therefore \quad P = \frac{3000 \times 34.64}{60} = 1732 \text{ N } \textbf{Ans.}$$

EXAMPLE 1.16. A circular roller of weight 100 N and radius 10 cm hangs by a TIE ROD AB = 20 cm and rests against a smooth vertical wall at C as shown in Fig. 1.21(a). Determine (i) force F in the TIE ROD and (ii) the reaction R_C at point C.

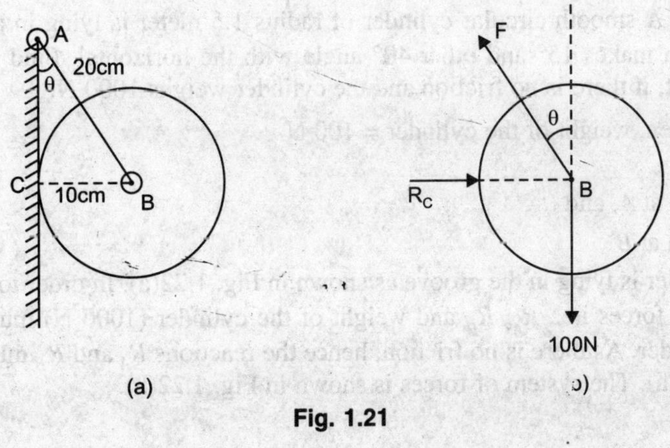

Fig. 1.21

SOLUTION: Given

Weight of the roller, $W = 100$ N

Radius of roller BC = 10 cm,

Length of TIE ROD, AB = 20 cm

From ΔABC, we get,

$$\sin\theta = \frac{\text{Perp.}}{\text{Diag.}} = \frac{10}{20} = 0.5$$

$$\therefore \qquad \theta = \sin^{-1}(0.50) = 30°$$

The Free Body Diagram of the roller is shown in Fig. 1.21(b) in which

R_C = Reaction at C

F = Force in the Tie Rod AB

Free body Diagram shows the equilibrium of the roller. Hence the resultant force in X-direction and Y-direction should be zero.

For $\Sigma H = 0$,

$$F \sin 30° - R_C \sin 90° + 100 \sin 180° = 0$$

or $$0.5\,F = R_C \qquad \text{...(i)}$$

For $\Sigma V = 0$

$$F \cos 30° - R_C \cos 90° + 100 \cos 180° = 0$$

or $$0.866F - R_C \times 0 + 100\,(-1) = 0$$

or $$0.866F = 100$$

$$\therefore \qquad F = \frac{100}{0.866} = 115.47 \text{ N } \textbf{Ans.}$$

But $$R_C = 0.5\,F = 115.47(0.5)$$

$$= 57.73 \text{ N } \textbf{Ans.}$$

EXAMPLE 1.17. A smooth circular cylinder of radius 1.5 meter is lying in a triangular groove, One side of which makes 15° and other 40° angle with the horizontal. Find the reactions at the surfaces of contact, if there is no friction and the cylinder weighs 1000 N.

SOLUTION: Given, weight of the cylinder = 100 N

Let,

R_A = Reaction at A, and

R_B = Reaction at B

The smooth cylinder is lying in the groove as shown in Fig. 1.22(a). In order to keep the system in equilibrium, three forces i.e., R_A, R_B and weight of the cylinder (1000 N) must pass through the centre of the cylinder. As there is no friction, hence the reactions R_A and R_B must be normal to the surfaces (Fig. 1.22a). The system of forces is shown in Fig. 1.22(b).

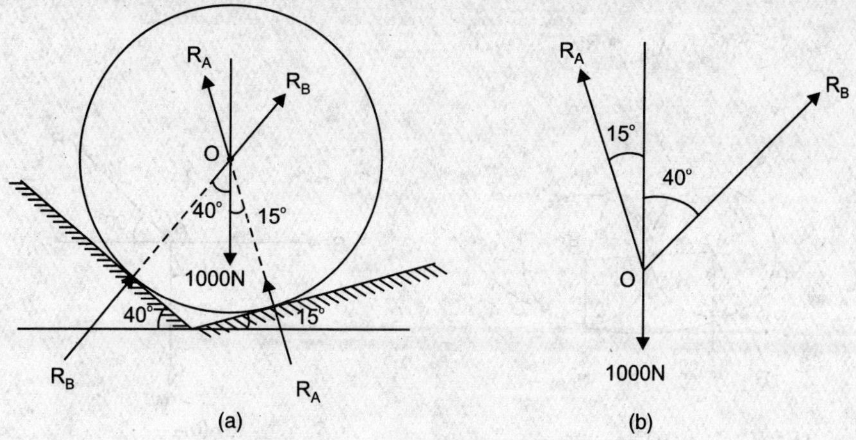

Fig. 1.22

Applying Lami's theorem, at point O,

$$\frac{R_A}{\sin(180° - 40°)} = \frac{R_B}{\sin(180° - 15°)} = \frac{100}{\sin(15° + 40°)}$$

or
$$\frac{R_A}{\sin 140°} = \frac{R_B}{\sin 165°} = \frac{100}{\sin 55°}$$

or
$$\frac{R_A}{0.64278} = \frac{R_B}{0.2588} = 122.077$$

$\therefore$
$$R_A = 122.077 \times 0.64278 = 78.47 \text{ N } \textbf{Ans.}$$
$$R_B = 122.077 \times 0.2588 = 31.59 \text{ N } \textbf{Ans.}$$

EXAMPLE 1.18. Two equal heavy spheres of 50 mm radius are in equilibrium within a smooth cup of 150 mm radius. Show that the reaction between the cup of one sphere is double than that between the two spheres.

SOLUTION: Given,

Radius of spheres = 50 mm
Radius of cup = 150 mm

The two spheres with centres A and B, lying in equilibrium, in the cup with O as centre are shown in Fig. 1.23(a). Let the two spheres touch each other at C and touch the cup at D and E respectively.

R = Reaction between sphere and cup
S = Reaction between two spheres at C.

From the Geometry of the figure, we find that OD = 150 mm and AD = 50 mm.

$\therefore$ OA = 100 mm

Similarly, OB = 100 mm. We also find that AB = 100 mm

$\therefore OAB$ is an equilateral triangle. Hence the system of forces (FBD) is shown in Fig. 1.23(b).

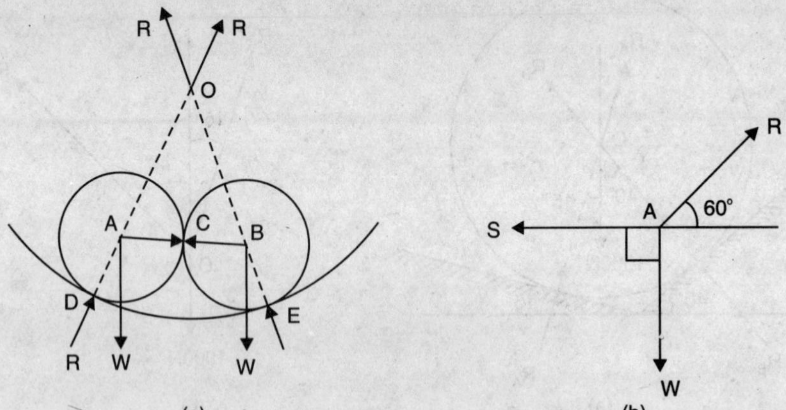

(a) (b)

Fig. 1.23

Applying Lami's Theorem

$$\frac{R}{\sin 90^\circ} = \frac{W}{\sin 120^\circ} = \frac{S}{\sin 150^\circ}$$

or
$$\frac{R}{1} = \frac{W}{0.866} = \frac{S}{0.5}$$

$\therefore$
$$0.5\,R = S$$

or
$$R = 2S$$

Hence the reaction between the cup and the sphere is double than that between the two spheres. **Ans**

EXAMPLE 1.19. **A smooth uniform ladder of length 2a and weight *W* rests on the ground and against a vertical wall and is prevented from slipping by a string of length *l* tied to its lower end and to the junction of the wall with the ground (Fig. 1.24). Find the tension of the string. Find also the tension when a man whose weight is twice that of ladder has ascended the ladder three fourth of the way up (2004).**

SOLUTION: From Fig. 1.24, we have

$$\cos\theta = \frac{\text{Base}}{\text{Diagonal}} = l/2a \qquad \text{...(i)}$$

From the right angled triangle *BCA*

$$(2a)^2 = l^2 + (AC)^2 \text{ or } 4a^2 = l^2 + (AC)^2$$

$\therefore$
$$AC = \sqrt{4a^2 - l^2} \qquad \text{...(ii)}$$

(a) Considering the equilibrium of ladder only; the various forces on the ladder are:

(i) Weight of the ladder, *W*

(ii) Tension in the string, *T*, in horizontal direction.

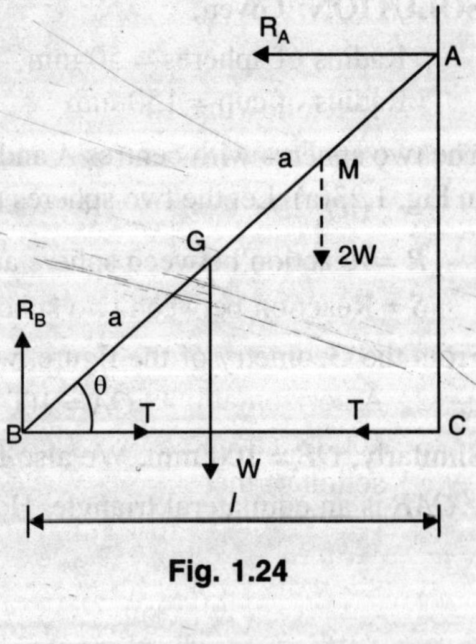

Fig. 1.24

(iii) Reaction of wall, R_A, in horizontal direction

(iv) Reaction of floor, R_B in vertical upward direction

Equations for equilibrium are:

$$\Sigma H = 0,\ \Sigma V = 0,\ \Sigma M = 0$$

$\therefore$ For $\Sigma H = 0$, we have $\quad R_A = T$ ...(iii)

and For $\Sigma V = 0$, $\quad R_B = W$ ...(iv)

For $\Sigma M_B = 0$,

$$W \times \frac{l}{2} = R_A \times A_C$$

or

$$\frac{Wl}{2} = R_A\sqrt{(4a^2 - l^2)}$$

$\therefore$

$$\frac{Wl}{2} \times \frac{1}{\sqrt{4a^2 - l^2}} = R_A = T$$

$\therefore$

$$T = \frac{Wl}{\sqrt{4a^2 - l^2}} \textbf{ Ans.}$$

(b) Considering the equilibrium of the ladder when the man of $2W$ weight has ascended the ladder three fourth of the way up (point M):

$$R_B = W + 2W = 3W \qquad \text{...(v)}$$

For $\Sigma M_B = 0$,

$$W \times \frac{l}{2} + 2W \times \frac{3l}{4} = R_A \times AC$$

or

$$2Wl = R_A\sqrt{4a^2 - l^2}$$

$\therefore$

$$R_A = T = \frac{2Wl}{\sqrt{4a^2 - l^2}} \textbf{ Ans.}$$

EXERCISE-1

1. The following forces act at a point O.
   (i) 20 N inclined at 30° towards East-North.
   (ii) 25N towards North.
   (iii) 30 N towards North-West
   (iv) 35 N inclined at 40° towards south-West.

   Find the magnitude and direction of the resultant force. **[Ans.** $R = 45.6$ N, $\theta = 47.7°$]

2. A horizontal line $ABCD$ is 12m long, where $AB = BC = CD = 4$m. Forces of 1000N, 1500 N, 1000N and 500N act at A, B, C and D respectively in downward direction. The lines of action of these forces make angles of 90°, 60°, 45° and 30° respectively with line AD.

   Find the magnitude, direction and position of the resultant force.

   [Ans. $R = 3765$ N, $\theta = 59.8°$, $x = 4.25$ m]

3. Three forces of $2P$, $3P$ and $4P$ magnitudes act along the three sides of an equilateral triangle of side 100 mm taken in order. Find the magnitude and position of the resultant force.

   [**Ans.** $R = 1.732\ P$, $x = 150$ mm]

4. Two men carry a weight of 2 kN by means of two ropes fixed to the weight. One rope is inclined at 45° and the other at 30° with their vertices. Find the tension in each rope.

   [**Ans.** $T_1 = 1.04$ kN, $T_2 = 1.46$ kN]

5. An electric light fixture weighing 15N hangs from a point C, by two strings AC and BC. The string AC is inclined at 60° to the horizontal and BC at 45° to the horizontal. Determine the forces in the strings AC and BC.

   [**Ans.** $T_1 = 1.0$ N, $T_2 = 7.8$ N]

CHAPTER 2

Structure

INTRODUCTION

If we consider the equilibrium of a girder supported on the walls, we see that total weight of the girder is acting through the supports of the girder on the walls. It is thus obvious, that walls must exert equal and upward reactions at the supports to maintain the equilibrium. The upward reactions offered by the walls, are known as support Reactions. As a matter of fact, the support reactions depend upon the type of loading and the support.

TYPES OF LOADING

1. Concentrated or Point Load
2. Uniformly distributed load, and uniformly varying load;

TYPES OF END SUPPORTS OF BEAMS

1. SIMPLY SUPPORTED BEAMS: It is a theoretical case, in which the end of the beam is simply supported over one of its support. In such a case the reaction is always vertical as shown in Fig. 2.1.

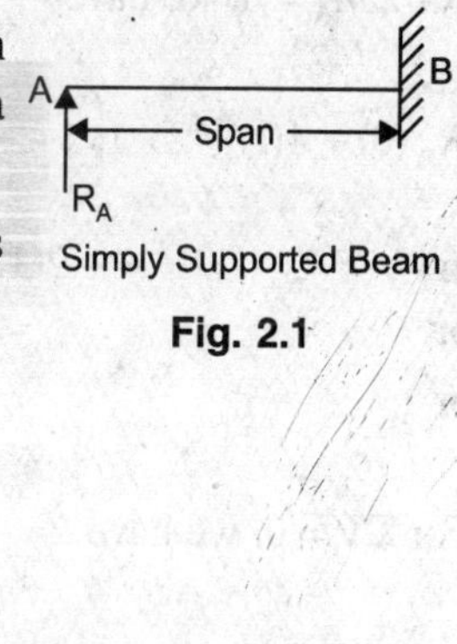

Simply Supported Beam

Fig. 2.1

EXAMPLE 2.1. A simply supported beam *AB* of span 5m is loaded as shown in Fig. 2.2 Find the reactions at *A* and *B*.

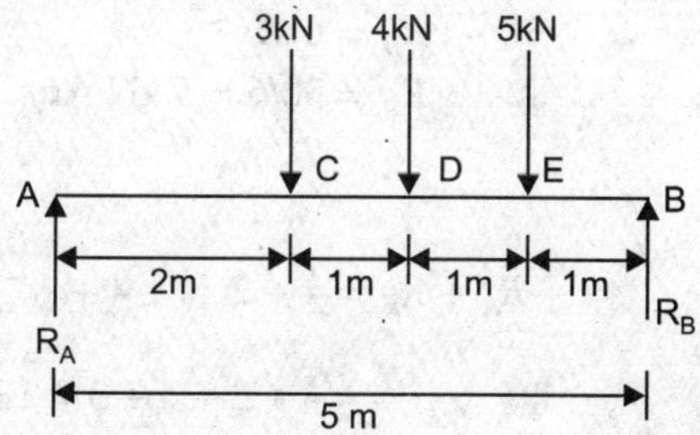

Fig. 2.2

SOLUTION: Given Span = 5m

Let, R_A = Reaction at *A*, and R_B = Reactions at *B*.

For $\Sigma M_A = 0$, we have

$$R_A \times O + 3(2) + 4(3) + 5(4) - R_B(5) = 0$$

or $\quad 5R_B = 6 + 12 + 20 = 38$

$\therefore \quad R_B = 38/5$

$= 7.60$ kN **Ans.**

For $\Sigma V = 0$, we have

$$R_A + R_B = 3 + 4 + 5 = 12$$

or $\quad R_A + 7.60 = 12$

$\therefore \quad R_A = 12 - 7.60 = 4.40$ kN **Ans.**

EXAMPLE 2.2. A simply supported beam *AB* of 6m span is subjected to loading as shown in Fig. 2.3. Find support reactions.

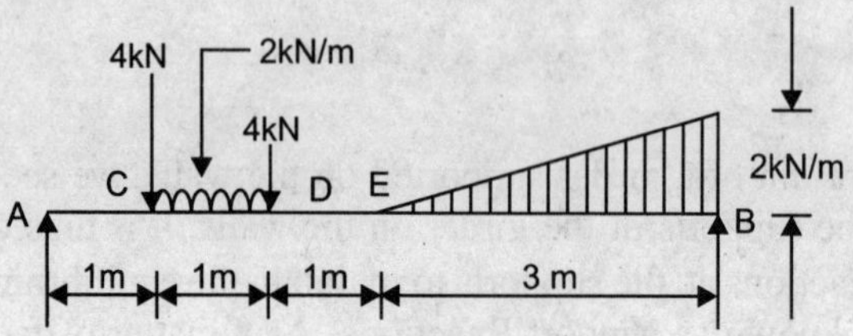

Fig. 2.3

SOLUTION: Given, Span = 6m
Let,

R_A = Reaction at A, and

R_B = Reaction at B

For $\Sigma M_A = 0$, we have

$$R_A(0) + 4(1) + 2\times 1\left(1+\frac{1}{2}\right) + 4(2) + \frac{0+2}{2}(3)\left(3+\frac{2\times 3}{3}\right) - 6R_B = 0$$

or $\quad 0 + 4 + 2(1.5) + 8 + 1(3)(5) - 6R_B = 0$

or $\quad 4 + 3 + 8 + 15 - 6R_B = 0$

or $\quad 30 - 6R_B = 0$

$\therefore \quad R_B = 30/6 = 5$ kN **Ans.**

For $\Sigma V = 0$, we have

$$R_A + R_B = 4 + 2(1) + 4 + \left(\frac{0+2}{2}\right)3$$

$= 4 + 2 + 4 + 3 = 13$ kN

$\therefore \quad R_A = 13 - R_B$

$= 13 - 5 = 8$ kN **Ans.**

OVER HANGING BEAMS: A beam having its end portion (or portions) extended in the form of a cantilever, beyond its support, as shown in Fig. 2.4, is known as an OVER HANGING BEAM. It may be noted that the beam may overhang on one of its sides or both the sides. In such cases, the reactions at both the supports will be vertical as shown in the Fig. 2.4.

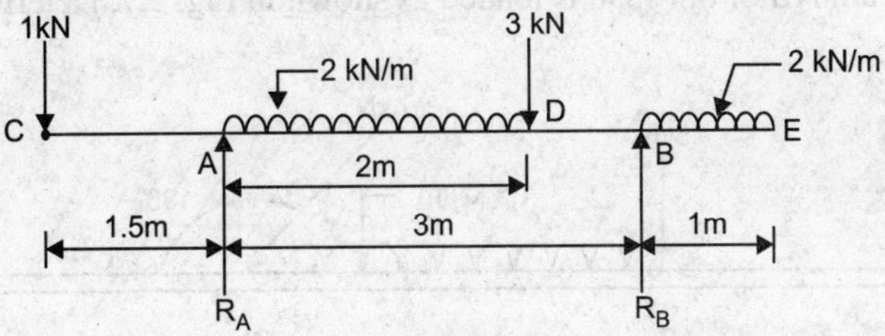

Fig. 2.4

EXAMPLE 2.3: A beam of span 3m, over hanging on both sides is loaded as shown in Fig. 2.4. Determine the reactions at the supports *A* and *B*.

SOLUTION: Given Span = 3m

Let,

R_A = Reaction at *A*, and

R_B = Reaction at *B*

For $\Sigma M_A = 0$, we have

$$-1\,(1.5) + R_A\,(0) + 2 \times 2\,(1) + 3\,(2) - R_B\,(3) + 1 \times (3.5) = 0$$

$$-1.5 + 4 + 6 - 3\,R_B + 3.5 = 0$$

or $$3\,R_B = 12$$

∴ $$R_B = 4 \text{ kN } \textbf{Ans}$$

For $\Sigma V = 0$, we have

$$R_A + R_B = 1 + 2 \times 2 + 3 + 1 \times 1$$

$$= 1 + 4 + 3 + 1 = 9 \text{ kN}$$

∴ $$R_A = 9 - R_B$$

$$= 9 - 4 = 5 \text{ kN } \textbf{Ans.}$$

ROLLER SUPPORTED BEAMS: In such a case, the end of the beam is supported on rollers, and the reaction on such an end is always normal to the support as shown in Fig. 2.5. All the steel trusses of the bridges, have one of their ends as supported on rollers.

The main advantage, of such a support, is that the beam can move easily towards left or right, on account of expansion or contraction, due to change in temperature.

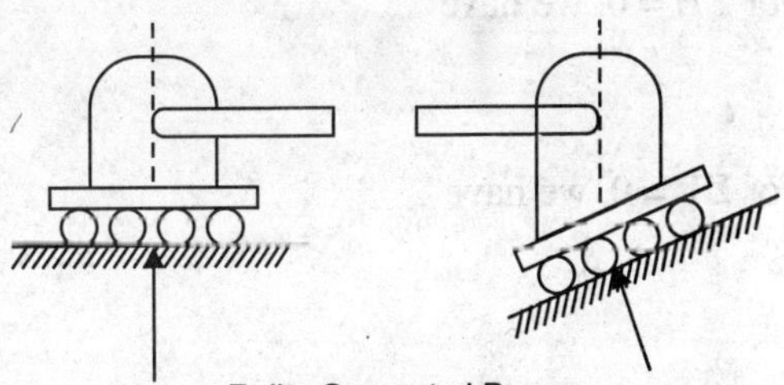

Roller Supported Beam

Fig. 2.5

HINGED BEAMS: In such a case, the end of a beam is hinged to the support as shown in Fig. 2.6. The reaction on such an end may be horizontal, vertical or inclined, depending upon the type of loading. All the steel trusses of the bridges have one of their end roller support, and the other hinged. The main advantage of such a support is that the beam remains stable. A beam can not be stable, if both of its ends are supported on rollers. Thus, one of the supports is made roller supported and the other hinged.

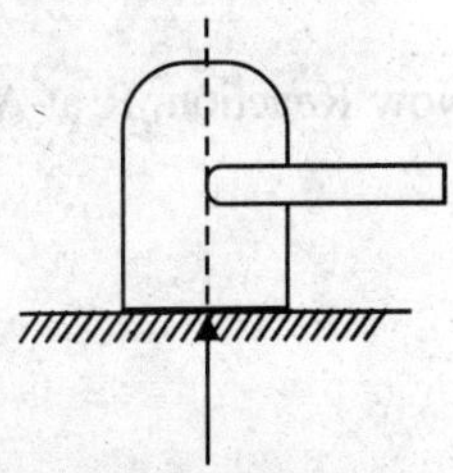

Hinged Beam

Fig. 2.6

EXAMPLE 2.4. A beam AB of 6m span is loaded as shown in Fig. 2.7. Determine the reactions at *A* and *B*.

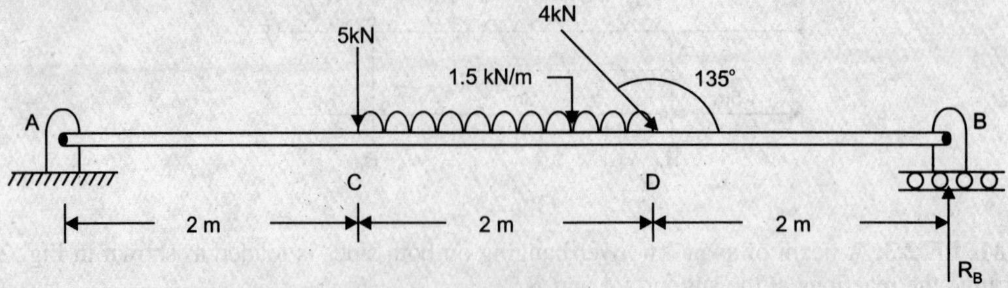

Fig. 2.7

SOLUTION: Given Span = 6m

Let,

R_A = Reaction at A, and

R_B = Reaction at B.

As the beam is supported on rollers at the right hand support (B), hence the reaction R_B will be vertical (because of horizontal support). As the beam is hinged at the left support (A) and it is also carrying inclined load, hence the reaction at this end will be resultant of horizontal and vertical forces, and thus will be inclined with the vertical.

For $\Sigma M_A = 0$, we have

$$R_A \times 0 + 5(2) + 1.5 \times 2\ (3) + 4 \sin 135°\ (4) - R_B\ (6)$$

or $$0 + 10 + 9 + 11.314 - 6R_B = 0$$

or $$6R_B = 30.32$$

$\therefore$ $$R_B = 5.05 \text{ kN } \textbf{Ans.}$$

For $\Sigma H = 0$, we have

$$R_H = 4 \cos 135°$$
$$= 2.83 \text{ kN}$$

For $\Sigma V = 0$, we have

$$R_A + R_B = 5 + 1.5(2) + 4 \sin 135°$$
$$= 10.83$$

$\therefore$ $$R_A = 10.83 - R_B$$
$$= 10.83 - 5.05$$
$$= 5.78 \text{ kN} \uparrow \text{(Vertical component)}$$

Now Reaction, R at A,

$$R = \sqrt{(\Sigma H)^2 + (\Sigma V)^2}$$
$$= \sqrt{(5.78)^2 + (2.83)^2}$$
$$= 6.44 \text{ kN}$$

$\therefore$ $$R = 6.44 \text{ kN } \textbf{Ans.}$$

Let, θ = Angle, which the reaction R at A makes with the vertical

Then,
$$\theta = \tan^{-1}\left(\frac{\Sigma H}{\Sigma V}\right)$$
$$= \tan^{-1}\left(\frac{2.83}{5.78}\right)$$
$$= \tan^{-1}(0.4896) = 25.1° \textbf{ Ans.}$$

EXAMPLE 2.5. A beam has hinged support at A and roller support at B as shown in Fig. 2.8. The beam is subjected to load as shown in Fig. 2.8. Determine the reactions at A and B.

SOLUTION : Given – span = 9 m

Let,

R_A = Reaction at A, and R_B = Reaction at B.

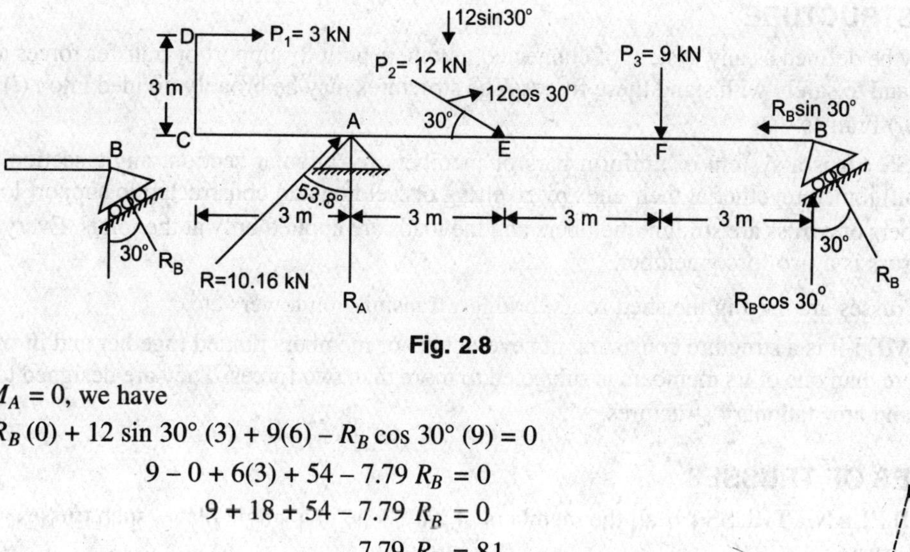

Fig. 2.8

For $\Sigma M_A = 0$, we have

$3(3) - R_B\,(0) + 12 \sin 30° \,(3) + 9(6) - R_B \cos 30° \,(9) = 0$

or $\quad 9 - 0 + 6(3) + 54 - 7.79\, R_B = 0$

or $\quad 9 + 18 + 54 - 7.79\, R_B = 0$

or $\quad 7.79\, R_B = 81$

$\therefore \quad R_B = 10.4$ kN **Ans.**

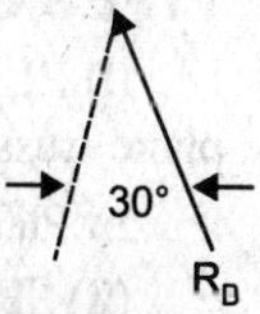

Fig. 2.9

For $\Sigma M_B = 0$, we have,

$3(3) + R_A(9) - 12 \sin 30°(6) - 9(3) - R_B \cos 30° \,(0) = 0$

or $\quad 9 + 9\,R_A - 36 - 27 = 0$

or $\quad 9R_A = 54$

$\therefore \quad R_A = 6$ kN (↑)

or Vertical component of reactions $R_B = R_B \cos 30° = 10.4(.866) = 9$ kN (↑)

$\therefore$ For $\Sigma M_B = 0$, we have,

$$R_A\,(V) + R_B(V) = 12 \sin 30° + 9$$
$$= 6 + 9 = 15 \text{ kN}$$

$$\therefore \quad R_A(V) = 6 + 9 - R_B\,(V)$$
$$= 6 + 9 - 9 = 6 \text{ kN } (\uparrow)$$

Horizontal Component of Reaction $R_B = R_B \sin 30°$
$$= 10.4\,(0.5) = 5.2 \text{ kN } (\leftarrow)$$

$\therefore$ Horizontal component of reaction R_A. $= (3 + 12 \cos 30°) - 5.2\,(\leftarrow)$
$$= 8.2 \text{ kN } (\rightarrow)$$

$$\therefore R = \sqrt{(\Sigma H)^2 + (\Sigma V)^2} = \sqrt{(8.2)^2 + (6)^2}$$
$$= 10.16 \text{ kN } \textbf{Ans.}$$

Let θ = angles, which the reaction at A makes with the vertical.

$$\therefore \quad \tan\theta = \frac{\Sigma H}{\Sigma V} = \frac{8.2}{6} = 1.3667$$

$$\therefore \quad \theta = \tan^{-1}(1.3667) = 53.8° \textbf{ Ans.}$$

2.1 STRUCTURE

It may be defined as any system of connected members built to support or transfer forces acting on them and to safely with stand these forces. The structures may be broadly divided into : (*i*) Trusses, and (*ii*) Frames.

TRUSS : It is a system of uniform bars or members (of circular section, angle section, channel section) joined together at their ends by rivetting or welding and constructed to support loads. The members of a truss are straight members and the loads are applied only at the joints. Every member of a truss is a two force member.

Trusses are used in the shed roofs, bridges, transmission towers etc.

FRAME : It is a structure consisting of several bars or members pinned together and in which one or more than one of its members is subjected to more than two forces. They are designed to support load and are stationary structures.

TYPES OF TRUSSES

(i) PLANE TRUSS : If all the members of a truss lie in a single plane, such trusses are called plane trusses.

In Plane trusses load acts along the plane of the frame, e.g. roof and bridge trusses.

(ii) SPACE TRUSS : If all the members of a truss do not lie in a single plane, then the truss is called space Truss, e.g. Transmission tower trusses.

CLASSIFICATION OF TRUSSES

The trusses can be classified into the following three categories depending upon the number in the truss:

(i) PERFECT TRUSS : A truss which has got just sufficient number of members to resist the loads without under going any appreciable deformation in its shape is called perfect truss. A triangular truss is the simplest perfect truss as shown in Fig. 2.10

1, 2, 3 → pin joints, (1), (2), (3) → Members

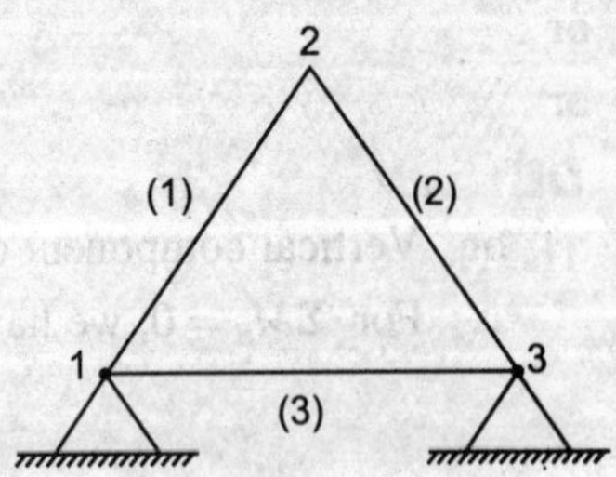

Fig. 2.10

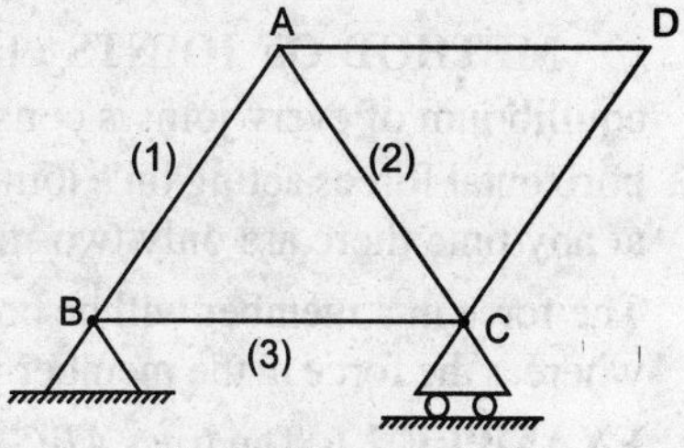

Perfect Truss

Fig. 2.11

If we add two members and one joint to the above truss as shown in Fig. 2.11, than the resultant truss will also be a perfect truss and so on.

The joints of a truss are also called Nodes, (KNOB or KNOT)

For a truss to be Rigid or Perfect, the relationship between its numbers of members and number of joints is $m + 3 = 2J$ ($\therefore m = 2J - 3$) ...(i)

m = Number of members in the truss

J = Number of Joints in the truss

Hence for a perfect truss :

No. of members required = Twice the no. of joints minus 3.

Fig. 2.12 (a)

Equation (i) i.e. $m = 2j - 3$ is a necessary condition for a truss to be perfect but not a sufficient condition.

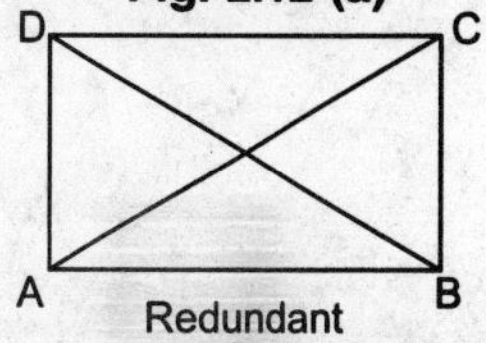

Redundant Truss

Fig. 2.12 (b)

The necessary and suficient condition for a truss to be perfect is that, it should retain its shape under the action of applied load.

(ii) DEFICIENT OR IMPERFECT TRUSS : A truss is said to be deficient or imperfect when it is unable to retain its shape under the action of applied loads. Fig. 2.12(a) (Refer)

Hence for deficient or imperfect truss;

$$m < 2j - 3$$

(iii) REDUNDANT TRUSS : If the number of members in a truss is more than that of a perfect truss, then it is called redundant truss as shown in Fig. 2.12(b)

For a redundant truss, $m > 2j - 3$

ANALYSIS OF TRUSS

Analysis of a trus means to calculate :

(a) The reactions at the supports.

(b) The forces in the members of the truss

ASSUMPTIONS IN THE ANALYSIS OF TRUSS : Following assumptions are made, while finding out the forces in the members of a perfect truss.

1. The end of the members are always assumed to be pin connected i.e. Hinged.
2. The loads on the truss are applied at the joints only.
3. Self weight of the members is assumed to be negligible.
4. Cross-section of the members is assumed to be uniform.

DETERMINATION OF AXIAL FORCES IN THE MEMBERS OF A TRUSS

The various methods are :

1. Method of joints
2. Method of sections
3. Graphical method

METHOD OF JOINTS : In this method, after determining the reactions at the supports, the equilibrium of every joint is considered. This means the sum of all the vertical forces as well as the horizontal forces acting on a joint is equated to zero. The joint should be selected in such a way that at any time there are only two members, in which the forces are unknown.

The force in a member will be compressive if the member pushes the joint to which it is connected, whereas the force in the member will be tensile if the member pulls the joint to which it is connected.

EXAMPLE 2.6. The truss *ABC*, shown in Fig. 2.13, has a span of 5 metres. It is carrying a load of 20kN at its apex. Find the forces in the members *AB*, *AC* and *BC*.

SOLUTION : First determine the reactions R_C and R_B.

For $\Sigma V = 0$,

we have,

$$R_C + R_B = 20 \text{ kN} \quad \text{...(i)}$$

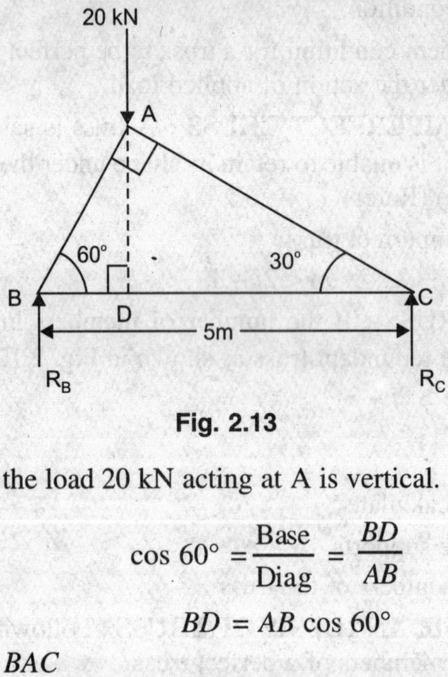

Fig. 2.13

$\because$ The line of action of the load 20 kN acting at A is vertical.

$$\therefore \quad \cos 60° = \frac{\text{Base}}{\text{Diag}} = \frac{BD}{AB}$$

$$\therefore \quad BD = AB \cos 60°$$

In a right angled triangle *BAC*

$$\because \quad \cos 60° = \frac{\text{Base}}{\text{Diag}} = \frac{AB}{BC} = \frac{AB}{5}$$

$$\therefore \quad AB = 5 \cos 60° \quad \text{...(ii)}$$

$$\therefore \quad BD = AB \cos 60° = 2.5 \cos 60° = 1.25 \text{ m}$$

Now taking moments about *B* i.e. for $\Sigma M_B = 0$

$$\therefore \quad R_B \times 0 + 20 \times 1.25 - R_C \times 5 = 0$$

or

$$5R_C = 20 \times 1.25$$

$$\therefore \quad R_C = 5 \text{ kN} \quad \text{...(iii)}$$

$$\because \quad R_B + R_C = 20$$

$$\therefore \quad R_B = 20 - R_C = 20 - 5 = 15 \text{ kN} \quad \text{...(iv)}$$

Now let us consider the equilibrium of the various joints.

JOINT B : (Refer Fig. 2.14)

Let the force F_{AB} is acting towards the joint B and F_{BC} is acting away from the joint B.

Now resolving the forces, acting on the joint B, vertically i.e.

For $\Sigma V = 0$,

$$-F_{AB}\sin 60^\circ + 15 = 0$$

or $$F_{AB}\sin 60^\circ = 15$$

$\therefore$ $F_{AB} = 15/0.866 = 17.32$ kN (Compressive)

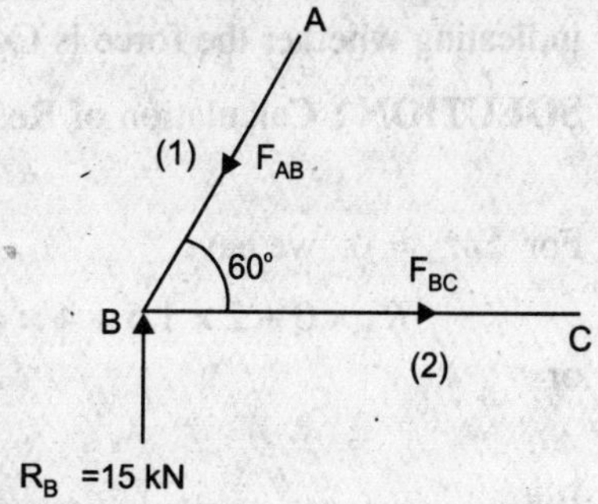

Fig. 2.14

As F_{AB} is pushing the joint B, hence this force will be compressive.

Now resolving the forces horizontally, i.e. for $\Sigma H = 0$

$$F_{BC} = F_{AB}\cos 60$$
$$= 17.32 \times 0.50 = 8.66 \text{ kN (Tensile)}$$

As F_{BC} is pulling the joint B, hence this force will be tensile.

JOINT C : Let (Refer Fig. 2.15)

F_{AC} = Force in member AC

F_{CB} = Force in member CB

The force F_{BC} has already been calculated in magnitude and direction, we have seen that force F_{BC} is tensile, hence it will pull the Joint C.

Now resolving the forces vertically, i.e. for $\Sigma V = 0$, we have

$$-F_{AC}\sin 30^\circ + 5 = 0$$

or $$F_{AC}\sin 30^\circ = 5$$

$\therefore$ $$F_{AC} = 5/0.5 = 10 \text{ kN (Compressive)}$$

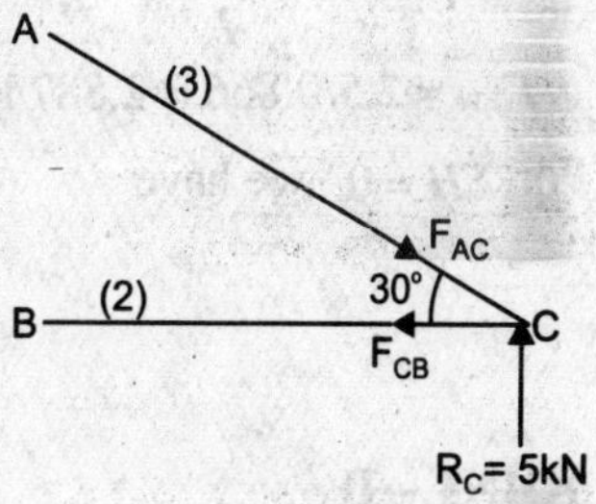

Fig. 2.15

As the force F_{AC} is pushing the joint C, hence it will be Compressive.

EXAMPLE 2.7. Fig. 2.16 shows a Warren Girder consisting of seven members each of 3 m length freely supported at its end points.

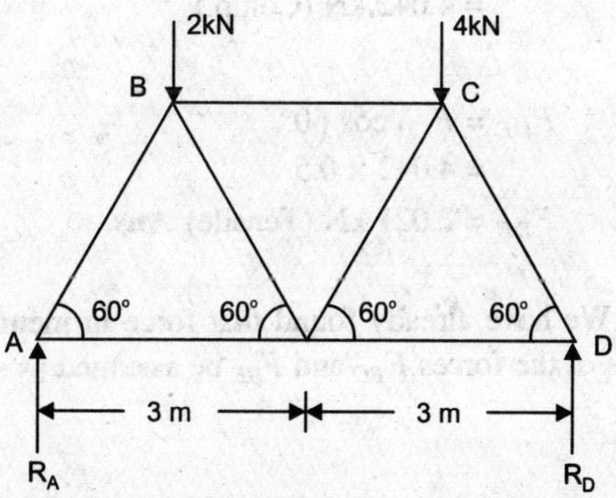

Fig. 2.16

The girder is loaded at *B* and *C* as shown. Find the forces in all the members of the girder, indicating whether the force is Compressive or Tensile.

SOLUTION : Calculation of Reactions (R_A, R_D)

$$R_A + R_D = 2 + 4 = 6 \text{ kN} \quad ...(i)$$

For $\Sigma M_A = 0$, we have,

$$R_A \times 0 + 2 \times 1.5 + 4 \times 4.5 - 6\, R_D = 0$$

or $$6R_D = 3 + 18 = 21$$

$\therefore$ $$R_D = 21/6 = 3.5 \text{ kN} \quad ...(ii)$$

But $$R_A + R_D = 6$$

$\therefore$ $$R_A = 6 - R_D = 6 - 3.5$$
$$= 2.5 \text{ kN} \quad ...(iii)$$

First of all, consider the joint *A*. Let the directions of F_{AB}. and F_{AE} be assumed as shown in Fig. 2.17

Now for $\Sigma V = 0$, we have

$$-F_{AB} \sin 60° + 2.5 = 0$$

or $$F_{AB} \sin 60° = 2.5$$

$\therefore F_{AB} = 2.5/0.866 = 2.887$ kN (Com.) **Ans.**

For $\Sigma H = 0$, we have

$$F_{AE} = F_{AB} \cos 60°$$
$$= 2.887 \times 0.5$$
$$= 1.444 \text{ kN (Tensile)} \textbf{ Ans.}$$

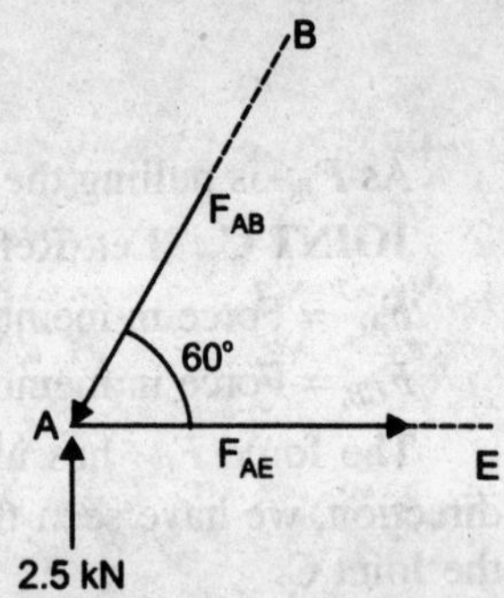

Fig. 2.17 Joint A

JOINT – D

Now consider the joint D. Let the directions of F_{CD} adn F_{ED} be as assumed in Fig. 2.18

For $\Sigma V = 0$, we have

$$-F_{CD} \sin 60° + 3.5 = 0$$

or $$F_{CD} \times 0.866 = 3.5$$

$\therefore$ $$F_{CD} = 3.5/0.866$$
$$= 4.042 \text{ kN (Comp.)}$$

For $\Sigma H = 0$, we have,

$$F_{DE} = F_{CD} \cos 60°$$
$$= 4.042 \times 0.5$$
$$F_{DE} = 2.021 \text{ kN (Tensile)} \textbf{ Ans.}$$

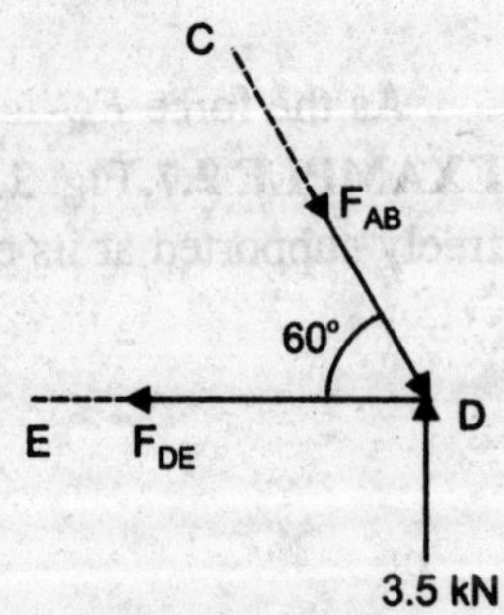

Fig. 2.18 Joint D

JOINT – B

Now consider Joint – B: We have already found that force in member *AB* i.e. F_{AB} = 2.887 kN (Comp.) Let the directions of the forces F_{BC} and F_{BE} be assumed as shown in Fig. 2.19.

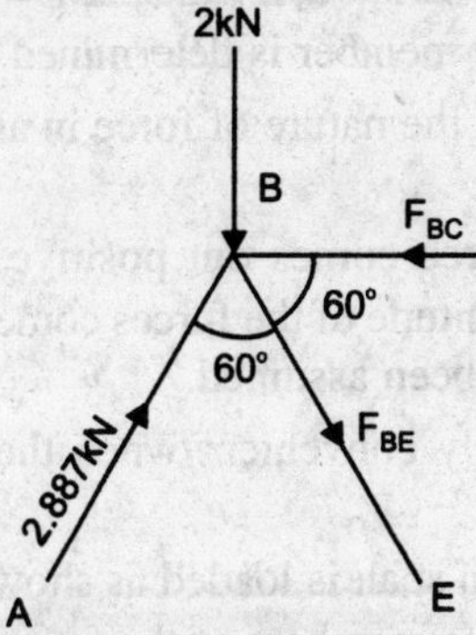

Fig. 2.19

For $\Sigma V = 0$, we have

$$2 - 2.887 \sin 60° + F_{BE} \sin 60° = 0$$

or $$2 - 2.50 + 0.886\, F_{BE} = 0$$

or $$-0.50 + 0.866\, F_{BE} = 0$$

or $$0.866\, F_{BE} = 0.50$$

$\therefore$ $$F_{BE} = \frac{0.50}{0.866} = 0.577 \text{ kN } \textbf{Ans.}$$

For $\Sigma H = 0$, we have

$$2.887 \cos 60° + F_{BE} \cos 60° - F_{BC} = 0$$

or $$2.887 \times 0.50 + 0.577 \times 0.50 = F_{BC}$$

or $$1.4435 + 0.2885 = F_{BC}$$

$\therefore$ $$F_{BC} = 1.732 \text{ kN (Compression)}$$

JOINT C

Now consider Joint – C. We have alrady found out that the forces in the members *BC* and *CD* (i.e. F_{BC} and F_{CD}) are 1.732 kN (comp.) and 4.042 kN (Comp.) respectively. Let the direction of P_{CE} be assumed as shown in Fig. 2.20.

Now for $\Sigma V = 0$, we have

$$F_{EC} \sin 60° - 4 + 4.4042 \sin 60° = 0$$

or $$0.866\, F_{EC} - 4 + 3.50 = 0$$

or $$0.866\, P_{EC} = 0.50$$

$\therefore$ $F_{EC} = 0.50/0.866 = 0.577$ kN (Comp.) **Ans.**

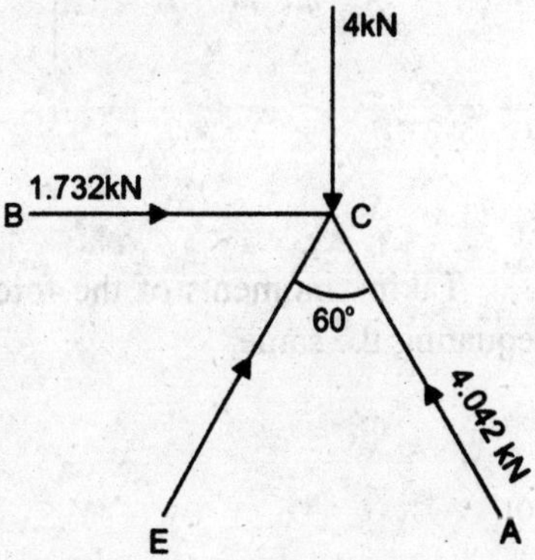

Fig. 2.20

METHOD OF SECTION : The various steps involved are:

1. The truss is split into two parts by passing an imaginary section.
2. The imaginary section has to be such that it does not cut more than three members in which the forces are to be determined.

3. The conditions of equilibrium, $\Sigma H = 0, \Sigma V = 0, \Sigma M = 0$, are applied for one part of the truss and unknown force in the member is determined.
4. While considering equilibrium, the nature of force in any member is chosen arbitrarily to be compressive or tensile.

If the magnitude of a particular force comes out positive, the assumption in respect of its direction is correct. However, if the magnitude of the forces comes out negative, the actual direction of the force is opposite to that what has been assumed.

The method of section is particularly convenient when the forces in a few members of the frame are required to be worked out.

EXAMPLE 2.8. A cantilever truss of 3m span is loaded as shown in Fig. 2.21. Find the forces in the various members of the framed truss by method of sections.

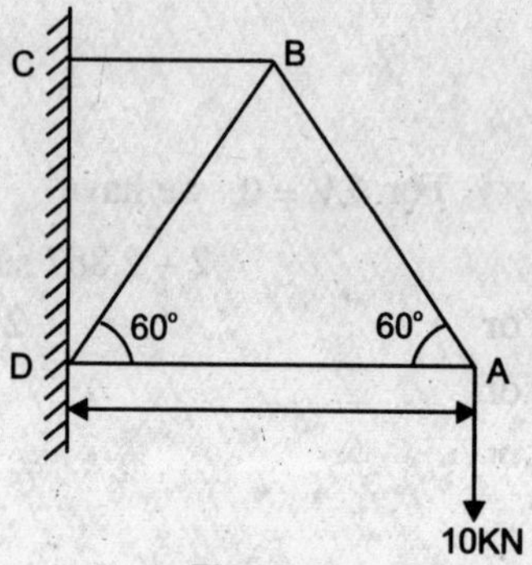

Fig. 2.21

SOLUTION : First of all, pass section (1 – 1) cutting the truss through the members *AB* and *AD*. Now consider the equilibrium of right part of the truss. Let the directions of the force F_{AB} and F_{AD} be assumed as shown in Fig. 2.22.

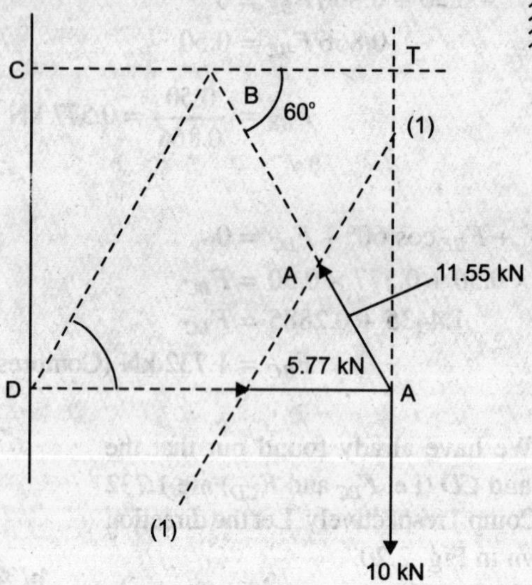

Fig. 2.22

Taking moments of the forces acting on right part of the truss only, about the joint D and equating the same,

$$3F_{AB} \sin 60° = 10 \times 3$$

or

$$F_{AB} = \frac{10 \times 3}{3 \times 0.866}$$

$$= 11.55 \text{ kN (Tension)}$$

For $\Sigma H = 0$,

$$F_{DA} = F_{AB} \cos 60°$$

$$= 11.55 \times 0.50$$

$\therefore \qquad F_{DA} = 5.77$ kN (Compressive)

$* \qquad \sin 60° = \text{Per/Diag.} = AT/AB = AT/3$

$\therefore \qquad AT = 3 \sin 60° \qquad$ ...(i)

Now pass section (2 – 2) cutting the truss through members *BC*, *BD* and *AD*. Now consider the equilibrium of the right part of the truss. Let the directions of the force F_{BC} and F_{BD} be assumed as shown in Fig. 2.23.

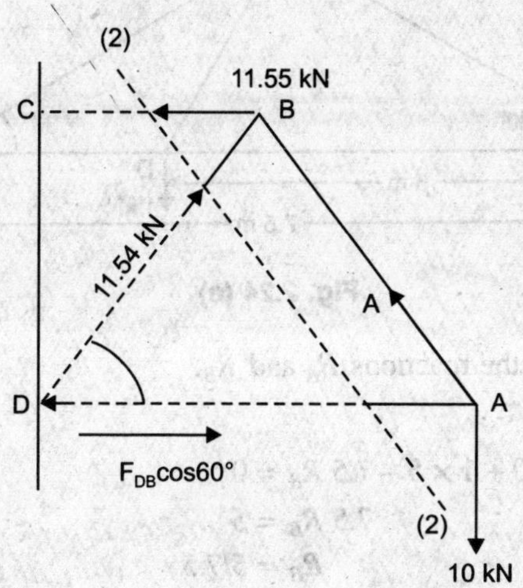

Fig. 2.23

Taking moments of the forces acting on right part of the truss only, about *D* and equating the same.

$$3 F_{BC} \sin 60° = 10 \times 3 \qquad (\because AT = 3 \sin 60°)$$

or
$$F_{BC} = \frac{10 \times 3}{3 \times 0.866} = 11.55 \text{ kN (Tension)}$$

$$F_{DA} = F_{BD} \cos 60°$$

or
$$5.77 = 0.50\, F_{BD}$$

$\therefore$
$$F_{DB} = 5.77/0.50$$
$$= 11.54 \text{ kN (Compressive)}$$ **Ans.**

GRAPHICAL METHOD

The force in perfect truss can also be determined by graphical Method. The analytical methods (such as method of joints and method of sections) give absolutely correct results, but some times it is not possible to get the results from Analytical methods. Then graphical method can be used conveniently to get the results. The graphical method also provides reasonable accurate results.

The naming of various members of a truss is done according to BOW's Notation. According to this notation a force is designated by two capital letters which are writen on either side of the line of action, as shown in Fig. 2.24. This force will be called *AB*.

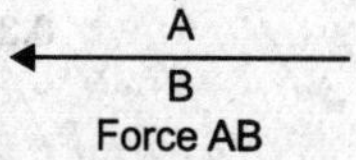

Fig. 2.24

The following steps are necessary for obtaining a graphical solution of a truss.

(i) Making a Space Diagram

(ii) Construction of Vector (Force) Diagram

(iii) Preparing a Force Table

EXAMPLE 2.9: A truss of span 7.5 m caries a point load of 1 kN at joint D as shown in Fig. 2.24(a). Find the reactions and forces in the member of the truss.

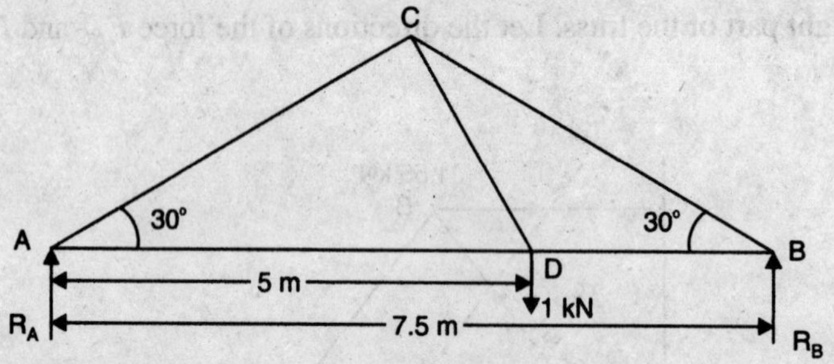

Fig. 2.24 (a)

SOLUTION : First determine the reactions R_A and R_B.

For $\Sigma M_A = 0$, we have,

$$R_A \times 0 + 1 \times 5 - 7.5\ R_B = 0$$

or $$7.5\ R_B = 5$$

$\therefore$ $$R_B = 5/7.5$$
$$= 0.667 \text{ kN}$$

$\therefore$ $$R_A + R_B = 1$$

$\therefore$ $$R_A = 1 - R_B$$
$$= 1 - 0.667$$
$$= 0.33 \text{ kN} \qquad \text{...(ii)}$$

SPACE DIAGRAM : Draw the given truss accurately on a suitable scale (say 1 cm = 1m). Load (1KN) and support reactions (0.333 kN, 0.667 kN) are also shown. Name the members of the truss *AC, CB, AD, CD* and *DB* according to BOW's Notation as *EI, EJ, IH, IJ* and *JG* respectively. Now construct the vector diagram as shown in Fig. 2.25.

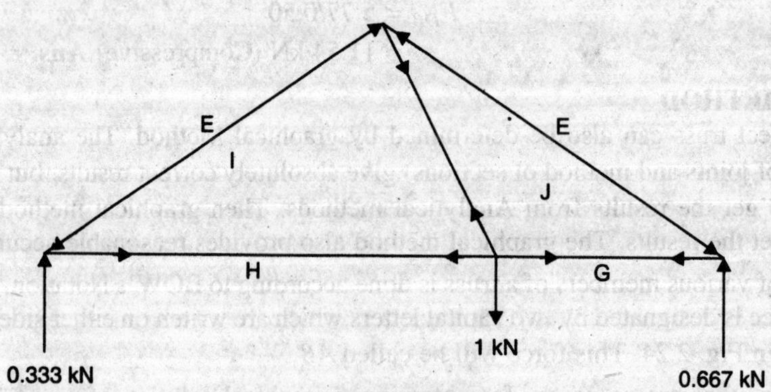

Space diagram

Fig. 2.25

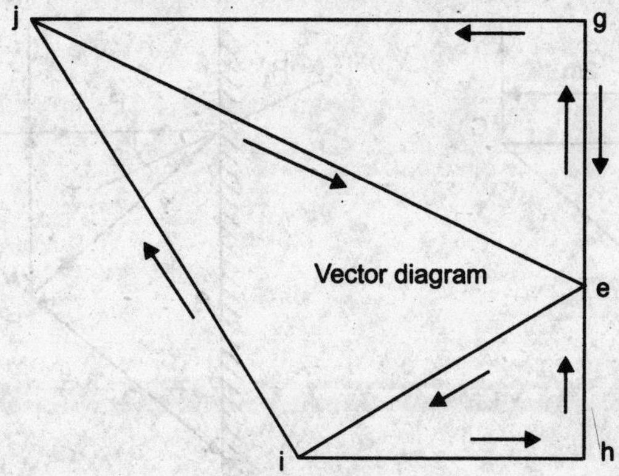

Fig. 2.26

VECTOR DIAGRAM : TAKE any point *g* and draw a Vertical load line *gh* down ward equal to load 1 kN to some suitable scale (say 1 cm = 0.1 kN). From *h* draw a vertical line *he* upward equal to 0.333 kN to the same scale to represent the reaction at *A*. The *e g* will represent the reaction R_B to the scale.

Now draw the vector diagram for joint *A*. From the point *h* of the load line *g h*, draw a line parallel to *HI* and another line parallel to *EI*, meeting the first line at *i*. Now *hei* is the vector diagram for joint *A*. Considering the real position of the vertical, i.e., towards *i* and *ih* towards *h*, mark the arrow in *EI* towards joint (Compressive) and for the member *IH*, away from the joint *A* i.e. tensile.

Now from the point *g*, draw a line parallel to *GJ* and from *e* another line parallel to *EJ*, meeting at *j*. Now *ejg* is the vector diagram for joint *B*. Join *ij* which should be parallel to *IJ*.

Now measure the various sides of the vector diagrams. The forces in the members are obtained by multiplying the scale factor to the corresponding sides of the vector diagram. The forces in the members are given in a tabular forms as

EXAMPLE 2.10: Reaction : $R_A = 0.333$ kN, $R_B = 0.667$ kN

S.No.	Members	Force	Nature
1	EI	0.63 kN	Compressive
2	IH	0.55 kN	Tensile
3	EJ	1.33 kN	Compressive
4	JG	1.13 kN	Tensile
5	IJ	1.16 kN	Tensile

Determine the forces in all the members of a cantilever truss shown in Fig. 2.27

SOLUTION: In this case the vector diagram can be drawn without knowing the reactions. First draw the space diagram as shown in Fig. 2.28. Vector diagram is shown in Fig. 2.29.

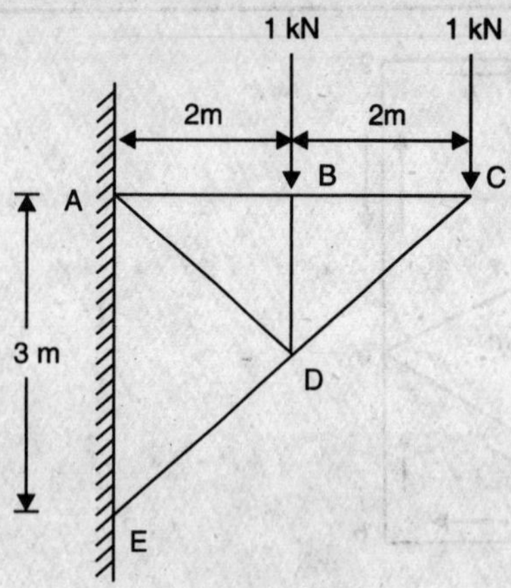

Fig. 2.27

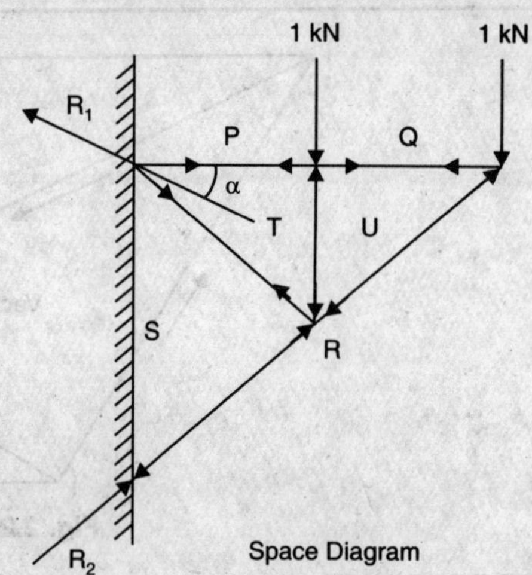

Space Diagram

Fig. 2.28

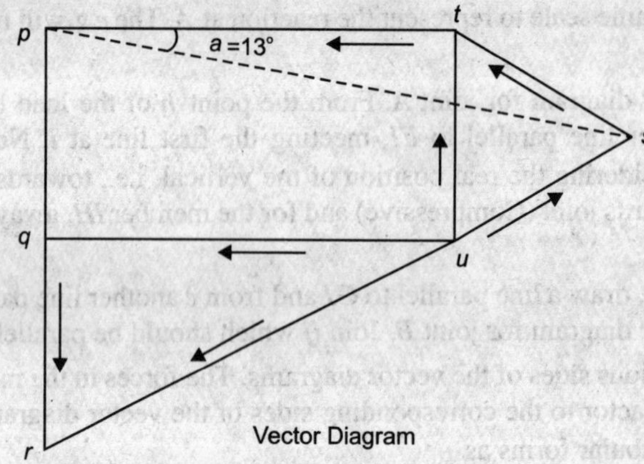

Fig. 2.29

S.No.	Members	Force	Nature
1	RU	1.660 kN	Compressive
2	UQ	1.440 kN	Tensile
3	RS	2.650 kN	Compressive
4	ST	0.840 kN	Tensile
5	TU	1.02 kN	Compressive
6.	PT	1.440 kN	Tensile

EXAMPLE 2.11: A cantilener truss is loaded and supported as shown in Fig. 2.30. Find the value of loads ρ which would produce an axial force of magnitude 3 kN in the member *AC*.

SOLUTION : In this case we need not to determine the support reactions.

The force in the members *AC* can be determined using the method of Sections.

Pass a section *mn* cutting the members *AC*, *CD* and *DF*. Consider the equilibrium of thc right hand portion of the truss.

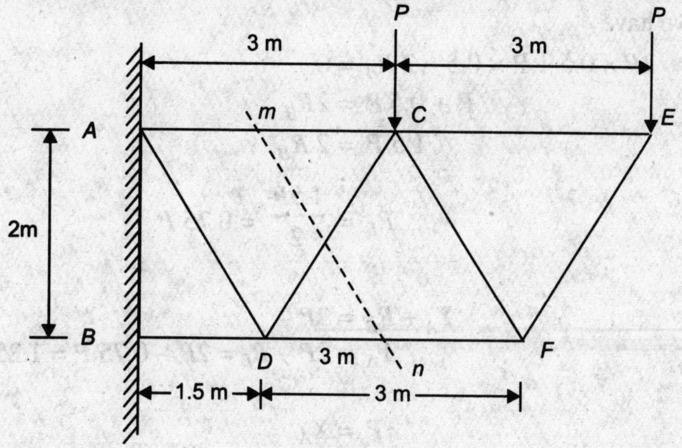

Fig. 2.30

Now taking moment about D i.e. for $\Sigma M_D = 0$, we have

$$P \times 1.5 + P \times 4.5 = F_{AC} \times 2$$

or
$$1.5\,P + 4.5\,P = 2\,F_{AC}$$

or
$$6P = 2\,F_{AC}$$

$\therefore$
$$3P = F_{AC}$$

But as per condition given in the question

$$F_{AC} = 3 \text{ kN}$$

$\therefore$
$$3P = 3 \text{ kN}$$

Hence $P = 1$ kN **Ans.**

EXAMPLE 2.12: Find the force in the member CF of the truss loaded and supported as shown in Fig. 2.31

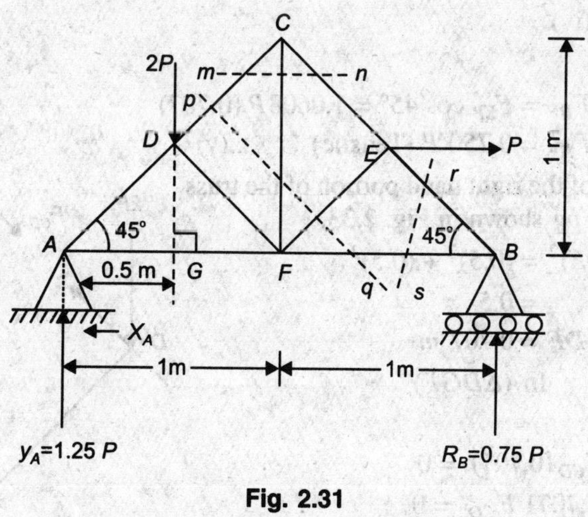

Fig. 2.31

SOLUTION :

Support Reactions : Consider the equilibrium of the entire truss as free body diagram.

For $\Sigma M_A = 0$, we have

$$2P \times 0.5 + P \times 0.5 - 2R_B = 0$$

or $$P + 0.5P = 2R_B$$

or $$1.5P = 2R_B$$

$$\therefore \quad R_B = \frac{1.5P}{2} = 0.75P \quad \text{...(i)}$$

For $\Sigma V = 0$

$$Y_A + R_B = 2P$$

or $$Y_A = 2P - R_B = 2P - 0.75P = 1.25P \quad \text{...(ii)}$$

For $\Sigma H = 0$,

$$P = X_A$$

$$\therefore \quad X_A = P \quad \text{...(iii)}$$

To find the force in the member *CF* let us consider the section through the line *mn*. Three members are cut but these are concurrent, so we can not solve for the three unknowns.

If we take the section through the line *pq*, then 4 members are cut.

So, first pass a section through *rs* cutting the members *BE* and *BF* as shown in Fig. 2.32

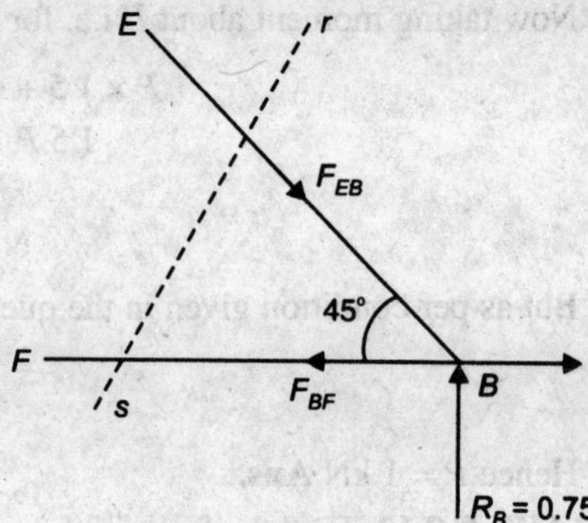

Fig. 2.32

For $\Sigma V = 0$, we have

$$F_{EB} \sin 45° = R_B = 0.75P$$

or $$F_{EB} \times 0.707 = 0.75P$$

$$\therefore \quad F_{EB} = \frac{0.75P}{0.707} = 1.0608P \text{ (Com.)} \quad \text{...(iv)}$$

For $\Sigma H = 0$, we have

$$F_{BF} = F_{EB} \cos 45° = 1.0608P\,(0.707)$$

$$\therefore \quad F_{BF} = 0.750P \text{ (Tensile)} \quad \text{...(v)}$$

Consider the equilibrium of the right hand portion of the truss as obtained by the section *pq* shown in Fig. 2.33.

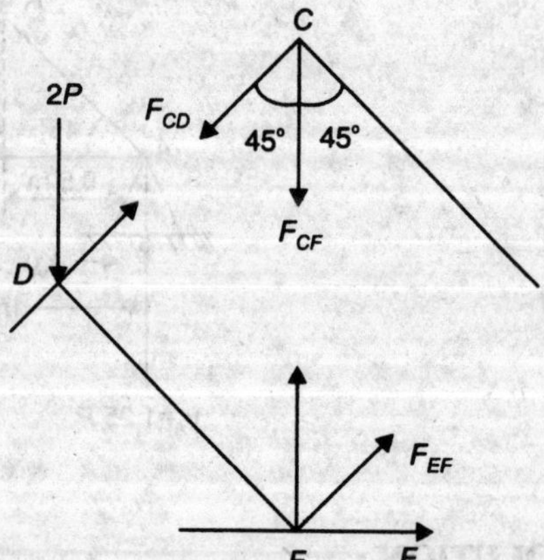

Fig. 2.33

$$\because \quad (DF)^2 = (0.5)^2 + (0.5)^2$$

$$= 0.5$$

$$\therefore \quad DF = 0.707\ m$$

In (ΔDGF)

For $M_F = 0$

$$-0.75P(1) + P(0.5) + F_{CD}(0.707) = 0$$

$$-0.25P + .7071 F_{CD} = 0$$

$$\therefore \quad F_{CD} = \frac{0.25P}{0.7071} = 0.354P \text{ (Comp.)}$$

For $M_C = 0$

$$-0.75\,P\,(1) + P\,(0.5) - F_{BF}\,(1) - F_{EF}\,(0.7071) = 0 \qquad (\because\ F_{BF} = 0.750\,P)$$

or $$-0.25\,P + 0.750\,P + F_{EF}\,(.7071) = 0$$

or $$0.50P = +\,F_{EF}\,(.7071)$$

$\therefore$ $$F_{EF} = \frac{0.50\text{ P}}{0.7071} = 0.7071\text{ P}$$

Taking moment about *A, i.e., for* $\Sigma M_A = 0$

$$-0.75\,P(2) + P\,(0.5) + F_{CF}\,(1) + F_{EF}\sin 45°(1) = 0$$

or $$-1.50P + 0.5P + F_{CF} + F_{EF}\,(1 \times 7.071) = 0$$

$$-P + F_{CF} + 0.707\,P\,(0.707) = 0$$

or $$-P + F_{CF} + 0.4999\,P = 0$$

or $$0.5P = F_{CF}$$

$\therefore$ $F_{CF} = 0.5\,P$ (Tensile) **Ans.**

EXAMPLE 2.13: A truss is loaded and supported as shown in Fig. 2.34. Determine the axial forces in the members *CE, CG* and *FG.*

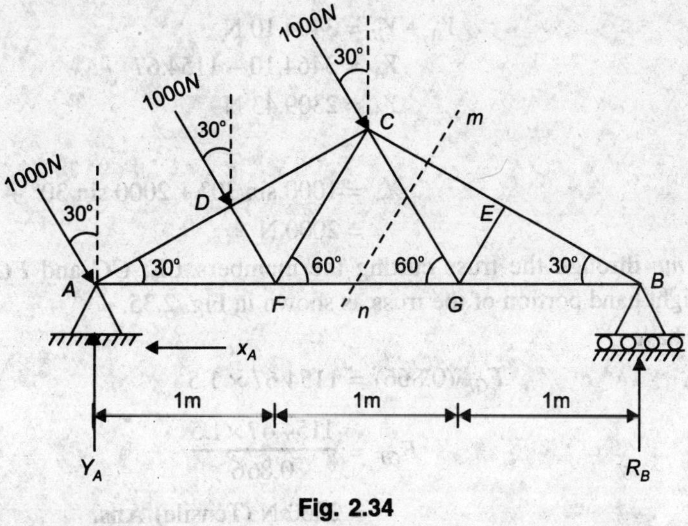

Fig. 2.34

SOLUTION : Support Reactions : Consider the equilibrium of the entire truss as a free body.

Taking moment about *A*, i.e. for $\Sigma M_A = 0$

$$2000 \times AD + 1000 \times AC = 3R_B$$

or $$2000\,(AF\cos 30°) + 1000\,(AG\cos 30°) = 3R_B$$

or $$2000\,(1 \times 0.866) + 1000\,(2 \times 0.866) = 3R_B$$

or $$3464 = 3R_B$$

$\therefore$ $$R_B = 3464/3$$

$$= 1154.67\text{ N}$$

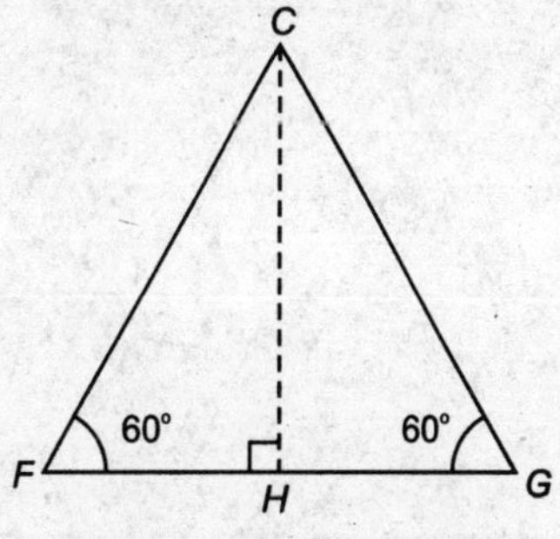

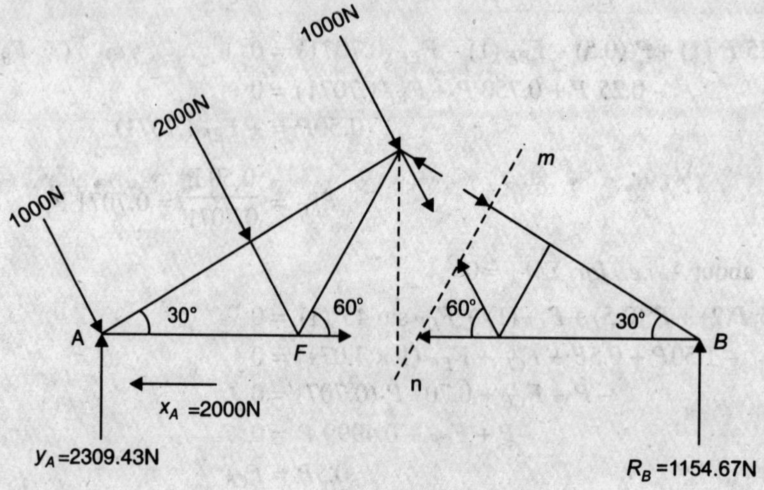

Fig. 2.35

For $\Sigma V = 0$

$$Y_A + R_B = 1000 \cos 30° + 2000 \cos 30° + 1000 \cos 30°$$

or $$Y_A + Y_B = 3464.10 \text{ N}$$

or $$Y_A = 3464.10 - 1154.67$$

$\therefore$ $$Y_A = 2309.43 \text{ N}$$

For $\Sigma H = 0$

$$X_A = 1000 \sin 30° + 2000 \sin 30° + 1000 \sin 30°$$
$$= 2000 \text{ N}$$

Pass a section *mn* through the truss cutting the members *CE*, *CG* and *FG*. Consider the equilibrium of the right hand portion of the truss as shown in Fig. 2.35.

For $M_C = 0$, we have

$$F_{GF} (0.866) = 1154.67 \times 1.5$$

$\therefore$ $$F_{GF} = \frac{1154.67 \times 1.5}{0.866}$$

$$= 2000 \text{ N (Tensile)}$$ **Ans.**

In right angled ΔCHF

$$(CF)^2 = (FH)^2 + (CH)^2$$
$$(1)^2 = (.5)^2 + (CH)^2$$
$$(1)^2 - (0.5)^2 = (CH)^2$$
$$\sqrt{0.75} = CH = 0.866 \ m$$

$\because$ $$\sin 30° = \frac{\text{Per}}{\text{Diag.}} = \frac{GE}{GB}$$

$\therefore$ $$GE = GB \sin 30°$$
$$= 1 \times \sin 30° = 0.5 \ m$$

For $M_G = 0$

$$F_{CE}\,(1 \times \sin 30°) = R_B\,(1)$$

or
$$0.50\,F_{CE} = 1154.67$$

∴
$$F_{CE} = 1154.67/0.50$$
$$= 2309.34 \text{ N (Comp) } \textbf{Ans.}$$

For $M_B = 0$

$$F_{CG}\ \sin 60°\ (1) = R_B \times 0$$

∴
$$F_{CG} = 0\ \textbf{Ans.}$$

EXAMPLE 2.14: Find the forces in the members of a cantilever truss shown in Fig. 2.36

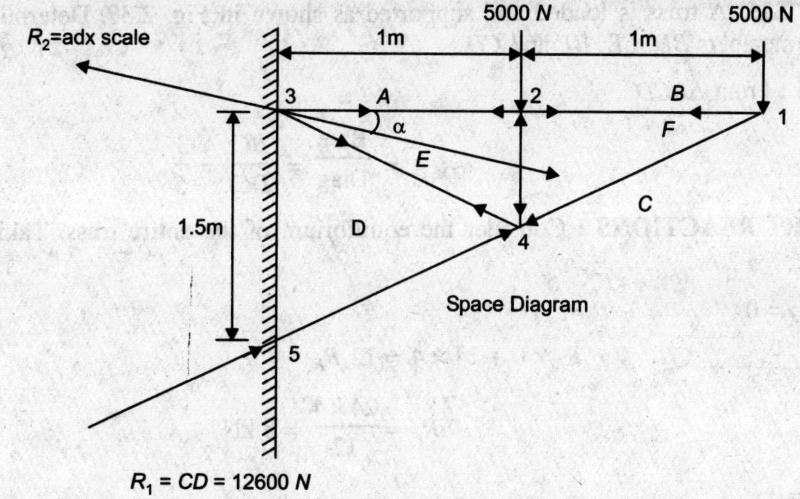

Fig. 2.36

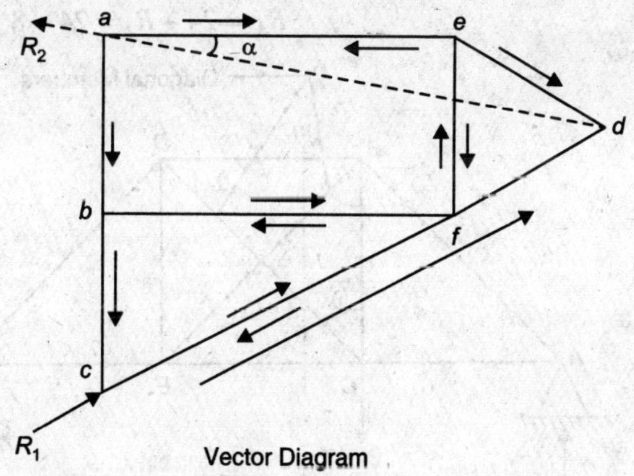

Fig. 2.37

S.No.	Members	Force	Nature
1	BF	6800 N	Tension
2	CF	8600 N	Compression
3	AE	6800 N	Tension
4	EF	5000 N	Compression
5	CD	12600 N	Compression
6.	DE	4100 N	Tension

EXAMPLE 2.15: A truss is loaded and supported as shown in Fig. 2.38. Determine the axial forces in the members *BD*, *CE*, *BE* and *CD*.

SOLUTION : From ΔBCD

$$\cos\theta = \frac{\text{Base}}{\text{Diag}} = \frac{BC}{DC} = \frac{3}{5}$$

SUPPORT REACTIONS : Consider the equilibrium of the entire truss. Taking moment about A.

$$\Sigma M_A = 0$$

$$R_A \times 0 + 24 \times 4 = 12\ R_F$$

$$\therefore \quad R_F = \frac{24 \times 4}{12} = 8\text{ kN}$$

For $\Sigma V = 0$

$$R_A + R_F = 24$$

$$\therefore \quad R_A = 24 - R_F = 24 - 8 = 16\text{ kN}$$

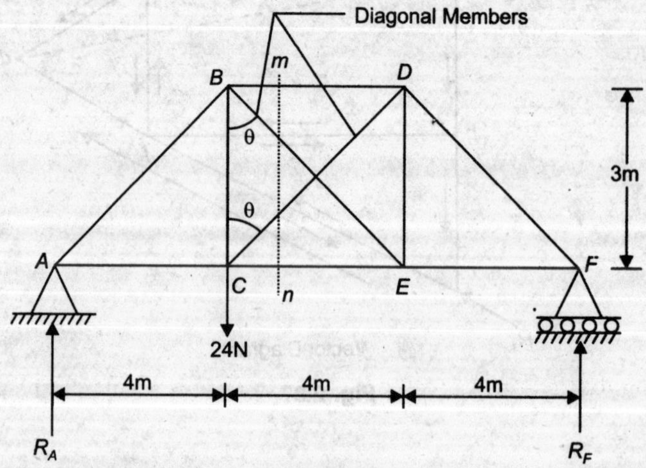

Fig. 2.38

Pass a section *m n*, which cuts *BD*, *BE*, *CD* and *CE* members. Consider the equilibrium of the left hand portion of the truss as shown in Fig. 2.39

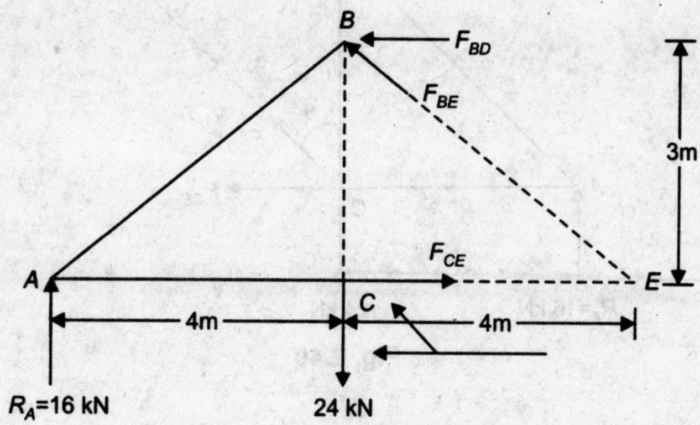

Fig. 2.39

Assume the member *BE* to be in compression and disregard the member *CD*.

For $\Sigma M_B = 0$

$$4R_A = (BC)F_{CE}$$

or $$4 \times 16 = 3\,F_{CE}$$

∴ $$F_{CE} = \frac{4\times16}{3}$$

$$= 21.33 \text{ kN (Tension)}$$

$$3F_{BD} + 24 \times 4 = 16 \times 8 \text{ (For } \Sigma M_E = 0)$$

∴ $$F_{BD} = \frac{(16\times8)-(24\times4)}{3} = 10.67 \text{ kN (Comp)}$$

For $\Sigma V = 0$

$$R_A + F_{BE}(\cos\theta) = 24$$

or $$16 + F_{BE}\left(\frac{3}{5}\right) = 24$$

or $$F_{BE} = (24-16)\left(\frac{5}{3}\right)$$

$$= \frac{8\times5}{3} = 13.33 \text{ kN (Comp)}$$

Now assuming the member *CD* to be in Tension and dis-regarding the member *BE*, as shown in Fig. 2.40.

For $\Sigma M_C = 0$

$$4R_A = 3F_{BD}$$

or $$4 \times 16 = 3\,F_{BD}$$

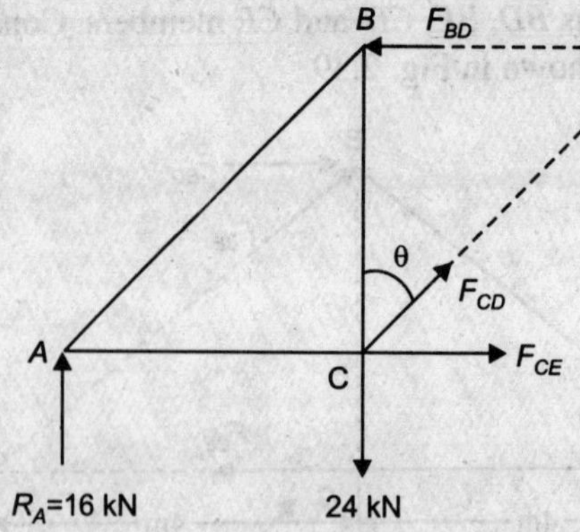

Fig. 2.40

$$\therefore \qquad F_{BD} = \frac{64}{3} = 21.33 \text{ kN (Comp.) } \textbf{Ans.}$$

For $\Sigma M_D = 0$

$$3F_{CE} + 24 \times 4 = 16 \times 8$$

$$\therefore \qquad F_{CE} = \frac{(16 \times 8) - (24 \times 4)}{3} = 10.66 \text{ kN (Tension) } \textbf{Ans.}$$

For $\Sigma V = 0$

$$F_{CD} \cos \theta + R_A = 24$$

or
$$F_{CD}\left(\frac{3}{5}\right) + 16 = 24$$

$$\therefore \qquad F_{CD} = (24 - 16)\frac{5}{3}$$

$$= \frac{40}{3} = 10.33 \text{ kN (Tension) } \textbf{Ans.}$$

Member *CD* is found to be in Tension. So this choice is correct. Hence the forces found in members *CE*, *BD* and *CD* are correct.

EXAMPLE 2.16. A plane truss is supported and loaded as shown in Fig. 2.41. Find the axial forces in members *CD*, *EF* and *CF* by method of sections.

SOLUTION : Support Reactions : Consider the equilibrium of the entire truss.

For $\Sigma M_A = 0$

$$R_A\,(0) + 30 \times 2 = 6\,R_B$$

$$\therefore \qquad R_B = 60/6 = 10 \text{ kN} \qquad \text{...(i)}$$

For $\Sigma V = 0$

$$R_A + R_B = 30$$

or
$$R_A = 30 - R_B = 30 - 10 = 20 \text{ kN}$$

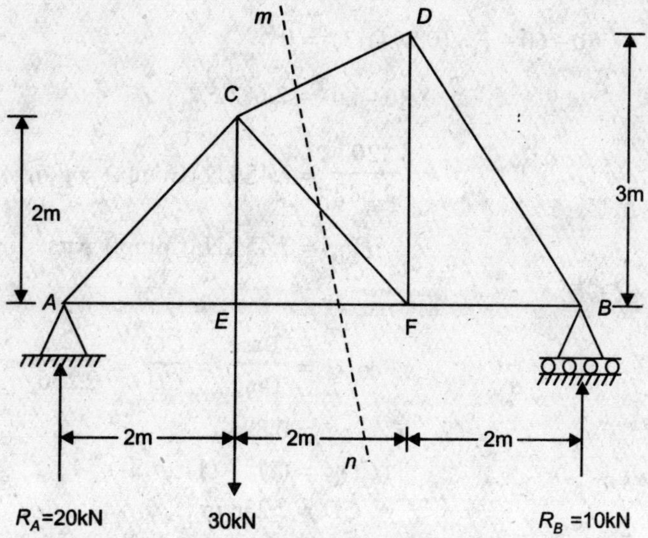

Fig. 2.41

Pass a section *mn* through the truss. Consider the equilibrium of the left hand portion of the truss as shown in Fig. 2.42

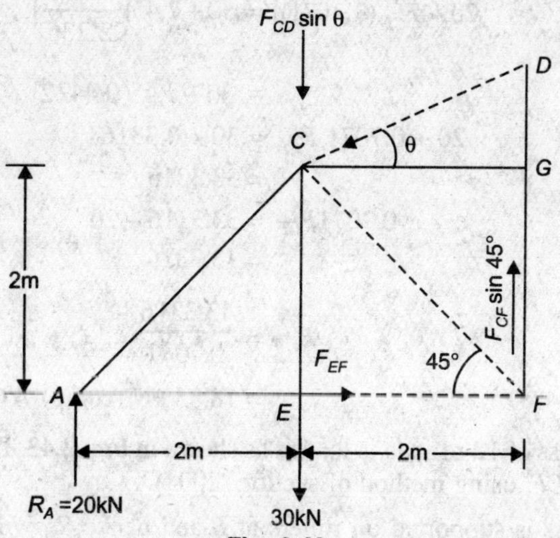

Fig. 2.42

For $\Sigma M_C = 0$

$$2R_A = E_{EF}\ (CE)$$

or
$$2 \times 20 = 2F_{EF}$$

∴
$$F_{EF} = 40/2 = 20 \text{ kN (Tension)} \textbf{ Ans.}$$

Now for $\Sigma M_F = 0$

$$4R_A - 30\times2 - F_{CD}\cos\theta\ (3) = 0$$

or
$$4\times20 - 30\times2 - 3F_{CD}\cdot\cos\theta = 0$$

or $$80-60-F_{CD}(0.894)(3)=0$$

or $$80-60 = 2.682\,F_{CD}$$

or $$\frac{20}{2.682} = 7.45 \text{ kN (Comp.)} = F_{CD}$$

$\therefore$ $$F_{CD} = 7.45 \text{ kN (Comp.) } \textbf{Ans.}$$

In right angled ΔCGD:

$$\cos\theta = \frac{\text{Base}}{\text{Diag.}} = \frac{CG}{CD} = \frac{2}{2.236}$$

$$= 0.894$$

$$(CD)^2 = (2)^2 + (1)^2$$

$\therefore$ $$CD = 2.236 \text{ m}$$

For $\Sigma V = 0$

$$R_A + F_{CF}\sin 45° = 30 + F_{CD}\sin\theta$$

or $$20 + F_{CF}(0.7071) = 30 + 7.45\left(\frac{1}{2.236}\right)$$

$$= 30 + 7.45(0.4422)$$

or $$20 + 0.7071\,F_{CF} = 30 + 3.3316$$

$$= 33.3316$$

or $$0.7071F_{CF} = 33.3116 - 20$$

$$= 13.3316$$

$\therefore$ $$F_{CF} = \frac{13.3316}{0.7071}$$

$$= 18.85 \text{ kN (comp) } \textbf{Ans.}$$

EXAMPLE 2.17. A truss of 12 m span is loaded as shown in Fig. 2.43. Determine the forces in the members *DG*, *DF* and *EF*, using method of section (2004).

SOLUTION : The truss is supported on rollers at *B* and hence R_B will be vertical. The truss is hinged at *A* and hence the support sections at *A* will consist of a horizontal section H_A and a vertical section R_A.

In $\Delta\, AEC$,

$$AC = AE\cos 30°$$

$$(\because \cos 30° = \text{Base/Diagonal} = AC/AE)$$

$\therefore$ $$AC = 4(0.866) = 3.464\ m$$

Now length,

$$AD = AC + CD = 2AC$$

$$= 2\,(3.464) = 6.928\ m$$

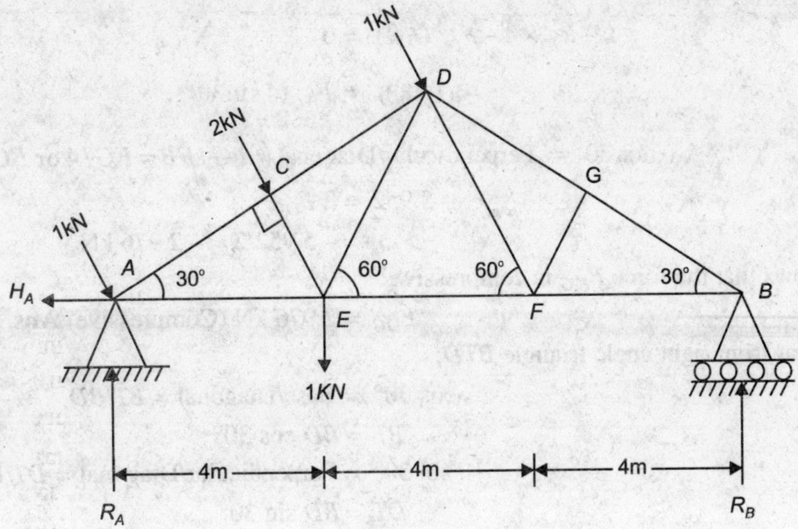

Fig. 2.43

Now taking moment about A i.e.,

for $\Sigma M_A = 0$

$$2 \times AC + 1 \times AD + 1 \times AE - R_B(12) = 0$$

or $$12\ R_B = 2\ (3.466) + 1(6.928) + 1 \times 4$$

or $$12\ R_B = 17.856$$

$\therefore$ $$R_B = \frac{17.856}{12} = 1.488 \text{ kN}$$

Now Draw a section line (1 – 1), passing through the members DG, DF and FE in which the forces are to be determined. Consider the equilibrium of right part of the truss. This part is shown in Fig. 2.44. Let F_{DG}, F_{FD} and F_{EF} are the forces in members DG, FD, and EF respectively. Let their directions are as assumed as shown in Fig. 2.44. Taking moments of all forces acting on right part about point F, we get,

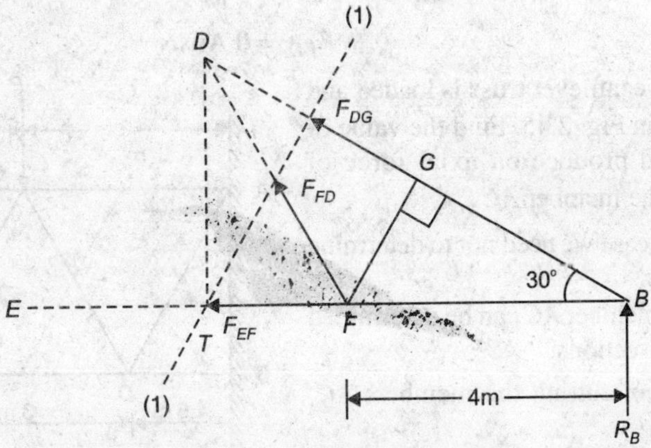

Fig. 2.44

$$-R_B \times 4 - F_{DG}(FG) = 0$$

or
$$-4(1.488) = F_{DG}(4\sin 30°)$$

$$(\because \sin 30^0 = \text{Perpendicular/Diagonal} = FG/FB = FG/4 \text{ or } FG = 4\sin 30^0)$$

or
$$-5.952 = 2\,F_{DG}$$

$\therefore$
$$F_{DG} = -5.952/2 = -2.976 \text{ kN}$$

–ve sign shows that the force F_{DG} is compressive

Hence
$$F_{DG} = 2.976 \text{ kN (Compressive)} \textbf{ Ans.}$$

We know that from right angle triangle *BTD*;

$\because$
$$\cos 30° = \text{Base/Diagonal} = BT/BD$$

$\therefore$
$$BT = BD\cos 30°$$

$\because$
$$\sin 30° = \text{Perpendicular/Diagonal} = DT/BD$$

$\therefore$
$$DT = BD\sin 30°$$

Now taking moment about point *D*, we get

$$-R_B(BT) + F_{EF}(DT) = 0$$

or
$$-R_B(BD\cos 30°) + F_{EF}(BD\sin 30°) = 0$$

or
$$-(1.488)(6.928\cos 30°) + F_{EF}(6.928\sin 30°) = 0$$

or
$$-(1.488)(5.999) + F_{EF}(3.464) = 0$$

or
$$-8.9265 + 3.464\,F_{EF} = 0$$

or
$$3.464\,F_{EF} = 8.9265$$

$\therefore$
$$F_{EF} = \frac{8.9265}{3.464} = 2.577 \text{ kN (Tensile)} \textbf{ Ans.}$$

For $M_B = 0$, we have

$$F_{FD}\sin 60^0(4) = R_B(0)$$

$\therefore$
$$F_{FD} = 0 \textbf{ Ans.}$$

EXAMPLE 2.18. A cantilever truss is loaded and supported as shown in Fig. 2.45. Find the value of load *P* which would produce on axial force of magnitude 3 kN in the member *AC*.

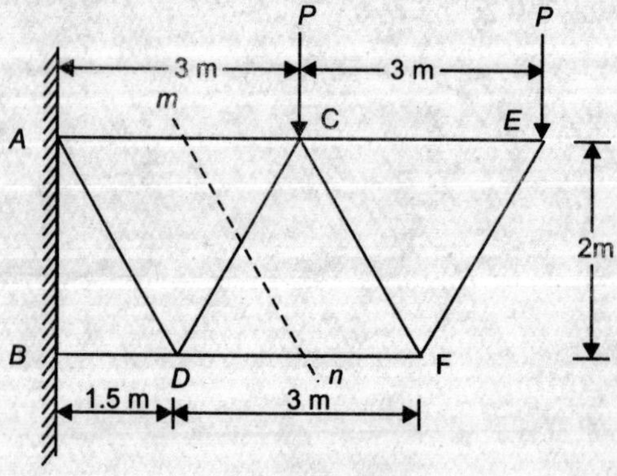

Fig. 2.45

SOLUTION: In this case we need not to determine the support reactions.

The force in the member *AC* can be determined using the method of sections.

Pass a section *mn* cutting the members *AC*, *CD* and *DF*

Consider the equilibrium of the right hand portion of the truss.

Now taking moment about D i.e.

for $\Sigma M_D = 0$, we have

$$P \times 1.5 + P \times 4.5 = F_{AC}\,(2)$$

or $$6P = 2F_{AC}$$

∴ $$3P = F_{AC}$$

But as per condition given in the question

$$F_{AC} = 3 \text{ kN}$$

∴ $$3P = 3 \text{ kN}$$

Hence $$P = 1 \text{ kN} \textbf{ Ans.}$$

EXAMPLE 2.19. A truss is loaded and supported as shown in Fig. 2.46 Find the axial forces in the members AB, EF and CD.

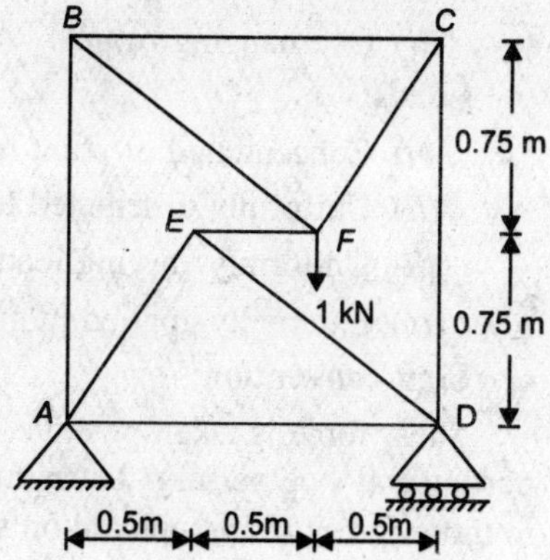

Fig. 2.46

SOLUTION : Pass a section 1 – 1 cutting the truss through the members AB, EF, and CD as shown in Fig. 2.47.

Now consider the equilibrium of the upper portion (dark) of the frame. Let the directions of the forces F_{AB}, F_{CD} be assumed as shown in Fig. 2.47.

Now consider joint F. We know that horizontal component of 1 kN load is zero.

Hence force in the member EF = 0 **Ans.**

Now taking moments of the forces acting on the upper portion of the frame only about the joint A, and equating the same, i.e.

for $\Sigma M_A = 0$, we have

$$F_{CD} \times 1.5 = 1 \times 1$$

or $$F_{CD} = 1/1.5 = 0.667 \text{ kN (Comp). } \textbf{Ans.}$$

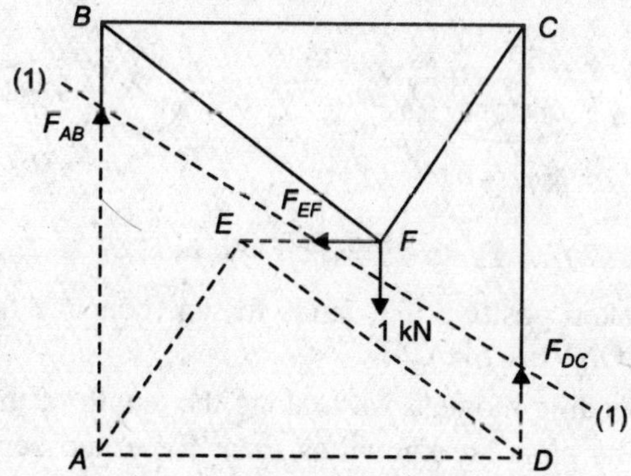

Fig. 2.47

EXAMPLE 2.20. What is a truss? Distinguish clearly between a perfect truss and an imperfect truss. Name the different methods employed for finding out forces in a truss.

SHEAR FORCE AND BENDING MOMENT DIAGRAMS

SHEAR FORCE : It is unblanced force on eiher side of a section.

BENDING MOMENT : The bending moment (B.M.) at a cross-section of a beam may be defined as the algebriac sum of the moments of the forces, to the right or left of the section.

KEY POINTS

Shear Force and Bending Moment Diagrams

Beam:

A beam is a horizontal structural member subjected generally to vertical loads.

(*i*) Cantilever beams

(*ii*) Simply supported bemas and

(*iii*) Overhanging beams.

Loads:

(*i*) Concentrated or point loads,

(*ii*) Uniformly distributed loads (U.D.L.),

(*iii*) Uniformly varying loads (U.D.L.),

(*iv*) Externally applied moments.

Sign convention:

Shear force is taken positive if it tends to move the left portion upward with respect to right portion and vice-versa. A better rule of sign, which is easier to remember is to give a positive sign to those forces acting upward on the LEFT PORTION.

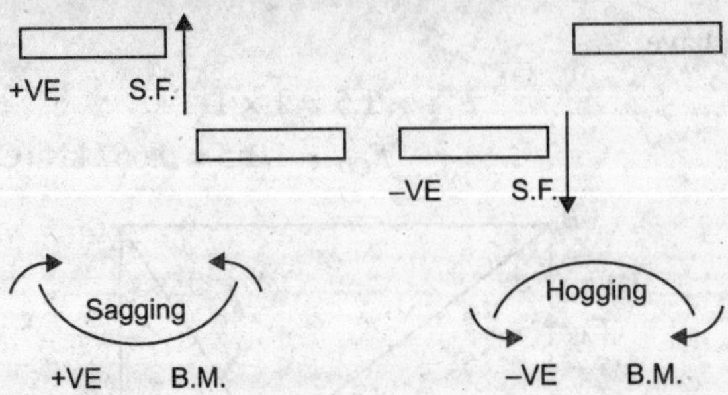

Fig. 2.47 (a)

Bending moment is taken positive if it tends to sag (concave form) the beam, and if it is negative it tends to hog (CONVEX SHAPE).

The shear force and bending moment vary, along the length of the beam and the variation is represented graphically. The plots are known as shear force and bending moment diagrams. In these diagrams, the abscissa indicates the position of the section along the beam, and the ordinate represents the value of S.F. and B.M. respectively. These plots help to determine the maximum value of each of these quantities.

EXAMPLE 2.21. Construct the shear force and bending moment diagrams for the cantilever loaded as shown in Fig. 2.48.

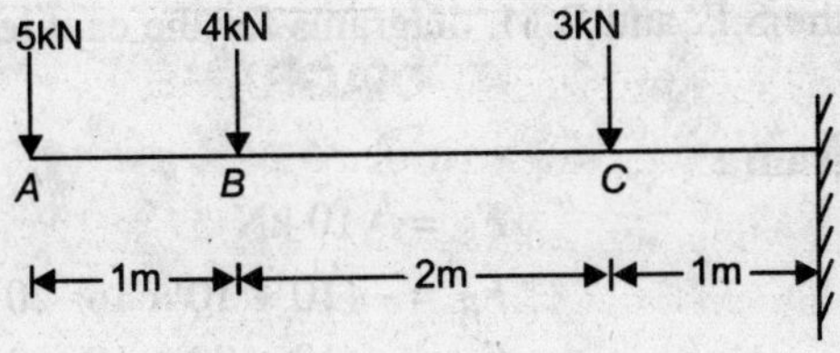

Fig. 2.48

SOLUTION :

S.F. Diagram : we know that :

$$F_A = -5 \text{ kN},$$
$$F_B = -(5+4)$$
$$= -9 \text{ kN}$$
$$F_C = -(9+3)$$
$$= -12 \text{ kN},$$
$$F_D = -12 \text{ kN}$$

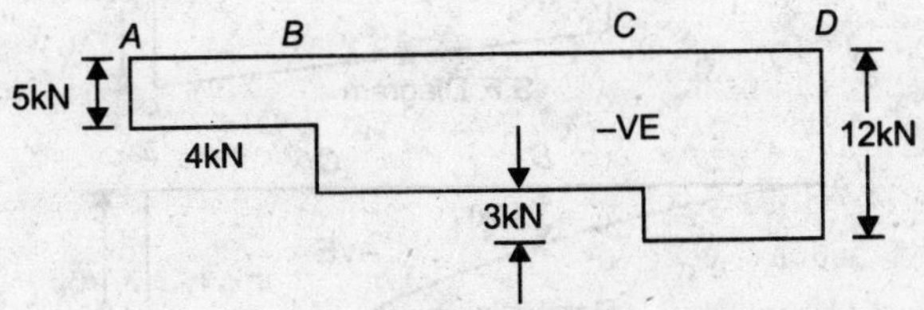

S.F. Diagram

For B.M. Diagram :

$$M_A = 0$$
$$M_b = (5 \times 1)$$
$$= -5 \text{ kN m}$$
$$M_c = -(5 \times 3) + (-4 \times 2)$$
$$= -23 \text{ kN m}$$
$$M_d = -(5 \times 4) + (-4 \times 3) + (-3 \times 1)$$
$$= -35 \text{ kN m}$$

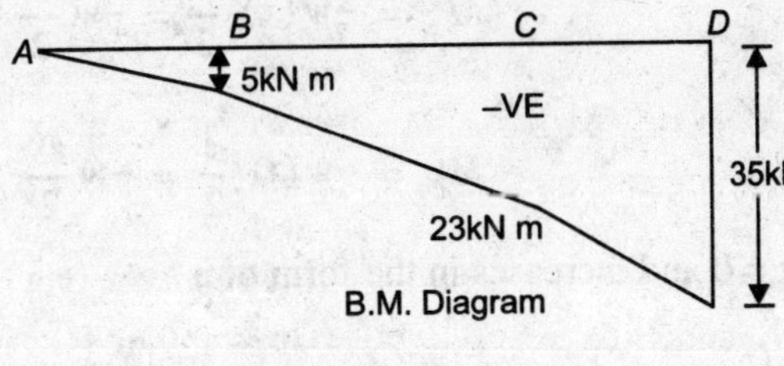

B.M. Diagram

EXAMPLE 2.22. Construct the S.F. and B.M. diagrams for the cantilever beam loaded as shown in Fig. 2.49.

SOLUTION : For S.F. Diagram :

$$F_A = -\ 10 \text{ kN}$$
$$F_B = -\ (10 + 10 \times 1 + 20) = -\ 40 \text{ kN}$$
$$F_C = -\ (10 + 20 + 10 \times 3) = -\ 60 \text{ kN}$$

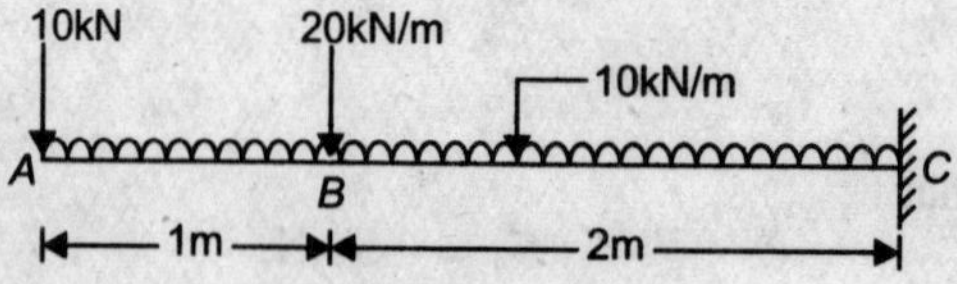

Fig. 2.49

The S.F. Diagram indicates the values of S.F. at salient points

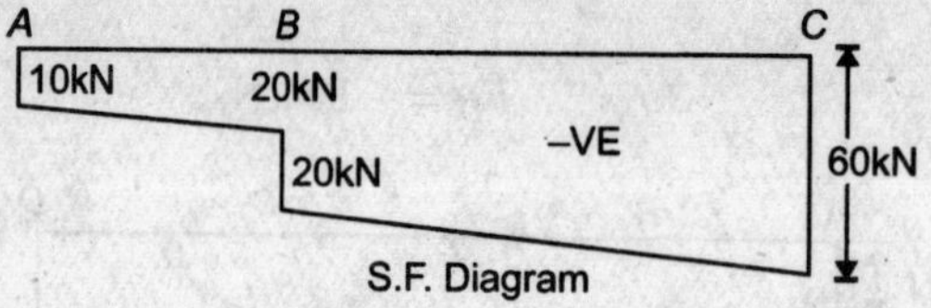

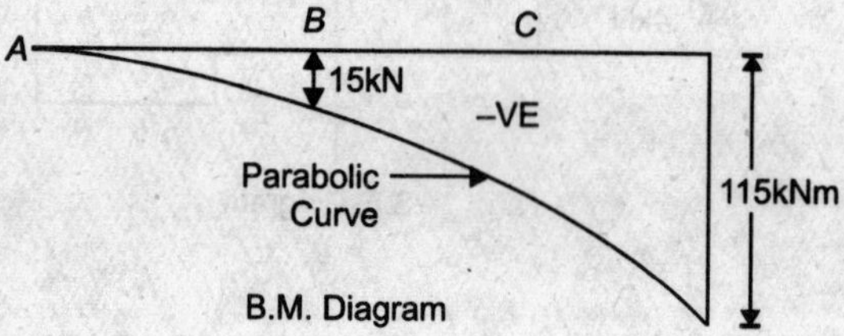

For B.M. Daigram :

$$M_A = 0$$
$$M_B = -\ (10 \times 1 + 10 \times 1 \times 0.5) = -\ 15 \text{ kN m}$$
$$M_C = -\ (10 \times 3 + 20 \times 2 + 10 \times 3 \times 1.5)$$
$$= -\ (30 + 40 + 45) = -\ 115 \text{ kN } m$$
$$M_A = 0,$$

$$M_x = -w\,(x)\cdot\frac{x}{2} = -w\,\frac{x^2}{2}$$

$$M_L = -w\,(\ell)\cdot\frac{\ell}{2} = -w\,\frac{\ell^2}{2}$$

B.M. at $A = 0$ (where $x = 0$ and increases in the form of a

Parabolic Curve to $-\dfrac{w\ell^2}{2}$ at C (where $x = \ell$) (Refer) Fig. 2.50.

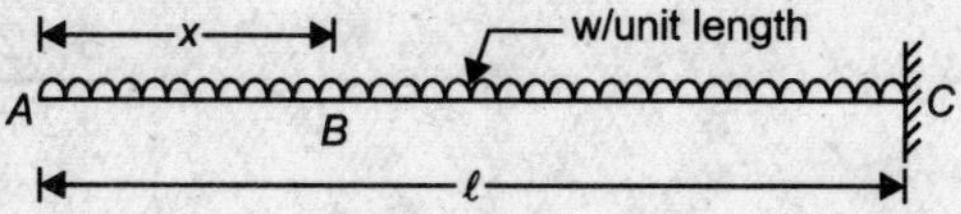

Fig. 2.50

EXAMPLE 2.23. A cantilever beam of 1.5 m span is loaded as shown in Fig. 2.51. Draw S.F. and B.M. Diagrams.

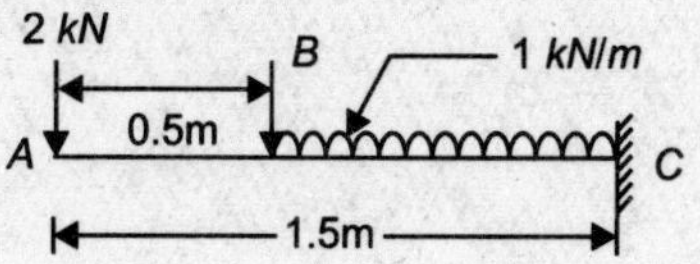

Fig. 2.51

SOLUTION : For S.F. Diagram :

$$F_A = -2 \text{ kN},$$

$$F_B = -2 \text{ kN}$$

$$F_C = -(2 + 1 \times 1)$$

$$= -3 \text{ kN}$$

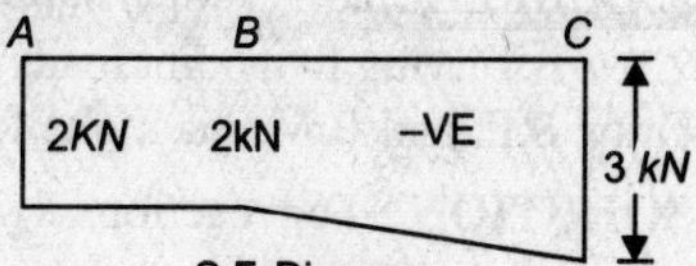

For B.M. Diagram :

$$M_A = 0$$

$$M_B = -(2 \times 0.5)$$

$$= -1 \text{ kN m}$$

$$M_C = -[(2 \times 1.5) + (1 \times 1)\, 1/2]$$

$$= -3.5 \text{ kN m}$$

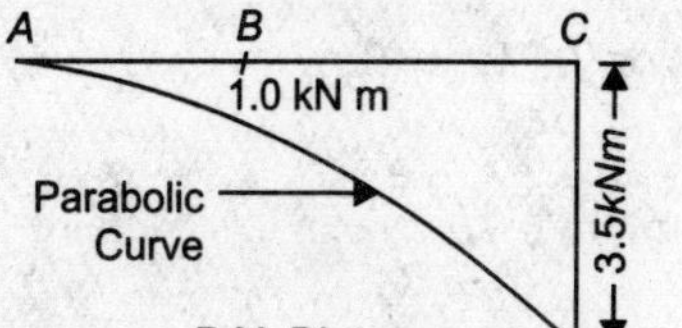

EXAMPLE 2.24. A cantilever beam of 2 m span is subjected to a gradually varying load from 2 kN/m to 5 kN/m as shown in Fig. 2.52. Draw S.F. and B.M. diagrams for the beam.

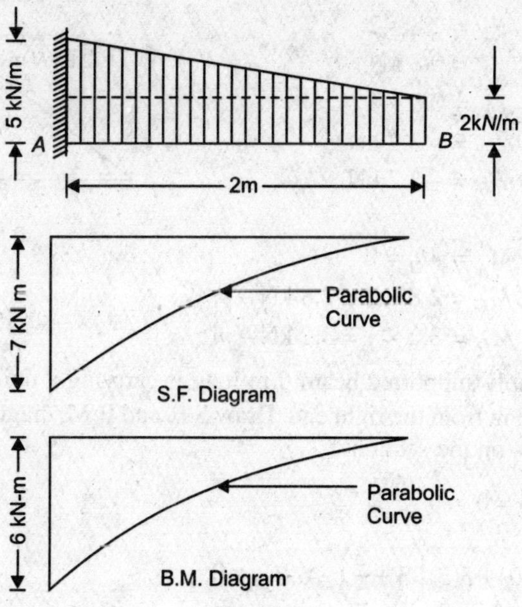

Fig. 2.52

SOLUTION : For S.F. Diagram :

$$F_B = 0$$

$$F_A = -\left[(2\times2)+\frac{3\times2}{2}\right] = -7 \text{ kN m}$$

For B.M. Diagram :

$$M_B = 0$$

$$M_A = -\left(2\times2\times\frac{2}{2}\right)+\frac{3\times2\times2}{2\times3}$$

$$= -6 \text{ kN m}$$

EXAMPLE 2.25. A simply supported beam *AB* of span 2.5 *m* is carying two point loads as shown in Fig. 2.53. Draw S.F. and B.M. diagrams for beam.

SOLUTION : For reactions R_A and R_B

$$R_A(0)+2\times1+4\times1.5-2.5R_B = 0$$

For $R\Sigma M_A = 0$

$$\therefore \quad R_B = \frac{8}{2.5} = 3.2 \text{ kN}$$

$$R_A = 2.8 \text{ kN}$$

$$F_A = R_A$$

$$= 2.8 \text{ kN},$$

$$F_C = 2.8 - 2$$

$$= 0.8 \text{ kN}$$

$$F_D = 0.8 - 4$$

$$= -3.2 \text{ kN}$$

$$F_B = -3.2 \text{ kN}$$

For B.M. Diagram

$$M_A = M_B = 0$$

$$M_C = 2.8 \times 1 = 2.8 \text{ kN} - m$$

$$M_D = 3.2 \times 1 = 3.2 \text{ kN} - m$$

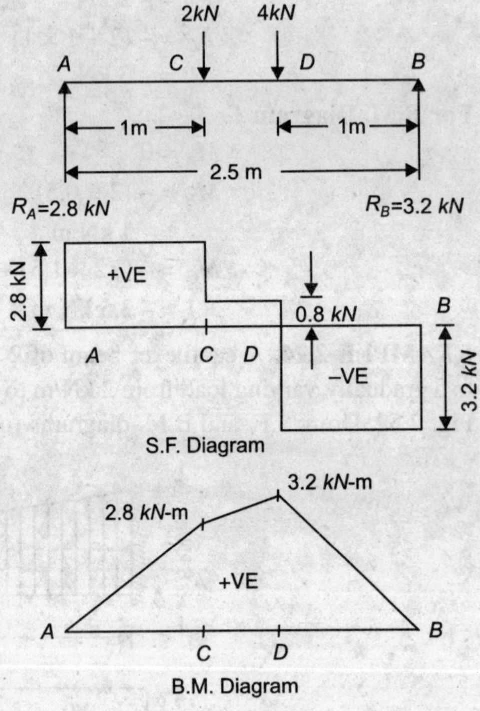

Fig. 2.53

EXAMPLE 2.26. A simply supported beam 6 m long is carrying a uniformly distributed load of 5 kN/m over a length of 3 m from the right end. Draw S.F. and B.M. diagrams for the beam and also calculate maximum B.M. on the section.

SOLUTION : For $\Sigma M_A = 0$

$$R_A(0)+5(3)\left(3+\frac{3}{2}\right)-6\,R_B = 0$$

$$\therefore \quad R_B = 11.25 \text{ kN}$$

$$R_A = 3.75 \text{ kN}$$

For S.F. Diagram :

$$F_A = R_A$$
$$= 3.75 \text{ kN}$$
$$F_C = 3.75 \text{ kN}$$
$$F_B = 3.75 - (5 \times 3)$$
$$= -11.25 \text{ kN}$$

For B.M. Diagram :

$$M_A = M_B = 0$$
$$M_C = 3.75 \times 3$$
$$= 11.25 \text{ kN-m}$$

We know that the maximum bending moment will occur at M, where the S.F. changes sign. Let x be the distance between C and M. Now from he geometry of the figure bewteen C and B, we find that,

$$\frac{x}{3.75} = \frac{3-x}{11.25}$$

or $$11.25\,x = (3-x)\,3.75$$

or $$x = 0.75\,m$$

$$M_{max.} = 3.75\,(3 + 0.75) - 5 \times 0.75 \times 0.75\,(0.5)$$
$$= 12.66 \text{ kN} - \text{m } \textbf{Ans.}$$

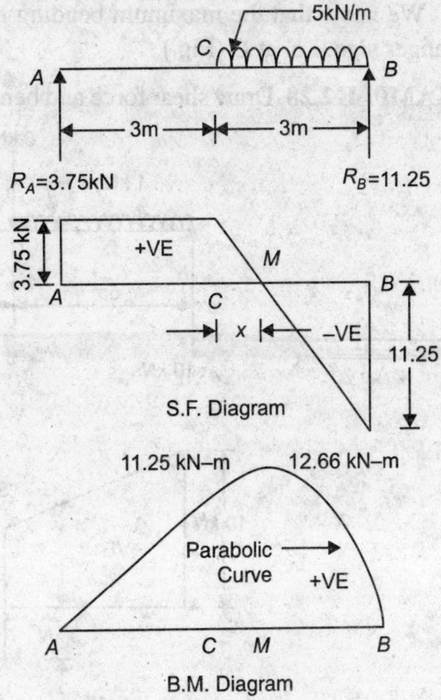

Fig. 2.54

EXAMPLE 2.27. A simply supported beam of 4 m span is carrying loads as shown in Fig. 2.55. Draw S.F. and B.M. diagrams for the beam.

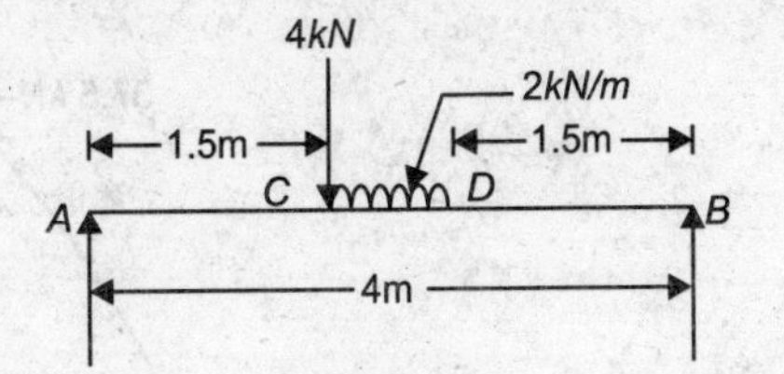

Fig. 2.55

SOLUTION : For $\Sigma M_A = 0$, we have

$$R_A(0) + 4(1.5) + 2 \times 1(1.5 + 1/2) - 4R_B = 0$$

$\therefore$ $$R_B = \frac{10}{4} = 2.5 \text{ kN}$$

$$R_A = 3.5 \text{ kN}$$

For S.F. Diagram :

$$F_A = R_A = 3.5 \text{ kN}$$
$$F_C = 3.5 - 4 = -0.5 \text{ kN}$$
$$F_D = -0.5 - (2 \times 1) = -2.5 \text{ kN}$$
$$F_B = -2.5 \text{ kN}$$

For B.M. Diagram :

$$M_A = M_B = 0$$
$$M_C = 3.5 \times 1.5 = 5.25 \text{ kN–m}$$
$$M_D = 2.5 \times 1.5 = 3.75 \text{ kN–m}$$

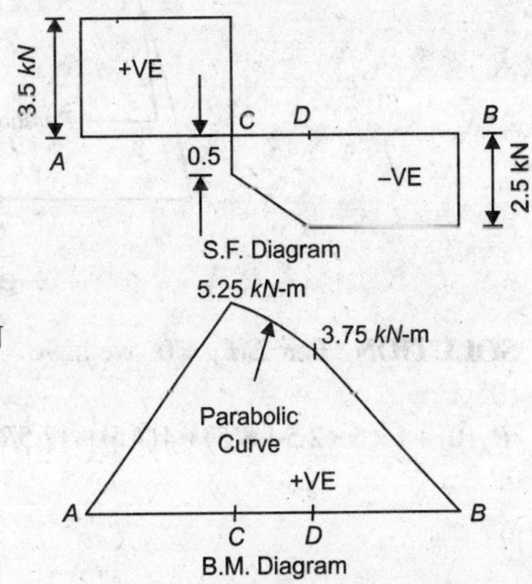

We know that the maximum bending moment will occur at C, where the shear force diagram changes sign, i.e. at C (Fig.)

EXAMPLE 2.28. Draw shear force and bending moment diagrams for the beam shown in Fig. 2.56.

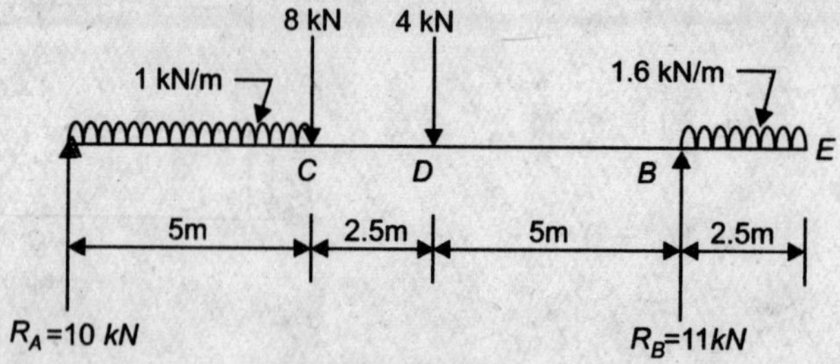

Fig. 2.56

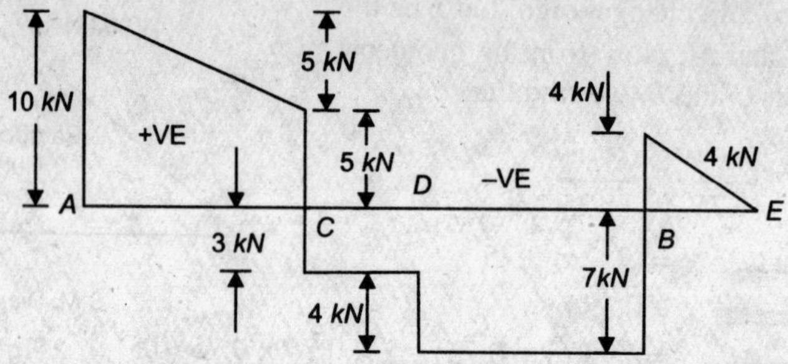

S. F. Diagram

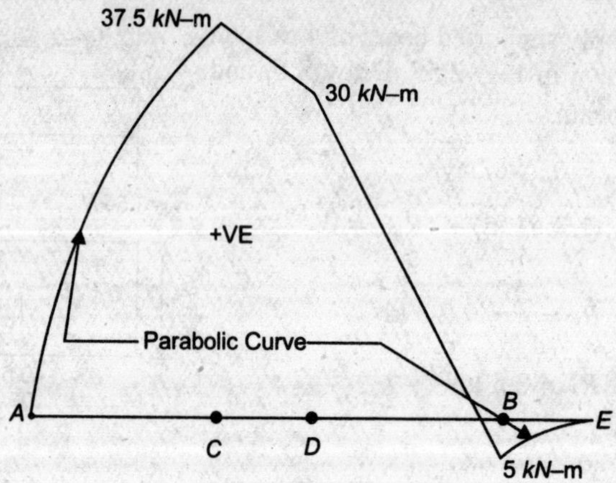

B.M. Diagram

SOLUTION : For $\Sigma M_A = 0$, we have

$$R_A(0) + 1 \times 5 \times 2.5 + 8(5) + 4(7.5) - 12.5R_B + 1.6 \times 2.5\left(12.5 + \frac{2.5}{7}\right) = 0$$

$$\therefore \qquad R_B = \frac{137.5}{12.5} = 11 \text{ kN}$$

$$R_A = 21 - 11 = 10 \text{ kN}$$

For S.F. Diagram :

$$F_A = R_A = 10 \text{ kN}$$
$$F_C = 10 - 1 \times 5 - 8 = -3 \text{ kN}$$
$$F_D = -3 - 4 = -7 \text{ kN}$$
$$F_B = -7 + 11 = 4 \text{ kN}$$
$$F_E = 4 - 1.6\,(2.5) = 0$$

For B.M. Diagram :

$$M_A = M_E = 0$$
$$M_C = 10 \times 5 - 1 \times 5 \times \frac{5}{2} = 37.50 \text{ kN} - \text{m}$$
$$M_D = 10 \times 7.5 - 8(2.5)$$
$$= 1 \times 5(2.5 + 2.5) = 30 \text{ kN} - \text{m}$$
$$M_B = 1.6 \times 2.5 \times \frac{2.5}{2} = 5 \text{ kN} - \text{m}$$

Maximum Bending Moment : The maximum bending moment will occur at *C* (+ve) and *B*(–ve) because the S.F. changes sign at both these points.

EXAMPLE 2.29. The shear force diagram (S.F.D.) of a simply supported beam is given in Fig. 2.57. Calculate the support reactions of the beam and also draw the bending moment diagram of the beam (UPTU - 2002).

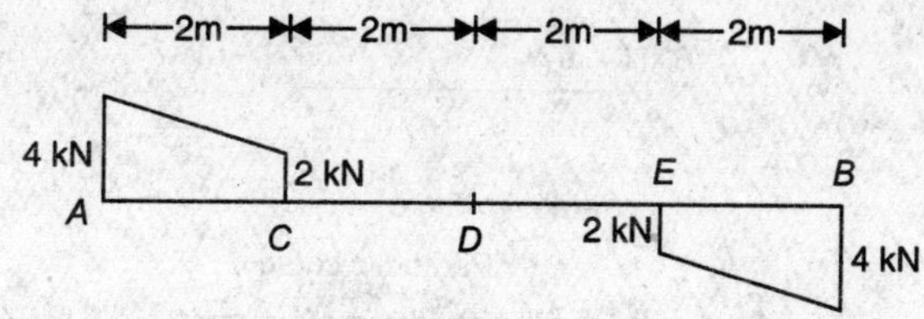

Fig. 2.57

SOLUTION: Given: Simply supported beam, let supported at the ends *A* and *B* and reactions be R_A and R_B. The shear force curve in the region *AC* and *EB* is an inclined straight line, it means the beam is loaded with U.D.L. in the region *AC* and *EB*. Let the intensity of UDL be w_1 and w_2 kN per *m* respectively.

For S.F.D.

$\therefore$ $$F_A = R_A = 4 \text{ kN};$$
$$F_B = R_B = 4 \text{ kN}$$
$$F_C = 4 - (w_1 \times 2 + 2) = 4 - 2 - 2w_1$$

$\therefore$ $$w_1 = 2/2 = 1 \text{ kN/m}$$
$$F_D = 0$$

Hence no load at *D*.

$$F_E = -2 \text{ kN} = \text{Vertical line}$$

Hence 2 kN point, load at E

$$F_B = -2 - (2w_2) + 4$$

or $$w_2 = 2/2 = 1 \text{ kN/m}$$

For B.M. Diagram :

$$M_A = M_B = 0$$
$$M_C = 4 \times 2 - 1 \times 2 \times 1$$
$$= 6 \text{ kN} - \text{m}$$
$$M_B = 0,\ M_E = 4 \times 2 - 1 \times 2 \times 1$$
$$= +6 \text{ kN} - \text{m}$$
$$M_E = 4 \times 6 - (1 \times 2 \times 5 + 2 \times 4)$$
$$= 6 \text{ kN-m}$$
$$M_D = 4 \times 4 - (1 \times 2 \times 3 + 2 \times 2)$$
$$= 6 \text{ kN} - \text{m}$$

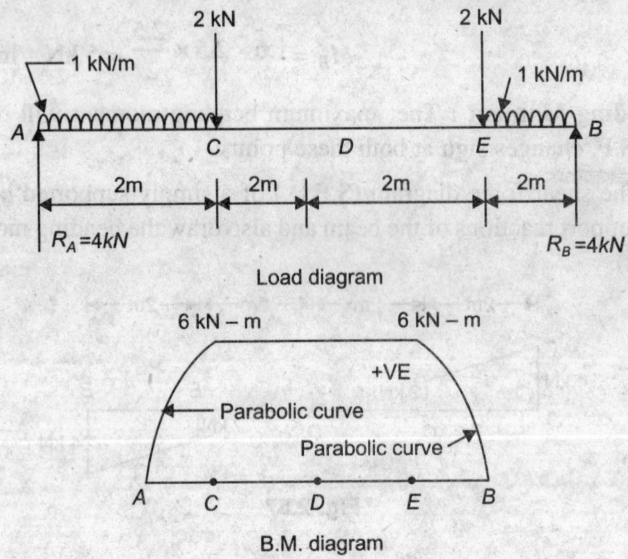

Fig. 2.58

EXAMPLE 2.30. The bending moment diagram (BMD) of a simply supported beam is given in Fig. 2.59(a). Calculate the support reactions of the beam and draw shear force diagram (2000).

SOLUTION: Given: Simply supported beam which is supported at ends A and B. The B.M.D. shown is a inclined straight line which means the beam is loaded with point loads. Let the intensity of loads at point C and B is w_1 and w_2 respectively.

Thus $$M_A = M_B = 0$$
$$M_C = R_A \times 1 = 7 \text{ kN} - \text{m}$$
$\therefore$ $$R_A = 7 \text{ kN}$$
$$M_D = R_B \times 1 = 5 \text{ kN} - \text{m}$$
$\therefore$ $$R_B = 5 \text{ kN} \qquad \because M_D = 5 \text{ kN} - \text{m}$$

$\therefore \quad R_A \times 2 - W_1 (1) = 5$

or $\quad 2 \times 7 - W_1 = 5$

$\therefore \quad W_1 = 9 \text{ kN} \quad$ ...(i)

For $\quad \Sigma V = 0,$

We have $\quad R_A + R_B = W_1 + W_2$

$7 + 5 = 9 + W_2$

$\therefore \quad W_2 = 12 - 9$

$= 3 \text{ kN} \quad$ ...(ii)

For S.F. Diagram $\quad F_A = R_A$

$= 7 \text{ kN}$

Refer Fig. 2.59(c)

$F_B = 7 - 9 = -2 \text{ kN}$

$F_D = -(2 + 3) = -5 \text{ kN}$

$F_B = -5 + 5$

$= 0 \text{ kN}$

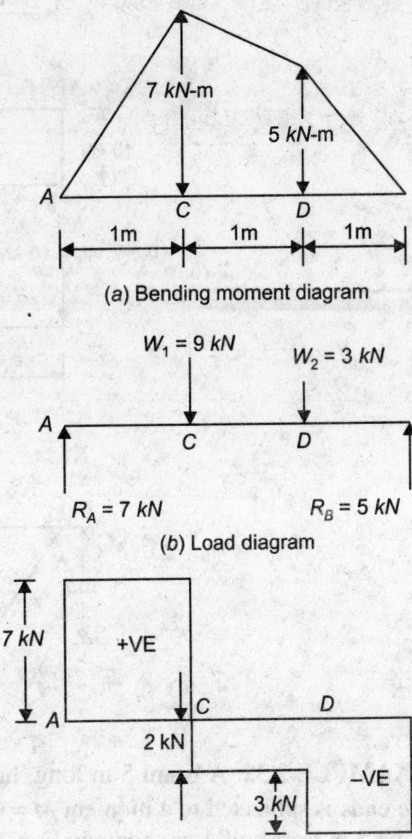

(a) Bending moment diagram

(b) Load diagram

(c) S. F. Diagram

Fig. 2.59

EXAMPLE 2.31. Shear force diagram of a simply supported beam at *A* and *B* is given in Fig. 2.60(*a*). Calculate support reactions and draw B.M.D. at the beam (03).

SOLUTION: Let R_A and R_B be the reactions at *A* and *B* respectively.

For S.F. Diagram: $\quad F_C = -W_1 = -10 \text{ kN}$

$\therefore \quad W_1 = 10 \text{ kN}$

$F_A = -W_1 + R_A = -10 + 10$

$= 0 \text{ kN}$

$\therefore \quad R_A = W_1 = 10 \text{ kN}$

$F_B = W_2 = 10 \text{ kN}$

$= -W_1 + R_A + R_B$

$= -10 + 10 + 10 = 10 \text{ kN}$

$F_B = R_B = 10 \text{ kN}$

$F_D = -W_2$

$= -W_1 + R_A + R_B - W_2 = 0$

$= -10 + 10 + 10 - W_2$

$\therefore \quad W_2 = 10 \text{ kN}$

For Bending Moment Diagram :

$M_C = M_D = 0$

$M_A = -10\,(a) = -10a$

$M_B = -10\,(a + b) + 10\,b$

$= -10\,a - 10b + 10\,b = -10\,a$

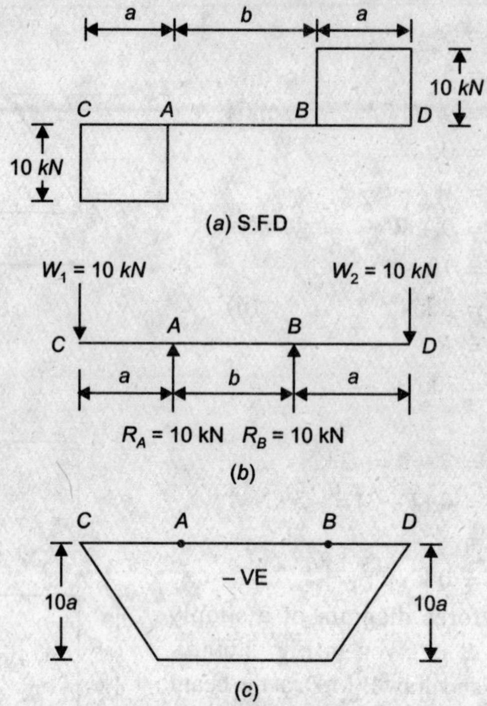

(a) S.F.D

(b)

(c)

Fig. 2.60

EXAMPLE 2.32. A beam 5 m long, hinged at both the ends is subjected to a moment $M = 60$ kN-m at a point 3 m from end A as shown in Fig. 2.61(*a*). Draw the shear force and bending moment diagrams.

(U.P.T.U., 07)

SOLUTION: For

$$\Sigma M_A = 0$$

$$RA \times 0 - 60 + 5\,R_B = 0$$

$$\therefore \quad R_B = 60/5 = 12 \text{ kN}$$

For $\Sigma V = 0$, we have

$$R_A - R_B = 0$$

or

$$R_A - 12 = 0$$

$$\therefore \quad R_A = 12 \text{ kN}$$

For S.F. Diagram, we have

$$FA = RA = 12 \text{ kN}$$

$$F_B = 12 - 12 = 0$$

S.F. remains constant between *A* and *B*

For B.M. Diagrams, we have

$$M_A = M_B = 0$$

$$M_C = 12 \times 3 - 60$$

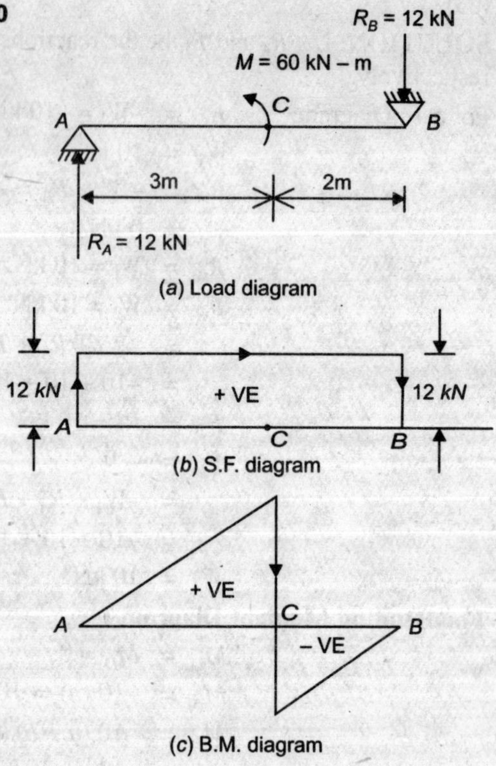

(a) Load diagram

(b) S.F. diagram

(c) B.M. diagram

Fig. 2. 61

$$M_C = (36 - 60) \text{ kN-m}$$
$$= -24 \text{ kN-m}$$

NOTE: Anti-clockwise moment of 60 kN-m will abruptly change the moment value from 36 kN- m to – 24 kN-m, at point *C*. (Fig. B.M.D.)

EXAMPLE 2.33. A simply supported beam is shown in Fig. 2.62(*a*). Draw S.F. and B.M. diagrams of the beam. **(U.P.T.U., 2004–05)**

SOLUTION: For symmetric U.D.L. we have

$$R_A = R_B = \frac{20 \times 18}{2} = 180 \text{ kN}$$

For S.F.D. we have,

$$F_A = R_A = 180 \text{ kN}$$

S.F. just left to

$$B = 180 - 20 \times 18 = -180 \text{ kN}$$
$$F_B = 180 - 180 = 0$$

S.F. is zero (changes sign) at 9 m from *A*

For B.M. Diagram, we have

$$M_A = M_B = 0$$
$$M_C = 180 \times 9 - (20 \times 9 \times 4.5)$$
$$= 810 \text{ kN} - \text{m}$$

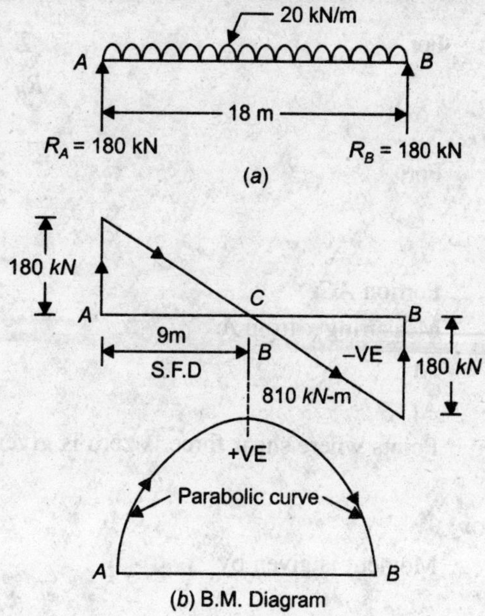

Fig. 2.62

EXAMPLE 2.34. Draw the SF and BM diagrams for the beam shown in Fig . 2.63 (a) and find out the position and magnitude of the maximum moment.

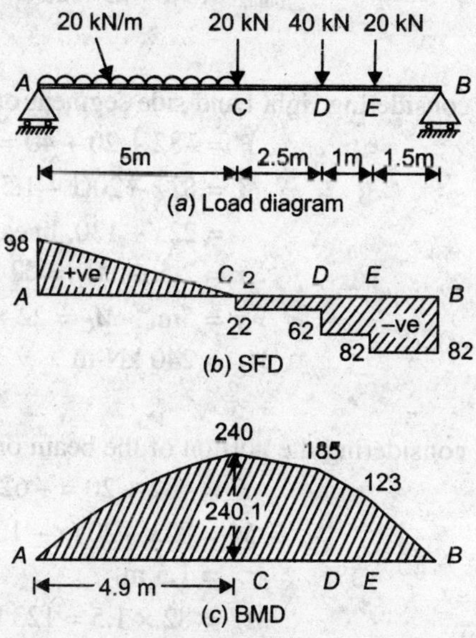

Fig. 2.63

For, $\Sigma M_A = 0$

$$R_B \times 10 = 20 \times 5 \times 2.5 + 20 \times 5 + 40 \times 7.5 + 20 \times 8.5$$

$\therefore$ $R_B = 82$ kN

For, $\Sigma V = 0$

$\therefore$ $R_A = 20 \times 5 + 20 + 40 + 20 - 82$

$R_A = 98$ kN

Portion *AC*:

Measuring x from *A*, $F = 98 - 20x$, linear variation

At $x = 0$, $F_A = 98$ kN

At $x = 5$m, $F_B = 98 - 100 = -2$ kN

Points where shear force is zero is given by,

$$0 = 98 - 20x$$

or $x = 4.9$ m

Moment is given by $M = 98\,x - 20\,x - x/2$, parabolic variation

At $x = 0$, $M_A = 0$

At $x = 5$ m, $M_B = 98 \times 5 - \dfrac{20 \times 5^2}{2} = 240$ kN-m

Maximum moment occurs at $x = 4.9$ m where

$$F = \frac{dM}{dx} = 0$$

$$M_{\max} = 98 \times 4.9 - 20 \times \frac{4.9^2}{2} = 240.1 \text{ kN-m}$$

Portion *CD*

Measuring x from *B* and considering right hand side segment of the beam,

$$F = -82 + 20 + 40 = -22\text{kN, constant}$$

$$M = 82x - 20(x - 1.5) - 40\,(x - 2.5)$$

$$= 22x + 130\text{, linear variation}$$

At $x = 2.5$ m, $M_D = 22 \times 2.5 + 130 = 185$ kN-m

At $x = 5$m, $M_C = 22 \times 5 + 130$

$\therefore$ $M_C = 240$ kN-m

Portion *DE*:

Measuring x from *B* and considering the portion of the beam on the right side of the section,

$$F = -82 + 20 = -62\text{ kN, constant}$$

$$M = 82x - 20\,(x - 1.5)\text{, linear variation}$$

At $x = 1.5$ m,

$$M_E = 82 \times 1.5 = 123\text{ kN-m,}$$

At $x = 2.5$, $M = 82 \times 2.5 - 20 \times 1$

$\therefore$ $M = 185$ kN-m

Portion *EB*:

Measuring *x* from *B* and considering the right hand side segment,

$$F = -82 \text{ kN, constant}$$

$$M = 82x, \text{ linear variation}$$

At $\quad x = 0, \quad M_B = 0$

At $\quad x = 1.5 \text{ m}, \quad M_B = 82 \times 1.5 = 123 \text{ kN-m}$ **Ans.**

SFD and BMD are shown in Fig. 2.64 (a) and (b) respectively, for the entire beam.

EXAMPLE 2.35. A beam of span 8 m has roller support at *A* and hinge support at *B* as shown in Fig. 2.64 (a). Draw *SF* and *BM* diagrams when the beam is subjected to an uniformly distributed load, a concentrated load and an externally applied moment as shown in the Figure.

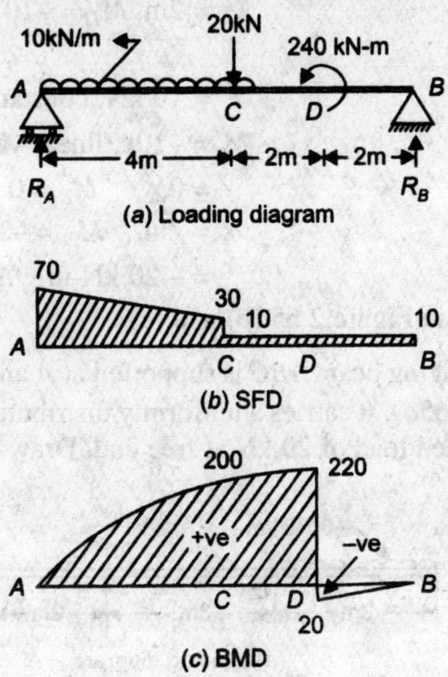

Fig. 2.64

For, $\quad \Sigma M_A = 0$

$$R_B \times 8 - 10 \times 4 \times 2 - 20 \times 45 + 240 = 0$$

$\therefore \quad R_B = -10 \text{ kN (upwards), and}$

$\quad R_B = 10 \text{ kN (downwards)}$

For, $\quad \Sigma V = 0$

$$R_A = 10 \times 4 + 20 + 10$$

$\therefore \quad R_A = 70 \text{ kN}$

Portion *AC*:

Measuring *x* from *A* and considering left hand side segment of the beam,

$$F = 70 - 10x, \text{ linear variation}$$

At, $\quad x = 0, F_A = 70 \text{ kN}$

At $\quad x = 4\text{m}, F_C = 70 - 40 = 30 \text{ kN}$

$$M = 70x - 10x\frac{x}{2}, \text{ parabolic variation}$$

At $x = 0, \quad M_A = 0$

At $x = 4\text{m}, M_C = 70 \times 4 - 10 \times 4 \times \frac{4}{2} = 200 \text{ kN-m}$

Portion *CD*:

Measuring *x* from *B*, $F = 10$ kN, constant

$M = -10x + 240$, linear variation

At $x = 4\text{m}, M_C = 200$ kN-m

At $x = 2\text{m}, M_D = -10 \times 2 + 240 = 220$ kN-m

Portion *DB*:

Measuring *x* from *B*, $F = 10$ kN, constant

$M = -10x$, linear variation

At $x = 0, \quad M_B = 0$

At $x = 2\text{m}, \quad M_D = -10 \times 2$

$= -20$ kN-m **Ans.**

SFD and *BMD* are shown in Figure 2.65 (b) and (c).

EXAMPLE 2.36. The overhanging beam *ABC* is supported at *A* and *B*, the span *AB* being 6 m. The overhang *BC* is 2m (see Fig. 2.65*a*). It carries a uniformly distributed load of 30 kN/m over a length of 3m from *A* and a concentrated load of 20 kN at free end. Draw *SF* and *BM* diagrams.

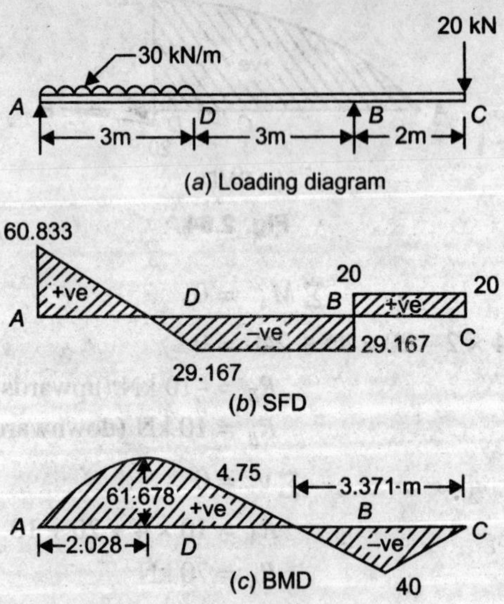

Fig. 2.65

For, $\sum M_A = 0$

$R_B \times 6 = 20 \times 8 + 30 \times 3 \times 1.5$

$\therefore \quad R_B = 49.167$ kN

For, $\sum V = 0$

$R_A = 30 \times 3 + 20 - 49.167$

$\therefore$ $R_A = 60.833$ kN

Portion AD:

Measuring x from A and considering left side segment,

$F = 60.833 - 30x$, linear variation

At $x = 0$, $F_A = 60.833$ kN

At $x = 3$ m,

$F_D = 60.833 - 30 \times 3$

$= -29.167$ kN

The point of zero shear is given by $0 = 60.833 - 30x$

or, $x = 2.028$ m

At section X-X, the moment is given by

$$M = 60.83 - 30\frac{x^2}{2}, \text{ parabolic variation}$$

At $x = 0$, $M_A = 0$

At $x = 3\text{m}$, $M_D = 60.833 \times 3 - 30 \times \frac{9}{2}$

$\therefore$ $M_D = 47.5$ kN-m

Maximum moment occurs at $x = 2.028$ m.

Since here $F = \frac{dM}{dx} = 0$ $\quad M_{\max} = 60.833 \times 2.021 - 30 \times \frac{2.028^2}{2}$

$= 61.678$ kN-m

Portion DB:

Measuring x from the free end C and considering right hand side segment,

$F = 20.0 - 49.167$

$= 29.167$ kN, constant

$M = -20x + 49.167\ (x - 2)$, lincar variation

At $x = 5\text{m}$, $M_D = -20 \times 5 + 49.167 \times 3$

$= 47.5$ kN-m

At $x = 2\text{m}$, $M_B = -20 \times 2 = -40$ kN-m

In this portion the bending moment changes the sign. The point of contraflexure is given by the expression.

$0 = -20x + 49.167\ (x - 2)$

i.e., $x = 3.71$ m from free end

Portion BC:

Measuring x from free end, $F = 20$ kN, constant

$M = -20x$, linear variation

At $\quad x = 0, \quad M_C = 0$

At $\quad x = 2\text{m}, \quad M_B = -40$ kN-m **Ans.**

Hence *SF* and *BM* diagrams are as shown in Fig. 2.66(b) and (c) respectively.

EXAMPLE 2.37. Draw shear force and bending moment diagrams for the overhanging beam shown in Fig. 2.66(a). Indicate the values at all salient points.

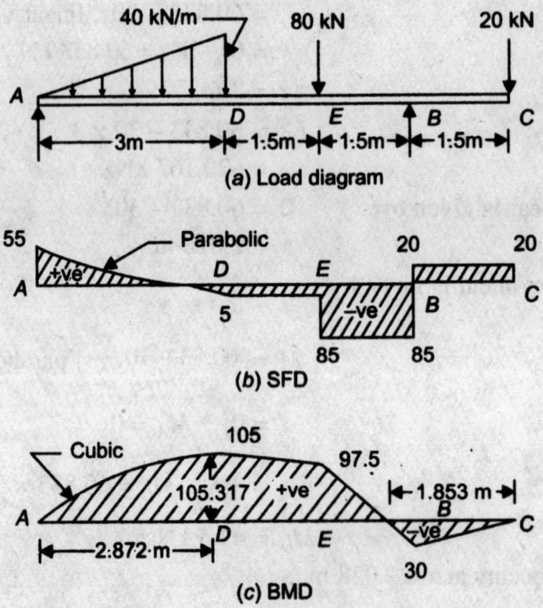

Fig. 2.66

For, $\quad \Sigma M_A = 0$

$$R_B \times 6 = \frac{1}{2} \times 3 \times 40 \times 2 + 80 \times 4.5 + 20 \times 7.5$$

$\therefore \quad R_B = 105$ kN

For, $\quad \Sigma V = 0$

$$R_A = \frac{1}{2} \times 3 \times 40 + 80 + 20 - 105$$

$\therefore \quad R_A = 55$ kN

Portion *AD*:

Measuring *x* from *A*, $\quad F = 55 - \frac{1x}{23} 40x$

$$= 55 - \frac{20}{3} x^2 \text{, parabolic variation}$$

At $\quad x = 0, \quad F_A = 55$ kN

At $\quad x = 3\text{m}, \; F_D = 55 - \frac{20}{3} \times 9$

$\therefore$ $$F_D = -5 \text{ kN}$$

Point where $SF = 0$ is given by $$0 = 55 - \frac{20}{3}x^2$$

i.e. $$x = 2.872 \text{ m}$$

Moment at Section X-X is given by $$M = 55x - \frac{1}{2} \times \frac{x}{3} 40 . x . \frac{x}{3}$$

$$= 55x - \frac{20}{9}x^3, \text{ cubic variation}$$

At $x = 0,\text{m} \quad M_A = 0$

At $x = 3\text{m}, \quad M_D = 55 \times 3 - \frac{20}{9} \times 3^3$

$\therefore$ $$M_D = 105 \text{ kN-m}$$

M is maximum at $x = 2.872$ where $SF = 0$.

$$M_{\max} = 55 \times 2.872 - \frac{20}{9} \times 2.872^3$$

$$= 105.317 \text{ kN-m}$$

Portion *DE*:

Measuring x from C and considering right hand segment of the beam.

$$F = 20 - 105 + 80 = -5 \text{ kN, constant}$$

$$M = -20x + 105(x - 1.5) - 80(x - 3), \text{ linear variation}$$

At $x = 4.5$ m, $M_D = -20 \times 4.5 \times 105 \times 3 - 80 \times 1.5$

$= 105$ kN-m

At $x = 3$, $M_E = 20 \times 3 \times 105 \times 1.5$

$= 97.5$ kN-m

Portion *BE*:

Measuring x from C, $\quad F = 20 - 105 = -85$ kN, constant

$$M = -20x + 105(x - 1.5), \text{ linear}$$

At $x = 3\text{m}, \quad M_E = -20 \times 3 + 105 \times 1.5 = 97.5$ kN-m

At $x = 1.5\text{m}, M_B = -20 \times 1.5 = -30$ kN-m

The point of contraflexure is given by $\quad 0 = -20x + 105(x - 1.5)$

$\therefore$ $$x = 1.853 \text{ m from } C$$

Portion *BC*:

Measuring x from C $\quad F = 20$ kN, constant

$$M = -20x, \text{ linear variation}$$

At $x = 0, M_C = 0$

At $x = 1.5, \quad MB = -30$ kN-m **Ans.**

Hence *SFD* and *BMD* are shown in Fig. 2.66 (b) and (c) respectively.

EXAMPLE. 2.38. Draw *BM* and *SF* diagrams for the beam shown in Fig. 2.68 (a), indicating the values at all salient points.

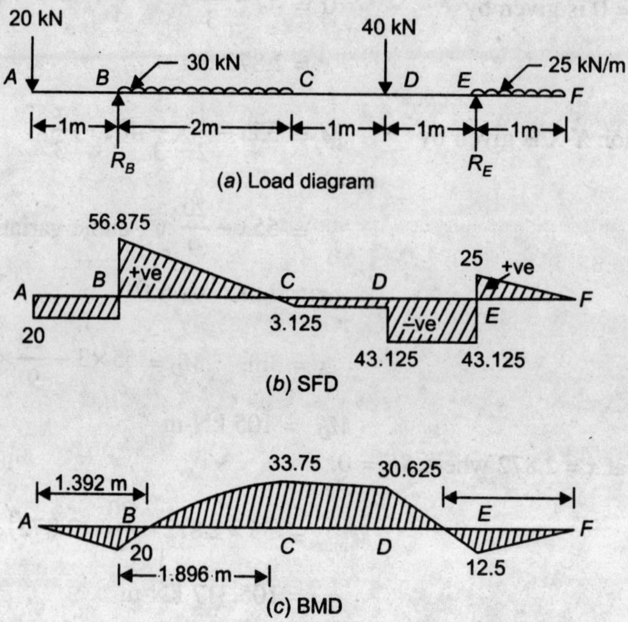

Fig. 2.67

For, $\Sigma M_A = 0$

$R_E \times 4 + 20 \times 1 - 30 \times 2 \times 1 - 40 \times 3 - 25 \times 1 \times 4.5 = 0$

$R_E = 68.125$ kN

For, $\Sigma V = 0$

$R_B = 20 + 30 \times 2 + 40 + 25 \times 1 - 68.125$

$R_B = 76.875$ kN

Portion *AB*:

Measuring *x* from *A*, $F = -20$ kN, constant

$M = -20x$, linear variation

At $x = 0$, $M_A = 0$

At $x = 1$ m, $M_B = -20$ kN-m

Portion *BC*:

Measuring *x* from *B*, $F = -20 + 76.875 - 30x$, linear variation

At $x = 0$, $F = 56.875$ kN

At $x = 2$ m, $F = -3.125$ kN

The point of zero shear force is given by $0 = -20 + 76.85 - 30x$

or $x = 1.896$ m from *B*.

At distance *x* from *B* the moment is given by

$$M = -20\,(x + 1) + 76.875\,x - 30x\,\frac{x}{2}$$

$$M = -20 + 56.875\,x - 15x^2, \text{ parabolic variation}$$

At $x = 0,\quad M_B = -20$ kN-m

At $x = 2\text{m},\quad M_C = -20 + 56.875 \times 2 - 15 \times 4$

$\therefore\quad M_C = 33.75$ kN-m

Maximum moment occurs where $SF = 0$, i.e., at $x = 1.896$ m

$\therefore\quad M_{max} = -20 + 56.875 \times 1.876 - 15 \times 18.96^2$

$= 33.913$ kN-m

The bending moment is changing its sign in this portion. Hence the point of contraflexure exists in this portion. It is given by

$$0 = -20 + 56.875\,x - 15x^2$$

$\therefore\quad x = 0.392$ m,

i.e., the point of contraflexure is at 1.392 m from the free end A.

Portion CD:

Measuring x from F,

Shear force $= 25 \times 1 - 68.125 - 40$

$= 3.125$ kN, constant

$M = -25 \times 1\,(x - 05) + 68.125\,(x - 1) - 40\,(x - 2)$, linear variation

At $x = 3\text{m},\quad M_C = 33.75$ kN-m

At $x = 2\text{m},\quad M_D = -25 \times 1.5 + 68.125$

$\therefore\quad M_D = 30.625$ kN-m

Portion DE:

Measuring x from fee end F,

Shear force $= 25 - 68.125$

$= -43.125$ kN, constant

$M = -25\,(x - 0.5) + 68.125\,(x - 1)$, linear variation

At $x = 2\text{m},\quad M_D = 30.625$ kN-m

At $x = 1\text{m},\quad M_E = -12.5$ kN-m

Portion EF:

Measuring x from free end F,

Shear force $\quad F = 25x$, linear variation

At $x = 0,\ F_F = 0$

At $x = 1\text{m},\quad F_E = 25$ kN

$$M = -25x, \frac{x}{2}, \text{ parabolic variation}$$

At $x = 0,\quad M_F = 0$

At $x = 1$ m, $\quad M_E = -12.5$ kN-m. **Ans.**

SF and *BM* diagrams are as shown in Fig. 2.68(b) and (c) respectively.

EXERCISE-2

1. A simply supported beam of 6m span is carrying a uniformly distributed load of 2 kN/m over a length of 3m from the right and *B*. Calculate the support reactions.

   [Ans. $R_A = 1.5$ kN, $R_B = 4.5$ kN]

2. A beam *AB* of 5m length, supported on the intermediate supports 3m apart, carries a uniformly distributed load of 0.6 kN/m. The beam also carries two concentrated loads of 3KN at left hand end *A*, and 5 kN at the right hand end *B*. Determine the location of the two supports. so that both the reactions are equal. **[Ans.** $x_1 = 1.45$m from *A*, $x_2 = 4.45$ m from *A*]

3. A beam *AB* of 6m length rests on two supports 4m apart whose right hand end is overhanging by 2 m. The beam carries a uniformly distributed load of 1 kN/m over the entire length of the beam. Determine the reactions at the two supports. **[Ans.** $R_A = 1.5$ kN, $R_B = 4.5$ kN]

4. Figure 2.70 shows a beam *ABCD* simply supported on a hinged support at *A* and at *D* on a roller support inclined at 45° with the vertical. Determine the horizontal and vertical components of reaction at support *A*. Show clearly the direction as well as magnitude of the resultant reaction at *A*.

   [Ans. $R_A = 1$ kN ↑ = 5.1 kN→, $R_D = 5$ kN ↑ = 5 kN →, $R_D = 7.07$ kN, $\theta = 78.7°$]

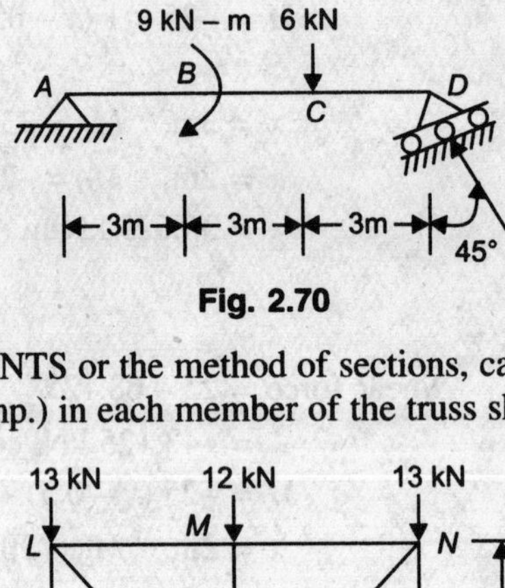

Fig. 2.70

5. Using the method of JOINTS or the method of sections, calculate the force (magnitude and nature i.e., tensile or comp.) in each member of the truss shown in Fig. 2.70.

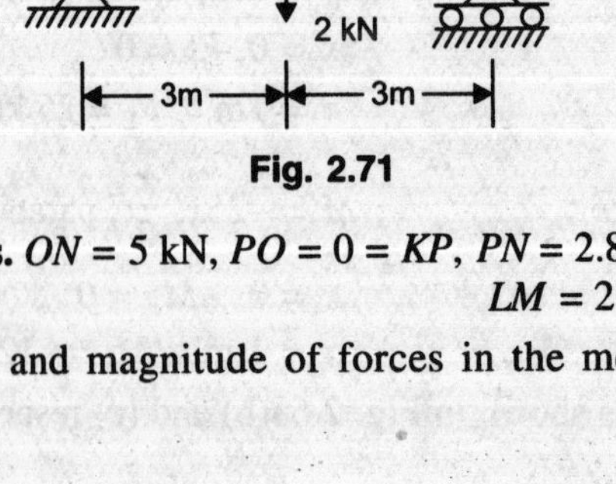

Fig. 2.71

[Ans. $ON = 5$ kN, $PO = 0 = KP$, $PN = 2.83$ kN, $MN = 2$ kN, $MP = 2$ kN, $LM = 2$ kN, $LP = 2.83$ kN, $KL = 5$ kN]

6. Determine the nature and magnitude of forces in the members of the truss shown in Fig. 2.72.

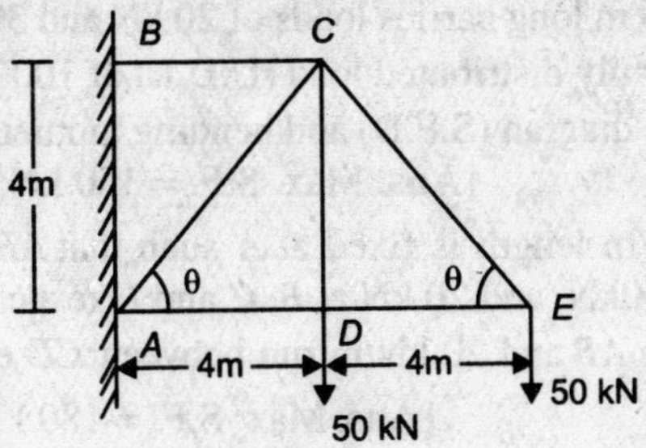

Fig. 2.72

[**Ans.** BC = 50 kN comp., CE = 70.71 kN – Tensile, DE = 50 kN – Comp.
AD = 50 kN – comp. CA = 141.42 kN – T, CD = 50 kN–Tensile]

7. **Determine the support reactions and nature and magnitude of forces in the members of the truss shown in Fig. 2.73.**

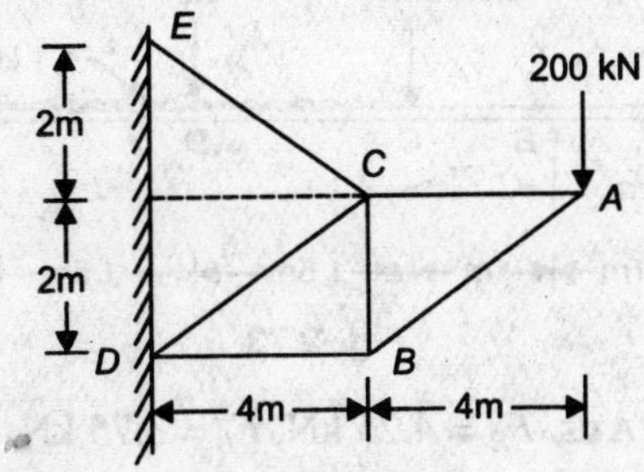

Fig. 2.73

[**Ans.** EF = 447.21 kN – T, CA = 400 kN – T, AB = 447.21 kN – C,
BD = 400 kN – C, CD = 0, CB = 200 kN – T]

8. **A trass is shown in Fig. 2.74. Find the forces in all the members of the truss and indicate whether it is in tension or compression.**

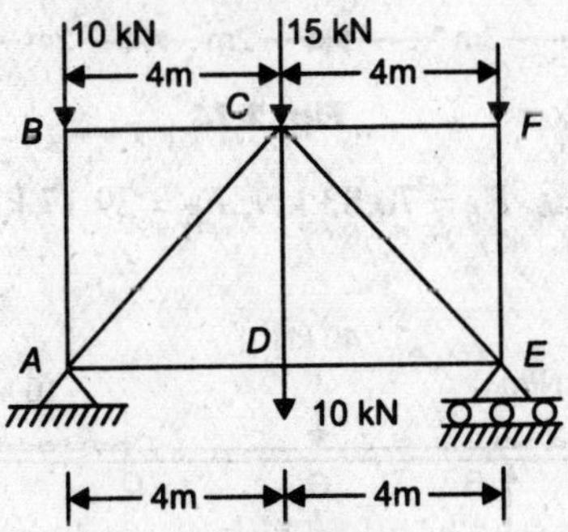

Fig. 2.74

[**Ans.** AD = 12.5 kN – T, DE = 12.5 kN – T, EF = 20 kN – C, FC =0, CB = 25 kN – T,
BA = 10 kN – C, AC = 35.35 kN – C, CE = 17.68 kN – C, CD = 10 kN – T]

9. **A cantilever 3m long carries loads 2 kN, 1.5 kN and 2.5 kN at free end, 1 m and 2 m from free end respectively. Draw S.F.D and B.M.D.**

[**Ans.** Max. S.F. = 6 kN, and Max. B.M. = –11.5 kN-m]

10. A horizontal cantilever 6 m long carries loads of 20 kN and 30 kN at 2m and 5m respectively from fixed end. A uniformly distributed load (U.D.L) of 100 kN is also spread over its entire length. Draw shear force diagran (S.F.D) and bending moment diagrams (B.M.D.) indicating maximum values. [**Ans.** Max. S.F. = 150 kN, and Max. B.M. = –490 kN-m]
11. A cantilever *ABCD* of 7m length is fixed at *A* such that *AB* = *BC* = 2m and *CD* = 3m. It carries loads of 50 kN, 30kN, and 20 kN at *B*, *C* and *D* respetively. In addition to it a U.D.L. of 10 kN/m run between *AB* and 20 kN/m run between *CD* exist. Draw S.F.D. and B.M.D.

    [**Ans.** Max. S.F. = 180 kN, Max. B.M. = – 710 kN - m]
12. A simply supported horizontal beam, 5m long carries concentrated loads of 70 kN, 90 kN, 50 kN and 80 kN at distances 1m, 3m, 4m and 4,5 m respectively from the left hand support. Find support reactions and draw S.F.D. and B.M.D.

    [**Ans.** R_A = 180 kN, R_B = 110 kN, and Max. B.M. = 190 kN under 90 kN load)
13. In all the problems given below draw SFD and BMD indicating values at salient point.

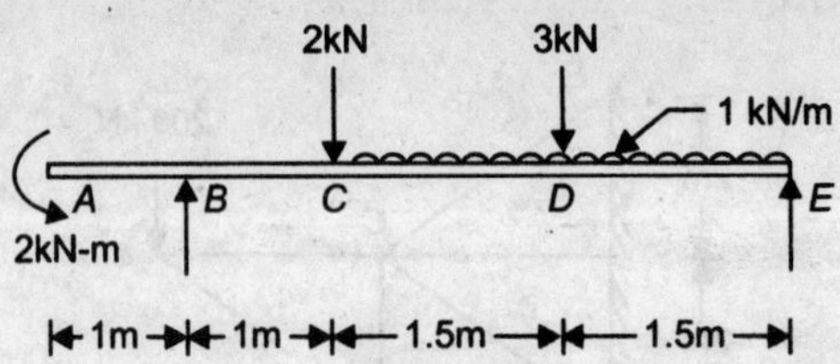

Fig. 2.73

[**Ans.** F_B = 4.25 kN, F_B = 3.75 kN, M_{max} = 4.5 kN-m at *D* Point of contraflexure at 1.47 m from *A*]

14.

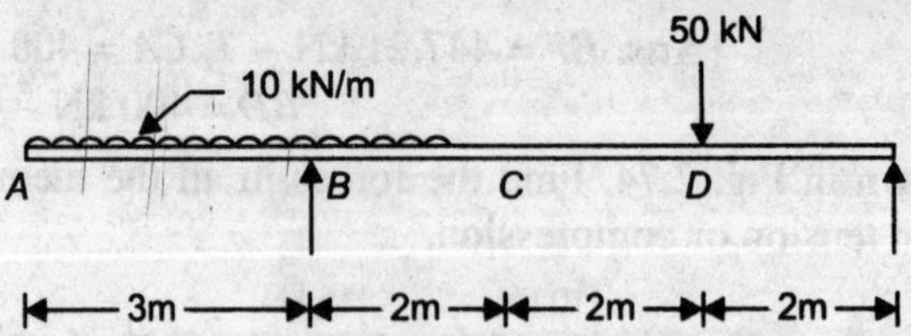

Fig. 2.74

[**Ans.** F_B= 70.83 kN, F_E = 29.17 kN, M_{max} = 45 kN-m at *B* Point of contraflexure at 4.313 m from *A*]

15.

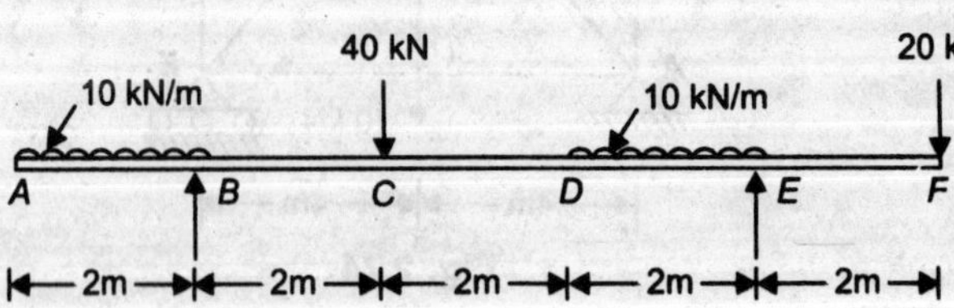

Fig. 2.75

[**Ans.** R_B = 46.67 kN, R_E = 53.33 kN, M_B = – 20 kN-m, M_E = –40 kN-m, M_C = 33.33 kN-m, Point of contraflexure: 2.75 m from *A* and 3.57 m from *F*]

16. 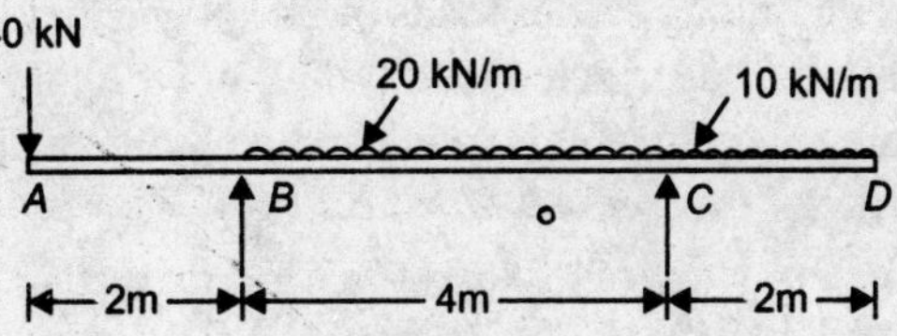

Fig. 2.76

[**Ans.** R_B = 95 kN, R_C = 45 kN, M_{max} = – 4.375 at 4.75 m from A No +ve moment any where]

17. 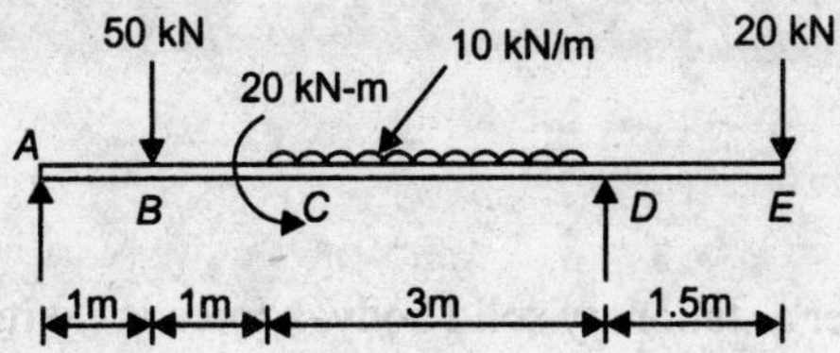

Fig. 2.77

18. **Determine load *P* such that reactions at supports *A* and *B* are equal in the beam shown in Fig.2.79. Draw *SF* and BM diagram marking the values at salient points.**

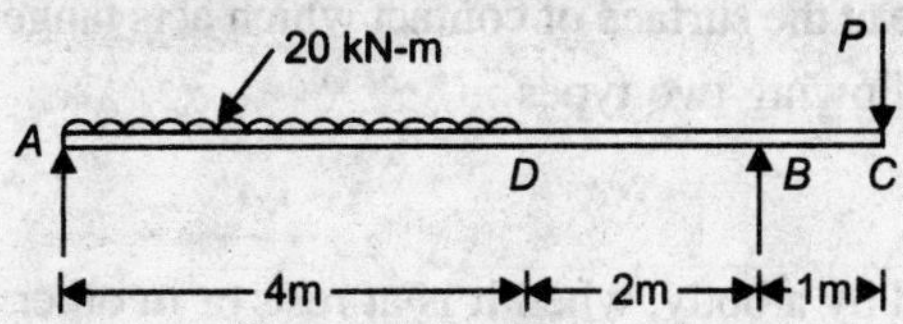

Fig. 2.78

[**Ans.** P = 20 kN, $R_A = R_B$ = 50 kN, M_{max} = 62.5 kN-m at 2.5 m from A,
Point of contraflexure 1.667 m from C]

CHAPTER 3

Friction

INTRODUCTION

When a solid body slides over a stationary solid body, a force is exerted at the surface of contact by the stationary body on the moving body. This force is called the force of friction, and always acts in the direction opposite to the direction of motion. Hence the property of the bodies by virtue of which a force is exerted by the stationary body on the moving body is called friction. Friction always acts parallel to the surface of contact and depends upon the nature of the surface of contact.

Hence Friction is a force at the surface of contact which acts tangential to the surface of contact.

The friction is of the following two types :

STATIC FRICTION

It is the friction experienced by a body, when it is at rest, or in other words, it is the friction when the body tends to move.

DYNAMIC FRICTION

It is the friction experienced by a body when it is in motion. It is also called kinetic friction. It is of the following two types :

1. **SLIDING FRICTION :** It is the friction, experienced by a body when it slides over another body.
2. **ROLLING FRICTION :** It is the friction, experienced by a body when it rolls over the other, or in other words, when balls or rollers are interposed between the two surfaces.
3. **DRY FRICTION :** The friction between dry surfaces in contact is called dry friction (solid friction)
4. **FLUID FRICTION :** The friction between two surfaces in the presence of fluid is called fluid friction.

LAWS OF DRY FRICTION (SOLID FRICTION)

1. The force of friction always acts in a direction, opposite to that in which the body tends to move.
2. The total friction that can be developed is proportional to the normal force transmitted across the surface of contact.

3. The magnitude of the limiting friction bears a constant ratio to the normal reaction between the two surfaces. Mathematically, F/R = constant, where F = limiting friction, and R = normal reaction.
4. The force of friction is independent of the area of contact between the two surfaces.
5. The force of friction depends upon the roughness of the surface.

DEFINITIONS

For defining the terms like co-efficient of friction (μ) and angle of friction, ϕ, consider a solid body placed on a horizontal plane surface as shown in Fig. 3.1.

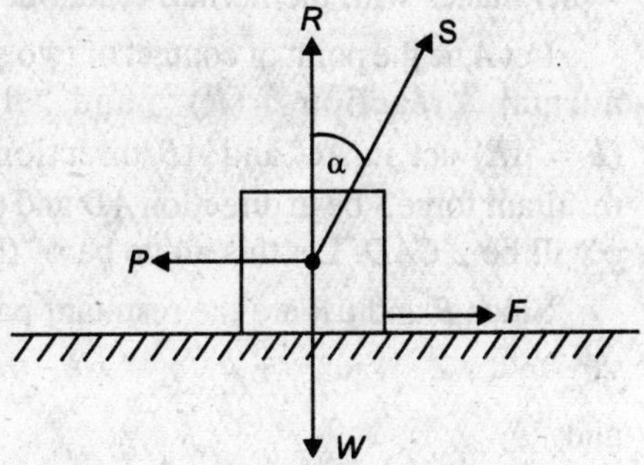

Fig. 3.1

This body is in equilibrium under the action of two forces. Its weight W is acting vertically down wards through its C.G. and the reaction of the surface *R* acting through the C.G. vertically upwards. As *R* is equal to *W*, the line of action of both *R* and *W* should be in one vertical direction. Let the body is pulled by a small force *P* acting on the body through its C.G. and parallel to horizontal surface. If *P* is not sufficient, the body will remains in equilibrium under the action of three forces *P*, *W* and the reaction of surface *S*. As all the three forces have to obey Lami's theorem, hence surface reaction will incline at an angle of α with *R*, instead of being vertical. If we take horizontal component of *S*, as *F* and vertical component *R*, then for equilibrium $P = F$ and $R = W$

where, $R = S\cos\alpha$ and $F = S\sin\alpha$ and $\dfrac{S\sin\alpha}{S\cos\alpha} = \dfrac{F}{R}$

$$\therefore \qquad \tan\alpha = \frac{F}{R}$$

If the magnitude of applied force *P* goes on increasing the angle α will also go on increasing to a limit and this limit of α (Maximum value of α) is indicated by ϕ and this limiting value of α is called angle of friction (i.e. ϕ).

As reaction *R* is always equal to the weight *W*, hence due to increase in applied force *P*, force *F* will also go on increasing and this force *F* (which is produced in opposite direction to *P*) is called force of friction. Hence force of friction is that force which prevents or tends to stop the sliding of one body over the other. This resisting force acts in a direction opposite to the direction of motion. It is also clear that maximum value of *F* is, $F = R\tan\phi$ where $\tan\phi = \mu$ and μ is called coefficient of friction.

$$\therefore \qquad F/R = \tan\phi \qquad \text{...(3.1)}$$

Hence limiting friction is the maximum friction force at the time when the motion is about to begin. The limiting force of friction is denotd by F.

If the magnitude of *F* is further increased the body will start moving, and the force of friction is called kinetic friction, and the friction force drops to some what low value.

ANGLE OF FRICTION (φ)

In equilibrium, if friction force (F) and normal reaction (R) are composed in one force then this composed force (S) is called resultant reaction. The angle between this resultant reaction (S) and normal reaction (R) is called angle of friction (φ). Hence angle of friction is defined as the angle (φ) which the resultant of normal reaction (R) and limiting friction ($f = \mu R$) makes with the normal reaction.

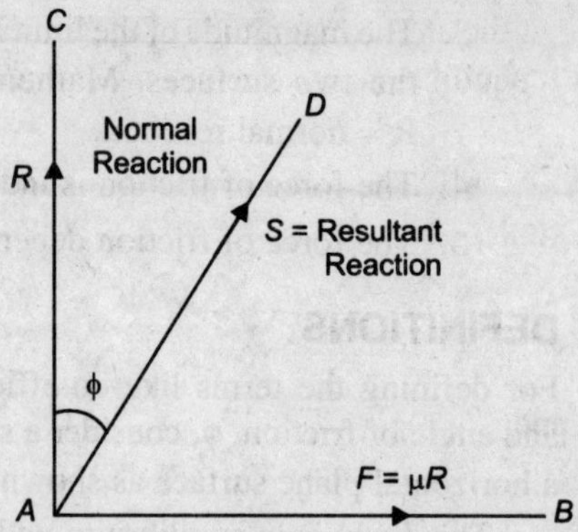

Fig. 3.2

Let A be the point of contact of two solid bodies at which normal reaction (R) and limiting friction ($F = \mu R$) act in AC and AB directions respectively. Let resultant force S be in direction AD and then angle of friction φ will be $\angle CAD$. Let this angle be φ. (Refer Fig. 3.2)

Since R and μR are the resultant parts of S

∴ $$\mu R = S \sin \phi$$

and $$R = S \cos \phi,$$

and $$\frac{\mu R}{R} = \frac{S \sin \phi}{S \cos \phi}$$

∴ $$\mu = \tan \phi \qquad \text{when, } \mu = \text{coefficient of friction,}$$

$$\therefore \mu = \tan^{-1}(\mu) \qquad \text{when, } \phi = \text{angle of friction}$$

Hence angle of friction is that angle whose tangent is equal to the coefficient of friction.

The angle between the resultant reaction S and normal reaction R is called angle of friction (φ).

COEFFICIENT OF FRICTION (μ)

It is defined as the ratio of the limiting force of friction (F) to the normal reaction (R) between two bodies. It is denoted by symbol μ. Thus

$$\mu = \frac{\text{limiting force of friction}}{\text{normal reaction}}$$

$$= \frac{F}{R}$$

∴ $$F = \mu R$$

The approximate values of static friction coefficients for pair of contacting surfaces are :

1. Wood on wood = 0.3 to 0.5
2. Metal on metals = 0.15 to 0.25
3. Wood on metals = 0.2 to 0.6

ANGLE OF REPOSE

Consider a block of weight W resting on an inclined plane OA making an angle α with the horizonal as shown in Fig. 3.3.

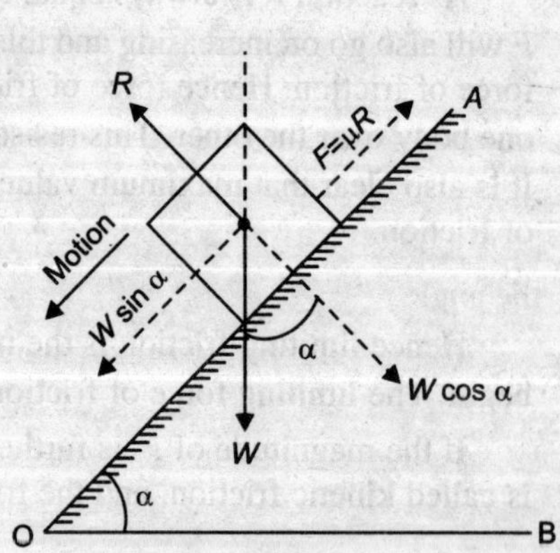

Fig. 3.3

Let the angle α be increased gradually till the block is just at the point of sliding. The block is then in equilibrium state under the influence of following forces :

(i) Weight W of the block acting vertically downwards.

(ii) Normal reaction R acting at right angle to the inclined plane, and

(iii) Limiting force of friction, $F = \mu R$, acting up the plane as the block is to slide downwards.

Resolving these forces along and perpendicular to the plane

$$\mu R = W \sin \alpha,$$

and

$$R = W \cos \alpha$$

or

$$\frac{\mu R}{R} = \frac{W \sin \alpha}{W \cos \alpha} = \tan \alpha$$

$\therefore$

$$\tan \alpha = \mu$$

i.e.

$$\mu = \tan \alpha \quad \text{...(i)}$$

In terms of anle of friction ϕ, the coefficient of friction is given as, $\mu = \tan \phi$.

$\therefore$

$$\tan \phi = \tan \alpha$$

or

$$\phi = \alpha \quad \text{...(ii)}$$

The angle α of the inclined plane at which the block is resting on it and is about to slide down the plane is called the angle of repose, and it is equal to the angle of friction between the block and the inclined plane.

CONE OF FRICTION

With reference to Fig. 3.4, the lines of action of normal reaction R and frictional force F meet at point O. The magnitude of total reaction, $S = \sqrt{F^2 + R^2}$ and it makes an angle ϕ with the normal reaction R. Obviously O is the vertex of a cone whose axis is R and semi-vertex angle is ϕ. Such a right circular cone is called the cone of friction.

It is worth while to point out that in case of impending motion, the friction force is maximum and the total reaction S lies on surface of the cone. When the friction force is less than the limiting friction, the total reaction S would lie within the cone. In that case, the forces acting on the body are not sufficient to cause motion. This aspect forms the working principle for self-locking mechanism.

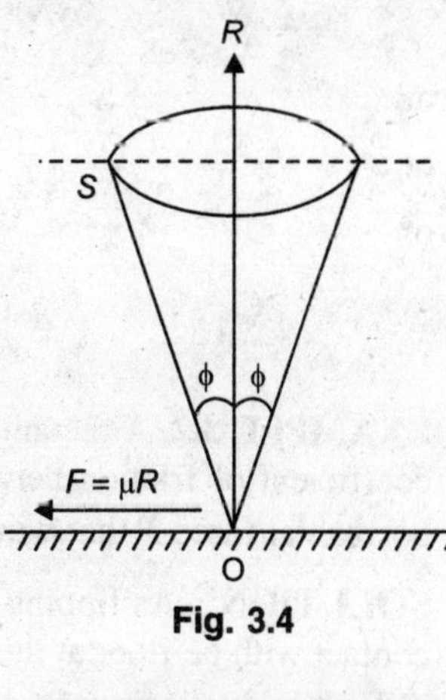

Fig. 3.4

Hence cone of friction is defined as a right circular cone with vertex as the point of contact of two bodies (or surfaces), axis in the direction of normal reaction (R) and semi-vertical angle equal to the angle of friction (ϕ).

In Fig. 3.4, O = Point of contact between two bodies.

R = Normal reaction and also axis of the cone of friction

ϕ = Angle of friction.

EXAMPLE 3.1. A wooden block of 5 kg mass rests on a horizontal plane. Determine the force required to (*a*) pull it, and (*b*) Push it. Assume the coefficient of friction, $\mu = 0.4$, and inclination of applied forces 15° to the horizontal.

SOLUTION : (a) Pull

Let P_1 be the force required to just pull it. Free body diagram is shown in Fig. 3.5 (a).

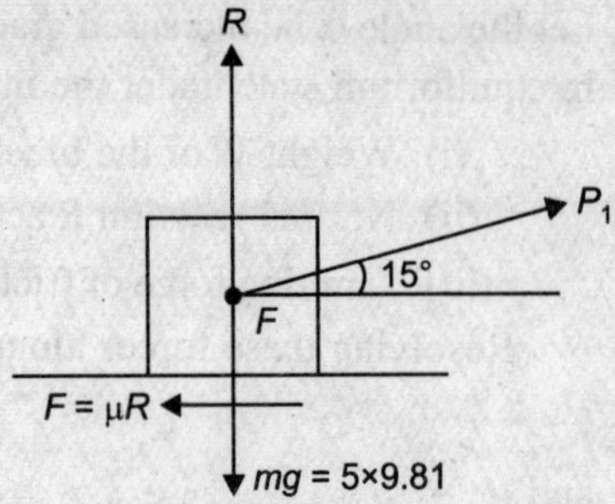

Fig. 3.5 (a)

Writing the equations of equilibrium :

For $\Sigma H = 0$, we have

$$P_1 \cos 15° = \mu R$$

$\therefore$ $$0.966 P_1 = 0.4\, R \quad ...(1)$$

For $\Sigma V = 0$, we have

$$R + P_1 \sin 15° = mg$$

or $$\frac{0.966 P_1}{0.4} + 0.259 P_1 = 5 \times 9.81$$

or $$2.415 P_1 + 0.249 P_1 = 49.05$$

or $$2.674 P_1 = 49.05$$

$\therefore$ $$P_1 = 49.05/2.654$$

$$= 18.34 \text{ N } \textbf{Ans.}$$

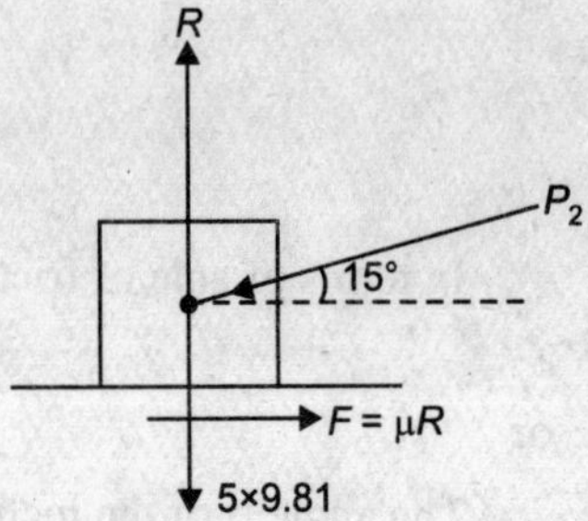

Fig. 3.5 (b)

(b) Push : Let P_2 be the required force. Writing equations of equilibrium with the help of free body diagram of Fig. 3.5(b)

For $\Sigma H = 0$, we have

$$P_2 \cos 15° = \mu R$$

or $$0.966 P_2 = 0.4 R$$

$\therefore$ $$R = 2.415\ P_2$$

For $\Sigma V = 0$, we have

$$R = P_2 \sin 15° + \text{mg}$$

or $$2.415\ P_2 = 0.2588\ P_2 + 5 \times 9.81$$

or $$2.415 P_2 - 0.2588 P_2 = 49.05$$

or $$2.1562 P_2 = 49.05$$

$\therefore$ $$P_2 = 49.05/2.1562$$

$$= 22.75 \text{ N } \textbf{Ans.}$$

EXAMPLE 3.2. A rectangular block *ABCD* of height *h*, width *b* and mass *m* rests on a floor. The coefficient of friction between the block and the floor is μ. What is the highest position for the horizontal force *P* that would permit it to just move the block without tipping.

SOLUTION : As tipping occurs, the block will just be lifted off the floor and shall maintain a contact with he floor at the edge *A*. So the normal reaction *R* and the frictional force μ*R* shall act at *A*. Free body diagram is shown in Fig. 3.6.

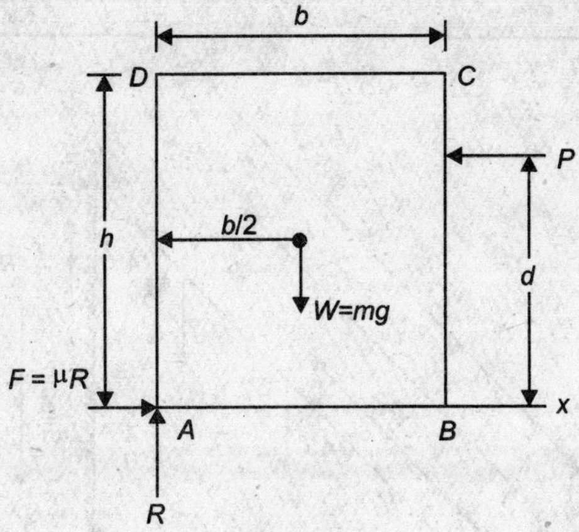

Fig. 3.6

Writing the equation of equilibrium,

For $\Sigma H = 0$,

$$\mu R = P \quad \text{...(i)}$$

For $\Sigma V = 0$,

$$R = mg \quad \text{...(ii)}$$

$\therefore$
$$P = \mu mg \quad \text{...(iii)}$$

For $\Sigma M_A = 0$

$$P \times d = mg \times \frac{b}{2}$$

or
$$\mu\, mg \times d = mg \times \frac{b}{2}$$

or
$$2\mu d = b$$

$\therefore$
$$d = b/2\mu \textbf{ Ans.}$$

EXAMPLE 3.3. A 7*m* long ladder, rests against a vertical wall, with which it makes an angle of 45°, and on a floor. If a man, whose weight is one half that of the ladder, climbs it, at what distance along the ladder will he be, when the ladder is about to slip?

The coefficient of friction between the ladder and the wall is 1/3 and that between the ladder and the floor is 1/2.

SOLUTION : Suppose the man climbs a length l of the ladder before slipping impends. Free body diagram is shown in Fig. 3.7.

Writing equations of equilibrium

For $\Sigma H = 0$

$$\frac{1}{2} R_A = R_B$$

$\therefore$
$$R_A = 2R_B \quad \text{...(i)}$$

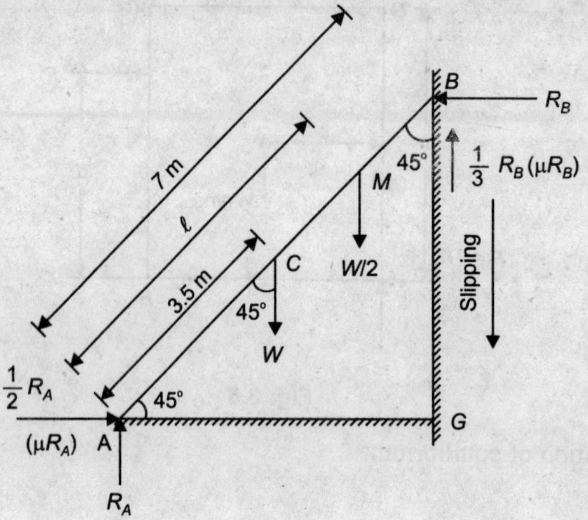

Fig. 3.7

For $\Sigma V = 0$

$$R_A + \frac{R_B}{3} = W + \frac{W}{2} \qquad \text{...(ii)}$$

or
$$2R_B + \frac{R_B}{3} = 1.5\ W$$

or
$$R_B = 0.6429W \qquad \text{...(iii)}$$

$$R_A = 2R_B = 1.2857W \qquad \text{...(iv)}$$

$$R_B(7 \sin 45°) + \frac{1}{3} R_B(7 \cos 45°) = W(3.5 \cos 45°) + \frac{W}{2}(\ell \cos 45°)$$

$$0.6429W(4.9497) + \frac{1}{3}(0.6429W)\ (4.9497) = W(2.4749) + \frac{W}{2}(\ell)\ (0.7071)$$

$$3.1822W + 1.0607W = 2.4749W + \frac{W}{2} \times 0.7071\ell$$

$$4.2429W - 2.4749W = 0.3536Wl$$

or
$$1.768W = 0.3536Wl$$

$\therefore$
$$l = 1.768/0.3536$$

$$= 5m \ \textbf{Ans.}$$

EXAMPLE 3.4. A body of weight 500 *N* is pulled up an inclined plane, by a force of 350*N*. The inclination of the plane is 30° to the horizontal and the force is applied parallel to the plane. Determine the coefficient of friction.

SOLUTION : Given

Weight of the body, $W = 500\ N$, Force applied, $P = 350N$, Inclination, $\alpha = 30°$

Let, μ = coefficient of friction, R = Normal reaction, $F = \mu R$ = Force of friction

The body is in equilibrium under the action of the forces shown in Fig. 3.8

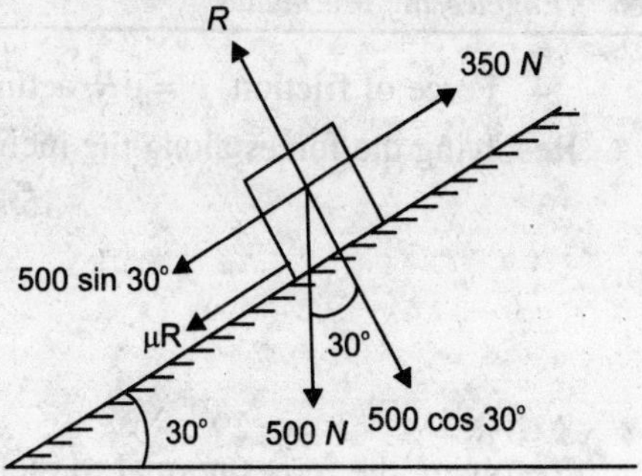

Fig. 3.8

Resolving the forces along the plane

$$500 \sin 30° + \mu R = 350 \quad ...(i)$$

Resolving the forces normal to the plane

$$R = 500 \cos 30°$$
$$= 500 \times 0.866 = 433\ N$$

Substituting he value of R in equation (i), we get

$$500 \sin 30° + \mu \times 433 = 350$$

or $\quad 500 \times 0.5 + 433\ \mu = 350$

or $\quad 433\ \mu = 350 - 250 = 100$

$\therefore \quad \mu = 100/433$

$= 0.23$ **Ans.**

EXAMPLE 3.5. (a) Define co-efficient of friction and limiting friction.

(b) Block A weighing $15N$ is a rectangular prism resting on a rough inclind plane as shown in Fig. 3.9(a). The block is tied up by a horizontal string which has a tension of $5N$. Find :

(i) Frictional Force on block

(ii) Normal reaction of inclined plane.

(iii) Coefficient of friction between the surfaces of contact.

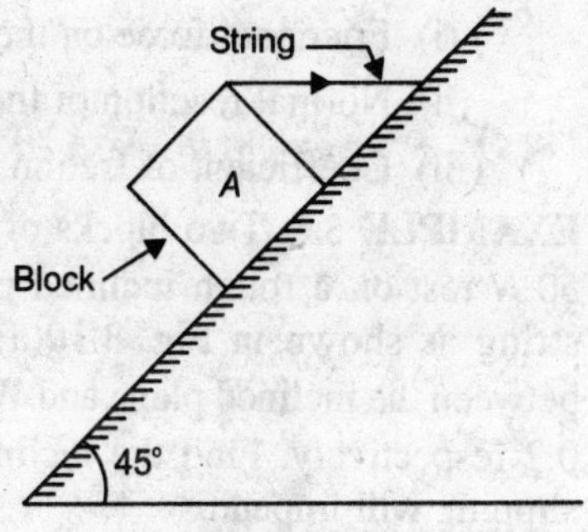

Fig. 3.9 (a)

SOLUTION : Given :

(i) Weight of block, $W = 15N$

(ii) Horizontal tension in the string, $T = 5N$

(iii) Inclination of plane, $\alpha = 45°$

Let, F = Frictional force, R = Normal reaction, and μ = coefficient of friction.

Since there is tension in the string which means if the string is removed, the block will slide down the plane. Hence force of friction ($F = \mu R$) will be acting in the upward direction.

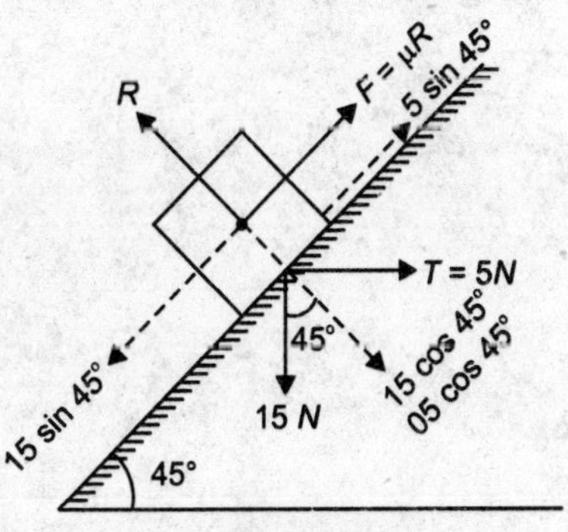

Fig. 3.9 (b)

The block A is in equilibrium under the action of forces shown in Fig. 3.9 (b). These froces are:

1. The weight of the block, $W = 15\ N$
2. Horizontal tension in the string, $T = 5N$
3. Normal reaction, R

4. Force of friction, $F = \mu R$, acting upwards.

Resolving the forces along the inclined plane,

$$15 \sin 45° = F + 5 \cos 45°$$

or $$F = 15 \sin 45° - 5 \sin 45°$$

∴ $$F = 15 \times 0.707 - 5 \times 0.707$$

$$= 10 \times 0.707 = 7.07\ N \qquad \text{...(i)}$$

Resolving the forces normal to inclined plane

$$R = 15 \cos 45° + T \cos 45°$$

$$= 15 \cos 45° + 5 \cos 45°$$

∴ $$R = 15 \times 0.707 + 5 \times 0.707$$

$$= 20 \times 0.707 = 14.14\ N$$

∴ $$F = \mu R$$

∴ $$\mu = F/R$$

$$= 7.07/14.14 = 0.5 \textbf{ Ans.}$$

Hence

(i) Frictional force on the block, $F = 7.07\ N$ **Ans.**

(ii) Normal reaction of the inclined plane, $R = 14.14\ N$ **Ans.**

(iii) Coefficient of frction, $\mu = 0.5$ **Ans.**

EXAMPLE 3.6. Two blocks of weight $W_1 = 50\ N$ and $W_2 = 50\ N$ rest on a rough inclined plane and are connected by a string as shown in Fig. 3.10(a). The coefficient of friction between the inclined plane and W_1 and W_2 are $\mu_1 = 0.3$ and $\mu_2 = 0.2$ respectively. Find the inclination of the plane for which slipping will impend.

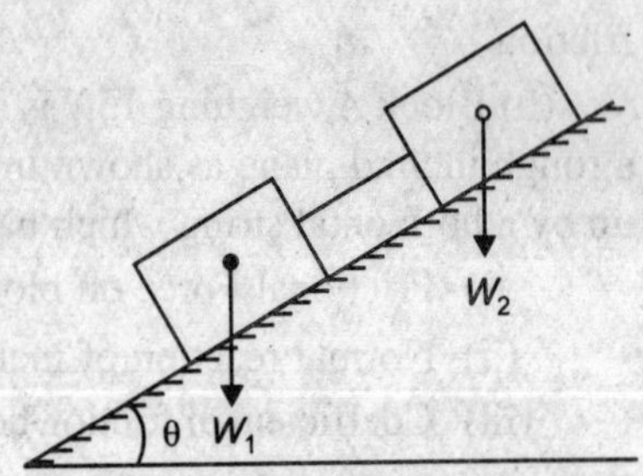

Fig. 3.10(a)

SOLUTION : Free body diagrams of the two blocks as shown in Fig. 3.10(b), where T is the tension in the string.

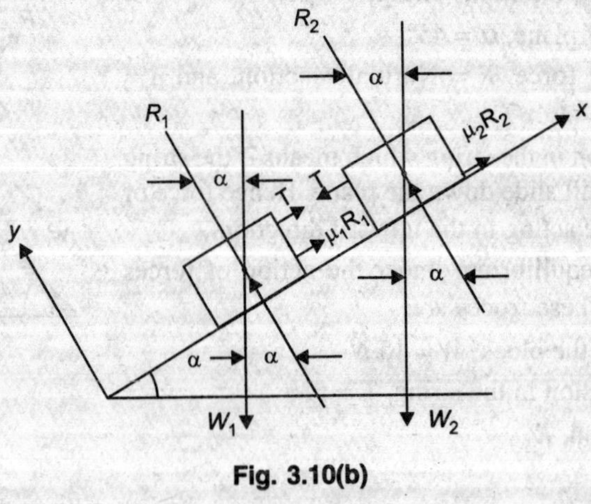

Fig. 3.10(b)

Consider the equilibrium of W_2

For $\Sigma X = 0$, (i.e. Along the plane)

$$\mu_2 R_2 = T + W_2 \sin\alpha \quad \text{...(i)}$$

For $\Sigma Y = 0$, (i.e. along the plane)

$$R_2 = W_2 \cos\alpha \quad \text{...(ii)}$$

Consider the equilibrium of W_1

For $\Sigma X = 0$,

$$\mu_1 R_1 + T = W_1 \sin\alpha \quad \text{...(iii)}$$

For $\Sigma Y = 0$,

$$R_1 = W_1 \cos\alpha \quad \text{...(iv)}$$

Add (*i*) and (*iii*)

$$\mu_1 R_1 + \mu_2 R_2 = W_1 \sin\alpha + W_2 \sin\alpha + T - T$$

or $$\mu_1 R_1 + \mu_2 R_2 = \sin\alpha(W_1 + W_2)$$

or $$\mu_1 (W_1 \cos\alpha) + \mu_2 (W_2 \cos\alpha) = \sin\alpha(W_1 + W_2) \quad \text{(Putting the value of } R_1 \text{ and } R_2\text{)}$$

or $$\cos\alpha(\mu_1 W_1) + \cos\alpha(\mu_2 W_2) = \sin\alpha(W_1 + W_2)$$

or $$\cos\alpha(\mu_1 W_1 + \mu_2 W_2) = \sin\alpha(W_1 + W_2)$$

or $$\frac{\mu_1 W_1 + \mu_2 W_2}{W_1 + W_2} = \frac{\sin\alpha}{\cos\alpha} = \tan\alpha$$

Putting $\mu_1 = 0.3$, $\mu_2 = 0.2$, $W_1 = 50\ N$, $W_2 = 50\ N$

$$\tan\alpha = \frac{0.3 \times 50 + 0.2 \times 50}{50 + 50}$$

or $$\tan\alpha = 0.25$$

$\therefore$ $$\alpha = \tan^{-1}(0.25) = 14° \textbf{ Ans.}$$

EXAMPLE 3.7. Two blocks are connected by a horizontal line *AB* and rest on two planes as shown in Fig. 3.11 What is the smallest weight W_A of the block *A* for which the equilibrium can exist? Assume the coefficient of friction for the block *A* and the horizontal surface to be 0.4 and the angle of friction for the block *B* on inclined plane is $\phi = 20°$ (2003).

SOLUTION : Given : $\mu_A = 0.4$, $W_B = 500N$

Let W_A = smallest weight of block *A*.

Considering the equilibrium of block *A*

Let *P* be the force of friction of block *A*, which is acting horizontally on the block *B*.

$P = \mu_A R_A = 0.4\ (W_A) = 0.4\ W_A$ ...(*i*)

We also know that the smallest force, which will hold the system in equilibrium or prevent the block *B* from sliding downwards.

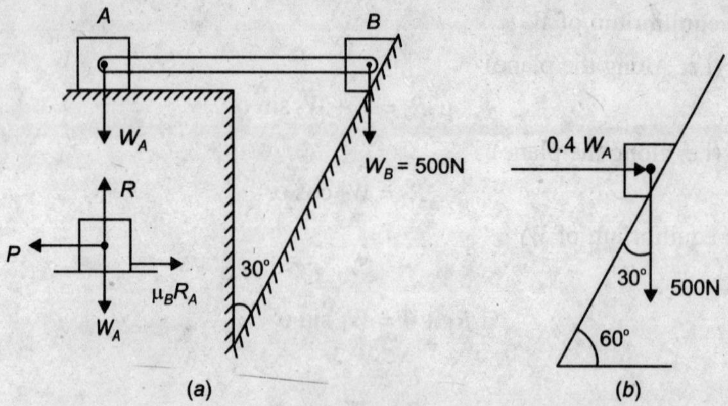

Fig. 3.11

This force ($P = .4\ W_A$) will be transmitted to block B through rod A.

$$\therefore \quad P = W_B \tan(\alpha - \phi)$$

$$(\because \tan\phi = \mu_B \text{ and } P = \mu_B . R_B = \tan\phi .\ W_B)$$

$$\therefore \quad 0.4\ W_A = W_B \tan(60° - 20°)$$

or $$0.4 \times W_A = 500 \text{ an } 40°$$

or $$0.4\ W_A = 500 \times 0.8391$$

$$\therefore \quad W_A = \frac{500 \times 0.8391}{0.4} = 1049N \textbf{ Ans}$$

EXAMPLE 3.8. Two blocks of weight W_1 and W_2 are connected by a string and rest on a horizontal plane as shown in Fig. 3.12. Find the magnitude and direction of the least force P that should be applied to the upper block to induce sliding. The coefficient of friction for each block is to be taken as μ.

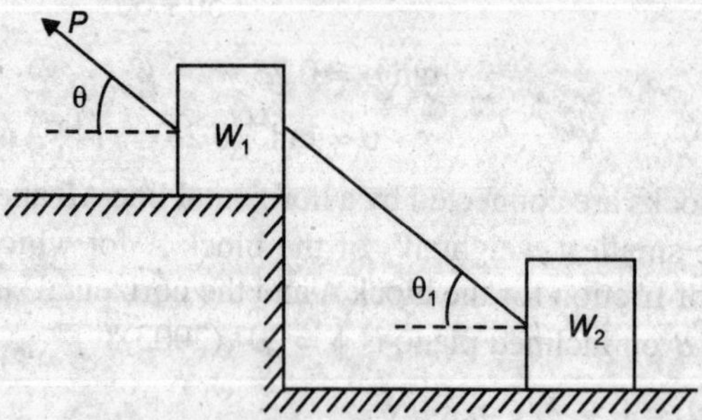

Fig. 3.12

SOLUTION : Let the force P makes an angle θ with the horizontal. Note that the angles θ_1 and θ are not known.

Free body diagram of each block is shown separately in Fig. 3.13. Let T be the tension in the string.

Writing the equations of equilibrium of block W_1 (Fig. 3.13b)

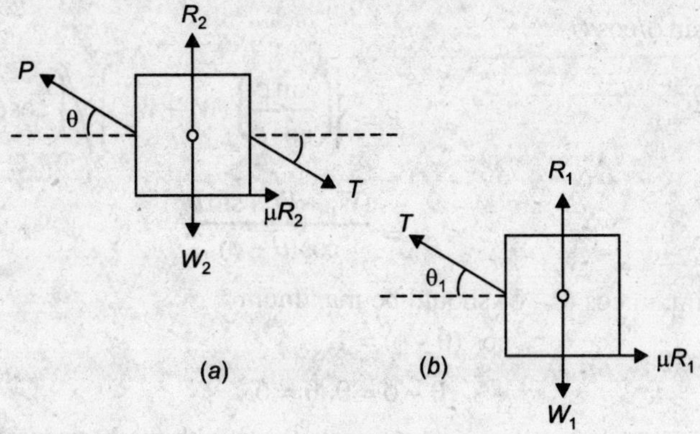

Fig. 3.13

For $\Sigma H = 0$,

$$\mu R_1 = T\cos\theta_1 \quad \text{...(i)}$$

For $\Sigma V = 0$,

$$T\sin\theta_1 + R_1 - W_1 \quad \text{...(ii)}$$

Now writing the equations of equilibrium, for block W_2

For $\Sigma H = 0$,

$$\mu R_2 = T\cos\theta_1 - P\cos\theta = 0 \quad \text{...(iii)}$$

For $\Sigma V = 0$,

$$R_2 + P\sin\theta - T\sin\theta_1 = 0 \quad \text{...(iv)}$$

There are four equations and six unknowns (R_1, R_2, T, P, θ_1, θ).

Let us eliminate T, R_1, R_2 and θ_1

From (i) and (ii) eliminating R_1

$$T = \frac{W_1\mu}{(\mu\sin\theta_1 + \cos\theta_1)} \quad \text{...(v)}$$

From (iii) and (iv) eliminating R_2

$$T = \frac{P(\cos\theta + \mu\sin\theta) - \mu W_2}{(\mu\sin\theta_1 + \cos\theta_1)} \quad \text{...(vi)}$$

Eliminating T from (v) and (vi)

$$\frac{W_1\mu}{(\mu\sin\theta_1 + \cos\theta_1)} = \frac{P(\cos\theta + \mu\cos\theta) - \mu W_2}{(\mu\sin\theta_1 + \cos\theta_1)}$$

$$\therefore \quad P = \frac{\mu(W_1 + W_2)}{(\cos\theta + \mu\sin\theta)}$$

But $\mu = \tan\phi = \sin\phi/\cos\phi$

$$P = \left\{\left(\frac{\sin\phi}{\cos\phi}\right)(W_1 + W_2)\right\} \Big/ \left(\cos\theta + \frac{\sin\phi}{\cos\phi}\cdot\sin\theta\right)$$

$$= \frac{(W_1 + W_2)\sin\phi}{\cos(\theta - \phi)}$$

For P to be minimum $\cos(\theta - \phi)$ should be maximum

$$\cos(\theta - \phi) = 1,$$

$$\theta - \phi = 0, \theta = \phi$$

$\therefore$ $P_{min} = (W_1 + W_2)\sin\theta$ and acts at an angle $\theta = \phi$ with the horizontal. **Ans.**

EXAMPLE 3.9. A body resting on a rough horizontal plane required a pull of 180 N inclined at 30° to the plane just to move it. It was found that a push of 220*N* inclined at 30° to the plane just moves the body. Determine the weight of the body and coefficient of friction (2004).

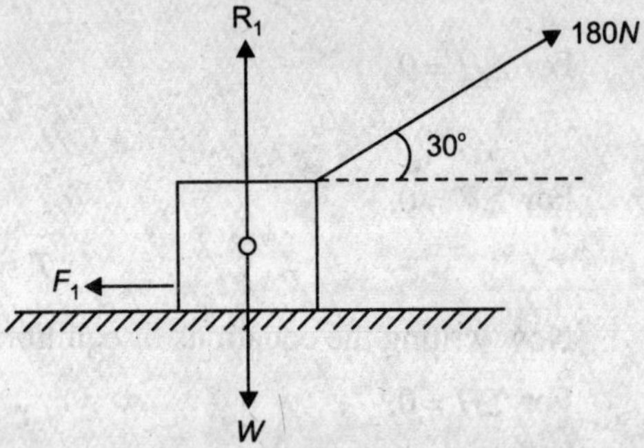

Fig. 3.14

SOLUTION : Given :

Pull = 180 *N*; Push = 220*N*, $\theta = 30°$

Let, W = Weight of the body in Newtons,

R = Normal reaction, and

μ = Coefficient of friction

First of all, consider a pull of 180*N* acting on a body. We known that in this case the force of friction F_1 will act towards left side as shown in Fig. 3.14.

Resolving the forces horizontally,

$$F_1 = 180\cos 30° = 155.8846\ N$$

and now resolving the forces vertically,

$$R_1 = W - 180\sin 30° = (W - 90)N$$

We know that force of friction $F_1 = \mu R_1$

$$\therefore \quad 155.8846 = \mu(W - 90) \quad \text{...(i)}$$

Now consider a push of 220*N* acting on the body. We know that in this case, the, the force of friction F_2 will act towards right side as shown in Fig. 3.15.

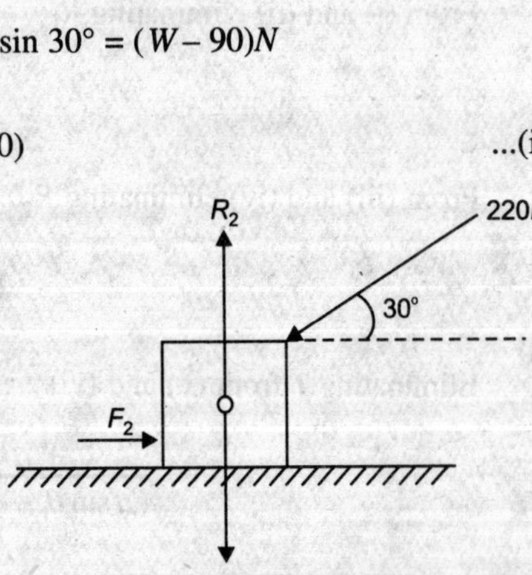

Fig. 3.15

Resolving the forces horizontally,

$$F_2 = 220\cos 30° = 190.526N$$

and now resolving the forces vertically,

$$R_2 = W + 220\sin 30° = (W + 110)N$$

We know that force of friction,

$$F_2 = \mu R_2$$

$$\therefore \quad 190.526 = \mu(W + 110) \quad \text{...(ii)}$$

Dividing equation (i) by (ii), we have,

$$\frac{155.885}{190.526} = \frac{\mu(W-90)}{\mu(W+110)}$$

$$= \frac{W-90}{W+110}$$

or $$155.885W + 17147.79 = 190.526W - 17147.34$$

or $$34.641W = 34295.13$$

$\therefore$ $$W = 34295.13/34.641$$

$$= 990.016N \textbf{ Ans.}$$

From equation (i)

$$155.8846 = \mu\,(990.016 - 90)$$

$\therefore$ $$\mu = 0.1732 \textbf{ Ans.}$$

EXAMPLE 3.10. A block of weight W rests on a rough inclined plane of inclination α with the horizontal. The block is subjected to a force P acting horizontal. Set up the following relations for the equilibrium of the block :

(i) $P = W\tan(\alpha - \phi)$ when the block is at the point of sliding down (2004).

(ii) $P = W\tan(\alpha + \theta)$ when the block is at the point of sliding up, when ϕ = Angle of friction.

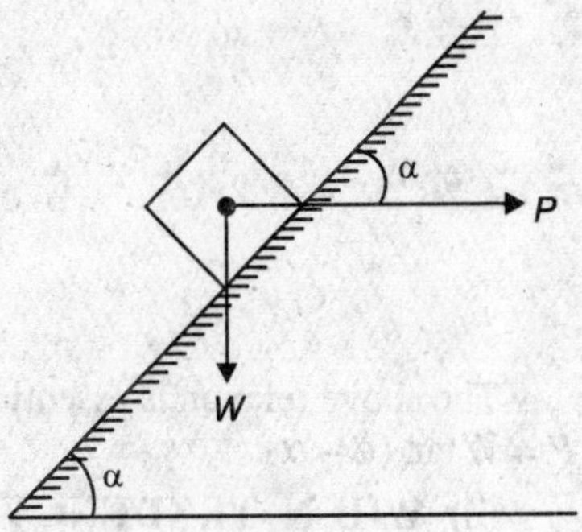

Fig. 3.16

SOLUTION : Refer Fig. 3.16, which shows the block of weight W resting on a rough inclined plane of inclination α with the horizontal. The block is subjected to a force P that acts horizontally.

(i) WHEN TENDENCY OF THE BLOCK IS TO MOVE DOWN THE PLANE (Fig. 3.17) : Since the block has impending motion down the plane, the friction force ($F = \mu R$) would act up the plane. The various forces which keep the block in equilibrium and as shown in free body diagram (Fig. 3.17) are :

(i) Weight W of the block

(ii) Reaction R of the plane

(iii) Tractive force P, and

(iv) Frictional force, $F = \mu R$

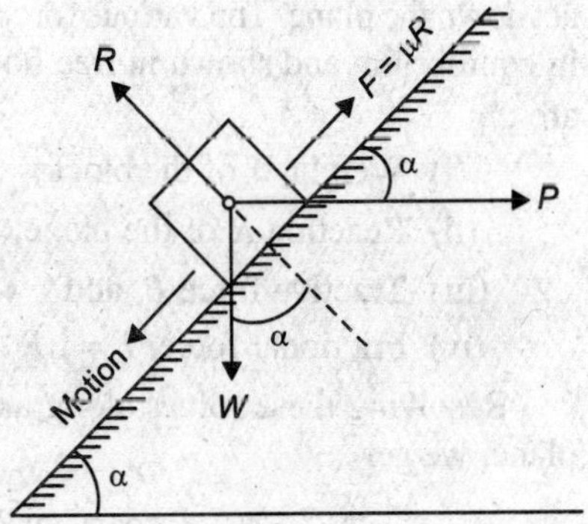

Fig. 3.17

Resolving these forces along and perpendicular to the plane, we get,

$$P\cos\alpha + \mu R - W\sin\alpha = 0$$

or $$P\cos\alpha = W\sin\alpha - \mu R$$

and $$R = W\cos\alpha + P\sin\alpha$$

$\therefore$ $$P\cos\alpha = W\sin\alpha - \mu(W\cos\alpha + P\sin\alpha)$$

or $$P\cos\alpha = W\sin\alpha - \mu W\cos\alpha - \mu P\sin\alpha$$

or $$P(\cos\alpha + \mu\sin\alpha) = W(\sin\alpha - \mu\cos\alpha)$$

$\therefore$ $$P = W\frac{\sin\alpha - \mu\cos\alpha}{\cos\alpha + \mu\sin\alpha}$$

Substituting $\mu = \tan\theta = \dfrac{\sin\theta}{\cos\theta}$ where θ is the angle of friction

$$P = W\frac{\sin\alpha - \dfrac{\sin\phi}{\cos\phi}\cos\alpha}{\cos\alpha + \dfrac{\sin\phi}{\cos\phi}\sin\alpha}$$

$$= W\frac{\sin\alpha\cos\phi - \sin\phi\cos\alpha}{\cos\alpha\cos\phi + \sin\alpha\sin\phi}$$

$\therefore$ $$P = W\frac{\sin(\alpha - \phi)}{\cos(\alpha - \phi)}$$

$$= W\tan(\alpha - \phi) \textbf{ Ans.} \quad \text{...(i)}$$

The above relation is essentially valid where $\alpha > \phi$. Increase $\phi > \alpha$, this relation takes the form $P = W\tan(\phi - \alpha)$.

(ii) WHEN TENDENCY OF BLOCK IS TO MOVE UP THE PLANE (Fig. 3.14b): Since the block has impending motion up the plane, the friction force would act down the plane. The various forces which keep the block in equilibrium and shown in free body diagram (Fig. 3.18) are :

(i) Weight *W* of the block,

(ii) Reaction *R* of the plane,

(iii) Tractive force *P*, and

(iv) Frictional force, $F = \mu R$

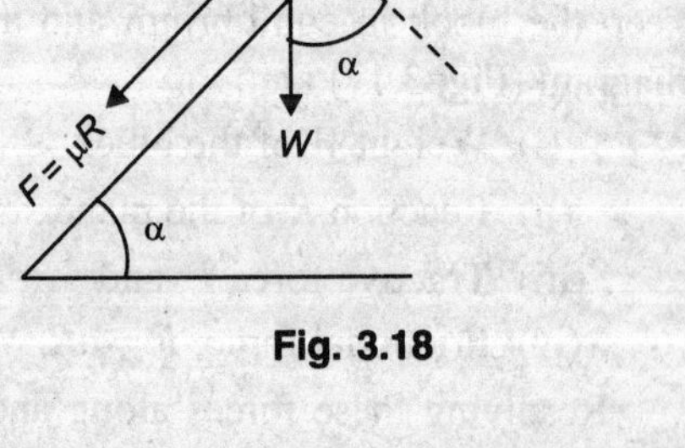

Fig. 3.18

Resolving these forces along and perpendicular to the plane, we get

$$P\cos\alpha - \mu R - W\sin\alpha = 0$$

$\therefore$ $$P\cos\alpha = W\sin\alpha + \mu R$$

and $$R - W\cos\alpha - P\sin\alpha = 0$$

$$\therefore \quad R = W \sin \cos\alpha + P \sin \alpha$$

$$\therefore \quad P\cos\alpha = W \sin \alpha + \mu(W \cos\alpha + P \sin\alpha)$$

$$= W \sin \alpha + \mu W \cos \alpha + \mu P \sin \alpha$$

or
$$P(\cos \alpha - \mu \sin \alpha) = W(\sin\alpha + \mu\cos\alpha)$$

$$\therefore \quad P = W\frac{\sin \alpha + \mu \cos\alpha}{\cos\alpha - \mu \sin \alpha}$$

Substituting $\mu = \tan\phi = \dfrac{\sin\phi}{\cos\phi}$ where ϕ is the anle of friction

$$\therefore \quad P = W\frac{\sin \alpha + \dfrac{\sin\phi}{\cos\phi}\cos\alpha}{\cos\alpha - \dfrac{\sin\phi}{\cos\phi}\sin\alpha}$$

$$= W\frac{\sin \alpha \cos\phi + \sin\phi\cos\alpha}{\cos\alpha\cos\phi - \sin\phi\sin\alpha}$$

$$P = W\frac{\sin(\alpha + \phi)}{\cos(\alpha + \phi)}$$

$$= W\tan(\alpha + \phi) \text{ **Ans.**}$$

ROPE AND BELT FRICTION

The transmission of power in factories from one rotating shaft to another that lies at a considerable distance is achieved through the belts and ropes.

With reference to Fig. 3.19, the pulley *A* which is keyed to the rotating shaft is called driver. The pulley that needs to be driven is known as follower. When the driver rotates it carries the belt because of friction that exists between the pulley and the belt. The frictional resistance develops all

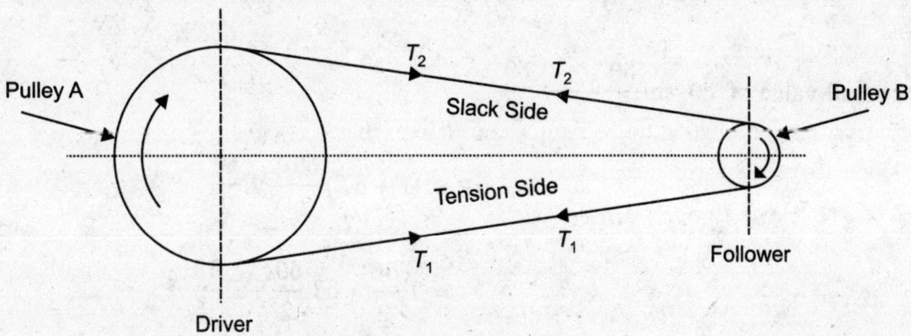

Fig. 3.19

along the contact surfaces. That makes the belt carry the follower which too starts rotating. The driving pulley pulls the belt from one side (called tension side) and delivers it to the other side (called slack side). The tension T_1 in the belt on the tension side is more than tension T_2 on slack slide.

RATIO OF TENSIONS (BELT FRICTION) : Fig. 3.20 shows a flexible belt resting on a stationary drum. The tension T_1 and T_2 are such that motion is impending between the belt and the drum. Considering impending motion of the belt to be counter clockwise relative to the drum, tension T_1 is more than T_2.

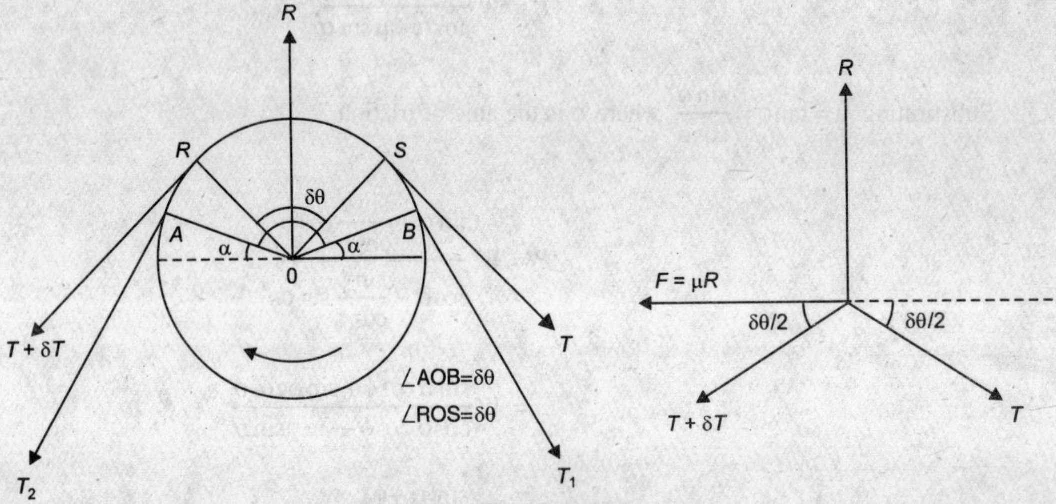

Fig. 3.20

Let attention be focussed on small segment *RS* of the belt which subtends an angle $\delta\theta$ at the centre. This segment *RS* is acted upon the following set of forces:

1. Tension T in the belt at S,
2. Tension $T + \delta T$ in the belt at R,
3. Normal reaction R and
4. Frictional force, $F = \mu R$

Considering equilibrium of the forces in the radial direction.

$$\mu R = (T + \delta T) \sin \frac{\delta\theta}{2} + T \sin \frac{\delta\theta}{2}$$

For small value of $\delta\theta$, $\sin \frac{\delta\theta}{2} \longrightarrow \frac{\delta\theta}{2}$

$$\mu R = (T + \delta T) \frac{\delta\theta}{2} + T \frac{\delta\theta}{2}$$

$$= T \frac{\delta\theta}{2} + \delta T \frac{\delta\theta}{2} + T \frac{\delta\theta}{2}$$

The term $\delta T \frac{\delta\theta}{2}$ is small in magnitude and can be neglected.

$$\therefore \quad R = T\delta\theta \quad \text{...(i)}$$

Considering equilibrium of forces in the tangential direction,

$$\mu R = (T + \delta T)\cos\frac{\delta\theta}{2} - \cos\frac{\delta\theta}{2}$$

For small value of $\delta\theta$; $\cos\frac{\delta\theta}{2} \longrightarrow 1$

$$HR = (T + \delta T) - T$$

$$\therefore \quad R = \frac{\delta T}{\mu} \quad \text{...(ii)}$$

From the expressions (i) and (ii)

$$T\delta\theta = \frac{\delta T}{\mu}$$

Separating the values and integrating within the limits $T = T_2$ at $\theta = 0$, and $T = T_1$ at $\theta = 0$, we get

$$\int_{T_2}^{T_1} \frac{\delta T}{T} = \mu \int_0^{\theta} \delta\theta, \log\frac{T_1}{T_2} = \mu\theta$$

$$\therefore \quad \frac{T_1}{T_2} = e^{\mu\theta} \quad \text{...(10.1)}$$

The value of $e = 2.718$ can be used for the numerical calculations

RATIO OF TENSIONS (ROPE AND V-BELT DRIVE): In the case of a rope or a belt drive, the rim of the pulley is grooved to accomodate the rope or the V-belt. The ratio of tensions is determined as follows :

Let 2α be the angle of the groove. The other notations used are the same as that used in the previous case of flat belt.

Free body diagram for an element *ab* of the belt, subtending an angle $d\theta$, is similar to the flat belt and is as shown in Fig. 3.21(c).

But the normal reaction and the frictional force are acting in a slightly different manner than in the case of the flat belt. This can be understood by considering a cross-section of the rope or the V-belt as shown in Fig. 3.21(a) and (b).

Where, dN_1 represent the normal reactions exerted by the slides of the groove on the belt or the rope and dN is the resultant of the normal reactions dN_1 acting on the belt.

$$dN = dN_1 \sin\alpha + dN_1 \sin\alpha$$

$$= 2dN_1 \sin\alpha$$

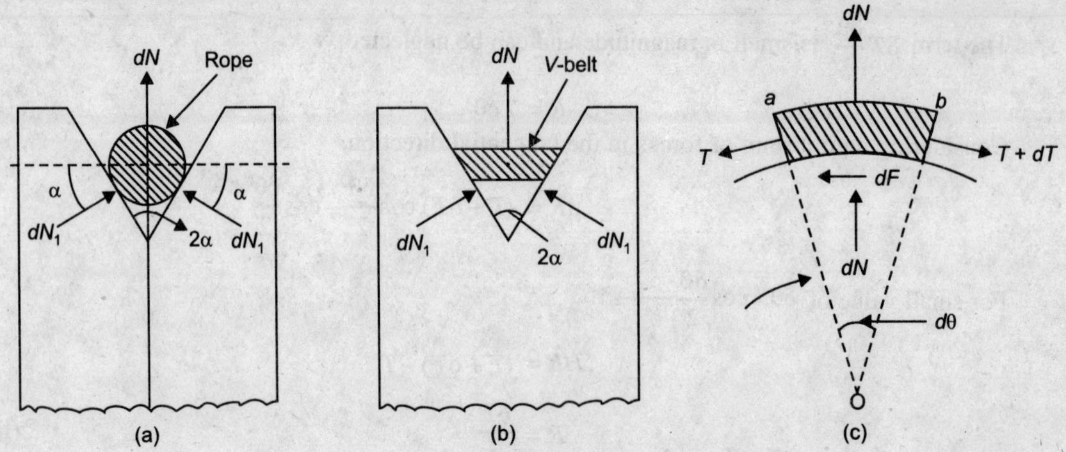

Fig. 3.21

or
$$dN_1 = \frac{dN}{2\sin\alpha} \quad \text{...(10.2)}$$

The friction force,

$$dF = \mu dN_1 + \mu dN_1 = 2\mu dN_1$$

$$dF = 2\mu \frac{dN}{2\sin\alpha} = \mu dN \text{cosec}\,\alpha$$

$$dF = (\mu \text{cosec}\,\alpha)\, dN \quad \text{...(10.3)}$$

Since for a flat belt we have obtained, $\frac{T_1}{T_2} = e^{\mu\theta}$

Hence for rope and V-belt drive,

$$\frac{T_1}{T_2} = e^{(\mu \text{cosec}\,\alpha)\theta} \quad \text{...(10.4)}$$

EXAMPLE 3.11. A belt supports two weights W_1 and W_2 over a pulley as shown in Fig. 3.22. If $W_1 = 1000\ N$, find the minimum weight W_2 to keep W_1 in equilibrium. Assume that the puley is locked and $\mu = 0.25$.

SOLUTION: Let the tensions in the belt be T_1 and T_2 as shown in Fig. (3.18) since the weight W_2 just checks the tendency of weight W_1 to move down, the tension on the side of W_1 is larger, that is $T_1 > T_2$, $\mu = 0.25$, $\theta = \pi$ and $W_1 = 1000\ N$ then W_2 = ?

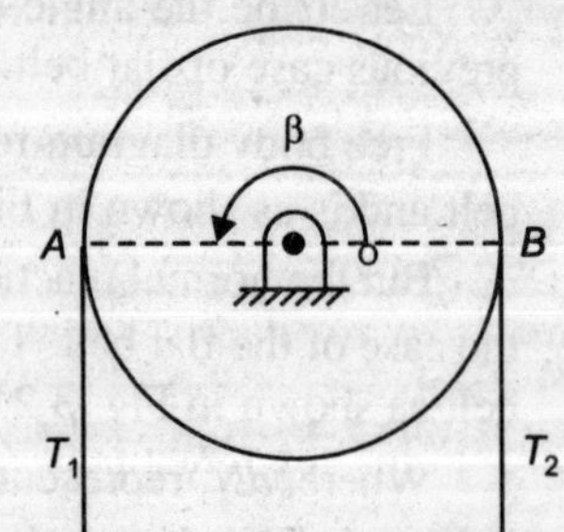

Fig. 3.22

Using the relation, $\frac{T_1}{T_2} = e^{\mu\theta}$,

we have
$$\frac{T_1}{T_2} = e^{\mu\theta}$$
$$= 2.781^{(0.25)\pi}$$
$$= 2.718^{(0.25)3.1416}$$
$$= 2.718^{0.7854}$$
$$\therefore \quad \frac{T_1}{T_2} = 2.193$$
But $T_1 = W_1 = 1000$ N

or $2.193\,(T_2) = T_1$

or $2.193T_2 = 1000$

$\therefore \quad T_2 = 1000/2.193 = 456\ N$

But $W_2 = T_2 = 456\ N$

$\therefore \quad W_2 = 456\ N$ **Ans.**

EXAMPLE 3.12. A rope is wrapped three turns around a cylinder as shown in Fig. 3.23. Determine the force required to just support a load of 1 kN. Coefficient of friction between the rope and the cylinder is 0.30.

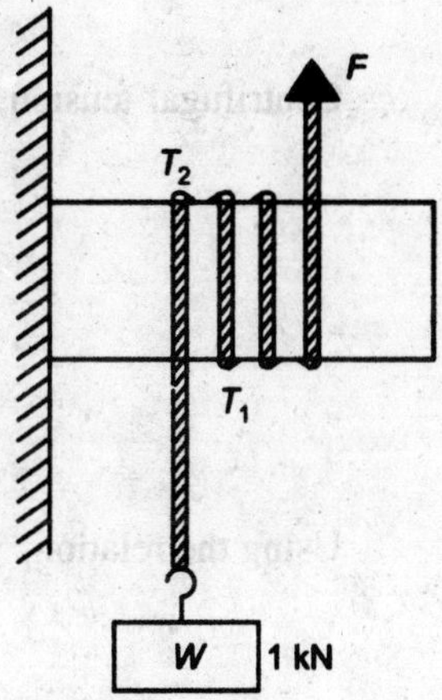

Fig. 3.23

SOLUTION : Angle of lap $\theta = 2\pi \times 3 = 6\pi$ radian for 3 turns of the rope.

The rope is wound on a surface with no groove, so $2\alpha = 180°$, and $\alpha = 90°$

$$\therefore \quad \operatorname{cosec}\alpha = \frac{1}{\sin\alpha} = \frac{1}{\sin 90} = 1$$

Using the relation $\frac{T_1}{T_2} = e^{(\mu\ \text{cosec})\theta}$

Where T_1 is the larger tension in that section of the rope which is about to slip. That is,

$$T_1 = W = 1KN = 1000 \text{ N}$$
and
$$T_2 = F$$
$$\therefore \quad \frac{1000}{F} = e^{(0.30 \times 1 \times 6\pi)}$$
$$= 2.718^{(0.30 \times 18.8496)}$$
$$= 2.718^{5.6549}$$

or $$\frac{1000}{F} = 285.52$$

or $$F = \frac{1000}{285.62}$$

$$= 3.50 \text{ N } \textbf{Ans.}$$

It can be seen here that a weigtht of 1000*N* can be checked from slipping down by applying a very small force (3.5*N*) because of the presence of frictional force.

EXAMPLE 3.13. Find the numer of ropes required to transmit 50 KW. The maximum permissible tension in the rope is 1500 *N*, velocity of the rope is 10 m/sec and the weight of the rope is 4N/m. Assume the angle of contact as 180° and pulley groove angle as 60°.

SOLUTION : Given :

$$T_{max} = 1500\text{N}, \theta = 180 = \pi \text{ radian}$$

$$2\alpha = 60°,$$

$$\alpha = 30°,$$

$$\mu = 0.2,$$

$$w = 4\text{N/m},$$

$$v = 10 \text{ m/sec}$$

Centrifugal tension,

$$T_c = \frac{W}{g}v^2 = \frac{4(10)^2}{9.81} = 40.77 \text{ N}$$

$$T_1 = T_{max} - T_c$$

$$= 1500 - 40.8$$

$$= 1459.20 \text{ N}$$

Using the relation, $\frac{T_1}{T_2} = e^{(\mu \text{ cosec } \alpha)\theta}$, we have

$$\frac{T_1}{T_2} = e^{(0.2 \text{ cosec } 30^0)\pi}$$

$$= 2.718^{(0.2\times 2)3.1415}$$

$$= 2.718^{1.257} = 3.5144$$

$\therefore$ $$\frac{T_1}{T_2} = 3.5144$$

$\therefore$ $$T_2 = \frac{T_1}{3.5144}$$

$$= \frac{1459.20}{3.5144} = 415.21 \text{ N}$$

Power transmited by single rope

$$P = (T_1 - T_2)\ v$$
$$= (1459.2 - 415.21)10$$
$$= 10.44 \text{ kW}$$

Number of ropes required to transmit 50 kW = 50/10.44 = 4.79.

∴ Whole number of ropes = 5 **Ans.**

DISC AND BEARING FRICTION

Power can be transmitted between two shafts *A* and *B* by virtue of the friction present between the two discs mounted on these shafts (Fig. 3.24).

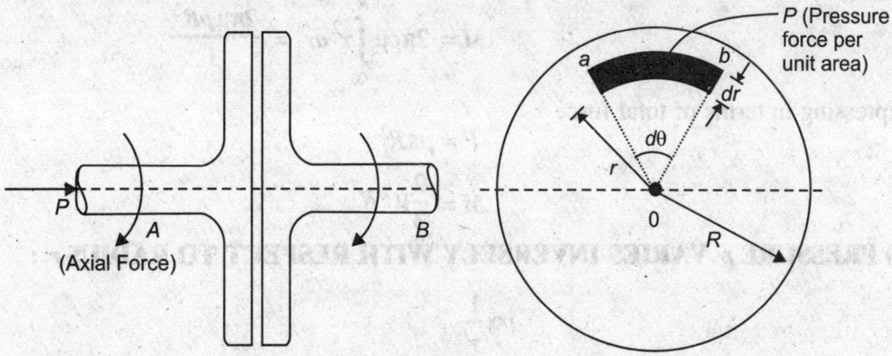

Fig. 3.24

Consider that each disc is of radius *R*, of area *A* and be under an axial force of *P*.

Consider an element *ab* of the disc at a distance *r* from the centre and of length $r(d\theta)$ having an area, $dA = rdrd\theta$

Let *p* be the force acting on the unit area of this element.

Total force acting on the element = pdA

Frictional force acting on the element,

$$dF = \mu(pdA) = \mu(p \cdot rdr.d\theta)$$

Moment caused by the frictional force of *dF* acting on the area *dA*, about the axis of the disc,

$$dM = (\mu prdrd\theta) = \mu pr^2 drd\theta$$

The moment caused by the entire frictional force at the contact surface,

$$M = \int_0^{2\pi}\int_0^{R} \mu pr^2 d\theta dr \qquad \begin{cases}\text{First evaluating the integral}\\ \text{with respect to } \theta.\end{cases}$$

$$= \int_0^{R}\int_0^{2\pi} \mu pr^2 drd\theta$$

$$M = 2\pi\mu \int_0^R pr^2 dr \qquad ...(10.5)$$

The integration with respect to r can be carried out if we know how 'p' varies with respect to radius r.

(a) PRESSURE p IS CONSTANT OR UNIFORM :

$$p = \text{constant}$$

$$= \frac{P}{\pi R^2} \qquad ...(10.6)$$

Therefore, equation (10.5) can be written as

$$M = 2\pi p\mu \int_0^R r^2 dr = \frac{2\pi\mu p R^3}{3}$$

Expressing in terms of total force

$$P = p\pi R^2 \qquad ...(10.7)$$

$$M = \frac{2}{3}\mu PR \qquad ...(10.8)$$

(b) PRESSURE p VARIES INVERSELY WITH RESPECT TO RADIUS r :

$$p \alpha \frac{1}{r}$$

or

$$p = \frac{k}{r} \qquad ...(10.9)$$

where k is a constant

Total pressure,

$$p = \int_0^R 2\pi r p\, dr = \int_0^R 2\pi r \frac{k}{r} dr = 2\pi k R$$

or

$$k = \frac{P}{2\pi R} \qquad ...(10.10)$$

From equation (10.9),

$$p = \left(\frac{P}{2\pi R}\right)\frac{1}{r}$$

Substituting for p in equation (10.5) gives

$$M = 2\pi\mu \int_0^R \left(\frac{P}{2\pi R r}\right) r^2 dr$$

$$= \frac{2\pi\mu P}{2\pi R}\int_0^R r\,dr = \frac{\mu P}{R}\cdot\frac{R^2}{2}$$

$$= \frac{\mu PR}{2} \qquad ...(10.11)$$

BEARING FRICTION : The moment M required to overcome the frictional resistance in the cases of thrust and conical pivot bearings can be calculated by the same method as discussed for the disc clutch. The results are as,

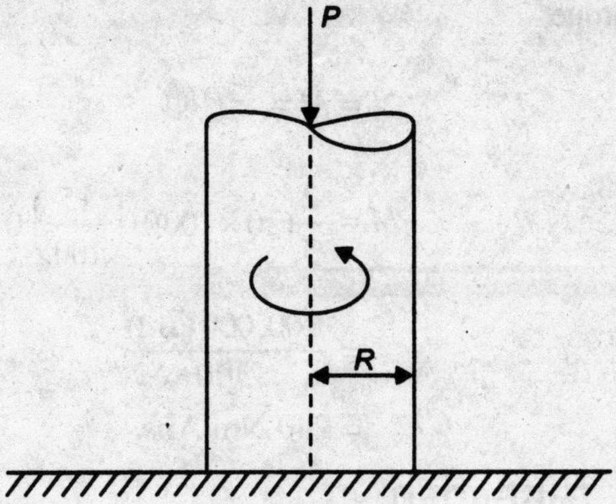

Thrust Bearing

Fig. 3.25

(i) THRUST BEARING : (Refer Fig. 3.25)

$$M = \frac{2}{3}\mu PR \quad \text{(If pressure is uniform)} \qquad ...(10.12)$$

$$M = \frac{\mu PR}{2}$$

(If pressure varies inversely with the radius) ...(10.13)

(ii) CONICAL PIVOT BEARING : (Refer Fig. 3.26)

$$M = \frac{2}{3} \cdot \frac{\mu P}{\sin\theta}\left(\frac{R_1^3 - R_2^3}{R_1^2 - R_2^2}\right)$$

(Pressure is uniform) ...(10.14)

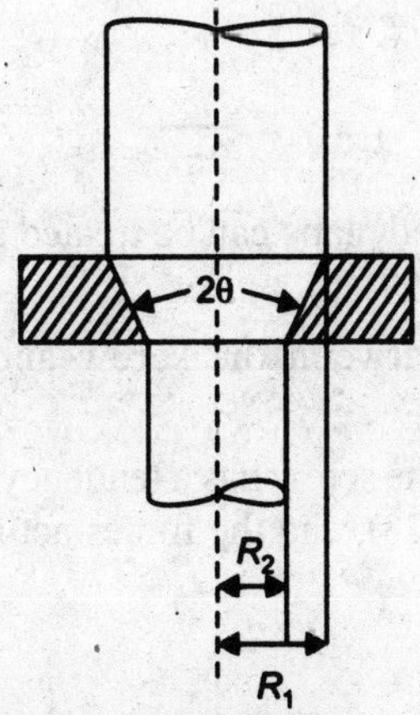

Conical Bearing

Fig. 3.26

EXAMPLE 3.14. The end of a vertical shaft of 30 cm diameter and weighing 20 kN rests on a flat surface. If the coefficient of friction between the surfaces is 0.12, find the frictional torque assuming constant pressure.

SOLUTION : Frictional Torque,

$$T = M = \frac{2}{3} PR\mu$$

$$\therefore \quad M = \frac{2}{3}(20 \times 1000)\left(\frac{15}{100}\right)0.12$$

$$= \frac{600,000\,(.12)}{300}$$

$$= 240 \text{ Nm } \textbf{Ans.}$$

FRICTION IN A SQUARE THREADED SCREW

Consider a screw jack consisting of square threaded screw and a base. The screw carries a load W which can be raised or lowered by turning a handle of length l with a force F.

Let,

r = Mean radius of the thread, and

p = Pitch of the thread.

The pitch is the axial distance measured between two consecutive threads.

The lead is the axial distance through which the screw advances in one turn.

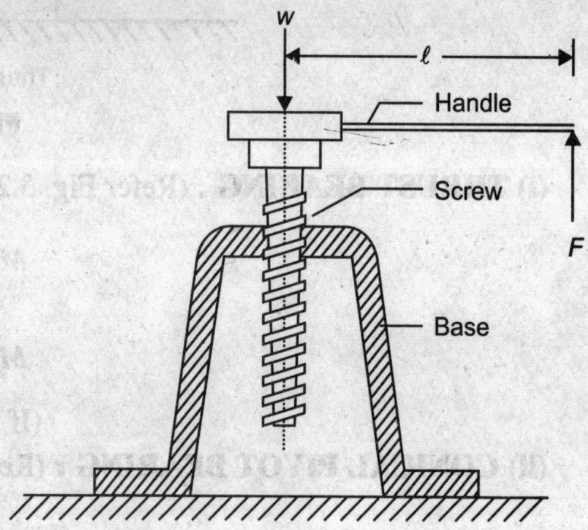

Fig. 3.27

Lead and pitch are equal in the case of a single threaded screw.

To analyse it mathematically, let us unwrap the threads on the nut (fixed in the base) and treat it as an inclined plane of inclination,

$$\tan\theta = \frac{p}{2\pi r} \qquad ...(10.15)$$

The screw moving upon this inclined plane can be treated as a body having weight equal to the load W supported by the screw (Fig. 3.27).

Let the coefficient of friction between the screw and base = μ, and angle of friction $\phi = \tan^{-1}\mu$.

(a) RAISING OF LOAD : When the screw has a tendency to move up friction acts downwards as shown in free body diagram (Fig. 3.28), and the forces acting are :

(i) Load W,

(ii) N, the normal reaction,

(iii) μN, the frictional force

(iv) P_1, the horizontal force acting at the surface of the screw.

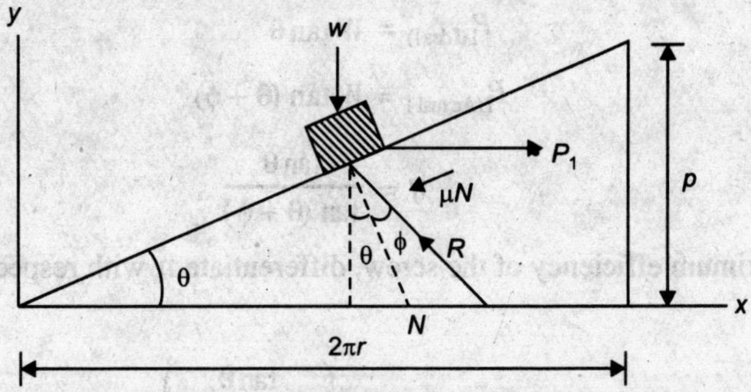

Fig. 3.28

R, the resultant reaction (of N and μN) is inclined at angle $(\theta + \phi)$ with the vertical.

Force P_1 is related to the force F applied to he handle by the relation,

$$F\ell = P_1 r$$

$$\therefore \quad P_1 = \frac{F\ell}{r} \qquad ...(10.16)$$

Writing the equations of equilibrium, for $\Sigma F_x = 0$

$$P_1 - R\sin(\theta + \phi) = 0$$

and for $\Sigma F_y = 0$

$$W - R\cos(\theta + \phi) = 0$$

$$\therefore \quad P_1 = R\sin(\theta + \phi)$$

and for $W = R\cos(\theta + \phi)$

Eliminating R,

$$\frac{P_1}{W} = \tan(\theta + \phi)$$

or

$$P_1 = W\tan\theta(\theta + \phi)$$

$$= W\frac{\tan\theta + \tan\phi}{1 - \tan 0 \tan\phi} \qquad ...(10.17)$$

where,

$$P_1 = \frac{F\ell}{r}$$

$$\text{Efficiency of the screw} = \frac{\text{Ideal effort (when friction is 0)}}{\text{Actual effort}}$$

$$P_{1(\text{Ideal})} = W\left(\frac{\tan\theta + 0}{1 - \tan\theta(0)}\right)$$

as $\mu = 0$,

so $\tan\phi = 0$

$$\therefore \qquad P_{1(\text{Ideal})} = W \tan\theta$$

$$P_{1(\text{Actual})} = W \tan(\theta + \phi)$$

$$\therefore \qquad \eta = \frac{\tan\theta}{\tan(\theta + \phi)} \qquad \text{...(10.18)}$$

To find the maximum efficiency of the screw, differentiate η with respect to θ and set it equal to 0 (zero)

$$\frac{d\eta}{d\theta} = \frac{d\left(\dfrac{\tan\theta}{\tan(\theta+\phi)}\right)}{d\theta} = 0$$

which on solving gives,

$$\theta = \frac{\pi}{4} - \frac{\theta}{2}$$

and

$$\eta_{\max} = \frac{1 - \sin\phi}{1 + \sin\phi} \qquad \text{...(10.19)}$$

θ is also known as the helix angle of the thread

(b) LOWERING OF LOAD : It can be proved that the effort P_2 required to lower the load W (Fig. 3.29) is given by,

$$P_{2(\text{Actual})} = W \tan(\theta - \phi) \qquad \text{...(10.20)}$$

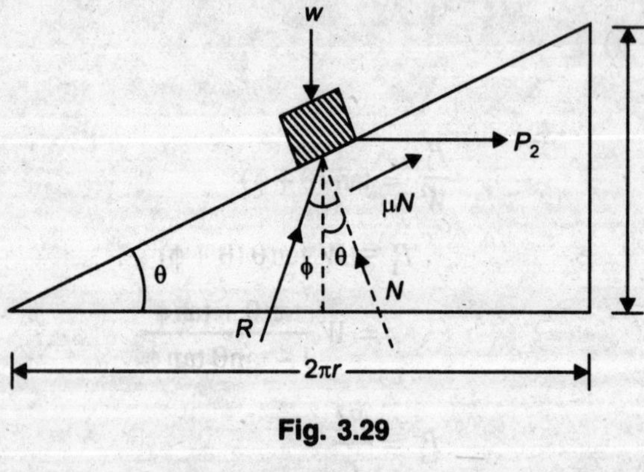

Fig. 3.29

SELF LOCKING : When the load W on the screw remains in place even after the effort is removed (when effort is zero) it is called self locking machine. For a screw to be self locking

$$\phi > \theta \qquad \text{...(10.21)}$$

EXAMPLE 3.15. A screw jack has square threads of mean diameter of 10 cm and a pitch of 1.25 cm. Determine the force that must be applied to the end of 50 cm lever (i) To raise, and (ii) to lower, a weight of 50 kN. Find the efficiency of the jack. Is it self locking? Assume $\mu = 0.20$

SOLUTION : Given :

$p = 1.25$ cm, $d = 10$ cm, $r = 5$ cm

$l = 50$ cm, $W = 50$ kN, $\mu = 0.20$

Helix angle,

$$\tan\theta = \frac{p}{2\pi r}$$

$$\tan\theta = \frac{1.25}{2\pi \times 5} = \frac{1.25}{31.416} = 0.0398$$

$$\therefore \quad \theta = \tan^{-1}(0.0398) = 2.28°$$

Angle of friction $\quad \phi = \tan^{-1}(\mu) = \tan^{-1}(.2) = 11.31°$

(i) TO RAISE THE LOAD : Effort required, $P_1 = W \tan(\theta + \phi)$

Taking the leverage, due to handle, into account, force F_1 required :

$$F_1 = W \tan(\theta + \phi)\frac{r}{\ell}$$

$$= 50,000 \tan(2.28° + 11.31°) \times \frac{0.05}{0.5}$$

$$F_1 = 50,000 \tan(\tan 13.59) \times 0.1$$

$$= 5000 \tan(13.59°) = 5000\,(0.2417)$$

$$\therefore \quad F_1 = 1208.70 \text{ N } \textbf{Ans.}$$

(ii) TO LOWER THE LOAD :

$$F_2 = W \tan(\theta - \phi)\frac{r}{\ell}$$

$$= 50000 \tan(2.28° - 11.31°) \times \frac{0.05}{0.5}$$

$$F_2 = 50000 \tan(-9.03°) \times 0.1$$

$$= -794.61N = -795 \text{ N } \textbf{Ans.}$$

FORCE REQUIRED IN OPPOSITE SENSE

$$\eta = \frac{\tan\theta}{\tan(\theta + \phi)}$$

$$= \frac{\tan 2.28°}{\tan(2.28° + 11.31°)}$$

$$= \frac{0.0398}{\tan(13.59°)} = \frac{0.0398}{0.2417}$$

$$\therefore \quad \eta = 0.1647 = 16.47\%$$

The screw is self locking **Ans.**

As $\theta = 2.28°, \phi = 11.31°$, so $\phi > \theta$ is satisfying the condition for a self locking machine.

The efficiency of the jack is 16.47% which is less than 50%, varifying further that it is a self locking machine.

EXAMPLE 3.16. Find out the number of turns a hauling rope must be wound round a rotating capstan lathe in order to haul a load of 3 MN up to a gradient of 1 in 30. Presume the following data:

Resistance due to rolling = 0.00375 per newton

Friction coefficient between the rope and drum = 0.35

Pull on the free end of the rope = 250 N

SOLUTION : The hauling is required up an inclined plane and for that T_1 has to be overcome the frictional resistance as well as effort component of the incline. That is

$$T_1 = 3 \times 10^6 \times 0.00375 + 3 \times 10^6 \times \frac{1}{30}$$

$$= 3 \times 10^6 \left(0.00375 + \frac{1}{30}\right) = 111250\text{N}$$

$$T_2 = 250\ N\ \text{(Given)}$$

Involving the relation, $\frac{T_1}{T_2} = e^{\mu\theta}$, we have

$$e^{\mu\theta} = \frac{111250}{250} = 445$$

or

$$\mu\theta = \log_e 445;$$

$$\therefore \quad \theta = \frac{\log_e 445}{0.35} = \frac{2.3 \log 445}{0.35} = 17.40 \text{ radians}$$

$$\text{Number of turns} = 17.40/2\pi$$

$$= 17.40/6.283 = 2.77$$

Hence number of turns to be given = 3 **Ans.**

EXAMPLE 3.17. A pulley is driven by a flat belt running at a speed of 450 m/min. The angle of lap is 760° and the coefficient of friction between the belt and pulley material is 0.3. If the maximum allowable tension in the belt is 800 N, calculate the net driving tension and power transmitted by the belt. Neglect the effect of centrifugal tension.

SOLUTION : Angle of

$$\text{lap} = 160° = \frac{160}{180} \times \pi = 2.79 \text{ radians}$$

If T_1 and T_2 are the tensions on the tight and slack side of the belt, then

$$\frac{T_1}{T_2} = e^{\mu\theta} = e^{0.3 \times 2.79} = e^{0.837}$$

$$= 2.718^{0.837} = 2.309$$

$$\therefore \quad T_2 = \frac{T_1}{2.309} = \frac{800}{2.309} = 346.47 \text{ N}$$

Effective turning force or net driving tension

$$= T_1 - T_2 = 800 - 386.47 = 453.53N$$

Work done = force × distance = $(T_1 - T_2) \times V$

$$= 453.53 \times \frac{450}{60} = 3401.47 \text{ N m/s}$$

Power transmitted by the belt is 3401.17 W = 3.40 kW Ans.

EXERCISE-3

1. State the Laws of Friction.
2. Define coefficient of Friction and Limiting Friction.
3. Derive an expression for the frictional torque required to overcome friction in the case of a Thrust Bearing assuming pressure to be uniform.
4. Derive the relation $T_1 / T_2 = e^{\mu\theta}$ for a belt drive.
5. Explain the term Angle of Friction.
6. How will you distinguish between Static friction and Dynamic friction.
7. A body of weight 300 N is lying on a rough horizontal plane having a coefficient of friction as 0.30. Find the magnitude of the force, which can move the body, while acting at an angle of 25° with the horizontal. **[Ans.** 87.1 N]
8. A body, resting on a rough horizontal plane, requires a pull of 180 N inclined at 30° to the plane, just to move it. It was found that a push of 220 N inclined at 30° to the plane just moves the body. Determine the weight of the body and the coefficient of friction.

   [Ans. W = 991. N, $\mu = 0.173$]
9. A body of weight 500 N is lying on a rough plane inclined at an angle of 25° with the horizontal. It is inclined at an angle of 25° with the horizontal. It is supported by an effort P parallel to the plane. Determine the minimum and maximum value of P, for which the equilibrium can exist, if the angle of friction is 20°. **[Ans.** $P_{min.}$ 46.4 N, $P_{max.} = 376.2$ N]
10. A load of 1.5 kN, resting on an inclined rough plane, can be moved up the plane by a force of 2 kN applied horizontally or by a force 1.25 kN applied parallel to the plane. Find the inclination of the plane and the coefficient of friction. **[Ans.** $\alpha = 36.8°$ and $\mu = 0.292$]
11. Find the force required to move a load of 300 N up a rough plane, the force being applied parallel to the plane. The inclination of the plane is such that when the same load is kept on a perfectly smooth plane inclined at the same angle, a force of 60 KN applied at an inclination of 30° to the plane, keeps the same load is equilibrium. Assume coefficient of friction between the rough plane and the load to be equal to 0.3. **[Ans.** P = 140.7 N]
12. A uniform lodder AB of 20 m length and weight W is supported by the horizontal floor at A and by a vertical wall at B. It makes an angle 45° with the horizontal. If a man, whose weight is one half that of the ladder, how much length x of the ladder he shall climb before the ladder slips?

If a boy now stands on the end *A* of the ladder, what must be his least weight *w* so that man may go on the top of the ladder? Assume, μ between the ladder and the wall = 1/3, μ between the ladder and the floor = 1/2. **[Ans.** x = 14.3 m and w = 0.25 W]

13. A screw Jack has a square threads of mean diameter 6 cm of helix angle 10° and coefficient of friction 0,30. Determine the force that must be applied to the end of 60 cm lever to (i) Raise, and (ii) Lower a weight of 3000 N. **[Ans.** P_1 = 75 N and P_2 = 18 N]
14. A uniform ladder of 3m long weighs 200 N. It is placed against a wall making an angle of 60° with the floor. The coefficient of friction between the wall and the ladder is 0.25 and that between the floor and the ladder is 0.35. The ladder, in addition to its weight, has to support a man of 1000 N at its top end *B*. Calculate:
    (i) The horizontal force P to be applied to ladder at the floor level to prevent slipping.
    (ii) The force *P* is not applied, what should be the minimum inclination of the ladder with the horizontal, so that there is no slipping of it with the man at its top.

[Ans. P_H = 183.5 N, and α = 68.9°]

CHAPTER 4

Centre of Gravity

GRAVITY

Gravity means the force of attraction by which a body is attracted towards the centre of earth. This force of attraction i.e. gravity depends upon (i) The mass of the body, and (ii) its distance from the centre of the earth. As the size of the body is very small in comparison to the size of the earth, it can very safely be assumed that all the forces of attraction are parallel and their resultant constitutes the weight of the body.

CENTRE OF GRAVITY

The point through which the resultant of the forces of attraction in a body passes whatever be the position in which it is suspended, is known as centre of gravity of the body. The centre of gravity is, therefore, defined as a point at which the whole weight of the body may be assumed to be acting. When the body is considered to be composed of a number of small weights each of which is acting vertically downwards the point where the resultant of these small weights act, will give the position of centre of gravity of the body. It is denoted by C.G. Every object has got one and only one, centre of gravity.

CENTROID

The centroid is defined as the point where the whole area of the plane figure is assumed to be concentrated. The word, "Centre of gravity" may be used for centroid but not the vice-versa. The term C.G. is used for solid bodies having mass.

CENTRE OF MASS

It is the point where the entire mass of a body may be assumed to be concentrated.

The centre of mass (C.M.) and centre of gravity (C.G.) of a body are different only when the gravitational field is not uniform and parallel. For most practical purposes they are assumed to be the same.

Information is given on next page for the position of centroid/centre of gravity of different laminas (plane sections) most commonly used in engineering practice.

1. For a rectangular section, C.G. lies at the intersection of diagonals, i.e. at the mid point of its breadth as well as depth (Fig. 4.1a)
2. For triangular section, C.G. lies at the point of intersections of the three medians. If height of triangle is h, then its C.G. is at a distane of $h/3$ from the base along vertical axis (Fig. 4.1b)
3. For a circular section, C.G. lies at the centre of circle (Fig. 4.1c)

4. The C.G. of the semi-circle of radius R is at a distance of $4R/3\pi$ from its base measured along vertical axis (Fig. 4.1d).
5. The C.G. of a sphere of radius R lies at a distance of R from every point.
6. For the hemisphere, C.G. would be at a distance of $3R/8$ from its base measured along the vertical axis (Fig. 4.1e).
7. The C.G. of a uniform rod is at its mid point (Fig. 4.1f).
8. A solid circular cone has its C.G. at a height of $h/4$ from its base and on its axis of symmetry (Fig. 4.1g).

$$\text{Volume} = \frac{\pi}{3} R^2 h$$

9. Solid cylinder: Its C.G. lies at a height of $h/2$ from the base and on the central axis. Surface Area = $2\pi Rh$ (Fig. 4.1h).

$$\text{Volume} = \frac{\pi}{4}(2R)^2 \cdot h = \frac{\pi}{4} \cdot 4R^2 h = \pi R^2 h$$

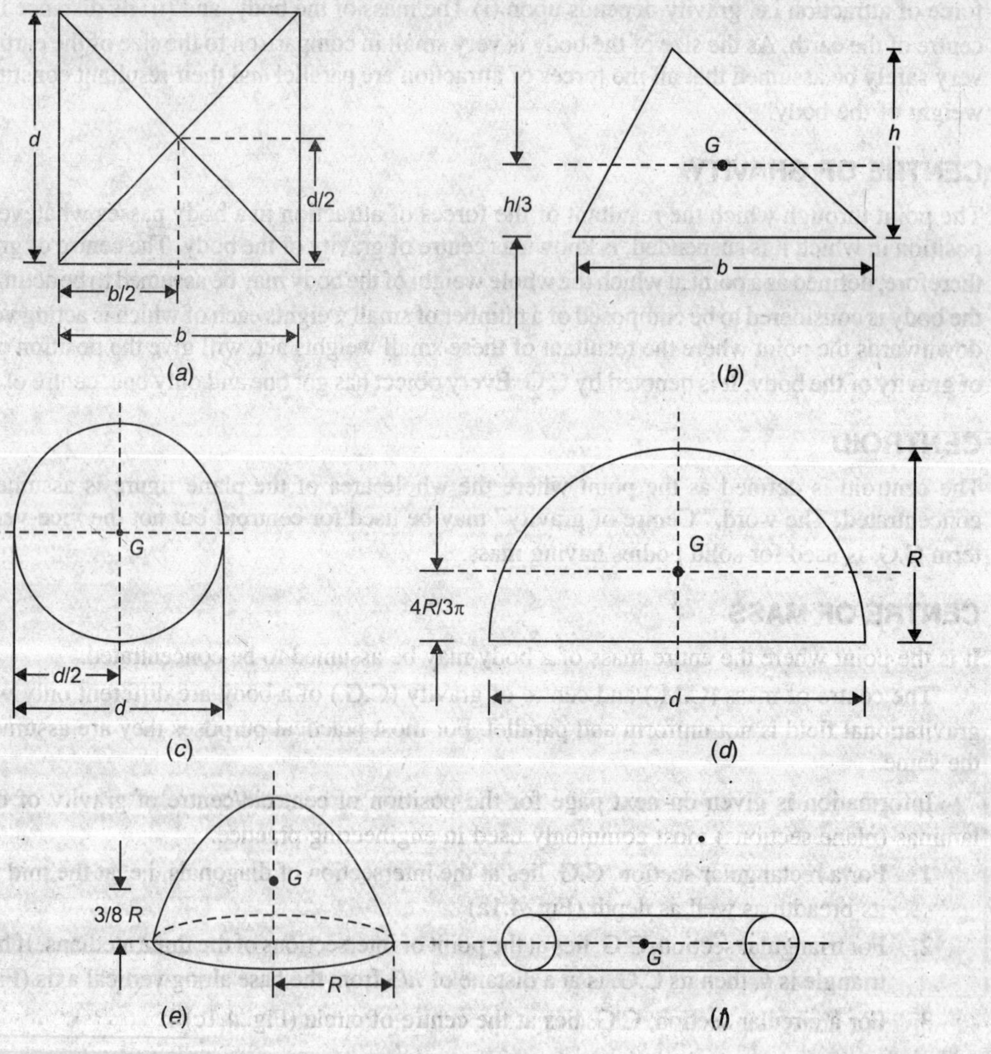

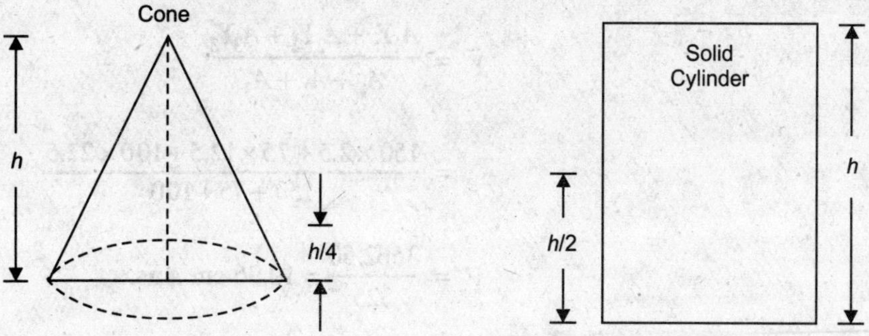

(g) (h)

Fig. 4.1

EXAMPLE 4.1. Determine the centroid of the cross-sectional area of an unequal I-section shown in Fig. 4.2.

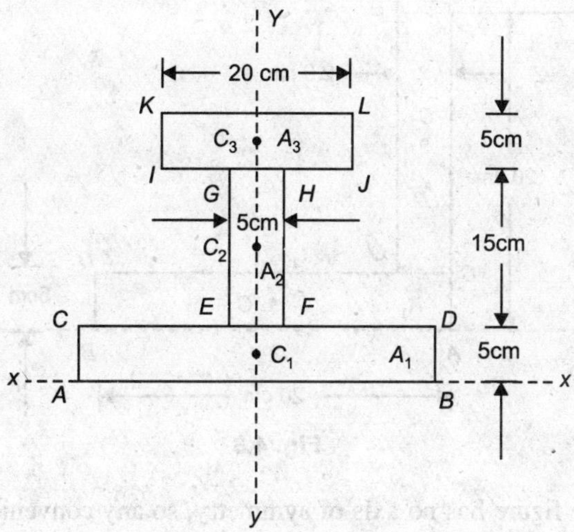

Fig. 4.2

SOLUTION: The figure is symmetrical about Y-Y axis. X-X axis may be chosen to coincide with the bottom edge *AB*.

The figure may be considered to be made up of three rectangles *ABCD*, *EFGH*, and *IJKL*.

Due to symmetry, centroid of the total figure lies on Y-Y axis.

S.No.	Area (cm²)	Y-coordinate of the centroid in cm
1.	$A_1 - 5 \times 30 = 150$	$Y_1 = 5/2 = 2.5$
2.	$A_2 = 5 \times 15 = 75$	$Y_2 = 5 + \frac{15}{2} = 12.5$
3.	$A_3 = 5 \times 20 = 100$	$Y_3 = 4 + 15 + \frac{5}{2} = 22.5$

$$\bar{Y} = \frac{A_1Y_1 + A_2Y_2 + A_3Y_3}{A_1 + A_2 + A_3}$$

$$= \frac{150 \times 2.5 + 75 \times 12.5 + 100 \times 22.5}{150 + 75 + 100}$$

$$\therefore \qquad \bar{Y} = \frac{3562.50}{325} = 10.96 \text{ cm } \textbf{Ans.}$$

EXAMPLE 4.2. Determine the centroid of the cross-sectional area of a z-section as shown in Fig. 4.3.

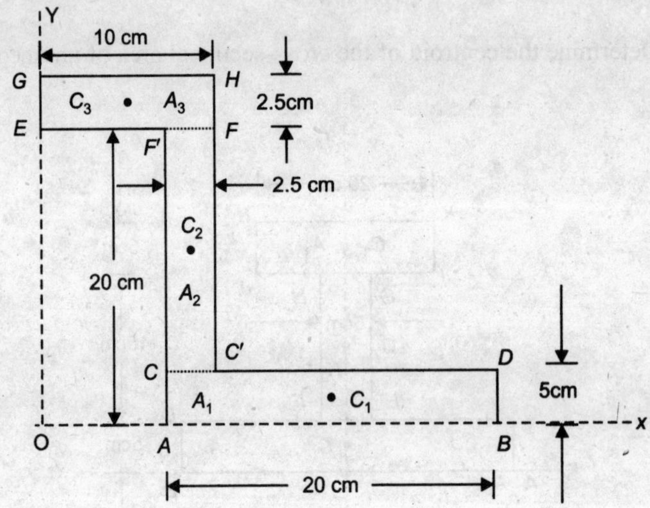

Fig. 4.3

SOLUTION: Since the figure has no axis of symmetry, so any convenient axis can be chosen as the axes of reference. Choosing one of the axes along the bottom edge *AB* and the other vertical edge *EG*.

Figure Rectangle	Area (cm²)	X co-ordinate of the centroid (cm)	Y-co-ordinate of the centroid (cm)
ABCD	$A_1 = 5 \times 20 = 100$	$7.5 + \frac{20}{2} = 17.5 = x_1$	$y_1 = \frac{5}{2} = 2.5$
CC′F′F′	$A_2 = 2.5 \times 15 = 37.50$	$7.5 + \frac{2.5}{2} = 8.75 = x_2$	$y_2 = 5 + \frac{15}{2} = 12.50$
EFGH	$A_3 = 2.5 \times 10 = 25$	$x_3 = \frac{10}{2} = 5$	$y_3 = 20 + \frac{2.5}{2} = 21.25$

$$\bar{x} = \frac{A_1x_1 + A_2x_2 + A_3x_3}{A_1 + A_2 + A_3}$$

$$\bar{x} = \frac{(100\times 17.5)+(37.5\times 8.75)+(25\times 5)}{100+37.50+25}$$

$$= \frac{2203.125}{162.50}$$

$$\therefore \quad \bar{x} = 13.56\ cm \textbf{ Ans.}$$

$$\bar{y} = \frac{A_1y_1 + A_2y_2 + A_3y_3}{A_1 + A_2 + A_3}$$

$$= \frac{(100\times 2.5)+(37.5\times 12.5)+(25\times 21.25)}{100+37.5+25}$$

$$= \frac{1250}{162.50}$$

$$\therefore \quad \bar{y} = 7.69\ cm \textbf{ Ans.}$$

Hence $\bar{x} = 13.56\ cm$, $\bar{y} = 7.69\ cm$ w.r.t to point O.

EXAMPLE 4.3. A square hole is punched out of a circular lamina, the diagonal of the square being radius of the circle. Find the C.G. of the remainder, if R is the radius of the circle.

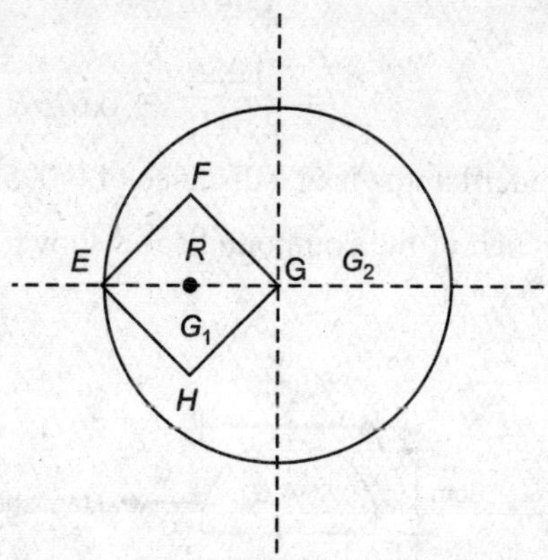

Fig. 4.4

SOLUTION: Let the C.G. of the circular lamina be at G from which a square $EFGH$, whose one end is at centre G of the circle and diagonal of the square $EG = R$ = Radius of the circle, has been removed.

Let the C.G. of the circle, square and remainder be at points G, G_1 and G_2 respectively. These three will be on a straight line i.e. axis of symmetry.

$\because$ Area of big circle $= \pi R^2$

$$\text{Area of punched portion} = \frac{\text{Diagonal} \times \text{diagonal}}{2}$$

$$= \frac{R \times R}{2} = \frac{R^2}{2}$$

$\therefore$ Area of remainder portion $= \pi R^2 - \dfrac{R^2}{2}$

$$= \frac{2\pi R^2 - R^2}{2} = \frac{6.283R^2 - R^2}{2}$$

$$\frac{5.283R^2}{2} = 2.6415R^2$$

Now C.G. of square *EFGH*, whose area is $0.5\,R^2$, is at G_1 and the C.G. of the remainder having an area of $2.6145R^2$ be at G_2.

$\therefore$ $$0.5R^2(GG_1) = 2.6415R^2(GG_2)$$

or $$0.5R^2(0.5R) = 2.6415R^2(GG_2)$$

or $$0.25R = 2.6415(GG_2)$$

$\therefore$ $$GG_2 = \frac{0.25R}{2.6415}$$

$$= \frac{0.25R}{2.6415} = 0.095R$$

Hence the C.G. of the remainder lamina is at a distance of $0.095R$ from the centre of the circle.

EXAMPLE 4.4. Determine the C.G. of the compound solid shown in Fig. 4.5

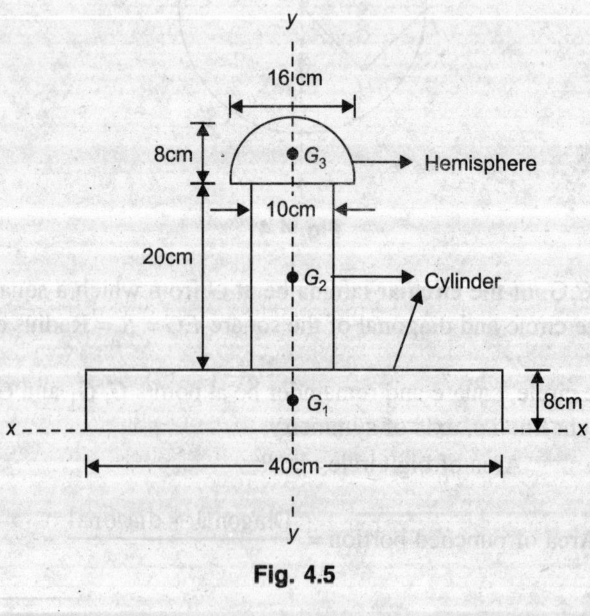

Fig. 4.5

SOLUTION: Volume of the bottom cylinder:

$$V_1 = \pi r_1^2 h_1 = \pi \times 20 \times 20 \times 8 = 3200\,\pi$$

$$Y_1 = \frac{8}{2} = 4 \text{ cm}$$

$$V_2 = \pi r_2^2 h_2$$

$$= \pi \times 5 \times 5 \times 20 = 500\,\pi$$

$$Y_2 = 8 + \frac{20}{2} = 18 \text{ cm}$$

$$V_3 = \frac{2}{3}\pi r_3^3$$

$$= \frac{2}{3}\pi \times 8 \times 8 \times 8 = 341.33\,\pi$$

$$Y_3 = 8 + 20 + \frac{3}{8} r_3$$

$$= 28 + \frac{3 \times 8}{8} = 31 \text{ cm}$$

The section is symmetrical about y-y axis i.e. vertical line passing through the axis of vertical cylinder.

Let the C.G. of the section will be at point *G* at a height of $\bar{y}$ from the base line x-x on y-y axis.

$$\therefore \qquad \bar{y} = \frac{V_1 Y_1 + V_2 Y_2 + V_3 Y_3}{V_1 + V_2 + V_3}$$

$$= \frac{3200\pi \times 4 + 500\pi \times 18 + 341.33 \times 31}{3200\pi + 500\pi + 341.33\pi}$$

$$\bar{y} = \frac{12800\pi + 900\pi + 10581.23\pi}{441.33\pi}$$

$$= \frac{32381.23\,\pi}{4041.33\,\pi} = 8.01 \text{ cm } \textbf{Ans.}$$

EXAMPLE 4.5. Locate the centroid of the shaded area obtained by removing a semi-circle of diameter *a* from a quadrant of a circle of radius *a*.

SOLUTION: To determine the centroid (x_c, y_c) of the shaded area let us consider that the shaded area is obtained by substracting the area of the semicircle of radius $a/2$ from the area of the quadrant of circle of radious *a*. In this sense, therefore, the area to be substracted is treated to be as negative area.

Reference axes are as shown in the Fig. 4.6. Different areas and coordinates of their centroids are tabulated on next page:

$$x_c = 0.349a \textbf{ Ans.}$$

$$y_c = \frac{A_1y_1 + A_2y_2}{A_1 + A_2}$$

$$y_c = \frac{\frac{\pi}{4}a^2\left(\frac{4a}{3\pi}\right) - \frac{\pi a^2}{8}\left(\frac{2a}{3\pi}\right)}{\frac{\pi a^2}{4} - \frac{\pi a^2}{8}}$$

$$y_c = \frac{\frac{a}{3\pi} - \frac{a}{12\pi}}{\frac{1}{8}} = \frac{2a}{\pi}$$

$$y_c = 0.636a \textbf{ Ans.}$$

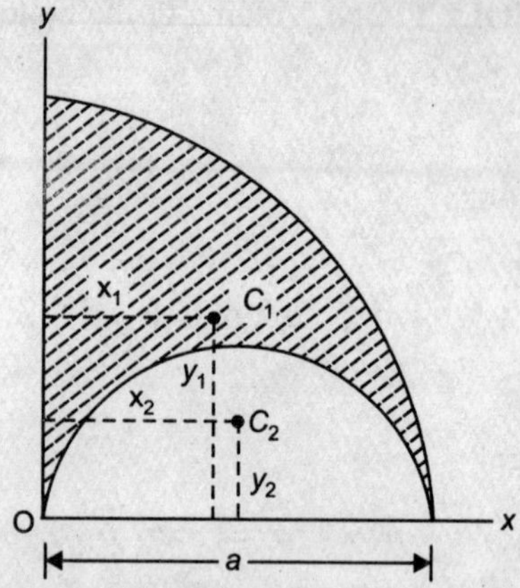

Fig. 4.6

DETERMINATION OF CENTROID AND CENTRE OF GRAVITY

INTEGRATION METHOD: By considering a plane figure to be made up of a number of small elements of length or area, we cannot generate the true shape of the figure. To truly generate shape of a figure, we have to make the size of these elements very very small and their number very large.

For example, the circumference of a circle can be generated only by a polygon having a large number of very very small sides.

Mathematically speaking, when the terms ΔL or ΔA occuring in the expressions of C.G. and centroid become infinitestimally small, these expressions (equations 4.1 to 4.6) can be written as

$$x_c = \frac{\int xdL}{\int dL} \qquad x_c = \frac{\int xdA}{\int dA} \qquad x_c = \frac{\int xdm}{\int dm}$$

$$y_c = \frac{\int xdL}{\int dL} \qquad y_c = \frac{\int xdA}{\int dA} \qquad y_c = \frac{\int xdm}{\int dm} \qquad ...(4.7)$$

where, dL, dA and dm denote the length, area and mass respectively of a differential element choosen and (x, y) the coodinates of its centroid. The integral $\int xdA$ is known as the first moment of area with respect to the y-axis. Similarly, the integral $\int ydA$ denotes the first moment of area with respect to the x-axis.

Above expressions can be integrated to determine the coodinates of centroid and C.G. as explained in the following section. Also, some important points regarding the choice of a differential element for setting up the integrals and choosing the axes of reference are discussed.

INTEGRATION METHOD

(a) CHOICE OF DIFFERENTIAL ELEMENT: In the determination of the coordinates of the centroid by integration method, a proper choice of the differential element can considerably ease and simplfiy the setting up and the valuation of the integrals of the type

$$x_c = \frac{\int x dA}{\int dA}, \quad y_c = \frac{\int x dA}{\int dA}$$

Consider an area *OAB* bounded by the curve $x^2 = ay$ and the straight line $y = a$ as shown in Fig. 4.7.

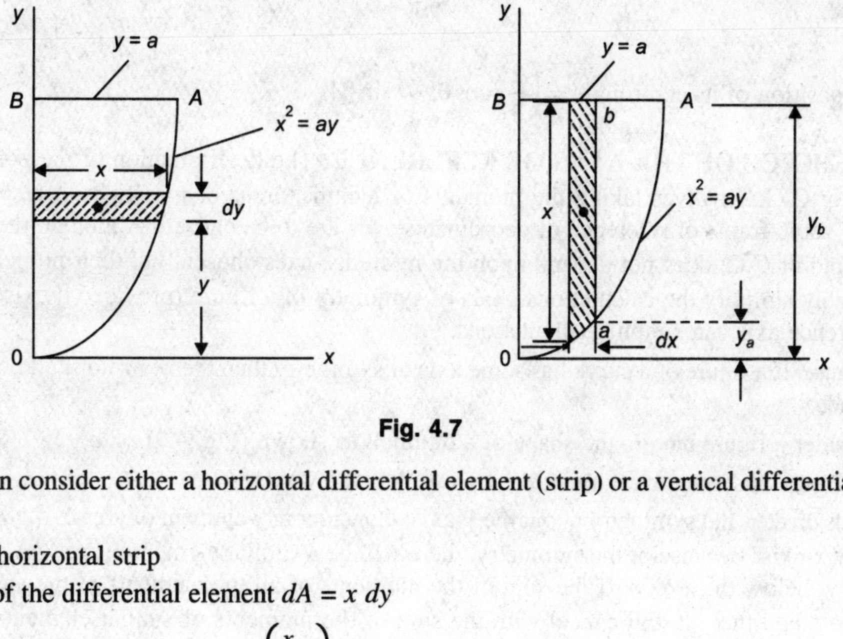

Fig. 4.7

We can consider either a horizontal differential element (strip) or a vertical differential element (strip).

For a horizontal strip

Area of the differential element $dA = x\, dy$

The position of its centroid is $\left(\frac{x}{2}, y\right)$

For a vertical strip

Area of the differential element $dA = y\, dx$ or $dA = (y_h - y_a)\, dx$

The position of its centroid is $\left(x, \frac{y_a + y_b}{2}\right)$

It may be noted that the point *a* lies on the curve *OA* and the point *b* on the straight line *AB*. It can be appreciated that of the two elements considered, the horizontal differential element is a better choice for evaluating the integral in the present situation.

TRIANGULAR ELEMENT: A triangular element can also be choosen in certain situations as shown in Fig. 4.8

Area of the element $dA = \frac{(rd\theta)r}{2}$

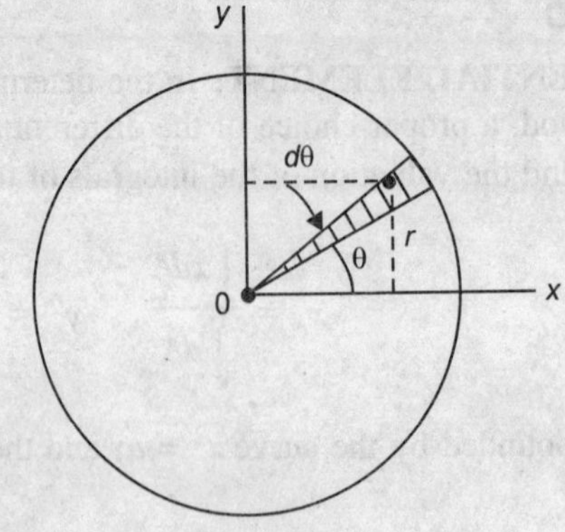

Fig. 4.8

The position of its centroid is $=\left(\frac{2}{3}r\cos\theta, \frac{2}{3}r\sin\theta\right)$

(b) CHOICE OF THE AXES OF REFERENCE: The determination of the position of the centroid or C.G., involves taking the moments of lengths, areas or masses with respect to some axes. So, some frame of reference or coordinates axes are to be chosen. Although, the location of the centroid or C.G. does not depend upon the reference axes chosen, but their proper choice can considerably simplify the calculations. Axis of symmetry of a figure (provided it exists) if chosen as a reference axis can simplify calculations.

Because, if a figure or a curve has some axis of symmetry then the centroid shall lie on this axis of symmetry.

Consider a figure having the shape of a dumbell as shown (Fig. 4.9).

The figure is symmetrical about the x as well as the y-axis.

Let us discuss the symmetry about the x-axis: Consider any element of area ΔA_1 at a distance y_1 above the x-axis. Because of the symmetry, there will be a similar element of area ΔA_1 situated at a distance y_1 below the x-axis. If the sum of the moments of all the elements of the area above the x-axis are taken then, it will cancel with the sum of the moments of similar elements of the area lying below the x-axis.

Thus, $y_c = 0$, or the centroid lies on the x-axis.

Similar argument is valid regarding the symmetry about the y-axis.

Thus $x_c = 0$, or the centroid lies on the y-axis.

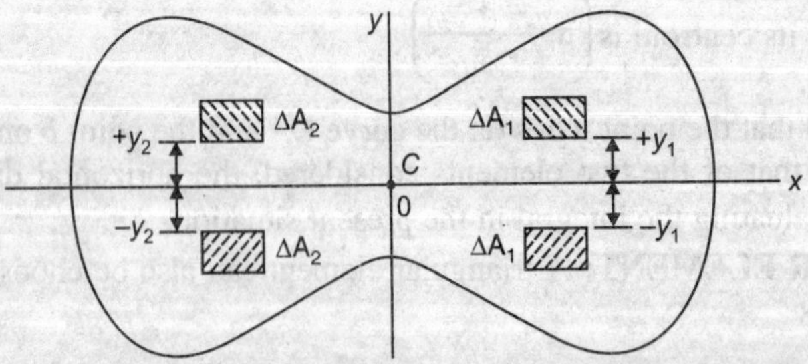

Fig. 4.9

CENTROID OF A COMPOSITE PLANE FIGURE

A composie area or a curve is one which can be considered to be made up of several pieces or components that represent familiar geometric shapes (e.g. rectangle, circle, triangle, semicircle, ellipse etc.) and for which the positions of individual centroids are known.

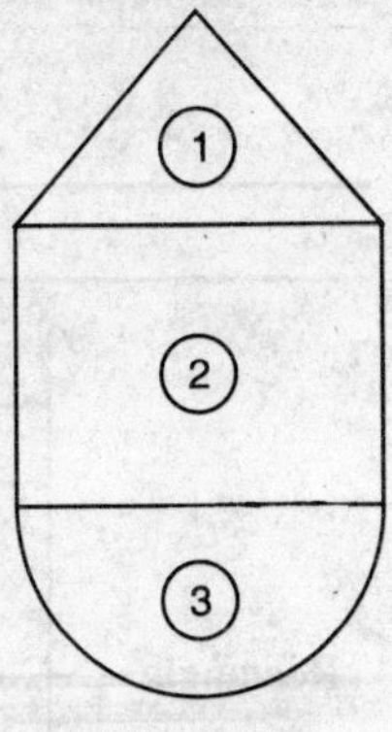

Fig. 4.10

The entire area shown in Fig. 4.10 can be considered to the made up of a triangle, rectangle and a semicircle.

To find the centroid of this area, divide the area into different component parts as discussed above (not into infinitesimal elements). Then, we can use the equation,

$$x_c = \frac{\sum \Delta A_i x_i}{\sum \Delta A_i}$$

$$y_c = \frac{\sum \Delta A_i y_i}{\sum \Delta A_i},$$

treating each component part as an element of area ΔA_1 and the distance of its centroid as (x_1, y_1).

The positions of the centroid of the component parts can be taken as standard results.

For example, for L-Section in Fig. 4.11(a)

$$x_c = \frac{A_1 x_1 + A_2 x_2}{A_1 + A_2},$$

$$y_c = \frac{A_2 x_2 + A_2 x_2}{A_1 + A_2}$$

If there is a hole or void (a non-existing area) then it may be treated as a negative area.

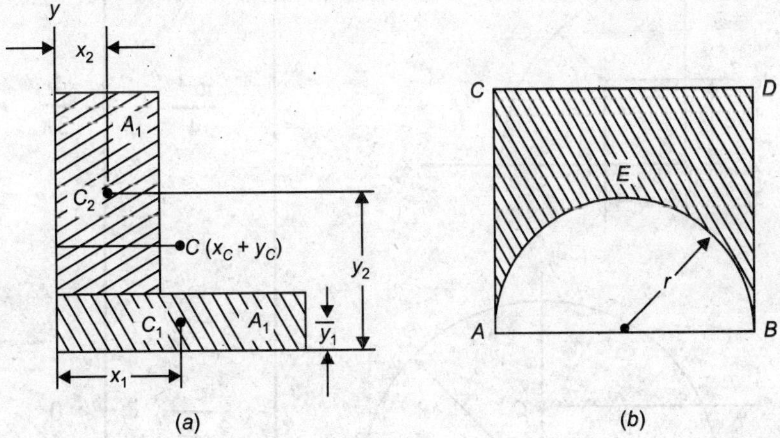

Fig. 4.11

In Fig. 4.11(b) hatched area, may be considered to be made up of a rectangular area *ABCD* and a negative area formed by a semicircle of radius *r*.

Table 4.1
Centroids of Various Shapes of Areas

Shape	Area	$x_c\bar{x}$	$y_c\bar{y}$
Rectangle 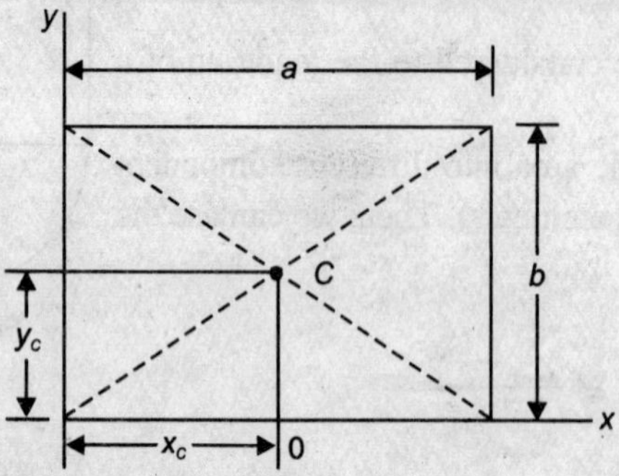	ab	$\frac{a}{2}$	$\frac{b}{2}$
Triangle 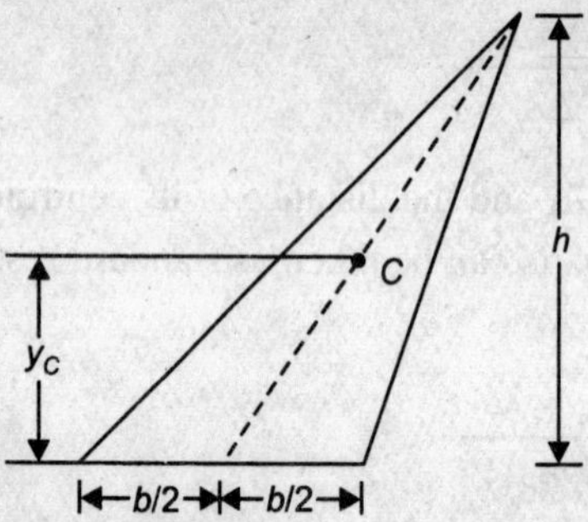	$\frac{bh}{2}$	–	$\frac{h}{3}$
Quarter-circle 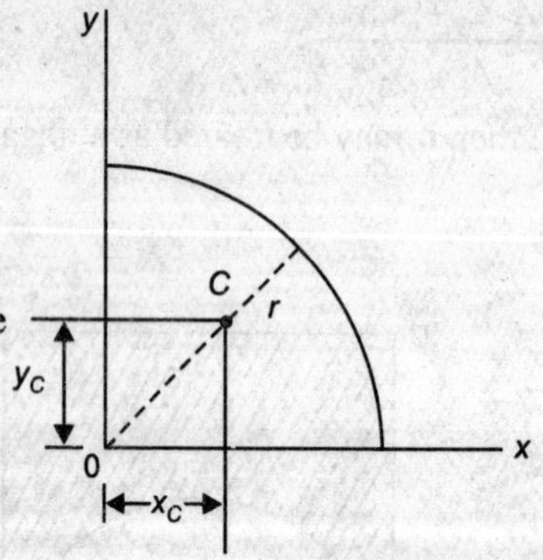	$\frac{\pi r^2}{4}$	$\frac{4r}{3\pi}$	$\frac{4r}{3\pi}$
Semi-circle 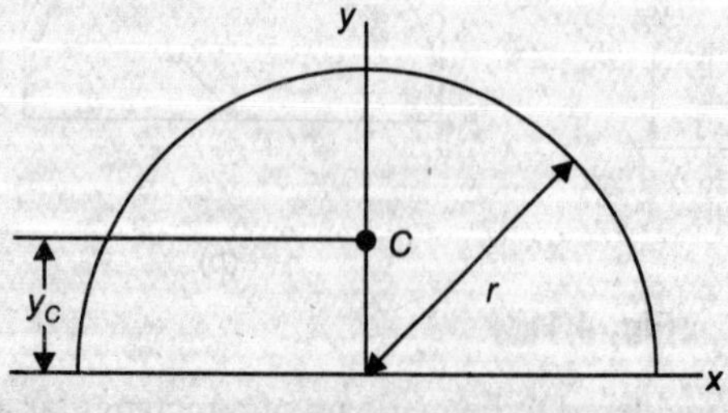	$\frac{\pi r^2}{2}$	0	$\frac{4r}{3\pi}$

Shape		Area	$x_c \bar{x}$	$y_c \bar{y}$
Circular sector	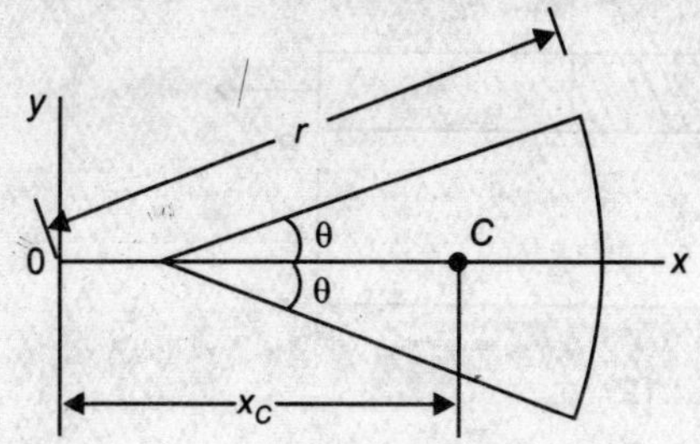	θr^2	$\frac{2r\sin\theta}{3\theta}$	0
Parabola	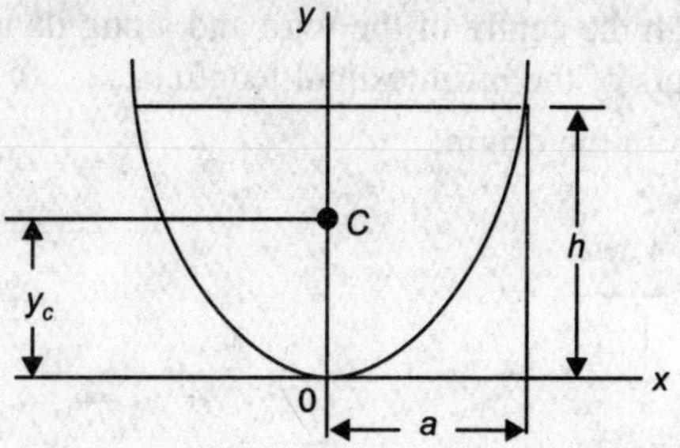	$4\frac{ah}{3}$	0	$\frac{3h}{5}$
General spander	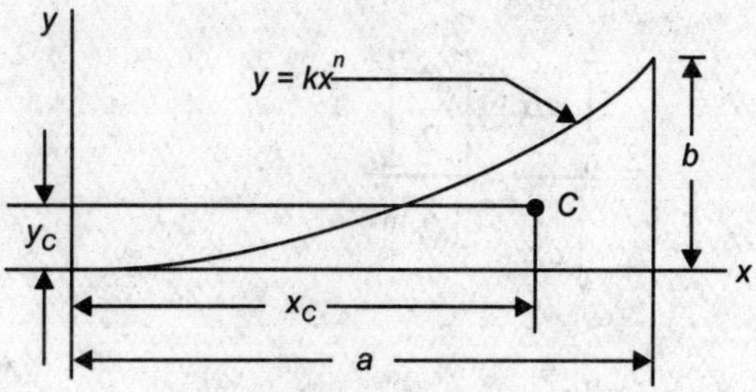	$\frac{ab}{n+1}$	$\left(\frac{n+1}{n+2}\right)a$	$\left(\frac{n+1}{2n+1}\right)\frac{1}{2}$
Hemisphere	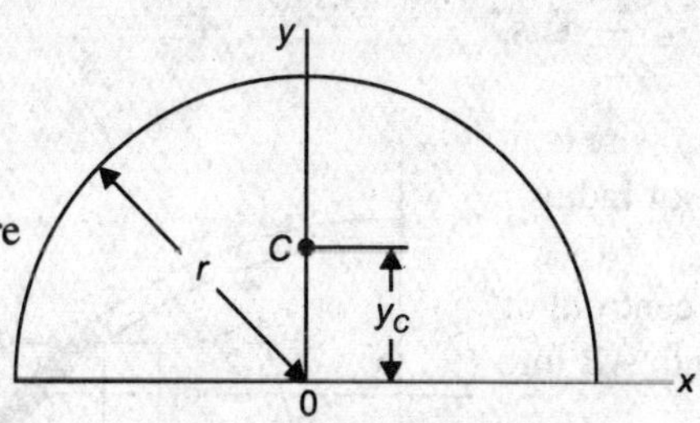	$\frac{2}{3}\pi r^3$	0	$\frac{3}{8}r$
Right circular cone	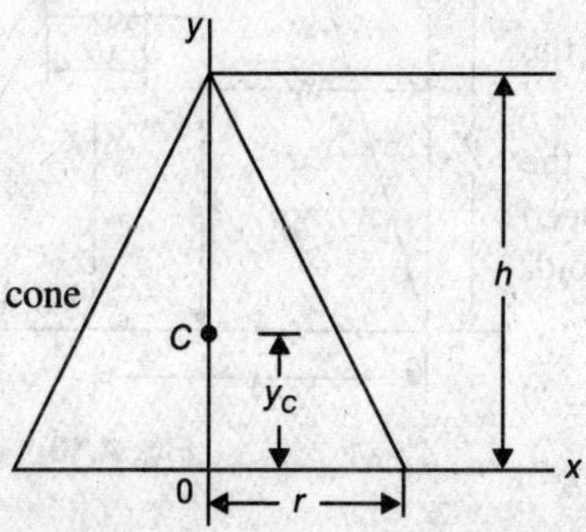	$\frac{1}{3}\pi r^2 h$	0	$\frac{h}{4}$

EXAMPLE 4.6. Find the centroid of a straight uniform wire of length L.

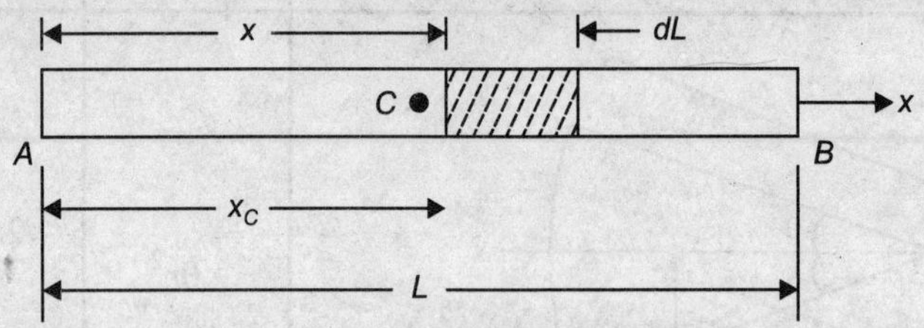

Fig. 4.12

SOLUTION: Choose the x-axis passing through the centre of the wire and along its length. Divide the length L of the wire into elements of the infinitesimal length dL.

Let us choose an element at a distance x from the origin.

$$x_c = \frac{\int x dL}{\int dL}$$

But
$$dL = dx$$

$$x_c = \frac{\int_0^L x dx}{\int_0^L dx} = \frac{\left[\frac{x^2}{2}\right]_0^L}{[X]_0^L}$$

$$x_c = \frac{L}{2} \textbf{ Ans.}$$

EXAMPLE 4.7. Find the centroid of a uniform wire bent in the form of a quadrant of the arc of a circle of radius r as shown in Fig. 4.13.

SOLUTION: Here we have to determine the centroid of the length of a curve, so let us divide the length AB into infinitesimal elements of length dL.

Choose the origin of coordinates at the centre of the circle O.

The figure is symmetrical about the line joining the origin to middle point of the length AB. Therefore, we need to determine only one of the coordinates of the centroid.

Let us determine y_c.

Consider an element of length dL at a distance (x, y) from the axes,

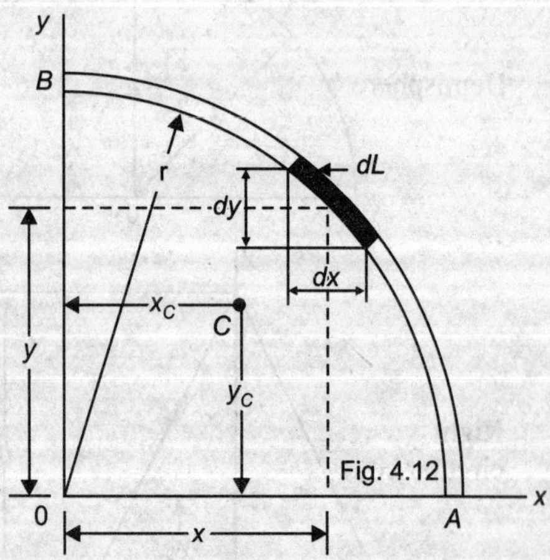

Fig. 4.13

$$y_c = \frac{\int y dL}{\int dL} \quad \text{...(i)}$$

Expressing dL in terms of x and y

$$dL = \sqrt{(dx)^2 + (dy)^2}$$

Equation of the circle is given by

$$x^2 + y^2 = r^2$$

Differentiating $\quad 2x\,dx + 2y\,dy = 0$

$$2x\,dx = -2y\,dy$$

$$dy = -\frac{x\,dx}{y}$$

As $\quad dL = \sqrt{(dx)^2 + (dy)^2}$

Therefore,

$$dL = \sqrt{(dx)^2 + \left(\frac{x}{y}dx\right)^2}$$

$$dL = \sqrt{\frac{y^2 + x^2}{y^2}}dx$$

$$dL = \frac{r}{y}dx$$

Substituting for dL in equation (i)

$$y_c = \frac{\int_0^r y \cdot \frac{r}{y}dx}{\int dL} = \frac{\int_0^r r\,dx}{\left(\frac{2\pi r}{4}\right)} = \frac{r[x]_0^r}{\frac{\pi r}{2}}$$

$$y_c = \frac{r^2}{\frac{\pi r}{2}}$$

or $\quad y_c = \frac{2r}{\pi}$ **Ans.**

Because of symmetry,

$$x_c = y_c = \frac{2r}{\pi} \text{ Ans.}$$

Now let us solve the same problem by using polar coordinates. Integral to be evaluated is

$$y_c = \frac{\int y dL}{\int dL}$$

Converting into polar coordinats, see Fig. 4.14

$$y = r \sin \theta$$

$$dL = rd\,\theta$$

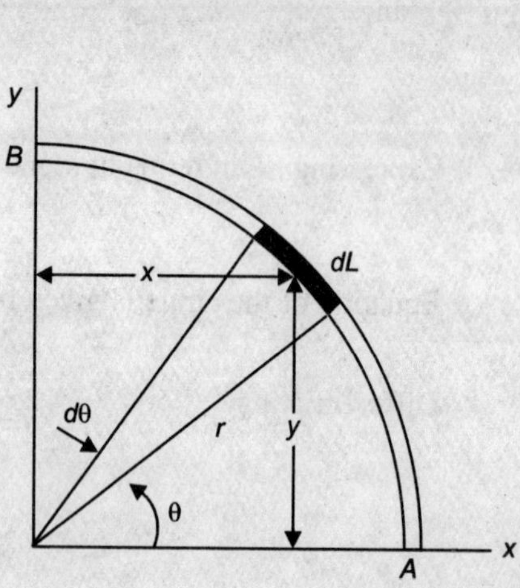

Fig. 4.14

$$y_c = \frac{\int_0^{\pi/2} (r \sin\theta)(rd\theta)}{\int_0^{\pi/2} rd\theta}$$

$$y_c = \frac{\int_0^{\pi/2} r^2 \sin\theta\, d\theta}{\int_0^{\pi/2} rd\theta}$$

$$= \frac{r^2 [\cos\theta]_0^{\pi/2}}{[\theta]_0^{\pi/2}}$$

$$y_c = \frac{r^2}{\frac{r\pi}{2}}$$

or $$y_c = \frac{2r}{\pi} \textbf{ Ans.}$$

Note here that working in polar coodinates considerably simplifies the evaluation of the integral because the polar coordinates best match the boundary of the figure.

EXAMPLE 4.8. Determine the coordinates of the centroid of a lamina in the shape of a circular sector of radius r and central angle 2α.

SOLUTION: Reference axes are as shown in Fig. 4.15. Note here that the figure is symmetrical about the x-axis therefore,

$$y_c = 0$$

Divide the area into infinitesimal triangular elements each of altitude r and base $rd\theta$. as shown in Fig. 4.15. Area of the triangular element *Oab* = 1/2 $(rd\theta)r$. Centroid of the triangular area *Oab* lies on the line joining *O* to the mid-point of *ab* and at a distance 2/3 r from *O*.

Distance x of the centroid from the y-axis = $2/3\ r \cos\theta$.

$$x_c = \frac{\int xdA}{\int dA}$$

$$= \frac{2\int_0^\alpha \left(\frac{2}{3} r\cos\theta\right)\left(\frac{r^2 d\theta}{2}\right)}{2\int_0^\alpha \frac{r^2 d\theta}{2}}$$

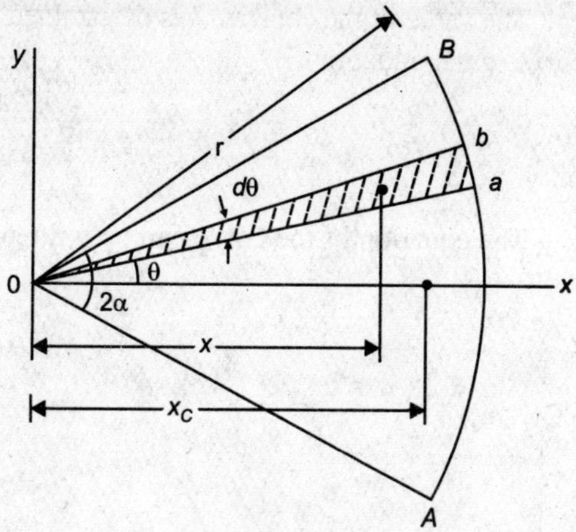

Fig. 4.15

$$x_c = \frac{\frac{r^3}{3}\int_0^\alpha \cos\theta\, d\theta}{\frac{r^2}{2}\int_0^\alpha d\theta}$$

$$= \frac{2r\,[\sin\theta]_0^\alpha}{3[\theta]_\theta^\alpha}$$

$$x_c = \frac{2r\sin\alpha}{3\alpha}\ \textbf{Ans.}$$

Centroid of a quadrant of a circle can be determined if we substitute

$$2\alpha = \frac{\pi}{2}$$

or $$\alpha = \frac{\pi}{4}$$

$$x_c = \frac{2r\sin\frac{\pi}{4}}{3\left(\frac{\pi}{4}\right)}$$

$$x_c = \sqrt{2}\,\frac{4r}{3\pi}\text{(Distance } OC\text{)}$$

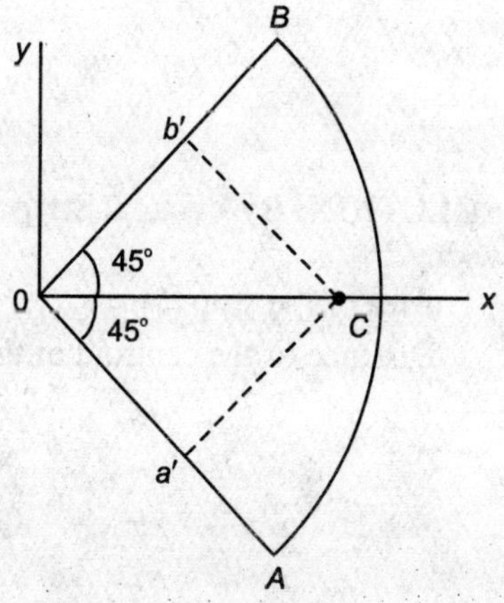

Fig. 4.16

Further, the position of centroid with respect to the radii OA and OB (as shown in Fig. 4.16) is

$$Oa' = \sqrt{2}\,\frac{4r}{3\pi}\cos 45^0 = \frac{4r}{3\pi}$$

$$Ob' = \sqrt{2}\,\frac{4r}{3\pi}\cos 45^0 = \frac{4r}{3\pi}$$

Note the difference in the values of the coordinates of the centroid for a (i) wire in the shape of quadrant of a circle (ii) lamina of the same shape, by comparing these results with the previous example.

EXAMPLE 4.9. Determine the centroid of the parabolic spandrel as shown in Fig. 4.17(a). The equation of the parabola is given by

$$y = kx^2 \qquad \text{...(i)}$$

SOLUTION: The equation of the parabola is

$$y = kx^2$$

The value of the constant k is determined by substituting the coordinates (a, b) at a point on the curve in the equation (i)

$$b = ka^2$$

or

$$k = \frac{b}{a^2}$$

The equation of the curve can be written as

$$y = \frac{b}{a^2}x^2$$

or

$$x = \frac{a}{\sqrt{b}}\sqrt{y}$$

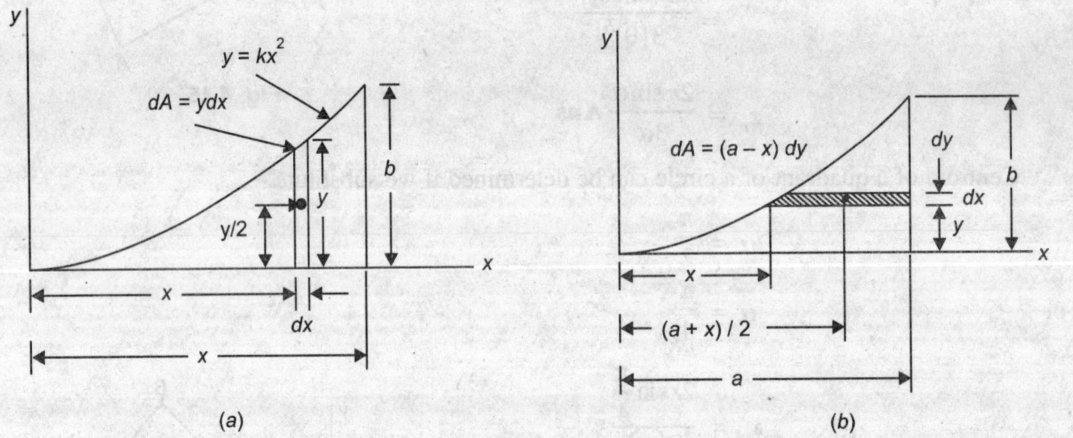

Fig. 4.17

SOLUTION: By Vertical Strip : Consider a vertical differential element (or strip) of height y and width dx.

Area of the strip $dA = v\,dx$.

Distance of the centroid of the strip from the y-axis $= x$

$$x_c = \frac{\int x\,dA}{\int dA} = \frac{\int x \cdot y\,dx}{\int y\,dx} = \frac{\int_0^a x\left(\frac{b}{a^2}x^2\right)dx}{\int_0^a \frac{b}{a^2}x^2\,dx}$$

$$x_c = \frac{\left[\dfrac{b^2}{a}\dfrac{x^4}{4}\right]_0^a}{\left[\dfrac{b^2}{a}\dfrac{x^3}{3}\right]_0^a}$$

$$x_c = \frac{3}{4}a \ \textbf{Ans.}$$

$$y_c = \frac{\int ydA}{\int dA}$$

Distance of the centroid of the strip from the x-axis $= y/2$

$$y_c = \frac{\int \frac{y}{2} ydx}{\int ydx} = \frac{\int_0^a \frac{1}{2}y^2 dx}{\int_0^a ydx} = \frac{\int_0^a \frac{1}{2}\left(\frac{b}{a^2}x^2\right)^2 dx}{\int_0^a \frac{b}{a^2}x^2\, dx}$$

$$y_c = \frac{\left[\dfrac{b^2}{2a^4}\dfrac{x^5}{5}\right]_0^a}{\left[\dfrac{b}{a^2}\dfrac{x^3}{3}\right]_0^a}$$

$$y_c = \frac{3}{10}b \ \textbf{Ans.}$$

SOLUTION: By Horizontal Strip. Consider a horizontal differential element strip) as shown in Fig. 4.17 (b).

Area of the strip $dA = (a - x)dy$.

Distance of the centroid of the element from the y-axis $= (a + x)/2$

$$x_c = \frac{\int xdA}{\int dA} = \frac{\int_0^h \left(\frac{a+x}{2}\right)(a-x)\, dy}{\int_0^b (a-x)\, dx}$$

$$x_c = \frac{\int_0^b \left(\frac{a^2 - x^2}{2}\right) dy}{\int_0^b (a - x)\, dy} = \frac{\frac{1}{2}\int_0^b \left(a^2 - \frac{a^2}{b} y\right) dy}{\int_0^b \left(a - \frac{a}{\sqrt{b}}\sqrt{y}\right) dy}$$

$$x_c = \frac{3 \times a^2 b}{4 \times ab}\, x_c = \frac{3}{4} a \textbf{ Ans.}$$

$$y_c = \frac{\int y dA}{\int dA} = \frac{\int_0^b y\,(a - x) dy}{\int_0^b (a - x) dy} = \frac{\int_0^b y \left(a = \frac{a}{\sqrt{b}}\sqrt{y}\right) dy}{\int_0^b \left(a - \frac{a}{\sqrt{b}}\sqrt{y}\right) dy}$$

$$y_c = \frac{3ab^2}{10 \times ab}$$

$$y_c = \frac{3b}{10} \textbf{ Ans.}$$

EXAMPLE 4.10. Determine the coordinates of the centroid of the shaded area formed by the intersection of a straight line and a parabola as shown in Fig. 4.18. The equation of the parabola is given by $y = x^2/a$ and of straight line by $y = x$.

SOLUTION: The straight line and the parabola

$$y = x \qquad \text{...(i)}$$

$$y = \frac{x^2}{a} \qquad \text{...(ii)}$$

intersect at the point O and A.]

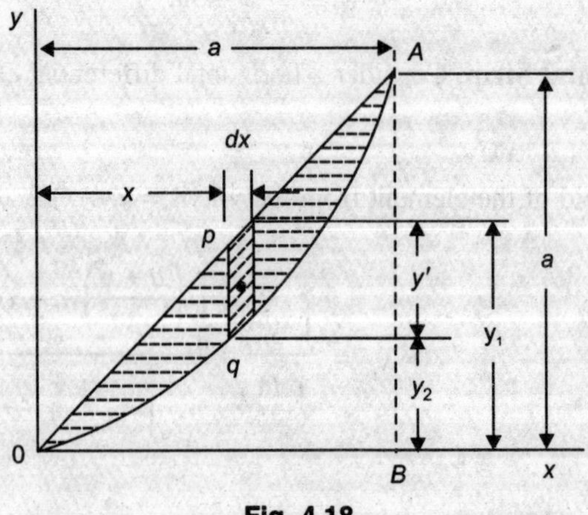

Fig. 4.18

Solving (i) and (ii) simultaneously the coordinates of the point O and A are, O, (0, 0) and A (a, a).

Divide the area into infinitesimal vertical strips. Consider a strip of height y' and width dx.

Area dA of the strip = $(pq)\ dx$

$$dA = y'dx$$

$$dA = (y_1 - y_2)\ dx$$

where y_1 is the coordinate of the point p which lies on the straight line OA and y_2 is the coordinate of the point q which lies on the parabole OA.

Using the equations (i) and (ii), y_1 and y_2 can be expressed in terms of x as

$$y_1 = x,$$

$$y_2 = \frac{x^2}{a}$$

Area of the vertical strip, $$dA = \left(x - \frac{x^2}{a}\right) dx$$

Distance of the centroid of the strip from the y-axis = x

$$x_c = \frac{\int x dA}{\int dA} = \frac{\int_0^a x\left(x - \frac{x^2}{a}\right) dx}{\int_0^a \left(x - \frac{x^2}{a}\right) dx}$$

$$x_c = \frac{\int_0^a \left(x^2 - \frac{x^3}{a}\right) dx}{\int_0^a \left(x - \frac{x^2}{a}\right) dx}$$

$$x_c = \frac{\left[\frac{x^3}{3} - \frac{x^4}{4a}\right]_0^a}{\left[\frac{x^2}{2} - \frac{x^3}{3a}\right]_0^a}$$

$$x_c = \frac{a}{2} \quad \textbf{Ans.}$$

$$y_c = \frac{\int y dA}{\int dA}$$

where, dA = Area of the strip = $(y_1 - y_2)\ dx$

$$y = \frac{y_1 + y}{2}$$

The distance of the centroid of the strip from the x-axis.

$$y_c = \frac{\int \left(\frac{y_1 + y}{2}\right)(y_1 - y_2)\, dx}{\int (y_1 - y_2)\, dx}$$

Using equations (i) and (ii), y_1 and y_2 can be expressed in terms of x as

$$y_1 = x, \quad y_2 = \frac{x^2}{a}$$

$$y_c = \frac{\int_0^a \frac{1}{2}\left(x - \frac{x^2}{a}\right)\left(a + \frac{x^2}{a}\right) dx}{\int_0^a \left(a - \frac{x^2}{a}\right) dx}$$

$$y_c = \frac{\frac{1}{2}\int_0^a \left(x^2 - \frac{x^4}{a^2}\right) dx}{\int_0^a \left(x - \frac{x^2}{a}\right) dx} = \frac{\frac{1}{2}\left[\frac{x^3}{3} - \frac{x^5}{5a^2}\right]_0^a}{\left[\frac{x^2}{2} - \frac{x^3}{3a}\right]_0^a}$$

$$y_c = \frac{2a}{5} \quad \textbf{Ans.}$$

Alternative Method: The problem can be solved by treating the shaded area as a composite area. That is,

Shaded Area = Area of the triangle OAB – Area under the curve $y = x^2/a$.

Area of triangle OAB and the location of its C.G. is listed. Area under the curve $y = x^2/a$ is the area of the spandrel ($n = 2$, $a = b = a$). The area and the location of its C.G. is also listed. Centroid of the composite area now can be determiend.

EXAMPLE 4.11. Locate the centroid of the shaded area obtained by removing a semicircle of diameter a from a quadrant of a circle of radius a.

SOLUTION: To determine the centroid (x_c, y_c) of the shaded area let us consider that the shaded area is obtained by substracting the area of the semicircle of radius $a/2$ from the area of the quadrant of circle of radius a. In this sense, therefore, the area to be substracted is treated to be as negative area.

Reference axes are as shown in the Fig. 4.19. Different areas and coodinates of their centroids are tabulated below:

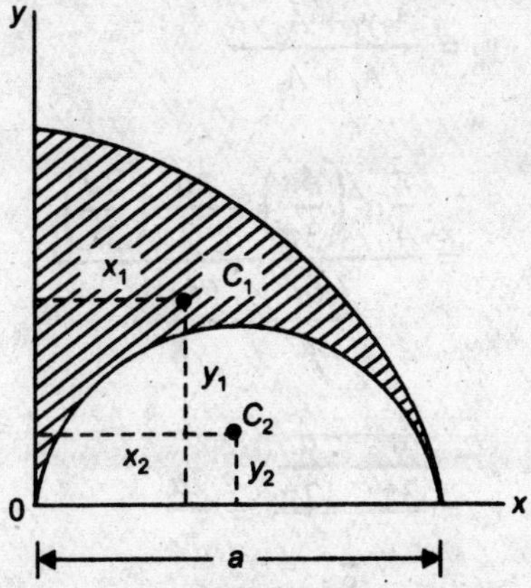

Fig. 4.19

Figure	Area	X co-ordinate of the centroid	Y-co-ordinate of the centroid
Quadrant of circle of radius = a	$A_1 = \frac{\pi}{4}a^2$	$x_1 = \frac{4a}{3\pi}$	$y_1 = \frac{4a}{3\pi}$
Semicircle of radius = $a/2$	$A = \frac{\pi(a/2)^2}{2}$ $A_2 = \frac{\pi a^2}{-8}$	$x_2 = \frac{a}{2}$	$y_2 = \frac{4}{3\pi}\left(\frac{a}{2}\right) = \frac{2a}{3\pi}$

Centroid of the composite area

$$x_c = \frac{A_1x_1 + A_2x_2}{A_1 + A_2}$$

$$x_c = \frac{\frac{\pi}{4}a^2\left(\frac{4a}{3\pi}\right) - \frac{\pi a^2}{8}\left(\frac{a}{2}\right)}{\frac{\pi a^2}{4} - \frac{\pi a^2}{8}}$$

$$x_c = \frac{\frac{a}{3\pi} - \frac{a}{16}}{\frac{1}{8}}$$

$$= 8a\left(\frac{1}{3\pi} - \frac{1}{16}\right)$$

$x_c = 0.349a$ **Ans.**

$$y_c = \frac{A_1 y_1 + A_2 y_2}{A_1 + A_2}$$

$$= \frac{\frac{\pi}{4} a^2 \left(\frac{4a}{3\pi}\right) - \frac{\pi a^2}{8}\left(\frac{2a}{3\pi}\right)}{\frac{(\pi a^2)}{4} - \frac{(\pi a^2)}{8}}$$

$$y_c = \frac{\frac{a}{3\pi} - \frac{a}{12\pi}}{\frac{1}{8}} = \frac{2a}{\pi}$$

$$\therefore \quad y_c = 0.636a \textbf{ Ans.}$$

EXAMPLE 4.12. Locate the centroid of the shaded area as shown in the Fig. 4.20 (2004).

SOLUTION: See Fig. 4.20

Let $\overline{x}$ = required distance of C.G. of the given portion of the area from *y*-axis, and

$\overline{y}$ = required distance of C.G. of the given portion of the area of from *x*-axis.

Then, $\overline{x} = \dfrac{a_1 x_1 + a_2 x_2 - a_3 x_3}{a_1 + a_2 - a_3}$, where

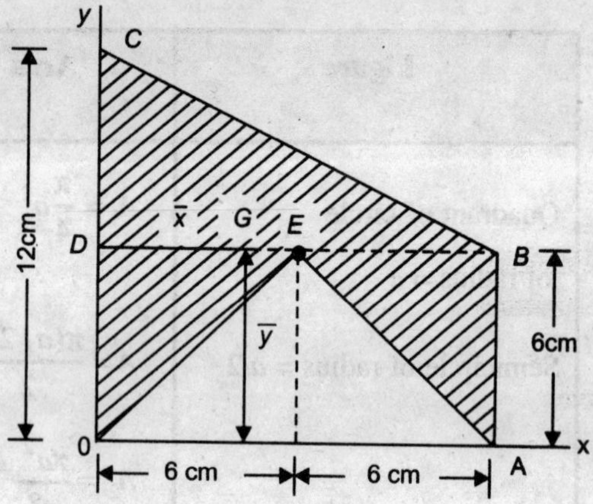

Fig. 4.20

$$a_1 = \text{Area } DBC = \frac{1}{2} DB \times DC = \frac{1}{2} \times 12 \times 6 = 36 \text{ cm}^2$$

$$a_2 = \text{Area } DBAO = OA \times OD = 12 \times 6 = 72 \text{ cm}^2$$

$$a_3 = \text{Area } OEA = \frac{1}{2} OA \times AB = \frac{1}{2} \times 12 \times 6 = 36 \text{ cm}^2$$

x_1 = Distance of C.G. of the area *DBC* from *y*-axis $= \dfrac{1}{3} \times DB = \dfrac{1}{3} \times 12 = 4\text{cm}$

x_2 = Distance of C.G. of the area *DBAO* from *y*-axis $= \dfrac{12}{2} = 6$ cm, and

x_3 = Distance of C.G. of he area *OEA* from *y*-axis = 60 cm

Now

$$\overline{x} = \frac{a_1 x_1 + a_2 x_2 - a_2 x_3}{a_1 + a_2 - a_3} = \frac{36 \times 4 + 72 \times 6 - 36 \times 6}{36 + 72 - 36} = 5 \text{ cm } \textbf{Ans.}$$

$$\overline{y} = \frac{a_1 y_1 + a_2 y_2 - a_3 y_3}{a_1 + a_2 - a_3}, \text{ where}$$

y_1 = Distance of C.G. of the area *CBD* from *x*-axis = $6+\frac{1}{3}\times 6$ = 8 cm

y_2 = Distance of C.G. of the area *DBAO* from *x*-axis = 6/2 = 3 cm

y_3 = Distance of C.G. of the aea *OEA* from *x*-axis = 6/3 = 2 cm

$$\bar{y} = \frac{a_1 y_1 + a_2 y_2 - a_3 y_3}{a_1 + a_2 + a_3} = \frac{36\times 8 + 72\times 3 - 36\times 2}{36+72-36} = 6\,\text{cm } \textbf{Ans.}$$

EXERCISE-4

1. Define the terms:
   (i) Centre of gravity,
   (ii) Centroid.
2. Find the centre of gravity of a *T*-section with flange 150 mm × 10 mm and web 150 × 10 mm.
   [**Ans.** 115 mm from the bottom of the web]
3. Find the centre of gravity of an inverted *T*-section with flange 60 mm × 10 mm and web 50 mm × 10 mm. [**Ans.** 18.6 mm from the bottom of the flange]
4. Find the centre of gravity of an *I*-section with top flange 100 mm × 20 mm, web 200 mm × 30 mm and bottom flange 300 mm × 40 mm.
   [**Ans.** 79 mm from the bottom of lower flange]
5. Find the centre of gravity from the back of the web of a channel section 300 mm × 10 mm × 20 mm (Thick). [**Ans.** 27.4 mm]
6. An I-section has the following dimensions.
   (i) Bottom flange = 300 mm × 100 mm
   (ii) Top flange = 150 mm × 50 mm
   (iii) Web = 300 m × 50 mm

   Determine the position of centre of gravity of the section. [**Ans.** $\bar{y}$ = 160.7 mm]
7. A body consists of right circular solid cone of height 40 mm and radius 30 mm placed on a solid hemisphere of radius 30 mm of the same material. Find the position of centre of gravity of the body. [**Ans.** $\bar{y}$ = 27.3 mm]

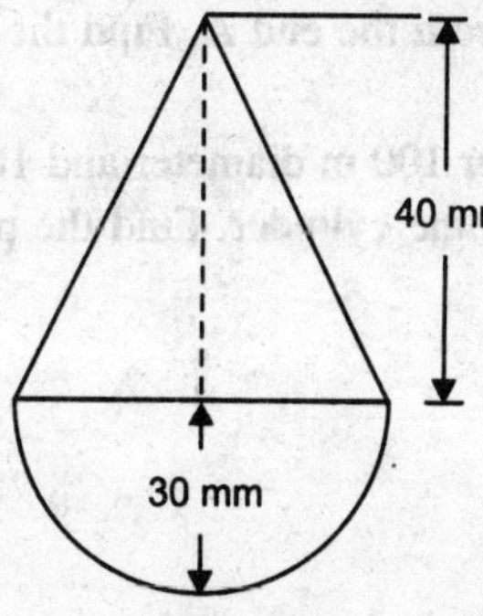

Fig. 4.21

8. A body consists of a cone and hemi-sphere of radius r fixed on the same base, rests on the table, the hemi-sphere being in contact with the table. Find the greatest height of the cone, so that the combined body may stand upright. **[Ans.** $h = 1.732\ r$**]**
9. A solid hemisphere of 20 mm radius supports a solid cone of same base and 60 mm height. Locate the centre of gravity of the composite section. **[Ans.** $\bar{y} = 54$mm**]**
10. A circular hole of 50 mm diameter is cut out from a circular disc of 100 mm diameter as shown in Fig. 4.22. Find the centre of gravity of the section from A.

[Ans. $\bar{x} = 41.7$ mm**]**

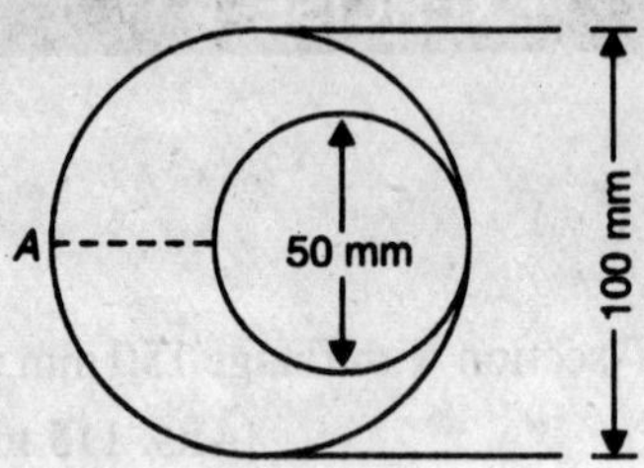

Fig. 2.22

11. Find the centre of gravity of a semi-circular section having outer and inner diameters of 200 mm and 160 mm respectively. **[Ans.** 57.5 mm from the base**]**
12. From a rectangular sheet of metal *ABCD*, in which *AB* = 400 mm and *BC* = 600 mm, a rectangular piece *ABX* is removed, such that *AX* = *BX* = 250 mm. Calculate distance of centroid of the remainder from side *AB*. **[Ans.** 335.7 mm from *AB* on centre line**]**
13. A thin uniform metal plate *ABCD* is 720 mm square. It is folded so that the side *AB* lies along the line joining mid points of *AD* and *BC*, and the folded part is pressed flat. Find the position of centre of gravity of the folded plate.

[Ans. 315 mm from *DC* on perpendicular bisecting *DC***]**

14. A cylindrical cane of diameter 160 mm and length 120 mm is closed at one end. Assume that weight of any part of the cane is proportional to its area,; find distance of C.G. of the cane from the centre of closed end. **[Ans.** 45 mm**]**
15. A uniform blank *AB* of length 3m and weighing 150 N is loaded with weight 360 N and 90 N, 300 mm and 1.8 m respectively from the end A. Find the point at which the plank may be supported by a single prop. **[Ans.** 3.825 m from *A***]**
16. A solid body is made up a cylinder 100 m diameter and 160 mm long and a hemisphere 50 mm radius is fixed on one end of the cylinder. Find the position of centre of gravity from plane end of the cylinder. **[Ans.** 97 mm**]**

CHAPTER 5

Moment of Inertia

INTRODUCTION

We are familiar with the fact that moment of a force about a point, is the product of a force (P) and perpendicular distance (x) between the point and the line of action of the force i.e. $P.x$. This moment is also called first moment of force. If this moment is again multiplied by perpendicular distance (x) between the point and the line of action of the force i.e. $(P x)x = Px^2$, then this quantity is called moment of the moment of a force or second moment of force or moment of inertia (briefly written as M.1)

Some times instead of force, the area or mass of a figure or body is taken into consideration, then the second moment is known as second moment of area or second moment of mass. But all such second moments are broadly termed as moment of inertia.

MOMENT OF INERTIA OF A PLANE AREA

Consider a plane area, whose moment of inertia is required to be found out. Split up the whole area into a number of small elements.

Let,

a_1, a_2, a_3 .... = Areas of small elements, and

x_1, x_2, x_3 .... = Distance of the elements from the line about which the moment of inertia is required to be found out.

Now the moment of inertia of the area,

$$I = a_1 x_1^2 + a_2 x_2^2 + a_3 x_3^2 + ... + \sum ax^2$$

UNITS OF MOMENT OF INERTIA

The units of moment of inertia of a plane area depend upon the units of the area and the length e.g.

1. If area is in m^2 and the length is also in m, the moment of inertia is expressed in m^4.
2. If area is in cm^2 and the length is also in cm, then moment of inertia is expressed in cm^4.
3. If the area is in mm^2 and the length is also in mm, then moment of inertia is expressed in mm^4.

MOMENT OF INERTIA

Consider a thin lamina of area A as shown in Fig. 5.1

Let x = Distance of C.G. of area A from the axis OY.

y = Distance of C.G. of area A from the axis OX.

Then moment of area about the axis OY = Area × perpendicular distance of C.G. of area from axis

$$OY = Ax \qquad ...(5.1)$$

Equation (5.1) is known as first moment of area about the axis OY. This first moment of area is used to determine the centre of gravity of the area.

If the moment of area given by the equation (5.1) i.e. Ax is again multiplied by the perpendicular distance between the C.G. of the area and axis OY (i.e. distance x) then the quantity $(Ax)x = Ax^2$ is known as moment of the moment of area or second moment of area or moment of inertia about the axis OY. This second moment of area is used in the study of mechanics of fluids and mechanic of solids.

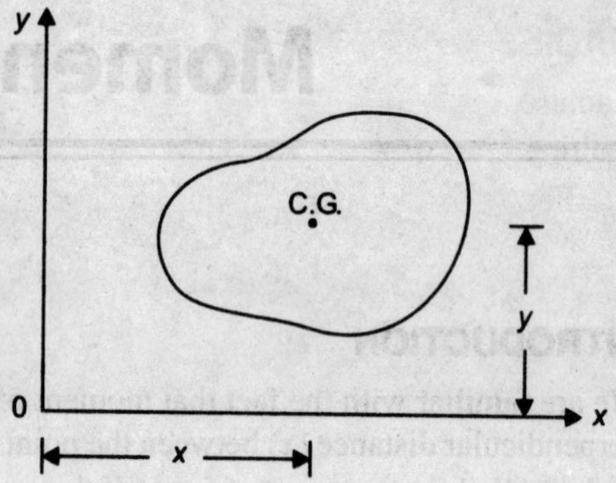

Fig. 5.1

Similarly, the moment of area or first moment of area about the axis $OX = Ay$.

And second moment of area or moment of inertia about the axis $OX = (Ay)y = Ay^2$

If instead of area, the mass m of the body is taken into consideration then the second moment is known as second moment of mass. This second moment of mass is also known as moment of inertia.

Hence moment of inertia when mass is taken into consideration about the axis $OY = mx^2$, and about the axis $OX = my^2$

Hence the product of area or mass and the square of the distance of the centre of gravity of the area or mass from an axis is known as moment of inertia of the area or mass about that axis. Moment of inertia is represented by I. The moment of inertia about OX axis is represented by I_{xx} whereas about the axis OY by I_{yy}.

Consider a plane area which is split up into small areas a_1, a_2, a_3 etc. Let the C.G. of the small areas from a given axis be at a distance of r_1, r_2, r_3 ... etc. as shown in Fig. 5.2

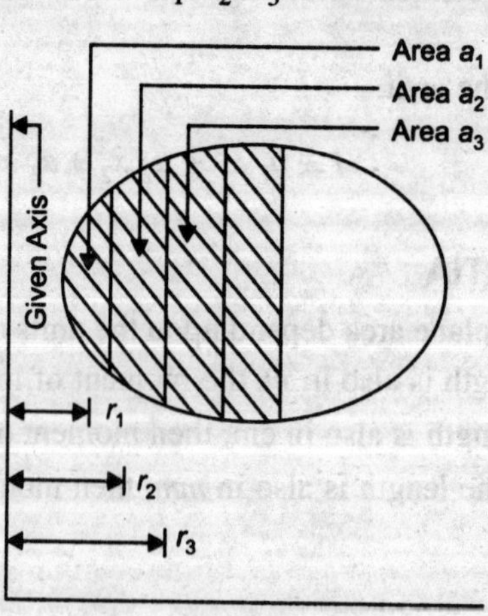

Fig. 5.2

Then the moment of inertia of the plane area about the given axis is given by,

$$I = a_1r_1^2 + a_2r_2^2 + a_3r_3^3 + ... \quad ...(5.2)$$

or

$$I = \sum ar^2 \quad ...(5.3)$$

RADIUS OF GYRATION

Radius of gyration of a body or a given lamina about an axis is a distance such that its square multiplied by the area gives moment of inertia of the area about the given axis.

For the Fig. 5.2, the moment of inertia about the given axis is given by the equation (5.2) as

$$I = a_1r_1^2 + a_2r_2^2 + a_3r_3^3 + ... \quad ...(i)$$

Let the whole mass or area of a body is concentrated at a distance k from the axis of reference, then the moment of inertia of the whole area about the given axis will be equal to Ak^2.

If $Ak^2 = I$, then k is known as radius of gyration about the given axis.

$$\therefore \quad k = \sqrt{\frac{I}{A}} \quad ...(5.3)$$

POLAR MOMENT OF INERTIA

The product of area or mass and the square of the distane of the centre of gravity of the area or mass from an axis perpendicular to the plane of the area is known as polar moment of inertia, and it is represented by J.

Consider a plane figure of area A in the $x-y$ plane as shown in Fig. 5.3. Divide this area A into infinitesimal areas.

Let dA be any element of the area situated at a distance x, y from the axes.

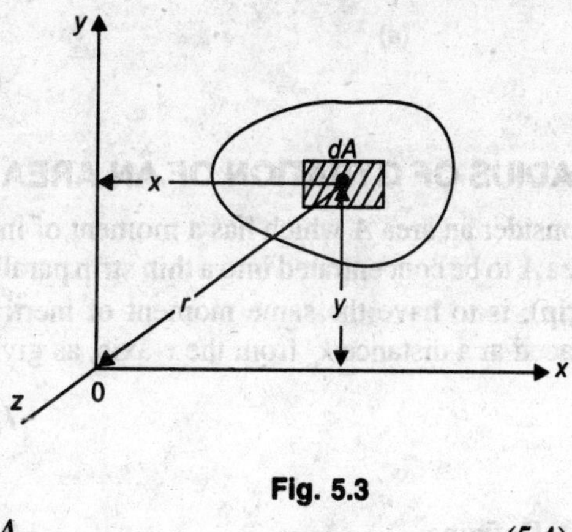

Fig. 5.3

The moment of inertia of the area A with respect to the x-axis (also called second moment of the area)

$$I_x = \int y^2 dA \quad ...(5.4)$$

The moment of inertia of the area A with respect to the y-axis (also called the second moment of the area).

$$I_y = \int x^2 dA \quad ...(5.5)$$

Integration should cover the entire area of the figure and its value shall depend upon the shape of the area and its orientation with respect to the axis.

Hence the moment of inertia of an area of a plane figure with respect to an axis perpendicular to the x-y plane and passing through a pole O (Z-axis) is called polar moment of inertia and is denoted by J.

$$\therefore \qquad J = \int r^2 \, dA \qquad \text{...(5.6)}$$

As
$$x^2 + y^2 = r^2$$

Hence,

$$J = \int (x^2 + y^2)\, dA = I_x + I_y$$

The moment of inertia of an area can be determined with respect to any axis. One commonly used axis is the centroidal axis. Any axis passing through the centroid of an area is called the centroidal axis. Two of them are centroidal *x*-axis and centroidal *y*-axis.

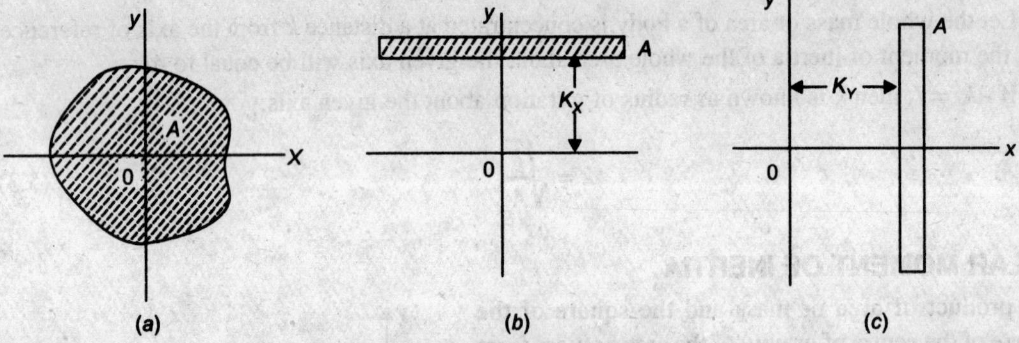

Fig. 5.4

RADIUS OF GYRATION OF AN AREA

Consider an area A which has a moment of inertia I_x with respect to the x-axis. Let us imagine this area A to be concentrated into a thin strip parallel to the x-axis (Fig. 5.4b). If this area A (concentrated strip), is to have the same moment of inertia (I_x) with respect to the x-axis, the strip should be placed at a distance k_x from the x-axis, as given by the relation.

$$I_x = k_x^2 A$$

Defining
$$k_x = \sqrt{\frac{I_x}{A}} \qquad \text{...(5.7)}$$

k_x is known as radius of gyration of the area with respect to x-axis and has a unit of length (m).
We can similarly define, radius of gyration with respect to y-axis

$$k_y = \sqrt{\frac{I_y}{A}} \qquad \text{...(5.8)}$$

Radius of gyration with respect to the polar axis,

$$k_0 = \sqrt{\frac{J_0}{A}} \qquad \text{...(5.8)}$$

As, $$J_0 = I_x + I_y$$

or $$A(k_0)^2 = A(k_x)^2 + A(k_y)^2,$$

we get $$k_0^2 = k_x^2 + k_y^2 \qquad ...(5.9)$$

THEOREM OF PERPENDICULAR AXIS

It states that if I_{xx} and I_{yy} be the moment of inertia of a plane section about two mutually perpendicular axes *x-x* and *y-y* in the plane of the section, then moment of inertia of the section I_{zz} about the axis *z-z*, perpendicular to the plane and passing through the inter-section of *x-x* and *y-y* is given by,

$$I_{zz} = I_{xx} + I_{yy} \qquad ...(5.10)$$

The moment of inertia I_{zz} is also known as polar moment of inertia (*J*).

PROOF: A plane section of area *A* and lying in plane *x-y* is shown in Fig. 5.5. Let *OX* and *OY* be two mutually perpendicular axes, and *OZ* be the perpendicular axis. Consider a small area *dA*.

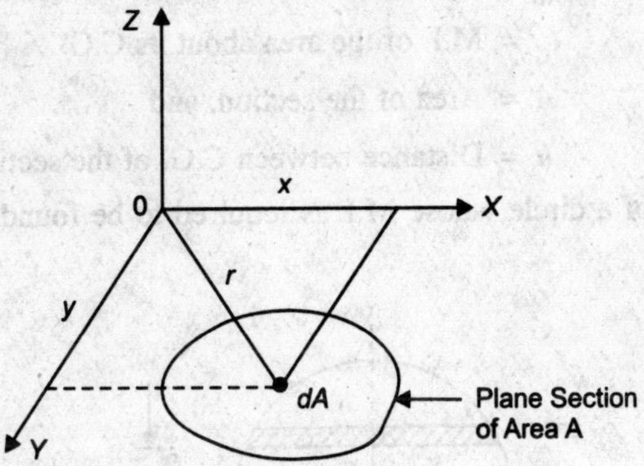

Fig. 5.5

Let

x = Distance of *dA* from axis *OY*

y = Distance of *dA* from axis *OX*

r = Distance of *dA* from axis *OZ*

Then,

$$r^2 = x^2 + y^2$$

Now moment of inertia of *dA* about *x*-axis

$$= dA \text{ (Distance of } dA \text{ from } x\text{-axis)}^2$$

$$= dA \times y^2$$

∴ Moment of inertia of total area *A* about *x*-axis, $I_{xx} = \sum dAy^2$

Similarly moment of inertia of total area *A* about *y*-axis, $I_{yy} = \sum dAx^2$

and moment of inertia of total area A about z-axis, $I_{zz} = \sum dAr^2$

or $$I_{zz} = \sum dA(x^2 + y^2) \qquad (\because r^2 = x^2 + y^2)$$

or $$I_{zz} = \sum dAx^2 + \sum dAy^2 = I_{yy} + I_{xx}$$

Hence $$I_{zz} = I_{xx} + I_{yy}$$

THEOREM OF PARALLEL AXIS

It states that if the moment of inertia of a plane area about an axis through its centre of gravity, be denoted by I_G, the moment of inertia of the area about axis AB, parallel to the first, and at a distance h from the centre of gravity is given by:

$$I_{AB} = I_G + Ah^2$$

where,

I_{AB} = M.I. of the area about an axis AB

I_G = M.I. of the area about its C.G.

A = Area of the section, and

h = Distance between C.G. of the section and axis AB.

PROOF: Consider a strip of a circle whose M.I. is required to be found out about a line AB as shown in Fig. 5.6.

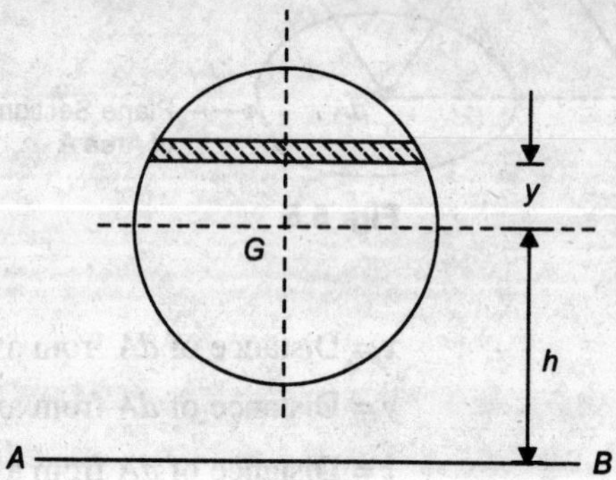

Fig. 5.6

Let,

δa = Area of strip

y = Distance of strip from the C.G. of the section.

h = Distance between C.G. of the section and the axis AB.

We known that M.I. of the strip about an axis passing through C.G. of the section = δay^2 and M.I. of the whole section about an axis passing through its C.G.,

$$I_G = \sum \delta a \cdot y^2 \qquad \text{...(i)}$$

∴ M.I. of the whole section about the axis *AB*,

$$I_{AB} = \sum \delta a\,(h+y)^2 = \sum \delta a\,(h^2+y^2+2hy)$$

$$= \sum h^2 \cdot \delta a + \sum y^2 \cdot \delta a + \sum 2hy \cdot \delta a = ah^2 + I_G + 0$$

It may be noted that

$$\sum h^2 \cdot \delta a = ah^2$$

and
$$\sum y^2 \cdot \delta a = I_G$$

(As per equation (i) above) and $\sum \delta a \cdot y$ is the algebriac sum of moments of all the areas, about an axis through C.G. of the section and is equal to $a\bar{y}$ where $\bar{y}$ is the distance between the section and the axis passing through the C.G., which, obviously, is zero.

EXAMPLE 5.1. Find the moment of inertia of a rectangular cross-section about its centroidal axes. Also find its moment of inertia about the base *AB*.

SOLUTION: The centroid of the rectangular area is at *O* and centroidal axis $X' - X$ and $Y' - Y$ are as shown in Fig. 5.7 and the area is symmetrical about both these axes.

Consider a rectangular section *ABCD* (Fig. 5.7).

Let, b = width of the section, and

h = Height of the section

Now consider a strip *PQ* of thickness dy parallel to $X' - X$ axis and at a distance y from it as shown in Fig. (5.7).

∴ Area of the strip = $b.dy$

M.I. of the strip about $X - X$ axis = Area × y^2

$= (b.dy)y^2 = b.y^2.dy$

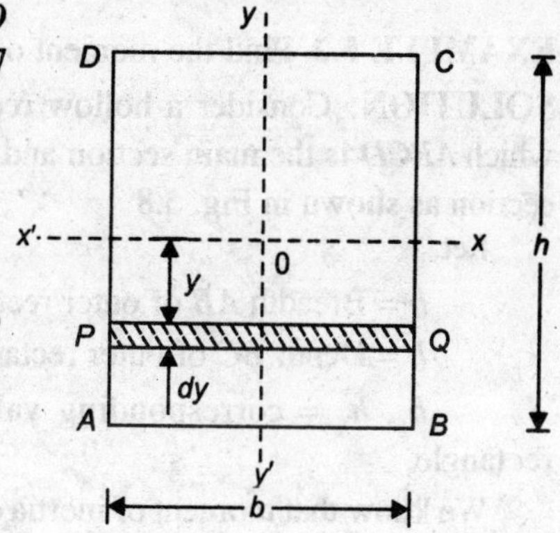

Fig. 5.7

The M.I. of the whole section can be found out by integrating for the whole length of the lamina i.e. $-\frac{h}{2}$ to $+\frac{h}{2}$.

$$\therefore \quad I_{xx} = \int_{-\frac{h}{2}}^{+\frac{h}{2}} b \cdot y^2 \cdot dy$$

$$= b\int_{-\frac{h}{2}}^{+\frac{h}{2}} y^2 \cdot dy$$

$$= b\left[\frac{y^3}{3}\right]_{-\frac{h}{2}}^{+\frac{h}{2}} = b\left[\frac{(h/2)^3}{3} - \frac{(-h/2)^3}{3}\right]$$

$$I_{xx} = \frac{bh^3}{12} \textbf{ Ans.}$$

Similarly by $I_{yy} = \dfrac{hb^3}{12}$ **Ans.**

MOMENT OF INERTIA ABOUT THE BASE: USING PARALLEL AXIS THEOREM

$$I_{AB} = I_G + ah^2 = I_{xx} + ah^2 = \frac{bh^3}{12} + b\cdot h\left(\frac{h}{2}\right)^2$$

$$= \frac{bh^3}{3} \textbf{ Ans.}$$

EXAMPLE 5.2. Find the moment of inertia of a hollow rectangular section.

SOLUTION: Consider a hollow rectangular section, in which *ABCD* is the main section and *EFGH* is the cut out section as shown in Fig. 5.8

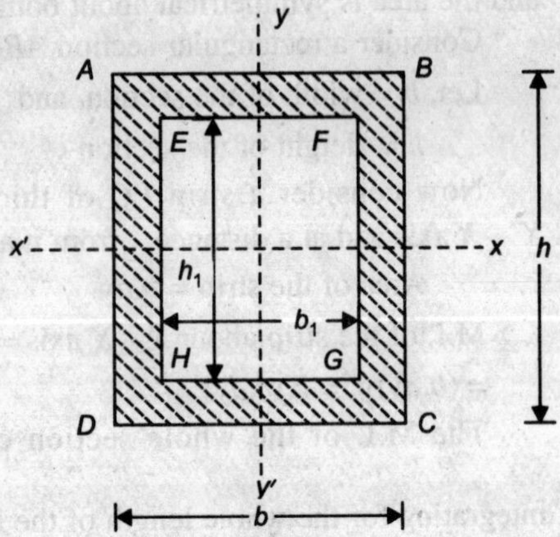

Fig. 5.8

Let,

b = Breadth *AB* of outer rectangle,

h = Depth *BC* of outer rectangle,

b_1, h_1 = corresponding values for the cut out rectangle.

We know that moment of inertia of the outer rectangle

ABCD about $X - X$ axis $= \dfrac{bh^3}{12}$

and moment of inertia of the cut out rectangle *EFGH* about

$X - X$ axis $= \dfrac{b_1h_1^3}{12}$

∴ M.I. of the hollow rectangular section about $X–X$ axis,

I_{xx} = M.I. of rectangle *ABCD* – M.I. of rectangle *EFGH*

or $$I_{xx} = \frac{bh^3}{12} - \frac{b_1h_1^3}{12} \textbf{ Ans.}$$

Similarly, $$I_{yy} = \frac{hb^3}{12} - \frac{h_1b_1^3}{12} \textbf{ Ans.}$$

EXAMPLE 5.3. Find the moment of inertia of a hollow rectangular section about its C.G. if the external dimensions are breadth 60 mm, depth 80 mm and internal dimensions are breadth 30 mm and depth 40 mm respectively.

SOLUTION: Given

$b = 60$ mm, $h = 80$ mm, $b_1 = 30$ mm, $h_1 = 40$ mm

We know that moment of inertia of the section about an axis passing through its C.G. and parallel to $X - X$ axis.

$$I_{xx} = \frac{bh^3}{12} - \frac{b_1h_1^3}{12}$$

$$= \frac{60(80)^3}{12} - \frac{30(40)^3}{12}$$

$$= 2560\times10^3 - 160\times10^3\ mm^4$$

$$= 2400\times10^3\ mm^4\ \textbf{Ans.}$$

Similarly,

$$I_{yy} = \frac{hb^3}{12} - \frac{h_1b_1^3}{12}$$

$$= \frac{80(60)^3}{12} - \frac{40(30)^3}{12}$$

$$= 1350\times10^3\ mm^4\ \textbf{Ans.}$$

EXAMPLE 5.4: Determine the moment of inertia of a circular area about the centroidal axes.

SOLUTION: The centroid of the circular area is its centre. The axes $X–X'$ and $Y–Y'$ passing through O are the centroidal axes.

Consider a circle $ABCD$ of radius r with centre O and $X–X'$ and $Y–Y'$ be two axes of reference through O as shown in Fig. 5.9.

Now consider an elementary ring of radius x and thickness dx.

Hence area of the ring, $da = 2\pi x.dx$ and M.I. of the ring about $X–X$ or $Y – Y$ axes

$$= \text{Area} \times (\text{Distance})^2 = 2\pi x.dx \times x^2 = 2\pi x^2.dx$$

Now M.I. of the whole section, about the central axis, can be found out by integrating the above equation for the whole radius of the circle i.e. from O to r. Hence,

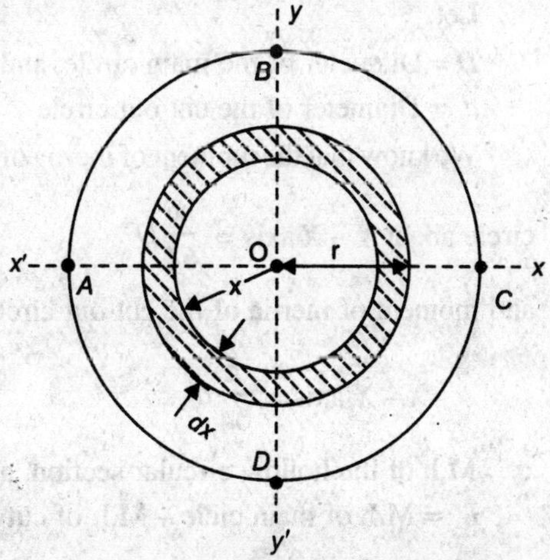

Fig. 5.9

$$I_{zz} = \int_0^r 2\pi x^3 \cdot dx$$

$$= 2\pi \int_0^r x^3 \cdot dx = \pi \left[\frac{x^4}{4}\right]_0^r = \frac{\pi}{2}(r)^4$$

$$\therefore \quad I_{zz} = \frac{\pi}{32} d^4 \quad \text{(Substituting } r = \frac{d}{2}\text{)}$$

We know from the theorem of perpendicular axis, that

$$I_{xx} + I_{yy} = I_{zz}$$

For circular area,

$$I_{xx} = I_{yy}$$

$$\therefore \quad I_{xx} + I_{xx} = I_{zz} \quad \text{and}$$

$$\therefore \quad I_{xx} = \frac{1}{2} I_{zz}$$

$$= \frac{1}{2} \times \frac{\pi}{32} d^4 = \frac{\pi}{64} d^4 \quad \textbf{Ans.}$$

EXAMPLE 5.5. Determine the moment of inertia of a hollow circular section about its centroidal axes.

SOLUTION: Consider a hollow circular section as shown in Fig. 5.10, whose moment of inertia is required to be found out.

Let,

D = Diameter of the main circle, and

d = Diameter of the cut out circle

We know that the moment of inertia of the main circle about $X - X$ axis = $\frac{\pi}{64} D^4$

and moment of inertia of the cut out circle about $X - X$ axis = $\frac{\pi}{64} d^4$

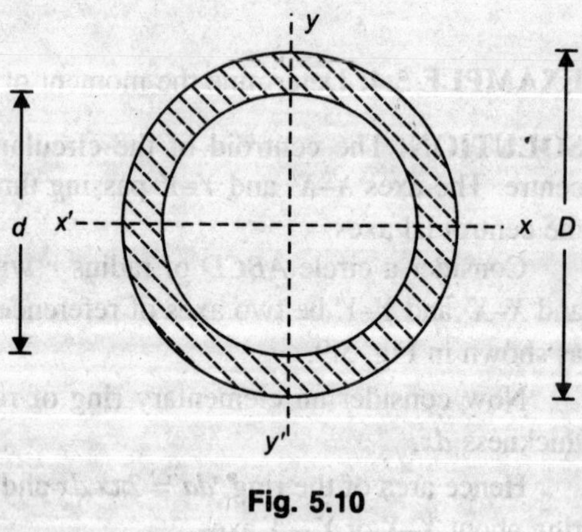

Fig. 5.10

$\therefore$ M.I. of the hollow circular section, about $X - X$ axis.

I_{xx} = M.I. of main cicle – M.I. of cut out circle.

$$= \frac{\pi}{64} D^4 - \frac{\pi}{64} d^4$$

$$= \frac{\pi}{64}(D^4 - d^4) \textbf{ Ans.}$$

Similarly,

$$I_{yy} = \frac{\pi}{64}(D^4 - d^4) \textbf{ Ans.}$$

EXAMPLE 5.6. **A hollow circular section has an external diameter of 80 mm and internal diameter of 60 mm. Find the moment of inertia about the horizontal axis passing through its centre.**

SOLUTION: Given:

$$D = 80 \text{ mm};$$

$$d = 60 \text{ mm}$$

We know that moment of inertia of the hollow circular section about the horizontal axis passing through its centre.

$$I_{xx} = \frac{\pi}{64}(D^4 - d^4)$$

$$= \frac{22[(80)^4 - (60)^4]}{7 \times 64}$$

$$= 1374 \times 10^3 \text{ mm}^4 \textbf{Ans.}$$

EXAMPLE 5.7. Determine the moment of inertia of a triangle with respect to its base.

SOLUTION: Consider a triangular section *ABC* whose moment of inertia is required to be found out. Let, *b* = base, and *h* = height

Now consider a small strip *PQ*, of thickness *dx* at a distance of *x* from *A* as shown in Fig. 5.11.

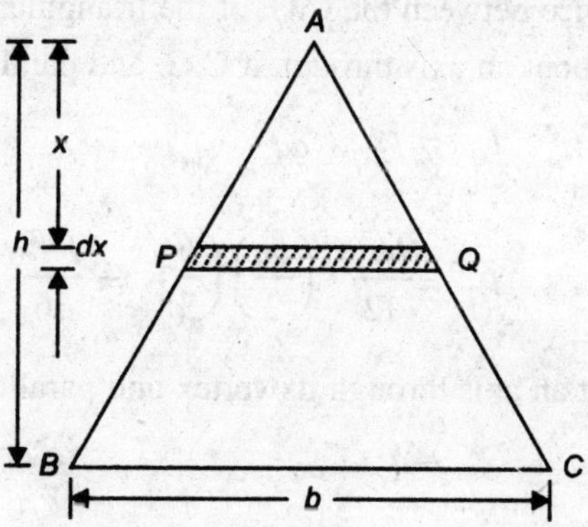

Fig. 5.11

From the geometry of the figure we find that the two triangles *APQ* and *ABC* are similar.

Therfore, $\frac{PQ}{BC} = \frac{x}{h}$

$$\therefore \qquad PQ = \frac{BC \cdot x}{h} = \frac{bx}{h} \qquad (\because\ BC = \text{base} = b)$$

Now area of strip $PQ = \dfrac{bx}{h} \cdot dx$

and M.I. of the strip about the base BC

$$= \text{Area} \times (\text{Distance})^2$$

$$= \frac{bx}{h} dx (h - x)^2 = \frac{bx}{h}(h - x)^2 dx$$

Now M.I. of the whole triangular section may be found out by integrating for the whole height of the triangle, i.e. from O to h.

$$I_{BC} = \int_0^h \frac{bx}{h}(h - x)^2 dx$$

$$= \frac{b}{h}\int_0^h x(h^2 + x^2 - 2hx)\, dx$$

$$= \frac{b}{h}\int_0^h (xh^2 + x^3 - 2hx^2)\, dx = \frac{b}{h}\left(\frac{x^2h^2}{2} + \frac{x^4}{4} - \frac{2hx^3}{3}\right)_0^h$$

$$= \frac{bh^3}{12} \qquad \text{...(i)}$$

We know that the distance between the C.G. of the triangular section and base BC, $d = h/3$.

$\therefore$ M.I of the section about an axis through it C.G. and parallel to $X - X$ axis,

$$I_G = I_{BC} - ad^2 \qquad (\because I_{xx} = I_G + ah^2)$$

$$\therefore \qquad I_G = \frac{bh^3}{12} - \left(\frac{bh}{2}\right)\left(\frac{h}{3}\right)^2 = \frac{bh^3}{36}$$

M.I, of the section about an axis through its vertex and parallel to the base

$$= I_G + ad^2$$

$$= \frac{bh^3}{36} + \left(\frac{bh}{2}\right)\left(\frac{2h}{3}\right)^2$$

$$= \frac{9bh^3}{36} = \frac{bh^3}{4}$$

EXAMPLE 5.8. An isosceles triangular section *ABC* has base width 8 cm and height 6 cm. Determine the moment of inertia of the section about the C.G. of the section and the base *BC*.

SOLUTION: Given:

$b = 8$ cm, $h = 6$ cm

Moment of inertia about the C.G. of the section.

We know that moment of inertia of a triangular section about its C.G.,

$$I_G = \frac{bh^3}{36} = \frac{8(6)^3}{36} = 48\ cm^4\ \textbf{Ans.}$$

MOMENT OF INERTIA ABOUT BASE BC

We know that moment of inertia of triangular section about the base *BC*,

$$I_{BC} = \frac{bh^3}{12} = \frac{8(6)^3}{12} = 144\ cm^4\ \textbf{Ans.}$$

MOMENT OF INERTIA OF A SEMI-CIRCULAR SECTION

SOLUTION: Consider a semi-circular section *ABC* whose moment of inertia is required to be found out as shown in Fig. 5.12

Let, r = radius of the semi-circle.

We know that moment of inertia of the semi-circular section about the base *AB* is equal to half of the moment of inertia of a circular section about *AC*. Therefore moment of inertia of the semicircular section *ABC* about the base *AC*,

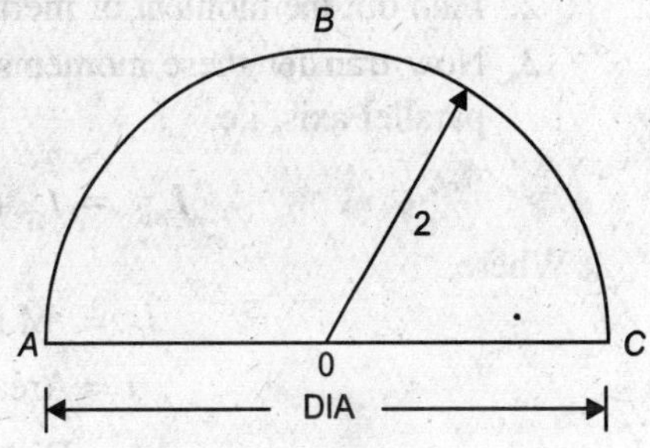

Fig. 5.12

$$I_{AC} = \frac{1}{2} \times \frac{\pi}{64} d^4$$

$$= \frac{1}{2} \times \frac{\pi}{64} (2r)^4 = \frac{\pi}{8} r^4$$

$(\because d = 2r)$

We also know that the area of a semicircular section $a = \dfrac{\pi r^2}{2}$ and distance between C.G. of the section and the base $AC, h = \dfrac{4r}{3\pi}$.

$\therefore$ M.I. of the section through its C.G. and parallel to $X - X$ axis.

$$I_G = I_{AC} - ah^2 = \frac{\pi}{8} r^4 - \frac{\pi r^2}{2}\left(\frac{4r}{3\pi}\right)^2$$

$$= \frac{\pi}{8} r^4 - \frac{8}{9\pi} r^4 = 0.11 r^4$$

and M.I of the section through its C.G. and parallel to $Y - Y$ axis $= \dfrac{\pi}{8} r^4 = 0.393 r^4$

EXAMPLE 5.9. Determine the moment of inertia of a semi-circular section of 10 cm diameter about its C.G. and parallel to $X-X$ axis and $Y-Y$ axis.

SOLUTION: Given:

$D = 10$ cm,

$\therefore \quad r = 5$ cm

M.I. OF THE SECTION ABOUT ITS C.G. AND PARALLEL TO $X-X$ AXIS:

We know that moment of inertia of a semicircular section about its C.G. and parallel to $X-X$ axis.

$$= 0.11r^4 = 0.11(5)^4 = 68.75\,cm^4 \textbf{ Ans}$$

M.I. OF THE SECTION ABOUT ITS C.G. AND PARALLEL TO Y - Y AXIS

We know that moement of inertia of a semicircular section about its C.G. and parallel to Y-Y axis

$$0.393\,r^4 = 0.393(5)^4 = 245.625 \text{ cm}^4 \textbf{ Ans.}$$

MOMENT OF INERTIA OF A COMPOSITE SECTION

The moment of inertia of a composite section may be found out as discussed below.

1. Split up the given section into plane area (i.e. rectangular, triangular, circular etc.)
2. Find out the moment of inertia of these areas about their respective centres of gravity.
3. Now transfer these moments of inertia about the required axis (AB) by the theorem of parallel axis, i.e.

$$I_{AB} = I_G + a \cdot h^2$$

Where,

I_G = M.I. of a section about its C.G. and parallel to the axis AB,

a = Area of section,

h = Distance between AB and C.G. of the section

4. The moment of inertia of the given section may now be obtained by the algebriac sum of the moments of inertia about the required axis.

EXAMPLE 5.10. Find the moment of inertia of a T-section shown in Fig. 5.13, about X-X and Y–Y axes through the C.G. of the section.

SOLUTION: First of all, let us find out C.G. of the section. As the section is symmetrical about Y–Y axis, therefore, its C.G. will lie on this axis. Split up the whole section into two rectangles, viz. (1) and (2) as shown in Fig. 5.13. Let bottom of the flange be the axis of reference.

(i) Rectangle – 1:

$$a_1 = 150 \times 50 = 7500\,mm^2,$$

$$y_1 = 150 + \frac{50}{2} = 175\,mm$$

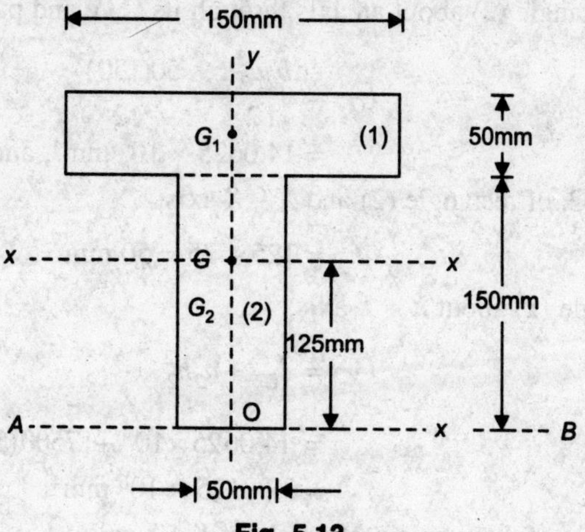

Fig. 5.13

(ii) Rectangle – 2:

$$a_2 = 150 \times 50 = 7500\, mm^2,$$

$$y_2 = \frac{150}{2} = 75\, mm$$

We know that distance between C.G. of the section and bottom of the flange.

$$\bar{y} = \frac{a_1 y_1 + a_2 y_2}{a_1 + a_2}$$

$$= \frac{(7500 \times 175) + (7500 \times 75)}{7500 + 7500} = 125 \text{ mm}$$

MOMENT OF INERTIA ABOUT X-X AXIS: We know that M.I. of rectangle (1) about an axis through its C.G. and parallel to $X - X$ axis,

$$I_{G_1} = \frac{b_1 d_1^3}{12} = \frac{150(50)^3}{12}$$

$$= 1.5625 \times 10^6\, mm^4,$$

and distance betwen C.G. of rectangle (1) and $X - X$ axis,

$$h_1 = 175 - 125 = 50 \text{ mm}$$

∴ M.I. of rectangle (1) about $X - X$ axis,

$$I_{X_1} = I_{G_1} + a_1 h_1^2$$

$$= 1.5625 \times 10^6 + [7500(50)^2]$$

$$= 20.3125 \times 10^6 \text{ mm}^4$$

Similarly, M.I. of rectangle (2) about an axis through its C.G. and parallel to $X - X$ axis.

$$I_{G_2} = \frac{b_2 d_2^3}{12} = \frac{50(150)^3}{12}$$
$$= 14.0625 \times 10^6 \text{ mm}^4, \text{ and}$$

Distance between C.G. of rectangle (2) and $X - X$ axis,

$$h_2 = 125 - 75 = 50 \text{ mm.}$$

Hence M.I. of rectangle (2) about $X - X$ axis.

$$I_{X_2} = I_{G_2} + a_2 h_2^2$$
$$= 14.0625 \times 10^6 + [7500(50)^2]$$
$$= 32.8125 \times 10^6 \text{ mm}^4$$

Now moment of inertia of the whole section about $X - X$ axis.

$$I_{xx} = 20.3125 \times 10^6 + 32.8125 \times 10^6$$
$$= 53.125 \times 10^6 \text{ mm}^4 \textbf{ Ans.}$$

M.I. ABOUT $Y - Y$ AXIS: We know that M.I. of rectangle (1) about $Y - Y$ axis.

$$I_{y_1} = \frac{d_1 b_1^3}{12} = \frac{50(150)^3}{12}$$
$$= 14.0625 \times 10^6 \text{ mm}^4, \text{ and}$$

M.I. of rectangle (2) about $Y - Y$ axis

$$I_{y_2} = \frac{d_2 b_2^3}{12} = \frac{150(50)^3}{12} = 1.5625 \times 10^6 \text{ mm}^4$$

$\therefore$ Moment of inertia of the whole section about $Y - Y$ axis.

$$I_{yy} = 14.0625 \times 10^6 + 1.5625 \times 10^6$$
$$= 15.625 \times 10^6 \text{ mm}^4 \textbf{ Ans.}$$

EXERCISE-5

1. Derive an equation for moment of inertia of the followiong sections about centroidal axis: (i) A rectangular section, (ii) A hollow rectangular section (iii) A circular section, and (iv) A hollow circular section.
2. A state and prove the theorem of perpendicular axis applied to moment of inertia.
3. Prove the parallel axis theorem in the determination of moment of inertia of areas.
4. A hollow semicircular section has its outer and inner diameters of 200 m and 120 mm respectively as shown in Fig. 5.14.

   Calculate its moment of inertia about, the base AB.

   [Ans. $I_{AB} = 34.21 \times 10^6$ mm^4**]**

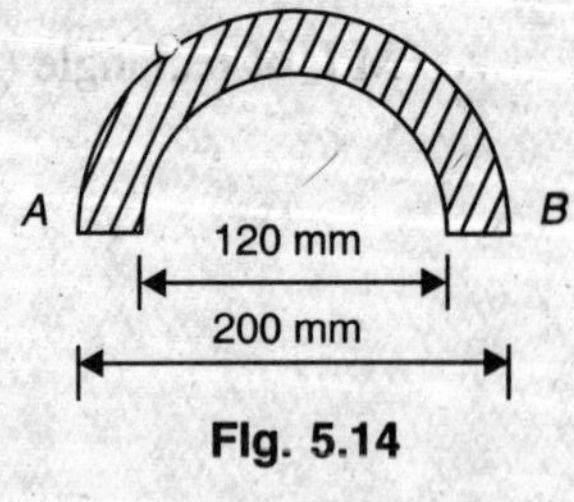

Fig. 5.14

5. Find the moment of inertia of a rectangular section 30 mm wide and 40 mm deep about *X-X* axis and *Y-Y* axis.

[**Ans.** $I_{XX} = 160 \times 10^3$ mm^4, $I_{YY} = 90 \times 10^3$ mm^4]

6. Find the moment of inertia of a hollow rectangular section about its centre of gravity, if the external dimensions are 40 mm deep and 30 mm wide and internal dimensions are 25 mm deep and 15 mm wide. [**Ans.** I_{XX} = 140470 mm4, I_{YY} = 82970 mm^4]

7. Find the moment of inertia of a circular section of 20 mm diameter through its centre of gravity. [**Ans.** 7854 mm^4]

8. Calculate the moment of inertia of a hollow circular section of external and internal diameters 100 mm and 80 mm respectively about an axis passing through its centroid.

[**Ans.** 2.898×10^6 mm^4]

9. A hollow triangular section shown in Fig. 5.15 is symmetrical about its vertical axis. Find the moment of inertia of the section about the base *BC*. [**Ans.** $I_{BC} = 12.84 \times 10^6$ mm^4]

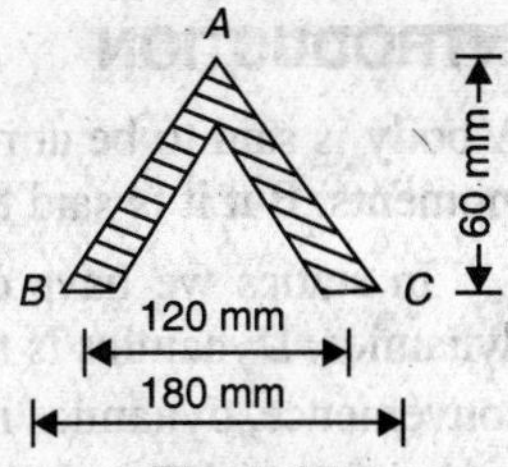

Fig. 5.15

10. Find the moment of inertia of a triangular section having 50 mm base and 60 mm height about an axis through its centre of gravty and base. [**Ans.** 300×10^3 mm^4, 381330 mm^4]

11. Find the moment of inertia of a semicircular section of 30 mm radius about is centre of gravity and parallel to *X-X* and *Y-Y* axes.

[**Ans.** 89100 mm^4, 381330 mm^4]

12. Find the moment of inertia of a hollow section shown in Fig. 5.16 about an axis passing through its centre of gravity or parallel to *X-X* axis. [**Ans.** $I_{XX} = 362.54 \times 10^6$ mm^4]

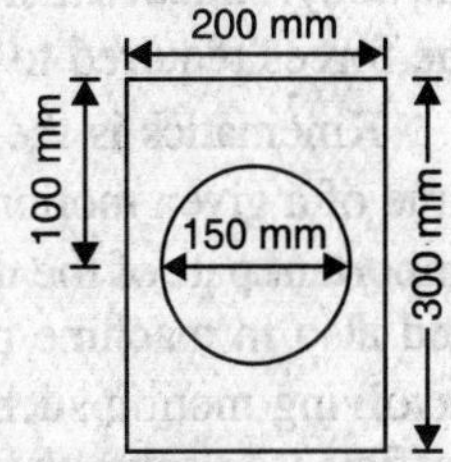

Fig. 5.16

13. Find the moment of inertia of a *T*-section having flange and web both 120 mm × 30 mm about *X-X* axis passing through the centre of gravity of the section. [**Ans.** 14.715×10^6 mm^4]

14. A cast iron *I*-section is 240 mm deep. The upper flange is 72 mm wide and 24 mm deep, the lower flange is 192 mm wide and 36 mm deep and web 30 mm thick, find $\bar{y}$ i.e. distance of centroid from the lowest edge and the second moment of area about X-X passing through centroid and perpendicular to web.

[**Ans.** $\bar{y}$ = 85.2 mm, $I_{xx} = 9.084 \times 10^7$ mm^4]

15. A T-section is of 150 mm × 150 mm × 50 mm. Determine I_{XX}, I_{YY} both passing through the centroid and the least value of section modulus about *X-X* axis.

16. A channel section 160 mm × 80 mm × 20 mm stands with the flanges horizontal. Determine I_{XX} and I_{YY} passing through the centroid of the section. Also find section modulus about *X-X*.

[**Ans.** $I_{XX} = 1.867 \times 10^7$ mm^4, $I_{YY} - 3.02 \times 10^6$ mm^4, $Z_{XX} = 2.33 \times 10^5$ mm^3]

CHAPTER 6

Kinematics of Particles

INTRODUCTION

A body is said to be at rest, if it occupies the same position with respect to its surroundings at all moments. But it is said to be in motion, if it changes its position, with respect to its surroundings.

In statics we have considered the bodies at rest and now we shall begin with the study of dynamics. Dynamics is the part of mechanics that deals with the analysis of bodies in motion. For convenience, dynamics is divided into two branches called kinematics and kinetics. Kinetics is the study of the relationship between the forces acting on a body, the mass of the body and motion of the body. Kinetics therefore, can be used to predict the motion caused by a given force or to determine the forces required to produce the prescribed motion.

Kinematics is the study of the relationships between displacement, velocity, acceleration and time of a given motion, without considering the forces that cause the motion. Kinematics forms an important part of the dynamics because of its application to problems in which forces are involved and also in machine parts where motion is involved. It is also observed that for many problems involving motion such as cam shafts, gears, connecting rods etc., the principles of kinematics are sufficient to solve the problems.

IMPORTNAT TERMS

1. SPEED: The speed of a body, may be defined as its rate of change of displacement with respect to its surroundings. The speed of a body is irrespective of its direction and is, thus, a scalar quantity.

2. VELOCITY: The velocity of a body may be defined as its rate of change of displacement, with respect to its surroundings, in a particular direction. As the velocity is always expressed in a particular direction, therefore, it is a vector quantity.

3. ACCELERATION: The acceleration of a body may be defined as the rate of change of its velocity. It is said to be positive, when the velocity of a body increases with time, and negative when the velocity decreases with time. The negative acceleration is also called Retardation. In general, the term acceleration is used to denote the rate at which the velocity changes. It may be uniform or variable.

4. UNIFORM ACCELERATION: If a body moves in such a way, that its velocity changes equal in magnitude in equal intervals of time, it is said to be moving with a uniform acceleration.

5. VARIABLE ACCELERATION: If a body moves in such a way, that its velocity changes unequal in magnitude in equal intervals of time, it is said to be moving with a variable acceleration.

6. DISTANCE TRAVERSED: It is the total distance moved by a body. Mathemetically, if the body is moving with a uniform velocity (v) then in t seconds, the distance traversed, $s = v\ t$.

RECTILINEAR MOTION

When a particle moves along a path which is a straight line, it is called rectilinear motion.

MOTION UNDER UNIFORM ACCELERATION

Consider a particle starting from O and moving along OX with a uniform acceleration as shown in Fig. 6.1. Let P be its position after t seconds.

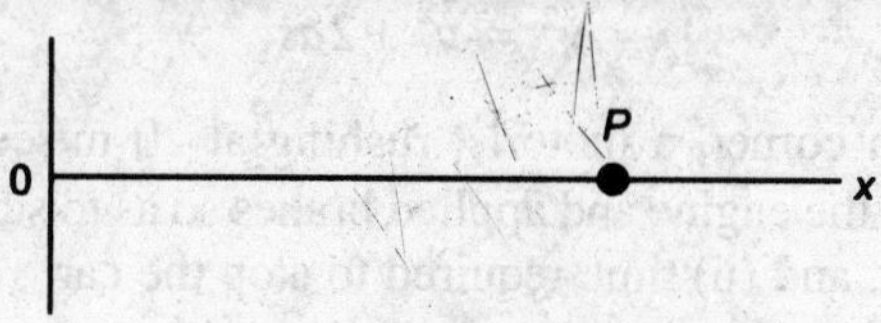

Motion Under Uniform Acceleration

Fig. 6.1

Let,

u = Initial velocity,

v = Final velocity

t = Time in seconds taken by the particle to change its velocity from u to v,

a = Uniform positive acceleration, and

s = Distance travelled in t seconds.

Since in t seconds, the velocity of the particle has increased steadily from u to v at the rate of a, therefore, total increase in velocity = $a.t.$

$$\therefore \quad v = u + a \cdot t \qquad \text{...(6.1)}$$

$$\text{Average velocity} = \frac{u+v}{2} \qquad \text{...(i)}$$

But distance travelled by the particle,

$$s = \text{Average velocity} \times \text{time}$$

$$= \left(\frac{u+v}{2}\right)t \qquad \text{...(ii)}$$

Substituting the value of v from equation (6.1), we get

$$s = \left(\frac{v+u+at}{2}\right)t = u \cdot t + \frac{1}{2}a \cdot t^2 \qquad \text{...(6.2)}$$

From equation (6.1), i.e., $v = u + at$ we find that

$$t = \frac{v-u}{a}$$

Substituting this value of t in equation (ii), we get

$$s = \left(\frac{u+v}{2}\right)\left(\frac{v-u}{a}\right)$$

$$= \frac{v^2 - u^2}{2a}$$

or $$v^2 - u^2 = 2as$$

$\therefore$ $$v^2 = u^2 + 2as \quad \text{...(6.3)}$$

EXAMPLE 6.1. On turning a corner, a motorist rushing at 20 m/sec, finds a child on the road 50 m ahead. He instantly stops the engine and applied brakes so as to stop the car within 10 m of the child. Calculate (i) retardation, and (ii) time required to stop the car.

SOLUTION: Given:

u = 20 m/sec;

v = 0;

s = 50 – 10 = 40 m

Let, a = Acceleration of the motorist

We know that,

$$v^2 = u^2 + 2as$$

or $$(0)^2 = (20)^2 + 2a(40) = 400 + 80a$$

$\therefore$ $$a = -\frac{400}{80} = -5 m/\sec^2 \textbf{ Ans.}$$

(Minus sign shows that the acceleration is negative i.e. retardation.)

TIME REQUIRED TO STOP THE CAR:

Let, t = Time required to stop the car.

We know that final velocity of the car,

$$v = u + at$$

or $$0 = 20 - 5 \times t \qquad (\because a = -5\, m/\sec^2)$$

$\therefore$ $$t = \frac{20}{5} = 4 \text{ sec. } \textbf{Ans.}$$

EXAMPLE 6.2. A Burglar's car had a start with an acceleration of 2 m/sec^2. A police vigilant party came after 5 seconds and continued to chase the burglar's car with a uniform velocity of 20 m/sec. Find the time taken, in which the police van will over take the burglar's car.

SOLUTION: Let, t = Time in seconds, taken by the police party, to overtake the burglar's car after reaching the spot.

First of all, consider the motion of the burglar's car. In this case, $u = 0$; $a = 2$ m/sec^2; $t_1 = (t + 5)$ sec.

We know that distance travelled by the burglar's car,

$$s = ut + \frac{1}{2}at^2$$

$$= 0(t+5) + \frac{1}{2}(2)(t+5)^2 = 0 + (t+5)^2$$

$\therefore$ $$s = (t+5)^2 \quad \text{...(i)}$$

Now consider the motion of police party. In this case, uniform velocity, $v = 20$ m/sec.

$\therefore$ Distance travelled by the police party,

s = velocity × time = 20 t

$\therefore$ $$s = 20t \quad \text{...(ii)}$$

For the police part to overtake he burglar's car, the two distances shown by equations (i) and (ii) should be equal.

$\therefore$ $$(t+5)^2 = 20t$$

or $$t^2 + 10t + 25 = 20t$$

or $$t^2 - 10t + 25 = 0$$

or $$(t-5)^2 = 0$$

or $$t - 5 = 0$$

$\therefore$ $t = 5$ sec. **Ans.**

EXAMPLE 6.3. A motorist takes 10 seconds to cover a distance of 20 m and 15 seconds to cover a distance of 40 m. Find the uniform acceleration of the car and its velocity at the end of 15 seconds.

SOLUTION: Given: When $t = 10$ sec; $s = 20$ *m*, when $t = 15$ sec, $s = 40$ m

UNIFORM ACCELERATION:

Let, u = Initial velocity of the car, and

a = Uniform acceleration.

We know that the distance travelled by the car in 10 seconds,

$$20 = ut + \frac{1}{2}at^2$$

$$= u(10) + \frac{1}{2}a(10)^2 = 10u + 150a$$

$\therefore$ $$20 = 10u + 50a \quad \text{...(i)}$$

Similarly distance travelled by the car is 15 seconds,

$$40 = u(15) + \frac{1}{2}a(15)^2 = 15u + 112.5a$$

or

$$80 = 30u + 225a \qquad \text{...(ii)}$$

Multiplying the equation (ii) by 3 we get,

$$60 = 30\,u + 150\,a \qquad \text{...(iii)}$$

Substracting equation (iii) from (ii)

$$75a = 20$$

$$\therefore \quad a = 20/75$$

$$= 0.267 \text{ m/sec}^2 \textbf{ Ans.}$$

VELOCITY AT THE END OF 15 SECONDS

Substituting the value of a in equation (ii), we get

$$80 = 30u + 225(0.267)$$

$$= 30u + 60.075$$

or

$$80 - 60.075 = 30\,u$$

$$\therefore \quad u = 19.925/30$$

$$= 0.664 \text{ m/sec.}$$

We know that the velocity of the car after 15 seconds.

$$v = u + at$$

$$= 0.664 + 0.267(15) = 4.672 \text{ m/sec. } \textbf{Ans.}$$

MOTION UNDER FORCE OF GRAVITY

It is a particular case of motion, under a constant acceleration of g where its value is taken as 9.80 m/sec^2. If there is a free fall under gravity, the expression for velocity and distance travelled in terms of initial velocity, time and gravity acceleration will be:

1. $v = u + gt$,
2. $s = ut + \frac{1}{2}gt^2$, and
3. $v^2 = u^2 + 2gs$

But if the motion takes place against the force of gravity, i.e., the particle is projected upwards, the corresponding equations will be:

1. $v = u - gt$,
2. $s = ut - \frac{1}{2}gt^2$, and
3. $v^2 = u^2 - 2gs$

In this case the value of g is taken as negative.

EXAMPLE 6.4. A stone is dropped into a well and the sound of splash is heard after 4 seconds. Assuming the velocity of sound to be 350 m/s, find the depth of the well.

SOLUTION: First of all, consider the downward motion of the stone.

Here, $u = 0$

Let, t = Time taken by the stone to reach the bottom of the well.

We know that the depth of the well,

$$s = ut + \frac{1}{2}gt^2$$

$$= 0(t) + \frac{1}{2} \times 9.8(t^2) = 4.9t^2 \qquad \text{...(i)}$$

and time taken by the sound to reach the top

$$= \frac{\text{Depth of the well}}{\text{speed}}$$

$$= \frac{s}{350} = \frac{4.9t^2}{350} \qquad \text{...(ii)}$$

Since the total time taken (i.e. stone to reach the bottom of the well and sound to reach the top of the well) is 4 seconds. Therefore,

$$t + \frac{4.9t^2}{350} = 4$$

or $$4.9t^2 + 360t = 1400$$

or $$4.9t^2 + 350t - 1400 = 0$$

If $$ax^2 + bx + c = 0\text{, then, } x = \frac{-b \pm \sqrt{b^2 - 4ac}}{2a}$$

Hence, $$t = \frac{-350 \pm \sqrt{(350)^2 - 4(4.9)(-1400)}}{2 \times 4.9}$$

$$t = 3.798 \text{ sec.}$$

Now substituting the value of t in equation (i)

$$s = 4.9(t^2)$$

$$= 4.9(3.798)^2 = 70.70 \text{ m } \textbf{Ans.}$$

EXAMPLE 6.5. A stone is dropped from the top of the tower 50m high. At the same time another stone is thrown up from the foot of the tower with a velocity of 25 m/sec. At what distance from the top and after how much time the two stones cross each other?

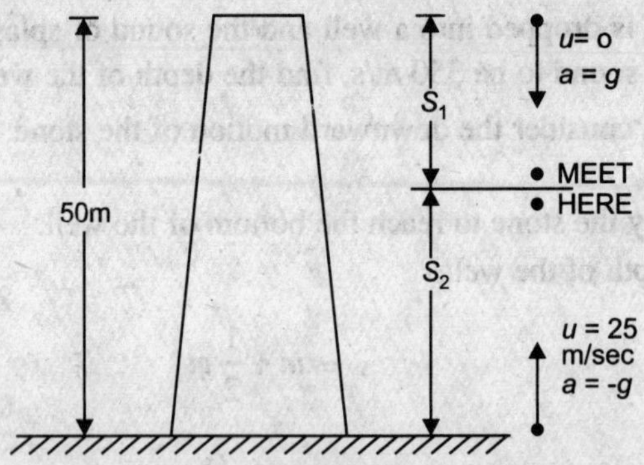

Fig. 6.2

SOLUTION: The condition for the two stones to cross each other is that the sum of the distances s_1 and s_2 travelled by the two stones at the time of crossing should be, $s_1 + s_2 = 50$ m

Using the relation,

$$s = ut + \frac{1}{2}gt^2$$

First stone,

$$s_1 = 0(t) + \frac{1}{2}gt^2 = \frac{1}{2}gt^2$$

Second stone,

$$s_2 = 25(t) - \frac{1}{2}gt^2 = 25t - \frac{1}{2}gt^2$$

$\therefore$ $$s_1 + s_2 = 50 = \frac{1}{2}gt^2 + 25t - \frac{1}{2}gt^2$$

or $$25t = 50$$

$\therefore$ $$t = 2 \text{ sec } \textbf{Ans.}$$

Now $$s_1 \text{ (from top)} = \frac{1}{2}gt^2$$

$$= \frac{1}{2} \times 9.80(2)^2 = 19.60\ m\ \textbf{Ans.}$$

EXAMPLE 6.6. A stone was thrown vertically upwards from the ground with a velocity of 100 m/s. After 2 seconds, another stone was thrown vertically upwards from the same place. If both the stones strike the ground at the same time, calculate the velocity with which the second stone was thrown.

SOLUTION: At the maximum height, the stones will have zero velocity. Accordingly considering upward motion of the first stone.

$\therefore$ $$v = u - gt$$

$\therefore$ $$0 = u - gt$$

or $$t = \frac{u}{g} = \frac{100}{9.8} = 10.20 \text{ sec}.$$

Thus the stone will take 10.20 seconds in ascending to maximum height. The time taken for return path will also be same.

$$\therefore \quad \text{Total time for flight} = 10.20 + 10.20 = 20.40 \text{ secs.}$$

FOR SECOND STONE:

$$\text{Time of flight} = 20.40 - 2 = 18.40 \text{ secs.}$$

$$\therefore \quad \text{Time taken to reach maximum height} = \frac{18.40}{2} = 9.20 \text{ secs.}$$

Then from the relation, $v = u - gt$

$$0 = u - 9.8\,(9.2)$$

Hence, $u = 90.16$ m/sec. **Ans.**

EXAMPLE 6.7. A cage descends in a mine shaft with an acceleration of 0.5 m/sec^2. After the cage has travelled 25 m, a stone is dropped from the top of the shaft. Determine (a) the time taken by the stone to hit the cage, and (b) distance travelled by the cage before impact (at the time of impact).

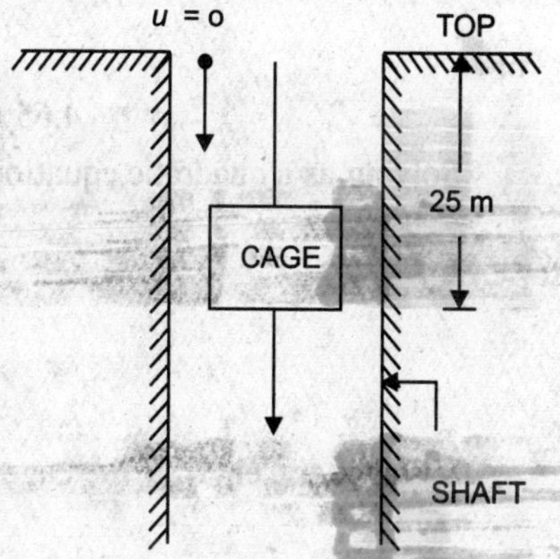

Fig. 6.3

SOLUTON: When the stone hists the elevator both elevator and stone must be at the same distance from the top of the shaft. Refer Fig. 6.3

(A) TIME TAKEN BY THE STONE TO HIT THE CAGE: First consider the motion of stone.

Let the time taken by the stone to hit the elevator = t

Here $u = 0$

We know that distance travelled by the stone before the impact,

$$s = ut + \frac{1}{2}gt^2$$

$$= 0(t) + \frac{1}{2}gt^2 = 4.9t^2 \quad \text{...(i)}$$

Now consider the motion of the cage for first 25 m

Here $u = 0$, $a = 0.5$ m/sec^2, $s = 25$ m

Let t_1 = Time taken by the cage to travel 25 m

We know that distance travelled by the cage,

$$25 = 0(t_1) + \frac{1}{2}(0.5)t_1^2 = 0.25t_1^2$$

$$\therefore \quad t_1 = \sqrt{\frac{25}{0.25}} = \sqrt{100} = 10 \text{ sec.}$$

It mean that the cage has travelled for 10 secs, before the stone was dropped. Therefore, total time taken by the cage before impact = (10 + t) secs.

We know that distance travelled by the cage in (10 + t) secs, by the relation,

$$s = ut + \frac{1}{2}at^2$$

$$s = 0(10+t) + \frac{1}{2}(0.5)(10+t)^2$$

$$= 0.25(10+t)^2 \qquad \text{...(ii)}$$

In order that the stone may hit the cage, both the distances must be equal. Hence equating (i) and (ii)

$$4.9\,t^2 = 0.25(10+t)^2 = 0.25(100+20t+t^2)$$

$$= 25 + 5t + .25t^2$$

or $\quad 4.65\,t^2 = 25 + 5t$

$\therefore \quad 4.65\,t^2 - 5\,t - 25 = 0$

Solving as a quadratic equation for t

$$\therefore \quad t = \frac{5 \pm \sqrt{(5)^2 + 4(4.65)(25)}}{2(4.65)}$$

$$= 2.92 \text{ sec } \textbf{Ans.}$$

Distance travelled by the cage before impact - equation (iii)

$$s = 0.25(10+t)^2 = 0.25(10+2.92)^2$$

$$= 41.7 \text{ m } \textbf{Ans.}$$

DISTANCE TRAVELLED IN THE nth SECOND

Consider the motion of a particle, starting from O and moving along OX as shown in Fig. 6.4

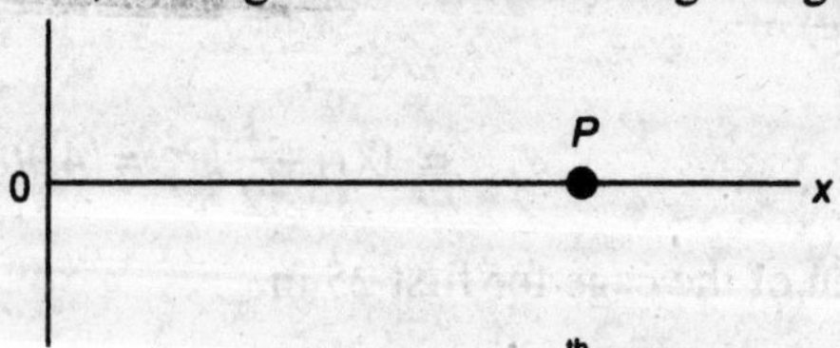

Distance Travelled in n^{th} Second

Fig. 6.4

Let,

u = Initial velocity of the particle

v = Final velocity

a = Constant positive acceleration

s_n = Distance (OX) travelled in n sec.

s_{n-1} = Distance (OP) travelled in $(n - 1)$ sec,

$s = (s_n - s_{n-1})$ = Distance (PQ) travelled in n^{th} sec,

n = No. of second

Substituting the values of $t = n$ and $t\,(n - 1)$ in general equation of motion $\left(s + ut + \frac{1}{2}at^2\right)$,

$$s_n = u \cdot n + \frac{1}{2}a(n)^2 \quad \text{...(i)}$$

and

$$s_{n-1} = u(n-1) + \frac{1}{2}a(n-1)^2 \quad \text{...(ii)}$$

Distance travelled in the nth sec,

$$s = s_n - s_{n-1}$$

$$= \left[\left(un + \frac{1}{2}a(n)^2\right)\right] - \left[u(n-1) + \frac{1}{2}a(n-1)^2\right]$$

$$= un + \frac{1}{2}an^2 - un + u - \frac{1}{2}a(n^2 + 1 - 2n)$$

$$= u - \frac{1}{2}a + an = u + a\left(a - \frac{1}{2}\right) = u + \frac{a}{2}(2n - 1)$$

Hence

$$s = u + \frac{1}{2}a(2n - 1) \quad \text{...(i)}$$

EXAMPLE 6.8. A body was thrown vertically down from a tower and traverses a distance of 40 metres during its 4th second of its fall. Find the initial velocity of the body.

SOLUTION: Given:

$s = 40$ m; $n = 4$, $a = g = 9.8$ m/sec^2

Let, u = Initial vclocity of the body.

We know that distance traversed by the body in the 4th second $(s) = u + \frac{a}{2}(2n - 1)$

$\therefore$

$$40 = u + \frac{a}{2}(2n - 1)$$

$$= u + \frac{9.8}{2}(2 \times 4 - 1) = u + 34.3$$

or

$$40 - 34.3 = u = 5.7 \text{ m/sec} \quad \textbf{Ans.}$$

MOTION UNDER VARIABLE ACCELERATION

A body, which does not move with a uniform acceleration, is said to be moving with a variable acceleration.

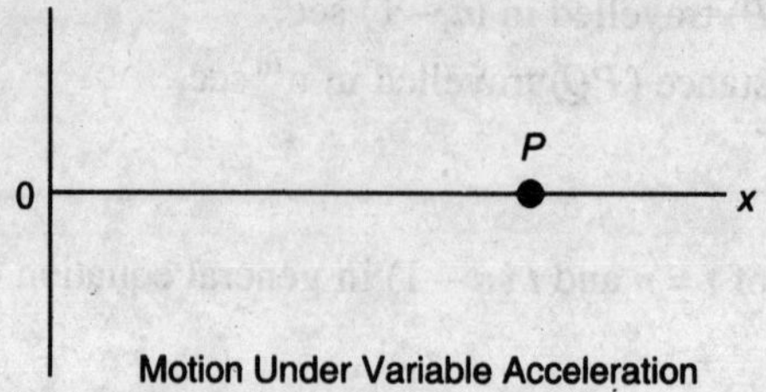

Motion Under Variable Acceleration

Fig. 6.5

VELOCITY AND ACCELERATION AT ANY INSTANT

Consider a body moving from *O* in the direction *OX*. Let *P* be its position at any instant as shown in Fig. 6.5

Let,

s = Distance travelled by the body

t = Time taken by the body, in seconds, to travel the distance s.

v = Velocity of the body, and

a = Acceleration of the body.

We know that the velocity of a body, is the rate of change of its position. Expressing it mathematically.

$$v = \frac{ds}{dt} \qquad ...(i)$$

Similarly, the acceleration of a body is the rate of change of its velocity. Expressing it mathematicaly i.e. differentiating the equation (i) with respect to t,

$$a = \frac{d^2 s}{dt^2} \qquad ...(ii)$$

$$a = \frac{dv}{dt} \qquad ...(iii)$$

$$a = v \cdot \frac{dv}{ds}$$

METHODS FOR VELOCITY, ACCELERATION AND DISPLACEMENT FROM A MATHEMATICAL EQUATION

The velocity, acceleration and displacement of a body, from a mathematical expression, may be found out by either of the following two methods:

1. By differentiation, or
2. By integration.

VELOCITY AND ACCELERATION BY DIFFERENTIATION

Some times, the given equation of motion is in terms of displacement (s) and time (t) e.g.,

$$s = 3t^3 + 2t^2 + 6t + 4 \qquad ...(i)$$

or $$s = 6 + 5t^2 + 6t^3 \quad \text{...(ii)}$$

or $$s = 2t^3 + 4t - 15 \quad \text{...(iii)}$$

Now differentiate both sides, of the equations, with respect to t.

$$\frac{ds}{dt} = 9t^2 + 4t + 6 \quad \text{...(i)}$$

$$\frac{ds}{dt} = 10t + 18t^2 \quad \text{...(ii)}$$

and, $$\frac{ds}{dt} = 6t^2 + 4 \quad \text{...(iii)}$$

The equations, so obtained by differentiation, will give us the velocity of the body (as the velocity of a body is the rate of change of its position). Again differentiate, both sides of the above equations, with respect to t,

$$\frac{d^2s}{dt^2} = 18t + 4 \quad \text{...(i)}$$

$$\frac{d^2s}{dt^2} = 10 + 36t \quad \text{...(ii)}$$

$$\frac{d^2s}{dt^2} = 12t \quad \text{...(iii)}$$

Theequations, so obtained by second differentiation, will give us the acceleration of the body (as the acceleration of the body is the rate of change of velocity).

EXAMPLE 6.9. A particle, starting from rest, moves in a straight line, whose equation of motion is given by: $s = t^3 - 2t^2 + 3$. Find the velocity and acceleration of the particle after 5 seconds.

SOLUTION: Given:

$$s = t^3 - 2t^2 + 3 \quad \text{...(i)}$$

VELOCITY AFTER 5 SECONDS:

Differentiate the above equation with respect to t,

$$\frac{ds}{dt} = 3t^2 - 4t \quad \text{...(ii)}$$

i.e., velocity, $$v = 3t^2 - 4t \qquad \left(\because \frac{ds}{dt} = \text{Velocity}\right)$$

Substituting, $t = 5$ in the above equations,

$$v = 3(5)^2 - 4(5)$$
$$= 75 - 20 = 55 \text{ m/sec } \textbf{Ans.}$$

ACCELERATION AFTER 5 SECONDS:

Again differentiating equation (ii) with respect to t,

$$\frac{d^2s}{dt^2} = 6t - 4 \qquad \text{...(iii)}$$

i.e. Acceleration, $a = 6t - 4$ $\quad \left(\because \frac{d^2s}{dt^2} = \text{Acceleration}\right)$

Now putting $t = 5$ in the above equation.

$$a = 6(5) - 4 = 30 - 4$$

$$= 26 \text{ m/s}^2 \textbf{ Ans.}$$

EXAMPLE 6.10. A car moves along a straight line whose equation of motion is given by $s = 12t + 3t^2 - 2t^3$, where s is in metres and t in seconds. Calculate.

(i) Velocity and acceleration at start, and

(ii) Acceleration, when velocity is zero.

SOLUTION: Given:

$$s = 12t + 3t^2 - 2t^3 \qquad \text{...(i)}$$

VELOCITY AT START:

Differentiating the above equation with repect to t,

$$\frac{ds}{dt} = 12 + 6t - 6t^2 \qquad \text{...(ii)}$$

i.e. velocity $v = 12 + 6t - 6t^2$ $\quad \left(\because \frac{ds}{dt} = v\right)$

Substituting $t = 0$ in the above equation

$$v = 12 + 6(0) - 6(0)^2$$

$$= 12 \; m/\text{sec} \textbf{ Ans.}$$

ACCELERATION AT START:

Again differentiating equation (ii) with respect to t,

$$\frac{dv}{dt} = 6 - 12t \qquad \text{...(iii)}$$

$$\left(\because \frac{dv}{dt} = a\right)$$

i.e. Acceleration, $a = 6 - 12t$

Now substituting $t = 0$ in above equation,

$$a = 6 - 12(0) = 6 \text{ m/sec}^2 \textbf{ Ans.}$$

ACCELERATION, WHEN VELOCITY IS ZERO

Putting $v = 0$ in the equation, $v = 12 + 6t - 6t^2$

$$12 + 6t - 6t^2 = 0$$

or $$t^2 - t - 2 = 0 \quad \text{(Dividing by } -6)$$

or $$t = 2 \text{ secs}$$

i.e. velocity of the car after 2 seconds will be zero.

Now substituting the value of $t = 2$ in equation (iii), i.e.

$$a = 6 - 12t = 6 - 12(2)$$

$$= 6 - 24 = -18 \text{ m/sec}^2 \textbf{ Ans.}$$

EXAMPLE 6.11. The equation of motion of a particle moving in a straight line is given by: $s = 18t + 3t^2 - 2t^3$ where, s is in metres and t in seconds. Find

(i) The velocity and acceleration at start,

(ii) The time, when the particle reaches its maximum velocity and

(iii) The maximum velocity of the particle

SOLUTION: Given:

$$s = 18t + 3t^2 - 2t^3 \quad \text{...(i)}$$

(i) VELOCITY AT START:

Differentiate equation (i) with respect to t,

$$\frac{ds}{dt} = 18 + 6t - 6t^2 \quad \text{...(ii)}$$

i.e. velocity,

$$v = 18 + 6t - 6t^2$$

Substituting, $t = 0$ in equation (ii)

$$v = 18 + 6(0) - 6(0)^2$$

$$= 18 \text{ m/sec } \textbf{Ans.}$$

ACCELERATION AT START:

Again differentiating equation (ii) with respect to t.

$$\frac{d^2 s}{dt^2} = 6 - 12t \quad \text{...(iii)}$$

i.e. Acceleration, $$a = 6 - 12t \quad \text{...(iv)}$$

Putting $t = 0$, in equation (iv).

$$a = 6 - 12(0)$$

$$= 6 \text{ m/sec}^2 \textbf{ Ans.}$$

(ii) TIME, WHEN THE PARTICLE REACHES ITS MAXIMUM VELOCITY

For maximum velocity, let us differentiate the equation of velocity ($v = 18 + 6t - 6t^2$) and equate to zero. The differentiation of the equation of velocity is given in equation (iii). Hence equating this equation (iii) to 0,

$$6 - 12t = 0$$

or $$t = 6/12 = 0.5 \text{ sec } \textbf{Ans.}$$

(iii) MAXIMUM VELOCITY OF THE PARTICLE

Substituting $t = 0.5$ sec. in equation (ii),

$$v = 18 + 6t - 6t^2$$
$$= 18 + 6\,(0.5) - 6(0.5)^2$$
$$= 19.50 \text{ m/sec } \textbf{Ans.}$$

VELOCITY AND DISPLACEMENT BY INTEGRATION

Some times, the given equation of motion is in terms of acceleration *a* and time *t*. e.g.

$$a = 4t^3 - 3t^2 + 5t + 6 \quad \text{...(i)}$$

$$\frac{dv}{dt} = t^3 + 8t \quad \text{...(ii)}$$

$$v \cdot \frac{dv}{ds} = 6 + 3t \quad \text{...(iii)}$$

$$\frac{d^2 s}{dt^2} = 4t - 8t^2 \quad \text{...(iv)}$$

$\frac{dv}{dt}$, $v \cdot \frac{dv}{ds}$, and $\frac{d^2 s}{dt^2}$ are the different forms of acceleration. If the variable acceleration is a function of *t*, then equation (i) or (ii) is used, but if it is a function of *s*, then equation (iii) or (iv) is used.

Now integrate both sides of the above equations, velocity,

$$v = \frac{t^4}{4} + \frac{8t^2}{2} + C_1 \quad \text{...(i)}$$

$$v = 6t + \frac{3t^2}{2} + C_1 \quad \text{...(ii)}$$

$$v = \frac{4t^2}{2} - \frac{8t^3}{3} + C_2 \quad \text{...(iii)}$$

where C_1 is the constant of first integration. The equation so obtained, will give us the velocity of the body. Again integrate both sides of the above equation.

Displacement,

$$s = \frac{t^5}{20} + \frac{8t^3}{t} + C_1 t + C_2 \quad \text{...(i)}$$

$$s = \frac{6t^2}{2} + \frac{3t^3}{6} + C_1 t + C_2 \quad \text{...(ii)}$$

$$s = \frac{4t^3}{6} - \frac{8t^4}{12} + C_1 t + C_2 \qquad ...(iii)$$

Where C_2 is the constant of second integration. The equation, so obtained, will give us the displacement of the body. This method of inegration is difficult as we have to find out the values of constants of integration i.e. C_1 and C_2.

EXAMPLE 6.12. A train starting from rest is uniformly accelerated. The acceleration at any instant is $\frac{10}{v+1}$ m/sec^2, where v is the velocity of the train in m/sec at the instant. Find the distance, in which the train will attain a velocity of 36 kmph.

SOLUTION : Given:

$$a = \frac{10}{v+1}$$

Rewriting the given equation,

$$v \cdot \frac{dv}{ds} = \frac{10}{v+1} \qquad \left(\because a = v \cdot \frac{dv}{ds}\right)$$

$\therefore$
$$v(v+1)dv = 10ds \qquad ...(i)$$

or
$$(v^2 + v)dv = 10ds$$

Integrating both sides of equation (i),

$$\frac{v^3}{3} + \frac{v^2}{2} = 10s + C_1 \qquad ...(ii)$$

Where C_1 is the first constant of integration. Substituting the values of $S = 0$ and $v = 0$ in equation (ii) $C_1 = 0$

Now substituting the value of $C_1 = 0$ in equation (ii), $\frac{v^3}{3} + \frac{v^2}{2} = 10s$

$\therefore$
$$2v^3 + 3v^2 = 60s \qquad ...(iii)$$

Now for the distance travelled by the train, substituting $v = 35$ km p.h. = 10 m/sec in equation (iii)

$$2(10)^3 + 3(10^2) = 60s$$

or
$$2000 + 300 = 60s$$

$\therefore$
$$s = 2300/60$$
$$= 38.33 \text{ m} \quad \textbf{Ans.}$$

EXAMPLE 6.13. The motion of a particle is given by: $a = t^3 - 3t^2 + 5$, where a is the acceleration in m/sec^2, and t is the time in seconds. The velocity of the particle at $t = 1$ second is 6.25 m/sec and the displacement is 8.8 metres. Calcuate the displacement and the velocity at $t = 2$ seconds.

SOLUTION: Given: $a = t^3 - 3t^2 + 5$

Rewriting the given equation,

$$\frac{dv}{dt} = t^3 - 3t^2 + 5 \qquad \left(\because a = \frac{dv}{dt}\right)$$

$$\therefore \quad dv = (t^3 - 3t^2 + 5)\, dt \qquad ...(i)$$

VELOCITY AT t = 2 SECONDS:

Integrating both sides of equation (i),

$$v = \frac{t^4}{4} - \frac{3t^3}{3} + 5t + C_1$$

$$= \frac{t^4}{4} - t^3 + 5t + C_1 \qquad ...(ii)$$

Wheren C_1 is the first constant of integration. Substituting the values of t = 1 sec. and v = 6.25m in equation (ii), i.e.,

$$6.25 = \frac{1}{4} - 1 + 5 + C_1 = 4.25 + C_1$$

$$\therefore \quad C_1 = 6.25 - 4.25 = 2$$

Substituting the value of C_1 in equation (ii),

$$v = \frac{t^4}{4} - t^3 + 5t + 2 \qquad ...(iii)$$

And now for velocity of the particle, substituting the value of t = 2 in the above equation,

$$v = \frac{(2)^4}{4} - (2)^3 + (5 \times 2) + 2$$

= 8 m/sec **Ans.**

Displacement at t = 2 Seconds:

Rewriting equation *(iii)*,

$$\frac{ds}{dt} = \frac{t^4}{4} - t^3 + 5t + 2 \qquad \left(\because v = \frac{ds}{dt}\right)$$

$$\therefore \quad ds = \left(\frac{t^4}{4} - t^3 + 5t + 2\right) dt$$

Integrating both sides of the above equation,

$$s = \frac{t^5}{20} - \frac{t^4}{4} + \frac{5t^2}{2} + 2t + C_2 \qquad ...(iv)$$

Where C_2 is the second constant of integration.

Substituting the values of t = 1 and s = 8.8 in equation (iv)

$$8.8 = \frac{1}{20} - \frac{1}{4} + \frac{5}{2} + 2 + C_2 = 4.3 + C_2$$

$$\therefore \quad C_2 = 8.8 - 4.3 = 4.5$$

Substituting the values of C_2 in equation (iv),

$s = \frac{t^5}{20} - \frac{t^4}{4} + \frac{5t^2}{2} + 2t + 4.5$ and now for displacement of the particle, substituting the value of $t = 2$ seconds in above equation,

$$s = \frac{32}{20} - \frac{16}{4} + \frac{20}{2} + 4 + 4.5 = 16.1 \text{ m } \textbf{Ans.}$$

EXAMPLE 6.14. A particle, starting from rest, moves in a straight line, whose acceleration is given by the equation: $a = 10 - 0.006\ s^2$ where a is in m/sec^2 and s in metres. Determine,

(i) The velocity of particle, when it has travelled 50 metres,

(ii) The distance travelled by the particle, when it comes to rest.

SOLUTION: Given: $a = 10 - 0.006\ s^2$

Rewriting the given equation

$$v \cdot \frac{dv}{ds} = 10 - 0.006s^2 \qquad \left(\because a = v \cdot \frac{dv}{ds}\right)$$

$$\therefore \quad v \cdot dv = (10 - 0.006s^2)\ ds \qquad \text{...(i)}$$

(i) VELOCITY OF THE PARTICLE, WHEN IT HAS TRAVELLED 50 METRES:

Integrating both sides, of equation (i),

$$\frac{v^2}{2} = 10\ s - \frac{0.006s^3}{3} + C_1$$

$$= 10\ s - 0.002s^3 + C_1$$

$$\therefore \quad v^2 = 20s - 0.004s^3 + 2C_1 \qquad \text{...(ii)}$$

Where C_1 is the first constant of integration. Substituting the values of $s = 0$ and $v = 0$ in equation (ii), $C_1 = 0$.

Substituting the value of C_1 in equation (ii)

$$v^2 = 20s - 0.004s^3 \qquad \text{...(ii)}$$

and now for the velocity of the particle, substituting $s = 50$m in equation (iii),

$$v^2 = 20(50) - 0.004(50)^3$$

$$= 1000 - 500$$

$$= 500$$

$$\therefore \quad v = \sqrt{500} = 22.36 \text{ m/sec } \textbf{Ans.}$$

(ii) DISTANCE TRAVELLED BY THE PARTICLE, WHEN IT COMES TO REST.

When the particle comes to rest, the velocity will be zero. Therefore substituting $v = 0$ in equation (iii).

$$20s - 0.004s^3 = 0$$

or $$s\,(20 - 0.004\,s^2) = 0$$

$\therefore$ $$s = 0 \qquad \text{When } s = 0\text{, the body is at its initial stage}$$

or $$20 - 0.004\,s^2 = 0$$

or $$0.004\,s^2 = 20$$

or $$s^2 = 20/0.004 = 5000$$

$\therefore$ $$s = \sqrt{5000} = 70.71 \text{ m } \textbf{Ans.}$$

EXAMPLE 6.15. A body moves along a straight line and its acceleration a which moves with time t is given by $a = 2 - 3t$. After 5 seconds from start of observations, its velocity is observed to be 20 m/sec. After 10 seconds, from the start of observation, the body was at 85 metres from the origin. Determine

(i) Its acceleration, velocity and distance from the origin at the start of observations;

(ii) The time after start of observation in which the velocity becomes zero and its distance from the origin.

SOLUTION: Given:

$$a = 2 - 3t \qquad \text{...(i)}$$

(i) ACCELERATION AT THE TIME OF START:

Substituting the value of $t = 0$ in equation (i)

$$a = 2 - 3(0)$$

$$= 2 \text{ m/sec}^2 \textbf{ Ans.}$$

VELOCITY AT THE TIME OF START:

Rewriting the given equation (i),

$$\frac{dv}{dt} = 2 - 3t \qquad \left(\because a = \frac{dv}{dt}\right)$$

$\therefore$ $$dv = (2 - 3t)dt \qquad \text{...(ii)}$$

Integrating both sides of equation (ii),

$$v = 2t - \frac{3t^2}{2} + C_1 \qquad \text{...(iii)}$$

Where C_1 is the first constant of integration. Substituting the values of $t = 5$ and $v = 20$ in equation (iii).

$$20 = 2(5) - \frac{3}{2}(5)^2 + C_1 = C_1 - 27.5$$

$\therefore$ $$C_1 = 20 + 27.5 = 47.5$$

Now substituting the value of C_1 in equation (iii)

$$v = 2t - \frac{3t^2}{2} + 47.5 \quad \text{...(iv)}$$

and now for velocity of body at the time of start, substituting $t = 0$ in equation (iv),

$$v = 2(0) - \frac{3(0)^2}{2} + 47.5$$

$$= 47.5 \text{ m/sec } \textbf{Ans.}$$

(ii) DISTANCE FROM THE ORIGIN AT THE START OF OBSERVATION

Rewriting equation (iv),

$$\frac{ds}{dt} = 2t - \frac{3t^2}{2} + 47.5 \qquad \left(\because v = \frac{ds}{dt}\right)$$

$$\therefore \quad ds = \left(2t - \frac{3t^2}{2} + 47.5\right) dt \qquad dt$$

Integrating both sides of the above equation,

$$s = \frac{2t^2}{2} - \frac{3t^3}{6} + 47.5t + C_2$$

$$= t^2 - \frac{t^3}{2} + 47.5t + C_2 \quad \text{...(v)}$$

Where C_2 is the second constant of integration. Now substituting the values of $t = 10$ and $s = 85$ in above equation,

$$85 = (10)^2 - \frac{(10)^3}{2} + 47.5 \times 10 + C_2 = 75 + C_2$$

$$\therefore \quad C_2 = 85 - 75 = 10$$

Now substituting the value of C_2 in equation (v)

$s = t^2 - \frac{t^3}{2} + 4.75t + 10$ and now for the distance from the origin at the time of start of observation, substituting $t = 0$ in the above equation, $s = 10$ m **Ans.**

(iii) THE TIME AFTER START OF OBSERVATIONS IN WHICH THE VELOCITY BECOMES ZERO

Substituting the value of $v = 0$ in equation (iv),

$$0 = 2t - \frac{3t^2}{2} + 47.5$$

or $\quad 3t^2 - 4t - 95 = 0$

(Multiplying both sides by – 2 and rearranging)

Solving it as a quadratic equation for t,

$$t = \frac{+4 \pm \sqrt{(4)^2 + 4 \times 3 \times 95}}{2 \times 3}$$

$$= 6.33 \text{ sec. } \textbf{Ans.}$$

EXAMPLE 6.16. Three marks *A, B* and *C* at a distance of 100 m each are made along a straight road. A car starting from rest and with uniform acceleration passes the mark *A* and takes 10 seconds to reach *B* and further 8 seconds to reach the mark *C*. Calculate the

(i) Magnitude of the acceleration of the car,

(ii) Velocity of car at *A*,

(iii) Velocity of car at *B*, and

(iv) Distance of the mark *A* from the starting point (2004).

SOLUTION: Given: Three marks *A, B,* and *C* along a straight road (Fig. 6.6) such that:

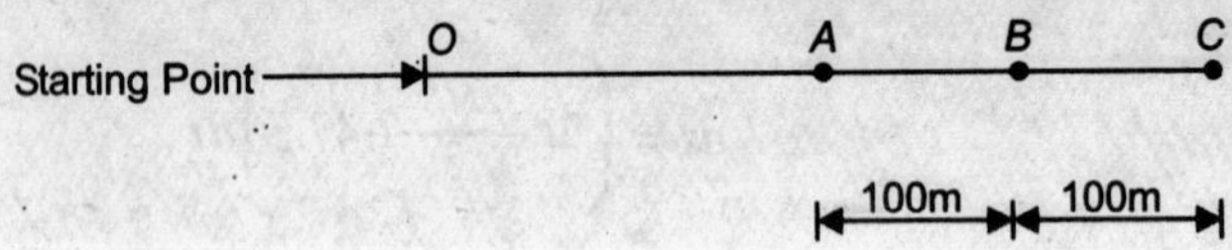

Fig. 6.6

Distances:

(i) $AB = 100$ m

(ii) $BC = 100$ m

As car starts from rest and with uniform acceleration.

Let the car starts from point O.

Time taken by car from *A* to *B*, $t_1 = 10$ sec

Time taken by car from *B* to *C*, $t_2 = 8$ sec

Let,

a = Acceleration of the car

v_A = Velocity of the car at *A*, and

v_B = Velocity of the car at *B*

FOR THE MOTION OF THE CAR FROM A TO B

Using the equation,

$$s = ut + \frac{1}{2}at^2$$

Where, distance, $s = 100$ m, time $t = 10$ sec, velocity, $u = v_A$

$$\therefore \quad 100 = v_A(10) + \frac{1}{2}a(10)^2$$

$$= 10v_A + 50a \quad \text{...(i)}$$

FOR THE MOTION OF THE CAR FROM A TO C:

Using the equation,

$$s = ut + \frac{1}{2}at^2$$

Where, Distance AC = Distance $(AB + BC)$ = 100 + 100 = 200 m

Time, t = Time from A to B + Time from B to C = 10 + 8 = 18 sec.

Velocity = v_A

$$\therefore \quad 200 = v_A(18) + \frac{1}{2}a(18)^2$$

or $$200 = 18v_A + 162a \quad ...(ii)$$

Multiplying equation (i) by 9 and equation (ii) by 5, we get,

$$900 = 90v_A + 450a \quad ...(iii) \quad \text{From equation (iii), and (iv)}$$

$$\_1000 = \_90v_A + \_810a \quad ...(iv)$$

$$-100 = -360\,a$$

or $$a = 100/360$$

$$= 0.278 \text{ m/sec}^2 \textbf{ Ans.}$$

Substituting the value of a in equation (i) we get,

$$100 = 10\,v_a + 50\,(.278)$$

$$= 10v_A + 13.889$$

or $$100 - 13.889 = 10v_A$$

or $$86.11 = 10v_A$$

$$\therefore \quad v_A = 86.11/10$$

$$= 8.611 \text{ m/sec. } \textbf{Ans.}$$

(iii) Velocity v_B of the car at B is obtained by considering the motion of the car from B to C and using the equation,

$$s = ut + \frac{1}{2}at^2$$

Where, Distance, BC = 100 m, Velocity, $u = v_B$

Acceleration, a = 0.278 m/sec^2

Time from B to C = 8 sec.

$$\therefore \quad 100 = v_B(8) + \frac{1}{2}(0.278)(8)^2$$

$$= 8v_B + 8.896$$

or $$100 - 8.896 = 8v_B$$

$$\therefore \quad v_B = 91.104/8$$

$$= 11.388 \text{ m/sec } \textbf{Ans.}$$

(iv) Distance of mark A from the starting point O is obtained by considering the motion of the car from O to A and using the equation $v^2 - u^2 = 2as$, where

u = Velocity, at 0 = 0, v = velocity at $A = v_A = 8.61$ m/sec

a = Acceleration of the car = 0.278 m/sec^2, s = distance OA

$\therefore \quad (8.61)^2 - (0)^2 = 2.(0.278)s$

or $\quad 74.1312 = 0.556\ s$

$\therefore \quad s = 74.1321/0.556$

$= 133.33$ m **Ans.**

EXERCISE-6

1. Distinguish clearly between speed and velocity.
2. Define clearly, (i) Positive acceleration and (ii) Negative acceleration
3. What is the difference between uniform acceleration and variable acceleration?
4. Prove the relationship, $s = ut + \frac{1}{2}at^2$ for a body, subjected to a uniformly accelerated motion.
5. Derive the relationship for the distance travelled by a body in the nth second.
6. What is the force of gravity? How does it effect the body, when: (i) It is allowed to fall downwards, and (ii) It is projected upwards.
7. A car starting from rest is accelerated at the rate of 0.4 m/s^2. Find the distance covered by the car in 20 seconds. **[Ans.** s = 80 m**]**
8. A train travelling at 27 Km. p.h. is accelerated at the rate of 0.5 m/s^2. What is the distance travelled by the train in 20 seconds? **[Ans.** s = 126 m**]**
9. A scooter starts from rest and moves with a constant acceleration of 1.2 m/s^2. Determine its velocity, after it has travelled for 60 meters. **[Ans.** v = 43.2 Km. p.h.**]**
10. A motor car takes 10 seconds to cover 30 meters and 12 seconds to cover 42 meters. Find the uniform acceleration of the car and its velocity at the end of 15 seconds.
    [Ans. a = 0.5 m/s^2, and v = 8m/s**]**
11. A train is uniformly accelerated and passes successive kilometre stones with velocities of 18 Km. p.h. and 36 Km. p.h. respectively. Calculate the velocity, when it passes the third kilometre stone. Also find the time taken for each of these two intervals of one kilometre.
    [Ans. v = 47.5 Km. p.h., t_1 = 133.3 secs, t_2 = 85.3 secs**]**
12. A car starts from rest and accelerates uniformly to a speed of 72 Km. p.h. over a distance of 500 m. Find acceleration of the car and time taken to attain this speed.
    [Ans. a = 0.4 m/s^2, and t = 50 secs**]**
13. A stone is thrown vertically upwards with a velocity of 29.4 m/s from the top of the tower 34.3 m high. Find the total time taken by the stone to reach the foot of the tower.
    [Ans. t = 7 secs**]**
14. A body is released from a great height falls freely towards earth. Another body is released from the same height exactly one second later. Find the separation between both the bodies, after two seconds of the release of second body. **[Ans.** $h_2 - h_1$ = 24.5 m**]**

15. A stone is thrown vertically upwards, from the ground, with a velocity 49 m/s. After 2 seconds, another stone is thrown vertically upwards from the same place. If both the stones strike the ground at the same time, find the velocity, with which the second stone was thrown upwards.

[Ans. u = 39.2 m/sec]

16. A body falling freely, under the action of gravity, passes two points 10 metres apart vertically in 0.2 second. From what height, above the higher point, did it start to fall?

[Ans. h = 122.5 m]

17. A particle, falling under gravity, falls 20 metres in a certain second. Find the time required to cover next 20 metres. **[Ans. t = 0.71 sec]**

18. A body was thrown vertically downwards from the top of a tower and traverses a distance of 40 metres during its 4th second of the fall. Find the initial velocity of the body.

[Ans. u = 5.7 m/sec]

19. The equation of motion of an engine is given by $s = 2t^3 - 6t^2 - 5$, where s is in metres and t in seconds. Calculate:

(i) Displacement and acceleration when velocity is zero; and

(ii) Displacement and velocity when acceleration is zero.

[Ans. $s_1 = -13$ m, $a_1 = 12$ m/s^2 and $s_2 = -9$m, $a_2 = -6$ m/s^2]

CHAPTER 7

Kinetics of Particles

KINETICS

Kinetics is the study of relationship between the forces acting on a body. Kinetics therefore can be used to predict the motion caused by a given force or to determine the forces required to produce the prescribed motion.

IMPORTANT TERMS

1. MASS : It is the matter contained by the body. The units of mass are kilogram, tonne etc.

2. WEIGHT : It is the force, by which the body is attracted towards the centre of the earth. The units of weight are same as those of force i.e. *N,KN, kgf, tf* etc.

3. MOMENTUM : It is the total motion possessed by a body. It can be expressed mathemetically as,

Momentum = mass × velocity

The units of momentum depends upon the units of mass and velocity. In S.I and M.K.S units, the mass is measured in kg, and velocity in m/sec, therefore, the units of momentum will be kg – m/ sec.

4. FORCE : It may be defined as an agent which produces or tends to produce, destroys or tends to destroy the motion. The units of force, like those of weight, are *N, kN, kgf, tf* etc.

5. INERTIA : It is an inherent property of a body, which offers reluctance or laziness to change its state of rest or uniform motion.

NEWTON'S SECOND LAW OF MOTION

It states that rate of change of momentum is directly proportional to the impressed force and takes place, in the same direction in which the force acts."

This law enables us to measure a force, and establishes the fundamental equation of dynamics. Let its velocity be changed while moving.

Let,

m = Mass of the body,

u = Initial velocity of the body,

a = Constant acceleration

t = Time in seconds required to change the velocity from u to v, and

p = Force required to change the velocity from u to v in t seconds.

∴ Initial momentum = mu, and

Final momentum = mv

∴ Rate of change of momentum = $\dfrac{mv - mu}{t}$

$$\frac{m(v-u)}{t} = ma \qquad \left(\because \frac{v-u}{t} = a\right)$$

According to Newton's second law of motion.

The rate of change of momentum is directly proportional to the impressed force.

$$\therefore \qquad P \propto ma = Kma$$

Where K is a constant of proportionality.

For the sake of convenience, the unit of force adopted is such that it produes unit aceleration to unit mass.

$$\therefore \qquad P = ma = \text{Mass} \times \text{Aceleration}$$

In S.I. and M.K.S. system of units, the unit of force is called Newton, briefly written as *N*. A Newton may be defined as the force, while acting upon a mass of 1 kg, produces an acceleration of 1 m/sec^2 in the direction in which it acts.

EXAMPLE 7.1. A vehicle of mass 500 kg, is moving with a velocity of 25 m/sec. A force of 200 N acts on it for 2 minutes. Find the velocity of the vehicle.

(i) When the force acts in the direction of motion, and

(ii) When the force acts in opposite direction of the motion

SOLUTION : Given : m = 500 kg, u = 25 m/sec, P = 200 N, t = 2 min = 120 secs.

(i) Force acts in directions of motion:

We know that acceleration of the vehicle,

$$a = P/m = 200/500 = 0.4 \text{ m/sec}^2$$

Velocity of the vehicle after 120 secs.

$$v_1 = u + at$$

$$= 25 + 0.4(120)$$

$$= 73 \text{ m/sec. } \textbf{Ans.}$$

(ii) Force acts in opposite direction of motion :

$$v_2 = u + at$$

$$= 25 + (-0.4 \times 120)$$

$$= -23 \text{ m/sec. } \textbf{Ans.}$$

Minus sign means that the vehicle is moving in reverse direction or in other words opposite to the direction in which the vehicle was moving before the force was made to act.

EXAMPLE 7.2. A car of 2.5 tonnes moves on a level road under action of 1 kN propelling force. Find the time taken by the car to increase its velocity from 36 km p.h. to 54 km. p.h.

SOLUTION : Given :

$m = 2.5\ t, P = 1$ kN, $u = 36$ km p.h. $= 10$ m/sec, $v = 54$ km/hr $= 15$ m/sec

Let, t = Time taken by the car to increase its speed. We know that acceleration of the car,

$a = P/m = 1\ (1000)/2.5\ (1000) = 0.4$ m/sec^2

and final velocity of the car, $v = 15 = u + at = 10 + 0.4t$

$$\therefore \quad t = \frac{15-10}{0.4}$$

$$= \frac{5}{0.4} = 12.5 \text{ sec. } \textbf{Ans.}$$

EXAMPLE 7.3. A body of mass 10 kg is moving over a smooth surface, whose equation of motion is given by the relation : $s = 5t + 2t^2$, where s is in metres and t in seconds. Find the magnitude of the force responsible for the motion.

SOLUTION : Given : $s = 5t + 2t^2$

Differentiating both sides of the above equation with respect to t,

$$ds/dt = 5 + 4t$$

Again differentiating both sides of the above equation with respect to t,

$$\frac{d^2 s}{dt^2} = 4$$

or acceleration, $a = 4$m/sec^2.

$\therefore$ Force responsible for the motion,

$$P = ma = 10 \times 4$$

$$= 40\ N \textbf{ Ans.}$$

MOTION OF A LIFT

Consider a lift (Elevator or cage) carrying some mass and moving with a uniform acceleration.

Let,

m = Mass carried by the lift in kg,

W = mg = Weight carried by the lift in newtons

a = Uniform acceleration of the lift, and

R = Reaction of the lift or tension in the cable, supporting the lift, in newtons.

1. WHEN THE LIFT IS MOVING UPWARDS : Net upwards force, which is responsible for the motion of the lift (Refer Fig. 7.1)

$$= R - W = R - mg \qquad \ldots(i)$$

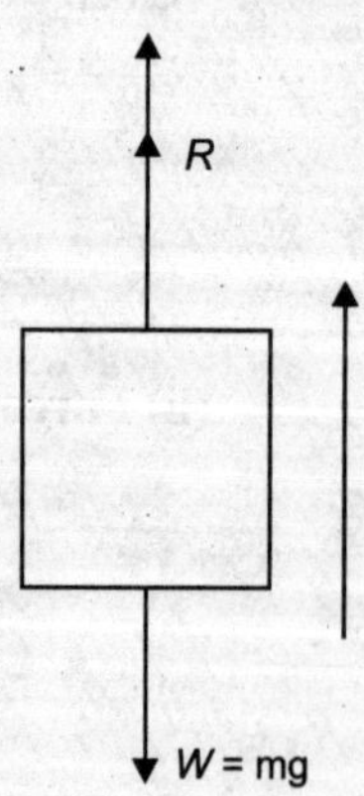

Fig. 7.1

We know that this force = Mass × Acceleration

$= ma$ ...(ii)

Equating (i) and (ii),

$$R - mg = ma$$

$$\therefore \quad R = ma + mg$$

$$= m(a+g) \qquad \text{...(iii)}$$

2. WHEN THE LIFT IS MOVING DOWNARDS : Net downward force, which is responsible for the motion of the lift (Refer Fig. 7.2)

$$= W - R = mg - R \qquad \text{...(iv)}$$

Now equating (ii) and (iv)

$$ma = mg - R$$

$$\therefore \quad R = mg - ma$$

$$= m(g-a) \qquad \text{...(v)}$$

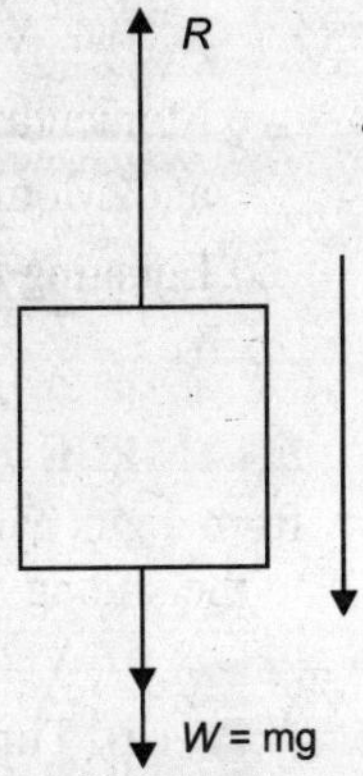

Lift Moving Downwards

Fig. 7.2

EXAMPLE 7.4. An elevator is required to lift a body of mass 65 kg. Find the acceleration of the elevator, which could cause a pressure of 800 N on the floor.

SOLUTION : Given : $m = 65$ kg; $R = 800$ N

We know that pressure caused on the floor $(R) = m(g + a)$

$$\therefore \quad 800 = 65\,(9.8 + a)$$

$$\text{or} \quad \frac{800}{65} - 9.8 = a$$

$$\therefore \quad a = 2.5 \text{ m/sec}^2$$ **Ans.**

EXAMPLE 7.5. An elevator of mass 500 kg is ascending with an acceleration of 3 *m*/sec^2. During this ascent its operator whose mass is 70 kg is standing on the scale placed on the floor. What is the scale reading? What will be the total tension in the cables of the elevator during this motion?

SOLUTION : Given :

$$m_1 = 500 \text{ kg},$$

$$m_2 = 70 \text{kg},$$

$$a = 3 \text{m/sec}^2$$

SCALE READING : We known that scale reading,

$$R_1 = m_2(g+a)$$

$$= 70(9.8+3) = 896 \text{ N}$$ **Ans.**

TOTAL TENSION IN THE CABLE OF ELEVATOR : We know that total tension in the cable of the elevator,

$$R_2 = (m_1 + m_2)(g + a)$$

$$= (500 + 70)(9.8 + 3)$$

$$= 7296 \text{ N}$$ **Ans.**

RECOIL OF GUN

According to Newton's third law of motion, when a bullet is fired from a gun, opposite reaction of the bullet is known a the recoil of gun.

Let,

M = Mass of the gun

V = velocity of the gun with which it recoils,

m = Mass of the bullet, and

v = Velocity of the bullet after explosion.

Momentum of the bullet after explosion = mv ...(i)

and, Momentum of the gun = MV ...(ii)

Equating (i) and (ii)

$$MV = mv \quad ...(iii)$$

EXAMPLE 7.6. A bullet of mass 200 gm, is fired horizontally with a velocity of 30 metres/sec, from a gun carried in a carriage, which together with the gun has a mass of 100 kg. The resistance to the sliding to the cariage over the ice, on which it rests, is 2 kgf. Find

(i) Velocity, with which the gun will recoil,

(ii) Time taken to do so.

SOLUTION : Given :

$$m = 200 \text{ gm} = 0.2 \text{ kg};$$
$$v = 30 \text{ m/sec},$$
$$M = 100 \text{ kg},$$
$$P = 2 \text{ kgf} = 2 \times 9.8 \text{ N}$$
$$= 19.60 \text{ N}$$

(i) VELOCITY WITH WHICH THE GUN WILL RECOIL :

$$V = \frac{mv}{M} = \frac{0.2 \times 30}{100}$$

$$= 0.06\ m/\text{sec } \textbf{Ans.}$$

(ii) DISTANCE IN WHICH THE GUN COMES TO REST : Here,

$$u = 0.06 \text{ m/sec};$$
$$v = 0$$

Let,

a= Retardation of the gun, and

s = Distance in which the gun comes to rest.

We know that resisting force to sliding of carriage (P)

$$19.60 = M_a = 100\ a$$

$$\therefore \quad a = \frac{19.60}{100} = 0.196 \text{ m/sec}^2$$

We know that,

$$v^2 = u^2 - 2as \qquad \text{(–ve sign due to retardation)}$$

$$\therefore \quad (0)^2 = (0.06)^2 - 2(0.196)s$$

$$= 0.0036 - 0.392\,s$$

$$\therefore \quad s = \frac{0.0036}{0.392} = 0.009\ m$$

$$= 9\ mm \textbf{ Ans.}$$

(iii) TIME TAKEN BY THE GUN IN COMING TO REST :

Let,

t = Time taken by the gun in coming to rest. We know that final velocity of the gun (v), $v = u–at$

i.e.

$$0 = u - at$$

$$= 0.06 - 0.196t$$

$$\therefore \quad t = \frac{0.06}{0.196} = 0.3 \text{ sec. } \textbf{Ans.}$$

MOTION OF A BOAT

We see that a boat boy always pushes the water with the help of sticks, which in turn, sets the boat in motion. It has also been experienced that if the boat is at rest and the boat boy runs on it and dives off into the water, the boat will also move backwards.

The movement of the boat may be easily found out by the application of the newton's third law of motion (i.e. by equating the momentum of the boat boy and the boat). Now consider a boat on which a boat boy runs and the dives off into the water.

Let,

M = Mass of he boat,

V = Velocity of the boat

m = Mass of the boat boy

v = Velocity of the boat boy

Momentum of the boat, after the boy jumps = $M.V.$ ...(i)

Momentum of the boat boy = mv ...(ii)

Equating (i) and (ii),

$$MV = mv \qquad \text{...(iii)}$$

EXAMPEL 7.7. Two men, standing on a floating boat, run in succession, along its length, with a speed of 4.2 m/sec relative to the boat and dive off from the end. The mass of each man is 80 kg and that of boat is 400 kg. If the boat was initially at rest, find the final velocity of the boat. Neglect water friction.

SOLUTION : Given :

v = 4.2 m/sec., Mass of each man = 80 kg = m, Mass of boat, M = 400 kg

Let,

V = Velocity of the boat after the second man dives off the boat

Note : When the first man dives off the boat, it will give some momentum to the boat as well as the second man (who is still standing on the boat). When the second man also dives off the boat, it will give some momentum to the boat. Hence total momentum gained by the boat is equal to the momentum given by first man plus the momentum given by the second man to the boat.

Now final momentum of the boat = $MV = 400\ V$ kg–*m*/sec. ...(i)

Momentum given by the first man to the boat

$$= m_1 v_1 = 80 \times 4.2$$

$$= 336\ kg - m/\sec$$

Momentum given by the second man to the boat

$$= m_2 v_2 = 80 \times 4.2$$

$$= 336\ kg - m/\sec$$

We know that final momentum of the boat = Momentum given by the first man + Momentum given by the second man

$$= 336 + 336$$

$$= 672 \text{ kg - m /sec} \quad ...(ii)$$

Equating (i) and (ii)

$$400\ V = 672$$

$$\therefore \quad V = \frac{672}{400} = 1.68\ m/\text{sec}. \textbf{ Ans.}$$

MOTION ON AN INCLINED SURFACE

Sometimes, a body instead of moving horizontally, under the action of applied force, moves up or down on an inclined surface. In such a case, the vertical component of the weight of the body will cause some acceleration to the motion of the body. Now consider a body sliding downwards on a smooth inclined surface as shown in Fig. 7.3

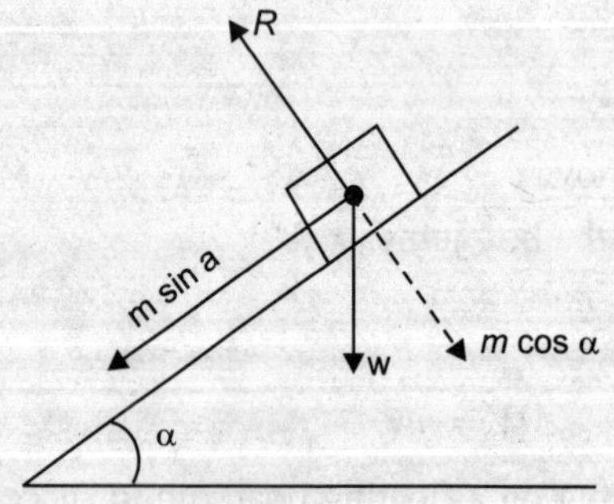

Motion on an inclined plane

Fig. 7.3

Let,

m = Mass of the body in absolute units in kg

W = Weight of the body in gravitational units in *kgf*, (equal to m kg).

α = Angle, at which the surface is inclined with the horizontal, and

a = Acceleration of the body due to inclined surface.

Since the surface is smooth, therefore it does not offer any resistance due to friction. Thus the force responsible for sliding the body (or in other words vertical component of the weight of the body).

$$P = W \sin\alpha = m \sin\alpha$$

We know that force = Mass × Acceleration

$$\therefore \quad m \sin\alpha = ma$$

$$\therefore \quad a = \sin a$$

Note : If the body is pushed upwards on a smooth inclined plane, the corresponding acceleration will be $-\sin\alpha$.

If the surface is not smooth (i.e. there is some friction betwen the body and the surface) then the force of friction will act in opposite direction of the motion of the body.

EXAMPLE 7.8. A vehicle of mass 200 tonnes has a frictional resistance of 5 *kgf* per tonne. Speed of the train, at the top of an inclined plane of 1 in 80, is 45 Km. p.h. Find the speed of the train after running down the incline for 1 km.

SOLUTION : Given :

$m = 200\ t$, Frictional resistance = 5 kgf/*t*.

$$\sin\alpha = \frac{1}{80} = 0.0125$$

$$u = 45 \text{ km.p.h.} = 12.5 \text{m/sec}$$

$$s = 1 km = 1000 m$$

We know that frictional resistance

$$= 5 \text{ kg}/t = 5 \times 200$$

$$= 1000 \text{ kg} f = 1\ tf$$

and force responsible for sliding = $m \sin\alpha$

$$= 200 \times 0.0125$$

$$= 2.5\ tf = 24.525 \text{ kN}$$

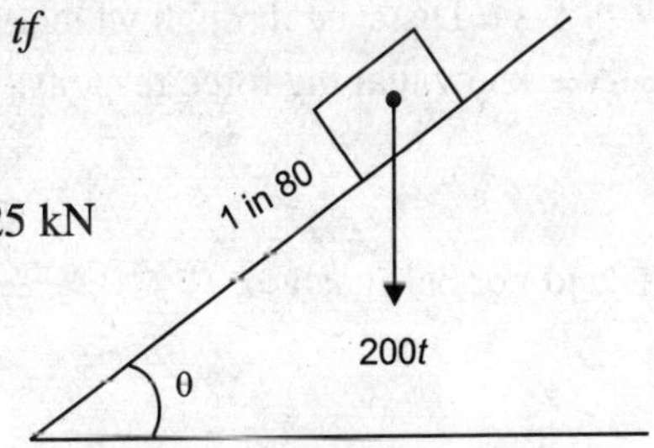

Fig. 7.4

$\therefore$ Available force

$$= 2.5 - 1.0$$

$$= 1.5\ tf$$

$$= 1.5 \times 9.8$$

$$= 14.7 \text{ kN}$$

$$24.5 - 9.8 = 14.7 \text{ kN}$$

and acceleration of the vehicle,

$$a = P/m = \frac{14.7}{200} = 0.0735\ m/\text{sec}^2$$

We know that,

$$v^2 = u^2 + 2as$$

$$= (12.5)^2 + 2(0.0735)100 = 303.25$$

$$\therefore \qquad v = \sqrt{303.25}$$
$$= 17.41\ m/\text{sec}\ \textbf{Ans.}$$

EXAMPLE 7.9. A body of mass 200 kg is initially stationary on a 15° inclined plane. What distance along the incline must the body slide before it reaches a speed of 10 m/sec? Take coefficient of friction between the body and the plane as 0.1

SOLUTION : Given :

$$m = 200\text{ kg};$$
$$u = 0,$$
$$a = 15°,$$
$$v = 10\text{m/sec}; \quad \mu = 0.1$$

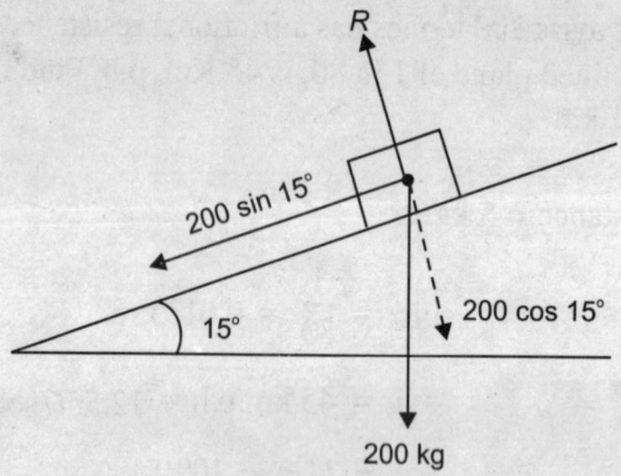

Fig. 7.5

Let,

s = Distance through which the body will slide.

We know that the force responsible for sliding

$$m \sin\alpha = 200 \sin 15° = 200(0.2588)$$
$$= 51.76\ kgf$$

and normal reaction,

$$R = 200 \cos 15° = 200(0.9659)$$
$$= 193.19\ kgf$$

$$\therefore \qquad \text{Force of friction} = \mu R = 0.1(193.19)$$
$$= 19.32\ kgf \text{ and}$$
$$\text{Available force} = 51.76 - 19.32$$
$$= 32.44\ kgf = 32.44 \times 9.8$$
$$= 317.91\ N$$

$\therefore$ Acceleration of the body,

$$a = \frac{P}{m} = \frac{317.91}{200} = 1.59\ m/\text{sec}^2$$

We know that,

$$v^2 = u^2 + 2as$$

$$(10)^2 = (0)^2 + 2(1.59)s = 3.18s$$

$$\therefore \quad s = \frac{100}{3.18} = 31.45\,m \textbf{ Ans.}$$

MOTION OF TWO BODIES CONNECTED BY A STRING PASSING OVER A SMOOTH PULLEY

Consider two bodies of masses m_1 and m_2 connected at the ends of a light inextansible string that passes over a smooth frictionless pulley (Fig. 7.6). If $m_1 > m_2$ mass m_1 moves downards (b) and the mass m_2 moves upwards (a).

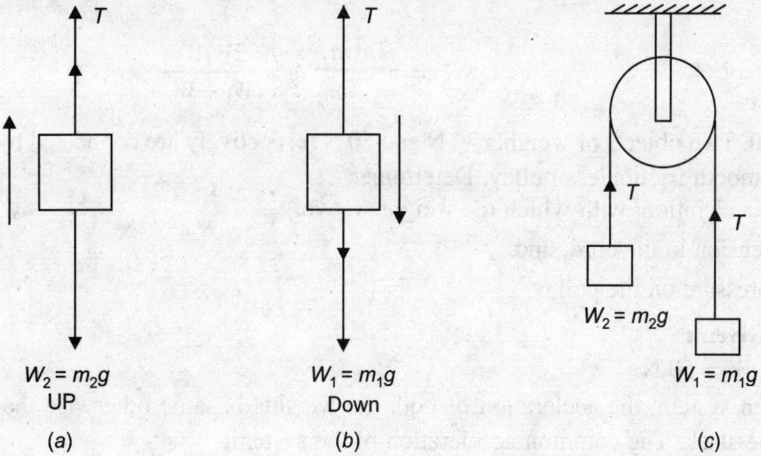

Fig. 7.6

It is to be noted that :

1. The acceleration of both the masses is same otherwise the cord would break or become slack.
2. For the smooth frictionless pulley and continuous cord, the tension induced in the string will be the same throughout.

With reference to free body diagram (*a*, *b*) the equation of motion for the two masses are as follows :

Downwards motion of mass m_1.

$$m_1 g - T = m_1 a \qquad \text{...(i)}$$

Upward motion of mass m_2,

$$T - m_2 g = m_2 a \qquad \text{...(ii)}$$

Adding expressions (i) and (ii)

$$m_1 g - m_2 g = m_2 a + m_1 a$$

$$= a(m_1 + m_2)$$

∴ Acceleration of the system,

$$a = \frac{m_1 - m_2}{m_1 + m_2} g = \frac{W_1 - W_2}{W_1 + W_2} g \qquad \text{...(iii)}$$

Upon substituting this value of acceleration a in expression (i), we get

$$m_1 g - T = m_1 \frac{m_1 - m_2}{m_1 + m_2} g$$

$$\therefore \qquad T = m_1 g \left[1 - \frac{m_1 - m_2}{m_1 + m_2}\right]$$

$$= m_1 g \times \frac{2m_2}{m_1 + m_2}$$

$$= \frac{2m_1 m_2}{m_1 + m_2} g = \frac{2W_1 W_2}{W_1 + W_2} \qquad \text{...(iv)}$$

EXAMPLE 7.10. Two objects of weights 30 N and 50 N respectively are connected by a light cord passing over a smooth frictionless pulley. Determine

(a) The acceleration, with which the weights move,

(b) The tension in the cord, and

(c) The pressure on the pulley.

SOLUTION : Given :

$W_1 = 30$ N, $W_2 = 50$ N

For the given system, the accleration of both the weights is same otherwise the cord would break or be come slack. The common acceleration of the system.

$$a = \frac{W_1 - W_2}{W_1 + W_2} g = \frac{50 - 30}{50 + 30} \times 9.80$$

$$= 2.45\, m/\text{sec}^2 \ \textbf{Ans.}$$

Further tension in the cord is same through out (because friction of the pulley is negligible) and is given by

$$T = \frac{2W_1 W_2}{W_1 + W_2} = \frac{2 \times 50 \times 30}{50 + 30} = 37.5\, N \ \textbf{Ans.}$$

Pressure (reaction) on the pulley,

$$R = T + T = 2T$$

$$= 2 \times 37.5 = 75\, N \ \textbf{Ans.}$$

EXAMPLE 7.11. A system of frictionless pulleys caries two weights hung by inextensible cords as shown in Fig. 7.7. Make calculations for the tension in the cords and acceleration of the weights.

Also calculate the displacement and velocity of weight W_1 after 4 seconds from start. Assume that the system is released from rest.

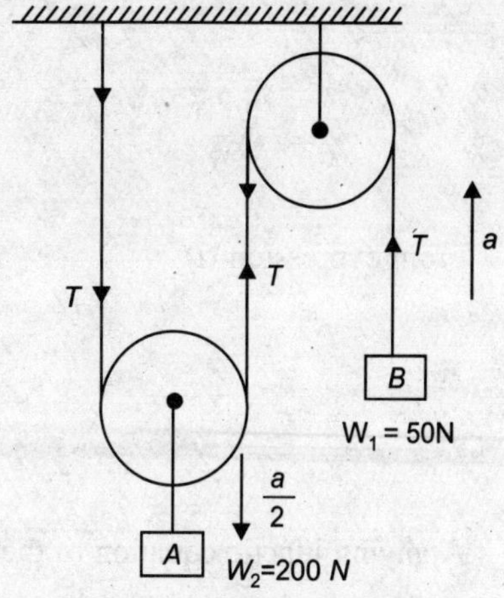

Fig. 7.7

SOLUTION : Since the pulleys are frictionless and the cord is continuous, the tension *T* induced in the cord will be same throughout.

It is evident from the given arrangement that when the weight W_1 travels a unit distance the W_2 weight travels half the distance. Acceleration is proportional to the distance travelled, and therefore if *a* is acceleration of weight W_1, the weight W_2 will have the acceleration equal to $a/2$. The weight W_1 moves upward and the weight W_2 moves downwards.

With reference to free body diagram (Fig. 7.8) the equations of motion for the two weights are as follows :

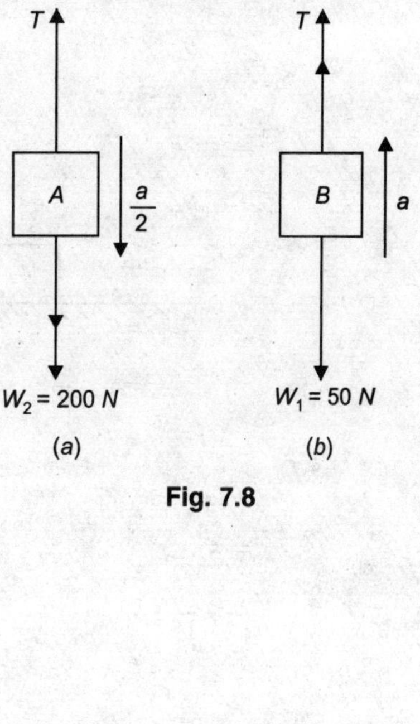

Fig. 7.8

$$T - m_1 g = m_1 a$$

or $$T - W_1 = \frac{W_1}{g} a$$

$\therefore$ $$T - 50 = \frac{50}{9.8} a$$

(upward motion of block B)

$\therefore$ $$T = 50 + \frac{50}{9.8} a \quad \text{...(i)}$$

Also, $$W_2 - 2T = m_2 \frac{a}{2}$$

or $$W_2 - 2T = \frac{W_2}{g} \cdot \frac{a}{2}$$

or $$W_2 = \frac{W_2}{g} \cdot \frac{a}{2} + 2T$$

$\therefore$ $$200 = \frac{200}{9.8} \cdot \frac{a}{2} + 2T$$

or $$200 = \frac{100}{9.8} a + 2T$$

or $$200 - \frac{100}{9.8} a = 2T$$

$\therefore$ $$T = 100 - \frac{50}{9.8} a \quad \text{...(ii)}$$

From expression (i) and (ii) we get

$$50 + \frac{50}{9.8} a = 100 - \frac{50}{9.8} a$$

or $$\frac{100}{9.8}a = 50$$

or $$a = \frac{50 \times 9.8}{100} = 4.9\, m/\sec^2$$

From expression (i)

$$T = 50 + \frac{50}{9.8}a$$

$$= 50 + \frac{50}{9.8} \times 4.9 = 75\, N$$

Applying kinetic equation to the motion of weight B $(W_1 = 50N)$

$$v = u + at$$

$$= 0 + 4.9 \times 4 = 19.6\, m/\sec \textbf{ Ans.}$$

$$s = ut + \frac{1}{2}at^2 = 0 + \frac{1}{2}(4.9)(4)^2$$

$$= 39.2\, m \textbf{ Ans.}$$

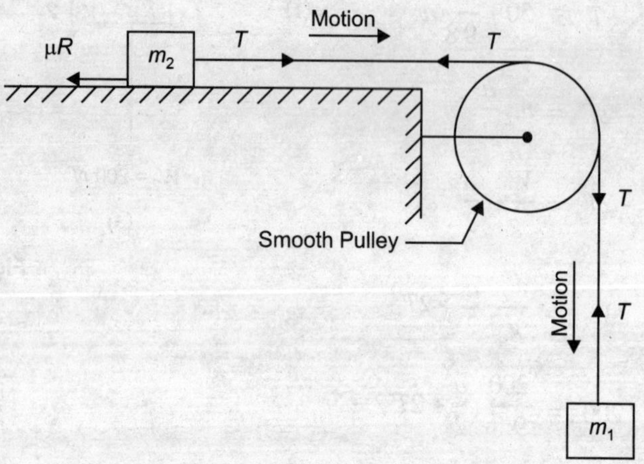

Fig. 7.9

MOTION OF TWO BODIES CONNECTED AT THE EDGE OF A HORIZONTAL SURFACE

Consider a block of mass m_2 resting on a rough horizontal surface. The block is attached to a light inextensible string which passes over a smooth frictionless pulley at the end of the surface. The portion of the string, beyond the pulley, hangs vertically down and carries a mass m_1 at the end (Refer Fig. 7.9). Let mass m_1 moves donwards and the mass m_2 moves along the surface of the plane. It is to be noted that:

(i) The acceleration of both masses is same otherwise the string will break or become loose.

(ii) For a smooth frictionless pulley and continuous string, the tension induced in the string is same throughout.

With reference to the free body diagrams (a, b,) Fig. 7.10(a and b), the equation of motion for the two masses are as follows :

Downward motion of mass m_1

$$m_1 g - T = m_1 a \qquad \text{...(i)}$$

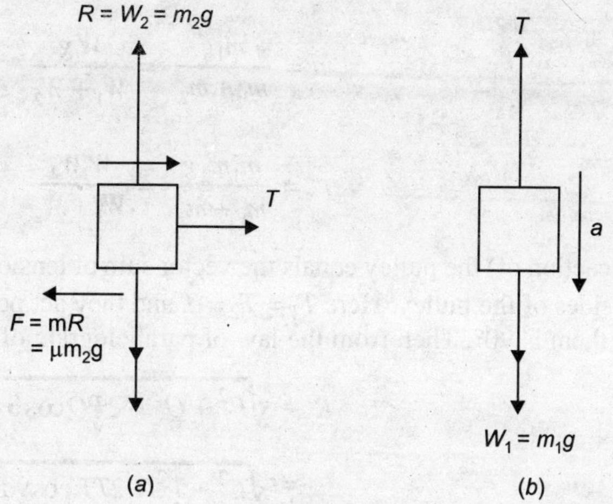

Fig. 7.10

Horizontal motion of mass m_2

$$T - \mu m_2 2g = m_2 a \qquad \text{...(ii)}$$

Where μ is the coefficient of friction between the block and the rough surface.

Adding expressions (i) and (ii)

$$m_1 g - \mu m_2 g = m_1 a + m_2 a$$

or

$$(m_1 - \mu m_2)g = (m_1 + m_2)a$$

∴ Acceleration of the system,

$$a = \frac{m_1 - \mu m_2}{m_1 + m_2} g = \frac{W_1 - \mu W_2}{W_1 + W_2} g \qquad \text{...(iii)}$$

Upon substitution of the value of acceleration a in expression (i), we get

$$m_1 g - T = m_1 \times \frac{m_1 g - \mu m_2 g}{m_1 + m_2}$$

$$T = m_1 g - m_1 \frac{m_1 g - \mu m_2 g}{m_1 + m_2}$$

∴

$$T = m_1 g\left(1 - \frac{m_1 - \mu m_2}{m_1 + m_2}\right)$$

$$= \frac{m_1 m_2 g(1+\mu)}{m_1 + m_2} \qquad \text{...(iv)}$$

$$= \frac{W_1 W_2 (1+\mu)}{W_1 + W_2}$$

For smooth horizontal surface, $\mu = 0$, and in that case the equations may be modified to :

$$a = \frac{m_1 g}{m_1 + m_2} = \frac{W_1 g}{W_1 + W_2} \qquad \text{...(v)}$$

$$T = \frac{m_1 m_2 g}{m_1 + m_2} = \frac{W_1 W_2}{W_1 + W_2} \qquad \text{...(vi)}$$

Pressure on (or reaction of) the pulley equals the vector sum of tension T_1 and T_2 induced in the string lying on both sides of the pulley. Here $T_1 = T_2 = T$ and they act perpendicular to each other, i.e. angle θ between them is 90°. Then from the law of parallelogram of forces,

$$R = \sqrt{P^2 + Q^2 + 2PQ\cos\theta}$$

$$= \sqrt{T^2 + T^2 + 2TT\cos 90^0}$$

Hence $$R = \sqrt{2T^2} = \sqrt{2}T \qquad \text{...(vii)}$$

Thus pressure on pulley is $\sqrt{2}$ times the tension induced in the string.

EXAMPLE 7.12. Find the acceleration of a solid body *A* of mass 10 kg, when it is being pulled by another body of mass 5 kg along a smooth horizontal plane as shown in Fig. 7.11. Also find the tension in the string, assuming the string to be inextensible.

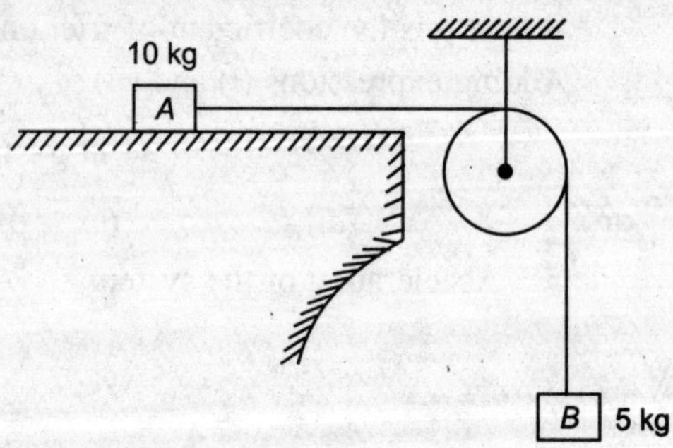

Fig. 7.11

SOLUTION : Given :

$m_1 = 5$ kg,

$m_2 = 10$ kg

(i) ACCELERATION OF BODY : We know that the acceleration of the body, *A*,

$$a = \frac{m_1 g}{m_1 + m_2} = \frac{5 \times 9.8}{5 + 10}$$

$= 3.27\ m/\text{sec}^2$ **Ans.**

(ii) TENSION IN THE STRING :

$$T = \frac{m_1 m_2 g}{m_1 + m_2} = \frac{5 \times 10 \times 9.8}{5 + 10}$$

$- 32.67\ N$ **Ans.**

EXAMPLE 7.13. A block of weight 10N is resting on a rough horizontal table 1.5 m from its edge. This block *A* is attached to a string which passes over a pulley at the end of the table. The portion of the string beyond the pulley hangs vertically down and carries a block *B* of weight 8*N* at the end. If the coefficient of friction between the block *A* and table is 0.2, make calculations for the acceleration of the system and pressure on the pulley. Neglect friction in the pulley and extension of the string.

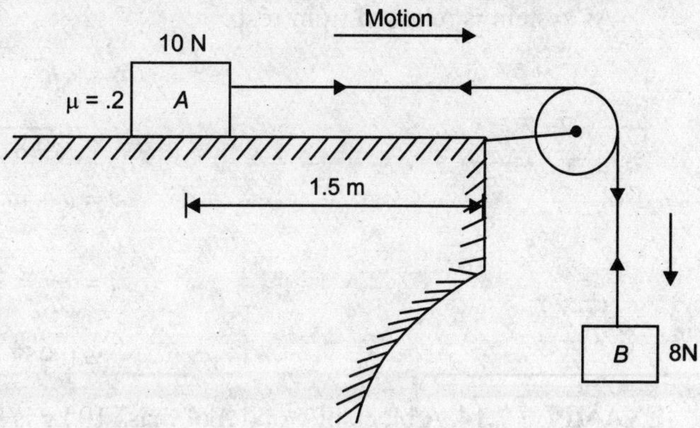

Fig. 7.12

If the system is released from rest, what time block *A* will take to fall over the edge?

SOLUTION : Given :

$$W_2 = 10N,$$

$$W_1 = 8N,$$

$$\mu = 0.2,$$

$$s = 1.5\ m$$

For the given system (Fig. 7.12) the accleration of both weights is same otherwise the string would break or become loose. The common acceleration of the system is

$$a = \frac{W_1 - \mu W_2}{W_1 + W_2} g$$

$$= \frac{8 - 0.2 \times 10}{8 + 10} 9.8$$

$$= 3.27 \text{ m/sec}^2 \textbf{ Ans.}$$

Further, tension in the cord is same throughout (because friction of pulley is negligible) and is given by,

$$T = \frac{W_1 W_2 (1 + \mu)}{W_1 + W_2} = \frac{8 \times 10(1 + 0.2)}{8 + 10}$$

$$= 5.33 \text{ N } \textbf{Ans.}$$

Pressure on the pulley = $\sqrt{2}T = \sqrt{2} \times 5.33 = 7.538$ N **Ans.**

Applying kinetic equations to motion for weight *A* (10*N*).

$$v^2 = u^2 + 2as,$$

$$u = 0$$

As system is released from rest

$$\therefore \quad v = \sqrt{2as} = \sqrt{2 \times 3.27 \times 1.5}$$

$$= \sqrt{9.81} = 3.13\, m/\text{sec}$$

Also, $$v = u + at = at$$

$$t = \frac{v}{a} = \frac{3.13}{3.27}$$

$$= 0.957 \text{ sec. } \textbf{Ans.}$$

EXAMPLE 7.14. A block of wood *A* of mass 10 kg is held on a rough horizontal table. An elastic string connected to the block passes over a smooth pulley at the end of the table and then under a second smooth pulley carrying a body *B* of mass = 5kg as shown in Fig. 7.13.

The other end of the string is fixed to a point above the second pulley. When 10 kg block is released it moves with an acceleration of *g*/9. Determine the value of coefficient of friction between the block and the table.

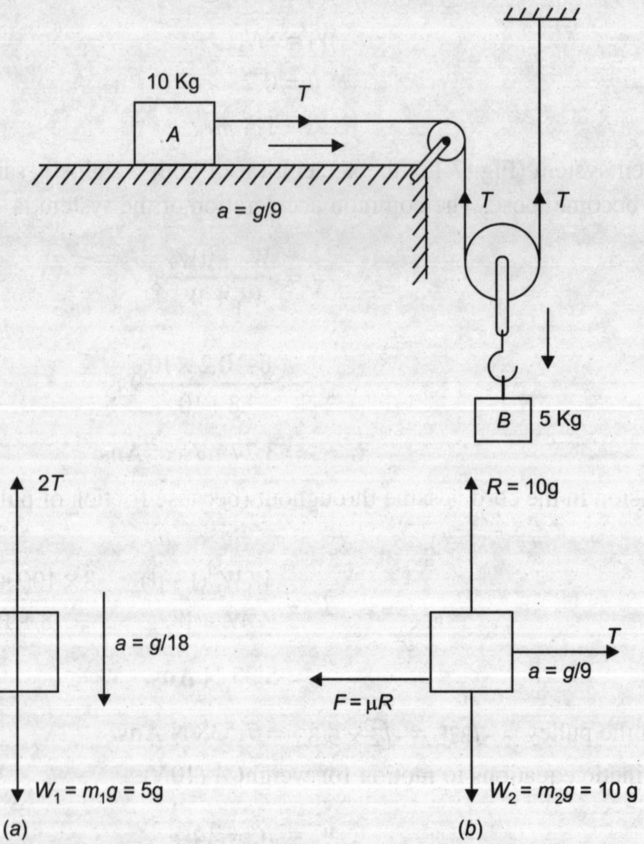

Fig. 7.13

SOLUTION : Given :

$$m_1 = 5 \text{ kg},$$

$$m_2 = 10 \text{ kg},$$

$$a_A = g/9$$

Let,

T = Tension in the string in Newtons

μ = Coefficient of friction between block A and table

HORIZONTAL MOTION OF BLOCK A :

$$T - \mu R = m_2 \frac{g}{9}$$

or $$T - \mu\,(m_2 g) = m_2 \frac{g}{9}$$

or $$T - \mu(10g) = \frac{(10g)}{9}$$

or $$T - 10\,\mu\, g = \frac{10g}{9}$$

$\therefore$ $$2T - 20\mu g = \frac{20g}{9} \quad ...(i)$$

VERTICAL DOWNWARD MOTION OF BLOCK B. The acceleration of this block will be half of that of the block A i.e. $g/18$.

We known that the forces acting on it are $m_1 g = 5g$ (Downwards) and $2T$ newtons (upwards).

$$5g - 2T = 5 \times \frac{g}{18}$$

or $$5g - 2T = 5 \times \frac{5g}{18} \quad ...(ii)$$

Adding equations (i) and (ii)

$$2T - 20\mu g = \frac{20g}{9} \quad ...(i)$$

$$5g - 2T = \frac{5g}{18} \quad ...(ii)$$

$$-20\mu g = \frac{20g}{9} + \frac{5g}{18} - 5g$$

$$-20\mu g = \frac{40g + 5g - 90g}{18} = -\frac{45g}{18}$$

$$\therefore \qquad \mu = \frac{45}{360} = 0.125 \textbf{ Ans.}$$

MOTION OF TWO BODIES CONNECTED BY A STRING, ONE HANGS FREE AND OTHER ON A ROUGH INCLINED PLANE

Consider two bodies of masses m_1 and m_2 connected at the ends of a light inextensible string that passes over a smooth frictionless pulley.

Let the mass m_1 hangs free and mass m_2 lies on a rough surface inclined at an angled α with the horizontal.

It is noted that :

(i) The acceleration of both the masses is same, otherwise the cord could break or become slack.

(ii) For a smooth frictionless pulley and continuous cord, the tension induced in the string will be same throughout.

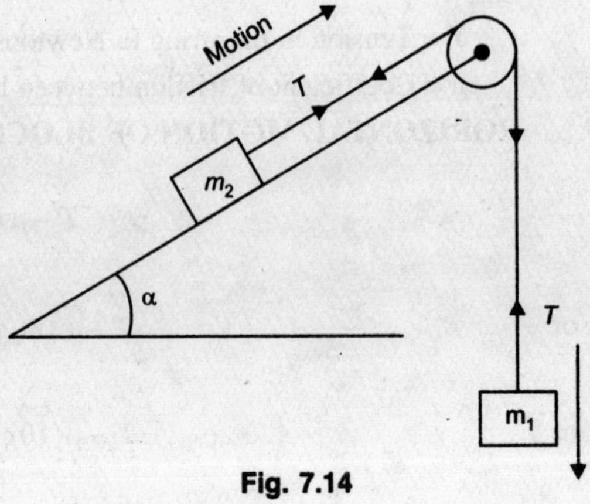

Fig. 7.14

Let mass m_1 moves downwards and the body of mass m_2 moves upwards along the inclined surface. Then with reference to free body diagrams (Fig. 7.15). the equations of motion for the two masses are as follows.

$$m_1 g - T = m_1 a \qquad \text{...(i)}$$

$$T - m_2 g \sin\alpha - \mu R_2 = m_2 a$$

$$T - m_2 g \sin\alpha - \mu m_2 g \cos\alpha = m_2 a \qquad \text{...(ii)}$$

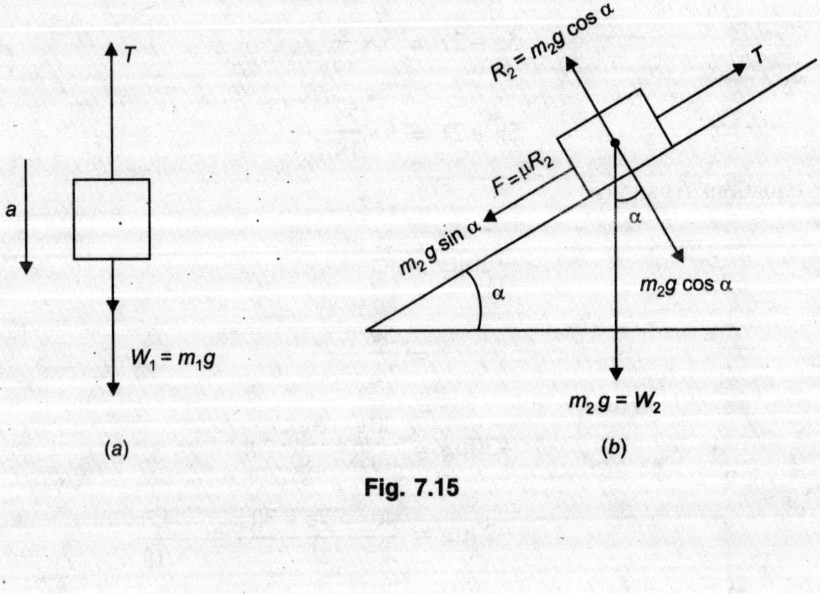

Fig. 7.15

Adding expression (i) and (ii)

$$m_1 g - m_2 g \sin\alpha - \mu m_2 g \cos\alpha = a(m_1 + m_2)$$

∴ Acceleration of the system,

$$a = \frac{m_1 - m_2 \sin\alpha - \mu m_2 \cos\alpha}{m_1 + m_2} g$$

$$= \frac{W_1 - W_2 \sin\alpha - \mu W_2 \cos\alpha}{W_1 + W_2} g$$

From expression (i) the tension T in the string is

$$T = m_1(g - a)$$

$$= m_1\left(g - \frac{m_1 g - m_2 g \sin\alpha - \mu m_2 g \cos\alpha}{m_1 + m_2}\right)$$

$$T = m_1\left(\frac{m_1 g + m_2 g - m_1 g + m_2 g \sin\alpha + \mu m_2 g \cos\alpha}{m_1 + m_2}\right)$$

$$T = \frac{m_1 m_2 (1 + \sin\alpha + \mu\cos\alpha)}{m_1 + m_2} g$$

$$= \frac{W_1 W_2 (1 + \sin\alpha + \mu\cos\alpha)}{W_1 + W_2}$$

For a smooth inclined surface, $\mu = 0$ and in that case

$$a = \frac{m_1 - m_2 \sin\alpha}{m_1 + m_2} g$$

$$= \frac{W_1 - W_2 \sin\alpha}{W_1 + W_2} g \qquad \text{...(iii)}$$

and

$$T = \frac{m_1 m_2 g(1 + \sin\alpha)}{m_1 + m_2}$$

$$= \frac{W_1 W_2 (1 + \sin\alpha)}{W_1 + W_2} \qquad \text{...(iv)}$$

Pressure on (or reaction of) the pulley equals the vector sum of tension T_1 and T_2 induced in the string lying on two sides of the pulley. Here $T_1 = T_2$ and the angle θ between them is $90 - \alpha$, then from the parallelogram law of forces,

$$R = \sqrt{P^2 + Q^2 + 2PQ\cos\theta}$$

$$= \sqrt{T^2 + T^2 + 2TT\cos(90-\alpha)}$$

$$R = \sqrt{2T^2(1+\sin\alpha)}$$

$$= T\sqrt{2(1+\sin\alpha)} \qquad \text{...(v)}$$

Thus the pressure on the pulley is $\sqrt{2(1+\sin\alpha)}$ times the tension induced in the string.

EXAMPLE 7.15. For the mass pulley system depicted in Fig. 7.16, the mass $m_2 = 5$ kg is placed on the inclined plane (smooth) of inclination α whereas mass m_1 is hanging free. If acceleration of the system is 1.5 m/sec^2, determine inclination of the plane, tension in the string and reaction at the pulley.

How the acceleration of the system would be effected if each mass is doubled?

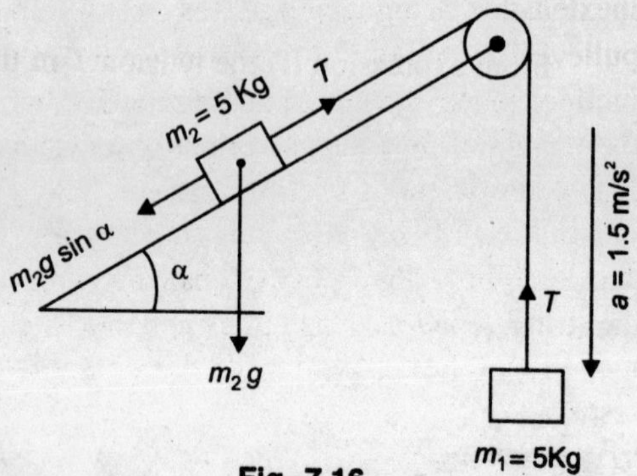

Fig. 7.16

SOLUTION : Considering the motion of mass $m_1 = 5$kg downwards.

$\therefore$ $$m_1g - T = m_1a$$

$\therefore$ $$5 \times 9.8 - T = 5 \times 1.5$$

or $$T = 5 \times 9.8 - 5 \times 1.5 = 41.5 \text{ N}$$

Hence tension, $T = 41.5$ N **Ans.**

2. Considering the motion of mass $m_2 = 5$ kg upwards along the plane.

$$T - m_2 g\sin\alpha = m_2 a$$

$\therefore$ $$41.5 - 5\times 9.8\sin\alpha = 5\times 1.5$$

or $$49\sin\alpha = 41.5 - 7.5$$

$\therefore$ $$\sin\alpha = \frac{34}{49} = 0.694$$

$\therefore$ $$\alpha = \sin^{-1}(0.694)$$

$$= 43.95^0 \textbf{ Ans.}$$

$\therefore$ Reaction at the pulley,

$$R = T\sqrt{2(1+\sin\alpha)}$$

$\therefore$ $$R = 41.5\sqrt{2(1+\sin 43.95^0)}$$

$$= 41.5(1.84)$$

$$= 76.38N \textbf{ Ans.}$$

$$\text{Acceleration, } a = \frac{m_1 - m_2 \sin\alpha}{m_1 + m_2} g$$

An examination of the above expression shows that acceleration of the system would remain uneffected when each mass is doubled.

Hence, acceleration, $a = 1.5$ m/sec^2

EXAMPLE 7.16. Two bodies of weights 50*N* and 10*N* are connected to the two ends of a light inextensible string which passes over a smooth pulley. The weight 10*N* is placed on a rough inclined plane of angle of inclination 20°, while the weight of 50*N* hangs vertically downward. If the coefficient of friction between body and the plane is 0.2, make calculations for the acceleration of the system, tension induced in the string, reaction at the pulley and the distance moved by the body in 3 seconds starting from rest.

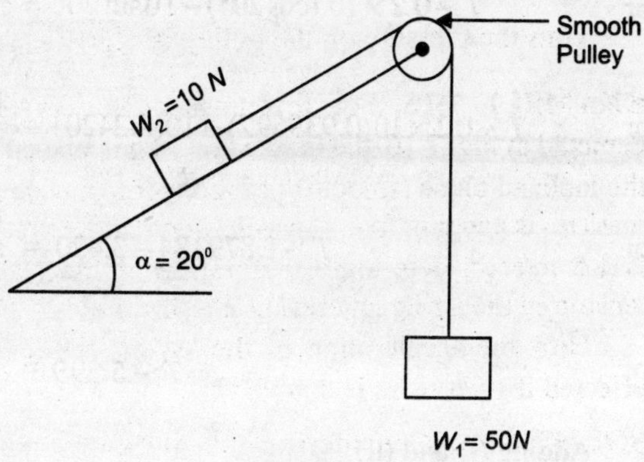

Fig. 7.17

SOLUTION : Refer Fig. 7.17

$W_1 = 50\ N$, $W_2 = 10$ N, $\mu = 0.2$ and $\alpha = 20°$

The acceleration of both the weights is equal and tension induced in the string is same throughout. The weight $W_2 = 10N$ is stated to move up the plane. Then with reference to the free body diagrams (a, b) of Fig. 7.18, the equations of motion for the two weights are as follows :

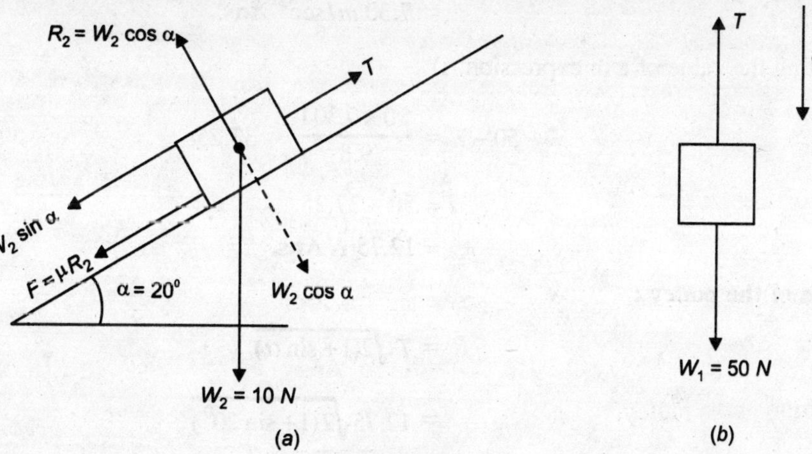

Fig. 7.18

1. For downward motion of weight, $W_1 = 50N$

$$W_1 - T = m_1 a$$

or

$$50 - T = \frac{50}{g} a \qquad \text{...(i)}$$

2. For upwards motion along rough inclined plane for weight, $W_2 = 10N$

$$T = \mu R_2 - W_2 \sin\alpha = m_2 a$$

or $$T - 0.2(W_2 \cos\alpha) - W_2 \sin\alpha = m_2 a$$

or $$T - 0.2 \times 10\,(\cos 20°) - 10 \sin 20° = \frac{10}{g} a$$

or $$T - 0.2 \times 10(0.939692) - 10(0.3420) = \frac{10a}{g}$$

or $$T - 1.879384 - 3.420 = \frac{10a}{g}$$

or $$T - 5.299 = \frac{10a}{g} \qquad \text{...(ii)}$$

Adding (i) and (ii)

$$44.701 = \frac{60a}{g}$$

$$\therefore \quad a = \frac{44.701 \times 9.8}{60}$$

$$= 7.30\ m/\sec^2 \ \textbf{Ans.}$$

Substituting the value of a in expression (i)

$$50 - T = \frac{50 \times 7.301}{9.8} = 37.25$$

$$\therefore \quad T = 50 - 37.25$$

$$= 12.75\ N\ \textbf{Ans.}$$

Reaction of the pulley :

$$R = T\sqrt{2(1 + \sin\alpha)}$$

$$= 12.75\sqrt{2(1 + \sin 20^0)}$$

$$= 20.89\ \text{N}\ \textbf{Ans.}$$

Applying kinematic equation to the motion of weight $W_2 = 10\ N$:

$$s = ut + \frac{1}{2}at^2 = 0 + \frac{1}{2} \times 7.301 \times (3)^2$$

$$= 32.85\ m\ \textbf{Ans.}$$

MOTION OF TWO BODIES CONNECTED OVER INCLINED PLANES.

Consider two blocks *A* and *B* of masses m_1 and m_2 respectively connected by a weightless inextensible rope passing over a frictionless pulley and placed on inclined planes making α_1 and α_2 angles with the horizontal as shown in Fig. 7.19

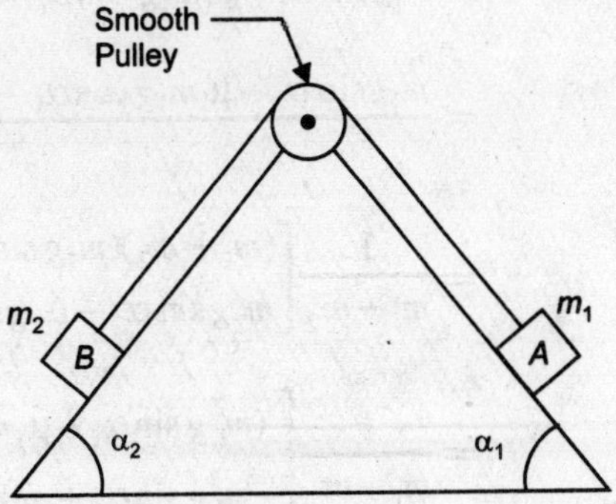

Fig. 7.19

It is to be noted that :

(i) The acceleration of both the weights is same otherwise the rope would break or become slack.

(ii) For smooth frictionless pulley and continuous cord, the tension induced in the string will be same throughout.

Let mass m_1 moves downwards. Then with reference to free body diagrams 7.20a, b the equations of motion for the two masses are as follows :

$$m_1 g \sin\alpha_1 - T - \mu_1 m_1 g \cos\alpha_1 = m_1 a \quad \text{...(i)}$$

$$T - m_2 g \sin\alpha_2 - \mu_2 m_2 g \cos\alpha_2 = m_2 a \quad \text{...(ii)}$$

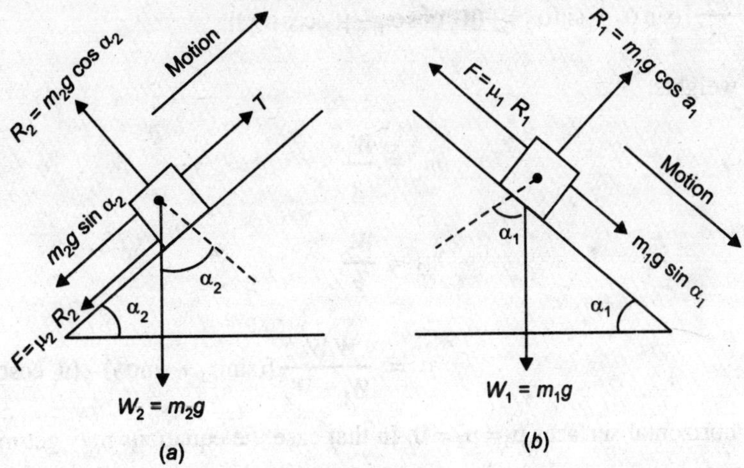

Fig. 7.20

Adding expressions (i) and (ii)

$$m_1 g \sin\alpha_1 - \mu_1 m_1 g \cos\alpha_1 - m_2 g \sin\alpha_2 - \mu_2 m_2 g \cos\alpha_2 = (m_1 + m_2)a$$

$$\therefore \quad a = \frac{m_1 g \sin\alpha_1 - m_2 g \sin\alpha_2 - \mu_1 m_1 g \cos\alpha_1 - \mu_2 m_2 g \cos\alpha_2}{m_1 + m_2} \quad \text{...(iii)}$$

$$a = \frac{W_1 \sin\alpha_1 - W_1 \sin\alpha_2 - \mu_1 W_1 \cos\alpha - \mu_2 W_2 \cos\alpha_2}{W_1 + W_2} g$$

From expression (i) the tension T in the string is

$$T = m_1 g \sin\alpha_1 - \mu_1 m_1 g \cos\alpha_1 = m_1 a$$

$$= \frac{m_1 g \sin\alpha_1 - \mu_1 m_1 g \cos\alpha_1 - m_1(m_1 g \sin\alpha_1 - m_2 g \sin\alpha_2 - \mu_1 m_1 g \cos\alpha_1 - \mu_2 m_2 g \cos\alpha_2)}{m_1 + m_2}$$

$$= \frac{1}{m_1+m_2}\begin{bmatrix}(m_1+m_2)(m_1 g \sin\alpha_1 - \mu_1 m_1 g \cos\alpha_1) - m_1(m_1 g \sin\alpha_1 - \\ m_2 g \sin\alpha_2 - \mu_2 g \sin\alpha_2 - \mu_1 m_1 g \cos\alpha_1 - \mu_2 m_2 g \cos a_2)\end{bmatrix}$$

$$= \frac{1}{m_1+m_2}\begin{bmatrix}(m_1^2 g \sin\alpha_1 - \mu_1 m_1^2 g \cos\alpha_1 + m_1 m_2 g \sin\alpha_1 - \mu_1 m_1 m_2 g \cos\alpha_1 \\ -m_1^2 g \sin\alpha_1 + m_1 m_2 g \sin\alpha_2 + \mu_1 m_1^2 g \cos\alpha_1 + \mu_2 m_1 m_2 \cos\alpha_2)\end{bmatrix}$$

$$= \frac{1}{m_1+m_2}(m_1 m_2 g \sin\alpha_1 + m_1 m_2 g \sin\alpha_2 - \mu m_1 m_2 g \cos\alpha_1 + \mu_2 m_1 m_2 \cos\alpha_2)$$

$$= \frac{1}{m_1+m_2}[g m_1 m_2(\sin\alpha_1 + \sin\alpha_2) - g m_1 m_2(\mu_1 \cos\alpha_1 - \mu_2 \cos\alpha_2)]$$

$$T = \frac{g m_1 m_2}{m_1+m_2}[(\sin\alpha_1 + \sin\alpha_2) - (\mu_2 \cos\alpha_1 - \mu_2 \cos\alpha_2)]$$

In terms of weights:

$$m_1 = \frac{W_1}{g}$$

and

$$m_2 = \frac{W_2}{g}$$

$\therefore$

$$T = \frac{W_1 W_2}{W_1 + W_2}[(\sin\alpha_1 + \sin\alpha_2) - (\mu_1 \cos\alpha_1 - \mu_2 \cos\alpha_2)]$$

For smooth horizontal surfaces $\mu_1 = \mu_2 = 0$. In that case the equations may get modified to :

$$a = \frac{W_1 \sin\alpha_1 - W_2 \sin\alpha_2}{W_1 + W_2} g$$

$$= \frac{m_1 \sin\alpha_1 - m_2 \sin\alpha_2}{m_1 + m_2} g$$

$$T = \frac{W_1 W_2 (\sin\alpha_1 + \sin\alpha_2)}{W_1 + W_2}$$

$$= \frac{m_1 m_2 (\sin\alpha_1 + \sin\alpha_2)}{m_1 + m_2} g$$

Pressure on (or reaction of) the pulley equals the vector sum of tension T_1 and T_2 induced in the string lying on two sides of the pulley. Here $T_1 = T_2 = T$ and the angle θ between them is 180 – (α_1 + α_2). Then from the parallelogram law of forces.

$$R^2 = P^2 + Q^2 + 2PQ\cos\theta$$

$$= T^2 + T^2 + 2TT\cos 180 - (\alpha_1 + \alpha_2)$$

$$R^2 = 2T^2 - 2T^2\cos(\alpha_1 + \alpha_2)$$

$$= 2T^2[1 - \cos(\alpha_1 + \alpha_2)]$$

$$= 2T^2 \times 2\sin^2\frac{\alpha_1 + \alpha_2}{2}$$

$$\therefore \quad R = 2T\sin\frac{\alpha_1 + \alpha_2}{2}$$

Thus the pressure on the pulley is 2 $\sin\frac{\alpha_1 + \alpha_2}{2}$ times the tension induced in the string.

EXAMPLE 7.17. Two smooth inclined planes whose inclinations with the horizontal are 30° and 20°, are placed back to back. Two bodies of 100 N and 60N are placed on them and are connected by a light inextensible string passing over a smooth pulley as shown in Fig. 7.21. Calculate the common acceleration of the system, tension in the string and pressure on the pulley.

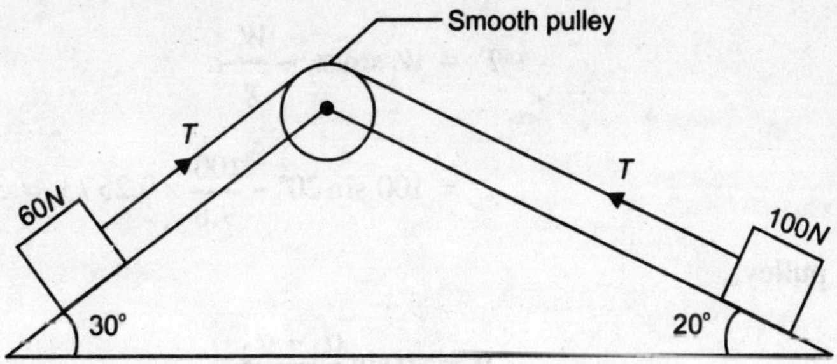

Fig. 7.21

SOLUTION : With reference to Fig. 7.21,

$$W_1 = 100 \text{ N},$$

$$W_2 = 60 \text{ N},$$

$$\alpha_1 = 20°,$$

$$\alpha_2 = 30°$$

Components of weights W_1 and W_2 along respective planes are : W_1 sin α_1 and W_2 sin α_2.

If W_1 moves downwards along the smooth plane with acceleration a and having tension T in the string them equations of motion for the two weights are as follows :

$$W_1 \sin\alpha_1 - T = m_1 a = \frac{W_1}{g} a \qquad \text{...(i)}$$

$$T - W_2 \sin\alpha_2 = m_2 a = \frac{W_2}{g} a \qquad \text{...(ii)}$$

Adding expressions (i) and (ii)

$$W_1 \sin\alpha_1 - W_2 \sin\alpha_2 = \frac{a}{g}(W_1 + W_2)$$

∴ Acceleration of the system

$$a = \frac{g(W_1 \sin\alpha_1 - W_2 \sin\alpha_2)}{W_1 + W_2}$$

$$= \frac{9.80(100 \sin 20^0 - 60 \sin 30^0)}{100 + 60}$$

∴

$$a = \frac{9.8(100 \times 0.342 - 60 \times 0.5)}{160}$$

$$= 0.2573\ m/\sec^2 \textbf{ Ans.}$$

From expression (i), Tension in the string

$$T = W_1 \sin\alpha_1 - \frac{W_1}{g} a$$

$$= 100 \sin 20° - \frac{100}{9.8} \times 0.2573 = 31.58\ N$$

Pressure on the pulley,

$$P = 2t \sin\frac{\alpha_1 + \alpha_2}{2}$$

$$P = 2T \sin\frac{20 + 30}{2}$$

$$= 2 \times 31.58 \sin 25$$

$$= 26.69 N \textbf{ Ans.}$$

IMPULSE

We know that product of mass and velocity (*mv*) is called momentum of the body, therefore

mu = Momentum of the body at the beginning, and

mv = Momentum of the body at the end of time *t*.

Thus, "The change in linear momentum per unit time is proportional to the impressed force and takes place in the direction of force".

Further,

$$F \times t = mv - mu$$

The product of force and the time during which its acts ($F \times t$) is called the impulse of force. Thus the impulse equals the change in momentum.

Moment and impulse are vector quantities with units kg-m/sec or Ns

The concept of impulse is useful in solving problems when a large force acts for a very short time, e.g., sudden blow of hammer striking a nail.

EXAMPLE 7.18. A cricket ball of mass 175 gm is moving with a speed of 36 km/hr. What average force will be required to stop the ball in 0.2 second.

SOLUTION : Initial speed of ball,

$$u = 36\ km/hr$$

$$= \frac{36 \times 1000}{3600} = 10 \text{ m/sec.}$$

From the impulse moment relation,

$$F \times t = m(v - u),$$

$$F \times 0.2 = \frac{175}{1000}(0 - 10)$$

$\therefore$ $$F = -8.75 \text{ N } \textbf{Ans.}$$

The negative sign indicates that the force F to be applied in a direction opposite to that in which the ball was moving.

EXAMPLE 7.19. A machine gun fires 180 bullets per minute. Each bullet has a mass of 50 gm and muzzle velocity of the bullet is 600 m/sec. Presuming the firing to be continuous, make calculations for the average reaction of the gun against the support.

SOLUTION : Time taken in firing one bullet,

$$t = \frac{60}{180} = 0.333s$$

From the impulse – Moment relation

$$F \times t = m(v - u),$$

or $$F \times 0.333 = \frac{50}{1000}(0 - 600)$$

$\therefore$ $$F = -90.1 \text{ N } \textbf{Ans.}$$

The negative sign indicates that this is the reaction of the gun on the bullet. The average reaction of the gun against the support will be numerically equal to it.

EXAMPLE 7.20. A pile hammer of 250 kg mass is made to fall freely on a pile from a height of 6m. If the hammer comes to rest in 0.012 second, determine the change in momentum, impulse and average froce.

SOLUTION : Since the initial velocity $u = 0$, the velocity with which the hammer falls on the pile is,

$$v = \sqrt{2gh} = \sqrt{2 \times 9.8 \times 6}$$

$$= \sqrt{117.6} = 10.84 \ m/\text{sec}.$$

$$\text{Change in Momentum} = \text{mass change in velocity}$$

$$= m(v - u)$$

$$= 250(10.84 - 0)$$

$$= 2710 \ Ns \ \textbf{Ans.}$$

As Impulse equals the change in Momentum

Hence Impulse = 2710 Ns **Ans.**

Further, Impulse represents the product of force and time during which it acts. Then,

$$F \times t = 2710$$

or

$$F(0.012) = 2710$$

Hence average force

$$F = \frac{2710}{0.012}$$

$$= 225.83 \ N \ \textbf{Ans.}$$

EXAMPLE 7.21. A glass marble whose weight is 0.2 N falls from a height of 12 m and rebounds to a height of 9m. The marble and the floor remain in contact for 0.2 second. Determine the Impulse and the average force between the marble and the floor.

SOLUTION : Velocity with which the marble strikes the floor

$$\sqrt{2gh} = \sqrt{2 \times 9.80 \times 12}$$

$$= \sqrt{235.2}$$

$$= 15.34 \text{ m/s (downwards)}$$

$$\text{velocity of rebound} = \sqrt{2 \times 9.8 \times 9}$$

$$= \sqrt{176.4}$$

$$= 13.28 \text{ m/s(upward)}$$

Impulse = Change in momentum = Change in velocity × Mass

$$= \frac{0.2}{9.8}(13.28 - (-15.34)) = 0.584 \ Ns$$

Since Impulse represents the product of force and the time during which it acts. Hence,

$$F \times t = 0.5841$$

or
$$F(0.2) = 0.5841$$

$\therefore$ Average force,
$$F = \frac{0.5841}{0.2}$$

$$= 2.92\ N\ \textbf{Ans.}$$

EXAMPLE 7.22. A hammer of mass 200 kg is made to fall freely from 2m height on the head of a pile of 1500 kg mass. The pile is driven 5 cm into the ground in one blow. Determine

(a) The common velocity of the pile and hammer after the impact

(b) Energy lost in impact, and

(c) The average resistance of the ground to penetration.

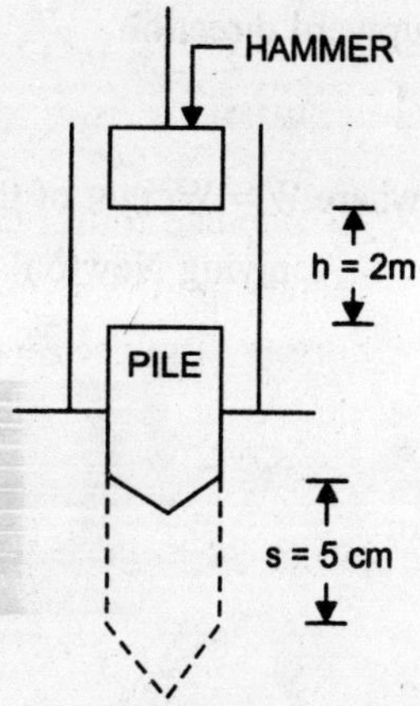

Fig. 7.22

SOLUTON : Let v be the velocity of the hammer when it reaches the pile. Then using the kinematic relation,

$$v^2 = u^2 + 2gh$$

$$v^2 - 0^2 = 2 \times 9.8 \times 2 = 39.2$$

$\therefore$
$$v = \sqrt{39.2} = 6.26\ \text{m/s}$$

Let v be the common velocity of total mass $(M + m)$ in motion after the impact. Then from the principle of conservation of momentum.

Momentum before impact = Momentum after impact

$$mv = (M + m)V$$

or
$$200 \times 6.26 = (1500 + 200)V = 1700V$$

$\therefore$
$$V = \frac{200(6.26)}{1700} = 0.736\ \text{m/sec.}\ \textbf{Ans.}$$

(b) Kinetic energy before Impact $= \frac{1}{2}mv^2$

$$= \frac{1}{2} \times 200(6.25)^2 = 3918.76\ \text{Nm}$$

Kinetic energy after impact $= \frac{1}{2}(M + m)V^2$

$$= \frac{1}{2}(1500 + 200)(0.736)^2 = 460.44\ \text{Nm}$$

$\therefore$ Loss in kinetic energy at impact $= 3918.76 - 460.44$

$= 3458.32$ Nm **Ans.**

(c) After penetration in the ground, the velocity of the system (pile + hammer) becomes zero. Hence using the kinematic relation $v^2 = u^2 + 2as,$ we have

$$0^2 - (0.736)^2 = 2a(0.05)$$

$$\therefore \quad a = 5.417\ m/\text{sec}^2 \text{ (Retardation)}$$

Let F_R be the average resistance exerted by the ground. Then net force acting on the system in upward direction

$$F_n = R_R - W,$$

where W = Weight of the hammer and pile.

Applying Newton's second law of motion,

$$F = ma$$

$$F_R - (1500 + 200)9.8 = (1500 + 200) \times 5.417$$

or

$$F_R - 1700(9.8) = 1700(5.417)$$

$$\therefore \quad F_R = 9208.9 + 16660$$

$$= 25868.9\ N \textbf{ Ans.}$$

EXAMPLE 7.23. A wooden block of weight 40N rests on a rough horizontal plane having friction coefficient μ = 0.35. The block is struck by a bullet travelling horizontally with a velocity of 750 m/sec and weighing 0.25 N. Workout the distance by which the block is displaced from its initial position.

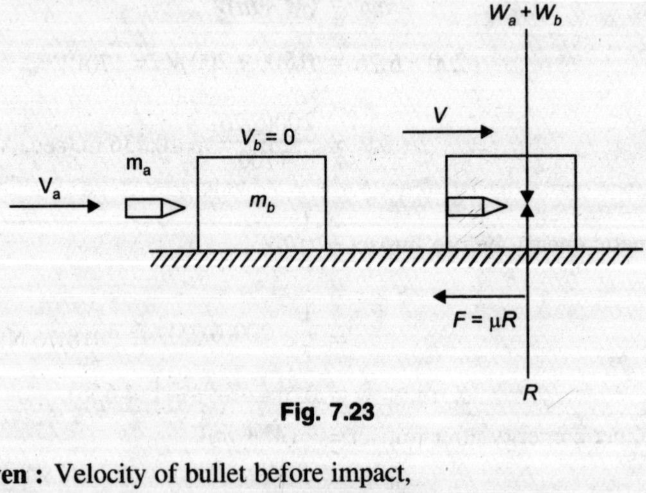

Fig. 7.23

SOLUTION : Given : Velocity of bullet before impact,

$$V_a = 750 \text{ m/s}$$

Velocity of block before impact,

$$V_b = 0$$

Mass of the bullet

$$m_a = \frac{0.25}{g} kg$$

Mass of the block,

$$m_b = \frac{40}{g} kg$$

Let us assume that the bullet after striking the block remains burried in the block and both move with a common velocity *v*.

Applying the principle of conservation of momentum,

Momentum before impact = Momentum after impact

$$m_a v_a + m_b V_b = (m_a + m_b)V$$

$$\frac{0.25}{9.8} \times 750 + \frac{40}{9.8} \times 0 = \left(\frac{0.25 + 40}{9.8}\right) V$$

or $$0.25 \times 750 = 40.25V$$

or $$\frac{0.25(750)}{40.25} = V$$

$$= \frac{187.5}{40} = 4.658 \text{ m/sec}$$

Normal reaction,

$$R = W_a + W_b$$

$$= 40 + 0.25 = 40.25N$$

Force of friction

$$F = \mu R = 0.35(40.25) = 14.088N$$

To find the distance travelled by the block apply the principle of work and energy.

Work done to over come the frictional force = Kinetic energy lost by the block with bullet embedded.

$$F \times s = \frac{1}{2}(m_a + m_b)V^2$$

or $$14.088s = 0.5\left(\frac{0.25 + 40}{9.8}\right)(4.658)^2$$

or $$14.088s = 44.556$$

∴ $$s = 3.163m \textbf{ Ans.}$$

CONSERVATION OF MOMENTUM

In a system, if the resultant force R is zero, the impulse moment equation (impulse = final momentum – initial momentum) reduces to final momentum = Initial momentum. The resultant force is zero, only when entire system is considered. When a person jumps off a boot, the action of a person is equal and opposite to the reaction of the boat. Hence the resultant force is zero in the system. If W_1 is the weight of a person and W_2 that of the boat, v is the velocity of the person and the boat before the person jumps out of the boat and v_1, v_2 are the velocities of person and the boat after jumping, then according to principle of conservation of momentum,

$$\frac{w_1 + w_2}{g} v = \frac{w_1}{g} v_1 + \frac{w_2}{g} v_2$$

or

$$(m_1 + m_2)v = m_1 v_1 + m_2 v_2$$

Similar equation holds good when we consider the system of a gun and a shell. Hence the principle of conservation of momentum may be stated as, the momentum is conserved in a system in which resultant force is zero. In other words, in a system if the resultant force is zero, Initial momentum will remain equal to final momentum. The conservation of momentum applies to entire system and not to individual elements of the system.

EXAMPLE 7.24. A 800 N man, moving horizontally with a velocity of 3 m/sec, jumps off the end of a pier into a 3200 N boat. Determine the horizontal velocity of the boat :

(a) If it had no velocity, and

(b) If it was approaching the pier with an initial velocity of 0.9 m/sec.

SOLUTION : WEIGHT OF THE MAN, $w_1 = 800$ N

Velocity with which the man is running, $v = 3$ m/sec

Weight of the system after the man jumps into boat = 800 + 3200 = 4000 N

(a) WHEN INITIAL VELOCITY OF THE BOAT = 0 :

Since the action of the man is equal to the reaction of the boat, the principle of conservation of momentum can be applied to the system consisting of man and boat.

$\because$ Iniital momentum = Final momentum

$$\therefore \quad \frac{800}{9.81}(3) + \frac{3200}{9.81}(0) = \frac{4000}{9.81}(v)$$

$$\therefore \quad v = 0.6 \text{ m/sec} \textbf{ Ans.}$$

(b) WHEN INITIAL VELOCITY OF THE BOAT

$= 0.9$ m/sec towards the pier

$= -0.9$ m/sec.

Now applying principle of conservation of momentum, we get,

$$\frac{800}{9.81}(3) + \frac{3200}{9.81}(-0.9) = \frac{4000}{9.81}(v)$$

$$\therefore \quad v = -0.12 \text{ m/sec} \textbf{ Ans.}$$

i.e velocity of boat and man will be 0.12 m/sec towards pier **Ans.**

EXAMPLE 7.25. A body of mass 10 kg is suspended by a string of length 1 m. It is struck by a bullet travelling horizontally with a velocity of 450 m/sec. The bullet weighs 30 gm and get embedded into the body after striking it. Determine the maximum angle through which the body swings.

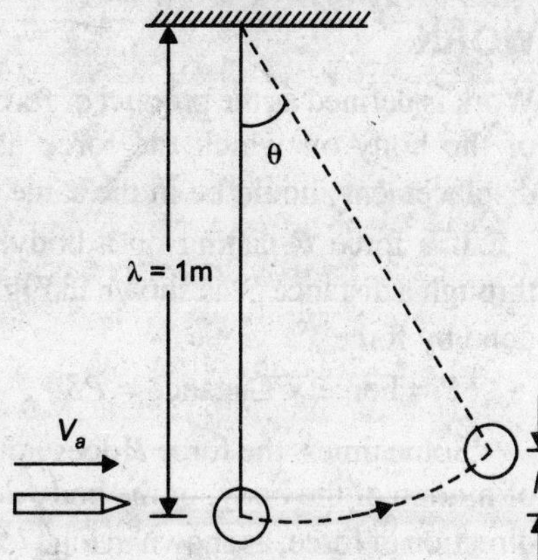

Fig. 7.24

SOLUTION : Refer Fig.7.24 which shows the given system with various parameters inserted.

Aplplying the principle of conservation of momentum

Momentum before Impact = Momentum after impact.

$$m_a V_a + m_b V_b = (m_a + m_b)V$$

Where V is the common velocity of the body and the bullet together after impact.

$$\therefore \quad \frac{30}{1000}(450) + 10(0) = \left(\frac{30}{1000} + 10\right)V$$

or $$13.50 = 10.0\,3V$$

$$\therefore \quad V = 1.3456 \text{ m/sec}$$

Now applying the principle of conservation of energy,

Loss of kinetic energy = Gain in potential energy

or $$\frac{1}{2}(m_a + m_b)V^2 = (m_a + m_b)gh$$

where h is the height to which the body rises.

or $$h = \frac{V^2}{2g}$$

$$= \frac{(1.346)^2}{2 \times 9.81} = 0.0923\ m$$

From Fig. 7.19,

$$\cos\theta = \frac{\text{base}}{\text{diagonal}}$$

$$= \frac{\ell - h}{\ell} = \frac{1 - h}{1}$$

or $$\cos\theta = 1 - 0.0923 = 0.9077$$

$$\therefore \quad \theta = \cos^{-1}(0.9077)$$

$$= 24.81° \ \textbf{Ans.}$$

WORK

Work is defined as the product of force and displacement of the body on which the force acts. The force and displacement should be in the same direction.

If a force P, acting on a body, causes to move it through a distance S, as shown in Fig. 7.25(a), then work done by force

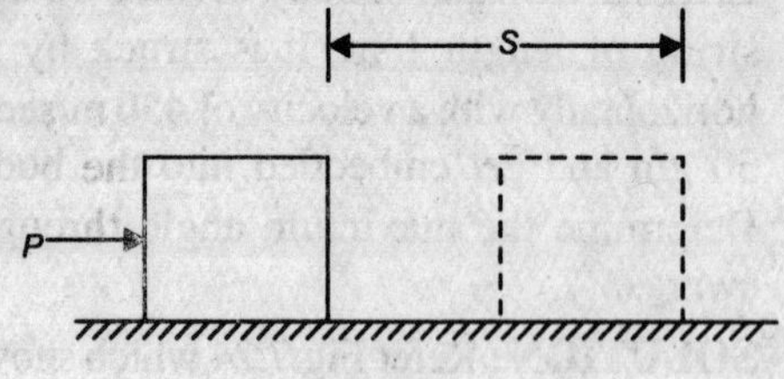

Fig. 7.25(a)

$$P = \text{Force} \times \text{Distance} = PS \qquad ...(i)$$

Some times, the force P does not act in the direction of motion of the body, or the body does not move in the direction of force, as shown in Fig. 7.25(b), then the work done on the body is given by :

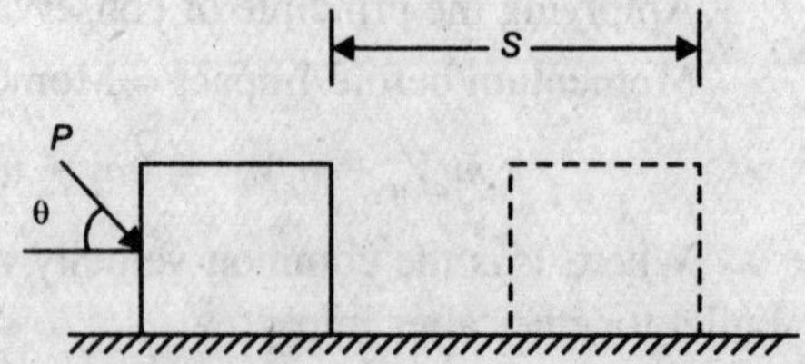

Fig. 7.25(b)

Work done = Component of the force in the direction of motion × Distance

$$P\cos\theta \times S = PS\cos\theta \qquad ...(ii)$$

Where, θ is the angle mae by the force with the direction of motion.

If $\theta = 90^0$, $\cos\theta = 0$, and hence work done will be zero. Hence, if the force and displacement are at right angle, then work done will be zero.

UNITS OF WORK

As work is the product of force and distance and in S.I. system, force is expressed in Newton (N), whereas the distance is expressed in metre (m), hence the unit of work is N – m.

The work done by a force of 1N on a body which moves a distance of 1 m, is called 1 N-m. This is also known as 1 Joule (J). Hence one N-m (1 Jolule) is the work done by a force of one Newton (1 N) on a body whose displacement is 1 m.

One kN-m is the work done by a force of 1 kN when it displaces the body through 1 m. It is also called kilo Joule (kJ). Mathematically

1 Joule = 1 N-m, and 1 Kilo Joule = kN - m.

EXAMPLE 7.26. A horse pulling a cart exerts a steady horizontal pull of 400 N and runs at the rate fo 6 km p.h. How much work is done by the horse in 5 minutes?

SOLUTION : Given :

$$P = 400\ N,$$
$$v = 6 \text{ km.p.h.} = 100 \text{ m/min},$$
$$t = 5 \text{ min.}$$

We know that distance travelled in 5 minutes

= speed × time

= 100 × 5 = 500 m ...(i)

and work done by the horse = Force × Distance

= 400 × 500

= 200 kN-m = 200 KJ **Ans.**

EXAMPLE 7.27. A spring is stretched by 50 mm by application of a force. Find the work done, if the force required to stretch 1 mm of the spring is 10 N.

SOLUTION : Given : Distance, $S = 50$ mm

We know that maximum force required to stretch the spring by 50 mm

$$= 10 \times 50$$
$$= 500 \text{ N}$$

$\therefore$ Average Force,

$$P = \frac{500}{2}$$
$$= 250 \text{ N}$$

and Work done,

$$W = \text{Average Force} \times \text{Distance}$$
$$= 250 \times 50$$
$$= 12500 \text{ N-mm}$$
$$= 12.5 \text{ N-m}$$
$$= 12.5 \text{ J } \textbf{Ans.}$$

WORK DONE BY A TORQUE

Fig. 7.26 shows a circular body, which can rotate about the point A. A tangential force P is applied at point B and the body moves through a small angle θ. Let R = Radius.

Now the distance moved by the force P in rotating the body through an angle θ is equal to the length of arc BC.

But length of arc $BC = R\theta$

As the body has moved a distance $R\theta$, the work will be done by the force on the body.

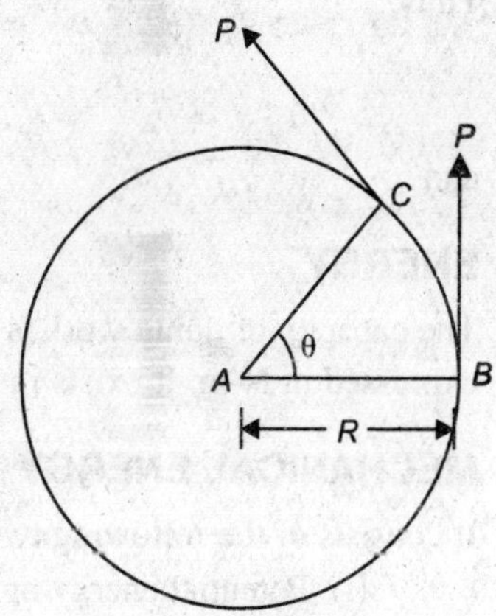

Fig. 7.26

$\therefore$ Work done $=$ Force $\times$ Distance moved

$$= P \times R \times \theta$$
$$= (P \times R)\theta$$

But $P \times R$ is equal to torque (T)

$$\therefore \quad \text{Work Done} = T \times \theta \quad \text{...(i)}$$

In this equation, θ should be taken in radians.

POWER DEVELOPED BY A TORQUE

Let, T = Torque, N = *R.P.M.* (Revolutions per minute)

Consider a body acted upon by a torque (T) and rotating at N r.p.m.

Now angle turned in one revolution $= 2\pi = 360°$

$\therefore$ Angle turned in N revolutions $= 2\pi N$

But N revolutions are performed in one minute.

$\therefore$ Angle turned in one minute = $2\pi N$

or Angle turned in one second = $\frac{2\pi N}{60}$

Now using the equation, work done = $T\theta$, we get,

Work done per second = $T \times$ Angle Turned in one second

$$= T \times \frac{2\pi N}{60} \text{ N m/sec}$$

But, Power = Work done per second $= T \times \frac{2\pi N}{60}$

$$= \frac{2\pi NT}{60} W \qquad ...(ii)$$

Hence Power is the rate of doing work and is obtained by dividing the work done by time. The unit of power is Watt (*W*), Kilowatt (kW) or Mega watt (*MW*). Watt represents a work equivalent of one Joule done per second.

$\therefore$ Power = Work done per unit time = J/sec.

Thus,

$$1W = 1 \text{ J/sec}$$
$$= 1 \text{ N–m/sec}$$
$$1 \text{ kW} = 10^3 \text{ W}$$

and

$$1 \text{ MW} = 10^6 \text{ W}$$

ENERGY

The capacity of doing work is known as energy. It is the product of power and time. The energy is expressed in N-m. It exists in many forms i.e., Mechanical, Electrical, Heat, Chemical, Light etc.

MECHANICAL ENERGY

It consists of the following two types :

(i) Potential energy or position energy or datum energy.

(ii) Kinetic energy

Depending upon the state of rest or that of motion, a body may possess any one or both of the above energies.

POTENTIAL ENERGY : It is also known as position energy or datum energy. It is the energy by virtue of position of a body with respect to any given reference or datum. A weight W lying on the top of a tower of height h possesses a potential energy of $W \times h$ with respect to the ground as the weight W is capable of doing $W \times h$ work if it falls on the ground.

A compressed spring has potential energy, because it can do work in recovering its original shape. Similarly, compressed air also possesses potential energy because it is capable of doing work when allowed to expand.

KINETIC ENERGY : The energy possessed by a body by virtue of its velocity or its motion is known as kinetic energy. It is represented by K.E.

The expression for kinetic energy is derived as follows :

Consider a body of mass m starting from rest.

Let it be subjected to an accelerating force F and after covering a distance S, its velocity becomes v.

$\therefore$ Initial velocity, $u = 0$

Now work done on the body = Force × Distance = FS ...(iii)

But Force = Mass × Acceleration

$$\therefore \quad F = m \times a$$

Substituting the value of F in equation (iii)

$$\text{Work done} = m \times a \times S = M\,(a \times S) \quad \text{...(iv)}$$

But from the equation of motion, we have

$$v^2 - u^2 = 2a \times S$$

or $$v^2 - 0^2 = 2a \times S \quad (\because u = 0)$$

or $$a \times S = \frac{v^2}{2}$$

Substituting the value of $a \times S$ in equation (iii)

$$\text{Work done} = m \times \frac{v^2}{2}$$

But work done on the body is equal to K.E. possessed by the body.

$$\therefore \quad K.E. = \frac{1}{2} m v^2 N - m \text{ (or Joule)}$$

WORK DONE IS EQUAL TO CHANGE IN KINETIC ENERGY : We know that,

$$P = m \times a \quad \text{...(iv)}$$

Where,

P = Resultant of all forces acting on a body,

m = Mass of the body, and

a = Acceleration in the direction of resultant force, $= v\dfrac{dv}{ds}$

Substituting the value of a in equation (iv), we get

$$P = m\left(v\frac{dv}{ds}\right)$$

or $$P \cdot ds = m \times v\, dv \quad \text{...(v)}$$

But $P \cdot ds$ is the work done by the resultant force P in displacing the body by small distance ds. The total work done by the resultant force P in displacing the body by a distance S is obtained by integrating the above equation (v). Hence integrating equation (ii) on both sides, we get,

$$\int_0^S P \cdot ds = \int_u^v m \times v \times dv$$

Where u is the initial velocity when distance is zero and v is the final velocity when distance is S.

$$\therefore \qquad P \cdot S = m \cdot \left[\frac{v^2}{2}\right]_u^v = \frac{m}{2}[v^2 - u^2]$$

$$= \frac{mv^2}{2} - \frac{mu^2}{2} \qquad ...(vi)$$

or Work done by resultant force = Change in kinetic energy

EXAMPLE 7.28. A man of mass 60 kg jumps in a swimming pool from a tower of height 20 m. He was found to go down in water by 2 m and then started rising. Find the average resistance of the water.

SOLUTION : Given :

Mass of man, $m = 60$ kg, Tower height, $h = 20$ m

Let P = Average resistance of the water in Newtons.

We know that potential energy of the man before jumping

$$= mgh = 60 \times 9.81 \times 20$$

$$= 11772 \; N-m. \qquad (i)$$

Work done by the average resitance of water

$$= P \times 2 = 2P \; N-m \qquad ...(ii)$$

Since the entire potential energy of the man is used in the work done by the water, therefore, equating (i) and (ii), we have,

$$11772 = 2P$$

$$\therefore \qquad P = \frac{11772}{2}$$

$$= 5886 \; N \; \textbf{Ans.}$$

EXAMPLE 7.29. A bullet of mass 80 gm and moving with a velocity of 300 m/sec is fired into a block of wood and it penetrates to a depth of 10 cm. If the bullet moving with the same velocity, was fired into a similar piece of wood 5 cm thick, with what velocity would it emerge? Find also the force of resistance assuming it to be uniform.

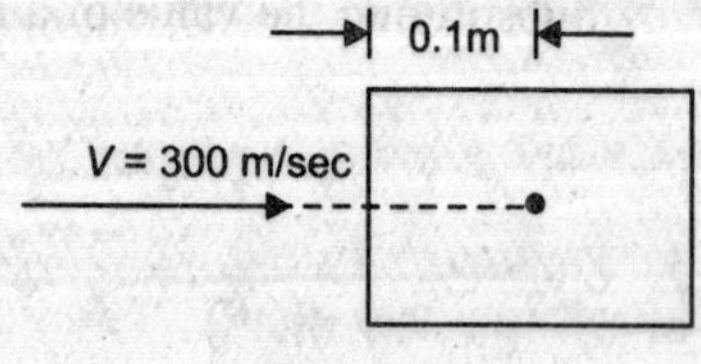

Fig. 7.27

SOLUTION : Given: (Refer Fig. 7.27)

Mass of the bullet, $m = 80$ gm $= 0.08$ kg,

Initial velocity of bullet, $u = 300$ m/sec

FIRST CASE : Penetration of the bullet, $S = 10$ cm $= 0.1\ m$

Final velocity of the bullet, $v = 0$

Let,

P = Force of resistance in Newton

The force of resistance will be acting in the opposite direction of motion of bullet.

The work done by the force of resistance = Force of resistance × Depth of penetration

$$= (-P)S = (-P)0.1$$

$$= 0.1P \quad \text{...(i)}$$

(–ve sign is due to opposite direction of force)

Change in K.E. of bullet $= \frac{1}{2}mv^2 - \frac{1}{2}mu^2$

$$= 0 - \frac{1}{2} \times 0.08 \times 300^2$$

$$= -3600 N - m \quad \text{...(ii)}$$

But change of K.E. of the bullet is equal to work done

∴ Change of K.E. of bullet = Work done by force of resistance

∴ $$-3600 = -0.1\ P$$

∴ $$P = \frac{3600}{0.1} = 36000\ N \textbf{ Ans.}$$

SECOND CASE : Velocity of bullet after 5 cm penetration

The force of resistance will be same i.e., $P = 36000\ N$

Now depth of penetration,

$$S = 5\text{cm} = 0.05\ m$$

∴ Work done by the resistance

$$= -P \times S = -36000 \times 0.05$$

$$= -1800\ N - m$$

(–ve sign is due to opposite direction of force)

Let,

v_1 = Velocity of bullet after 5 cm penetration.

∴ Change of K.E. of bullet after penetration

$$= \frac{1}{2}mv_1^2 - \frac{1}{2}mu^2$$

$$= \frac{1}{2} \times 0.08 \times v_1^2 - \frac{1}{2} \times 0.08 \times 300^2$$

$(\because \mu = 300\ m/\text{sec})$

But change in K.E. is equal to work done

$$\therefore \quad \frac{1}{2}\times 0.08(v_1^2)-\frac{1}{2}\times 0.08(300)^2 = -1800$$

or $$0.04v_1^2 - 3600 + 1800 = 0$$

or $$0.04v_1^2 = 1800$$

or $$v_1^2 = \frac{1800}{0.04} = 45000$$

$$\therefore \quad v_1 = (45000)^{1/2}$$

$$= 212.132\, m/\text{sec} \textbf{ Ans.}$$

LAW OF CONSERVATION OF ENERGY

It states that the energy can neither be created nor destroyed though it can be transformed from one form to another form. The second statement of this laws is :

"The total energy possessed by a body remains constant provided no energy is added to or taken from it".

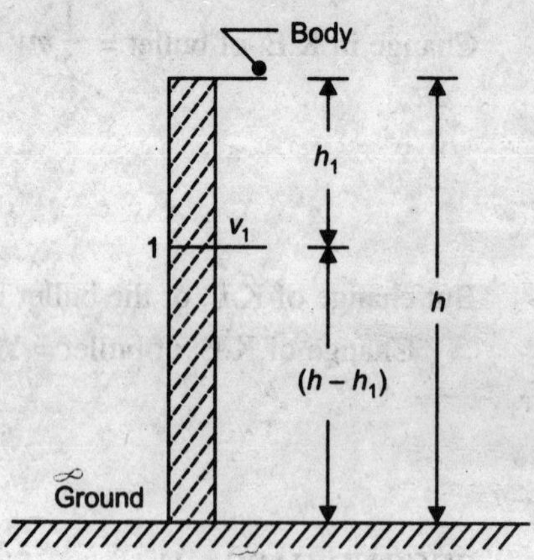

Fig. 7.28

Fig. 7.28 shows a body resting on the top of a tower.

Let,

W = Weight of body

m = Mass of body = $\frac{W}{g}$

h = Height of the tower

Let us find the potential energy and kinetic energy of the body at the top of tower

Potential energy of the body with respect to ground = Wh ...(i)

K.E. of the body

$$= \frac{1}{2}mv^2 = 0 \qquad (\because v = 0)$$

$\therefore$ Total energy at the top of tower = Potential Energy + K.E.

$$= Wh + O = Wh$$

Suppose the body falls down by a height h_1 to the position 1 as shown in Fig. 7.28. Let v_1 is the velocity at position 1.

Using equation $v^2 - u^2 = 2gh$, we get

$$v_1^2 - 0^2 = 2gh_1 \qquad (\because u = 0, h = h_1)$$

or $$v_1^2 = 2gh_1$$

$\therefore$ K.E. of the body at position 1

$$= \frac{1}{2}mv_1^2 = \frac{1}{2}m(2gh_1)$$

$$= mgh_1 = Wh_1 \qquad ...(i)$$

$$(\because W = mg)$$

Potential energy at position 1,

= $W \times$ Height of body at 1 with reference to ground

$$= W(h - h_1) \qquad ...(ii)$$

$\therefore$ Total Energy at position 1

= Potential energy + Kinetic energy

$$= W(h - h_1) + Wh_1$$

$$= Wh - Wh_1 + Wh_1 = Wh \qquad ...(iii)$$

And it is the same energy, the body was possessing at the top of the tower.

Similarly it can be proved that total energy of the body on the ground will be equal to '*Wh*'.

EXAMPLE 7.30. A train of mass 500×10^3 kg starts from rest and accelerates uniformly to a speed of 90 km per hour in 50 seconds. The total frictional resistance to motion is 15 kN. Determine

(a) Maximum power required,

(b) The power required to maintain the speed of 90 km/hour.

SOLUTION : Initial velocity of the train, $u = 0$

Final velocity of the train, v = 90 Km/hour = 25 m/sec

Time taken = 50 seconds

Using the relation, $v = u + at$

$$a = \frac{v - u}{t} = \frac{25 - 0}{50}$$

$$= 0.5\, m/\sec^2$$

Force required to accelerate the train = Mass × Acceleration of the train

$$= 500 \times 10^3 \times 0.5$$

$$= 250 \times 10^3 \text{ N}$$

Frictional force present = 15×10^3 N

Total force required = Force required to over come friction + Force required to accelerate the train

$$= 15 \times 10^3 + 250 \times 10^3$$

$$= 265 \times 10^3 \text{ N}$$

(a) Maximum power required at

t = 50 sec;

v = 25 m/sec

$\therefore$ $$\text{Max. Power} = F \times v$$
$$= 265 \times 10^3 \times 25$$
$$= 6.625 \text{ MW } \textbf{Ans.}$$

(b) At any time after 50 seconds, the force required only to overcome the frictional resistance of 15×10^3N

$\therefore$ $$\text{Power required} = Fv = 15 \times 10^3 \times 25$$
$$= 375 \text{ kW } \textbf{Ans.}$$

EXAMPLE 7.31. A truck weighing 20 KN is travelling at 45 km/hr on a level road.It is brought to rest in 20 metre, what is the average force of resistance acting on the truck?

SOLUTION : Given : Weight of the truck,

$$W = 20\ KN$$
$$= 20 \times 10^3\ N$$

Speed of the truck, u = 45 km/hour = 12.5 m/sec

$\therefore$ Initial velocity of the truck, u = 12.5 m/sec

Final velocity of th truck, $v = 0$

$$\text{Change in K.E. of the truck} = \frac{1}{2}mv^2 - \frac{1}{2}mu^2$$
$$= 0 - \frac{1}{2}mu^2$$
$$= -\frac{1}{2}\left(\frac{W}{g}\right)u^2$$
$$= -\frac{1}{2}\left(\frac{20000}{9.81}\right)(12.5)^2$$
$$= -159.2761 \times 10^3\ Nm \qquad \text{...(i)}$$

The truck is brought to rest, in a distance of 20 m

$\therefore$ Distance travelled = 20m

Let,

P = Average force of resistance which is acting in the opposite direction of motion

Work done by force of resistance = $(-P) \times$ Distance

$$= -P\,(20) = -20\,P \qquad \text{...(ii)}$$

But work done is equal to change in K.E.

$\therefore$ Equating the equations (i) and ii),

$$-20P = -159.276 \times 10^3$$

$\therefore$ $$P = \frac{159276}{20} = 7963.8\ N\ \textbf{Ans.}$$

EXAMPLE 7.32. A bullet of mass 10 gm is fired into a body of mass 1 kg, which is suspended by a string 1m long. The bullet gets embedded in the body and due to the impact, the body swings through an angle of 18.2°. Find the velocity of the bullet.

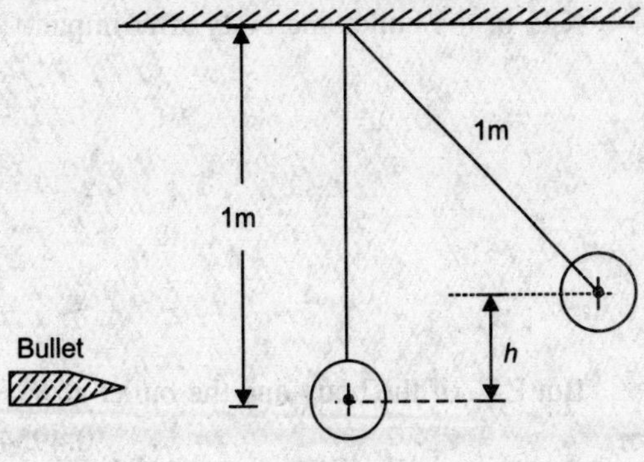

Fig. 7.29

SOLUTION : Given : Mass of bullet 10 gm = 0.01 kg (Refer Fig. 7.29)

Mass of body M = 1 kg, Length of string, L = 1 m, Angle of swing $\theta = 18.2°$

Let,

u = Velocity of bullet

V = Common velocity of bullet and body.

Initial velocity of body = 0

The moment of the bullet and body before impact $= m \times u + M \times$ Initial velocity of the body

$$= 0.01u + 1(0)$$

$$= 0.01u \; kgm/\text{sec} \qquad \text{...(i)}$$

Bullet gets embedded in the body and both of them move together with common velocity.

The momentum of bullet and body after impact

$$= (M+m)V = (1+0.01)V$$

$$= 1.01V kgm/\text{sec} \qquad \text{...(ii)}$$

Equating (i) and (ii), we get,

$$0.01u = 1.01V \qquad \text{...(iii)}$$

Now let us apply the law of conservation of energy.

The potential energy of the body and bullet at B = K.E. of body and bullet after impact.

Let us first find the height 'h' to which the body with bullet rises after impact.

$$\because \quad \cos\theta = \frac{\text{base}}{\text{diagonal}} = \frac{1-h}{1}$$

or $$1 - h = 1\cos\theta$$

or $$-h = 1\cos\theta - 1$$

$$\therefore \quad h = 1 - 1\cos\theta = 1 - 1(\cos 18.2°)$$

$$\therefore \quad h = 1 - 0.94997 = 0.05\ m$$

The potential energy of the body and bullet at B = Total weight of the bullet and body × h

$$= [(M+m)g]h$$

$$= (1+0.01)(9.81)(0.05)$$

$$= 0.4954\ Nm \qquad \text{...(iv)}$$

K.E. of the bullet and body after impact

$$= \frac{1}{2}(M+m)V^2$$

$$= \frac{1}{2}(1+0.01)V^2$$

$$= 0.505V^2 \qquad ...(v)$$

But P.E. of the body and the bullet at B = *K.E.* of the body and bullet after impact

or $$0.4954 = 0.505\ V^2$$

or $$V^2 = \frac{0.4954}{0.505} = 0.98099$$

$\therefore$ $$V = \sqrt{0.98099}$$

$$= 0.990449\ m/sec$$

Substituting this value in equation (iii), we get

$$0.01u = 1.01\ V$$

or $$0.01u = 1.01\ (0.98099)$$

$$= 1.00035$$

$\therefore$ $$u = \frac{1.00035}{0.01} = 100 \text{ m/sec } \textbf{Ans.}$$

EXAMPLE 7.33. A bullet of mass 10 gm moving with a velocity of 100 m/sec hits a 1 kg bob of a simple pendulum horizontally (Fig. 7.30). Find the maximum angle through which the pendulum string 1m long may swing if,

(a) The bullet gets embedded in the bob,

(b) The bullet rebounds from the surface of the bob with a velocity of 20 m/sec, and

(c) The bullet escapes from the other end of the bob with a velocity of 20 m/sec (2004).

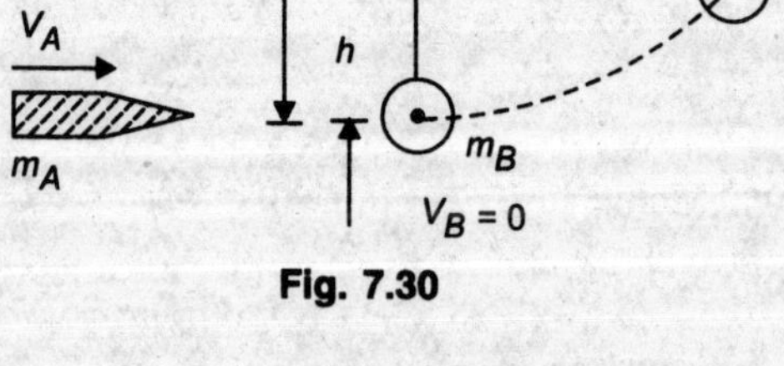

Fig. 7.30

SOLUTION : Given :

$$m_a = 10 \text{ gm} = 0.01 \text{ kg},$$
$$V_a = 100 \text{ m/sec},$$
$$m_b = 1 \text{ kg},$$
$$V_b = 0$$

Momentum of the bullet and the bob before impact,

$$m_a v_a + m_a v_b = 0.01 \times 100 + 0$$

$$= 1\ kg\ m/sec \qquad ...(i)$$

(a) BULLET GETS EMBEDDED IN THE BOB : Let the common velocity be v'.

Momentum after impact of the bullet and bob

$$= m_a v' + m_b v'$$

$$= (0.01 + 1)v' = 1.01v' \qquad \text{...(ii)}$$

As the momentum is conserved, equating (i) and (ii)

$$1 = 1.01v'$$

$$\therefore \qquad v' = \frac{1}{1.01} = 0.99\, m/\text{sec} \qquad \text{...(iii)}$$

Applying the principle of conservation of energy, the height h to whcih bob rises is given by

$$\underset{(K.E.)}{\frac{1}{2}(m_a + m_b)(v_1^1)^2} = \underset{(P.E.)}{(m_a + m_b)gh}$$

$$\text{or} \qquad h = \frac{(v')^2}{2g}$$

$$= \frac{1}{2} \times \frac{(0.99)^2}{9.81} = 0.05\, m$$

The angle θ by whcih the bob swings corresponding to the value of $h = 0.05$ m

$$\cos\theta = \frac{\ell - h}{\ell}$$

$$\text{or} \qquad \theta = \cos^{-1}\left(\frac{\ell - h}{\ell}\right)$$

$$= \frac{1 - 0.05}{1.0} = 0.95 = 18.2° \ \textbf{Ans.}$$

(b) Let the velocity of the bullet after rebound be v_a'

$$\therefore \qquad v_a' = -20\, m/\text{sec}$$

Momentum after impact = $m_a v_a' + m_b v_b'$

$$= -0.01 \times 20 + 1(v_b') \qquad \text{...(iv)}$$

Equating (i), and (iv)

$$1 = -0.2 + v_b'$$

$$\text{and} \qquad v_b' = 1.2 \text{ m/sec}$$

The bob after the impact attains a velocity $v_b' = 1.2$ m/sec and will rise to a height that can be determined using the principle of conservation of energy.

$$h = \frac{(v_b')^2}{2g} = \frac{(1.2)^2}{2\times 9.81} = 0.073\ m$$

The corresponding angle of swing, $\theta = \cos^{-1}\left(\frac{1-0.073}{1.0}\right) = 22.09°$ **Ans.**

(c) WHEN THE BULLET PIERCES AND ESCAPES WITH VELOCITY

$$v_a = 20\ m/\text{sec}$$

$$\text{Moment after impact} = m_a v_a' + m_b v_b'$$

$$= 0.01\times 20 + 1\times v_b' \quad \text{...(v)}$$

Equating (i) and (iv)

$$1 = 0.2 + v_b'$$

$$\therefore \quad v_b' = 1 - 0.2 = 0.8\ m/\text{sec}$$

The bob after the impact attains a velocity, $v_b' = 0.8\ m/\text{sec}$ and will rise to a height that can be determined using the principle of conservation of energy,

$$h = \frac{(v_b')^2}{2g}$$

and

$$h = \frac{(0.8)^2}{2\times 9.81} = 0.036\ m$$

The angle of swing, corresponding to the height,

$$\theta = \cos^{-1}\left(\frac{1-0.0326}{1}\right)$$

$$= \cos^{-1}(0.9674) = 14.67°\ \textbf{Ans.}$$

IMPACT OF BODIES

A collision between two bodies is said to be impact, if the bodies are in contact for a short interval of time and exert very large force on each other during this short period. On impact, the bodies deform first and then recover due to elastic properties and start moving with different velocities. Generally the velocities of colliding bodies before impact and afteı impact are considered.

DEFINITIONS :

(i) LINE OF IMPACT : The common normal to the colliding surfaces is known as line of impact.

(ii) DIRECT IMPACT : If the motion of two colliding bodies is directed along the line of impact, the impact is said to be direct impact.

(iii) OBLIQUE IMPACT : If the motion of one or both the colliding bodies is not directed along the line of impact, the impact is known as oblique impact.

(iv) CENTRAL IMPACT : If the mass centres of colliding bodies are on the line of impact, the impact is called central impact.

(v) ECCENTRIC IMPACT : Even if mass centre of one of the colliding bodies is not on the line of impact, the impact is called eccentric impact.

LAW OF CONSERVATION OF MOMENTUM

It states that if the resultant of the external forces acting on a system is zero, the momentum of the system remains constant. This means that the total momentum of the system before collision is equal to the total momentum of the system after collision. The system may consist of one body or two bodies or more.

DIRECT IMPACT OF TWO BODIES

Two bodies A and B are moving in a horizontal line before collision with velocities u_1 and u_2 in the same direction i.e. along x-axis (Fig. 7.31). If u_1 is greater than u_2, the body A will strike the body B and collision will take place. Let C is the point of collision of the two bodies (Fig. 7.32). The point C is also known as the point of contact. The line joining the centres of these two bodies and passing through the point of contact is known as line of impact. Hence the line $O_1 - C - O_2$ is called line of impact.

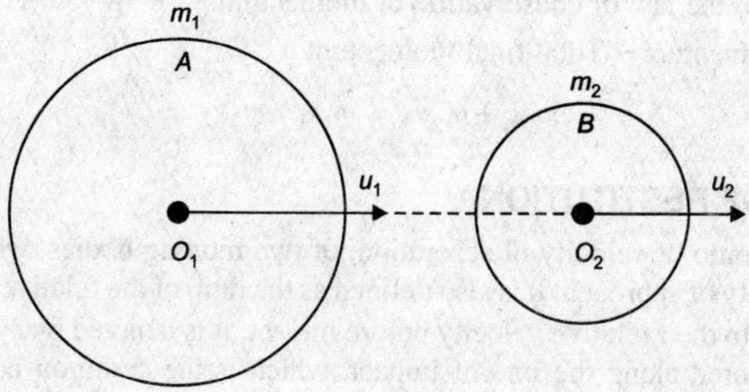

Fig. 7.31

The collision between two bodies is known as direct impact if the two bodies before impact, are moving along the line of impact. The two bodies shown in Fig. 7.31 and 7.32 are having a direct impact.

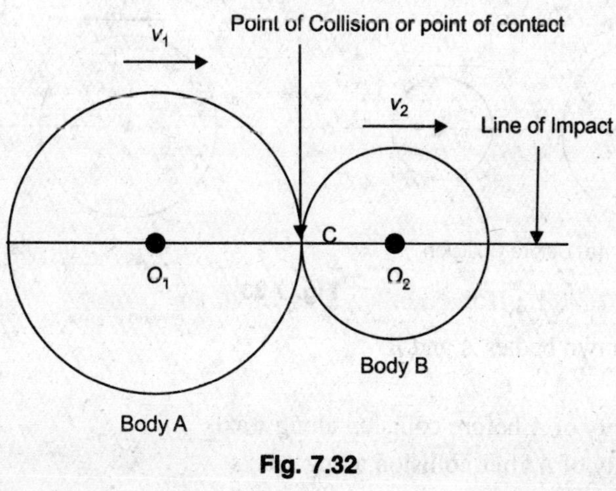

Fig. 7.32

Let,

m_1 = Mass of body A

u_1 = Initial velocity of body A, i.e., the velocity of body A before collision along x-axis.

v_1 = Final velocity of body A (after collision) along x-axis.

m_2, u_2 and v_2 are the mass of body B, velocity of body B before collision and velocity of the body B after collision along x-axis respectively.

The momentum of body A before collision = Mass × Velocity = m_1u_1

The momentum of the body B before collision = m_2u_2

∴ Total initial momentum i.e. momentum before collision

$$= m_1u_1 + m_2u_2 \quad \text{...(i)}$$

Similarly, total final momentum i.e. momentum after collision = Mass of body A × Final velocity of A + Mass of body B × Final velocity of body B

$$m_1v_1 + m_2v_2 \quad \text{...(ii)}$$

But according to the law of conservation of momentum.

Total initial momentum = Total final momentum

$$m_1u_1 + m_2u_2 = m_1v_1 + m_2v_2 \quad \text{...(iii)}$$

COEFFICIENT OF RESTITUTION

It is defined as the ratio of velocity of seperation, of two moving bodies, which collide with each other, to their velocity of approach. It is also defined as the ratio of the relative velocities of colliding bodies after impact to their relative velocity before impact. It is denoted by symbol 'e'. The relative velocities are measured along the line of impact, which is the common normal to the colliding surfaces.

According to Newton's law of collision of elastic bodies, "the velocity of separation, of the two moving bodies which collide with each other, bears a constant ratio to their velocity of approach", and the constant of proportionality is kown as co-efficient of restitution.

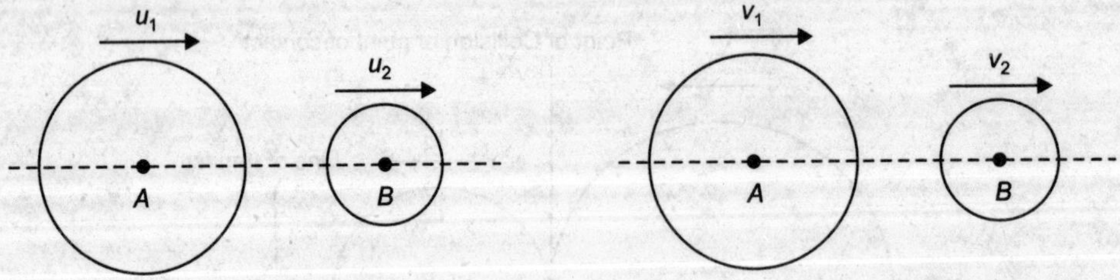

(a) Before Collision (b) After Collision

Fig. 7.33

Fig. 7.33 shows two bodies A and B

Let,

u_1 = Velocity of A before collision along x-axis

v_1 = Velocity of A after collision along x-aixs

u_2 = Velocity of B before collision along x-axis

v_2 = Velocity of B before collision along x-axis'

The body A will collide with body B if the velocity of A is more than that of B. Hence velocity of approach or relative velocity of colliding bodies before impact = Initial velocity of A – Initial velocity of B $= u_1 - u_2$.

After collision, the separation of two bodies will take place if final velocity of B is more than that of A.

Hence velocity of separation or relative velocity of colliding bodies after impact

= Final velocity of B – Final velocity of A = $v_2 - v_1$

Now according to Newton's Law of collision of elastic bodies,

Velocity of separation ∝ Velocity of approach

or $$(v_2 - v_1) \propto u_1 - u_2$$

or $$(v_2 - v_1) = e(u_1 - u_2)$$

Where e is the constant of proportionality and is known as co-efficient of restitution

$$\therefore \quad e = \frac{v_2 - v_1}{u_1 - u_2} \qquad \text{...(.23.1)}$$

For most of the bodies, the value of e lies between 0 and 1. For perfectly elastic bodies, $e = 1$ and for perfectly plastic bodies, $e = 0$.

To determine the velocities after impact i.e., velocity v_1 and v_2 the equation (23.1) is not sufficient to determine the two unknowns. One more equations is needed. This equation is law of conservation of momentum i.e. total initial momentum is equal to total final momentum $(m_1u_1 + m_2u_2 = m_1v_1 + m_2v_2)$.

EXAMPLE 7.34. Ball A of mass 1 kg moving with a velocity of 2 m/sec, strikes directly on a ball B of mass 2 kg at rest. The ball A after striking, comes to rest. Find the velocity of ball B after striking and coefficient of restitution.

SOLUTION : Given : Mass of ball A, $m_1 = 1$ kg,

Initial velocity of ball A, $u_1 = 2$ m/sec

Mass of ball B, $m_2 = 2$ kg

Initial velocity of ball B, $u_2 = 0$

Final velocity of ball A, $v_1 = 0$

Hence it is a case of direct impact

Let,

v_2 = Velocity of ball B after impact, and

e = Coefficient of restitution

Total initial momentum = $m_1u_1 + m_2u_2 = 1\times 2 + 2\times 0 = 2\,kg\,m/s$

Total final momentum = $m_1v_1 + m_2v_2 = 1\times 0 + 2\times v_2 = 2v_2$ kg m/s

According to the law of conservation of momentum,

Total initial momentum = Total final mmentum,

or $$2 = 2v_2$$

∴ $$v_2 = \frac{2}{2} = 1 \text{ m/sec } \textbf{Ans.}$$

Co-efficient of restitution,

$$e = \frac{v_2 - v_1}{u_1 - u_2} = \frac{1-0}{2-0}$$

$$= 0.5 \textbf{ Ans.}$$

EXAMPLE 7.35. Direct central impact occurs between a 300 *N* body moving to the right with a velocity of 6 m/sec and 150 *N* body moving to the left with a velocity of 10 m/sec. Find the velocity of each body after impact if the coefficient of restitution is 0.8

SOLUTION : Referring Fig. 7.34; initial velocity of 300 *N* body, $u_1 = 6$ m/sec.

Initial (Before Impact) velocity of 150*N* body, $u_2 = -10$ m/sec.

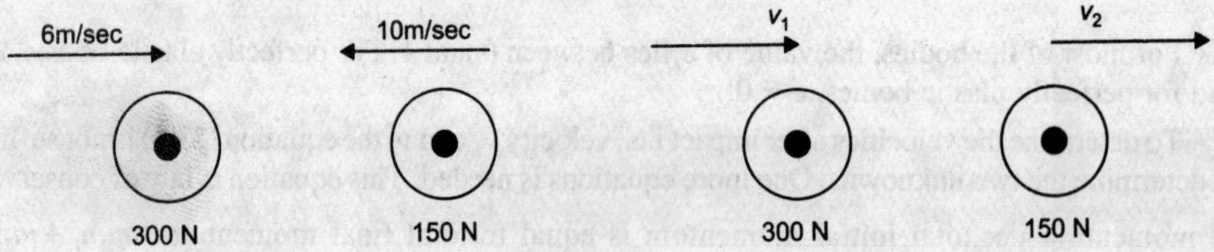

(*a*) Before Impact (*b*) After Impact

Fig. 7.34

Left final (after impact) velocity of :

(i) 300 *N* body = v_1 m/sec, and

(ii) 150 *N* body = v_2 m/sec

Now from the principle of conservation of momentum.

$$w_1u_1 + w_2u_2 = w_1v_1 + w_2v_2$$

or $$300(6) + 150(-10) = 300v_1 + 150v_2$$

or $$1800 - 1500 = 300\,v_1 + 150\,v_2$$

or $$300 = 300\,v_1 + 150\,v_2$$

∴ $$2v_1 + v_2 = 2 \qquad \text{...(i)}$$

From the definition of coefficient of restitution, we have

$$e\,(u_1 - u_2) = v_2 - v_1$$

or $$0.8\,(6 + 10) = v_2 - v_1$$

∴ $$v_2 - v_1 = 0.8\,(16) = 12.8 \qquad \text{...(ii)}$$

From (i) and (ii) expressions, we get

$$3v_1 = -10.8$$

$$\therefore \quad v_1 = -3.6 \text{ m/sec } \textbf{Ans.}$$

But

$$v_2 = 12.8 + v_1$$
$$= 12.8 + (-3.6)$$
$$= 9.2 \text{ m/sec } \textbf{Ans.}$$

EXAMPLE 7.36. An 80*N* body moving to the right at a speed of 3 m/sec strikes a 10*N* body that is moving to the left at a speed of 10 m/sec. The final velocity of 10*N* body is 4 m/sec to the right. Calculate the coefficient of restitution and the final velocity of 80*N* body.

SOLUTON : Given :

$$w_1 = 80N,$$
$$w_2 = 10N,$$
$$u_1 = 3 \text{ m/sec},$$
$$u_2 = -10 \text{ m/sec},$$
$$v_1 = ?,$$
$$v_2 = 4 \text{ m/sec}.$$

Applying the principle of conservation of momentum to the colliding bodies, we get,

$$\frac{w_1}{g}u_1 + \frac{w_2u_2}{g} = \frac{w_1v_1}{g} + \frac{w_2v_2}{g}$$

or

$$w_1\mu_1 + w_2u_2 = w_1v_1 + w_2v_2$$

$$\therefore \quad 80 \times 3 + 10(-10) = 80\, v_1 + 10 \times 4$$

or

$$240 - 100 = 80v_1 + 40$$

or

$$100 = 80\, v_1$$

$$\therefore \quad v_1 = 1.25 \text{ m/sec}$$

$\therefore$ Final velocity of 80*N* body,

$$v_1 = 1.25 \text{ m/sec } \textbf{Ans.}$$

From the definition of coefficient of restitution, we get

$$e(u_1 - u_2) = v_2 - v_1$$

or

$$e(3+10) = 4 - 1.25$$

or

$$13e = 2.75$$

$$\therefore \quad e = \frac{2.75}{13}$$
$$= 0.212 \textbf{ Ans.}$$

EXAMPLE 7.37. A ball M_1 of mass 1 kg traverses a frictionless tube falling through a height of 1.5 m. It then strikes a ball M_2 of mass 2 kg hanging from a cord 1.5 m long. Determine the height to which this ball M_2 will rise assuming the impact to the perfectly elastic.

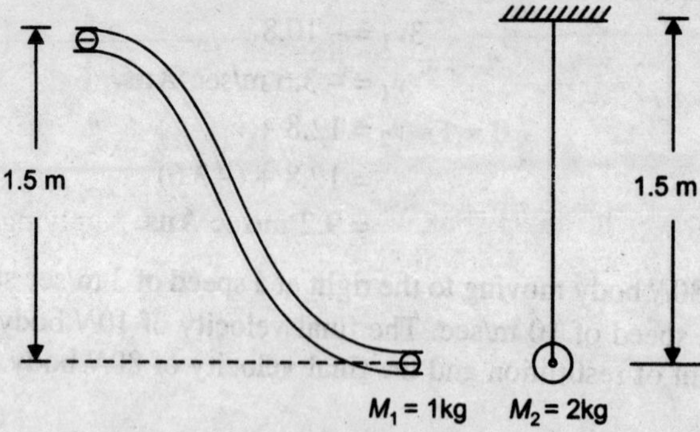

Fig. 7.35

SOLUTION : (Refer Fig. 7.35)

$\because$ $$v^2 = u^2 + 2gh$$

or $$v^2 = 0^2 + 2gh$$

$\therefore$ $$v = \sqrt{2gh} \quad \text{(when } u = 0\text{)}$$

$\therefore$ Velocity of 1kg mass ball falling through 1.5 m height,

$$u_1 = \sqrt{2gh} = \sqrt{2 \times 9.81 \times 1.5}$$

$$= \sqrt{29.43} = 5.4249\ m/\sec \quad \text{...(i)}$$

Velocity of 2 kg mass ball before impact, $u_2 = 0$

Let the velocities of 1 kg and 2kg balls after impact be v_1 and v_2 respectively.

By the principle of momentum,

$$m_1u_1 + m_2u_2 = m_1v_1 + m_2v_2$$

or $$1(5.4249) + 2(0) = 1(v_1) + 2(v_2)$$

$\therefore$ $$v_1 + 2v_2 = 5.4249 \quad \text{...(i)}$$

From the principle of coefficient of restitution, we have

$$e(u_1 - u_2) = v_2 - v_1$$

But $e = 1$ (As the impact is perfectly elastic)

$\therefore$ $$u_1 - u_2 = v_2 - v_1$$

or $$v_2 - v_1 = 5.4249 \quad \text{...(ii)}$$

From the equations (i) and (ii) we have,

$$v_1 + 2v_2 = 5.4249 \quad \text{...(i)}$$
$$v_2 - v_1 = 5.4249 \quad \text{...(ii)}$$
$$\overline{3v_2 = 10.8498}$$

$$\therefore \qquad v_2 = \frac{10.8498}{3}$$

$$= 3.6166\ m/\text{sec}$$

Let h be the height to which hanging ball will rise after impact. Applying work energy equation, we have change in kinetic energy = Work done

Hence,
$$0 - \frac{1}{2} \times 2v_2^2 = -2\,(9.81)\,h$$

or
$$-\frac{1}{2}(2)\,(3.6166)^2 = -19.62\,h$$

or
$$-\,13.07979 = -\,19.62\,h$$

$$\therefore \qquad h = 0.666\ m \ \textbf{Ans.}$$

EXAMPLE 7.38. The masses of two balls are in ratio of 2 : 1 and their respective velocities are in ratio of 1 : 2, but in opposite direction before impact. If the coefficient of restitution be 5/6, prove that after impact, each ball will move back with 5/6th of its original velocity.

SOLUTION : Given :

$$m_1 = 2M,$$
$$m_2 = M,$$
$$u_1 = 1U,$$
$$u_2 = -\,2U$$

and
$$e = 5/6$$

Let,

v_1 = Final velocity of the first ball, and

v_2 = Final velocity of the second ball

We know that,

$$m_1u_1 + m_2u_2 = m_1v_1 + m_2v_2$$

$$\therefore \qquad 2M(U) + M(-2U) = 2M(v_1) + M(v_2)$$

or
$$0 = 2Mv_1 + Mv_2$$

$$\therefore \qquad v_2 = -2v_1 \qquad \text{...(i)}$$

We know that,

$$v_2 - v_1 = e(u_1 - u_2)$$

$$= \frac{5}{6}[U - (-2U)] = \frac{5}{2}U \qquad \text{...(ii)}$$

Substituting the value of v_2 from equation (i)

$$-2v_1 - v_1 = \frac{5}{2}U$$

or $$-3v_1 = \frac{5}{2}U$$

$\therefore$ $$v_1 = -\frac{5}{6}U$$

Minus sign indicates that the direction of v_1 is opposite to that of U. Hence the first ball will move back with 5/6th of its original velocity **Ans.**

Now substituting the value of v_1 in equation (i)

$$v_2 = -2v_1$$

$$= -2\left(-\frac{5}{6}U\right)$$

$$= \frac{5}{6}(2U)$$

Plus sign indicates that the direction of v_1 is opposite to that of U. Hence the second ball will also move back with 5/6th of its original velocity **Ans.**

EXAMPLE 7.39. A sphere of mass 2 kg is released from rest and strikes a block of mass 2.5 kg resulting on a horizontal surface. How far the block will move after the impact? Assume $e = 0.75$ and coefficient of friction between the block and the floor is 0.25 (Fig. 7.36).

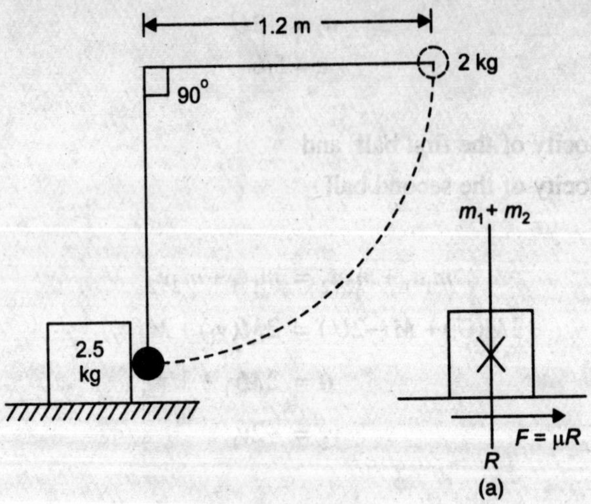

Fig. 7.36

SOLUTION : Given :

$$m_1 = 2 \text{ kg},$$
$$m_2 = 2.5 \text{ kg},$$
$$e = 0.75,$$
$$u = 0.25,$$
$$h = 1.2\text{m},$$

then $$s = ?$$

Velocity of 2 kg mass sphere falling through 1.2 m height,

$$u_1 = \sqrt{2gh}$$

$$= \sqrt{2\times9.8\times1.2}$$

$$= 4.8522\, m/\text{sec} \quad ...(i)$$

Velocity of 2 kg mass before impact, $u_2 = 0$

Let the velocities of 2 kg and 2.5 kg masses after impact be v_1 and v_2 respectively.

By the principle of momentum,

$$m_1u_1 + m_2u_2 = m_1v_1 + m_2v_2$$

$\therefore$ $$2(4.8522) + 2.6(0) = 2(v_1) + 2.5(v_2)$$

or $$9.7043 = 2v_1 + 2.5\,v_2 \quad ...(ii)$$

From the principle of coefficient of restitution, we have,

$$e(u_1 - u_2) = v_2 - v_1$$

or $$0.75(u_1 - u_2) = v_2 - v_1$$

or $$1.50(u_1 - u_2) = 2v_2 - 2v_1$$

or $$1.5(4.8522 - 0) = 2v_2 - 2v_1$$

$$7.2783 = 2v_2 - 2v_1 \quad ...(iii)$$

$$9.7044 = 2v_1 + 2.5v_2 \quad ...(ii)$$

$$16.9827 = 4.5v_2$$

Adding (ii) and (iii), we have

$\therefore$ $$v_2 = \frac{16.9827}{4.5}$$

$$= 3.774\, m/\text{sec}$$

$\because$ Normal reaction, $R = (m_1 + m_2)g$.... (Fig. 7.36(a)

$\therefore$ Force of Friction,

$$F = \mu R = \mu(m_1 + m_2)g$$

$$= 0.25(4.5)9.81 = 11.036N \quad ...(iv)$$

Now work done to overcome the frictional force = Kinetic energy lost by the block with sphere

$\therefore$ $$F.S. = \frac{1}{2}(m_1 + m_2)v_2^2$$

or $$11.036 \times S = \frac{1}{2}(2 + 2.5)(3.744)^2$$

or $$11.036\,(S) = 32.047$$

$\therefore$ $$S = 2.90 \text{ m } \textbf{Ans.}$$

LOSS OF KINETIC ENERGY DURING IMPACT

When two bodies collide with each other, the loss of kinetic energy take place due to impact. This loss of energy may be obtained by finding out the kinetic energy of the two bodies before and after the impact. The loss of kinetic energy during impact is equal to the difference of two kinetic energies.

Consider two bodies *A* and *B* having a direct impact.

Let,

m_1 = Mass of the first body,

u_1 = Velocity of the first body before impact,

v_1 = Velocity of first body after impact,

m_2, u_2 and v_2 = corresponding values of mass, initial velocity and final velocity of second body,

E_L = Loss of Energy,

e = Coefficient of restitution.

Kinetic energy of the first body before impact.

$$= \frac{1}{2} m_1 u_1^2$$

Kinetic energy of the second body before impact

$$= \frac{1}{2} m_2 u_2^2$$

$\therefore$ Total K.E. of the two bodies before impact

$$= \frac{1}{2} m_1 u_1^2 + \frac{1}{2} m_2 u_2^2 \qquad \text{...(i)}$$

Similarly, total K.E. of the two bodies after impact

$$= \frac{1}{2} m_1 v_1^2 + \frac{1}{2} m_2 v_2^2 \qquad \text{...(ii)}$$

$\therefore$ Loss of K.E. during impact

= Total K.E. before impact – Total K.E. after impact

$$= \left(\frac{1}{2} m_1 u_1^2 + \frac{1}{2} m_2 u_2^2\right) - \left(\frac{1}{2} m_1 v_1^2 + \frac{1}{2} m_2 v_2^2\right) \qquad \text{...(iii)}$$

EXAMPLE 7.40. A bullet of mass 100 gm is fixed into a freely suspended target of mass 10kg. Due to impact, the bullet gets embedded in the target and the target with bullet moves with a velocity of 7m/sec. Find the velocity of the bullet and the loss of kinetic energy.

SOLUTION : Given : Mass of bullet, m_1 = 100 gm = 100/1000 = 0.1 kg

Mass of target, m_2 = 10 kg

Common velocity of bullet and target = 7 m/sec

Initial velocity of the target, $u_2 = 0$

Let,

u_1 = Initial velocity of bullet

E_L = Loss of kinetic energy due to impact

Total momentum before impact

$$m_1u_1 + m_2u_2 = 0.1(u_1) + 10(10) = 0.1u_1 \quad \text{...(i)}$$

Total momentum after impact

$$= (m_1 + m_2)\,(\text{common velocity})$$

$$= (0.1+10)\,(7)$$

$$= 70.7 \text{ kg m/sec} \quad \text{...(ii)}$$

Equating the total momentum before impact to the total momentum after impact, we get

$$0.1\,u_1 = 70.7$$

$$\therefore \quad u_1 = \frac{70.7}{0.1}$$

$$= 707 \; m/\sec \; \textbf{Ans.}$$

To find the loss of kinetic energy due to impact, find the total kinetic energy before impact and after impact.

Total K.E. before impact

$$= \frac{1}{2}m_1u_1^2 + \frac{1}{2}m_2u_2^2$$

$$= \frac{1}{2}(0.1)\,(707)^2 + \frac{1}{2}(10)\,(0)^2$$

$$= 24992.45 \; Nm \quad \text{...(i)}$$

$$\text{Total K.E. after impact} = \frac{1}{2}(m_1 + m_2)V^2$$

$$= \frac{1}{2}(0.1 + 10)\,(7)^2$$

$$= 0.5(10.1)\,(7)^2$$

$$= 247.45 \; Nm \quad \text{...(ii)}$$

$\therefore$ Loss of K.E. = K.E. before impact – K.E. after impact

= 24992.45 – 247.45

= 24745 *Nm* **Ans.**

DIRECT IMPACT OF A BODY ON A FIXED PLANE

The fixed plane is at rest before impact and after impact. The mass of the fixed plane is very large. Consider a body having a direct impact on a fixed plane.

Let,

u = Initial velocity of the body,

v = Final velocity of the body

e = Coefficient of restitution

The velocity of approach between body and fixed plane

= Initital velocity of body – Velocity of fixed plane = $u - 0 = u$

The velocity of separation

= Final velocity of body – Velocity of fixed plane = $v - 0 = v$

Coefficient of restitution is given by,

e = Velocity of separation/Velocity of approach = v/u

$$\therefore \quad v = eu \qquad ...(25.1)$$

IMPORTANT CASES :

(a) A BODY IS FALLING ON A FLOOR FROM SOME HEIGHT :

Let,

H = Height from which the body is falling

u = Velocity with which the body strikes the floor.

This velocity u may be obtained by using the equation

(Final velocity)^2 – (Initial velocity)^2 = 2 gH

Initial velocity of the body = 0

Final velocity of the body = u

$$u^2 - (0)^2 = 2gH$$

or
$$u = \sqrt{2gH} \qquad ...(25.2)$$

(b) A BODY IS FIRST PROJECTED UPWARDS AND THEN STRIKES THE FLOOR: When the body is projected upwards with some initial velocity, the body will reach the greatest height and then will return to the ground with the same velocity with which it was projected.

EXAMPLE 7.41. A ball of mass 500 gm is dropped on a horizontal plane from a height of 18m. The ball rebounds due to impact with the horizontal fixed plane to a height of 8m. Find the coefficient of restitution between the fixed plane and the ball.

SOLUTION : Given : Mass of the ball, m = 500 gm = 0.5 kg.

Height from which the ball is dropped, H = 18 m

The velocity with which the ball strikes the plane is given by equation (25.2)

$$u = \sqrt{2gH} = \sqrt{2 \times 9.81 \times 18} = \sqrt{353.16} = 18.7926\ m/\text{sec} \qquad ...(i)$$

Height to which the ball rebounds, h = 8 m

This means that after the impact, the ball rises to a height of 8m. At the highest point, the velocity will be zero. The velocity of the ball after impact, may be obtained by using the relation.

(Final Velocity)^2 – (Initial velocity)^2 = $2gh$

Let,

v = Velocity of the ball after impact

Then,

$$v = \sqrt{2gh} = \sqrt{2 \times 9.81 \times 8}$$

$$= \sqrt{156.96} = 12.5284\ m/sec \quad ...(i)$$

The coefficient of restitution is given by the equation (25.1), as

$$v = eu$$

or $$12.5284 = e\ (18.7926)$$

∴ $$e = 12.5284 / 18.7926 = 0.67\ \textbf{Ans.}$$

EXAMPLE 7.42. A ball is dropped from a height of 14m on a smooth horizontal plane, from which it rebounds to a height of 10 m. The ball again strikes the plane and rises to an unknown height. Find;

1. Unknown height of the second rebound, and
2. The coefficient of restitution.

SOLUTION : Given : Height from which ball is dropped, $H = 14m$

Height to which the ball rebounds in the first case, $h = 10m$

∴ The velocity with which the ball strikes the plane for the first time is given by ,

$$u = \sqrt{2gH} = \sqrt{2 \times 9.81 \times 14}$$

$$= \sqrt{274.68} = 16.57\ m/sec \quad ...(i)$$

The velocity of ball after first impact is given by,

$$v = \sqrt{2gh} = \sqrt{2 \times 9.81 \times 10}$$

$$= \sqrt{196.2} = 14.007 \text{ m/sec} \quad ...(ii)$$

The coefficient of restitution is given by equation,

$$v = eu$$

or $$14.007 = e\ (16.57)$$

$$e = \frac{14.007}{16.57} = 0.845\ \textbf{Ans.}$$

THE HEIGHT OF THE SECOND REBOUND :

Let,

h_2 = Height of second rebound.

Height from which the ball strikes the plane for the second time, h = 10 m

The velocity, with which the ball strikes the plane second time, is given by

$$u_1 = \sqrt{2gh} = \sqrt{2 \times 9.81 \times 10}$$

$$= \sqrt{196.2} = 14.007\ m/sec \quad ...(iii)$$

The velocity with which the ball rebounds second time is given by,

$$v_1 = \sqrt{2gh_2} = \sqrt{2 \times 9.81 \times h_2}$$

Again using the equation, $v_1 = eu_1$

or $$\sqrt{2 \times 9.81 \times h_2} = 0.845(14.007)$$

Squaring we get,

$$2 \times 9.8 \times h_2 = (0.845)^2 (14.007)^2$$

or $$19.62\, h_2 = 140.089$$

$$\therefore \quad h_2 = \frac{140.089}{19.62}$$

$$= 7.14 \text{ m } \textbf{Ans.}$$

EXERCISE-7

1. State the laws of motion. Discuss the first law in the light of second law.
2. Explain clearly the term 'RECOIL OF GUN'. How will you find the velocity of the bullet?
3. A constant retarding force of 50 N is applied to a body of mass 20 kg moving initially with a velocity of 15 m/s. How long the body will take to stop? **[Ans.** $t = 6$ sec**]**
4. A multiple unit electric train has 800 tonnes mass. The resistance to motion is 100 N per tonne of the train mass. If the electric motors can provide 200 KN tractive force, how long does it take to accelerate the train to a speed of 90 km.p.h. from rest. ($t = 1166.7$ secs)
5. An elevator of mass 2500 kg is moving vertically downwards with a constant acceleration. Starting from rest, it travels a distance of 35 m during an interval of 10 seconds. Find the cable tension during this time. Neglecting all other resistances to motion, what are the limits of cable tension? **[Ans.** $R_1 = 22.75$ KN, $R_2 = 24.5$ KN, $R_3 = 0$**]**
6. An elevator of gross mass 500 kg starts moving upwards with a constant acceleration, and acquires a velocity of 2 m/s, after travelling a distance of 3 m. Find the pull in the cables during the accelerated motion. **[Ans.** $R = 5235$ N**]**
7. A bullet of 10 gm mass is fired horizontally with a velocity of 1000 m/s from a gun of mass 50 kg. Find (i) Velocity with which the gun will recoil, and (ii) Force necessary to bring the gun to rest in 250 mm. **[Ans.** $R_2 = 0.2$ m/s, 4 N**]**
8. A truck is moving down at 10° inclination when the driver applies brakes, with the result that the truck decelerates at a steady rate of 1 m/s^2. Investigate whether a 500 kg mass placed on the truck will slide or remain stationary relative to the truck. Assume coefficient of friction between the truck surface and load as 0.4. **[Ans.** Force of friction 1930 N is more than slipping force 1350.6 N Hence load will not slip**]**
9. Determine the tension is the string and acceleration of blocks A and B weighing 1500 N and 500 N connected by an inextensible string as shown in Fig. 7.37. Assume pulleys as frictionless and weightless. **[Ans.** $T = 642.89$ N, $a = 1.401$ m/sec^2**]**

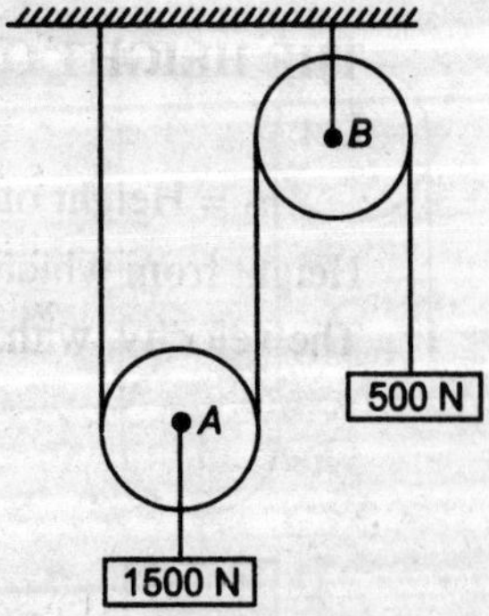

Fig. 7.37

10. A pile hammer weighing 20 kN drops from a height of 750 mm on a pile of 10 kN. The pile penetrates 100 mm per blow. Assume that the motion of the pile is resisted by a constant force, find the resistance to penetrate of the ground. **[Ans.** R = 130 kN]
11. A pile hammer, weighing 15 kN drops from a height of 600 mm on a pile of 7.5 kN. How deep does a single blow of hammer drive the pile of the resistance of the ground to the pile is 140 KN? Assume that ground resistance is constant. **[Ans.** s = 51 mm]
12. A bullet weighs 0.5 N and moving with a velocity of 400 m/sec hits a centrally 30 N block of wood moving away at 15 m/sec and gets embedded in it. Find the velocity of the bullet after the impact and the amount of kinetic energy lost.

    [Ans. v = 21.31 m/sec, K.E. Lost = 3715.47 J]
13. A bullet weighing 0.3 N and moving at 600 m/sec penetrates 40 N body and emerges with a velocity of 180 m/sec. How far and how long will the block move, if the coefficient of friction between the body and horizontal floor is 0.3. **[Ans.** s = 1.686 m, and t = 1.07 sec.]
14. A bullet weighing 0.3 N is fired horizontally into a body weighing 100 N which is suspended by a string 0.8 m long. Due to this impact the body swings through an angle of 30°. Find the velocity of the bullet and the loss in the energy of the system.

    [Ans. V = 342.82 m/sec, Energy loss = 1791.66J]
15. Determine the tension in the strings and the velocity of 1500 N block shown in Fig. 7.37 five seconds after starting from (i) Rest, (ii) Starting with a downward velocity of 3 m/sec. Assume pulleys as weightless and frictionless.

    [Ans. v = 7.007 m/sec, T_1 = 642.86N, T_2 = 655.96 N]
16. A 10 N ball traverses a frictionless tube, shown in Fig. 7.38, falling through a height of 2 m. It then strikes a 20 N ball hung from a rope 1.2 m long. Determine the height to which the hanging ball will rise: (i) If the collision is perfectly elastic, (ii) If the coefficient of restitution is 0.7. **[Ans.** h_1 = 0.889 m, h_2 = 0.642 m]

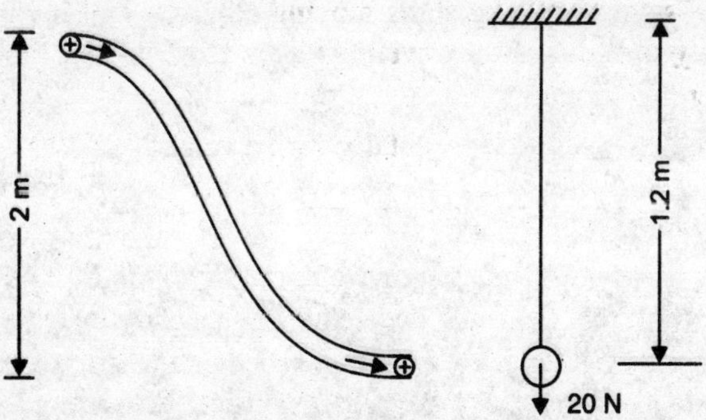

Fig. 7.38

17. A 10 N sphere shown in Fig. 7.39 is released from rest, when θ = 90°. The coefficient of restitution between the sphere and the block is 0.70. If the coefficient of friction between the block and the horizontal surface is 0.3, determine how far the block will move after impact.

    [Ans. s = 0.934 m]

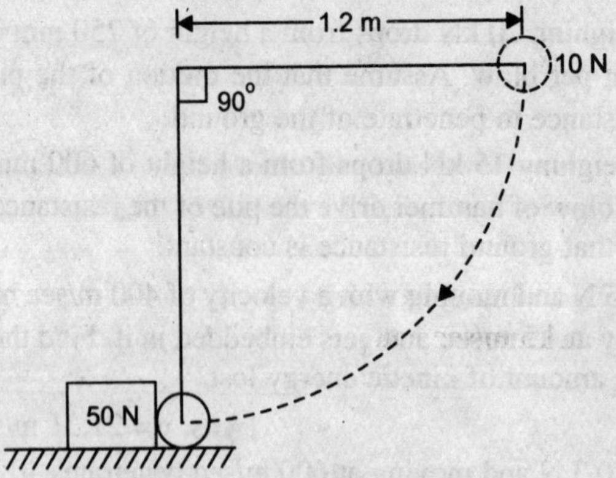

Fig. 7.39

18. A sphere of weight 10 N moving at 3 m/sec collides with another sphere of weight 50 N moving in the same line at 0.6 m/sec. Find the loss of kinetic energy during impact and show that the direction of motion of the first sphere is reversed after the impact. Assume coefficient of restitution as 0.75. **[Ans.** $v_1 = -0.5$ m/sec, $v_2 = 1.3$ m/sec, Loss of K.E. = 1.07 J]

19. Direct central impact occurs between a 300 N body moving to the right with a velocity of 6 m/sec and 150 N body moving to the left with a velocity of 10 m/sec. Find the velocity of each body after impact if the coefficient of restitution is 0.8.
[Ans. $v_1 = -4.133$ m/sec, and $v_2 = 10.267$ m/sec]

CHAPTER 8

Kinematics of Rigid Bodies

CONCEPT OF RIGID BODY

The physical bodies deform although slightly, under the action of loads or external forces. But in many situations this deformation is negligibly small to affect the results. So, the assumption of a rigid body shall mean that the body does not deform or the distance between any two points of the body does not change under the action of an applied force.

TYPES OF RIGID BODY MOTION

A rigid body can perform the various types of motion - from a simple translation to quite complex motions. Here we shall limit our study to the plane motion of rigid body. In the plane motion of a rigid body all the particles of the body move in parallel planes. The motion of the body, therefore, can be represented by the motion of any one of such parallel planes or by a representative plane figure instead of a three dimensional object.

The various types of plane motion can be grouped as follows:

1. TRANSLATION: A rigid body is said to have a translatory motion if an imaginary straight line drawn on the body remains parallel to its original position, during the motion. The particles constituting the rigid body move in parallel planes and travel the distance. During translation, the particles have the same velocity and acceleration.

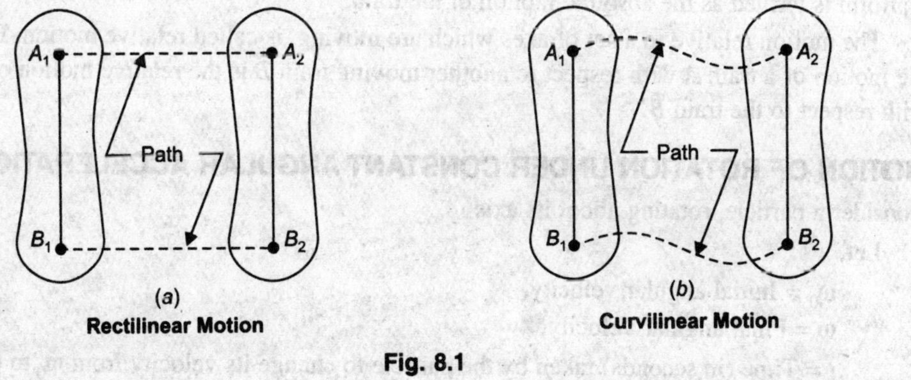

(a) Rectilinear Motion

(b) Curvilinear Motion

Fig. 8.1

If the path traced by the particles during motion is a straight line then the motion is said to be rectilinear translation. If the particle traces a curved path, the motion is called curvilinear translation. Refer Fig. 8.1 (a) and (b).

2. ROTATION: The body rotates about a fixed point and all the particles constituting the body move in a circular path. The fixed point about which the body rotates is called the point of rotation, and the axis passing through the point of rotation is called the axis of rotation. A point lying on the axis of rotation has a zero velocity and zero acceleration. In this case all the particles of the rigid body move in concentric circular paths. The point of rotation may be inside the body (Fig. 8.2a) or outside the body (Fig. 8.2 b).

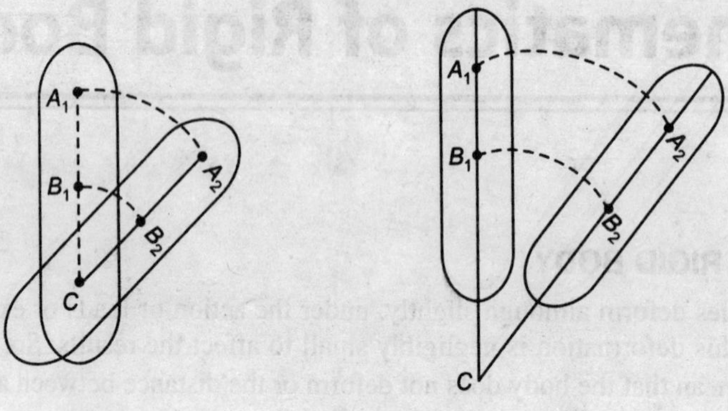

Fig. 8.2

3. GENERAL PLANE MOTION (COMBINED MOTION OF TRANSLATION AND ROTATION): There exist certain situations where a body possesses both motions of translation and rotation simultaneously at a particular instant. Examples of such a combined motion are:

1. Motion of a roller without slipping.
2. Motion of the wheel of a locomotive train, truck and car etc.
3. A rod sliding against a wall at one end and floor at the other end.

The combination of rotation and translation motion is usually referred to as general plane motion.

4. ABSOLUTE MOTION: The motion of a particle with respect to a fixed frame of reference is called the absolute motion of the particle. For example, the motion of a train with respect to the platform is termed as the absolute motion of the train.

The motion relative to a set of axes which are moving, is called relative motion. For example, the motion of a train *A* with respect to another moving train *B* is the relative motion of the train *A* with respect to the train *B*.

MOTION OF ROTATION UNDER CONSTANT ANGULAR ACCELERATION

Consider a particle, rotating about its axis

Let,

ω_0 = Initial angular velocity,

ω = Final angular velocity,

t = Time (in seconds) taken by the particle to change its velocity from ω_0 to ω.

α = Constant angular acceleration in rad/sec^2.

θ = Total angular displacement in radians.

Since in t seconds, the angular velocity of the particle has increased steadily from ω_0 to ω at the rate of the α rad/sec^2, therefore

$$\omega = \omega_0 + 2t \qquad \text{...(8.1)}$$

And average angular velocity $= \dfrac{\omega_0 + \omega}{2}$

We know that the total angular displacement,

$$\theta = \text{Average velocity} \times \text{Time}$$

$$= \left(\frac{\omega_0 + \omega}{2}\right) t \text{ rad.} \qquad \text{...(8.2)}$$

Substituting the value of ω from equation (8.1)

$$\theta = \frac{\omega_0 + (\omega_0 + \alpha \cdot t)}{2} t$$

$$= \frac{2\omega_0 + \alpha \cdot t}{2} t \text{ rad}$$

$$= \omega_0 t + \frac{1}{2} \alpha t^2 \text{ rad} \qquad \text{...(8.3)}$$

and from equation (8.1), we find that $t = \dfrac{\omega - \omega_0}{\alpha}$

Substituting this value of t in equation (8.2)

$$\theta = \left(\frac{\omega_0 + \omega}{2}\right)\left(\frac{\omega - \omega_0}{\alpha}\right)$$

$$= \frac{\omega^2 - \omega_0^2}{2\alpha}$$

$$\therefore \quad \omega^2 = \omega_0^2 + 2\alpha\theta \qquad \text{...(8.4)}$$

RELATION BETWEEN LINEAR MOTION AND ANGULAR MOTION

S.No.	Particular	Linear Motion	Angular Motion
1	Initial velocity	u	ω_0
2	Final velocity	v	ω
3	Constant Acceleration	a	α
4	Total distance traversed	s	θ
5	Formula for final velocity	$v = u + at$	$\omega = \omega_0 + \alpha t$
6	Formula for distance traversed	$s = ut + \frac{1}{2}at^2$	$\theta = \omega_0 t + \frac{1}{2}\alpha t^2$

7	Formula for final velocity	$v^2 = u^2 + 2as$	$\omega^2 = \omega_0^2 + 2\alpha\theta$
8	Differential formula for velocity	$v = \dfrac{ds}{dt}$	$\omega = \dfrac{d\theta}{dt}$
9	Differential formula for acceleration	$v = \dfrac{dv}{dt}$	$\alpha = \dfrac{d\omega}{dt}$

CIRCULAR MOTION (FIXED AXIS ROTATION)

When a body moves along a circular path, its motion is called circular motion. During such a motion, the centre of the rotation of the body remains fixed. The shafts, pulleys and fly wheels etc. undergo circular motion when they rotate about their geometric axis. The terms associated with circular motion are:

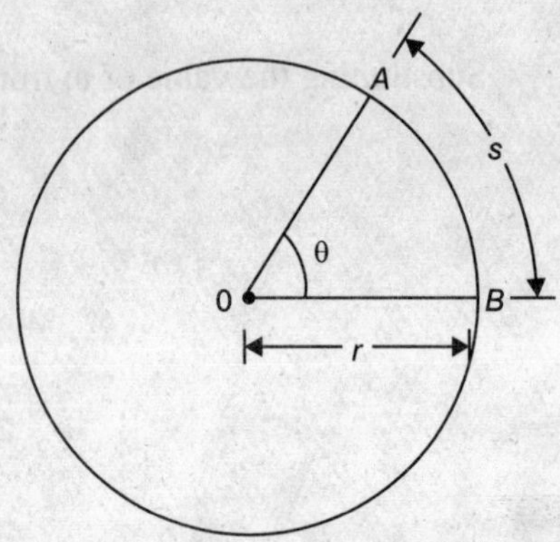

Fig. 8.3

(a) ANGULAR DISPLACEMENT: The displacement of a body in rotation is called angular displacement, and it is measued in terms of the angle through which the body moves from the initial state. With reference to Fig. 8.3, a body starts from initial position *A* and while moving in circular path reaches the position *B* after a certain time interval. Then $\angle AOB = \theta$ is a measure of angular displacement of the body. This displacement has magnitude as well as direction, and apparently displacement is a vector quantity. The direction of rotation either clock-wise or anti-clockwise.

Angular displacement θ can be measured in radians, degrees or revolutions. Various units of angular displacement are connected by the relation:

1 Revolution = 2π Radians = 360 degrees

(b) ANGULAR VELOCITY: The rate of change of angular displacement of a body with respect to time is called angular velocity. If a body traverses angular distance $d\theta$ over a time of interval dt, then the average angular velocity ω, is

$$\omega = \frac{d\theta}{dt}$$

The unit of angular velocity for *r* defining its magnitude is usually taken as radians per second (rad/s). Many times the angular velocity is expressed in terms of revolutions per minutes (r.p.m.). If the body turns *N* rev/min, then

Number of revolutions per second = N/60

In one revolution, the angular displacement of the body is 360 degrees or 2π radians.

Angle traversed by the body in one second = (Angle covered in one revolution) (Number of revolutions per second)

$$= 2\pi \times \frac{N}{60} = \frac{2\pi N}{60}$$

But the angle traversed by the body in one second is a measure of angular velocity ω. Then,

$$\omega = \frac{2\pi N}{60} \text{ rad/sec}$$

(c) ANGULAR ACCELERATION: The rate of change of angular velocity of a body with respect to time is called angular acceleration.

Angular acceleration = Rate of change of angular velocity

$$\alpha = \frac{d\omega}{dt} = \frac{d}{dt}\left(\frac{\theta}{t}\right) = \frac{d^2\theta}{dt^2}$$

The angular acceleration is some times expressed as

$$\alpha = \frac{d\omega}{dt} = \frac{d\omega}{d\theta} \times \frac{d\theta}{dt}$$

$$= \omega \cdot \frac{d\omega}{d\theta} \qquad \left(\because \frac{d\theta}{dt} = \omega\right)$$

The unit of angular acceleration for defining its magnitude is usually taken as radian per second per second (rad/sec^2).

RELATIONSHIP BETWEEN CIRCULAR MOTION AND LINEAR MOTION

When a body moves from A to B (Fig. 8.4), the distance travelled by it is s. If r is the distance of the body from centre of rotation, then $s = r\theta$.

and $$\frac{ds}{dt} = \frac{d}{dt}(r\theta) = \frac{r\,d\theta}{dt} \qquad (\because r \text{ is constant})$$

Noting that ds/dt = Linear velocity v and

$\frac{d\theta}{dt}$ = Angular velocity ω, we may write

⇒ $$v = \omega r$$

That is, the linear velocity is r-times the angular velocity.

When the expression is differentiated with respect to time, we get,

$$\frac{dv}{dt} = \frac{d}{dt}(\omega r) = \frac{r\,d\omega}{dt}$$

Since $\frac{dv}{dt}$ = Linear acceleration a and $\frac{d\omega}{dt}$ = Angular acceleration α,

we may write

$$a = \alpha r$$

That is, the linear acceleration is r-times the angular acceleration.

It is worth while to point out that when a body moves along a curved path (curvilinear motion), the linear velocity is referred to as tangential velocity. Further the body under goes tangential and normal components of acceleration given by

Tangential acceleration,

$$a_t = \alpha r \qquad ...(8.5)$$

Normal acceleration,

$$a_n = \frac{v^2}{r} = \omega^2 r \qquad ...(8.6)$$

The tangential acceleration is due to change in magnitude of the velocity and the normal acceleration is due to change in direction of the body.

Fig. 8.4 illustrates these components for any point P. The normal component is directed towards the centre of the circle. The total acceleration a is the vector sum of two components,

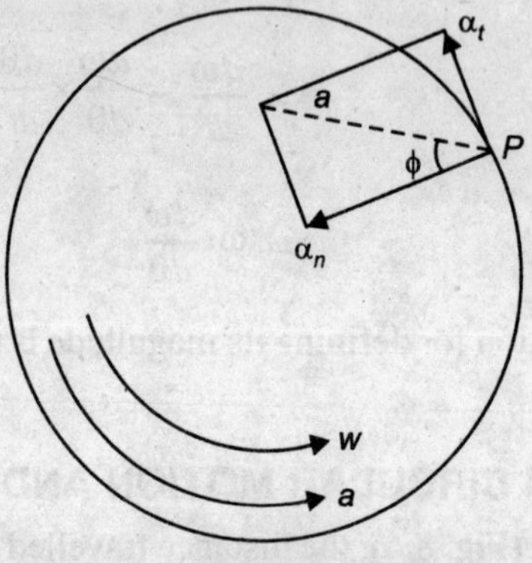

Fig. 8.4

$$a = \sqrt{\alpha_n^2 = \alpha_t^2} \qquad ...(8.7)$$

and the angle between the total acceleration and the radius is,

$$\phi = \tan^{-1}\left(\frac{\alpha_t}{\alpha_n}\right) \qquad ...(8.8)$$

EXAMPLE 8.1. A wheel increases its speed from 45 r.p.m. to 90 r.p.m. in 30 seconds. Find

(i) Angular acceleration of the wheel; and

(ii) Number of revolutions made by this wheel in these 30 seconds.

SOLUTION: Given:

$$\omega_0 = 45 \text{ r.p.m.}$$

$$= \frac{2\pi N}{60} = 2\pi \times \frac{45}{60} = 1.5\,\pi \text{ rad/sec;}$$

$$\omega = 90 \text{ r.p.m.}$$

$$= \frac{2\pi N}{60} = \frac{2\pi 90}{60}$$

$$= 3\pi \text{ rad/sec}, \qquad t = 30 \text{ sec.}$$

(i) ANGULAR ACCELERATION OF THE WHEEL

Let,

α = Angular acceleration of the wheel .

We know that final velocity, $\omega = \omega_0 + \alpha t$

Hence,

$$3\pi = 1.5\pi + \alpha(30)$$

or

$$3\pi - 1.5\pi = 30\alpha$$

$$\therefore \quad \alpha = \frac{1.5\pi}{30}$$

$$= 0.1571 \text{ rad/sec}^2 \textbf{ Ans.}$$

(ii) NO. OF REVOLUTIONS MADE BY THE WHEEL IN 30 SECONDS.

We know that, total angle turned by the wheel.

$$\theta = \omega_0 t + \frac{1}{2}\alpha t^2$$

$$= 1.5\pi(30) + \frac{1}{2}(0.1571)(30)^2$$

$$= 212.067 \text{ rad}$$

$$\therefore \quad \theta = \frac{212.067}{2\pi}$$

$$= 33.75 \text{ rev. } \textbf{Ans.} \qquad (\because 1 \text{ rev} = 2\pi \text{ rad})$$

EXAMPLE 8.2. A flywheel rotates freely on frictionless bearings at 240 rev/.min. How many revolutions will it make in 10 seconds after the start? Proceed to determine the angular speed if this wheel turns 500 revolutions in 15 seconds.

SOLUTION: There will be no resistance to the motion in frictionless bearings. Obviously the wheel will then rotate with constant (uniform) velocity for which $\theta = \omega t$ (as $\alpha = 0$).

(i) Given:

$$\omega_0 = 240 \text{ rev/min;}$$

$$t = 10 \text{ seconds} = \frac{10}{60} \text{ min}$$

$$\therefore \quad \theta = \omega_0 t$$

$$= 240 \times \frac{10}{60}$$

$$= 40 \text{ revolutins } \textbf{Ans.}$$

$$= 40 \times 2\pi = 251.33 \text{ radians}$$

(ii) Given: $\theta = 500$ revolutions; $t = 15$ seconds $= \frac{15}{60}$ min

From the expression,

$$\theta = \omega_0 t + \frac{1}{2}\alpha t^2$$

$$\omega = \frac{\theta}{t} = \frac{500}{\left(\frac{15}{60}\right)}$$

$$= 2000 \text{ rev/min}$$

$$= \frac{2000 \times 2\pi}{60} = 209.44 \text{ rad/s } \textbf{Ans.}$$

EXAMPLE 8.3. The speed of a flywheel changes from 10 rad/s to 30 rad/s in 5 seconds time. Determine the angular acceleration of the wheel.

How many revolutions the wheel would turn to attain a speed of 600 rev/min?

SOLUTION: Using the kinematic relation $\omega = \omega_0 + \alpha t$, we have

Angular acceleration,

$$\alpha = \frac{\omega - \omega_0}{t}$$

$$= \frac{30 - 10}{5} = 4 \text{ rad/sec}^2$$

(i) Given:

$$\omega = \frac{2\pi N}{60} = \frac{2\pi \times 600}{60}$$

$$= 62.83 \text{ rad/sec}$$

From the relation, $\omega^2 = \omega_0^2 + 2\alpha\theta$, total angular

Displacement,

$$\theta = \frac{\omega^2 - \omega_0^2}{2\alpha}$$

$$= \frac{(62.83)^2 - (10)^2}{2 \times 4} = 480.95 \text{ radians}$$

$\because$ 2π radian = 1 revolution

$\therefore$ $$480.95 \text{ radians} = \frac{1 \times 480.95}{2\pi} = 76.55 \text{ revolutions}$$

Hence total revolutions made by the wheel = 76.55 **Ans.**

EXAMPLE 8.4. A grinding wheel is attached to a shaft of an electric motor of rated speed 1800 r.p.m. when power is switched on, the unit attains the rated speed in 5 sec and when the power is switched off the unit coasts to rest in 90 seconds. Assuming uniformly accelerated motion, determine the number of revolution the unit turns

(i) To attain the rated speed, and

(ii) To come to rest

SOLUTION: Given:

$$\because \quad N = 1800 \text{ r.p.m.}$$

$$\therefore \quad \omega = \frac{2\pi N}{60} = \frac{2\pi \times 1800}{60}$$

$$= 60\,\pi \text{ (rad/s)}$$

Hence $\omega = 60\,\pi$, $\omega_0 = 0$, $t = 5$ sec.

Using the relation,

$$\omega = \omega_0 + \alpha t$$

or

$$60\pi = 0 + 5\alpha$$

$$\therefore \quad \alpha = \frac{60\pi}{5}$$

$$= 12\pi \text{ rad/sec}^2$$

Using the expression, $\omega^2 = \omega_0^2 + 2\alpha\theta$, we have,

$$(60\pi)^2 = (0)^2 + 2\,(12\pi)\,\theta$$

or

$$\theta = \frac{(60\pi)^2}{24\pi}$$

$$= 150\,\pi \text{ radians}$$

$\because$ 2π raidans = 1 revolution

Hence revolutions turned

$$= \frac{150\pi}{2\pi} = 75 \textbf{ Ans.}$$

(ii) NUMBER OF REVOLUTIONS TO COME TO REST: $\omega_0 = 60\,\pi$, $\omega = 0$, $t = 90\,s$

Using the relation,

$$\omega = \omega_0 + \alpha t$$

$$0 = 60\pi + \alpha(90)$$

$$\therefore \quad \alpha = -\frac{60\pi}{90}$$

$$= -\frac{2\pi}{3} \text{ rad/sec}^2$$

since $$\omega^2 = \omega_0^2 + 2\alpha\theta$$

or $$(0)^2 = (60\pi)^2 + 2\left(-\frac{2\pi}{3}\right)\theta$$

$\therefore$ $$\theta = \frac{(60\pi)^2 \times 3}{4\pi}$$

$$= 2700\pi \text{ radians}$$

$\because$ 2π radians = 1 revolution

Hence revolutions turned = $\frac{2700\pi}{2\pi}$ = 1350 **Ans.**

EXAMPLE 8.5. The piston of an engine is stated to make 360 strokes per minute. Determine the angular and linear speed of a point on the periphery of 1.8 m diameter flywheel fitted to the crank shaft of the engine.

SOLUTION: Since corresponding to two strokes of the piston, there is one revolution of the crank shaft.

Hence number of revolutions made by the crack shaft = 360/2 = 180 rev/min.

Since the flywheel is rigidly fixed to the crank shaft.

Hence number of revolutions made by the flywheel = 180 rev/min.

$\therefore$ Angular speed of the flywheel,

$$\omega = \frac{2\pi N}{60} = \frac{2\pi(180)}{60}$$

$$= 6\pi = 18.84 \text{ rad/s } \textbf{Ans.}$$

Since the linear velocity and angular velocity are connected by the relation: $v = \omega r$

$\therefore$ Linear speed,

$$v = 18.84\left(\frac{1.8}{2}\right)$$

$$= 16.96 \; m/\text{sec } \textbf{Ans.}$$

EXAMPLE 8.6. A 5 m long bar of small cross-section rotates in the horizontal plane about a vertical axis through one end. It accelerates uniformly from 1000 rev/min to 1500 rev/min in 5 seconds interval. Make calculations for the linear velocity of its mid point at the begining and end of the time interval.

SOLUTION: Let the subscripts *b* and *e* denote the begining and end of the time interval.

The linear velocity and the angular velocity are connected by the relation, $v = \omega r$

$\therefore$ $$v_b = \omega_b r = \frac{2\pi \times 1000}{60} \times \frac{5}{2}$$

$$= 261.799 \text{ m/sec } \textbf{Ans.} \qquad \left(\because \omega = \frac{2\pi N}{60}\right)$$

$$v_e = \omega_e r = \frac{2\pi \times 1500}{60} \times \frac{5}{2}$$

$$= 392.699 \text{ m/sec } \textbf{Ans.}$$

Note: The angular velocity is same for any point of the bar whereas the linear velocity depends on the radius of the point (whose velocity is needed) from the centre of rotation.

EXAMPLE 8.7. A flywheel 0.5 m in diameter accelerates uniformly from rest to 360 rpm in 12 seconds. Determine the

(i) Velocity, and

(ii) Acceleration of a point on the rim of the flywheel 1 second after it has started from rest.

SOLUTION:

$$\omega_0 = 0;$$

$$\omega = \frac{2\pi N}{60} = \frac{2\pi(360)}{60}$$

$$= 37.699 \text{ rad/sec}$$

From the kinematic relation, $\omega = \omega_0 + \alpha t$, we have

Angular acceleration,

$$\alpha = \frac{\omega - \omega_0}{t} = \frac{37.699}{12}$$

$$= 3.14 \text{ rad/sec}^2$$

Angular velocity of the wheel 1 second after starting

$$\omega = \omega_0 + \alpha t = 0 + 3.14 \times 1$$

$$= 3.14 \text{ rad/sec}$$

The linear velocity and the angular velocity are connected by the relation,

$$v = \omega r$$

Hence linear speed,

$$v = 3.14 \times \frac{0.5}{2} = 0.785 \text{ m/sec}$$

The linear velocity will be tangential to the rim.

The components of the acceleration are.

Tangential acceleration

$$\alpha_t = \alpha r = 3.14 \times \frac{0.5}{2}$$

$$= 0.785 \text{ m/sec}^2$$

Normal acceleration,

$$\alpha_n = \omega^2 r = (3.14)^2 \times \frac{0.5}{2}$$

$$= 2.46 \text{ m/sec}^2$$

Magnitude of total acceleration,

$$\alpha = \sqrt{\alpha_t^2 + \alpha_n^2} = \sqrt{(0.785)^2 + (2.46)^2}$$

$$= 2.5822 \text{ m/sec}^2$$

Let ϕ be the angle between the total acceleration vector and the radius, then

$$\phi = \tan^{-1}\frac{\alpha_t}{\alpha_n}$$

$$= \tan^{-1}\left(\frac{0.785}{2.46}\right) = 17.72° \textbf{ Ans.}$$

EXAMPLE 8.8 A shaft supported between two bearings carries a wheel of 1.5 m diameter. A constant moment is applied at the rim of the wheel and it attains a speed of 120 revolutions per minute in 10 minutes from rest. Determine

(a) The peripheral velocity of the wheel,

(b) The angular acceleration of the wheel, and

(c) The number of revolutions made by the wheel.

SOLUTION: Angular velocity,

$$\omega = \frac{2\pi N}{60} = \frac{2\pi(120)}{60}$$

$$\therefore \qquad \omega = 12.566 \text{ rad/sec}$$

Radius of the wheel, $r = 1.5/2 = 0.75$ m

The angular and peripheral velocities are connected by the relation, $v = \omega r$

Hence peripheral speed of the wheel, $v = \omega r$

$$\therefore \qquad v = 12.566 \times 0.75$$

$$= 9.495 \text{ m/sec } \textbf{Ans.}$$

(b) From the kinematic relation, $\omega = \omega_0 + \alpha t$, we have

Angular acceleration,

$$\alpha = \frac{\omega - \omega_0}{t} = \frac{12.566 - 0}{10 \times 60}$$

$$= 0.0209 \text{ rad/sec}^2$$

(c) From the kinematic relation,

$$\omega^2 = \omega_0^2 + 2\alpha\theta$$

Angular displacement,

$$\theta = \frac{\omega^2 - \omega_0^2}{2\alpha} = \frac{(12.566)^2 - (0)^2}{2(0.0209)}$$

$$= 3778 \text{ rad}$$

Since 2π radians = 1 revolution

Hence 3778 radians = $\frac{3778}{2\pi}$ = 601.28 revolutions **Ans.**

Hence total number of revolutions made by the wheel = 601 **Ans.**

EXMPLE 8.9. The motion of a gear is defined by the relation $\theta = 2t^3 - 5t^2 + 8t + 20$ where θ is in radians and t is in seconds.

Determine the angular diplacement, the angular velocity and the angular acceleration at time $t = 5$ seconds.

SOLUTION: Given that,

$$\theta = 2t^3 - 5t^2 + 8t + 20 \quad \text{...(i)}$$

Differentiating, the above expression with respect to t,

We have

$$\frac{d\phi}{dt} = 6t^2 - 10t + 8$$

or
$$\omega = 6t^2 - 10t + 8 \quad \text{...(ii)}$$

Where, $\omega = \frac{d\phi}{dt}$ is the angular velocity of the rotating gear

Differentiating the identity (ii) with respect to t,

$$\frac{d\omega}{dt} = 12t - 10$$

or
$$\alpha = 12\,t - 10 \quad \text{...(iii)}$$

Where α = Angular acceleration of the rotating gear.

Then at $t = 5$ seconds we have

Angular displacement,

$$\theta = 2t^3 - 5t^2 + 8t + 20$$

or
$$\theta = 2(5)^3 - 5(5)^2 + 8(5) + 20$$

$$= 250 - 125 + 40 + 20$$

$$= 185 \text{ radians } \textbf{Ans.}$$

Angular velocity,

$$\omega = 6t^2 - 10t + 8$$

$$= 6(5)^2 - 10(5) + 8$$

$$= 108 \text{ rad/sec } \textbf{Ans.}$$

Angular acceleration,

$$\alpha = 12t - 10 = 12(5) - 10$$

$$= 50 \text{ rad/sec}^2 \textbf{ Ans}$$

GENERAL PLANE MOTION (COMBINED MOTION OF TRANSLATION AND ROTATION)

We have familiar with plane motion or motion of translation. We are also conversant about motion of rotation. But some times, a body has, simultaneously, a motion of rotation as well as translation, such as wheel of a car, a sphere rolling (without slipping) on the ground etc. Such a motion is having the combined effect of rotation and translation.

Motion of a rigid link

Consider a rigid link *AB*, which moves from its initial position *AB* to its final position A_1B_1. It is clear from Fig. 8.5 (a) that the link neither has, wholly a motion of translation nor wholly rotational but a combination of the two.

If we split up the motion of the link *AB*, we will find that the link has first motion of translation from *AB* to A_1B_1' and then the motion of rotation about A_1, till it occupies the final position A_1B_1 (Fig. 8.5b). The motion of link *AB* may also be considered to be first motion of rotation from *AB* to *AB′* about *A*, and then motion of translation from *AB′ to* A_1B_1 (Fig. 8.5c).

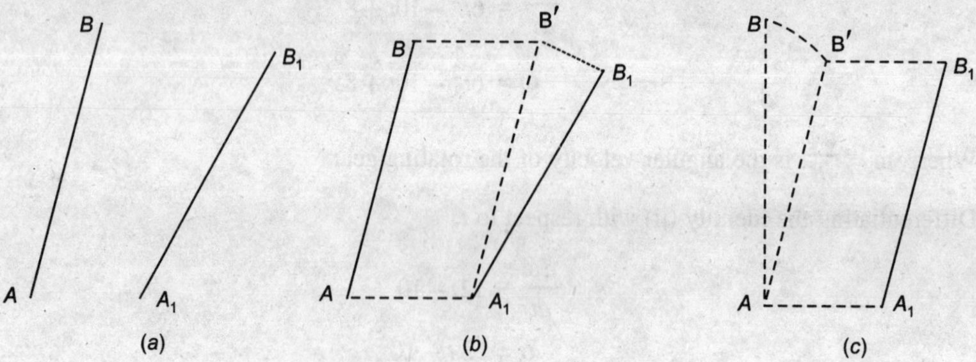

Fig. 8.5

The problems of composite motion involved in the plane motion of bodies can be handled by two methods:

1. Instantaneous centre method.
2. Analytical equation method

INSTANTANEOUS CENTRE METHOD

It is clear by the above description that the link can move from position *AB* to A_1B_1 by having composite motion consisting of translation and rotation. If this movement or displacement could be accomplished by a pure rotational motion of the link about some centre, this centre is called instantaneous centre. Instantaneous centre of course changes with the change in position of the link. The locus or patch covered by instantaneous centre is called as centroide. The position of instantaneous centre of rotation may be determined as given below.

Let the link *AB* in a short interval of time changes its position from *AB* to A_1B_1. The point *A* of the link has moved to point A_1, when the point *B* of the link has moved to the point B_1 (Fig. 8.6). Draw the right bisectors of chord AA_1 and chord BB_1. Let *CD* is the right bisector of AA_1, whereas the *EF* is the right bisector of BB_1. Let these two bisectors meet at point *I*. Then the point *I* is the instantaneous centre of rotation of link AB. This means the link AB as a whole has rotated about I.

Let, V_A = Linear velocity of point A

V_B = Linear velocity of point B

ω = Angular velocity of link AB about I

This means the angular velocity of point A and B about I will be ω.

We know that

Linear velocity = Angular velocity × r

∴ Linear vlocity of point A is given by,

V_A = Angular velocity of point A about I × Distance of A from centre of rotation (i.e. from I) = $\omega \times IA$

$$\therefore \qquad \omega = \frac{V_A}{I_A} \qquad \text{...(i)}$$

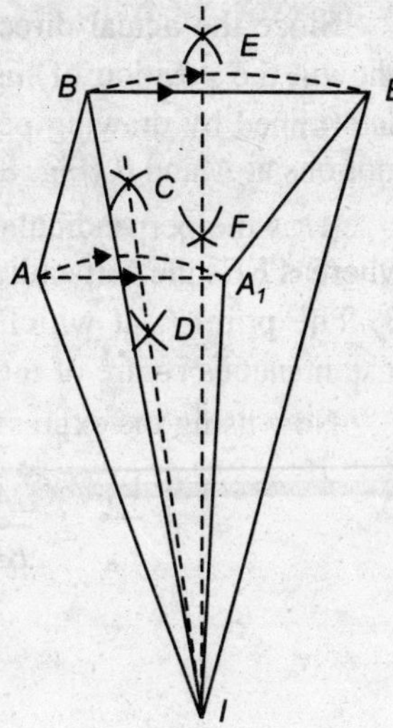

Fig. 8.6

Similarly, the linear velocity of point B is given by

V_B = Angular velocity of point B about I × Distance of B from cente of rotation (i.e. from I) = $\omega \times BI$

$$\therefore \qquad \omega = \frac{V_B}{I_B} \qquad \text{...(ii)}$$

Equating equations (i) and (ii), we get,

$$\frac{V_A}{I_A} = \frac{V_B}{I_B}$$

or

$$\frac{V_A}{V_B} = \frac{I_A}{I_B} \qquad \text{...(8.1)}$$

The direction of the velocity at A will be at right angle to IA whereas the velocity at B will be at right angle to BI.

Thus, if the directions of velocities at A and B are known, then the instantaneous centre of AB is obtained by drawing perpendiculars to the direction of velocities at A and B. The point, where these two perpendiculars meet, is the instantaneous centre.

EXAMPLE 8.10. A link AB is moving in a vertical plane. At a certain instant when the link is inclined at 30° to the horizontal, the point A is moving horizontally at 4m/sec, while B is moving vertically upwards. Find the velocity of B.

SOLUTION: Given:

Inclination of link AB with horizontal = 30°

Horizontal velocity of A, V_A = 4 m/sec

Let,

V_B = velocity of B in vertical upward direction.

Since the actual directions of motion of A and B are known, the position of instantaneous centre can be easily determined by drawing perpendiculars to the directions of motions at A and B (Fig. 8.7).

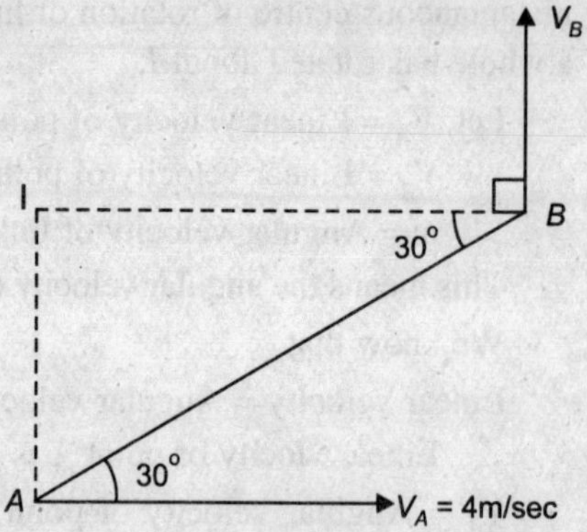

Fig. 8.7

AI is the perpendicular to the direction of motion of A whereas BI is the perpendicular to the direction of motion of B. The point I, at which these perpendiculars meet, is instantaneous centre of the link AB.

Now using the expression (8.1), we get

$$\frac{V_A}{V_B} = \frac{IA}{BI} = \tan 30^\circ$$

$$\left(\text{In } \Delta AIB, \tan 30^\circ = \frac{AI}{BI}\right)$$

or
$$\frac{4}{V_B} = 0.577$$

or
$$0.577\ V_B = 4$$

$\therefore$
$$V_B = \frac{4}{0.577} = 6.932 \text{ m/sec } \textbf{Ans.}$$

METHODS USED TO DETERMINE THE INSTANTANEOUS CENTRE

Depending on the given situation, following are some of the methods used to determine the instantaneous centre:

1. Let v_A and ω be linear and angular velocities of a point A on a rigid body (Fig. 8.8). Since ω and v_a are connected by the expression $v = \omega r$, the instantaneous centre I, then lies at a distance $\frac{v_a}{\omega}$ along the perpendicular to the direction of velocity v_a at point A.

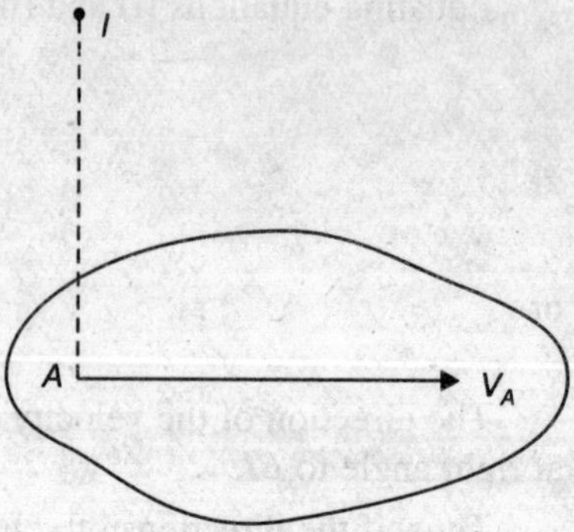

Fig. 8.8

$$I_A = \frac{v_a}{\omega} \qquad ...(i)$$

2. Let V_A and V_B be the linear velocities at point A and B on a rigid body. These velocities are directed along the direction AA' and BB' respectively. The instantaneous centre I is then be the point of intersection of the lines erected perpendicular to the direction of velocities at the given points.

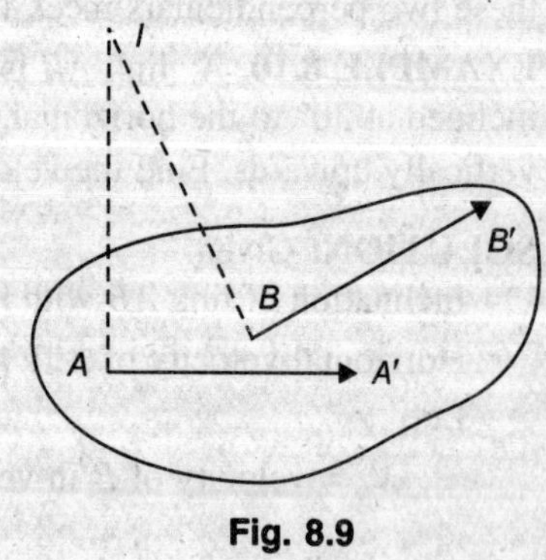

Fig. 8.9

Then,

$V_A = \omega \times IA$ and $V_B = \omega \times I_B$, where ω = Angular velocity with which the body shall appear to rotate about the instantaneous centre I.

3. Consider a solid circular cylinder in contact with two horizontal conveyer belts running with different velocities in the same or opposite directions (Fig. 8.10).

The instantaneous centre is found by determining the point of intersection of line *AB* with the line joining the extremities of the velocities vectors (FIg. 8.11). It is to be noted that when the velocities V_A and V_B are in the same direction (i), *I* lies outside *AB* and divides it externally in the ratio V_A to V_B.

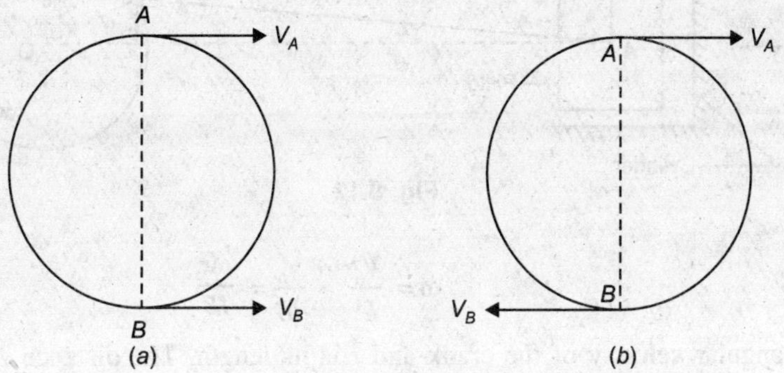

Fig. 8.10

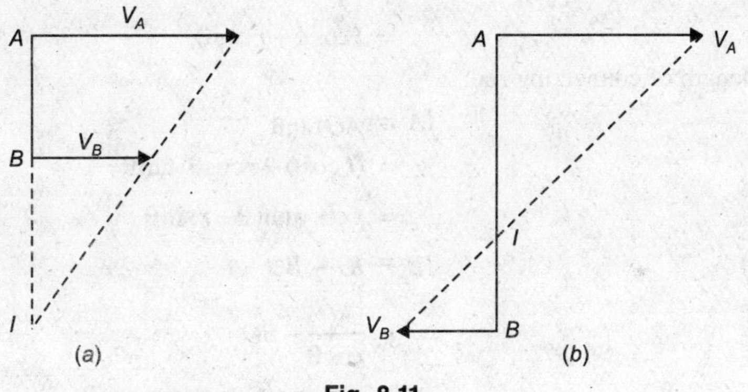

Fig. 8.11

When the velocities V_A and V_B are in opposite directions, *I* lies between *A* and *B*, and divides *AB* internally in the ratio V_A to V_B.

Every point on the cylinder shall appear to rotate about the instantaneous centre *I* with an angular velocity ω, therefore,

$$\omega = \frac{V_A}{I_A} = \frac{V_B}{I_B} \qquad \text{...(ii)}$$

4. Piston connecting rod assembly (Fig. 8.12). The point *B* moves in a circle whose centre is *O*, and the direction of V_B is perpendicular to *OB*. The velocity V_A of the piston, at any instant, must be horizontal. The instantaneous centre *I* of the connecting rod *AB* is the point of intersection of perpendiculars to V_a and V_B through *A* and *B* respectively. Then angular velocity ω_{ab} of the connecting rod about *I*, is;

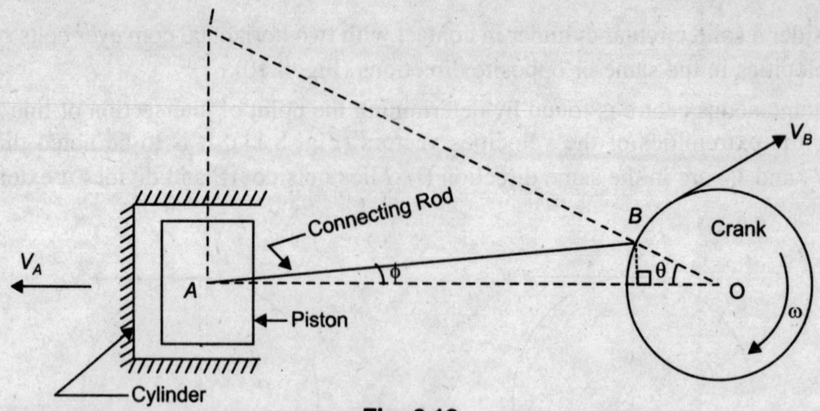

Fig. 8.12

$$\omega = \frac{V_a}{IA} = \frac{V_b}{IB} = \frac{\omega r}{IB} \quad \text{...(i)}$$

where ω is the angular velocity of the crank and r is its length. The distance IA and IB can be located as under:

$$AO = AC + CO = AB\cos\phi + BO\cos\theta$$

$$= \ell\cos\phi + r\cos\theta$$

where, l is the length of connecting rod.

$$IA = AO\tan\theta$$

$$= (\ell\cos\phi + r\cos\theta)\tan\theta$$

$$= \ell\cos\phi\tan\theta + r\sin\theta \quad \text{...(ii)}$$

$$IB = IO - BO$$

$$= \frac{AO}{\cos\theta} - BO$$

$$= \frac{\ell\cos\phi + r\cos\theta}{\cos\phi} - r$$

$$= \frac{\ell\cos\phi}{\cos\theta} + r - r = \frac{\ell\cos\phi}{\cos\theta} \quad \text{...(iii)}$$

From the expressions (i), (ii), (iii), the velocity V_a of the piston can be written as

$$V_a = \frac{IA}{IB}V_b$$

$$= \frac{\ell\cos\phi\tan\theta + r\sin\theta}{\ell\cos\phi/\cos\theta} \times \omega r$$

$$= \left(\cos\theta\tan\theta + \frac{r\sin\theta\cos\theta}{\ell\cos\phi}\right)\omega r$$

Applying sine rule to ΔOAB,

$$\frac{OB}{\sin\phi} = \frac{AB}{\sin\theta}; \quad \frac{r}{\sin\phi}$$

$$= \frac{\ell}{\sin\theta}; \quad \frac{r}{\ell} = \frac{\sin\phi}{\sin\theta}$$

Then,

$$V_a = \omega(r\sin\theta + r\cos\theta\tan\phi)$$

$$= \omega(\ell\sin\phi + r\cos\theta\tan\phi) \qquad \text{...(8.2)}$$

EXAMPLE 8.11. The crank of reciprocating engine is rotating at 210 r.p.m. The lengths of the crank and connecting rod are 20 cm and 100 cm respectively. Find the velocity of point A (piston), when crank has turned through an angle of 45° with the horizontal (Fig. 8.13).

SOLUTION: Given: Rotation of crank, $N = 210$ r.p.m.

∴ Angular velocity of crank,

$$\omega = \frac{2\pi N}{60} = \frac{2\pi(210)}{60}$$

$$= 22 \text{ rad/sec}$$

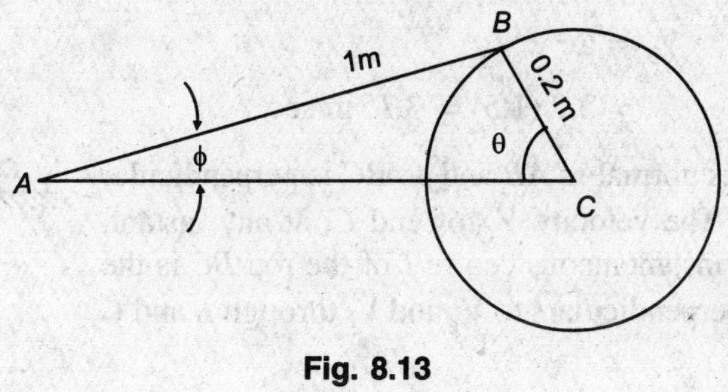

Fig. 8.13

Crank length or radius,

$$r = 20 \text{ cm} = 0.20 \text{ m}$$

Length of connecting rod,

$$l = 100 \text{ cm} = 1.0 \text{ m}$$

Angle turned by crank, $\theta = 45°$.

The velocity of point A, i.e. V_a can be calculated analytically by using equation 8.2,, i.e.

$$V_a = \omega(\ell\sin\phi + r\cos\theta\tan\phi)$$

Let us first calculate the angle ϕ.

Applying the sine rule for the triangle ABC (Fig. 8.13)

$$\frac{BC}{\sin\phi} = \frac{AB}{\sin\theta}$$

$$\therefore \qquad \sin\phi = \frac{BC\sin\theta}{AB}$$

$$= \frac{0.2}{1.0}\sin 45^\circ = 0.1414$$

$$\therefore \qquad \phi = \sin^{-1}(0.1414)$$

$$= 8.13^\circ$$

Using equation 8.2, we get

$$V_a = \omega(\ell\sin\phi + r\cos\theta\tan\phi)$$

$$= 22(1\times 0.1414 + 0.2\times\cos 45^\circ\times\tan 8.13^\circ)$$

$$V_a = 22\ (0.1414 + 0.2 \times .7071 \times 0.1428)$$

$$= 22\ (0.1414 + 0.02019)$$

$$V_a = 3.55 \text{ m/sec } \textbf{Ans.}$$

EXAMPLE 8.12. At the instant (Fig. 8.14) the rod *AB* is rotating clockwise at 2.5 rad/sec. If end *C* of the rod *BC* is free to move on a horizontal surface, make calculatios for the angular velocity of rod *BC* and the velocity of its end point *C*.

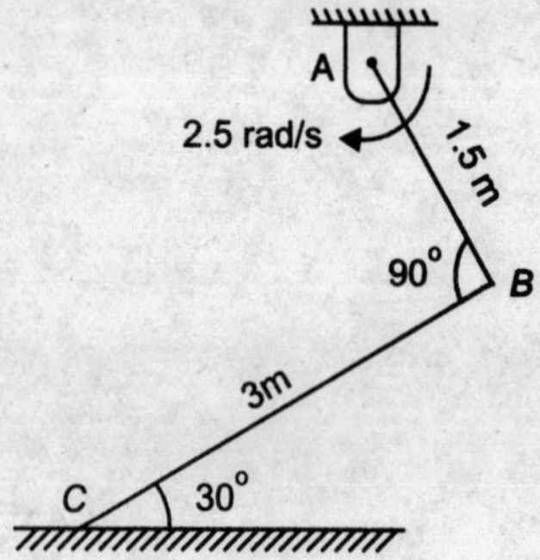

Fig. 8.14

SOLUTION: Velocity of end *B*,

$$V_b = \omega r$$

$$= 2.5\ (1.5) = 3.75 \text{ m/sec}$$

The direction of V_b is normal to *AB* and as *BC* is perpendicular to *AB*, it lies along *BC*. The velocity V_C of end *C*, at any instant, must be horizontal. The instantaneous centre *I* of the rod *BC* is the point of intersection of perpendiculars to V_b and V_c through *B* and *C* respectively (Fig. 8.15).

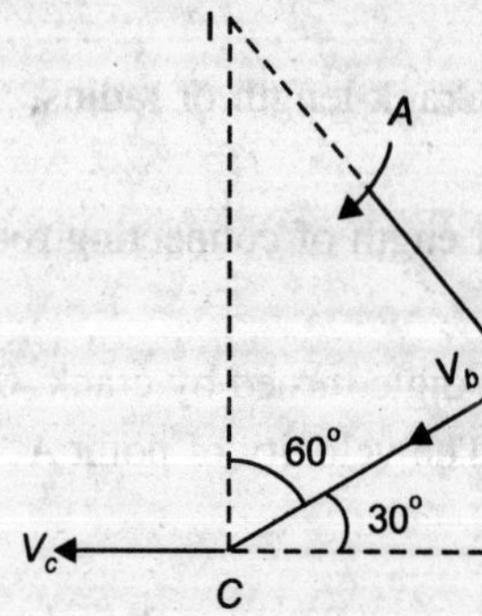

Fig. 8.15

$$IC = \frac{BC}{\cos 60^\circ}$$

$$= \frac{3}{0.50} = 6m$$

$$IB = IC\sin 60^\circ$$

$$= 6 \times 0.866 = 5.196 \text{ m}$$

Angular velocity of rod *BC*,

$$\omega = \frac{V_b}{IB} = \frac{V_c}{IC}$$

$$= \frac{3.75}{5.196} = 0.722 \text{ rad/sec (clockwise) } \textbf{Ans.}$$

$$V_c = \omega(IC) = 0.722(6)$$

$$= 4.33 \text{ m/sec. } \textbf{Ans.}$$

EXAMPLE 8.13. In a reciproacting engine mechanism (Fig. 8.16) the length of the crank OB and connecting rod AB are 30 cm and 1 m respectively. If the crank rotates at a constant angular velocity of 200 rev/min, determine

(i) Angular velocity of connecting rod, and

(ii) The velocity of piston when the crank makes an angle of $\theta = 45°$ with the horizontal

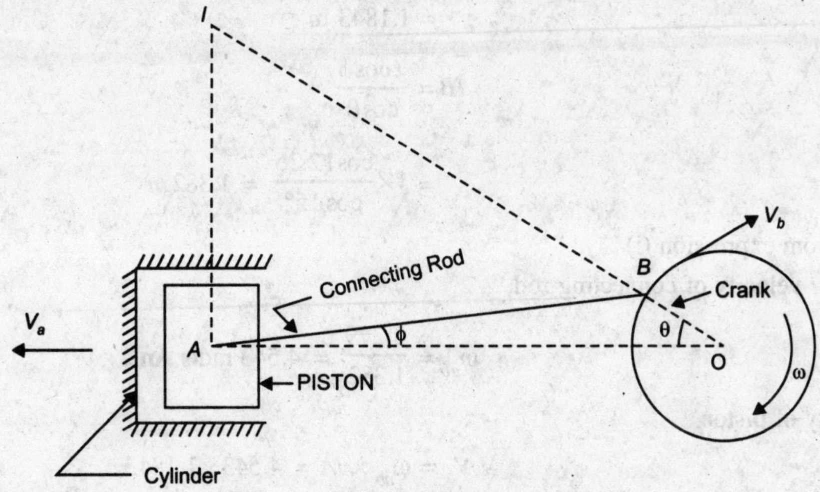

Fig. 8.16

SOLUTION: Angular velocity of the crank $= \dfrac{(2\pi N)}{60} = \dfrac{(2\pi \times 200)}{60}$

$$= 20.93 \text{ rad/sec.}$$

$$V_b = \omega r$$

$$= 20.93 \times 0.3$$

$$= 6.279 \text{ m/sec}$$

The point B moves in a circle whose centre is O, and the direction of V_a is perpendicular to OB. The velocity V_a of the piston, at any instant must be horizontal. The instantaneous centre I of the connecting rod AB is the point of intersection of perpendiculars to V_a and V_b through A and B respectively. Then angular velocity ω_{ab} of the connecting rod about I is,

$$\omega_{ab} = \frac{V_a}{IA} = \frac{V_b}{IB} = \frac{\omega r}{IB} \qquad ...(i)$$

Let θ be the angle between the connecting rod AB and the line AO. Then applying sine rule to ΔOAB.

$$\frac{OB}{\sin\phi} = \frac{AB}{\sin\theta}$$

$$\sin\phi = \frac{OB}{AB}\sin\theta = \frac{0.3}{1}\sin 45° = 0.2121$$

$$\therefore \qquad \phi = 12.25° \qquad \text{...(ii)}$$

The distance *IA* and *IB* are worked out from the relations:

$$IA = \ell\cos\phi\tan\theta + r\sin\theta$$

$$= (1\times\cos 12.25°\times\tan 45°) + 0.3\sin 45°$$

$$= 0.9772 + 0.2121$$

$$= 1.1843 \text{ m}$$

and

$$IB = \frac{\ell\cos\phi}{\cos\theta}$$

$$= 1\times\frac{\cos 12.25}{\cos 45°} = 1.382\, m$$

Then from expression (i)

Angular velocity of connecting rod,

$$\omega_{ab} = \frac{6.279}{1.382} = 4.543 \text{ rad/s } \textbf{Ans.}$$

Velocity of piston

$$V_a = \omega_{ab}\times IA = 4.543\times 1.1843$$

$$= 5.38 \text{ m/ sec } \textbf{Ans.}$$

EXAMPLE 8.14. A cylinder of diameter 3m rolls without slipping along a horizontal surface *PQ* as shown in Fig. 8.17. If its centre has a uniform velocity of 30 m/sec, determine the velocities of the points *B* and *D* lying on the rim of the cylinder.

SOLUTION: When the cylinder rolls without slipping, its point of contact with the horizontal surface at any instant has zero velocity. Thus the point *A* is instantaneously at rest and every other point on the cylinder has angular velocity about *A*.

Hence *A* is instantaneous centre of the cylnider. Then,

$$V_c = \omega\times AC;$$

$$V_B = \omega\times AB$$

$$V_d = \omega\times AD$$

Angular velocity of the cylinder,

$$\omega = \frac{V_c}{AC} = \frac{30}{3/2} = 20 \text{ rad/sec}$$

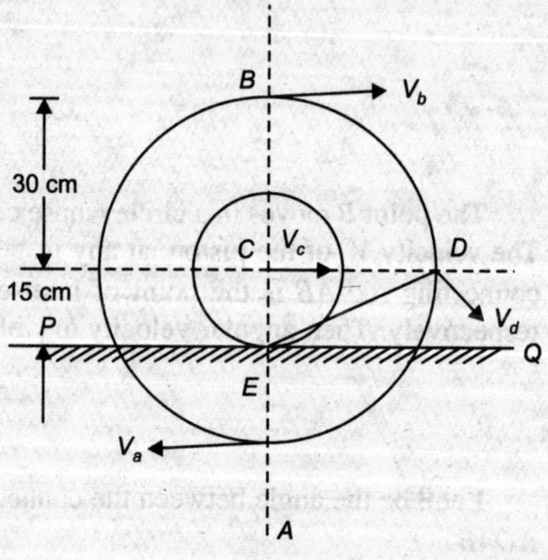

Fig. 8.17

Distance

$$AD = \sqrt{(DC)^2 + (AC)^2}$$

$$= \sqrt{(1.5)^2 + (1.5)^2} = 2.121 \text{ m}$$

∴ Velocity of point B;

$$V_b = \omega(AB) = 20(3)$$

$$= 60 \text{ m/sec } \textbf{Ans.}$$

Velocity of point D;

$$V_d = \omega(AD) = 20(2.121)$$

$$= 42.42 \text{ m/sec } \textbf{Ans.}$$

EXAMPLE 8.15. A flywheel 0.5 m in diameter accelerates uniformly from rest to 360 r.p.m. in 12 seconds. Determine,

(i) The velocity, and

(ii) Acceleration of a point on the rim of the wheel 1 second after it has started from rest.

SOLUTION: $\omega_0 = 0$,

$$\omega = \frac{2\pi N}{60} = \frac{2\pi(360)}{60}$$

$$= 37.699 \text{ rad/sec}$$

From the kinematic relation, $\omega = \omega_0 + \alpha t$, we have,

Angular acceleration,

$$\alpha = \frac{\omega - \omega_0}{t} = \frac{37.699}{12} = 3.14 \text{ rad/sec}^2$$

Angular velocity of the wheel 1 second after starting

$$\omega = \omega_0 + \alpha t = 0 + 3.14(1)$$

$$= 3.14 \text{ rad/sec}$$

The linear velocity and angular velocity are connected by the relation, $v = \omega r$.

Hence linear speed,

$$v = \omega r = 3.14 \times \frac{0.5}{2}$$

$$= 0.785 \text{ m/sec } \textbf{Ans.}$$

The linear velocity will be tangential to the rim

The components of acceleration are

Tangential acceleration,

$$\alpha_t = \alpha r = 3.14 \times \frac{0.5}{2}$$

$$= 0.785 \text{ m/sec}^2$$

Normal acceleation,

$$\alpha_n = \omega^2 r = (3.14)^2 \times \frac{0.5}{2}$$
$$= 2.46 \text{ m/sec}^2$$

Magnitude of total acceleration,

$$\alpha = \sqrt{\alpha_t^2 + \alpha_n^2}$$
$$= \sqrt{(0.785)^2 + (2.46)^2}$$
$$= 2.5822 \text{ m/sec}^2$$

Let ϕ be the angle between the total acceleration vector and the radius, then

$$\phi = \tan^{-1}\left(\frac{\alpha_t}{\alpha_n}\right) = \tan^{-1}\left(\frac{0.785}{2.46}\right)$$
$$= 17.72° \textbf{ Ans.}$$

EXAMPLE 8.16. An army vehicle travelling at 45 kph has its wheels of 1m diameter. **Find the** velocity of the top of the wheel relative to a person

(i) Sitting in the carriage; and

(ii) Standing on the ground

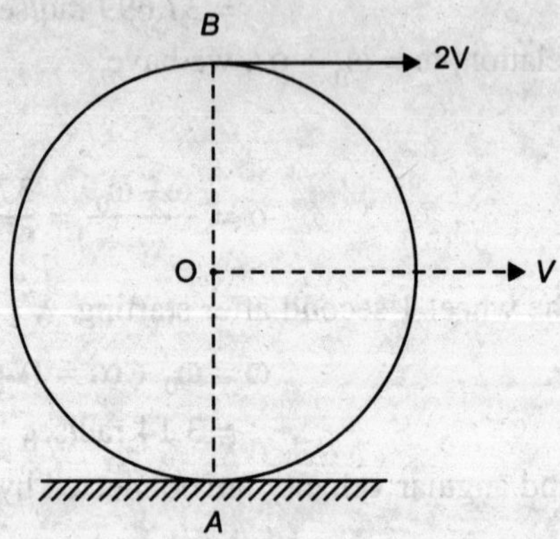

Fig. 8.18

SOLUTION: Given:

$$V = 45 \text{ km. p.h.} = \frac{45 \times 1000}{60 \times 60}$$
$$= 12.5 \text{ m/sec}$$
$$d = 1\text{m},$$
$$r = 0.5 \text{ m}$$

(i) VELOCITY OF THE TOP OF THE WHEEL RELATIVE TO THE PERSON SITTING IN THE CARRIAGE (Refer Fig. 8.18)

We know that the velocity of the top of the wheel (*B*) i.e. highest point of the wheel will be subjected to a resultant velocity of $2V$ and will act perpendicular to *OB*

$$= 2V = 2 \times 12.5$$

$$= 25 \text{ m/sec} \quad ...(i)$$

and velocity of the person sitting in the carriage

$$V = 12.5 \text{ m/sec} \quad ...(ii)$$

∴ Velocity of the top of the wheel relative to the person sitting in the carriage

$$= 25 - 12.5$$

$$= 12.5 \text{ m/sec } \textbf{Ans.}$$

(ii) VELOCITY OF THE TOP OF THE WHEEL RELATIVE TO THE PERSON STANDING ON THE GROUND

We know that velocity of the person standing on the ground = 0

∴ Velocity of the top of the wheel relative to the person standing on the ground

$$= 25 - 0$$

$$= 25 \text{ m/sec } \textbf{Ans.}$$

FOUR BAR MECHANISM

Fig. 8.19 shows a four bar mechanism, which consists of a fixed link *AD*, two movable links *AB* and *CD*, rotating about points *A* and *D* respectively, and a connecting link *BC* (which is also known as coupler *BC*). Let the link *AB* is rotating at a uniform angular velocity and it is required to find the corresponding motions of the two links *BC* and *CD*.

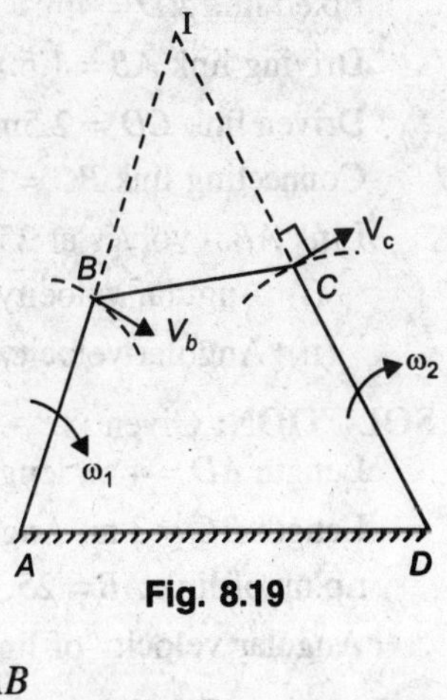

Fig. 8.19

Let,

ω_1 = Angular velocity of link *AB*, rotating about *A* in clockwise direction. The value of W_1 is given.

ω_2 = Angular velocity of link *CD*, rotating about *D*. The value of ω_2 is to be calculated.

ω_0 = Angular velocity of link *BC*. The value of ω_0 is also to be calculated.

V_b = Linear velocity of point *B* in the direction perpendicular to *AB*

$$= \omega_1 \times AB \quad ...(i)$$

V_c = Linear velocity of point *C* in direction perpendicular to *CD*

$$= \omega_2 \times CD \quad ...(ii)$$

The link *AB* and link *CD* are having motion of rotation, whereas the link *BC* is having motion of translation as well as rotation. The instantaneous centre of link *BC* for the given position is determined by drawing normals to the directions of velocity V_b and V_c. The normal to the direction V_b is the line *AB* whereas the normal to the direction V_c is line *CD*. Hence produce line *AB* and *DC*. The intersection of these lines gives the point *I* i.e. instantaneous centre for the link *BC*.

Then linear velocity at B is given by,

$$V_b = \omega_0 \times BI \qquad ...(iii)$$

and, linear velocity at C is gien by,

$$V_c = \omega_0 \times CI \qquad ...(iv)$$

Equating equations (i) and (ii), we get

$$\omega_1 \times AB = \omega_0 \times BI$$

$$\therefore \quad \omega_0 = \frac{\omega_1 \times AB}{BI} \qquad ...(8.3)$$

In the above equation (8.3), the values of ω_1 and AB are given. The value of BI is obtained from Fig. 8.20. Hence ω_0 (Angular velocity of link BC) can be determined. Again equating equations (ii) and (iv) we get,

$$\omega_2 \times CD = \omega_0 \times CI$$

$$\therefore \quad \omega_2 = \frac{\omega_0 \times CI}{CD} \qquad ...(8.4)$$

In the above equation value of CD is given, value of CI is obtained from Fig. 8.20 and the value of ω_0 is known from equation (8.3). Hence the value of ω_2 (Angular velocity of link CD) can be determined.

EXAMPLE 8.17. Fig. 8.20 shows a pin-joined four bar linkage having the following diamensions.

Fixed link AD = 4m;

Driving link AB = 1.5 m,

Driven link CD = 2.5m,

Connecting link BC = 3 m, Angle BAD = 60°

Link AB revolves at 25 r.p.m. Determine

(i) Angular velocity of link CD, and

(ii) Angular velocity of link BC.

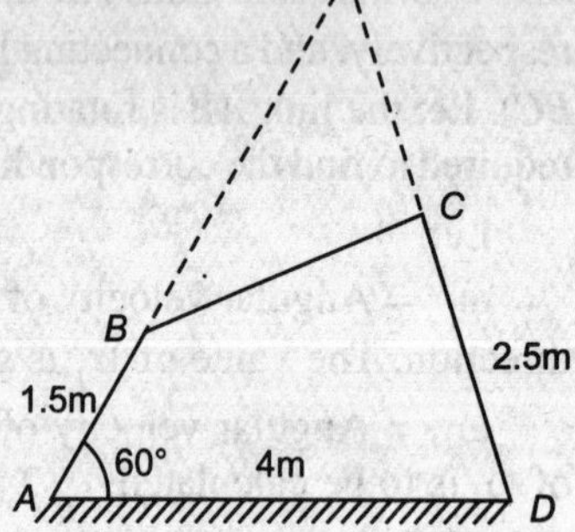

Fig. 8.20

SOLUTION: Given :

Length AD = 4 m, length AB = 1.5m, length CD = 2.5 m

Length BC = 3 m, Angle BAD = 60°,

r.p.m. of link AB = 25.

$\therefore$ Angular velocity of link AB,

$$\omega_1 = \frac{2\pi N}{60} = \frac{2\pi(25)}{60} = 2.619 \text{ rad/sec}$$

Draw the link mechanism to a suitable scale as shown in Fig. (8.20). The instantaneous centre I of the link BC is obtained by producing line AB and DC. Now measure the distance CI and BI from (Fig. 8.20)

By measurement, CI = 3m, and BI = 4.65 m.

First calculate the angular velocity of link BC

Let,

ω_0 = Angular velocity of link BI

Using the equation (8.3),

$$\omega_0 = \frac{\omega_1 \times AB}{BI} = \frac{2.619(1.5)}{4.65} = 0.845 \text{ rad/sec } \textbf{Ans.}$$

The angular velocity of link CD (i.e. ω_2) is obtained by using equation (8.4),

$$\omega_2 = \frac{\omega_0 \times CI}{CD} = \frac{0.845(3)}{2.5} = 1.014 \text{ rad/sec } \textbf{Ans.}$$

EXAMPLE 8.18. In a reciprocating pump, the lengths of connecting rod and crank is 1125 mm and 250 mm respectively. The crank is rotating at 420 r.p.m. Find the velocity, with which the piston will move, when the crank has turned through an angle of 40° from inner dead centre.

SOLUTION: Given: l = 1125 mm = 1.125m, r = 250 mm = 0.25 m, N = 420 r.p.m.; θ = 40°

We know that angular velocity of the crank,

$$\omega = \frac{2\pi N}{60} = \frac{2\pi \times 420}{60}$$

$$= 14\pi = 43.98 \text{ rad/sec}$$

and velocity of B,

$$V_b = \omega.r. = 43.98 \times 0.25 = 11 \text{ m/sec}$$

Now let us locate the position of the instantaneous centre of the rod BC (Fig. 8.21) as discussed below:

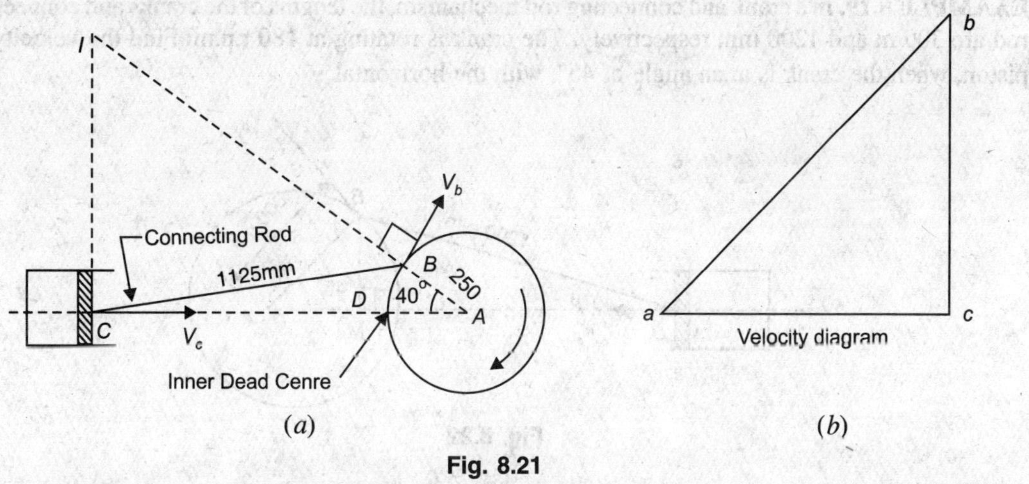

Fig. 8.21

1. Select a suitable point A, and draw a circle with A as centre and 0.25 m radius to some suitable scale to represent crank of the pump.
2. Through A, draw horizontal line meeting at D on the circumference of the crank, representing the inner dead centre. Extend the line AD.
3. Draw a line AB such that angle BAD is equal to 40°.
4. With B as radius cut off BC equal to 1.125 m to the scale on the horizontal line through A, representing the connecting rod of the pump.

5. Extend the line *AB*, and through *C* draw a line at right angles to *AC*, meeting the extended line *AB* at *I*, which is the instantaneous centre of the rod *BC*.
6. Measuring the diagram to scale, we find,
   $IB = 1.45$m and $IC = 1.1$ m
   We know that velocity of *C*:

$$V_c = \frac{V_b \times I_c}{IB} = \frac{11 \times 1.1}{1.45} = 8.345 \text{ m/sec}$$

Value of V_c can also be determined with the help of velocity diagram as discussed below:

First of all, draw the space diagram of reciprocating pump as shown in Fig. 8.21. Now proceed as discussed below:

1. Take some suitable point a and draw a horizontal line representing the direction of motion of the piston i.e. V_c.
2. Through *a*, draw another line *ab* representing the direction of motion of *B* i.e. V_b, which is at 40° with the horizontal.
3. Now cut off *ab* equal to 11 m/sec to some suitable scale.
4. Through *b*, draw *bc* perpendicular to the connecting rod.
5. Now *ac* gives the velocity of piston to the scale. By measurement, we find that velocity of piston,

$$V_c = A_c = 8.3 \text{ m/sec } \textbf{Ans.}$$

EXAMPLE 8.19. In a crank and connecting rod mechanism, the lengths of the cranks and connecting rod are 300 m and 1200 mm respectively. The crank is rotating at 180 r.p.m. Find the velocity of piston, when the crank is at an angle of 45°, with the horizontal.

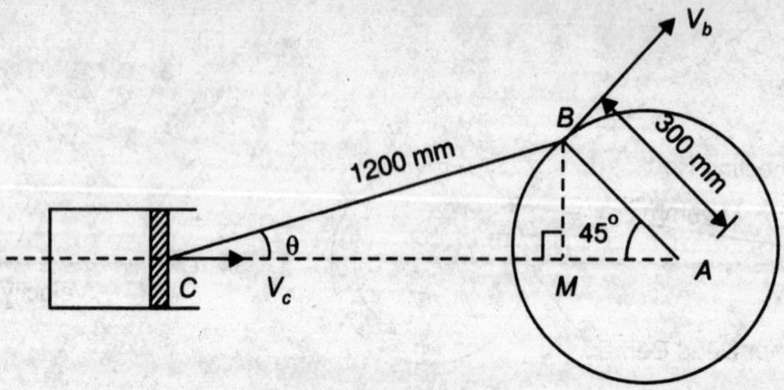

Fig. 8.22

SOLUTION: Given: $l = 1200$ mm $= 1.2$ *m*, $r = 300$ mm $= 0.3$ m, $N = 180$ r.p.m.; $\theta = 45°$

Angular velocity of the crank,

$$\omega = \frac{2\pi(180)}{60} = 18.85 \text{ rad/sec}$$

From the geometry of the figure, we find that,

$$\sin\phi = \frac{\text{Perp.}}{\text{Diagn.}} = \frac{BM}{BC}$$

$$= \frac{AB \sin 45}{BC} = \frac{0.3\ (0.7071)}{1.2}$$

$$= 0.1768$$

$$\therefore \qquad \phi = \sin^{-1}(0.1768)$$

$$= 10.18°$$

We know that velocity of the piston,

$$V_c = \omega\ (l \sin \phi + r \cos \theta \times \tan \phi)$$

$$= 18.85\ (1.2 \sin 10.18° + 0.3 \cos 45° \times \tan 10.18°)$$

$$= 18.85\ (1.2 \times 0.1768 + 0.3 \times 0.7071 \times 0.1796)$$

$$= 18.85\ (0.21216 + 0.03809)$$

$= 4.72$ m/sec **Ans.**

EXAMPLE 8.20. The crank *AB* in a mechanism shown in Fig. 8.23 rotates at 5 rev/sec is 300 mm long. The link *CB* is 600 mm long, and piston *C* moves in horizontal guides. Find for the position shown

(i) Velocity of piston *C*

(ii) Angular velocity of the connecting rod *AB*, and

(iii) Velocity of a point *D* at the centre of *AB*.

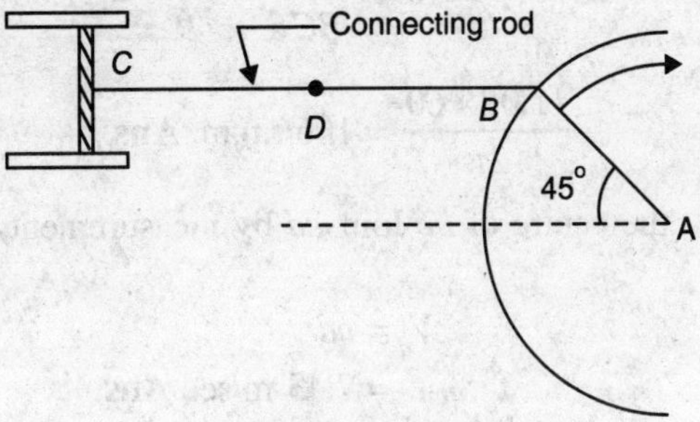

Fig. 8.23

SOLUTION: Given: $l = 600$ mm $= 0.6$ m, $r = 300$ mm $= 0.3$ m, $N = 5$ rev/sec

We know that angular velocity of the crank,

$$\omega = 2\pi N = 2\pi(5)$$

$$= 31.4159 \text{ rad/sec.}$$

and velocity of *B*,

$$V_b = \omega r = 31.4159\ (0.3)$$

$$= 9.4248 \text{ m/sec}$$

First of all draw the space diagram for the mechanism as shown in Fig. 8.24 (a). Now draw the velocity diagram as shown in Fig. 8.24(b) and as discussed below:

1. Take some suitable point *a*, and draw a horizontal line representing the direction of motion of the piston (i.e. V_c).
2. Through a draw a line *ab* repreenting the direction of motion *B* (i.e. V_b) which is at 45° with the horizontal.

3. Now cut off *ab* equal to 9.4 m/sec to some suitable scale.
4. Through *b*, draw *bc* perpendicular to the connected rod (which is vertical).
5. Now *ac* gives the velocity of the piston to the scale.

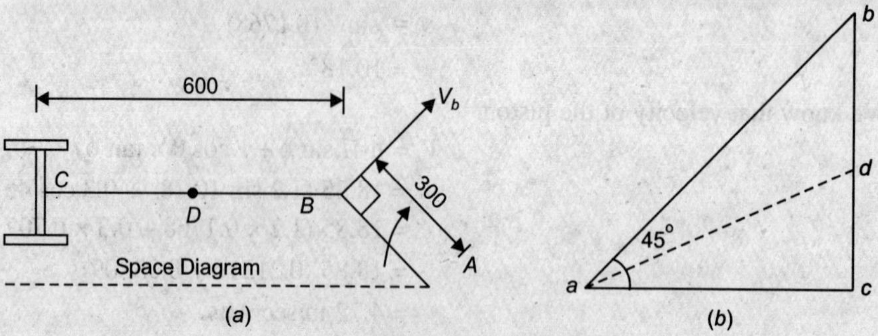

Fig. 8.24

By measurement, we find the velocity of the piston, $V_c = ac = 6.65$ m/sec **Ans.**

By measurement, we also find that $bc = 6.65$ m/sec

∴ Angular velocity of connecting rod,

$$\omega = \frac{bc}{BC} = \frac{6.65}{.6} = 11.08 \text{ rad/sec}$$

$$\frac{11.08 \times 60}{2\pi} = 106 \text{ r.p.m. } \textbf{Ans.}$$

Now locate a point *d* at the centre of *bc* Join *ad* by measurement, we also find that velocity of *D*,

$$V_d = ad$$
$$= 7.43 \text{ m/sec } \textbf{Ans.}$$

EXAMPLE 8.20. Three links are hinged together to form a triangle as shown in Fig. 8.25.

At a certain instant, the point *A* is moving towards the mid point of *BC* with a velocity of 5 m/sec, and *B* is moving at perpendicular direction to *AC*. Find the velocity of *C*.

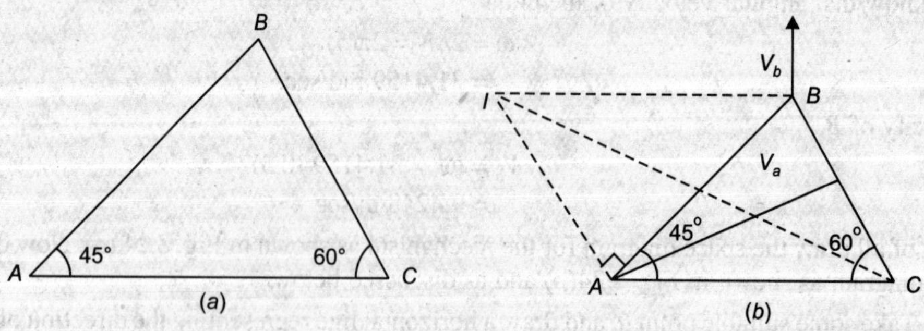

Fig. 8.25

SOLUTION: Given: Velocity of A, $v_a = 5$ m/sec.

First of all, let us locate the position of instantaneous centre of the points A and B graphically as shown in Fig. 8.25 (b). and as discussed below:

1. Draw a triangle ABC with the given data.
2. Now draw the lines indicating the directions of motions of the points A (towards mid-point of BC) and B at right angles to AC.
3. Now draw perpendiculars at A and B on the directions of motion of V_a and V_b.
4. Let these perpendiculars meet at I, which is the instantaneous centre of the link AB and BC.
5. Now join IC and draw a line at right angles to IC indicating the direction of motion of point C.

Measuring the diagram to some scale, find that $IA = 2.6$ and $IC = 5.4$ cm.

We know that,

$$\frac{V_c}{V_a} = \frac{IC}{IA} = \frac{5.4}{2.6} = 2.08$$

Hence velocity at C,

$$V_C = V_a(IC) = 5(2.08) = 10.38 \text{ m/sec}$$

Hence velocity of $C = 10.38$ m/sec **Ans.**

EXERCISE-8

1. A wheel rotating about a fixed axis at 20 r.p.m. is uniformly accelerated for 70 seconds during which it makes 50 revolutions. Find the (i) Angular velocity at the end of this interval, and (ii) time required for the velocity to reach 100 revolutions per minute.
   [**Ans.** $\omega = 6.8816$ rad/sec. and $t = 122.497$ sec.]
2. A flywheel, which accelerates at uniform velocity is observed to have made 100 revolutions to increase its velocity from 120 r.p.m. to 160 r.p.m. If the flywheel originally started from rest, determine (i) The value of acceleration, (ii) Time taken to increase the velocity from 120 r.p.m. to 160 r.p.m. and (iii) Revolution made in reaching a velocity of 160 r.p.m., starting from rest. [**Ans.** $\alpha = 0.0977$ rad/sec^2, $t = 42.86$ secs, $\theta' = 228.57$ revolutions]
3. Power supply was cut off to a power driven wheel when it was rotating at a speed of 900 r.p.m. It was observed to come to rest after making 360 revolutions. Determine the angular retardation and time it took to come to rest. [**Ans.** $\alpha = -1.9635$ rad/sec^{2}and $t = 48$ secs]
4. A wheel rotating about fixed axis at 20 r.p.m. is uniformly accelerated for 70 seconds during which time it makes 50 revolutions. Find (i) Angular velocity at the end of this interval, (ii) Time required for the speed to reach 100 revolutions per minute.
   [**Ans.** $\omega = 6.8816$ rad/sec, and $t = 122.497$ secs]
5. The armature of an electric motor rotates at 2000 r.p.m. at the instant when power is cut off. Calculate the average angular deceleration if it comes to rest in 10 seconds. Find how many complete revolutions the armature makes during this period. [**Ans.** $N = 167$ revolutions]

6. In a 4-bar mechanism *ABCD*, the two points *A* and *D* are fixed while the links AB and CD can rotate about the fixed points *A* and *D* as shown in Fig. 8.26. Find graphically or otherwise, the velocity of *B* and angular velocity of link *AB*, when the link *CD* rotates at 240 r.p.m. in the clockwise direction.

[**Ans.** V_B = 18.3 m/sec, 700 r.p.m.]

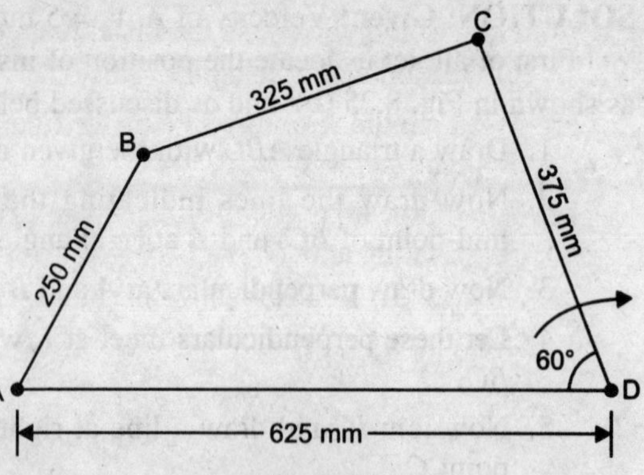

Fig. 8.26

7. In a reciprocating engine mechanism at a instant when the crank makes an angle of 45° with the line connecting piston and crank shaft, and from inner dead centre, the velocity of piston is found to be 4 m/sec. The length of the connecting rod is 1 m and crank radius is 30 cm. Determine (i) Angular speed of the crank in revolutions/min., (ii) Angular velocity of the connecting rod, and (iii) Acceleration of piston.

[**Ans.** N = 147 r.p.m., ω_P = 3.36 rad/sec, a_P = 51 m/sec^2]

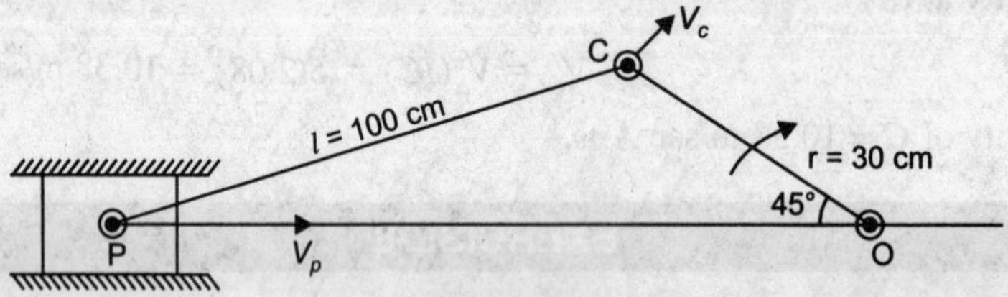

Fig. 8.27

8. In a 4-bar mechanism *ABCD*, points *A* and *C* are fixed points 37.5 cm apart and *AB, CD* are bars 75 cm and 87.5 cm long respectively which are connected by a rod *BD* which is 62.5 cm long. The bars move in one plane. If *AB* rotates with a uniforn speed of 60 r.p.m., determine (i) The velocity of *D* when *AB* is perpendicular to *AC* and also when it makes 10° on either side of the perpendicular, (ii) The instantaneous centres of the bar *BD* and its angular velocity in three positions. [**Ans.** 5.112 m/sec, 5.226 m/sec, 2.274 rad/sec in three positions]
9. In a crank and connecting rod mechanism, the crank is 300 mm long and the connecting rod 1500 mm long. If the crank rotates uniformly at 300 r.p.m., find the velocity of the cross-head when the crank is inclined at 30° with the inner dead centre. [**Ans.** 5.39 m/sec]
10. The lengths of connecting rod and crank in a reciprocating engine are 1000 mm and 225 mm respectively. The crank is rotating at 360 r.p.m. Find the velocity of cross head, when the crank has turned through 30° with the line joining the centres. [**Ans.** 5.19 m/sec]
11. The crank and connecting rod of a steam engine are 0.5 m and 2 m respectively. The crank makes 180 r.p.m. in the clockwise direction. When the crank has turned 45° from the inner dead centre, determine (i) Velocity of piston, and (ii) Angular velocity of the connecting rod.

[**Ans.** 8.15 m/sec, 32.5 r.p.m.]

12. Explain the term Instantaneous Centre.
13. Derive a relation for the velocity of a piston in a crank and connecting rod mechanism.

14. **How would you locate the Instantaneous centre of a rigid link moving with combined motion of rotation and translation?**

15. **What are the various methods for finding out the velocity of piston of a reciprocating pump? Explain them.**

16. **A reciprocating engine mechanism is shown in Fig. 8.28. The crank *OA* is of length 15 cm and rotating at 600 r.p.m. The connecting rod *AB* is 70 cm long. Find (i) Angular velocity of the rod, (ii) Velocity of piston *B*, (iii) Velocity of point *C* on the connecting rod at a distance 20 cm from *A*, when θ = 45°.**

[Ans. ω_{ab} = 9.64 rad/sec, V_b = 7.67 m/sec, and V_c = 8.4 m/sec]

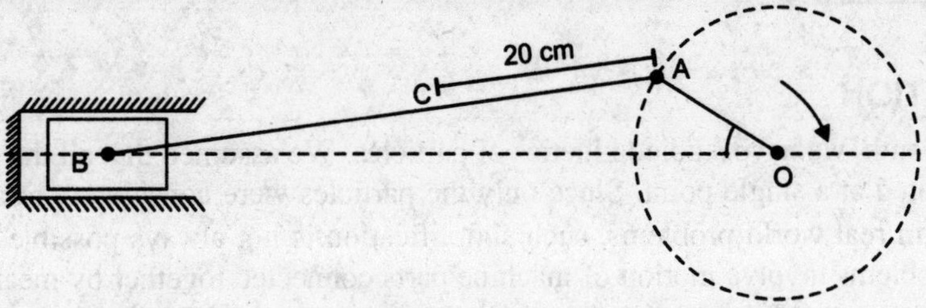

Fig. 8.28

CHAPTER 9

Kinetics of Rigid Bodies

INTRODUCTION

In chapter seventh, we have studied kinetics of particles. We assumed that all the mass of the body was concentrated at a single point. Since only the particles were considered, rotation of the body was ignored. In real world problems, such simplification is not always possible. In machine tool structures, problems involve motion of machine parts connected together by means of links, gears and several other type of connections. In such cases, the motion of one point relative to the other point in the same body becomes important. Hence it is necesary to consider the rotation of the body in such cases.

RIGID BODY

A rigid body is a collection of particles that are held together by internal forces such that the distances between them remain constant. Hence, a rigid body is one in which the distance between any two points does not change due to an application of external force on it. If a rigid body has a motion and acceleration in any direction, each particle of the body will have the same acceleration in that direction.

In this chaper, we shall study the relations betwen the applied forces and the corresponding motion of translation, rotation or both, of the rigid body. We shall study the problems that can be idealized as plane motion problems. For this, we shall assume the body as a thin slab with its mass centre lying in the plane of study. The forces acting on the body can be projected on the plane and their effects can be found out. A variety of engineering problems can be idealized as the plane motion problems.

Let a system of forces be act on a rigid body (idealized into a plane) as shown in Fig. 9.1 (a). The resultant of the force system may be any one of the following:

1. Resultant force $\sum P$, passing through the mass centre of the body, as shown in Fig. 9.1 (b).
2. A resultant couple L, acting on the body (Fig. 9.1 c)
3. A resultant force $\sum P$ acting at some distance from the mass centre of the body i.e., a resultant force $\sum P$ acting at mass centre of the rigid body accompained by a resultant couple L (Fig. 9.1 d).

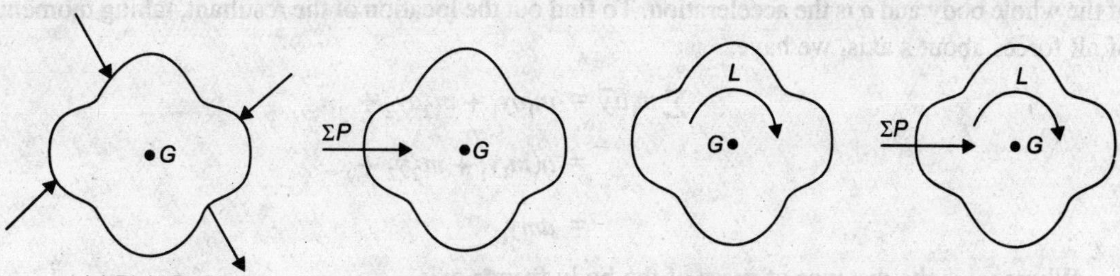

Fig. 9.1

Case – 1, produces the motion of translation which may be rectilinear or curvilinear.

Case – 2, produces the motion of rotation which may be centroidal i.e., about *G*, or non-centroidal i.e., about any other point.

Case – 3, produces a general plane motion which is a motion of combined translation and rotation.

The problems of kinetics of rigid bodies can also be solved by the three methods used for particle kinetics. These methods are:

1. Force, mass and acceleration method (inertia force method).
2. Work and energy method
3. Impulse and momentum method

These methods will now be discussed in detail along with the motion of translation, rotation and plane motion one by one.

TRANSLATION

If a rigid body has a motion of translation, every line of the body remains parallel to its original position at all the times. The translation may be rectilinear or curvilinear.

Consider a rigid body idealized into a thin slab having a motion of translation in or parallel to *XOY* plane, and having an acceleration of $a_x = a$ in *x* direction. By identification of a rigid body, all the particles will have the same acceleration. We can apply Newton's law of motion, viz., $\sum P = ma$ or in general, $\sum P_x - ma_x$ and $\sum P_y - ma_y$, to this rigid body. These equations determine the magnitude and sense of the resultant in terms of mass and acceleration but they do not locate the point of application of the resultant force. To locate the resultant of the force, we shall use *D*'Alembert's principle.

According to *D*'Alembert's principle, the resultant vector of the external forces acting on a rigid body is equal to the resultant of m_a vectors of the particles of the body.

Let a particle of the body lying at co-ordinate (x_1, y_2) has a mass m_1. Its m_a vector will be $m_1 a$. The *ma* vectors of all the particles from a system of parallel forces, the resultant of which is $\Sigma m_1 a = ma$, where *m* is the mass

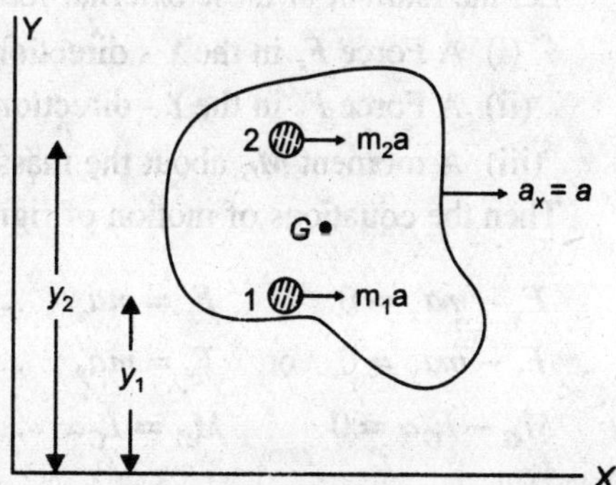

Fig. 9.2

of the whole body and a is the acceleration. To find out the location of the resultant, taking moments of all forces about z axis, we have,

$$\sum m_1 a\bar{y} = m_1 a y_1 + m_2 a y_2 + ...$$

$$= a(m_1 y_1 + m_2 y_2 + ...$$

$$= amy_G$$

Where y_G is the distance of mass of the body from z axis.

Also, $\sum m_1 a = ma$

$$\therefore \qquad \bar{y} = y_G$$

We may state that the resultant of the ma vectors pass through the mass centre of the body.

According to D'Alembert's principle, the resultant of the external forces acting on the body also should pass through the mass centre of the body. Thus if the moments of all the external forces are taken about the mass centre, there sum should be zero. We then have $\sum M_G = 0$.

If the external forces are inclined, their components in X and Y directions may be used. We then have,

$$\sum (M_G)_x = 0,$$

and $$\sum (M_G)_y = 0$$

We have the scalar equations of motion of translation as follows:

$$\sum P_x = ma_x,$$

$$\sum P_y = ma_y$$

and $$\sum (M_G)_x = \sum (M_G)_y = 0$$

If the rigid body has a motion of curvilinear translation, the above equations are valid.

EQUATIONS OF MOTION

Consider a rigid body of mass m in plane motion under the action of the applied external forces.

Let the rsultant of these external forces reduces to:

(i) A Force F_x in the X - direction

(ii) A Force F_y in the Y - direction

(iii) A moment M_G about the mass centre

Then the equations of motion of rigid body become:

$$F_x - ma_x = 0 \qquad F_x = ma_x \qquad ...(9.1)$$

$$F_y - ma_y = 0 \quad \text{or} \quad F_y = ma_y \qquad ...(9.2)$$

$$M_G - I_G\alpha = 0 \qquad M_G = I_G\alpha \qquad ...(9.3)$$

From the above equations it can be concluded that for a rigid body in plane motion we can write three equations of motion as:

(i) Two equations for the translatory motion of its mass centre due to external forces F_x and F_y.,
$F_x = ma_x$, and $F_y = ma_y \rightarrow$ translatory motion.

(ii) One equation for the rotary motion of the body, due to moment M_G of the external forces about the axis through the mass centre and perpendicular to the plane of motion,
$M_G = I_G\,\alpha \rightarrow$ Rotary motion
F_x , F_y and M_G represent the resultant of applied external forces.

RELATION BETWEEN THE TRANSLATORY MOTION AND ROTARY MOTION OF A BODY IN PLANE MOTION

To explain this point, consider the specific case of the plane motion of a right circular cylinder on a horizontal surface as shown in Fig. 9.3.

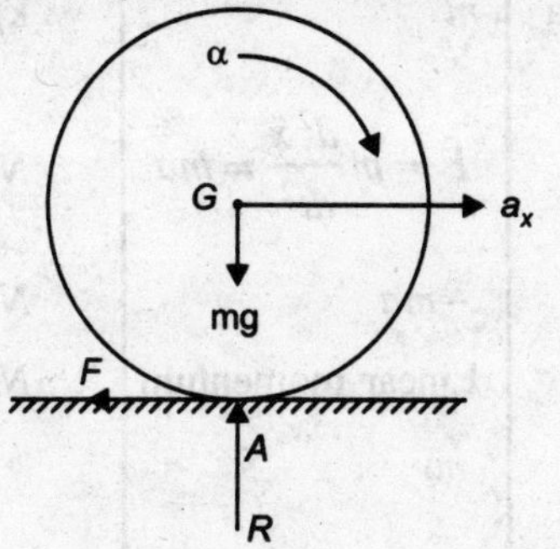

Fig. 9.3

Let the mass of the cylinder be m, R the normal reaction and F the force of friction acting on the cylinder. The acceleration of its mass centre G be a_x and angular acceleration α. The cylinder may (a) roll without slipping, (b) may slip without rolling, and (c) may roll as well as slip.

(a) THE CYLINDER ROLLS WITHOUT SLIPPING: In this case, the forward motion of the mass centre is related to its angular motion. The distance travelled and the angle turned by the body are related as

$$x = \theta r = \omega r = \alpha r$$

or

$$a_x = \alpha r$$

And the frictional force F is such that,

$F \leq \mu R$ (Less than μR)

(b) THE CYLINDER SLIPS WITHOUT ROLLING: There is no rotary motion involved in $F = uR$

(c) THE CYLINDER ROLLS AS WELL AS SLIPS: In this case translatory and rotary motions are independent of each other, and $F = uR$.

RELATION BETWEEN RECTILINEAR MOTION AND ROTATIONAL MOTION

Table 9.1

S.No.	Quantity	Rectilinear		Rotational	
		Symbol	Unit	Symbol	Unit
1	Velocity	$v=\dfrac{dx}{dt}$	m/sec	$\omega=\dfrac{d\theta}{dt}$	rad/sec
2	Acceleration	$a=\dfrac{d^2x}{dt^2}$	m/sec^2	$\alpha=\dfrac{d^2\theta}{dt^2}$	rad/sec^2
3	Displacement	x	m	θ	rad
4	Mass moment of inertia	m	kg	M.I.	kgm^2
5	Effort: Force, torque	$F=m\dfrac{d^2x}{dt^2}=ma$	N	Torque, $T = I\alpha$	Nm
6	Inertia: Force, couple	$-ma$	N	Couple = $-I\alpha$	Nm
7	Momentum	Linear momentum mv	Ns	Angular momentum $I\omega$	Nms
8	Kinetic energy	$K.E=\frac{1}{2}mv^2$	J	$K.E.=\frac{1}{2}I\omega^2$	J
9	Work	$\int F\,dx$	J	$\int T\,d\theta$	J
10	Spring constant	K	N/m	K_t	$\dfrac{Nm}{rad}$

KINETICS OF ROTARY MOTION

Below are given some brief out lines of the different aspect of kinetics of rotary motion.

(i) ROTARY MOTION: Motion of a rigid body, in which the particles move in a circular path, is called rotary motion. The particles continue repeating the same path and have a fixed centre of rotation.

(ii) TORQUE: It is turning moment of a force on a body on which it acts. Torque equals the product of force and perpendicular distance between the line of action of force and point of rotation. With reference to Fig. 9.4.

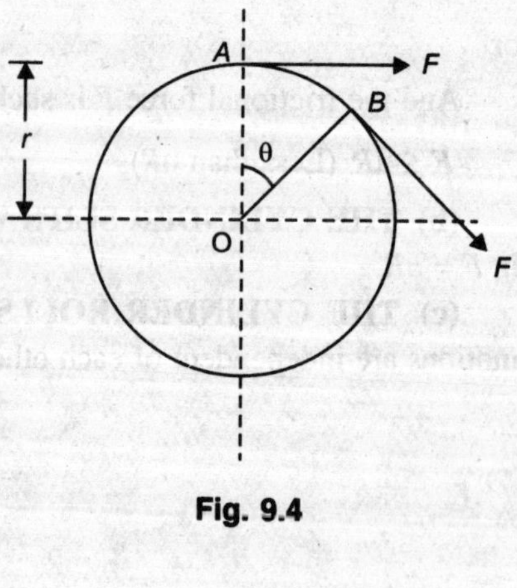

Fig. 9.4

If F is in Newtons (N) and r in metres (m), then the unit of torque will be Nm.

When the body pivoted at point O rotates through a small angle θ (measured in radians), the point A shifts to B.

Work done by the tangential force F in rotating the body from A to B = Force × distance moved = $F \times$ length of arc $AB = F \times r\,\theta = (F \times r)\theta = T\theta$.

Thus the work done by the torque is given by the product of torque and the angular displacement.

In one rotation $\theta = 2\pi$. If the body turns N revolutions per minute, then the angular displacement per second is $\frac{2\pi N}{60}$.

$$\therefore \quad \text{Work done} = T \times \frac{2\pi N}{60} \text{ Nm/sec}$$

$$\therefore \quad \text{Power of the system} = \frac{2\pi NT}{60} \text{ watt} \quad ...(9.4)$$

(ii) TORQUE AND ANGULAR MOMENTUM: The product of mass momentum of Inertia and the angular velocity of a rotating body is known as moment of momentum or angular momentum.

∴ Angular momentum

$$I\omega \quad ...(9.5)$$

Further, the rate of change of angular momentum of a rotating body is proportional to the external torque applied on the body and takes place in the direction of the torque i.e.,

$T \propto$ Rate of change of angular momentum

$$T \propto \frac{d}{dt}(I\omega)$$

$$T \propto I\frac{d\omega}{dt} = KI\alpha \quad ...(9.6)$$

Where, $\alpha = \frac{d\omega}{dt}$ = Angular accelerations, and k is a constant of proportionality

Take unit torque (T = 1) to produce unit angular acceleration (α = 1) in a body of unit mass moment of inertia (I = 1), we get k = 1 and the expression (9.6) can be written as

$$T = I\alpha \quad ...(9.7)$$

(iii) MOMENT OF INERTIA AND RADIUS OF GYRATION: The moment of inertia I of a body is the second moment of all elemental areas or masses comprising the body.

For a circular lamina of mass m and radius r, $I = \frac{1}{2}mr^2$

For a solid sphere of mass m and radius r, $I = \frac{2}{5}mr^2$, and

For a uniform bar of mass m and length l, $I = \frac{ml^2}{12}$

The radius of gyration k is defined as the distances of the point, from the axis of reference where the whole mass of the body is assumed to be concentrated so as the moment of inertia about the given axis does not change.

The moment of inertia of a body in terms of radius of gyration, is given by:

$$I = mk^2$$

or

$$k = \sqrt{\frac{I}{m}}$$

For a circular lamina:

$$k = \sqrt{\frac{mr^2}{2m}} = \frac{r}{\sqrt{2}} = 0.707\ r$$

For a solid sphere:

$$k = \sqrt{\frac{2}{5} \cdot \frac{mr^2}{m}}$$

$$= \sqrt{\frac{2}{5}}r = 0.63r$$

(iv) KINETIC ENERGY DUE TO ROTATION: With reference to Fig. 9.5, a rigid body of mass m rotates about point O with constant angular velocity ω.

K.E. of an elementary mass

$$= \frac{1}{2} dmV^2 = \frac{1}{2} dm(\omega r)^2$$

$$= \frac{1}{2} \omega^2 r^2 dm$$

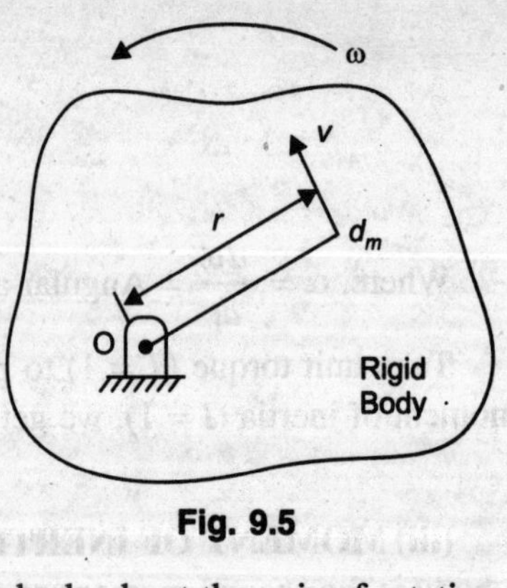

Fig. 9.5

K.E. of the whole body

$$= \int \frac{1}{2} \omega^2 r^2 dm$$

$$= \frac{1}{2} \omega^2 \int r^2\ dm$$

The quantity $\int r^2\ dm$ represents the moment of inertia of the body about the axis of rotation.

$\therefore$ K.E. of a rotating body $= \frac{1}{2} I\omega^2$

Work done equals the change in kinetic energy and therefore

$$\text{Work done} = T\theta$$

$$= \frac{1}{2} I(\omega_2^2 - \omega_1^2)$$

(v) KINETIC ENERGY IN PLANE MOTION: The plane motion of a rigid body consists of rectilinear motion and a rolling motion without slipping. Then, total kinetic energy of the body = K.E. in translation + K.E. in rotation

$$= \frac{1}{2}mV^2 + \frac{1}{2}I\omega^2$$

$$= \frac{1}{2}mV^2 + \frac{1}{2}(mk^2)\left(\frac{V}{r}\right)^2$$

$$= \frac{mv^2}{2}\left(1+\frac{k^2}{r^2}\right)$$

(vi) PRINCIPLE OF CONSERVATION OF ENEGY: The sum of the potential and kinetic energy of a rigid body under the conservation forces remains constant.

(vii) WORK AND ENERGY PRINCIPLE: Work done = Change in kinetic energy

The work done results both from linear and angular displacements from the initial and final positions. That is

$$\text{Work done} = Fs + T\theta$$

The change in kinetic energy resulting from translation and rotation between the initial and final states is

$$\frac{1}{2}m\,(V_2^2 - V_1^2) + \frac{1}{2}I\,(\omega_2^2 - \omega_1^2)$$

(viii) For a rigid body in plane motion (combination of translation and rotation), the equations of motion are:

$$\left.\begin{aligned}\sum F_x &= ma_x\\ \sum F_y &= ma_y\end{aligned}\right\}\text{Translation motion}$$

and

$$\sum M_G = I_G\alpha \rightarrow \text{Rotary motion}$$

Where suffix G refers to the mass centre of the body.

EXAMPLE 9.1. A uniform homogeneous cylinder of 100 mm radius has a mass of 0.10 kg. This cylinder rolls without slipping along a level horizontal surface with a translation velocity of 20 cm/ sec. Determine its total kinetic energy.

SOLUTION: Kinetic energy due to translation,

$$(K.E.)_t = \frac{1}{2}mV^2 = \frac{1}{2}(0.10)(0.2)^2$$

$$= 2\times10^{-3}\text{ Nm}$$

Kinetic energy due to rotation,

$$(K.E.)_r = \frac{1}{2}I\omega^2$$

$$= 0.5\left(\frac{mr^2}{2}\right)\frac{V}{r}$$

$$= 0.5\left(\frac{0.10 \times 0.100^2}{2}\right)\frac{0.200}{0.100}$$

$$= 0.5(5 \times 10^{-4})2$$

$$= 5 \times 10^{-4} \text{ Nm}$$

$\because$ Mass moment of inertia,

$$I = \frac{mr^2}{2}$$

$$= \frac{0.10(0.10)^2}{2}, \text{ and}$$

Angular velocity,
$$\omega = \frac{V}{r} = \frac{0.200}{0.100}$$

$$= 2 \text{ rad/sec}$$

$\therefore$ Total kinetic energy = $(K.E.)_t + (K.E)_r$

$$2 \times 10^{-3} + 5 \times 10^{-4} = 2.5 \times 10^{-3} \text{ Nm } \textbf{Ans.}$$

EXAMPLE 9.2. A string of 5 m length has been wrapped round the shaft of a wheel to determine its moment of inertia about its axis. A constant pull of 80N is applied to a string and observations indicate that the wheel turns 200 rev/min at the instant the string leaves the axle. Calculate the moment of inertia of the wheel.

SOLUTION: Work done in pulling the string

= Force applied × distance moved

= 80 ×5 = 400 Nm

Angular velocity of the wheel,

$$\omega = \frac{2\pi N}{60} = \frac{2\pi(200)}{60} = 29.49 \text{ rad/sec}$$

Now from the work – energy co-relation of a rotating system,

Work done = Kinetic energy of the wheel

$$400 = \frac{1}{2}I\omega^2 = \frac{1}{2}I(20.94)^2$$

$\therefore$ Moment of inertia of the wheel,

$$I = \frac{400 \times 2}{(20.94)^2} = \frac{800}{438.48}$$

$$= 1.824 \text{ kgm}^2 \textbf{ Ans.}$$

EXAMPLE 9.3. A flywheel of mass 3000 kg and radius of gyration 0.8 m looses its speed from 350 rpm to 250 rpm in 2 minutes. Make calculations for

(a) The torque acting on the wheel,

(b) Change in the kinetic energy and

(c) Angular momentum of the wheel during the given period.

SOLUTION: Initial angular velocity,

$$\omega_0 = \frac{2\pi N_0}{60} = \frac{2\pi(350)}{60} = 36.65 \text{ rad/sec}$$

Final angular velocity,

$$\omega = \frac{2\pi N}{60} = \frac{2\pi(250)}{60} = 26.18 \text{ rad/sec}$$

Then from the relation, $\omega = \omega_0 + \alpha t$

Angular acceleration,

$$\alpha = \frac{\omega - \omega_0}{t} = \frac{26.18 - 36.65}{2 \times 60} = -0.08725 \text{ rad/s}^2$$

Torque,

$$T = I\alpha = mk^2 \alpha$$
$$= 3000\,(0.8)^2\,(-0.08725)$$
$$= -167.52 \text{ Nm } \textbf{Ans.}$$

The negative sign means that the torque is of retarding nature.

(b) Change in kinetic energy $= \frac{1}{2}I\omega^2 - \frac{1}{2}I\omega_0^2$

$$= 0.5I(\omega^2 - \omega_0^2)$$
$$= 0.5\,mk^2\,(\omega^2 - \omega_0^2)$$
$$= 0.5\,(3000)\,(.8)^2\,(26.18^2 - 36.65^2)$$
$$= 960\,(685.39 - 1343.22)$$
$$= 960\,(-657.83)$$
$$= -6.315 \times 10^5 \; Nm \textbf{ Ans.}$$

The negative sign implies for decrease in kinetic energy

(c) Change in angular momentum

$$= I\omega - I\omega_0 = I(\omega - \omega_0)$$
$$= mk^2\,(\omega - \omega_0)$$
$$= 3000\,(0.8)^2\,(26.18 - 36.50)$$
$$= -20102.4 \text{ Nm/sec } \textbf{Ans.}$$

Negative sign implies for decrease in angular momentum.

EXAMPLE 9.4. A flywheel 800 kg mass and 0.8 m radius of gyration is rotating at 200 rev/min. Determine its,

(i) Kinetic energy,

(ii) Torque, and

(iii) Average power required to give the wheel a speed of 200 rev/min in 70 revolutions.

SOLUTION: Angular velocity of wheel,

$$\omega = \frac{2\pi N}{60} = \frac{2\pi(200)}{60}$$

$$= 20.94 \text{ rad/sec}$$

Moment of Inertia of flywheel,

$$I = mk^2 = 800(0.8)^2$$

$$\therefore \quad I = 512 \text{ kgm}^2$$

(i) Kinetic energy of the fly wheel

$$= \frac{1}{2}I\omega^2 = 0.5(512)(20.94)^2$$

$$= 112252 \text{ Nm } \textbf{Ans.}$$

(ii) Let T be the torque required to give a speed of 200 rev/min in 70 revolutions, i.e., $2\pi(70)$ radians.

From the work – Energy relation of rotating system.

Change in kinetic energy = work done

= Torque × Angular displacement

$$\therefore \quad 112252 = T(2\pi \times 70)$$

or

$$T = \frac{112252}{140\pi} = 255.22 \text{ Nm}$$

$$\text{Average speed of the flywheel} = \frac{0+200}{2} = 100 \text{ rev/min}$$

$$\text{Time taken to make 70 revolutions} = \frac{70}{100}\times 60 = 42 \text{ sec}$$

$$\text{Work done/sec} = \frac{112252}{42} = 2672.67 \text{ Nm/sec}$$

Hence average power = 2672.67 W = 2.673 kW **Ans.**

EXAMPLE 9.5. A grinding wheel has a rated speed of 1500 r.p.m. and can be assumed to be a disc of 0.5 m radius and of uniform thickness. It weighs 300 N. It is made to turn at 1500 r.p.m. and then allowed to decelerate uniformly due to bearing friction. It was deserved to come to rest in 120 seconds. Determine

(i) The number of revolutions that it shall excute before coming to rest, and

(ii) The frictional torque

SOLUTION: $N = 1500$ r.p.m.

$$\therefore \quad \omega_0 = \frac{2\pi N}{60} = \frac{2\pi(1500)}{60} = 157.0796 \text{ rad/sec}$$

$$\omega \text{ (Final)} = 0$$

and
$$t = 120 \text{ sec.}$$

Using the relation,

$$\omega = \omega_0 + \alpha t$$

$$\alpha = \frac{\omega - \omega_0}{t}$$

$$\alpha = \frac{0 - 157.0796}{120} = -1.309 \text{ rad/sec}^2$$

Hence angular deceleration, $\alpha = -1.309$ rad/sec^2

Using the relation,

$$\omega^2 = \omega_0^2 + 2\alpha\theta$$

$$(0)^2 = (157.0796)^2 + 2(-1.309)\theta$$

$$0 = 24674.001 - 2.618\,\theta$$

$$\therefore \quad \theta = 24674.001/2.618$$

$$= 9424.752 \text{ radians}$$

Number of revolutions = $9424.752/2\pi = 1500$

Hence number of revolutions before coming to Rest = 1500 **Ans.**

(ii) Frcitional Torque

$$M = I_G \alpha$$

$$I_G = \frac{1}{2} mr^2 = 0.5\left(\frac{300}{9.81}\right)(0.5)^2 = 3.8226 \ kgm^2$$

$$\therefore \quad M = I_G \alpha = 3.8226(-1.309)$$

$$= -5 \text{ Nm } \textbf{Ans.}$$

EXAMPLE 9.6. A right circular cylinder of mass m and radius r is suspended from the chord that is wound around its circumference (Fig. 9.6). if the cylinder is allowed to fall freely, determine the acceleration of its mass centre G and the tension induced in the chord.

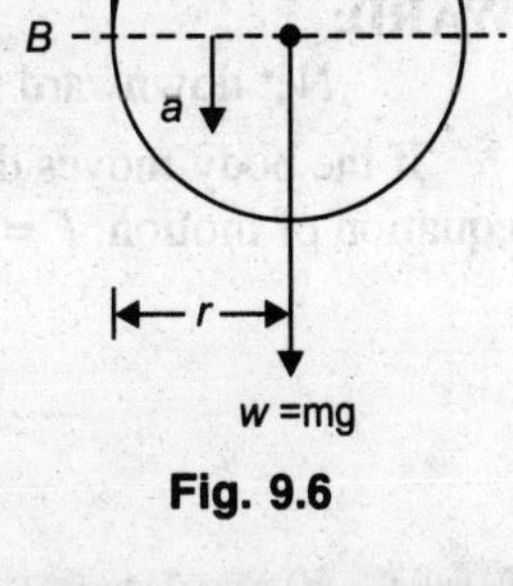

Fig. 9.6

SOLUTION: The cylinder is acted upon by the following forces:

(i) Weight of cylinder $W = mg$ that acts at the point of its centre of gravity G.

(ii) Tension T induced in the chord.

For a rigid body in plane motion (combination of translation and rotation), the equations of motion are:

$$\sum F_x = ma_x \quad : \text{Here no force acts in } x\text{-direction}$$

$$\sum F_y = ma_{xy} \quad : mg - T = ma \qquad \text{....(i)}$$

$$\sum M_G = I_G\alpha, \text{ and } Tr = I_G\alpha$$

For a cylinder, the moment of inertia about the mass centre, $I_G = \frac{1}{2}mr^2$, and in the absence of slip, the angular acceleration α and linear acceleration a are related as $a = \alpha r$. That gives:

$$Tr = \frac{1}{2}mr^2\left(\frac{a}{r}\right);$$

$$T = \frac{1}{2}ma \qquad \text{...(ii)}$$

Eliminating T from expressions (i) and (ii), we get

$$mg - \frac{1}{2}ma = ma$$

or $$mg = \frac{3}{2}ma$$

or $$g = \frac{3}{2}a$$

$\therefore$ $$a = \frac{2}{3}g \qquad \text{...(iii)}$$

Further from expression (i) $mg - T = ma$

or $$mg - ma = T$$

or $$m(g - a) = T$$

$\therefore$ $$T = m(g - a)$$

$$= m\left(g - \frac{2}{3}g\right) = \frac{mg}{3}$$

EXAMPLE 9.7. A body of weight 10N is suspended by a light rope wound round a pulley of weight 50N and radius 30 cm. The other end of the rope is fixed to the periphery of the pulley. If the weight is moving donwards, make calculations for the acceleration of 10N weight and tension in the string.

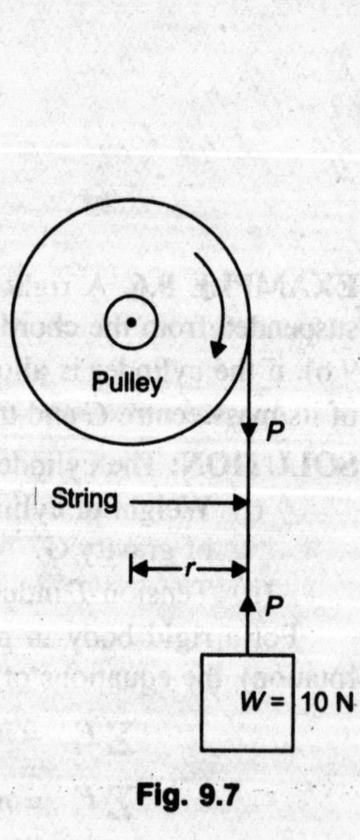

Fig. 9.7

SOLUTION: For the arrangement refer Fig. 9.7

(i) CONSIDER THE MOTION OF 10 N WEIGHT DOWN WARD:

Net downward force on the body = $W - P$

If the body moves downward with an acceleration a, then from the equation of motion, $F = ma$, we have

$$W - P = \frac{W}{g}a \qquad \text{...(i)}$$

(ii) CONSIDER THE MOTION OF PULLEY

Torque on the pulley, $T = I\alpha$

But $T = Pr$; and $\alpha = \dfrac{a}{r}$, hence we get

$$Pr = I\left(\frac{a}{r}\right)$$

and

$$P = I\left(\frac{a}{r^2}\right)$$

If the pulley is considered as solid

$$I = \frac{w}{g}\cdot\frac{r^2}{2}$$

where w = weight of the pulley

$$\therefore \quad P = I\left(\frac{a}{r^2}\right) = \frac{\omega}{g}\cdot\frac{r^2}{2}\cdot\frac{a}{r^2}$$

$$= \frac{\omega a}{2g} = \frac{\omega}{2g}a \qquad \text{...(ii)}$$

From the expressions (i) and (ii) we get,

$$W - \frac{\omega}{2g}a = \frac{W}{g}a$$

$$W - \frac{a}{g}\left(\frac{\omega}{2} - W\right) = 0$$

or

$$W = \frac{a}{g}\left(\frac{\omega}{2} + W\right)$$

or

$$Wg = a\left(W + \frac{\omega}{2}\right)$$

$$\therefore \quad a = \frac{Wg}{W + \frac{\omega}{2}}$$

Now from expression (i)

$$W - P = \frac{W}{g}\cdot\frac{Wg}{W + \frac{\omega}{2}} = \frac{2W^2}{2W + \omega}$$

or

$$P = W - \frac{2W}{2W + \omega}$$

$$= \frac{2W^2 + Ww - 2W^2}{2W + w} = \frac{Ww}{2W + w}$$

Substituting the given data, we get:

(i)

$$a = \frac{Wg}{W+\frac{w}{2}} = \frac{10\times 9.81}{10+\frac{50}{2}}$$

$$= \frac{98.10}{35} = 2.803 \text{ m/sec}^2 \textbf{ Ans.}$$

(ii) Tension induced in the string,

$$P = \frac{Ww}{2W+w}$$

$$= \frac{10\times 50}{2\times 10+50} = \frac{500}{70} = 7.14 \text{ N } \textbf{Ans.}$$

EXAMPLE 9.8. Two bodies of weight 600 N and 500 N respectively are connected to the two ends of a chord which passes over a pulley of 100 cm diameter. The pulley may be assumed as a solid disc having mass 100 kg and 50 cm radius of gyration about its axis of rotation.

Make calculations for the torque which need to be applied to the pulley to raise the 600 N body with an acceleration of 1 m/sec^2.

Neglect friction in the bearings of the pulley.

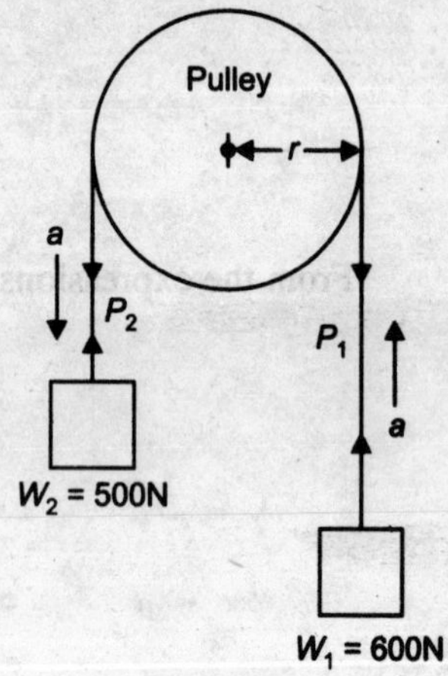

Fig. 9.8

SOLUTION: For the arrangement refer Fig. 9.8

(i) CONSIDER THE MOTION OF WEIGHT W_1: Let the weight W_1 is being raised upwards with an acceleration *a*.

Net upward force on weight $W_1 = P_1 - W_1$

From the equation of motion, $F = ma$

$$P_1 - W_1 = \frac{W_1}{g}a$$

$$\therefore \quad P_1 = \frac{W_1}{g}a + W_1$$

$$= \frac{600\times 1}{9.81} + 600 = 661.16\ N$$

(ii) CONSIDER THE MOTION OF WEIGHT W_2: The weight W_2 is being lowered with an acceleration a

Net downward force on weight $W_2 = W_2 - P_2$

Now from the equation of motion, $F = ma$, we have

$$W_2 - P_2 = \frac{W_2}{g}a$$

or $$W_2 - \frac{W_2 a}{g} = P_2$$

$\therefore$ $$P_2 = W_2 - \frac{W_2 a}{g}$$

$$= 500 - \frac{500 \times 1}{9.81} = 449.03\ N$$

(iii) CONSIDER THE MOTION OF PULLEY: Moment of inertia of the pulley,

$$I = mk^2 = 100(0.5)^2 = 25\ kgm^2$$

Angular acceleration of the pulley,

$$\alpha = \frac{a}{r} = \frac{1}{.5} = 2 \text{ rad/sec}$$

Torque due to rotation of pulley,

$$T_1 = I\alpha = 25 \times 2 = 50\ Nm$$

Torque acting on pulley due to difference in pulls in the two ropes,

$$T_2 = (P_1 - P_2)\ r$$
$$= (661.16 - 449.03)\ (0.5)$$
$$= 106.065\ Nm$$

Hence torque which should be applied to the pulley

$$= T_1 + T_2 = 50 + 106.065$$
$$= 156.065 \text{ Nm } \textbf{Ans.}$$

D'ALEMBERT'S PRINCIPLE AND DYNAMIC EQUILIBRIUM

Introduction

In this chapter analysis of kinetic problems of a body in plane motion using D'Alembert's principle are explained. Dynamic problem can be converted into a static equilibrium problem by applying D'Alembert's principle. This is done by introducing an additional force and then the usual equations of static equilibrium are used to get the solution.

NEWTON'S SECOND LAW OF MOTION

D'Alembert's principle is in fact an application of Newton's second law to a moving body. According to Newton's second law the rate of change of momentum is directly proportional to the impressed force and takes place in the direction, in which the force acts. The above definition leads to statement that force is directly proportional to product of mass and acceleration and unit of force is so selected that constant of proportionality reduces to unity. Hence, finally Newton's second law reduces to the statement, Force = mass × acceleration.

Instead of single force, if a system of forces acts on a particle, the above statement reduces to resultant force is equal to the: *the product of mass and acceleration in the direction of the resultant force*. Mathematically

$$R = m\,a \qquad \text{(i)}$$

where, R is the resultant of forces acting on the particle. Hence many time Newton's second law is stated as: a particle acted upon by an unbalanced system of forces has an acceleration directly proportional and in line with the resultant force.

D'ALEMBERT'S PRINCIPLE

French mathematician Jean le Rondd' Alembert proved in 1743 that the Newton's second law of motion is applicable not only to the motion of a particle but also to the motion of a body and looked at equation. (i) from different angle. The equation $R = ma$ may be written as, $R - ma = 0$ ...(ii)

The term '$-ma$' may be looked as a force of a magnitude $m \times a$, applied in the opposite direction of motion and is termed as the inertia force or reverse effective force. D'Alembert looks at equation (ii) *as an equation of equilibrium with the inertia force of the body*. This is known as D'Alembert's principle.

Let the body shown in Fig. 9.9 be subjected to a system of forces causing the body to move with an acceleration a in the direction of the resultant. Then apply a force equal to ma in the reversed direction of acceleration as shown in Fig. 9.10. Now according to D'Alembert's principle, the equations of equilibrium $\sum x = 0$ and $\sum y = 0$ may be used for the system of forces shown in Fig. 9.10.

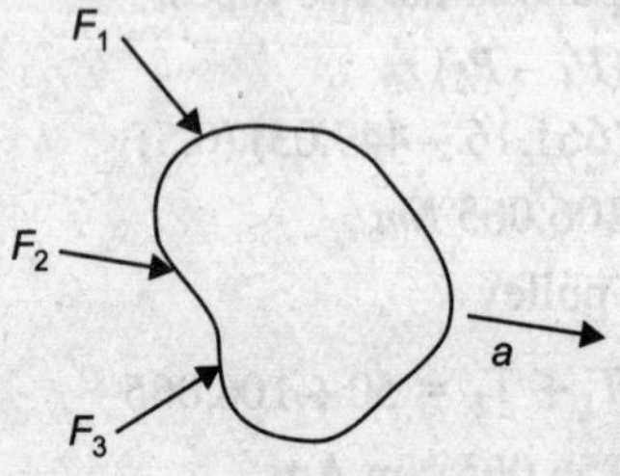

Fig. 9.9

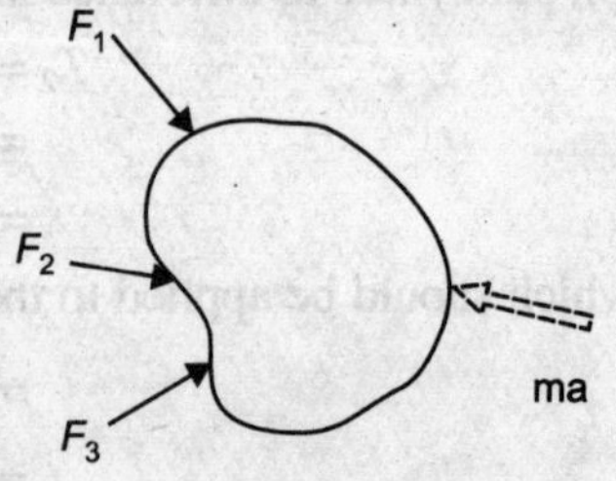

Fig. 9.10

The inertia force *-ma* has a physical meaning. According to Newton's first law of motion, a body continues to be in the state of rest or of uniform motion in a straight line unless acted by an external force. That means every body has a tendency to continue in its state of rest or of uniform motion. This tendency is called inertia. Hence inertia force is the resistance offered by a body to the change in its state of rest or uniform motion.

Many engineers prefer to use D'Alembert's principle, since just by applying a reverse effective force, the moving body can be treated as a body in equilibrium and can be analysed using equations of static equilibrium.

EXAMPLE 9.9. A man weighing W Newton entered a lift which moves with an acceleration of a m/sec^2. Find the force exerted by the man on the floor of lift when

(a) lift is moving downward

(b) lift is moving upward

SOLUTION:

(a) When the lift is moving downward, the inertia force $ma = \frac{w}{g} a$, should be applied in upward direction as shown in Fig 9.11(a).

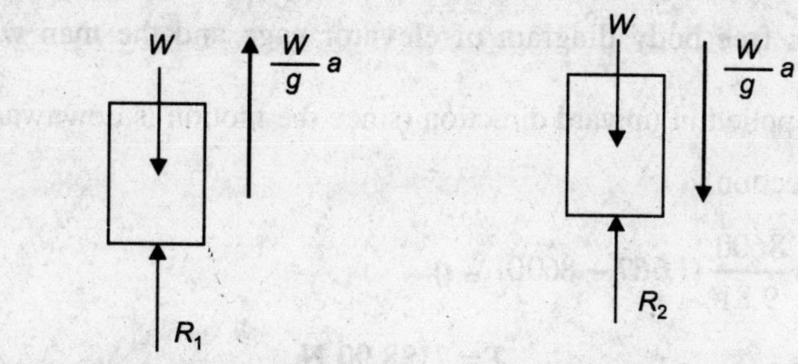

(a) Lift moving downword (b) Lift moving upward

Fig. 9.11

For the lift, $\sum V = 0$, gives

$$R_1 - W + \frac{W}{g} a = 0$$

$$R_1 = W\left(1 - \frac{a}{g}\right) \qquad \text{...(i)}$$

(b) When lift is moving upwards, inertia force $\frac{W}{g}$ a should be applied in the downward direction as shown in Fig. 9.11 (b). Applying the equation, of equilibrium, we get,

$$R_2 - W - \frac{W}{g} a = 0$$

$$R_2 = W\left(1 - \frac{a}{g}\right) \qquad \text{...(ii)}$$

Thus when lift is moving with acceleration downward, the man exerts less force on the floor of the lift and while moving upward he exerts more force. From equations (1) and (2) it may be observed that if the lift moves with uniform velocity then the acceleration a is zero and hence the man exerts force equal to his own weight on the lift.

EXAMPLE 9.10. An elevator cage of a mine shaft weighing 8 kN, when empty, is lifted or lowered by means of a wire rope. Once a man weighing 600 N, entered it and lowered with uniform acceleration such that when a distance of 187.5 m was covered, the velocity of the cage was 25 m/sec. Determine the tension in the rope and the force exerted by the man on the floor of the cage.

SOLUTION:

In this problem

Initial velocity $u = 0$

Final velocity $v = 25\text{m/sec}$

and distance covered, $s = 187.5$ m

Using the equation of motion, $v^2 - u^2 = 2as$

we get, $25^2 - 0 = 2a\,(187.5)$

or $a = 1.667 \text{ m/sec}^2$

Fig. 9.12 (a) shows free body diagram of elevator cage and the man with inertia force $\frac{W}{g}a = \frac{8000 + 600}{9.81} \cdot a$ applied in upward direction (since the motion is downward). Summing up the forces in vertical direction,

$$T + \frac{8600}{9.81}(1.667 - 8600) = 0$$

$$\therefore \qquad T = 7138.90 \text{ N}$$

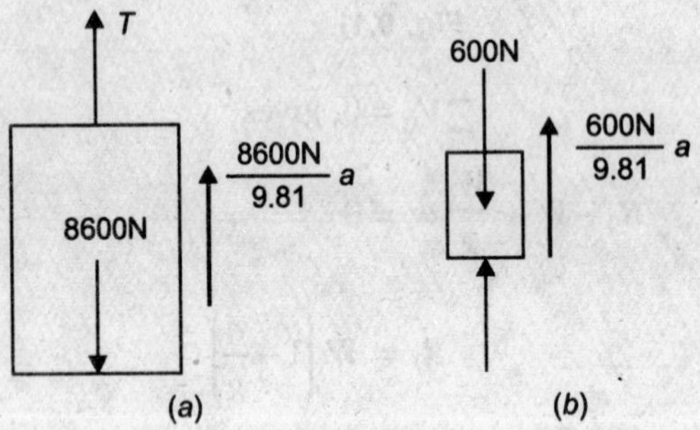

Fig. 9.12

Fig. 9.12 (b) shows the free body diagram of the man along with inertia force $\frac{600}{9.81}a$ applied in upward direction. Sum of the vertical forces should be zero. That is,

$$\Sigma V = 0 \quad \text{gives}$$

$$R + \frac{600}{9.81}a - 600 = 0$$

i.e.
$$R + \frac{600}{9.81} \times 1.667 - 600 = 0$$

or
$$R = 498.06 \text{ N} \quad \textbf{Ans.}$$

EXAMPLE 9.11. A motorist travelling at a speed of 70 km.p.h. suddenly applies brakes and halts after skidding 50 m. Determine:

1. The time required to stop the car;
2. The coefficient of friction between the tyres and the road.

SOLUTION:

Initial velocity $\quad u = 70 \text{ km.p.h.} = \frac{70 \times 1000}{60 \times 60} = 19.44 \text{ m / sec}$

Final velocity $\quad v = 0$

Displacement $\quad s = 50 \text{ m}$

Using the equation of linear motion $\quad v^2 = u^2 + 2as,$

we get $\quad 0 = 19.44^2 + 2a \times 50$

$a = -3.78 \text{ m/sec}^2$ i.e., retardation is 3.78 m/sec^2.

Using the relation $v = u + at$, we get $0 = 19.44 - 3.78\,t$

$\therefore$ $t = 5.14$ sec **Ans.**

Inertia force must be applied in the opposite direction of acceleration, which means, it should be applied in the direction of motion while retarding. Fig. 9.13 shows the free body diagram of the motor along with inertia force.

Σ Forces normal to road $= 0$

$$N = W$$

From the law of friction, $F = \mu N = \mu W$

Σ Forces in the direction of motion = 0, gives

$$F = \frac{w}{9.81} 3.78$$

$$\mu w = \frac{w \times 3.78}{9.81}$$

$\therefore$ $\mu = 0.385$ **Ans.**

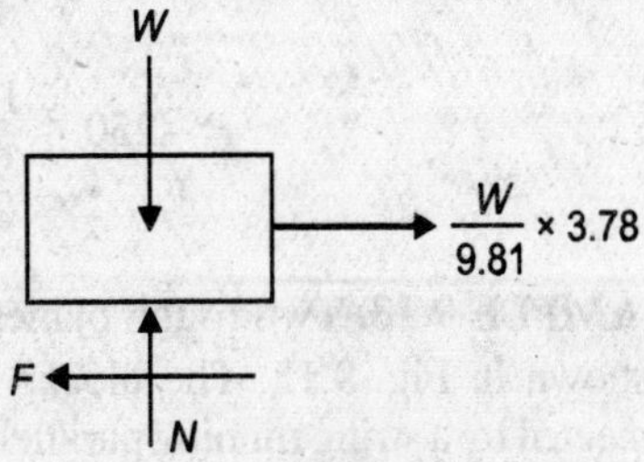

Fig. 9.13

EXAMPLE 9.12. A 750 N crate rests on a 500 N cart. The coefficient of friction between the crate and the cart is 0.3 and between cart and the road is 0.2. If the cart is to be pulled by a force *P* (Ref. Fig. 9.14 (a) such that the crate does not slip, determine: (a) The maximum allowable magnitude of *P* and (b) The corresponding acceleration of the cart.

SOLUTION:

Let the maximum acceleration be a, at which 750 N crate is about to slip. Hence frictional force will have limiting value (= μN). Consider the free body diagram of crate along with inertia force, shown in Fig. 9.14 (b).

$$\Sigma V = 0$$

$$N = W = 750 \text{ Newton}$$

Frictional force $F = \mu N = 0.3 \times 750$

$$= 225 \text{ N}$$

$$\Sigma H = 0$$

$$225 = \frac{750}{9.81} a$$

$\therefore$ $a = 2.943 \text{ m/sec}^2$

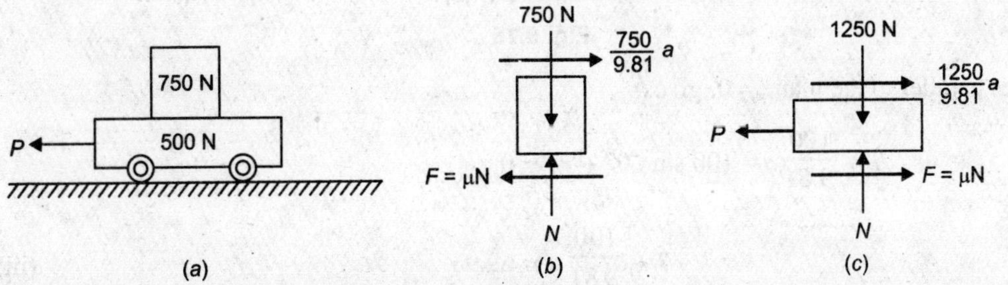

Fig. 9.14

Consider now dynamic equilibrium of crate and the cart shown as a single body in Fig. 9.14(c).

$$\Sigma V = 0$$

$$N = 1250 \text{ Newton}$$

$$\text{Frictional force} = \mu N = 0.2 \times 1250 = 250 \text{ Newton}$$

$$\Sigma H = 0$$

$$P - 250 - \frac{1250}{9.81} \times 2.943 = 0$$

$$P = 625 \text{ N} \quad \textbf{Ans.}$$

EXAMPLE 9.13. Two rough planes inclined at 30° and 60° to horizontal are placed back to back as shown in Fig. 9.15. The blocks of weights 50 N and 100 N are placed on the faces and are connected by a string running parallel to planes and passing over a frictionless pulley. If the coefficient of friction between planes and blocks is 1/3, find the resulting acceleration and tension in the string.

SOLUTION:

Let the assembly move down the 60° plane by an acceleration 'a' m/sec². Free body diagrams of 100 N and 50 N blocks along with inertia forces are shown in Figs. 9.15(b) and 9.15 (c) respectively.

Consider the block weighing 100 N.

Σ Forces normal to the plane = 0, gives

$$N_1 = 100 \cos 60° = 50 \text{ N} \qquad \text{...(i)}$$

From the law of friction,

$$F_1 = \mu N = \frac{1}{3} \times 50 = 16.67 \text{ N} \qquad \text{...(ii)}$$

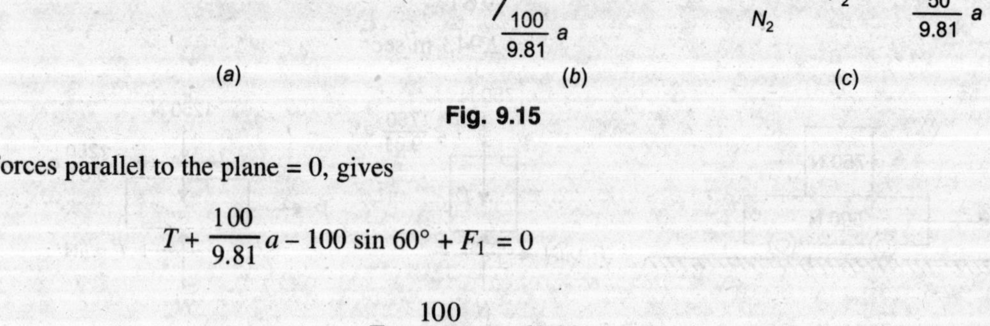

Fig. 9.15

Σ Forces parallel to the plane = 0, gives

$$T + \frac{100}{9.81}a - 100 \sin 60° + F_1 = 0$$

$$T + \frac{100}{9.81}a = 69.93 \qquad \text{...(iii)}$$

since $F_1 = 16.67$

Now consider 50 N block:

Σ forces normal to plane = 0 gives

$$N_2 = 50 \cos 30° = 43.30 \text{ N} \qquad ...(iv)$$

From the law of friction, $F_2 = \mu N_2$

$$= \frac{1}{3} \times 43.3 = 14.33 \text{ N} \qquad ...(v)$$

Σ Forces parallel to 30° plane = 0

$$\frac{50}{9.81} a + F_2 + 50 \sin 30° - T = 0$$

$$\frac{50}{9.81} a - T = -39.43 \qquad ...(vi)$$

since $F_2 = 14.43$

Adding equations (3) and (6) we get,

$$\left(\frac{100}{9.81} + \frac{50}{9.81}\right) a = 69.93 - 39.43$$

or $a = 1.9947$ m/sec^2 **Ans.**

From eqn, (3), $T = 69.93 - 100/9.81 \times 1.9947 = 49.6$ N **Ans.**

EXAMPLE 9.14. Two bodies weighing 300 N and 450 N are hung to the ends of a rope passing over an ideal pulley as shown in Fig. 9.16 (a). With what acceleration the heavier body comes down? What is the tension in the string?

SOLUTION: Let a be the acceleration with which the system moves and T be the tension in the string.

Free body diagrams of 300 N block and 450 N blocks along with inertia forces are shown in Figs. 9.16 (b) and 9.16 (c).

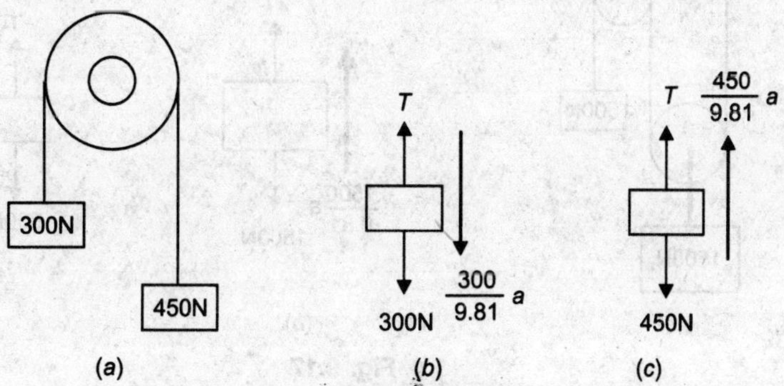

Fig. 9.16

Consider the body weighing 300 N

$$\Sigma V = 0$$

$$T - \frac{300}{9.81}a - 300 = 0$$

i.e.,
$$T - \frac{300}{9.81}a = 300 \quad ...(i)$$

Considering the body weighing 450 N, we get

$$T + \frac{450}{9.81}a = 450 \quad ...(ii)$$

Subtracting eqn (i) from eqn. (ii) we get

$$\frac{450}{9.81}a + \frac{300}{9.81}a = 450 - 300$$

$$a = 1.962 \text{ m/sec}^2 \quad \textbf{Ans.}$$

Substituting this value in eq. (i) we get,

$$T = 300 + \frac{300}{9.81} \times 1.962$$

i.e.
$$T = 360 \text{ N} \quad \textbf{Ans.}$$

EXAMPLE 9.15. Determine the tension in the string and accelerations of blocks *A* and *B* weighing 1500 N and 500 N connected by an inextensible string as shown in Fig. 9.17 (a). Assume pulleys as frictionless and weightless.

SOLUTION: In this pulley system, it may be observed that if 1500 N block moves downward by distance x, 500 N block moves up by $2x$. Hence if acceleration of 1500 N block is a that of 500 N block is $2a$. The free body diagrams of 1500 N block and 500 N blocks are shown in Fig. 9.17 (b) and (c), along with inertia forces. According to D'Alembert's principle the system of forces shown in Fig. 9.17 (b) and (c) may be treated to be in equilibrium.

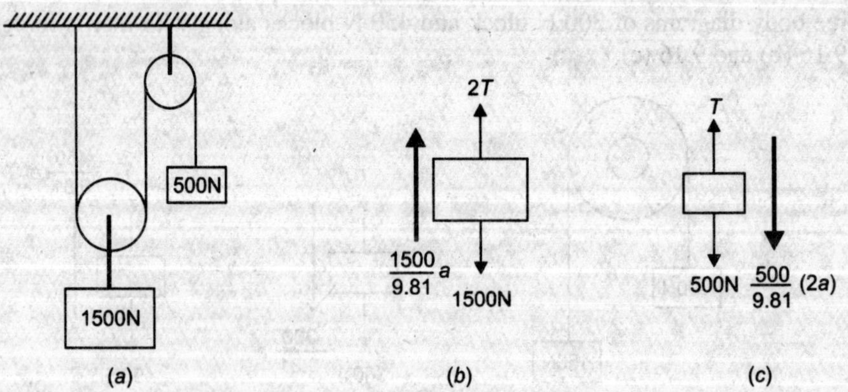

Fig. 9.17

Considering 1500 N block, we get,

$$2T + \frac{1500}{9.81}a = 1500 \quad ...(i)$$

Considering 500 N block, we get,

$$T - \frac{500}{9.81}(2a) = 500 \qquad \text{...(ii)}$$

From eqns. (i) and (ii), we get,

$$\left(\frac{1500}{9.81} + \frac{2000}{9.81}\right) a = 500$$

$\therefore$ $a = 1.401$ m/sec² **Ans.**

Substituting it in (i), we get $2T = 1500 - \frac{1500}{9.81} \times 1.401$

$T = 642.89$ N **Ans.**

EXERCISE-9

1. A wheel has a 5.4 m long string wrapped round its shaft. The string is pulled with a constant force of 98 N and it is observed that the wheel is rotating at 3 r.p.m., when string leaves the axle. Find the moment of inertia of the wheel about its axis. [**Ans.** $I = 2.98$ kg–m²]
2. A solid cylindrical pulley of mass 800 kg, having 0.8 m radius of gyration and 2 m diameter, is rotated by an electric motor, which exerts a uniform torque of 60 KN–m. A body of mass 3000 kg is to be lifted by a wire wrapped round the pulley. Find (i) Acceleration of the body, and (ii) Tension in the rope. [**Ans.** $a = 8.71$ m/sec², and $T = 55.53$ KN]

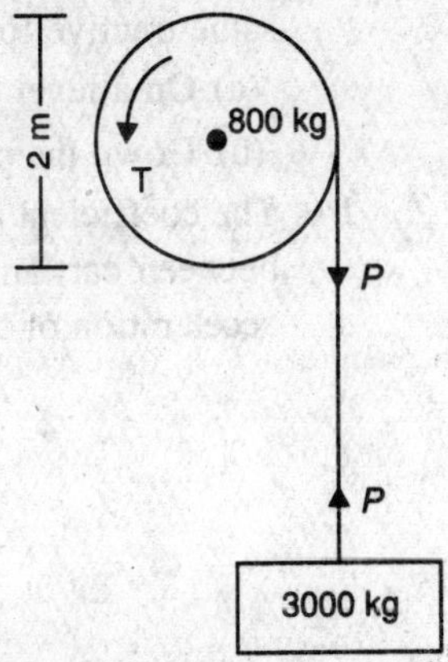

3. A gyroscope wheel weighing 1.5 kg and having a radius of gyration 30 cm is spinning about its axle at a rate of 240 r.p.m. The axle is held horizontal and is supported by a pivot at one end which is 10 cm from the centre of mass of the wheel. Calculate the angular velocity of the precession of the wheel. [**Ans.** $\omega_p = .43$ rad/sec]
4. Two bodies of masses 15 kg and 5 kg are attached to the two ends of a flexible rope, which is passes over a pulley of mean radius 200 mm having a mass of 10 kg and radius of gyration 150 mm. Find the acceleration of the masses and pulls on either side of the rope. [**Ans.** $a = 3.82$ m/sec², $P_1 = 89.7$ N, and $P_2 = 68.1$ N]
5. Two bodies A and B of masses 800 kg and 600 kg are attached at the ends of a flexible rope. The rope passes over a pulley of 800 mm diameter. The pulley has a mass of 100 kg with a radius of gyration as 400 mm about its axis of rotation.

   Find the torque, which must be applied to the pulley to raise the 800 kg body with an acceleration of 1 m/sec². Neglect friction of the spindle. [**Ans.** $T_2 - T_1 = 1384$ N–m]
6. A light rope passing round a pulley of mass 60 kg, radius 300 mm and radius of gyration 200 mm, has two masses 8 kg and 2 kg attached to its ends. If the rope does not slip as the pulley rotates, determine the acceleration of the two masses and the pulls in the two ropes. [**Ans.** 0.48 m/sec², 74.6 N and 61.7 N]

7. Two masses of 100 kg and 40 kg are supported by a rope of negligible mass passing over a solid disc pulley. If the mass of the pulley is 50 kg, find the acceleration of the 100 kg mass and the pulls in the two strings. [**Ans.** 3.56 m/sec^2, 624 N, and 534.4 N]
(For solid disc pulley of radius r, $k^2 = 0.5\ r^2$ and mass moment of inertia, $I = Mk^2 = 50 \times 0.5\ r^2 = 25r^2$)
8. A sphere rolls down a plane inclined at 30° to the horizontal. Find the minimum value of the coefficient of friction between the sphere and the plane, so that the sphere may roll without slipping. [**Ans.** μ = .165]
9. Find the time taken by a solid cylinder of radius 600 mm and initially at rest to roll down a distance 19.2 m on a plane inclined at 30° with the horizontal. Take g = 9.81 m/sec^2. [**Ans.** t = 3.5 secs.]
10. A train of mass 300 tonnes is brought to rest in 200 m by a braking force equal to 500 N per tronne weight of the train. There is also a resistance due to friction and air acting parallel to the track of 70 N per tonne weight. How much work is done in bringing the train to rest? [**Ans.** W = 34200 KJ]
11. Find the power required to derive a lift when raising a mass of 2 tonnes at a speed of 1.5 m/sec. If the efficiency of the lift is 70 percent. [**Ans.** Input power = 42 KW]
12. A mine cage weighs 12 kN and can carry a maximum load of 20 kN. The average frictional resistance of the slide guys is 500 N. What constant cable tension is required to give a loaded cage an upward velocity of 3m/sec, from rest in a distance of 3m? [**Ans.** 37.393 kN]
13. A train weighing 3000 kN is moving up a slope 2 in 100 with an acceleration of 0.04 m/sec^2. Tractive resistance is 6N/kN. Determine the acceleration of the train if it moves with the same tractive force:
(a) On a level track;
(b) Down the plane inclined at 2 in 100 [**Ans.** 0.2362 m/sec^2; 0.4324 m/sec^2]
14. The coefficient of friction between the crate and the cart shown in Fig. 9.18 is 0.25 and that between cart and the road is 0.15. If the cart is pulled by a force of 500 N determine the acceleration of the cart. Check whether there is slipping of the crate at this state.

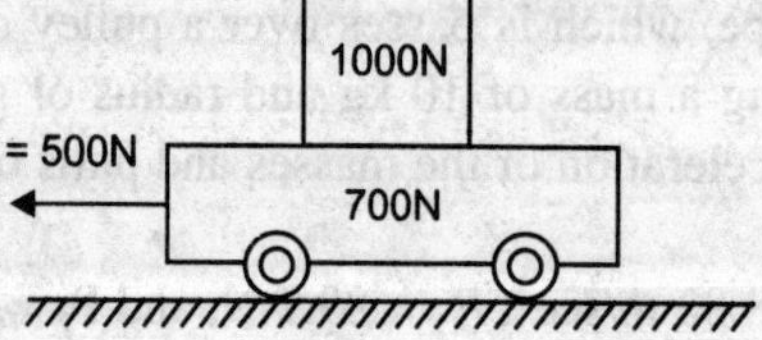

Fig. 9.18

[**Ans.** a = 1.4138 m/sec^2; No slipping]
15. A block weighing 2500 N rests on a level horizontal plane which has a coefficient of friction 0.20. This block is pulled by a force of 1000 N, which is acting at an angle of 30° to the horizontal. Find the velocity of the block, after it moves 30m, starting from rest. If the force of 1000 N is then removed, how much further will it move?
[**Ans.** v = 10.478 m/sec; s = 27.961 m]

16. In what distance will body 1 shown in Fig. 9.19 attains a velocity of 3m/sec starting from rests? Take coefficient of friction between the blocks and plane as 0.2. Assume pulley is smooth. What is the tension in the chord?

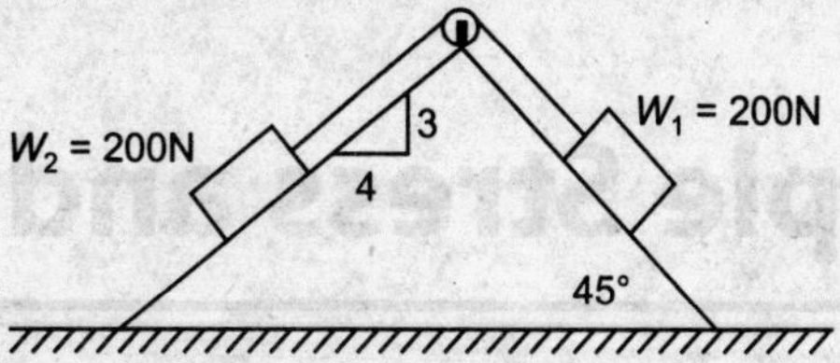

Fig. 9.19

[**Ans.** s = 12.953 m; T = 159.08 N]

17. Two blocks of weight W_1 and W_2 are connected by inextensible wire passing over a smooth pulley as shown in Fig. 9.20. If W_1 is greater than W_2, find the tension in the string and the acceleration of the system.

$$\left[\textbf{Ans. } a = g\left(\frac{W_1 - W_2}{W_1 + W_2}\right); T = \frac{2W_1 W_2}{W_1 + W_2}\right]$$

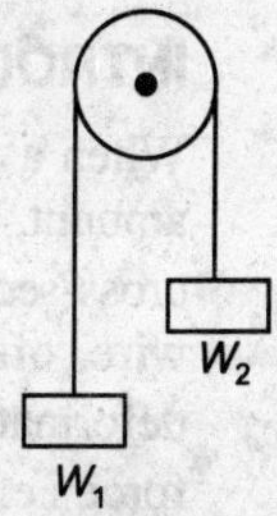

Fig. 9.20

18. Find the acceleration of the three weights shown in Fig. 9.21. Assume pulleys are frictionless. Find also the tension in the cables.

[**Ans.** Acceleration of 200 N block = 3.45 m/sec^2, 40 N block = 0.098 m/sec^2, 40 N block = 0.795 m/sec^2 Tension in upper cable = 129.73 N, Tension in lower cable = 64.85 N]

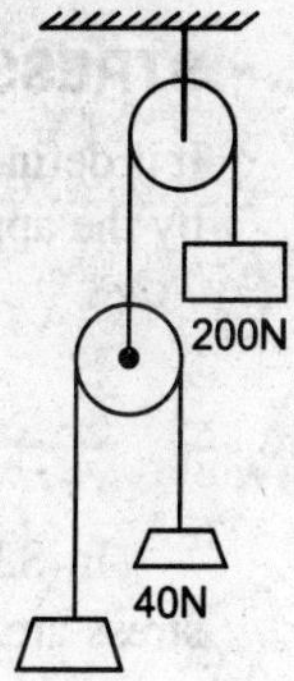

Fig. 9.21

19. The weights of the three blocks shown in Fig. 9.22 are W_A = 100N, W_B = 200 N and W_C =200 N. Coefficient of friction between block A and the floor is 0.2., that between floor and block C is 0.25. Assuming pulleys as weightless and smooth, find the acceleration of each block.

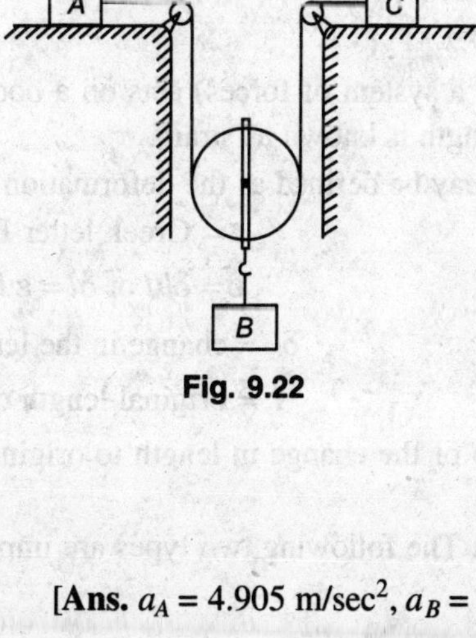

Fig. 9.22

$$\left[\textbf{Hint: } a_B = \left(\frac{a_A + a_C}{2}\right)\right]$$

[**Ans.** a_A = 4.905 m/sec^2, a_B = 2.943 m/sec^2, a_C = .981 m/sec^2]

CHAPTER 10

Simple Stress and Strain

INTRODUCTION

When a load is attached to a thin hanging wire, it elongates and the load moves downward. The amount, by which the wire elongates, depends upon the amount of load, and the nature, as well as cross-sectional area of wire material. The cohesive force, between the molecules of the hanging wire, offers resistance against the deformation, and the force of resistance increases with the deformation. The process of deformation stops when the force of resistance is equal to the external force i.e. the load attached. When the force of resistance, offered by the molecules, is less than the external force then the deformation will continue until failure takes place.

STRESS

It is defined as restoring force (internal force of resistance) per unit area, developed at every section, by the application of External forces. It is the ratio of force to the cross-sectional area, i.e. stress,

σ = Force/area = P/A, where, σ = Greek letter Sigma

P = Load or force acting on a body in Newton

A = Cross - sectional area of the body in mm^2

In S.I. system, the unit of stress is PASCAL (Pa) which is equal to $1N/m^2$. Bigger units of stress are Mega Pascal (MPa) and Giga Pascal (GPa) equal to N/mm^2 and kN/mm^2.

STRAIN

Whenever a single force (or a system of forces) acts on a body, it undergoes some deformation. This deformation per unit length is known as strain.

Mathematically, strain may be defined as the deformation per unit length, i.e. strain,

ε = Greek letter Epsilon

$$\varepsilon = \delta l / l \text{ or } \delta l = \varepsilon . l.$$

Where, δl = change in the length of the body

l = original length of the body.

As the strain is the ratio of the change in length to original length, hence it is dimensionless quantity.

TYPE OF STRESSES: The following two types are important.

Fig 10.1: Tensile stress

Fig. 10.2: Compressive stress

TENSILE STRESS: When the section is subjected to two equal and opposite pulls (P–P) and the body tends to increase its length (Fig. 10.1), the stress induced is called tensile stress. The corresponding strain is called tensile strain. As a result of the tensile stress, the cross-sectional area of the body gets reduced.

COMPRESSIVE STRESS: When the section is subjected to two equal and opposite pushes (P-P) and the body tends to shorten its length (Fig. 10.2), the stress induced is called compressive stress. The corresponding strain is called compressive strain. As a results of compressive stress ,the cross-sectional area of the body gets reduced.

ELASTIC LIMIT : When ever some external system of forces acts on a body, it undergoes some deformation. If the external forces, causing deformation, are removed, the body springs back to its original position. For a given section there is a limiting value of force upto and within which, the deformation entirely disappears on the removal of force. The value of stress corresponding to this limiting force is called elastic limit of the material.

Beyond the elastic limit, the material gets into plastic stage and in this stage the deformation does not entirely disappear, on the removal of force But as a result of this , there is a residual deformation even after the removal of force.

HOOKE'S LAW : When a material is loaded, within elastic limit, the stress is proportional to the strain. Mathematically, stress/strain = E = constant

Hooke's Law equally holds good for tension as well as compression.

MODULUS OF ELASTICITY OR YOUNG'S MODULUS : When ever a material is loaded, within elastic limit, the stress is proportional to strain. Mathematically,

$\sigma \propto \varepsilon$ or $\sigma = E.\varepsilon$ or $E = \sigma/\varepsilon$ or stress/strain = E

E = A constant of proportionality known as modulus of elasticity or young's modulus.

SHEAR STRESS : It exists between two parts of a body in contact when each part exerts equal and opposite force on each other laterally in a direction tangential to their surface of contact.

Fig. 10.3 (a) shows a section of rivet subjected to equal and opposite forces P–P causing sliding of the plates by shearing off the rivet section, one over the other. From the Fig. it is clear that the resisting force of the rivet must be equal to P. Hence shearing stress τ is given by, τ = total tangential force / area of cross section of rivet = P/A.

τ = Tau

Tensile stress and compressive stress are known as Direct stresses and the Shearing stress as Tangential stress.

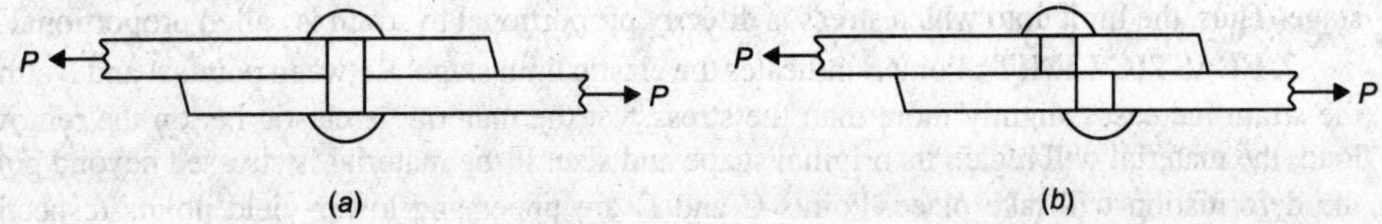

Fig 10.3: Shear stress

SHEAR STRAIN : Consider a cube of length l, fixed at the bottom face AB. Let force P be applied at the face CD, tangentially to the face AB. As a result of force, let the cube be distorted from *ABCD* to *ABC′D′* through an angle ϕ (Fig. 10.4). We know that,

Shear Strain = Deformation / Original length

$= CC'/l = \phi$, and shear stress, $\tau = P/AB$

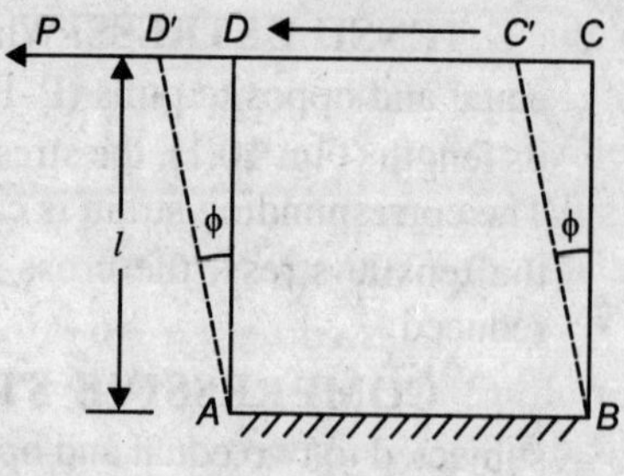

Fig. 10.4

STRESS-STRAIN CURVE FOR DUCTILE MATERIALS

A material is said to be ductile in nature, if it elongates appreciably before fracture. One such material is mild steel. The tensile test of mild steel is carried out on a specimen of uniform cross-section throughout its gauge length. The specimen is gripped between two grips (jaws) of the tensile testing machine, with which gradually increasing load is applied. The load and extension in the gauge length (50 mm) of the specimen are observed. A graph is drawn between Load and Extension i.e. stress and strain (Fig. 10.5).

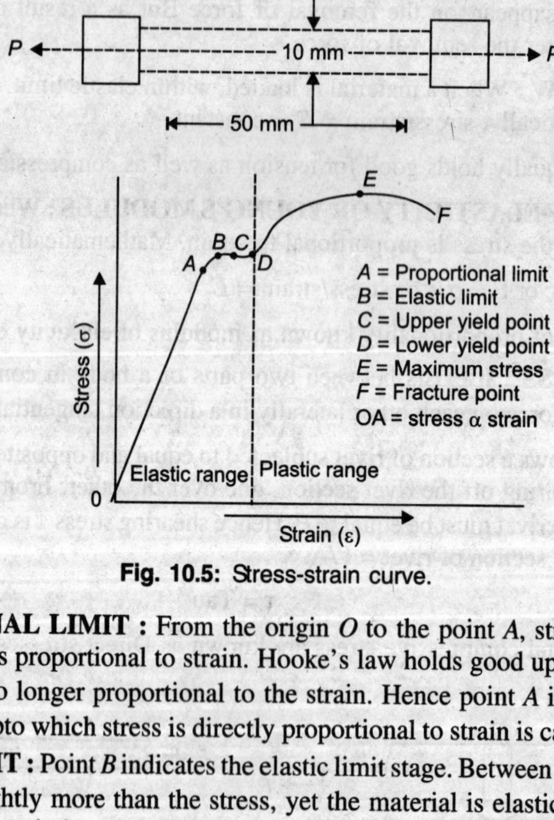

Fig. 10.5: Stress-strain curve.

1. PROPORTIONAL LIMIT : From the origin *O* to the point *A*, stress strain diagram is a straight line i.e. stress is proportional to strain. Hooke's law holds good upto this point *A*. Beyond point A, the stress is no longer proportional to the strain. Hence point *A* is the proportional limit stage. Thus, the limit upto which stress is directly proportional to strain is called proportional limit.

2. ELASTIC LIMIT : Point *B* indicates the elastic limit stage. Between points *A* and *B* although the strain increases slightly more than the stress, yet the material is elastic i.e. on the removal of load, the material will regain its original shape and size. If the material is stressed beyond point B, the deformation will take place. Points C and D are upper and lower yield points respectively. Between points *B* and *C*, the strain increases more rapidly than the stress. At this (C) the dial, which gives the reading of the load suddenly becomes stationary for few seconds to point D. Beyond point D, the load again starts increasing but the elongation increases at faster rate than load upto point E. Hence E indicates maximum or ultimate stress point. The bar of specimen begins to form a local neck. Point F is the breaking point. The extension remains continuous even with lesser load and fracture occurs at point F.

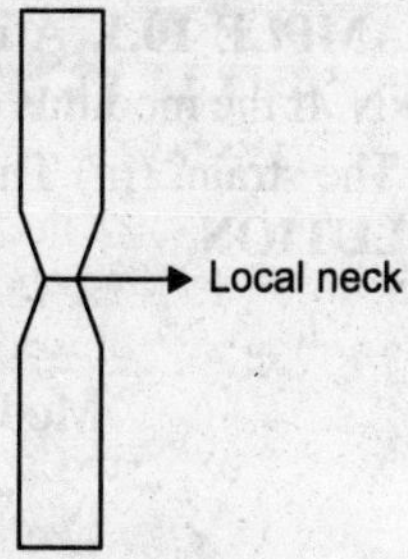

Fig. 10.6

The stress corresponding to the peak load is called ultimate tensile stress or ultimate tensile strength or tensile strength. The stress corresponding to the load when the specimen ruptures is called rupture strength.

3. ULTIMATE STRESS : The ratio of maximum load to the original cross-sectional area of a bar is called ultimate stress.

$$\therefore \quad \text{Ultimate stress} = \frac{\text{Maximum load}}{\text{Original cross - sectional area}}$$

4. PERCENTAGE ELONGATION : The ratio of percentage increase in gauge length to the original gauge length is called the percentage elongation.

$$\therefore \quad \text{Percentage elongation} = \frac{L_1 - L_0}{L_0} \times 100$$

Where, L_0 = original gauge length

L_1 = final gauge length after fracture

5. WORKING STRESS : The greatest stress to which a material is ever subjected is called the working stress.

$$\therefore \quad \text{Working stress} = \text{Ultimate stress / Factor of safety}$$

6. FACTOR OF SAFETY : The ratio of ultimate stress to working stress is called factor of safety.

$$\therefore \quad \text{Factor of safety} = \text{Ultimate stress/Working stress}$$

The factor of safety is also known as factor of ignorance. It is decided by experience and depends upon the number of factors such as nature of loading, degree of safety, degree of economy required, permanency of design, material used, etc. For cast iron, concrete, wood etc. the value of factor of safety may be taken as 4 to 6.

7. BREAKING STRESS : The ratio of load at the breaking or fracture point and original cross-sectional area of a material is called breaking stress.

$$\therefore \quad \text{Breaking stress} = \text{load at breaking point/original cross-sectional area}$$

8. PERCENTAGE REDUCTION IN AREA : The ratio of the percentage decrease in cross-sectional area to the original cross-sectional area is called the percentage reduction in area after rupture.

$$\therefore \quad \text{Percentage reduction in area} = \frac{A_0 - A_1}{A_0} \times 100$$

Where, A_0 = Original cross-sectional area

A_1 = Final cross-sectional area

EXAMPLE 10.1. A rod 20 mm in diameter and 2.5 meter long is subjected to an axial pull of 35 kN. If the modulus of elasticity of the material of the rod is 200 GN/m^2, determine (i) The stress, (ii) The strain, (iii) The elongation of the rod.

SOLUTION. Diameter of the rod (d) = 20 mm

Length of the rod (l) = 2.5 m = 2500 mm

Modulus of Elasticity (E) = 200 GN/m^2

$$= \frac{200 \times 10^6 \times 10^3}{1000 \times 1000} = 200 \text{ kN/mm}^2$$

Axial Pull (P) = 35 kN = 35 × 1000 N

We know that

(i) Stress
$$\sigma = \frac{\text{Load}}{\text{Area}} = \frac{P}{A} = \frac{35000}{\frac{\pi}{4}d^2} = \frac{35000 \times 7 \times 4}{22 \times 20 \times 20}$$

$$= 111.41 \text{ N/mm}^2. \textbf{ Ans.}$$

(ii) Strain
$$\varepsilon = \frac{\sigma}{E} = 111.41 / 200 \times 10^3 = 0.000557. \textbf{ Ans.}$$

(iii) Elongation
$$\delta l = l \times \text{strain} = l.\varepsilon = 2500 \times 0.000557$$
$$= 1.39 \text{ mm. } \textbf{Ans.}$$

STRESS - STRAIN CURVE FOR BRITTLE MATERIALS

Materials which show very small elongation before they fracture are called brittle materials. The shape of the curve for a brittle material is shown in Fig. 10.7.

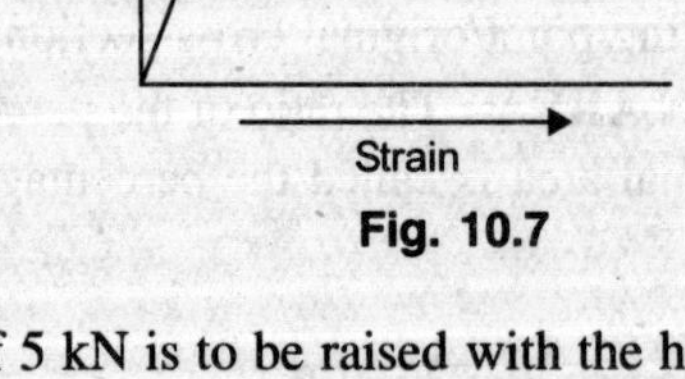

Fig. 10.7

EXAMPLE 10.2. A load of 5 kN is to be raised with the help of a steel wire. Find the minimum diameter of the steel wire if the stress is not to exceed 100 MPa.

SOLUTION. Given Load (P) = 5 kN = 5 × 10^3 N

Stress (σ) = 100 MPa = 100 N/mm^2

Let, d = diameter of the wire in mm

We know that the stress in the steel wire $(\sigma) = \dfrac{P}{A}$

$\therefore \quad 100 = (5 \times 10^3)/(\pi d^2)/4 = (6.366 \times 10^3)/d^2$

$\therefore \quad d^2 = (6.366 \times 10^3)/100 = 63.66$ or $d = (63.66)^{1/2}$

$\therefore \quad d = 7.98$ say 8 mm. **Ans.**

STRESS Vs STRENGTH

Stress : Every material is elastic in nature. That is why, whenever some external system of forces acts on a body, it undergoes some deformation. As the body undergoes deformation, it sets up some resistance to deformation. This resistance per unit area to deformation is known as stress. Mathematically stress may be defined as the force per unit area, i.e. $\sigma = P/A$

Where, σ = intensity of stress (written as stress)

P = load or force acting on the body

A = cross-sectional area of the body

In S.I. units, the units of stress are N/mm^2, kN/mm^2, MN/mm^2, and GN/mm^2 depending upon units of force.

Strength : The strength of a material is its ability to resist the application of force without rupture. In service the material may have to withstand tension, compression or shear force. The strength of a material is measured by loading it in a testing machine. The ultimate strength is the load necessary to fracture one square cm of the cross-section of the material. The tenacity is the ultimate strength in tension. Ultimate strength and tenacity are always expressed in stress units.

EXAMPLE 10.3. In an experiment, a steel specimen of 13 mm diameter was found to elongate 0.2 mm in 200 mm gauge length when it was subjected to a tensile force of 26.8 kN. If the specimen was tested within elastic limit, what is the value of young's modulus for the steel specimen?

SOLUTION: Given

Diameter (d) = 13 mm

Elongation (δl) = 0.2 mm

Length (l) = 200 mm

Force (P) = 26.8 kN

Let, E = value of Young's modulus for the steel specimen

Cross-sectional area $A = \dfrac{\pi}{4}d^2 = \dfrac{\pi}{4}(13)^2$

$= 132.73 \text{ mm}^2$

$$E = \frac{\sigma}{\varepsilon} = \frac{P/A}{\delta l / l} = \frac{P.l}{A\delta l}$$

$$= \frac{26.8 \times 200}{132.73 \times 0.2} = \frac{5360}{26.546}$$

$$E = 201.91 \text{ kN/mm}^2$$
$$= 201.91 \text{ GPa} \quad \textbf{Ans.}$$

EXAMPLE 10.4. A bar of 20 mm in square cross-section is subjected to a tensile load of 100 kN and the measured extension over a length of 200 mm was found to the 0.16 mm. The contraction in the lateral direction was 0.005 mm. Calculate the modulus of rigidity.

SOLUTION. Given

Cross-sectional area of bar $A = 20 \times 20 \text{ mm}^2$

Tensile load $P = 100$ kN

Length of bar $l = 200$ mm

Extension of bar $\delta l = 0.16$ mm

Contraction in lateral direction = 0.005 mm

$$\text{Now linear (longitudinal strain) } \varepsilon = \frac{\delta l}{l} = \frac{0.16}{200}$$
$$= 0.008$$

$$\text{Stress, } \sigma = \frac{P}{A} = \frac{100,000}{20 \times 20}$$
$$= 250 \text{ N/mm}^2$$

$$\text{Young's modulus of elasticity } E = \frac{\sigma}{\varepsilon} = \frac{250}{0.008}$$
$$= 312500 \text{ N/mm}^2$$

$$\text{Lateral strain} = \frac{\text{Contraction in lateral direction}}{\text{Length in lateral direction}}$$

$$= \frac{0.005}{20} = 0.00025$$

$$\text{Poisson's ratio, } \frac{1}{m} = \frac{\text{Lateral strain}}{\text{Longitudinal strain}}$$

$$= \frac{0.00025}{0.0008} = 0.3125$$

But, $$E = 2G\left(1 + \frac{1}{m}\right)$$

Hence $$312500 = 2G\,(1 + 0.3125)$$
$$= G\,(2 + 0.625)$$

$\therefore$ $$G = 312500/2.625$$
$$= 119.048 \text{ kN/mm}^2 \quad \textbf{Ans.}$$

EXAMPLE 10.5. A specimen of a material having original diameter equal to 13 mm and gauge length of 50 mm is tested under tension, the final diameter being 9 mm at fracture and the gauge at fracture being 70 mm. During testing it is found that yielding occurs at a load of 35 kN (lower yield point) and the maximum load that the specimen can take is 60 kN (ultimate load). The specimen fractures or breakes under a load of 30 kN. Find :

(i) Yield strength

(ii) Ultimate tensile strength

(iii) Breaking strength

(iv) % elongation

(v) % reduction in area

(vi) Young's modulus if load corresponding to any point on a linear portion of the stress-strain (load-extension) curve is 25 kN corresponding to an extension of 0.0315 mm.

SOLUTION:

$$\text{Original area of cross-section, } A = \frac{\pi}{4}d^2 = \frac{\pi}{4}\left(\frac{13}{1000}\right)^2$$

$$= 0.1325 \times 10^{-3} \text{ m}^2$$

$$\text{Yield strength} = \frac{\text{Load at Yielding}}{\text{Original x-sectional area}}$$

$$= \frac{35 \times 10^3}{0.1325 \times 10^{-3}} = 264 \text{ MPa } \textbf{Ans.}$$

$$\text{Ultimate strength} = \frac{\text{Ultimate load}}{\text{O.C.S. area}} = \frac{60 \times 10^3}{0.1325 \times 10^{-3}}$$

$$= 452 \text{ MPa } \textbf{Ans.}$$

$$\text{Breaking strength} = \frac{\text{Breaking load}}{\text{O.C.S. area}} = \frac{30 \times 10^3}{0.1325 \times 10^{-3}}$$

$$= 226 \text{ MPa } \textbf{Ans.}$$

$$\text{Percentage elongation} = \frac{L_1 - L_0}{L_0} \times 100 = \frac{70 - 50}{50} \times 100 = 40\% \textbf{ Ans.}$$

$$\text{Percentage reduction in area} = \frac{A_0 - A_1}{A_0} \times 100 = \frac{\pi/4(13)^2 - \pi/4(9)^2}{\pi/4(13)^2} \times 100$$

$$= 52\% \textbf{ Ans.}$$

$$\text{Young's modulus, } E = \text{Stress/strain}$$

$$= [(20 \times 10^3)/0.1325 \times 10^{-3}] / 0.0315/50$$

$$= (20 \times 10^3 \times 50) / (0.1325 \times 10^{-3} \times 0.0315)$$

$$= 239 \times 10^9 \text{ N/m}^2 = 239 \text{ GPa } \textbf{Ans.}$$

EXAMPLE 10.6. An automolite component (Fig. 10.8) is subjected to a tensile load of 160 kN. Determine total elongation of the component if modulus of elasticity is 200 GPa.

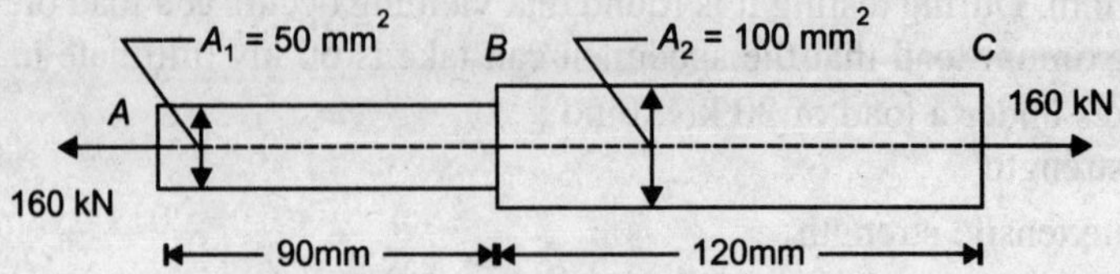

Fig. 10.8

SOLUTION:

$$\text{Elongation, } \delta l = \frac{P}{E}\left(\frac{l_1}{A_1}+\frac{l_2}{A_2}\right) = \frac{160\times10^3}{200\times10^3}\left(\frac{90}{50}+\frac{120}{100}\right)$$

$$\therefore \quad \delta l = 0.8(1.8 + 1.2)$$

$$= 2.4 \text{ mm. } \textbf{Ans.}$$

EXAMPLE 10.7. A metallic rectangular rod 1.5 m long and 40 mm wide and 25 mm thick is subjected to an axial tensile load of 120 kN. The elongation of the rod is measured as 0.9 mm. Calculate the stress, strain and modulus of elasticity. **(UPTU, 2004)**

SOLUTION:

$$\text{Stress } \sigma = \frac{\text{Load}}{\text{Area}} = \frac{120\times10^3}{40\times25}$$

$$= 120 \text{ N/mm}^2 \ \textbf{Ans.}$$

Strain = change in length/original length

or

$$\varepsilon = \frac{\delta l}{l} = \frac{0.9}{1.5\times10^3} = 0.006 \ \textbf{Ans.}$$

$$\because \quad \text{Modulus of elasticity} = \frac{\text{Stress}}{\text{Strain}}$$

$$\therefore \quad E = \frac{\sigma}{\varepsilon} = \frac{120}{0.0006} = 2\times10^5 \text{ N/mm}^2.$$

EXAMPLE 10.8. The following data refers to a mild steel tensile test

(i) Diameter of test piece = 16 mm
(ii) Gauge length = 80 mm
(iii) Load at yield point = 64 kN
(iv) Maximum load = 100 kN
(v) Load at breaking point = 70 kN

Calculate

(i) Yield strength
(ii) Ultimate strength

(iii) Strength at breaking point

(iv) Why is the breaking point strength lower than the ultimate strength?

(UPTU, 2003–04)

SOLUTION: Area of test piece,

$$A = \frac{\pi}{4}d^2 = \frac{22}{7\times 4}(16)^2 = 201.06 \text{ mm}^2$$

(i) Yield strength = Load at yield point/area

$$= (64 \times 10^3)/201.06$$
$$= 318.31 \text{ N/mm}^2 \textbf{ Ans.}$$

(ii) Ultimate strength = Maximum load/Area

$$= \frac{100\times 10^3}{201.06} = 497.36 \text{ N/mm}^2 \textbf{ Ans.}$$

(iii) Breaking strength = Load at breaking point/Area

$$= \frac{70\times 10^3}{201.06} = 348.15 \text{ N/mm}^2 \textbf{ Ans.}$$

(iv) Breaking point strength is lower than the ultimate strength because original diameter of the test piece has been taken throughout the calculations.

If the diameter of neck is considered for calculation, the breaking strength will be more than ultimate strength.

EXAMPLE 10.9. Find the stresses in three parts and total extension of the bar for an axial pull of 40 kN. Take $E = 2 \times 10^5$ N/mm^2. **(UPTU, 2005-6)**

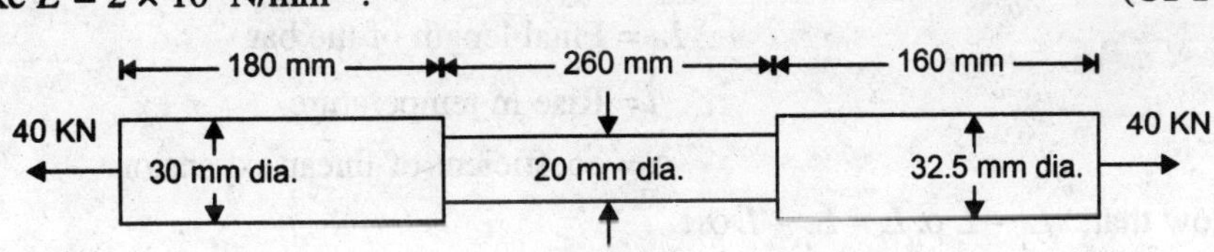

Fig. 10.9

SOLUTION. Stresses in three parts

$$\sigma_{AB} = \frac{40\times 10^3}{\frac{\pi}{4}(30)^2} = 56.59 \text{ N/mm}^2$$

$$\sigma_{BC} = \frac{40\times 10^3}{\frac{\pi}{4}(20)^2} = 127.4 \text{ N/mm}^2$$

$$\sigma_{CD} = \frac{40\times10^3}{\frac{\pi}{4}(32.5)^2} = 48.22 \text{ N/mm}^2$$

$\because$ Total extension = sum of extension in all the 3 parts

$\therefore$
$$\delta l = (\delta l)_{AB} + (\delta l)_{BC} + (\delta l)_{CD}$$

$$\left[\because \frac{\sigma}{\varepsilon} = E \text{ or } \frac{\sigma}{\delta l / l} = E,\ \frac{\sigma l}{\delta l} = E\ \therefore\ \delta l = \frac{\sigma l}{E}\right]$$

$$\delta l = \left(\frac{\sigma L}{E}\right)_{AB} + \left(\frac{\sigma L}{E}\right)_{BC} + \left(\frac{\sigma L}{E}\right)_{CD}$$

$$= \frac{1}{E}\ (56.59 \times 180 + 127.4 \times 260 + 48.22 \times 160)$$

$$= \frac{1}{2\times10^5}\ (56.59\times180 + 127.4\times260 + 48.22\times160)$$

$$= 0.255 \text{ mm}$$

Hence $\delta l = 0.255$ mm.

TEMPERATURE STRESSES: Due to temperature changes, dimensions of the material change. If these changes in dimensions are prevented, stresses are set up in the material.

STESSES DUE TO CHANGE IN TEMPERATURE : If a bar is heated (which has been prevented by end grips from expanding) external forces P–P will be exerted by the end grips causing compressive strain and the bar will have to offer compressive stresses to resist the forces P–P

If, L = Initial length of the bar

L_1 = Final length of the bar

t = Rise in temperature

α = coefficient of linear expansion

We know that, $L_1 - L\ \alpha\ L,\ \ L_1 - L\ \alpha\ t$

$\therefore$
$$L_1 - L = \alpha L t \text{ or } \frac{L_1 - L}{L} = \alpha t \text{ or } \varepsilon = \alpha t \qquad ...(1)$$

Hence compressive strain imposed by the grips,

$$\varepsilon = \alpha t \qquad ...(i)$$

But $\frac{\sigma}{\varepsilon} = E$ or $\sigma = \varepsilon E$ or $\frac{P}{A} = \varepsilon E$ ...(ii)

or
$$P = \varepsilon AE = EA\ \alpha t \qquad ...(iii)$$

$\therefore$
$$\sigma = \varepsilon\ \alpha\ t \qquad ...(3)$$

Hence push exerted by the end grips, $P = E\ A\ \alpha\ t$ ...(2)

If the grips yield by an amount δ, then expansion prevented $= L\ \alpha\ t - \delta\ (\because\ L_1 - L = L\ \alpha\ t)$

$$\therefore \quad L_1 - L = L\,\alpha\,t - \delta \text{ or } \frac{(L_1 - L)}{L} = \alpha t - \frac{\delta}{L}$$

$$\therefore \quad \varepsilon = \alpha t - \frac{\delta}{L} \quad \text{...(4)}$$

and
$$P = EA\left(\alpha t - \frac{\delta}{L}\right) \quad \text{...(5)}$$

EXAMPLE 10.10. A rail of steel 10 m long is at temperature of 10°C and is in the unstressed condition. Calculate the stress set up when the temperature of the rail increases to 70°C, assuming that no provision is made for expansion of rail. Take $\alpha = 0.000012$ per K and $E = 200$ GN/m². If there is a gap of 1 mm at 10°C, what is the stress set up?

SOLUTION. Stress set up when there is

(i) No provision of expansion

$$\sigma_1 = E\,\alpha(t_2 - t_1) = 200 \times 10^9\,(0.000012)\,(70 - 10)$$

$$= 200 \times 10^3 \times 12 \times 60$$

$$= 144 \text{ M N/m}^2 \textbf{ Ans.}$$

(ii) 1 mm GAP at 10°C

$$\varepsilon = \alpha t - \frac{\delta}{L} = 0.000012(60) - \frac{10^{-3}}{10} = 0.00062$$

$$\because \quad \frac{\sigma}{\varepsilon} = E \;\therefore\; \sigma_2 = \varepsilon.E = 0.00062\,(200 \times 10^9)$$

$$= 0.62 \times 200 \times 10^6$$

$$= 124 \text{ MN/m}^2 \textbf{ Ans.}$$

STRAIN ENERGY : When ever some load is attached to a hanging wire, it extends and the load moves downwards by an amount equal to the extension of the wire. When the load moves downwards it loses its potential energy. This energy is absorbed or stored in the stretched wire, which may be released by removing the load. On removing the load, the wire will spring back to its original position. This energy , which is absorbed in a body, when strained within its elastic limit is known as strain energy. This strain energy is always capable of doing some work (strain energy = work done).

RESILIENCE : It is a common term used for the total strain energy stored in a body. Some times the resilience is also defined as the capacity of a strained body for doing work (when it springs back) on the removal of straining force.

PROOF RESILIENCE : It is also a common term, used for maximum strain energy, which can be stored in a body. This happens when the body is stressed up to the elastic limit. The corresponding stress is known as proof stress.

MODULUS OF RESILIENCE : The proof resilience per unit volume of a material, is known as modulus of resilience.

TYPES OF LOADING : A load may act in following ways :

1. Gradually

2. Suddenly
3. With impact

Strain energy stored in a body when the load is :

1. **GRADUALLY APPLIED :** Modulus of resilience = strain energy per unit volume =

$$\frac{\sigma^2}{2E}$$

2. **SUDDENLY APPLIED :** $\sigma = \frac{2P}{A}$

   It means that the stress induced in this case is twice the stress induced when the same load is applied gradually.

3. **APPLIED WITH IMPACT :** $\sigma = \sqrt{\frac{2EPh}{Al}} = \frac{P}{A}\left[1 + \sqrt{1 \pm \frac{2AEh}{Pl}}\right]$

EXAMPLE 10.12. Calculate the strain energy stored in a bar 2 m long, 50 mm wide and 40 mm thick when it is subjected to a tensile load of 60 kN. Take E as 20 GPa.

SOLUTION. Given : Length of bar (l) = 2 m = 2×10^3 mm

Width of bar (b) = 50 mm

Thickness of bar (t) = 40 mm

Tensile load on bar (P) = 60 kN = 60×10^3 N

Modulus of elasticity (E) = 200 GPa = 200×10^3 N/mm^2

We know that stress in a bar, $\sigma = \frac{P}{A} = \frac{60 \times 10^3}{50 \times 40} = 30$ N/mm^2

Strain energy stored in a bar, $U = \frac{\sigma^2}{2E} V = \frac{(30)^2 (2 \times 10^3 \times 50 \times 40)}{2(200 \times 10^3)}$

$= 9 \times 10^3$ N-mm

$= 9$ kN - mm

EXAMPLE 10.13. An axial pull of 20 kN is suddenly applied on a steel rod 2.5 m long and 1000 mm^2 in cross-section. Calculate the strain energy, which can be absorbed in the rod. Take E = 200 GPa.

SOLUTION. Given:

Axial pull on the rod (P) = 20 kN = 20×10^3 N

Length of rod (l) = 2.5 m = 2.5×10^3 mm

Cross-sectional area of rod (A) = 1000 mm^2

Modulus of Elasticity (E) = 200 GPa = 200×10^3 N/mm^2

We know that stress in the rod, when the load is suddenly applied,

$$\sigma = 2\times\frac{P}{A} = 2\times\frac{20\times10^3}{1000} = 40 \text{ N/mm}^2$$

and volume of rod,

$$V = \text{L.A.}$$
$$= 2.5 \times 10^3\ (1000) = 2.5 \times 10^6 \text{ mm}^3$$

∴ Strain energy which can be absorbed in the rod,

$$U = \frac{\sigma^2}{2E}V = \frac{(40)^2\times(2.5\times10^6)}{2(200\times10^3)}$$
$$= 10 \times 10^3 \text{ N-mm}$$
$$= 10 \text{ kN-mm. } \textbf{Ans.}$$

EXAMPLE 10.14. A steel rod of 28 mm diameter is 2.5 m long. Find the maximum instantaneous stress and work done at maximum elongation when an axial load of 50 kN is suddenly applied to it. Also calculate the maximum dynamic force in the rod. Take E = 200 GPa.

SOLUTION. Given : Diameter of rod (d) = 28 mm

Length of rod (l) = 2.5 m = 2.5×10^3 mm

Axial load on the rod (P) = 50 kN = 50×10^{-3} N

Modulus of elasticity (E) = 200 GPa = 200×10^3 N/mm^2

MAXIMUM INSTANTANEOUS STRESS: We know that cross-sectional area of the rod, $A = \frac{\pi}{4}d^2 = \frac{\pi}{4}(28)^2 = 615.8 \text{ mm}^2$ and maximum instantaneous stress, when the load is suddenly applied, $\sigma_{max} = 2\times\frac{P}{A} = \frac{2\times50\times10^3}{615.8} = 162.4 \text{ N/mm}^2 = 162.4 \text{ MPa}$ **Ans.**

WORK DONE AT MAXIMUM ELONGATION : We know that maximum elongation,

$$\delta l = \frac{\sigma_{max}\times l}{E} = \frac{162.4\times2.5\times10^3}{200\times10^3}$$
$$= 2.03 \text{ mm}$$

and

$$\text{Work done} = \text{F.D.} = P\,\delta l = (50 \times 10^{-3})\ 2.03$$
$$= 101.5 \times 10^3 \text{ N-mm} = 101.5 \text{ N–m}$$

MAXIMUM DYNAMIC FORCE $= A.\sigma_{max} = 615.8 \times 162.4 = 100 \times 10^3 \text{ N} = 100\text{kN}$ **Ans.**

EXAMPLE 10.15. A 2m long alloy bar of 1500 mm^2 cross-sectional area and hangs vertically and has a collar securely fixed at its lower end. Find the stress induced in the bar, when a weight of 2 kN falls from a height of 100 mm on the collar. Table E = 120 GP$_a$. Also find the strain energy stored in the bar.

SOLUTION. Given:

Length of bar (l) = 2m = 2×10^3 mm;

Cross sectional area of bar (A) = 1500 mm^2;

Weight falling on collar of bar (p) = 2 kN = 2×10^3 N;

Height from which weight falls (h) = 100 mm, and

Modulus of Elasticity, E = 120 GPa = 120×10^3 N/mm^2.

We know that in this case, extension of the bar will be small and negligible as compared to the height (h) from where the weight falls on the collar (due to small value of weight i.e., 2 kN and large value of h i.e., 100 mm). Therefore stress induced in the bar,

$$\sigma = \sqrt{\frac{2EPh}{A.l}} = \sqrt{\frac{2 \times (120 \times 10^3)(2 \times 10^3)\,100}{1500\,(2 \times 10^3)}}$$

$$= 126.5 \text{ N/mm}^2 = 126.5 \text{ MP}_a \textbf{ Ans.}$$

STRAIN ENERGY STORED IN THE BAR

Volume of bar, V = l.A = (2×10^3) 1500 = 3×10^6 mm^3

Strain energy in the bar,
$$U = \frac{\sigma^2 V}{2E} = \frac{(126.5)^2}{2\,(120 \times 10^3)} \times 3 \times 10^6$$

$$= 200 \times 10^3 \text{ N–mm} = 200\text{N-m } \textbf{Ans.}$$

EXAMPLE 10.16. A steel bar 3m long and 2500 mm^2 in area hangs vertically, which is securely fixed on a collar at its lower end. If a weight of 15 kN falls on a collar from height of 10 mm, determine the stress developed in the bar. What will be the strain energy stored in the bar? Take E = 200 MPa.

SOLUTION. Given:

Length of bar (l) = 3m = 3×10^3 mm,

Area of bar (A) = 2500 mm^2,

Weight falling on collar of bar (P) = 15 kN = 15×10^3N,

Height from which weight falls (h) = 10mm, and

Modulus of Elasticity (E) = 200 GPa = 200×10^3N/mm^2.

Stress developed in the bar: We know that in this case, extension of the bar will be considerable as compared to the height (h) from where the weight falls on the collar (due to large value of weight i.e., 15 kN and a small value of h = 10 mm)

$\therefore$ Stress developed in bar,
$$\sigma = \frac{P}{A}\left[1 + \sqrt{1 + \frac{2AEh}{Pl}}\right]$$

$\therefore$
$$\sigma = \frac{15 \times 10^3}{2500}\left[1 + \sqrt{1 + \frac{2 \times 2500\,(200 \times 10^3)\,10}{(15 \times 10^3)(3 \times 10^3)}}\right]$$

$$= 6\,(1 + 4.9) = 95.4 \text{ N/mm}^2$$

$$= 95.4 \text{ MPa } \textbf{Ans.}$$

STRAIN ENERGY STORED IN THE BAR

Volume of the bar, $V = l.A = (3 \times 10^3)\ 2500 = 7.5 \times 10^6\ mm^3$ and strain energy stored in the bar.

$$U = \frac{\sigma^2}{2E} V$$

$$= \frac{(95.4)^2 \times 7.5 \times 10^6}{2\,(200 \times 10^3)} = 170.6 \times 10^3 \text{ N–mm}$$

$$= 170.6 \text{ N–m } \textbf{Ans.}$$

EXAMPLE 10.17. A copper bar of 12 mm diameter gets stretched by 1 mm under a steady load of 4 kN. What stress would be produced in the bar by a weight 500 N, the weight falls through 80 mm before striking the collar rigidly fixed to the lower end of the bar? Take Young's Modulus for the bar material 100 GPa.

SOLUTION. Given:

Diameter of bar (d) = 12 mm;

Change in length of bar (δl) = 1 mm,

Load on bar (P_2) = 4 kN = 4×10^3 N,

Weight falling on collar (P_2) = 500 N,

Height from which weight falls (h) = 80 mm, and

Modulus of Elasticity (E) = 100 GPa = 100×10^3 N/mm²

Let, l = length of copper bar,

We know that cross-sectional area of the bar, $A = \frac{\pi}{4} d^2 = \frac{\pi}{4} (12)^2 = 113.1$ mm², and stretching of the bar $(\delta l) = P.l)/A.E$.

$$\therefore \qquad \delta l = \frac{P.l}{A.E} = \frac{(4 \times 10^3)\,l}{113.1\,(100 \times 10^3)}$$

$$= \frac{l}{2.83 \times 10^3}$$

$$\therefore \qquad l = 1\,(2.83 \times 10^3) = 2.83 \times 10^3 \text{ mm}$$

We know that stress produced in the bar by the falling weight,

$$\sigma = \frac{P^2}{A}\left(1 + \sqrt{1 + \frac{2AEh}{P_2 l}}\right)$$

$$= \frac{500}{113.1}\left(1 + \sqrt{1 + \frac{2 \times 113.1\,(100 \times 10^3)\,80}{500\,(2.83 \times 10^3)}}\right)$$

$$\sigma = 4.42\ (1 + 35.77) = 162.52\ \text{N/mm}^2$$

$$= 162.52\ \text{MPa}\ \textbf{Ans.}$$

EXAMPLE 10.18. Obtain the relation for Strain Energy Stored in a Body, When The load is Gradually Applied.

In this case the loading starts from zero and increases gradually till the body is fully loaded. Consider a metallic bar subjected to gradual load.

Let, P = Load gradually applied

A = Cross-sectional area of the bar

l = Length of bar

E = Modulus of Elasticity of the bar material

δl = Deformation of the bar due to load

Since the load applied is gradual, and varies from zero to P, therefore, the average load is $P/2$.

$\therefore$ Work done = Force × Distance moved

= Average load × Deformation

$$= \frac{P}{2} . \delta l = \frac{P}{2} (\varepsilon . l) \qquad (\because \delta l = \varepsilon . l)$$

$$= \frac{1}{2} \sigma . \varepsilon\ A . l \qquad (\because P = \sigma A)$$

$$= \frac{1}{2}\ (\text{stress} \times \text{strain} \times \text{volume})$$

$$= \frac{1}{2}\left(\sigma . \frac{\sigma}{E} . Al\right) \qquad \left(\because \varepsilon = \frac{\sigma}{E}\right)$$

$$= \frac{1}{2} \times \frac{\sigma^2}{E} \times Al = \frac{\sigma^2}{2E} \times V \qquad (\because Al = \text{Volume} = V)$$

Since the energy stored is also equal to the workdone, therefore strain energy stored, $U = \frac{\sigma^2}{2E} V$.

We also know that modulus of resislience,

= strain energy per unit volume

$$= \sigma^2/2E \qquad ...(1)$$

EXAMPLE 10.19. Show that in a bar, subjected to an axial load, the instantaneous stress due to sudden application of a load is twice the stress caused by the gradual application of load.

SOLUTION. Strain Energy Stored in a Body When Load is Suddenly Applied.

Let, P = Load applied suddenly,

A = Cross-sectional area of the bar

l = Length of bar

E = Modulus of Elasticity of the bar material

δl = Deformation of the bar, and

σ = Stress induced by the application of the sudden load

Since the load is applied suddenly, therefore the load (P) is constant throughout the process of deformation of the bar.

$\therefore$ Work done = Force × Distance

= Average load × Deformation

$= P.\ \delta l$

We know that strain energy stored, $U = \dfrac{\sigma^2}{2E} Al$

Since the energy stored is equal to workdone, therefore

$$\frac{\sigma^2}{2E} Al = P.\ \delta l = P \frac{\sigma}{E} l \qquad \left(\because \delta l = \frac{\sigma}{E}.\ l\right)$$

$$\therefore \qquad \sigma = \frac{2P}{A}$$

It means that stress induced in this case is twice the stress induced when the same load is applied gradually. Once the stress (σ), is obtained, the corresponding instantaneous deformation (δl) and the strain energy may be found out as usual.

EXAMPLE 10.20. Obtain a relation for the stress induced is a body, if a load P is applied with an impact.

SOLUTION. Strain Energy Stored in a Body, When The Load is Applied with Impact: When a load falls through a distance on a platform, it will be the case of a **Load Applied with Impact.**

Now consider a bar subject to a load applied with impact as shown in Fig. 10.10.

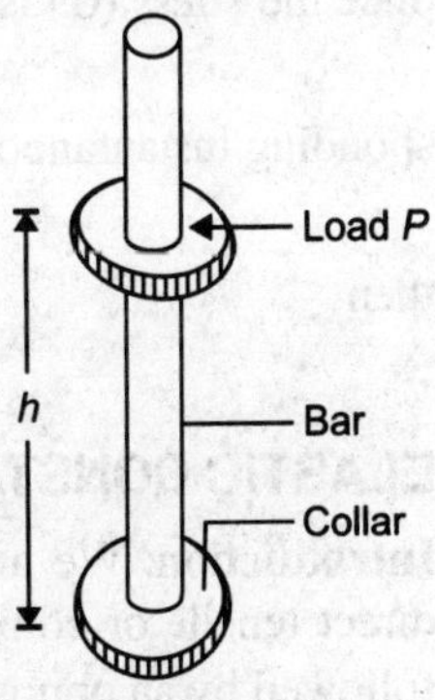

Fig. 10.10. Impact load.

Let, P = Applied load with impact,

A = Cross-sectional area of the bar

l = Length of bar

E = Modulus of Elasticity of the bar material

δl = Deformation of the bar, and

σ = Stress induced due to impact load, and

h = Height through which the load will fall, before impact on the collar of the bar

$$\therefore \qquad \text{Work done} = \text{Load} \times \text{Distance moved}$$

$$= P(h + \delta l) \qquad \text{...(1)}$$

and energy stored,

$$U = \frac{\sigma^2}{2E} Al \qquad \text{...(2)}$$

Since energy stored is equal to the work done,

$$\therefore \qquad \frac{\sigma^2}{2E} Al = P(h + \delta l) = P\left(h + \frac{\sigma}{E}.l\right) \qquad \left(\because \delta l = \frac{\sigma}{E}.l\right)$$

$$= Ph + \frac{P\sigma l}{E}$$

$$\therefore \qquad \sigma^2\left(\frac{Al}{2E}\right) - \sigma\left(\frac{Pl}{E}\right) - Ph = 0$$

Now multiplying both sides by $\left(\frac{E}{Al}\right)$.

$$\frac{\sigma^2}{2} \quad \sigma\left(\frac{P}{A}\right) \quad \frac{PEh}{Al} = 0$$

This is a quadratic equation. We know that

$$\sigma = \frac{P}{A} \pm \sqrt{\left(\frac{P}{A}\right)^2 + \left(4 \times \frac{1}{2}\right)\left(\frac{PEh}{Al}\right)}$$

once the stress (σ) is obtained, the corre-

$$= \frac{P}{A}\left[1 \pm \sqrt{1 + \frac{2AEh}{Pl}}\right]$$

sponding instantaneous deformation (δl) may be found out when δl is very small as compared to h, then

$$\sigma = \sqrt{\frac{2EPh}{Al}}$$

ELASTIC CONSTANTS

Introduction. We are familiar about the axial deformation of a body, when it is subjected to a direct tensile or compressive stress. It has been found, that the axial, strain of a body is always followed by an opposite kind of strain at right angle to it. Thus there is always a set of two types of strains in a body, when subjected to a direct stress.

1. PRIMARY OR LINEAR STRAIN: When ever some external force acts on a body, it undergoes some deformation. The deformation of the bar per unit length in the direction of force, i.e., $\delta l/l$ is known as PRIMARY OR LINEAR STRAIN.

2. SECONDARY OR LATERAL STRAIN: If we study the deformation of a bar of length l and diameter d subjected to a tensile force, we will find that bar has extended through a length δl, which will be followed by the decrease of diameter from d to $(d - \delta d)$. Similarly, if the bar is subjected to a compressive force, the length of the bar will decrease by δl which will be followed by the increase of diameter from d to $(d + \delta d)$.

It is thus obvious that every direct stress is always accompanied by a strain in its own direction and an opposite kind of strain in every direction at right angles to it. Such a strain is known as SECONDARY OR LATERAL STRAIN.

POISSON'S RATIO: The ratio of lateral strain to longitudinal strain is called Poisson's Ratio.

∴ Poisson's ratio = Lateral strain / Longitudinal strain

$$= A \text{ constant} = \frac{1}{m} = \mu$$

∴ Lateral strain $= \dfrac{1}{m} \times \varepsilon = \mu\varepsilon$

EXAMPLE 10.21. A steel bar 2 m long, 40 mm wide and 20 mm thick is subjected to an axial pull of 160 kN in the direction of its length. Find the changes in length, width and thickness of the bar. Table E = 200 GPa and Poisson's ratio = 0.3.

SOLUTION. Given: Length (l) 2m = 2×10^3 mm; Width (b) = 40mm;; Thickness (t) = 20 mm; Axial pull (P) = 160 kN = 160×10^3 N; Modulus of Elasticity (E) = 200 GPa = 20×10^3 N/mm^2,and Poisson's ration (1/m) = 0.3.

We know that $\dfrac{P}{A} / \dfrac{\delta l}{l} = E = \dfrac{Pl}{A.\delta l}$ or $EA\delta l = Pl$

$$\therefore \qquad \delta l = \frac{Pl}{AE}$$

$$\therefore \qquad \delta l = \frac{Pl}{AE} \frac{\left(160 \times 10^3\right)\left(2^2 \times 10^3\right)}{\left(40 \times 20\right)\left(200 \times 10^3\right)}$$

$$= 2 \text{ mm Ans.}$$

CHANGE IN WIDTH

We know that linear strain,

$$\varepsilon = \delta l / l = 2/2 \times 10^3 = 0.001, \text{ and}$$

$$\text{Lateral strain} = \frac{1}{m}\varepsilon = \mu\varepsilon = 0.3 \times 0.001$$

$$= 0.0003.$$

∴ Change in width, $\delta b = b \times \text{lateral strain} = 40 \times 0.0003$

$$= 0.012 \text{ mm } \textbf{Ans.}$$

CHANGE IN THICKNESS

We also know that change in thickness.

$$\delta l = l \times \text{lateral strain} = 20 \times 0.0003$$
$$= 0.006 \text{ mm } \textbf{Ans.}$$

EXAMPLE 10.22. A metal bar 50 mm × 50 mm in section is subjected to an axial compressive load of 500 kN. If the contraction of a 200 m gauge length was found to be 0.5 mm and the increase in thickness 0.04 mm, find the values of young's modulus and poisson's ration for the bar material.

SOLUTION: Given:

Width (b) = 50 mm;

Thickness (t) = 50 mm;

Axial compressive load (P) = 500 kN = 50 × 10^3 N;

Length (l) = 200 mm; change in length (δl) = 0.5 mm, and

Change on thickness (δt) = 0.04 mm.

VALUE OF BAR MATERIAL'S YOUNG'S MODULUS

Let, E = value of young's modulus for the bar material.

We know the contraction of the bar,

$$\delta l = \frac{P.l}{A.E} \text{ or } 0.5 = \frac{\left(50 \times 10^3\right) 200}{(50 \times 50)\, E} = \frac{40 \times 10^3}{E}$$

or

$$E = \frac{40 \times 10^3}{0.5}$$
$$= 80 \text{ GPa } \textbf{Ans.}$$

VALUE OF POISSON'S RATIO FOR THE BAR MATERIAL

Let, $\frac{1}{m}$ = Value of Poisson's ration for the bar material

We know that linear strain, $\varepsilon = \delta l \,/\, l = 0.5/200 = 0.0025$ and lateral strain = $\frac{1}{m}$ × linear strain

$= \frac{1}{m} \times 0.0025$.

We know that increase in thickness (δt) = t × Lateral strain

$$\therefore \quad 0.04 = 50 \times \frac{1}{m} \times 0.0025 = \frac{0.125}{m}$$

$$\therefore \quad \frac{1}{m} = \frac{0.04}{0.125} = 0.32 \textbf{ Ans.}$$

VOLUMETRIC STRAIN

When a body is subjected to a single force or a system of forces, it undergoes some changes in its dimensions and this change in dimensions of a body will cause some changes in its volume. The ratio of change in volume, to original volume, is known as VOLUMETRIC STRAIN, Mathematically.

Volumetric strain = Change in volume/original volume

$$\therefore \quad \varepsilon_V = \frac{\delta V}{V} = \varepsilon\left(1 - \frac{2}{m}\right)$$

LONGITUDINAL STRAIN: When a bar is subjected to an axial tensile force, there is an axial deformation in the length of the bar. Thus the strain or deformation produced in the direction of the applied force is called the LONGITUDINAL STRAIN.

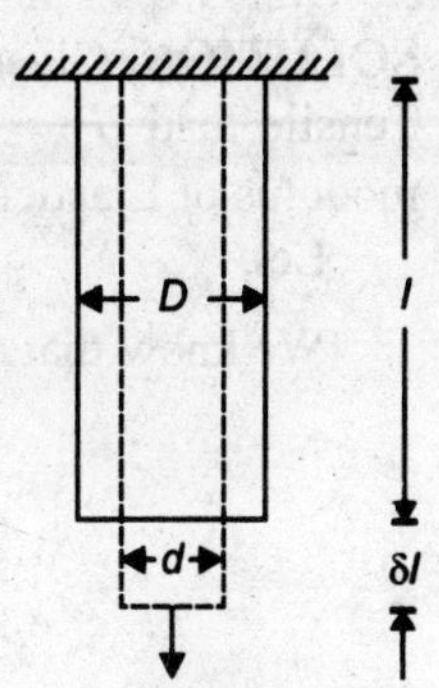

Fig. 10.11

$$\therefore \quad \text{Longitudinal strain} = \frac{\text{Increase in Length}}{\text{Original Length}} = \frac{\delta l}{l}$$

$$= \frac{\sigma}{E}\left(1 - \frac{2}{m}\right)$$

LATERAL STRAIN: When the bar is subjected to axial loads, the strain produced perpendicular to the axis is called LATERAL STRAIN.

$$\text{Lateral strain} = \frac{\text{Reduced dia. of bar}}{\text{Original dia. of bar}} = \frac{D - d}{D}$$

NOTE: If the longitudinal strain is tensile, the lateral strain will be compressive and if the longitudinal stress is compressive, the lateral strain will be tensile.

BULK OR VOLUME MODULUS OF ELASTICITY: The ratio of the NORMAL STRESS to the VOLUMETRIC STRAIN is called BULK or VOLUME MODULUS OF ELASTICITY. Hence

Bulk or Volume modulus of Elasticity = Normal stress/ Volumetric strain

$$K = \frac{\sigma_n}{\varepsilon_V}, \quad K = \frac{mE}{3(m-2)}$$

RELATION BETWEEN *E*, *G* AND *K*: $E = 2G\left(1 + \frac{1}{m}\right) = \frac{9\,KG}{3\,K + G}$

$$= 26\,(1 + \mu)$$

E, *G* and *K* are known as ELASTIC CONSTANTS OR ELASTIC MODULE and their values are different for different materials.

Hence, Modulus of Elasticity, $\quad E = \frac{\sigma_t}{\varepsilon_t} = \frac{\sigma_C}{\varepsilon_c} = 3\,K\left(3 - \frac{E}{G}\right)$

Modulus of Rigidity, $\quad G = \frac{\sigma_s}{\varepsilon_s} = \frac{mE}{2(m+1)}$

Bulk or Modulus of Elasticity, $K = \dfrac{\sigma_n}{\varepsilon_V}$

$$G = \frac{E}{2(1+\mu)}, \quad K = \frac{mE}{3(m-2)}$$

EXAMPLE 10.23. A steel bar 2m long, 20 mm wide and 13 mm thick is subjected to a tensile load of 30 kN. Find the increase in volume, if Poisson's ration is 0.25 and Young's modulus is 200 GPa.

SOLUTION. Given: length (l) = 2m = 2×10^3 mm; Width (b) = 20 mm; Thickness (t) = 15 mm; Tensile load (P) = 30 kN = 30×10^3 N; Poisson's Ratio (1/m) = 0.25 or m = 4; and young's modulus of Elasticity (E) = 200 GPa = 200×10^3 N/mm^2.

Let, δV = Increase in volume of the bar,

We know that original volume of the bar,

$$V = \text{l.b.t} = (2 \times 10^3) \times 20 \times 15$$

$$= 600 \times 10^3 \text{ mm}^3$$

and

$$\frac{\delta V}{V} = \frac{P}{btE}\left(1 - \frac{2}{m}\right) = \frac{30 \times 10^3 \left(1 - \frac{2}{4}\right)}{20 \times 15 \left(200 \times 10^3\right)} = 0.00025$$

$\therefore$ $\delta V = 0.00025 \times V = 0.00025\ (600 \times 10^3) = 150 \text{ mm}^3$ **Ans.**

EXAMPLE 10.24. A copper bar 250 mm long and 50 mm × 50 mm in cross-section is subjected to an axial pull in the direction of its length. If the increase in volume of the bar is 37.5 mm^3, find the magnitude of the pull. Take $m = 4$, and $E = 100$ GPa.

SOLUTION. Given:

Length (l) = 250 mm;

Width (b) = 50 mm;

Thickness (t) = 50 mm;

Increase in volume (δV) = 37.5 mm^3; m = 4; and

Modulus of Elasticity (E) 100 GPa = 100×10^3 N / mm^2.

Let, P = Magnitude of the pull in kN

We know that original volume of the bar,

$$V = l.b.t = 250 \times 50 \times 50 = 625 \times 10^3 \text{mm}^3$$

and

$$\frac{\delta \text{V}}{\text{V}} = \frac{P}{btE}\left(1 - \frac{2}{m}\right)$$

$$= \frac{P\left(1 - \frac{2}{4}\right)}{50 \times 50 \left(100 \times 10^3\right)}$$

or $$\frac{37.5}{625\times10^3} = \frac{P}{500\times10^6}$$

$$\therefore \quad P = \frac{37.5\left(500\times10^6\right)}{625\times10^3} = 30\times10^3\ N$$

$$= 30 \text{ kN } \textbf{Ans.}$$

EXAMPLE 10.25. A steel bar 50 mm × 50 mm in section is 1.2 m long. It is subjected to an axial pull of 200 kN. What are the changes in length, width and volume of the bar, if the value of Poisson's ration is 0.3. Take E as 200 GPa.

SOLUTION. Given:

Width (b) = 50 mm;

Thickness (t) = 50 mm;

Length (l) = 1.2 m = 1.2×10^3 mm;

Axial pull (P) = 200 kN = 200×10^3 N,

Poisson's ration (1/m) = 0.3; and

Modulus of elasticity (E) = 200 GPa = $200\text{X } 10^3 \text{N/mm}^2$.

CHANGE IN LENGTH: We know that change in length,

$$\delta l = \frac{Pl}{AE} = \frac{200\times10^3\left(1.2\times10^3\right)}{(50\times50)\left(200\times10^3\right)}$$

$$= 0.48 \text{ mm } \textbf{Ans.}$$

CHANGE IN WIDTH: We know that linear strain,

$$\varepsilon = \delta l / l = 0.48 / 1.2 \times 10^3$$

$$= 0.004$$

and $$\text{Lateral strain} = \frac{1}{m}.\varepsilon = 0.3 \times 0.0004$$

$$= 0.00012$$

$\therefore$ Change in width, $$\delta b = b \times \text{Lateral strain} = 50 \times 0.00012$$

$$= 0.0006 \text{ mm Ans.}$$

CHANGE IN VOLUME: We know that volume of the bar,

$$V = \text{l.b.t} = (1.2\times10^3)\times50\times50$$

$$= 3\times10^6 \text{ mm}^3$$

and $$\frac{\delta V}{V} = \frac{P}{btE}\left(1-\frac{2}{m}\right) = \frac{200\times10^3\left[1-2\,(0.3)\right]}{50\times50\left(200\times10^3\right)}$$

$$= 0.00016$$

$\therefore$ $$\delta V = 0.00016\ V = 0.00016\ (3 \times 10^6)$$
$$= 480\ \text{mm}^3 \ \textbf{Ans.}$$

EXAMPLE 10.26. If the values of modulus of elasticity and Poisson's ration for an alloy body are 150 GPa and 0.25 respectively, determine the value of bulk modulus for the alloy.

SOLUTION. Given:

Modulus of Elasticity (E) = 150

GPa = 150×10^3N/mm^2, and

Poissons' ratio (1/m) = 0.25 or m = 4.

We know that value of the bulk modulus for the alloy,

$$K = \frac{mE}{3\,(m-2)} = \frac{4\left(150 \times 10^3\right)}{3(4 \quad 2)}$$

$$= 100 \times 10^3\ \text{N/mm}^2$$

$$= 100\ \text{GPa} \ \textbf{Ans.}$$

EXAMPLE 10.27. For a given material, young's modulus is 120 GPa and modulus of rigidity is 40 GPa. Find the bulk modulus and lateral contraction of a round bar of 50 mm diameter and 2.5 m long, when stretched 2.5 mm. Take poissons' ration as 0.25.

SOLUTION. Given:

Young's modulus (E) = 120 GPa = 120×10^3 N/mm^2;

Modulus of rigitidy (G) = 40 GPa = 40×10^3 N/mm^2;

Diameter (d) = 50 mm;

Length (l) = 2.5 mm = 2.5×10^3 mm;

Linear stretching or change in length (δl) = 2.5 mm, and

Poisson's ration (1/m) = 0.25 or m = 4.

BULK MODULUS OF THE BAR: We know that bulk modulus of the bar,

$$K = \frac{mE}{3\,(m-2)} = \frac{4\left(120 \times 10^3\right)}{3(4-2)}$$

$$= 80 \times 10^3\ \text{N/mm}^2$$

$$= 80\ \text{GPa} \quad \textbf{Ans.}$$

LATERAL CONTRACTION OF THE BAR

Let, δd = Lateral contraction (or change in dia.) of the bar

We know that Linear strain,

$$\varepsilon = \frac{\delta l}{l} = \frac{2.5}{2.5 \times 10^3} = \frac{1}{1000}$$

$$= 0.001$$

and Lateral strain, $\delta d/d = \dfrac{1}{m}\varepsilon = 0.25 \times 0.001$

$$= 0.25 \times 10^{-3}$$

$\therefore$ $\delta d = d\,(0.25 \times 10^{-3}) = 50\,(0.25 \times 10^{-3})$

$$= 0.0125 \text{ mm} \quad \textbf{Ans.}$$

Example 10.28. An alloy specimen has a modulus of elasticity of 120 GPa and modulus of rigidity of 45 GPa. Determine the Poisson's ratio of the material.

SOLUTION. Given:

Modulus of Elasticity (E) = 120 GPa = 120×10^3 N/mm²; and

Modulus of Rigidity (G) = 45 GPa.

Let, $1/m$ = Poisson's ratio of the material

We know that modulus of rigidity, $G = (mE) / 2(m + 1)$

$\therefore$ $$45 = \frac{m \times 120}{2(m+1)} = \frac{120\,m}{2m+2}$$

$$= \frac{60m}{m+1}$$

or $$45m + 45 = 60\,m$$

or $$60m - 45m = 45$$

or $$15m = 45$$

$\therefore$ $$m = 45/15 = 3$$

$\therefore$ $$\frac{1}{m} = \frac{1}{3} \quad \textbf{Ans.}$$

EXAMPLE 10.29. In an experiment, a bar of 30 mm diameter is subjected to a pull of 60 kN. The measured extension on gauge length of 200 mm is 0.09 mm and the change in diameter is 0.0039 mm. Calculate the Poisson's ration and the values of the three moduli.

SOLUTION. Given:

Diameter (d) = 30 mm;

Pull (P) = 60 kN = 60×10^3 N;

Length (l) = 200 mm;

Extension (δl) = 0.09 mm; and

Change in diameter (δd) = 0.0039 mm.

POISSON'S RATION: We know that Linear Strain,.

$$\varepsilon = \delta l/l = 0.09/200 = 0.00045$$

and Lateral strain, $= \delta d/d = 0.0039/30 = 0.00013$

We also know that Poisson's ratio, $1/m$ = Lateral strain/ Linear strain

$= 0.00013 / 0.00045$

$= 0.289$ **Ans.**

VALUES OF THREE MUDULI:

Let, E = Value of young's modulus

We know that area of bar, $A = \frac{\pi}{4} d^2 = \frac{\pi}{4}(30)^2$

$= 706.9 \text{ mm}^2$

and extension of the bar $\delta l = (P.l) / (A.E.)$

or $$0.09 = \frac{(60 \times 10^3)\, 200}{706.9\, E}$$

or $$0.09 = \frac{17 \times 10^3}{E}$$

$\therefore$ $E = 17 \times 10^3/0.09 = 188.9 \times 10^3 \text{N/mm}^2$

$= 188.9$ GPa **Ans.**

We know that from the value of Poisson's ratio, $m = \frac{1}{0.289} = 3.46$, and value of modulus of rigidity, $G = \frac{mE}{2(m+1)}$

$$\therefore \quad G = \frac{3.46(188.9 \times 10^3)}{2(3.46+1))} = 73.3 \times 10^3 \text{N/mm}^2$$

$= 73.3$ GPa **Ans.**

We know that value of bulk modulus,

$$K = \frac{mE}{3(m-2)} = \frac{3.46(188.9 \times 10^3)}{3(3.46-2)}$$

$= 149.2 \times 10^3$ N./mm^2

$= 149.2$ GPa **Ans.**

EXAMPLE 10.30. A bar of 25 mm diameter is subjected to a pull of 60 kN, the measured extension over a gauge length 250 mm is 0.15 mm and change in diameter is 0.004 mm. Calcualte the modulus of Elasticity, modulus of rigidity and Poisson's ratio. **(U.P.T.U. II Sem: 2005-06)**

SOLUTION. Given: $d = 25$ mm, $L = 250$ mm, $\delta l = 0.15$ mm, $\delta d = 0.004$ mm, $P = 60$ kN

Longitudinal strain $= \delta l/l = 0.15/250$

$= 0.0006$

$$\text{Lateral strain} = \text{Change in dia/ Original dia.} = \delta d/d$$
$$= 0.004/25$$
$$= 0.00016$$
$$\text{Poisson's Ratio, } \mu = \text{Lateral strain/Longitudinal strain}$$
$$\therefore \quad \mu = 0.00016/0.0006$$
$$= 0.267 \quad \textbf{Ans.}$$
$$\text{Stress, } \sigma = P/A = (60 \times 10^3) / (22/7 \times 4)(25^2)$$
$$= 122.213 \text{ N/mm}^2$$
$$\text{Modulus of Elasticity, } E = \text{Stress/strain} = 122.23 \text{ N} / 0.0006$$
$$\therefore \quad E = 203718.32 \text{ N/mm}^2$$
$$= 2.04 \times 10^5 \text{ N/mm}^2 \quad \textbf{Ans.}$$
$$\text{Modulus of Rigidity, } G = \frac{E}{2(1+\mu)}$$
$$= \frac{203718.32}{2(1+0.267)}$$
$$\therefore \quad G = 80393.97 \text{ N/mm}^2$$
$$= 80.39397 \text{ kN/mm}^2 \quad \textbf{Ans.}$$

EXAMPLE 10.31: For a given material the modulus of rigidity is 0.43×10^5 N/mm^2 and the young's modulus is 1.10×10^5 N/mm^2. Find the bulk modulus and the lateral contraction of a round bar of 45 mm diameter and 2.5 m length stretched by 2.5 mm. **(U.P.T.U., 2006)**

SOLUTION. Given: $G = 0.43 \times 10^5$ N/mm^2, $E = 1.1 \times 10^5$ N/ mm^2, $d = 45$ mm, $\delta l = 2.5$ mm, $l = 2.5$ m $= 2.5 \times 10^3$ mm.

$$E = 2G(1 + \mu)$$
$$\therefore \quad 1.1 \times 10^5 = 2 \times 0.43 \times 10^5 (1 + \mu)$$
$$\therefore \quad \mu = 0.279$$

Again,
$$E = 3K\left(3 - \frac{E}{G}\right)$$

or
$$1.1 \times 10^5 = 3K\,\frac{3 - 1.1 \times 10^5}{0.43 \times 10^5}$$

$\therefore$ Bulk Modulus,
$$K = 82982 \text{N/mm}^2$$
$$= 82.982 \text{kN/mm}^2 \quad \text{Ans.}$$

Longitudinal (Axial) strain
$$\delta l/l = 2.5/2.5 \times 10^3$$
$$= 0.001$$

$\because$ Poisson's Ratio = Lateral strain/Axial strain

$\because$ Lateral strain = 0.279×0.001

$= 0.000279$

$\because$ Lateral strain = Change in diameter/Original diameter

$\because$ Contraction of round bar = L.S × O.D. = 0.000279×45

$= 0.012555$ mm **Ans.**

EXAMPLE 10.32. A 2m long rectangular bar of 7.5 cm × 5 cm is subjected to an axial tensile load of 1000 kN. The bar gets elongated by 2mm in length and decreases in width by 10×10^{-6} m. Determine the modulus of Elasticity E and Poisson's ratio μ of the material of the bar.

(U.P.T.U.: 2002-2003)

SOLUTION. Given: l = 2m, cross-section of bar = 7.5 cm × 5cm.

Normal stress, $\sigma = P/A = (1000 \times 1000)/7.5 \times 5 \times 10^2$

$= 266.7 \text{ N/mm}^2$

Linear strain = Change in length/Original length = $\delta l/l$

$= 2 \times 10^{-3}/2 = 0.001$

Modulus of Elasticity, E = Stress/strain

$= \sigma/E = 266.67/0.001$

$= 2.67 \times 10^5 \text{ N/mm}^2$ **Ans.**

Lateral strain = Decrease in width/Original width

$= (10 \times 10^{-6})/(7.5\ 5\ 10^{-2})$

$= 1.333 \times 10^{-4}$

Poisson's ratio, μ = Lateral strain/Linear strain

$= (1.333 \times 10^{-4})/0.001$

$= 0.1333$ **Ans.**

EXAMPLE 10.33. A steel bar of 25 mm diameter and 0.5 m long is subjected to a tensile stress of 180 MPa. Determine the change in volume if young's Modulus of elasticity, E = 210 MPa and Poissons' Ratio, μ = 0.3. **(U.P.T.U., II SEM. 2003-04)**

SOLUTION. Given: d = 25 mm, l = 0.5 m = 500 mm, tensile stress, σ_t = 180 MPa = 180 N/mm², Young's Modulus of Elasticity E = 210 MPa = 210 N/mm², Poisson's Ratio, m = 0.3.

$\therefore$ Stress/strain = E

or $\sigma/\varepsilon = E$

$\because$ $\varepsilon = \sigma/E = 180/210 = 0.857$

$\because$ $\varepsilon = \delta l/l$

$\because$ $\delta l = \varepsilon . l = 0.857 \times 500 = 428.5$ mm

$$\text{Poisson's ratio} = \frac{\text{Lateral strain}}{\text{Linear strain}}$$

$\therefore$ Lateral stain $= \mu \times \varepsilon$

$$= 0.3 \times .857 = 0.257$$

But lateral strain = Change in dia./Original diameter

$\therefore$ Change in diameter = Lateral strain × O.D $= 0.257 \times 25 = 6.4275$ mm

$\therefore$ Final diameter of the bar $= 25 - 6.4275 = 18.57$ mm

Final length of the bar $= 500 + 428.5 = 928.5$ mm

Change in volume = Initial volume – Final volume

$$= \frac{\pi}{4}(25)^2 \times 500 - \frac{\pi}{4}(18.57)^2 \times 928.5$$

$$= -6038.5 \text{ mm}^2 \quad \textbf{Ans.}$$

–ve sign means decrease in VOLUME OF THE BAR.

EXERCISE-10

1. State Hook's law. Distinguish between limit of proportionality and Elastic limit.
2. Differential between (i) Force and stress, (ii) Tensile stress and Compressive stress.
3. Sketch stress-strain diagrams for the specimen of (i) Mild steel (ductile material), and (ii) cast iron (Brittle material) and define each term used in them.
4. Explain the terms (i) Modulus of rigidity, (ii) Modulus of elasticity, (iii) Shear stress, (iv) Shear strain, and (v) Bulk modulus.
5. Find the expression for strain energy stored in a body when load is applied suddenly.
6. Define in brief: (i) Factor of safety, (ii) Poisson's ratio, (iii) Lateral strain, (iv) Longitudinal strain, and (v) Volumetric strain.
7. Distinguish between (i) Stress and strength, (ii) Stress and strain, (iii) Tensile and shear stress, (iv) Force and stress, (v) Ductility and brittleness, and (vi) Tensile and compressive stress.
8. Define (i) Resilience, (ii) Proof resilience, and (ii) Modulus of resilience.
9. A tensile axial load of 10 kN is applied to a mild steel member 4 m long having 4cm^2 cross-sectional area. Find (i) Stress, (ii) Strain, (iii) Elongation of the member, if E, for m.s. is 2×10^5 N/mm^2.
10. A bar shown in Fig. 10.12 is subjected to axial loads of 40 kN. It has 3 sections of diameters 25 mm, 20 mm and 25 mm and lengths 160 mm, 240 mm and 160 mm respectively. The applied load causes an extension of 0.3 mm. Determine the Modulus of Elasticity, E of the material.

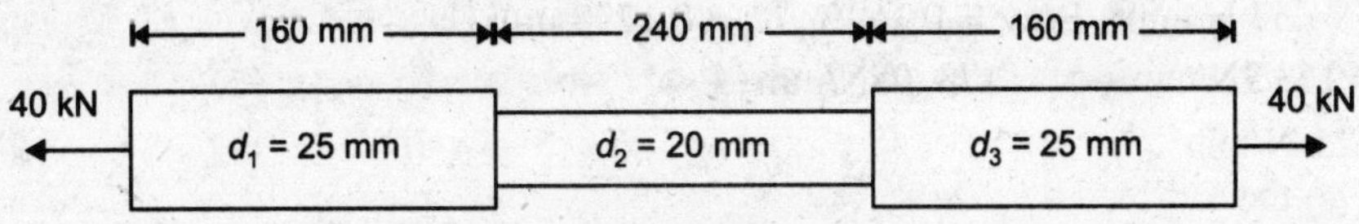

Fig. 10.12

11. A standard tensile test specimen gave the following results during the test on U.T.M. Load at yield point = 66 kN, Maximum load = 96 kN, Load at fracture = 68 kN. Distance between gauge points at fracture = 108 mm and minimum dia. at fracture = 9.25 mm. Gauge length = 80 mm, Initial diameter = 16 mm at the test section. Determine, (ii) Upper yield stress, (ii) Ultimate tensile strength, (iii) Percentage elongation, (iv) Percentage reduction is area after fracture, and (v) Nominal and Real stresses at fracture.
12. A tensile load of 40 kN is applied on a bar of 20 mm diameter with 200 mm gauge length. Elongation due to this load is 0.13 mm and corresponding contraction in diameter is 0.0037 mm. Find Poisson's ratio and three elastic constants.
13. A steel bar of 25 mm diameter and 500 mm length is subjected to a tensile stress of 200 MPa. Determine the change in volume of the bar if E_s = 210 MPa, and V = 0.3.
14. A steel bar of uniform section 40 × 25 mm and length 1.5 m is subjected to a gradually applied load of 100 kN. Calculate proof resilience and modulus of resilience if the elastic limit of the material of the bar is 160 N/mm^2.
15. A bar having a collar at its lower end is fixed at the top. A 120 N load falls on the collar from a height of 50 mm. Find the instantaneous stress in the bar and also its corresponding extension if the diameter of the bar is 30 mm. What is the error in percentage if the extension of bar is neglected.
16. A mild steel bar is fixed at the upper end and carries a collar at the lower end. A weight of 3 kN falls on the collar through a height of 20 cm. If another weight of 30 kN falls through the height of 2 cm. Find stresses in the rod in both situations. Take $E = 2 \times 10^5$ N/mm^2.
17. A steel bar is stretched so that it experiences a shear stress of 60N/mm^2. Find the strain energy per unit volume stored in the material due to shear stress. Take $G = 8 \times 10^4$ N/mm^2
18. A bar of 12 cm^2 area and 3 m length carries a collar at its lower end and its upper end is fixed. A weight drops on the collar from a certain height so that the extension of the bar is 1.5 mm. Calculate the value of suddenly applied load which causes this extension. Assume $E = 2 \times 10^5$ N/mm^2.

ANSWERS

9. σ = 25N/mm^2, ε = 0.000125, and δl = 0.5 mm
10. $E = 1.888778 \times 10^5$ N/mm^2
11. σ_y = 3278 MPa, σ_u = 477.6 MPa, 35%, 66.57%, σ_f = 328.3 MPa, σ_{True} = 1011.4 MN/m^2 = 1011.4 MPa
12. *P.R.* = 0.285, $E = 1.95883 \times 10^5$ N/mm^2 $G = 0.76219 \times 10^5$ N/mm^2, and $K = 1.51847 \times 10^5$ N/mm^2
13. 36.175%
14. 0.914×10^5 N/mm^2, 0.0609 N/mm^2
15. σ_i = 94.57 N/mm^2, Error = 0.169%, δl_i = 0.1798 mm
16. σ_1 = 163.3N/mm^2, σ_2 = 178 .95N/mm^2
17. 0.0225 N/mm^2
18. W = 60 kN

CHAPTER 11

Pure Bending of Beams

INTRODUCTION

A beam is a structural member on which external loads acts at right angles to its longitudinal axis. When a beam is subjected to a constant bending moment, without being subjected to shear then it is said to be in a state of SIMPLE BENDING OR PURE BENDING.

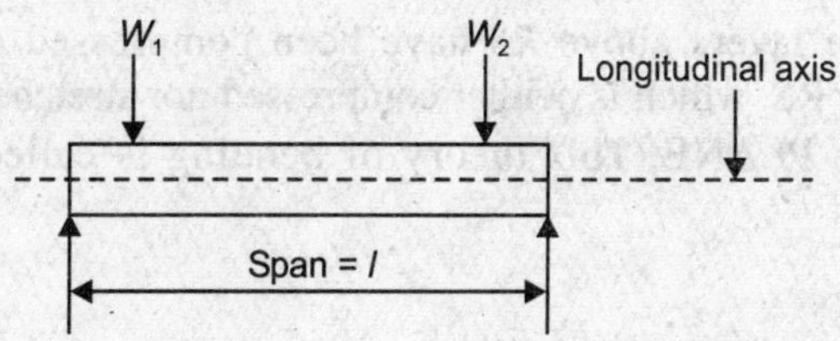

Fig. 11.1

As a matter of fact, the bending moment at a section tends to bend or deflect the beam and the internal stresses resist its bending. The process of bending stops, when energy cross section sets up full resistance to the bending moment. The resistance offered by the internal stresses, to the bending, is called BENDING STRESS and the relevant theory is called the THEORY OF SIMPLE BENDING.

ASSUMPTIONS IN THE THEORY OF SIMPLE BENDING

The following asssumptions are made in the theory of simple bending:

1. The material of the beam is perfectly homogeneous (i.e., of the same kind throughout) and isotropic (i.e., of equal elastic properties in all directions).
2. The beam material is stressed within its elastic limit and thus, obeys Hook's law.
3. The transverse section, which were plane before bending remain plane after bending also.
4. Each layer of the beam is free to expand or contract, independently, of the layer above or below it.
5. The value of E (Young's modulus of elasticity) is the same in tension and compression.
6. The beam is in equilibrium i.e., there is no resultant pull or push in the beam section.

THEORY OF SIMPLE BENDING: Consider a small length dx of a simple supported beam subjected to a bending moment M Fig. 11.2 (a). Now consider two sections *AB* and *CD*, which are normal to the axis of the beam *RS.* Due to action of the bending moment, the beam as a whole will bend as shown in Fig. 11.2 (*b*).

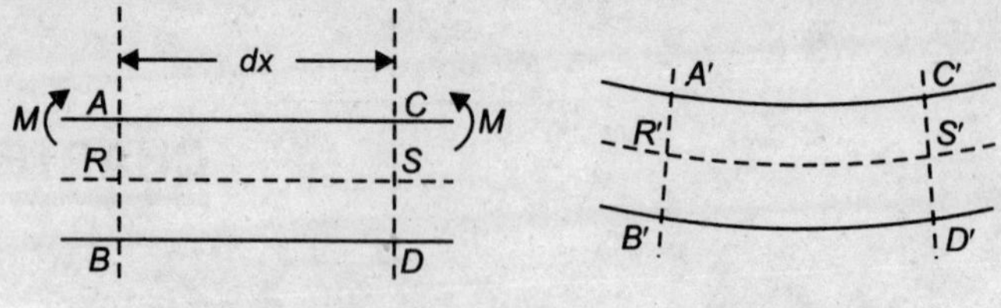

(a) Before Bending (b) After Bending

Fig. 11.2

Since we are considereing a small length of dx of the beam, therefore the curvature of the beam in this length, is taken to be as circular. The layers of the beam, whcih were originally of the same length do not remain of the same length any more. The top layer of the beam *AC* has suffered compression and reduced to *A′C′*. As we proceed towards the lower layers of the beam, we find that the layer's have no doubt suffered compression, but to lesser degree; untill we come across the layer *RS* which has suffered no change in its length, though bent into *R′S′*. If we further proceed towards the lower layers, we find the layers have suffered TENSION as a result of which the layers are stretched. The amount of extension increses as we proceed lower, until we come across the lower most layer *BD* which has been stretеched to *B′D′*.

Now we see that the layers above *RS* have been compressed and those below *RS* have been stretched. This layer RS, which is neither compressed nor stretched, is known as NEUTRAL LAYER OR NEUTRAL PLANE. This theory of bending is called THEORY OF SIMPLE BENDING.

BENDING STRESS

Consider a portion of uniform beam subjected to pure bending.

A fibre such as AB at a distance y from the neutral axis as shown in Fig. 11.3 is chosen.

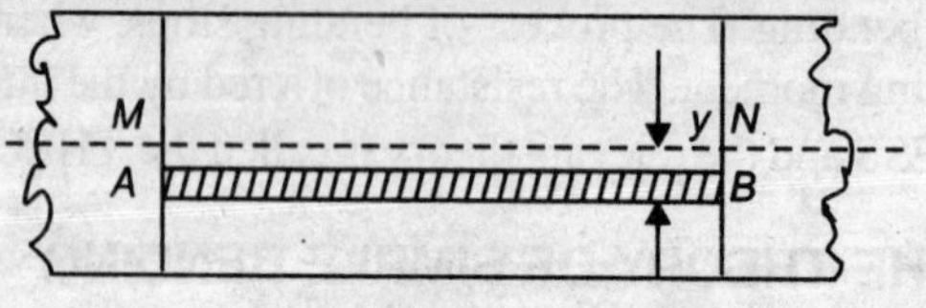

Before bending

Fig. 11.3

After bending it has elongated and is shown by A_1B_1 (Fig. 11.4).

Let R be the radius of the neutral surface after bending, making an angle θ at the point O.

Now, $MN = R\theta$

$$A_1B_1 = (R + y)\,\theta$$

Strain in the fibre at a distance y from the neutral axis

$$= \frac{\text{Increase in length}}{\text{Original length}} = \frac{A_1B_1 - AB}{AB}$$

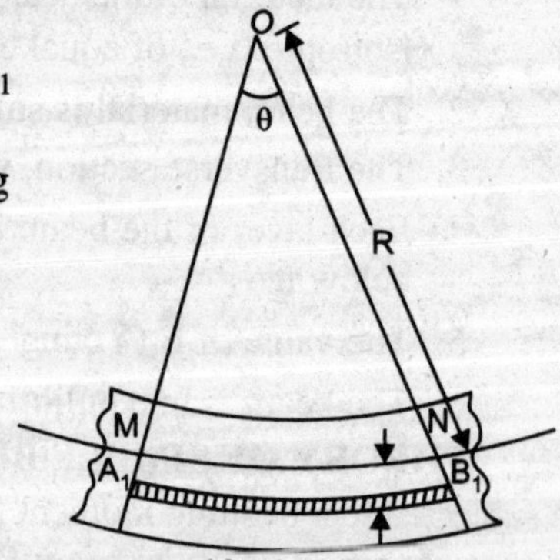

After bending

Fig. 11.4

$$= \frac{(R+y)\theta - R\theta}{R\theta} \qquad [\because AB = MN = R\,q]$$

$$= \frac{[R+y \quad R]\theta}{R\theta} = \frac{y}{R}$$

But $$E = \frac{\text{Stress}}{\text{Strain}}$$

Hence, $$\text{Strain} = \frac{\text{Stress}}{E} = \frac{\sigma}{E}$$

or $$\frac{\sigma}{E} = \frac{y}{R}$$

$$\Rightarrow \quad \frac{\sigma}{y} = \frac{E}{R} \qquad ...(1)$$

∴ Stress intensity in any fibre is proportional to the distance of the fibre from the neutral axis.

MOMENT OF RESISTANCE

Now we know that the bending stress at any point in the cross section is proportaionl to its distance from the neutral axis,. Also the portion of the beam which is above the neutral axis will experience compressive stress while the portion below the neutral axis will be subjected to tensile stress.

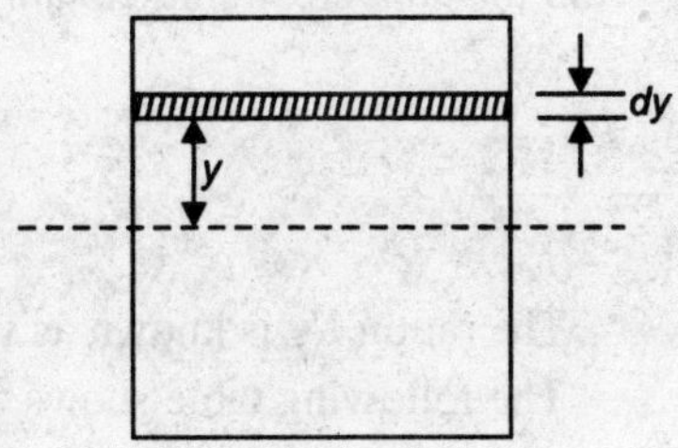

Fig. 11.5

These compressive and tensile forces form a couple at any cross-section whose moement, is called moment of resistance (M.R.). It must be equal to the external bending moment at the section of the beam. Consider a small elemental area A at a distance y from the neutral axis, the stress on the element is (Fig. 11.5)

$$\sigma = \frac{E}{R}\cdot y$$

$$\text{Force on the element} = \text{stress} \times \text{area} = \frac{E}{R} y \,.\, dA$$

$$\text{Moment of this force about the neutral axis} = \frac{E}{R} y \,.\, DA \,.\, y = \left(\frac{E}{R}\right) y^2\, dA\,.$$

$$\text{Total moment of resistance} = \int \frac{E}{R} y^2\, dA$$

$$M = \int \frac{E}{R} y^2\, dA$$

But $\int y^2\, dA$ = total moment of inertia of the entire cross section about the netural axis or the second moment of the elemental area dA.

i.e.,
$$\int y^2\, dA = I$$

$$M = \frac{E}{R}\int y^2\, dA = \frac{E}{R} I$$

$$\frac{M}{I} = \frac{E}{R} \qquad \text{...(2)}$$

Combining equation (1) and equation (2)

$$\frac{M}{I} = \frac{\sigma}{y} = \frac{E}{R}$$

which is called the bending equatioin, or Bernoulli-Euler bending equation.

SECTION MODULUS

From the above bending equation $\quad \frac{\sigma}{y} = \frac{M}{I}$

$$\Rightarrow \qquad \sigma = \frac{M}{I} \times y = \frac{M}{(I/y)} \quad \therefore \quad \sigma = \frac{M}{Z}$$

The ration I/y is known as section modulus and is denoted by Z.

The following table shows the properties of some common cross-sections.

Section	Area (A)	Moment of Inertia (I)	Section Modulus [$Z = (I/y)$]
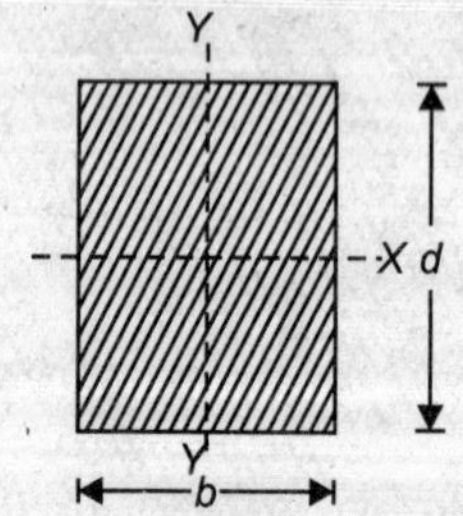	bd	$I_{xx} = \frac{bd^3}{12}$ $I_{yy} = \frac{bd^3}{12}$	$Z_{xx} = \frac{bd^2}{6}$ $Z_{xx} = \frac{bd^2}{6}$
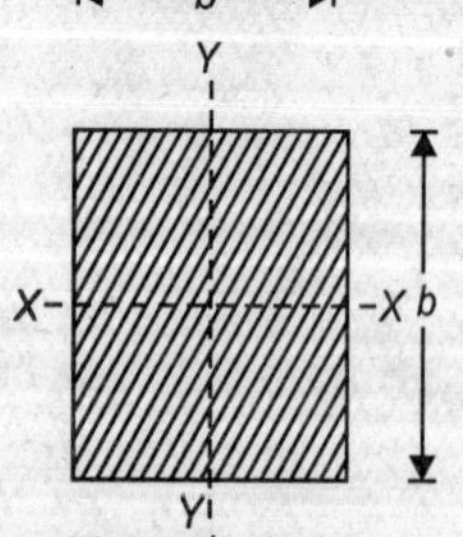	b^2	$I_{xx} = I_{yy} = \frac{b^4}{12}$	$Z_{xx} = Z_{yy} = \frac{b^3}{6}$

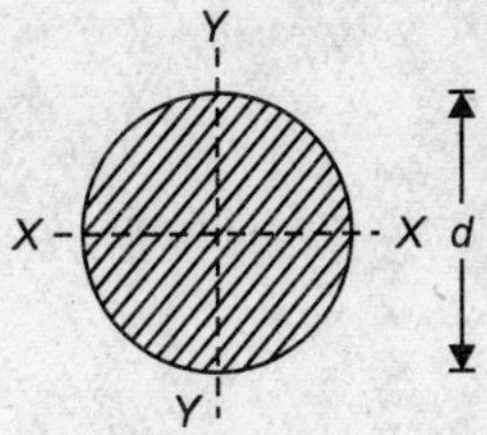	$\dfrac{\pi d^2}{4}$	$I_{xx} = I_{yy} = \dfrac{\pi d^4}{64}$	$Z_{xx} = Z_{yy} = \dfrac{\pi d^3}{32}$
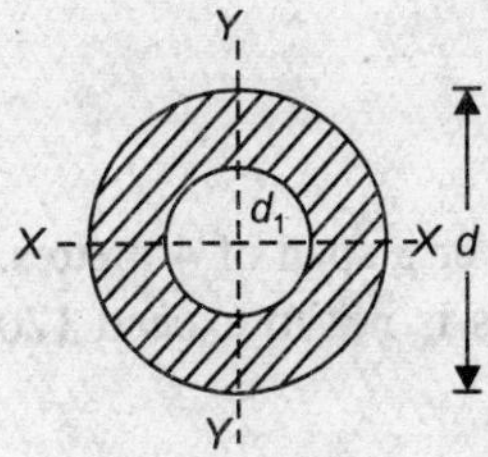	$\dfrac{\pi}{4}\left(d^2 - d_1^2\right)$	$I_{xx} = I_{yy} = \dfrac{\pi}{64}\left(d^4 - d_i^4\right)$	$Z_{xx} = Z_{yy} = \dfrac{\pi}{32}\left(\dfrac{d^4 - d_1^4}{d}\right)$
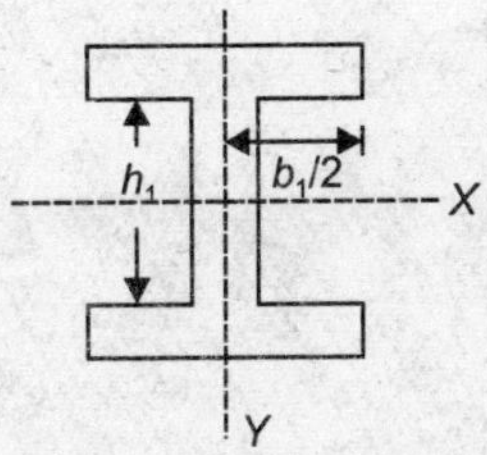	$bh - b_1 h_1$	$I_{xx} = \dfrac{bh^3 - b_1 h_1^3}{12}$	$Z_{xx} = \dfrac{bh^3 - b_1 h_1^3}{bh}$

Example 11.1. A rectangular beam 60 mm wide and 150 mm deep is simply supported over a span of 6 m. If the beam is subjected to central point load of 12 kN, find the maximum bending stress induced in the beam section.

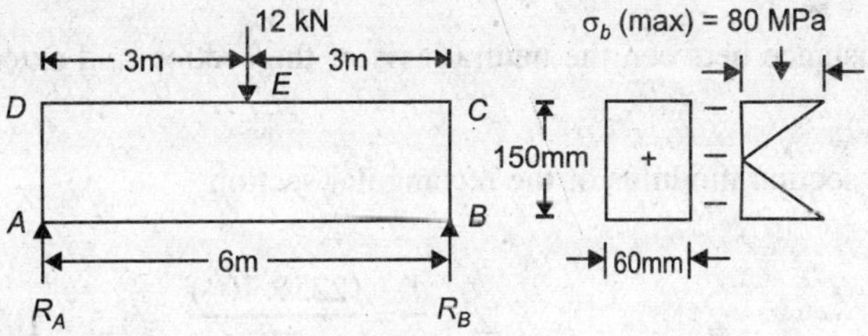

Fig. 11.6

SOLUTION. Give: Width (b) = 60 mm, Depth (d) = 150 mm, Span (l) = 6 m = 6×10^3 mm, Load (W) = 12 KN = 12×10^3 N.

For $\sum V = 0$, we have $R_A + R_B = 12$, and $R_A = R_B = 12/2 = 6$ kN $= 6 \times 10^3$ N.

Due to central point load, the maxium bending moment at the centre, i.e.,

$$M_E = 6 \times 10^3 \times 3 \times 10^3$$

$$= 18 \times 10^6 \text{ N} - \text{mm} \quad \text{...(1)}$$

Section modulus of the rectangular section,

$$Z = (bd^2)/6$$

$$\therefore \qquad Z = \frac{60 \times (150)^2}{6}$$

$$= 225 \times 10^3 \text{ mm}^3$$

Maximum bending stress, $$\sigma_{max} = \frac{M}{Z} = \frac{18 \times 10^6}{225 \times 10^3}$$

$$= 80 \text{ N/mm}^2$$

$$= 80 \text{ MPa } \textbf{Ans.}$$

EXAMPLE 11.2. A rectangular beam 30 mm deep is simply supported over a span of 4 metres. What uniformly distributed load the beam may carry, if the bending stress is not to exceed 120 MPa. take $I = 225 \times 10^6$ mm^4 (Fig. 11.7).

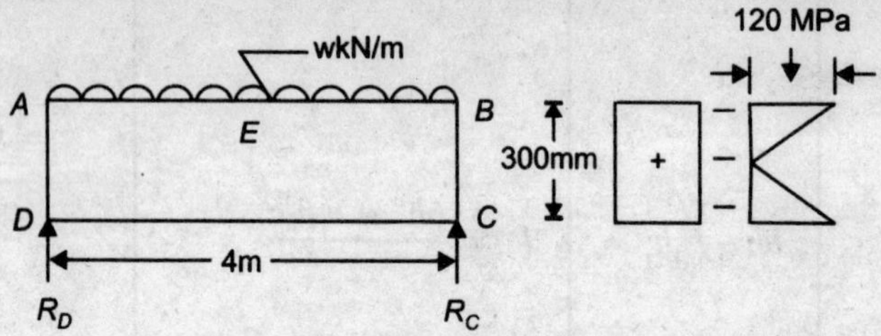

Fig. 11.7

SOLUTION. Given Depth (d) = 300 mm, span (l) = 4 m = 4×10^3 mm. Maximum bending stress (σ_{max}) = 120 MPa = 120 N/mm^2, and moment of inertia of the beam section (I) = 225×10^6 mm^4

Let, W = uniformly distributed load the beam can carry

We know that distance between the neutral axis of the section and external figure, $y = \frac{d}{2} = \frac{300}{2} = 150$ mm and section modulus of the rectangular section.

$$Z = \frac{I}{y} = \frac{(225 \times 10^6)}{150} = 1.5 \times 10^6 \text{ mm}^3$$

Moment of resistance, $$M = \sigma_{max} \times Z = 120\,(1.5 \times 10^6)$$

$$= 180 \times 10^6 \text{ N-mm}$$

We know that maximum bending moment at the centre (E) of the simply suported beam subjected to a uniformly distributed load (W) i.e. $M_E = (w\,l^2)/8$

$$\therefore \qquad 180 \times 10^6 = \frac{W(4 \times 10^3)^2}{8} = 2 \times 10^6\, w$$

$$\therefore \qquad w = \frac{180}{2} = 90 \text{ N/mm} = 90 \text{ kN/m.}$$

EXAMPLE 11.3. A timber beam of rectangular section supports a load of 20 kN uniformly distibuted over a span of 3.6 m. If depth of beam section is twice the width and maximum stress is not to exceed 7 MPa, find the dimensions of the beam section (Fig. 11.8).

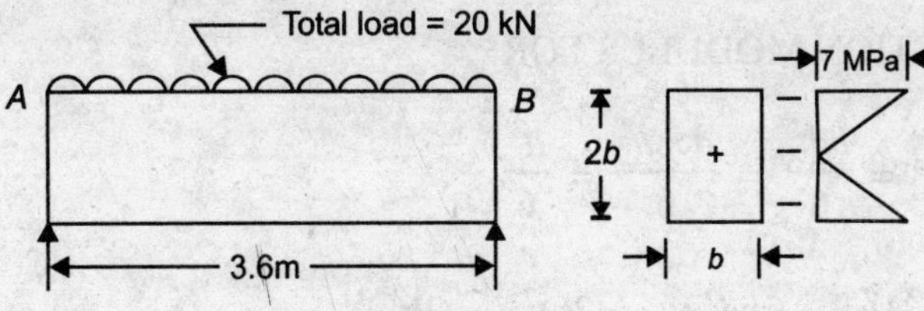

Fig. 11.8

SOLUTION. Total load (W) = 20 kN = 20×10^3 N, Span (l) = 3.6 m = 3.6×10^3 mm depth of beam (d) = 2 b, σ_{max} = 7 MPa = 7 N/mm^2

We know that section modulus of rectangular section, $Z = \frac{bd^2}{6} = \frac{b(2b)^2}{6} = \frac{2b^3}{3}$ and maximum bending moment at the centre of a simply supported beam subjected to a uniformly distributed load,

$$M = \frac{wl^2}{8} = \frac{wl}{8} = \frac{(20\times10^3)(3.6\times10^3)}{8}$$

$$= 9 \times 10^6 \text{ N-mm}$$

$\because$ Maximum bending stress, $\sigma_{max} = \frac{M}{Z} \quad \therefore 7 = \frac{M}{Z}$

or
$$7 = \frac{9\times10^6}{\frac{2b^3}{3}} = \frac{13.5\times10^6}{b^3}$$

or
$$b^3 = \frac{13.5\times10^6}{7} = 1.93 \times 10^6$$

$\therefore$
$$b = (1.93 \times 106)^{1/3} = 124.50 \text{ mm}$$

and
$$d = 2b = 249 \text{ mm} \quad \textbf{Ans.}$$

EXAMPLE 11.4. There beams have the same length, the same allowable stress and the same bending moment. The cross-section of the beam are

(i) A sqaure

(ii) A rectangle with depth twice the width

(iii) A circle

as shown in Fig. 11.9.

Find the ratios of weights of the circular and the rectangular beams with respect ot the square beam.

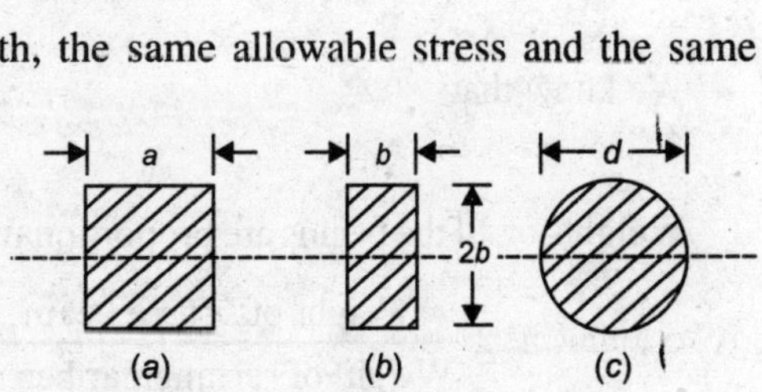

Fig. 11.9

SOLUTION. Square, rectangular and circular sections are shown in Fig. 11.9(a), (b) and (c)

Let, a = side of square beam, b = width of rectangular beam, $2b$ = depth of rectangular beam, and d = diameter of circular section.

Since all the three beams have the same allowable stress (σ) and bending moment (M), therefore the modulus of section(Z) of the three beams must be equal $\left(\sigma = \dfrac{M}{Z}\right)$.

We know that SECTION MODULUS FOR :

(i) Square beam : $z_1 = \dfrac{bd^2}{6} = \dfrac{a \times a^2}{6} = \dfrac{a^3}{6}$ ...(1)

(ii) Rectangular beam: $z_2 = \dfrac{bd^2}{6} = \dfrac{b(2b)^2}{6} = \dfrac{2b^3}{3}$ ...(2)

(iii) Circular beam : $z_3 = \dfrac{(\pi d^3)}{32}$ ...(3)

Equating equations (i) and (ii) $\dfrac{a^3}{6} = \dfrac{2b^3}{3}$ or $a^3 = \dfrac{6 \times 2b^3}{3} = 4b^3$

$\because \quad a^3 = 4b^3$

$\therefore \quad b^3 = \dfrac{1}{4}a^3$

and $\quad b = a(.25)^{1/3}$

$= 0.63\,a$ ...(4)

Now equating equations (1) and (3), $\dfrac{a^3}{6} = \dfrac{\pi d^3}{32}$

$\therefore \quad a^3 = \dfrac{6 \times \pi \times d^3}{32} = \dfrac{3\pi d^3}{16}$

and $\quad d^3 = \dfrac{16a^3}{3\pi}$

$= 1.697654\,a^3$

We know that $\quad \therefore d = a(1.697644)^{1/3}$

$= 1.196\,a$ ...(5)

Weights of all the beams are proportional to the cross-sectional areas of their sections. Therefore

$$\frac{\text{Weight of square beam}}{\text{Weight of rectangular beam}} = \frac{\text{Area of square beam}}{\text{Area of rectangular beam}}$$

$$\frac{a(a)}{b(2b)} = \frac{a^2}{2b^2} = \frac{a^2}{2(0.63a)^2} = \frac{1}{0.79} \quad \textbf{Ans.}$$

$$\frac{\text{Weight of square beam}}{\text{Weight of circular beam}} = \frac{\text{Area of square beam}}{\text{Area of circular beam}}$$

$$\frac{a^2}{\frac{\pi}{4}d^2} = \frac{a^2}{\frac{\pi}{4}(1.19a)^2} = \frac{1}{1.11} \textbf{ Ans.}$$

Section Modulus : It is defined as the ratio of moment of inertia (*I*) of a section about the neutral axis to the distance of the outer most layer from the neutral axis. It is denoted by symbol Z

$$\therefore \quad \text{Section modulus } Z = \left(\frac{I}{y_{max}}\right)$$

where I = Moment of inertia about neutral axis

y_{max} = distance of the outermost layer from the neutral axis

from
$$\frac{M}{I} = \frac{\sigma}{y}$$

Stess σ will be maximum when y is maximum

Hence,
$$\frac{M}{I} = \frac{\sigma_{max}}{y_{max}}$$

$$M = \sigma_{max} \cdot \frac{I}{y_{max}} = \sigma_{max} \cdot Z$$

$$\therefore \quad M = \sigma_{max} . Z$$

Where M is maximum B.M. or moment of resistance offered by the section. M is maximum when Z is maximum. Hence section modulus (Z) represents the strength of the secion.

(i) Section modulus of hollow rectangular section (Fig. 11.10)

$$I = \frac{BD^3}{12} - \frac{bd^3}{12} = \frac{1}{12}(BD^3 - bd^3)$$

$$y_{max} = \frac{D}{2}$$

$$\therefore \quad Z = \frac{I}{y_{max}}$$

$$= \frac{(1/12)(BD^3 - bd^3)}{D/2}$$

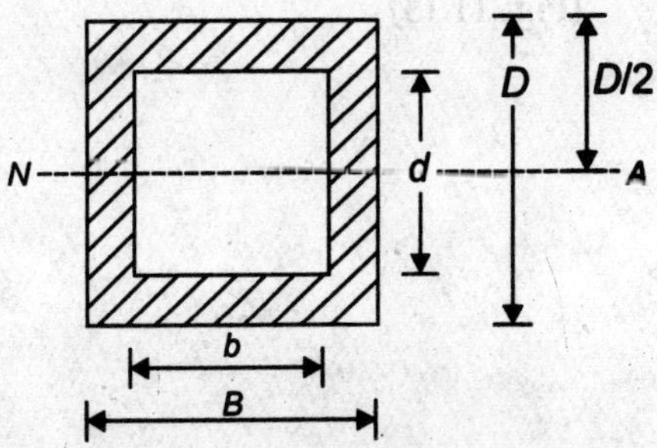

Fig. 11.10

$$Z = \frac{(BD^3 - bd^3)}{6D}$$

(ii) Circular section (Fig. 11.11)

$$I = \frac{\pi}{64} d^4, \; y_{max} = \frac{d}{2}$$

$$Z = \frac{I}{y_{max}} = \frac{\frac{\pi}{64} d^4}{d/2} = \frac{\pi}{32} d^3$$

$$Z = \frac{\pi}{32} d^3$$

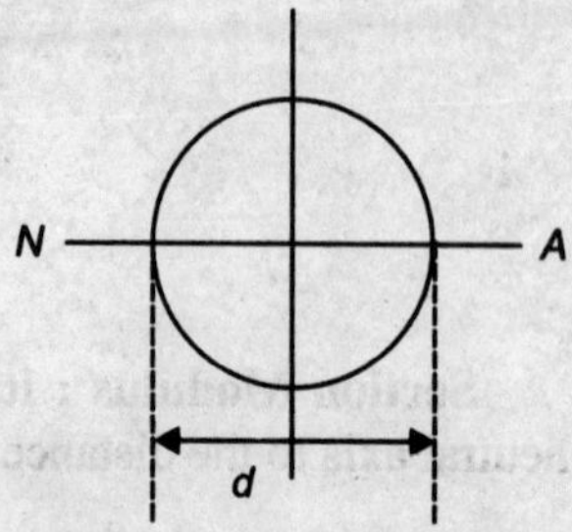

Fig. 11.11

(iii) Hollow circular section (Fig. 11.12)

$$I = \frac{\pi}{64}(d_0^{\,4} - d_1^{\,4}), \; v = \frac{d_0}{2}$$

$$Z = \frac{I}{y_{max}} = \frac{\frac{\pi}{64}(d_0^{\,4} - d_i^{\,4})}{d_0/2} = \frac{\pi}{32 d_0}(d_0^{\,4} - d_i^{\,4})$$

$$Z = \frac{\pi}{32 d_0}(d_0^{\,4} - d_1^{\,4})$$

$$= \frac{\pi}{32 d_0} d_0^{\,4} \left[1 - \left(\frac{d_i}{d_0}\right)^4\right]$$

$$Z = \frac{\pi}{32} d_0^3 \; (1 - k^4)$$

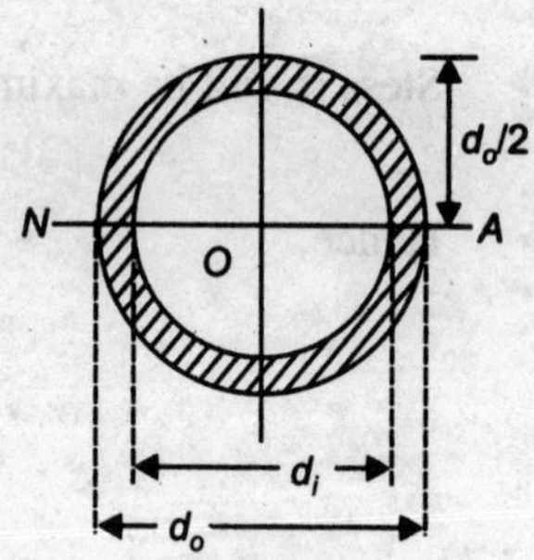

Fig. 11.12

Where $k = \frac{d_i}{d_0}$

(iv) Rectangular section (Fig. 11.13)

$$I = \frac{bd^3}{12}, \; y = \frac{d}{2}$$

$$Z = \frac{I}{y_{max}} = \frac{\frac{bd^3}{12}}{d/2} = \frac{bd^2}{6}$$

$$Z = \frac{bd^2}{6}$$

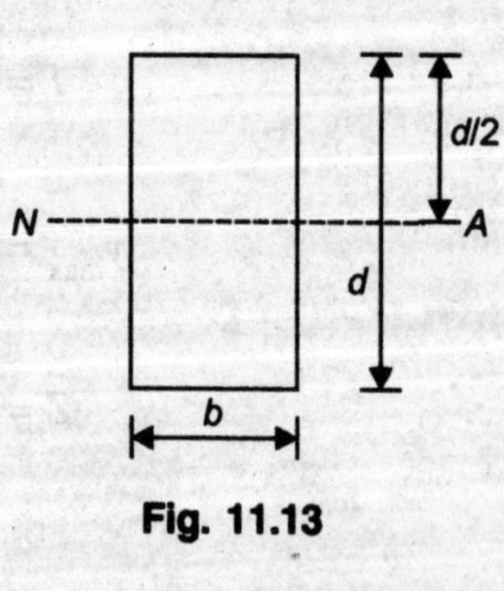

Fig. 11.13

EXAMPLE 11.5. The moment of inertia of a beam section 50 cm deep is 69490 cm^4. Find the longest span over which a beam of this section, when simply supported, could carry a uniformly distributed load of 50 kN per meter run. The maximum flange stress in the material is not to exceed 110 N/mm^2 (Fig. 11.14)

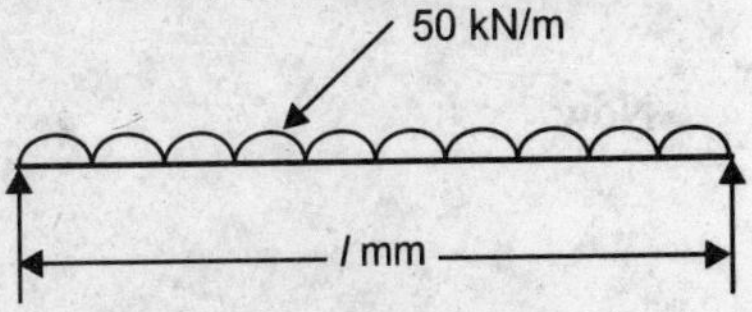

Fig. 11.14

SOLUTION:

$$d = 50 \text{ cm} = 500 \text{ mm}$$

$$I = 69490 \text{ cm}^4 = 69490 \times 10^4 \text{ mm}^4$$

$$w = 50 \text{ kN/m} = 50 \times 10^3 \text{ N/m} = 50 \text{ N/mm}$$

$$\sigma = 110 \text{ N/mm}^2$$

Now $$M = \frac{wl^2}{8} = 50 \times l \times \frac{l}{8} \quad (l \text{ is in mm})$$

$$= \frac{50}{8} l^2 = \frac{25}{4} l^2 \text{ N.mm}$$

Using $$\frac{M}{I} = \frac{\sigma}{y} \Rightarrow \sigma = \frac{M \times y}{I} \quad [y = d/2 = 250 \text{ mm}]$$

$$110 = \frac{25}{4} l^2 \times \frac{250}{69490 \times 10^4}$$

$$110 = l^2 \times 2.24852 \times 10^{-6}$$

$$l = \sqrt{\frac{110}{2.24852 \times 10^{6}}}$$

$$= \sqrt{(48920960)}$$

$$= 6994.352 \text{ mm.} = 6.994 \text{ m}$$

$$l \simeq 7 \text{ m.}$$

EXAMPLE 11.6. Moment of inertia of a symmetrical section of a beam about its neutral axis is 2640 cm^4 and its depth is 20 cm. Determine the longest span over which, when simply supported, the beam would carry a UDL of 6 kN/m run without stresses due to bending exceeding 120 MN/m^2 (Fig. 11.15).

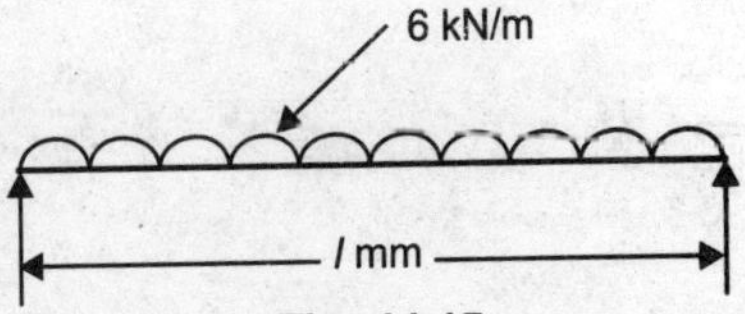

Fig. 11.15

SOLUTION.

$$w = 6 \text{ kN/m} = 6 \times 10^3 \text{ N/m} = 6 \text{ N/mm}$$

$$I = 2640 \text{ cm}^4 = 2640 \times 10^4 \text{ mm}^4$$

$$d = 20 \text{ cm} = 200 \text{ mm}$$

$$\sigma = 120 \text{ MN/m}^2 = 120 \text{ N/mm}^2$$

Now $$y = \frac{d}{2} = \frac{200}{2} = 100 \text{ mm}$$

$$M = \frac{wl^2}{8} \text{ N.mm}$$

$$= \left[\frac{6}{8} \times l \times l\right] \text{ N.mm}$$

$$= \frac{3}{4} l^2 = 0.75\, l^2 \text{ N.mm}$$

$$\frac{M}{I} = \frac{\sigma}{y} \Rightarrow \sigma = \frac{M \times y}{I}$$

$$\Rightarrow \quad 120 = \frac{0.75 l^2 \times 100}{2640 \times 10^4}$$

$$l = \sqrt{\frac{2640 \times 10^4 \times 120}{0.75 \times 100}}$$

$$= 6499.2307 \text{ mm} = 6.499 \text{ m}$$

$\therefore$ $l \simeq 6.5$ m **Ans.**

EXAMPLE 11.7. The beam of symmetrical I-section shown in figure 11.16 is simply supported over a span of 9 m. If the maximum permissible stress is 75 N/mm², what concentrated load can be carried at a distance of 3 m form one support? ($I = 31 \times 10^6$ mm⁴)

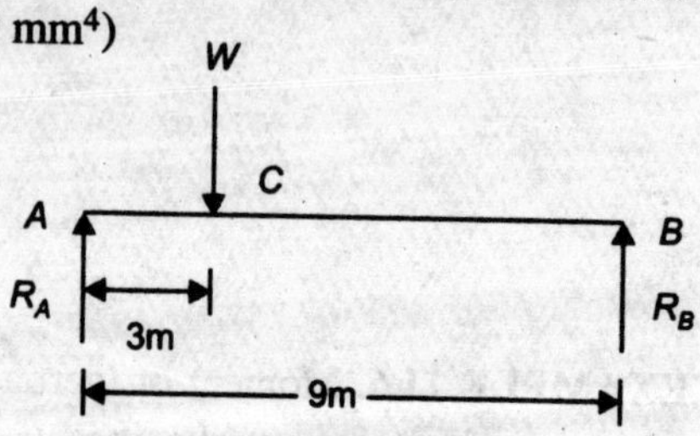

Fig. 11.16

SOLUTION.

$$l = 9 \text{ m}$$

$$\sigma = 75 \text{ N/mm}^2$$

Now for $$\Sigma M_A = 0$$

$$R_B \times 9 = W \times 3$$

$$\Rightarrow \quad R_B = \frac{3W}{9} = \left(\frac{W}{3}\right)$$

$$M = M_C = R_B \times 6$$

$$= (W/3) \times 6 = 2W \text{ N.m.}$$

$$= 2000\, W \text{ N–mm}$$

(As for simply supported beam, B.M. at the ends = 0).

$$I = 31 \times 10^6 \text{ mm}^4$$

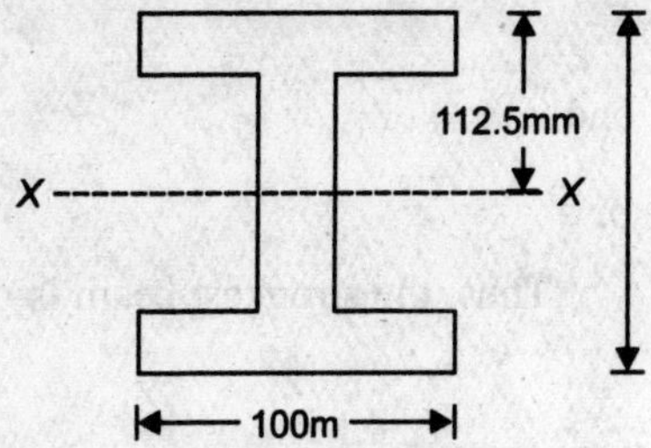

Fig. 11.17

from Fig.11.17 $y = \dfrac{d}{2} = 112.5$ mm

Using bending equation $\dfrac{M}{I} = \dfrac{\sigma}{y}$

$$\Rightarrow \quad \sigma = \frac{M \times y}{I} = \frac{2000W \times 112.5}{31 \times 10^6} \text{ N.mm}$$

But $\sigma = 75$ N/mm^2 (givne)

equating the two values $\dfrac{2000W \times 112.5}{31 \times 10^6} = 75$

$$W = 10333.333 \text{ N}$$

$$W = 10.33 \text{ kN}$$

EXAMPLE 11.8. Find the dimension of the strongest rectangular beam that can be cut out of a log of 200 mm diameter.

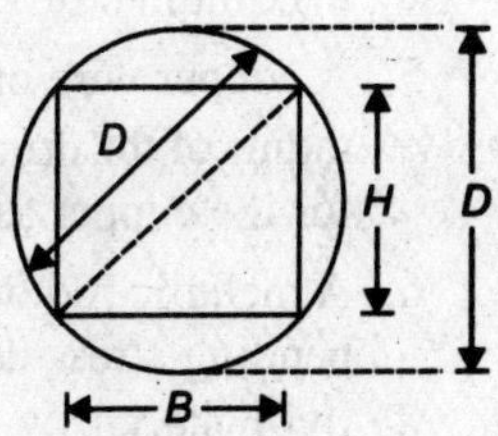

Fig. 11.18

SOLUTION. (Refer Fig. 11.18) $D^2 = B^2 + H^2$

(Let the strongest beam of H mm depth and B mm width that can be cut out of the log)

and $\dfrac{M}{I} = \dfrac{\sigma}{y}$

or $M = \sigma Z$

Strongest beam is one that can take the maximum M for given allowable σ.

Hence, for the strongest beam, Z has to be maximum

i.e. $Z = \dfrac{BH^2}{6} = \dfrac{B(D^2 - B^2)}{6}$ (since $B^2 + H^2 = D^2$)

For Maximum 'Z' $\left.\begin{array}{l}\dfrac{dZ}{dB} = 0 \\ \dfrac{dZ}{dH} = 0\end{array}\right\}$

i.e., $\dfrac{dz}{dB} = \dfrac{1}{6}(D^2 - 3B^2) = 0$

or $D^2 = 3B^2$

or $B = \dfrac{D}{\sqrt{(3)}} = 0.577\, D$

and $$H^2 = D^2 - B^2 = D^2 - \frac{D^2}{3} = \frac{2}{3}D^2$$

or $$H = 0.816\ D$$

Thus, the strongest beam is of
$$B = 0.577\ D = 115.4 \text{ mm width and}$$
$$H = 0.816\ D = 163.2 \text{ mm depth}$$
Ans.

EXERCISE-11

1. Define the term, BENDING STRESS and explain the THEORY OF SIMPLE BENDING.
2. State the assumptions made in the THEORY OF SIMPLE BENDING.
3. Prove the relations, $\frac{M}{I} = \frac{\sigma}{y} = \frac{E}{R}$
4. A steel wire of 5 mm diameter is bent into a circular shape of 5 m radius. Determine the maximum stress induced in the wire. Take $E = 200$ GPa.
5. A copper wire of 2 mm diameter is required to be wound around a drum. Find the minimum radius of the drum, if the stress in the wire is not to exceed 80 MPa. Take modulus of elasticity for the copper as 100 GPa.
6. A metallic rod of 10 mm diameter is bent into a circular form of radius 6 m. If the maximum bending stress developed in the rod is 125 MPa, find the value of Young's modulus for the rod material.
7. A cantilever beam is rectangular in section having 80 mm width and 120 mm depth. If the cantilever is subjected to a point load of 6 kN at the free end and the bending stress is not to exceed 40 MPa, find the span of the cantilever.
8. A rectangular beam 60 mm wide and 150 mm deep is subjected to a uniformly distributed load of 4.5 KN/m, find the maximum bending stress induced in the beam.
9. A rectangular beam 200 m deep is simply supported on a span of 2 m. Find the uniformly distributed load the beam can carry if the bending stress is not to exceed 30 MPa. Take *I* for the beam as 8×10^6 mm^4
10. A beam made of C.I. having a secton of 50 mm external diameter and 25 mm internal dia. is supported at two points 4 m apart. The beam carries a concentrated load of 100 N at its centre. Find the maximum bending stress induced in the beam .
11. A hollow square section with outer and inner diamensions of 50 mm and 40 mm respectrively is used as cantilever of span 1 m. How much concentrated load can be applied at the free end of the cantilever, if the maximum bending stress is not to exceed 35 MPa?
12. A hollow steel tube having external and internal diameters of 100 mm and 75 mm respectigely is simply supported over a span of 5 m. The tube carries a concentrated load of *W* at a distance of 2 m from one of the supports. What is the value of *W*, if the maximum bending stress is not to exceed 100 MPa.
13. A cast iron water pipe of 500 mm inside diameter and 20 mm thick is supported over a span of 10 meters. Find the maximum stress in the pipe metal, when the pipe is running full. Take density of cast iron as 70.6 KN/m^3 and that of water as 9.8 kN/m^3.

14. Calculate the cross-sectional dimensions of the strongest rectangular beam, that can be cut out of a cylindrical log of wood whose diameter is 500 mm.
15. A rectangular beam, simply supported over a span of 4 m, is carrying a uniformly distributed load of 50 kN/m. Find the dimensions of the beam, if depth of beam section is 2.5 times its width. Take maximum bending stress in the beam section as 60 MPa.

ANSWERS

4. $\sigma_{max} = \frac{E}{R} y = 100 \text{ N/mm}^2 = 100 \text{ MPa}$

5. $R = \frac{y}{\sigma_{max}} \times E = 1.25 \text{ m} \because \frac{\sigma_b}{y} = \frac{E}{R}$

6. $E = \frac{\sigma_{max}}{y} \times R = 150 \times 10^3 \text{ N/mm}^2 = 150 \text{ GPa}$

7. $l = 1.28 \text{ m} \because m = wl$, and $\sigma_{max} = \frac{M}{Z}$

8. $\sigma_{max} = \frac{M}{Z} = 40 \text{ N/mm}^2 = 40 \text{ MPa}$

9. $w = 4.8$ kN/m

10. $\sigma_{max} = \frac{My}{I} = 8.64 \text{ N/mm}^2$

11. $W = 430.5$ N

12. $W = 5.6$ kN

13. $\sigma_{max} = \frac{M}{Z} = 12.9 \text{ N/mm}^2 = 12.9 \text{ MPa}$

14. 288.5 mm × 408.5 mm

15. 125 mm, 300 mm

CHAPTER 12

Torsion

INTRODUCTION

In workshops and Factories, a Turning Force is always applied to transmit energy by rotation. This turning force is applied either to the rim of a pulley, keyed to the shaft or at any other suitable point at some distance from the axis of the shaft. The product of this TURNING FORCE AND THE DISTANCE between the point of application of the force and the axis of the shaft is known as TORQUE, TURNING MOMENT OR TWISTING MOMENT, and the shaft is said to be subjected to TORSION. Due to this TORQUE, cross-section of the shaft is subjected to the some SHEAR STRESS.

A circular shaft is said to be in a state of PURE TORSION when it is subjected only to TWISTING MOMENT (TORQUE) and not having direct axial force or BENDING MOMENT.

Torsion equation: $$\frac{T}{J} = \frac{\tau}{r} = \frac{G\theta}{l}$$

where

T = TORQUE in N-mm

J = POLAR MOMENT OF INERTIA, mm^4

τ = SHEAR STRESS at radius r, N/mm^2

r = Radius of the circular shaft in mm

G = Modulus of Rigidity of the shaft material N/mm^2

θ = Angle of twist in radian

l = Length of the shaft-mm

$\frac{T}{J} = \frac{G\theta}{l}$ is known as STIFFNESS EQUATION

$\frac{T}{J} = \frac{\tau}{r}$ is known as STRENGTH EQUATION

From $$\frac{T}{J} = \frac{G\theta}{l}; \quad \theta = \frac{Tl}{GJ}$$

GJ is known as TORSIONAL RIGIDITY

POLAR MOMENT OF INERTIA: $J = \dfrac{\pi d^4}{32}$ for solid shaft

$$J = \frac{\pi}{32}\left(D^4 - d^4\right) \quad \text{for hollow shaft}$$

POWER TRANSMITTED BY SHAFT:

$$P = (2\pi NT)/60,$$

where N = RPM of the shaft,

T = Torque in N-m

P = Power transmitted, W

STRENGTH OF A SOLID SHAFT $T = \dfrac{\pi}{16}\tau D^3$ N-mm

STRENGTH OF HOLLOW SHAFT $T = \dfrac{\pi}{16}\tau\left(\dfrac{D^4 - d^4}{D}\right)$ N-mm

D = External diameter

d = Internal diameter

EXAMPLE 12.1. A circular shaft of 50 mm diameter is required to transmit torque from one shaft to another. Find the safe torque, which the shaft can transmit, if the shear stress is not to exceed 40 MPa.

SOLUTION. Given: Diameter of the shaft (D) = 50 mm, Maximum shear stress (τ) = 40 MPa = 40 N/mm^2.

We know that the safe torque, which the shaft can transmit

$$T = \frac{\pi}{16}\tau D^3$$

$$= \frac{22}{7 \times 16} \times 40 \times (50)^3$$

$$= 981747.70 \text{ N-mm}$$

$$\therefore \quad T = 0.982 \times 10^6 \text{ N-mm}$$

$$= 0.982 \text{ kN-m} \quad \textbf{Ans.}$$

EXAMPLE 12.2. A solid shaft (steel) is to transmit a torque of 10 kN-m. If the shearing stress is not to exceed 45 MPa, find the minimum diameter of the shaft.

SOLUTION. Given: Torque (T) = 10 kN-m = 10 × 10^6 N-mm and the maximum shearing stress (τ) = 45 MPa = 45 N/mm^2.

Let, D = Minimum dia. of the shaft in mm

We know that torque transmitted by the shaft (T),

$$T = \frac{\pi}{16} \tau D^3$$

$$\therefore \quad 10 \times 10^6 = \frac{22}{7 \times 16} 45 \times D^3$$

$$= 8.836\ D^3$$

$$\therefore \quad D^3 = (10 \times 10^6)/8.836$$

$$= 1.132 \times 10^6$$

$$\text{or} \quad D = 1.04 \times 10^2$$

$$= 104 \text{ mm} \quad \textbf{Ans.}$$

EXAMPLE 12.3. A hollow shaft of external and internal diameter of 80 mm and 50 mm is required to transmit torque from one end to the other. What is the safe torque it can transmit if the allowable shear stress is 45 MPa?

SOLUTION. Given: External diameter (D) = 80 mm, Internal diameter (d) = 50 mm, and allowable shear stress (τ) = 45 MPa = 45 N/mm^2.

We know that the torque transmitted by hollow shaft,

$$T = \frac{\pi}{16} \tau \left(\frac{D^4 - d^4}{D} \right)$$

$$= \frac{\pi}{16} \times 45 \left[\frac{(80)^4 - (50)^4}{80} \right]$$

$$= 3.83 \times 10^6 \text{ N-mm}$$

$$= 3.83 \text{ kN-m} \quad \textbf{Ans.}$$

EXAMPLE 12.4. A circular shaft of 60 mm diameter is running at 150 r. p.m. If the shear stress is not to exceed 50 MPa, find the power which can be transmitted by the shaft.

SOLUTION. Given: Diameter of the shaft (D) = 60 mm; Speed of the shaft (N) = 150 r.p.m.; Maximum shear stress (τ) = 50 MPa = 50 N/mm^2.

We know that the torque transmitted by the shaft.

$$T = \frac{\pi}{16} \tau D^3$$

$$= \frac{\pi}{16} \times 50\, (60)^3$$

$$= 2.12 \times 10^6 \text{ N-mm}$$

$$= 2.12 \text{ kN-m}$$

Power which can be transmitted by the shaft

$$P = \frac{2\pi NT}{60} = \frac{2\pi \times 150 \times 2.12}{60}$$

$$= 33.3 \text{ kW} \quad \textbf{Ans.}$$

EXAMPLE 12.5. A hollow shaft of external and internal diameters as 100 mm and 40 mm is transmitting power at 120 r.p.m. Find the power of the shaft can transmit, if the shearing stress is not to exceed 50 MPa.

SOLUTION. Given: External diameter (D) = 100 mm, Internal diameter (d) = 40 mm, Speed of the shaft (N) = 120 r.p.m and allowable shear stress (τ) = 50 MPa = 50 N/mm^2.

We know that torque the shaft can transmit

$$T = \frac{\pi}{16} \tau \left(\frac{D^4 - d^4}{D} \right)$$

$$= \frac{\pi}{16} \left[\frac{(100)^4 - (40)^4}{100} \right] = 9.56 \times 10^6 \text{ N-mm}$$

$$= 9.56 \text{ kN-m} \quad \text{...(1)}$$

Power the shaft can transmit.

$$P = \frac{2\pi NT}{60} = \frac{2\pi \times 120 \times 9.56}{60}$$

$$= 120 \text{ kW} \quad \textbf{Ans.}$$

EXAMPLE 12.6. A solid steel shaft has to transmit 100 kW at 160 r.p.m. Taking allowable shear stress as 70 MPa, find the suitable diameter of the shaft. The maximum torque transmitted in each revolution exceeds the mean by 20%.

SOLUTION. Given: Power (P) = 100 kW; Speed of the shaft (N) = 160 r.p.m.; Allowable shear stress (τ) = 70 MPa = 70 N/mm^2 and Maximum torque (T_{max}) = 1.2 T_{mean}.

Let D = Diameter of the shaft in mm

We know that power transmitted by the shaft,

$$P = \frac{2\pi NT}{60}$$

$$\therefore \quad 100 = \frac{2\pi \times 160 \times T}{60}$$

$$= 16.8\, T$$

$$\therefore \quad T = 100/16.8 = 5.95 \text{ kN-m}$$

$$= 5.95 \times 10^6 \text{ N-mm}$$

and maximum torque,

$$T_{max} = 1.2\, T_{mean} = 1.2\, (5.95 \times 10^6)$$

We know that maximum $= 7.14 \times 10^6$ N-mm

$$\text{Torque } (T_{max}) = \frac{\pi}{16} \tau D^3$$

or
$$7.14 \times 10^6 = \frac{\pi}{16} \times 70 \times D^3 = 13.7\, D^3$$

or
$$D^3 = 7.14 \times 10^6 / 13.7$$
$$= 0.521 \times 10^6$$

∴
$$D = (0.52 \times 10^6)^{1/3} = 0.8 \times 10^2$$
$$= 80 \text{ mm} \quad \textbf{Ans.}$$

EXAMPLE 12.7. Calculate the maximum torque that a shaft of 125 mm diameter can transmit, if the maximum angle of twist is 1° in a length of 1.5 m. Take G = 70 GPa.

SOLUTION. Given:

Diameter of shaft (D) = 125 mm,

Angle of twist (θ) = 1° = $\pi/180$ rad.

Length of shaft (λ) = 1.5 m = 1.5×10^3 mm and

Modulus of rigidity (G) = 70 GPa = 70×10^3 N/mm^2.

Let T = Maximum torque the shaft can transmit.

We know that polar moment of inertia of a solid circular shaft,

$$J = \frac{\pi}{32} D^4 = \frac{\pi}{32} 125^4$$
$$= 24 \times 10^6 \text{ mm}^4$$

and the relation for torque transmitted by the shaft,

$$\frac{T}{J} = \frac{G\theta}{l}$$

∴
$$\frac{T}{24 \times 10^6} = \frac{(70 \times 10^3)\pi/180}{1.5 \times 10^3}$$
$$= 0.814$$

Hence,
$$T = 0.814\,(24 \times 10^6) = 19.5 \times 10^6 \text{ N-mm}$$
$$= 19.5 \text{ kN-m} \quad \textbf{Ans.}$$

EXAMPLE 12.8. Find the angle of twist per meter length of a hollow shaft of 100 mm external and 60 mm internal diameter, if the shear stress is not to exceed 35 MPa, Take G = 85 GPa.

SOLUTION. Given: Length of the shaft (l) = 1 m = 1×10^3 mm; External diameter (D) = 100 mm; Internal dia. (d) = 60 mm; Maximum shear stress (τ) = 35 MPa = 35N/mm^2 and Modulus of rigidity (G) = 85 GPa = 85×10^3 N/mm^2.

$$1° = \pi/180 \text{ rad}$$

$$1 \text{ Radian} = 180/\pi$$

Let, θ = Angle of twist in the shaft

We know that torque transmitted by the shaft,

$$T = \frac{\pi}{16} \times \tau \left[\frac{D^4 - d^4}{D}\right]$$

$$= \frac{\pi}{16} \times 35 \left[\frac{(100)^4 - (60)^4}{100}\right]$$

$$= 5.98 \times 10^6 \text{ N-mm}$$

We also know that polar moment of inertia of a hollow circular shaft,

$$J = \frac{\pi}{32}\left(D^4 - d^4\right)$$

$$= \frac{\pi}{32}\left[(100)^4 - (60)^4\right]$$

$$= 8.55 \times 10^6 \text{ mm}^4$$

and angle of Twist,

$$\frac{T}{J} = \frac{G\theta}{l}$$

or

$$\frac{5.98 \times 10^6}{8.55 \times 10^6} = \frac{\left(85 \times 10^3\right)\theta}{1 \times 10^3} = 85\theta$$

$$\therefore \quad \theta = \frac{5.98 \times 10^6}{\left(8.55 \times 10^6\right) 85} = 0.008 \text{ rad}$$

$$= .008 \times \frac{180}{\pi} = 0.458°$$

$$= 0.5° \quad \textbf{Ans.}$$

EXAMPLE 12.9. A solid shaft of 120 mm diameter is required to transmit 200 kW at 100 r.p.m. If the angle of twists not to exceed 2°, find the length of the shaft. Take modulus of rigidity for the shaft material as 90 GPA.

SOLUTION. Given. Diameter of Shaft (D) = 120 mm, Power (P) = 200 kW, Speed of the shaft (N) = 100 r.p.m., Angle of twist (θ) = $2\pi/180$ rad, and modulus of rigidity (G) = 90 GPA = 90×10^3 N/mm^2.

Let T = Torque transmitted by the shaft, and

l = Length of the shaft

We know that power transmitted by the shaft,

$$P = \frac{2\pi NT}{60}$$

$$\therefore \quad 200 = \frac{2\pi \times 100 \times T}{60} = 10.5\ \text{T}$$

$$\therefore \quad T = \frac{200}{10.5}$$

$$= 19.0 \text{ kN-m} = 19 \times 10^6 \text{ N-mm}$$

We know that polar moment of inertia of a solid shaft,

$$J = \frac{\pi}{32} D^4$$

$$= \frac{\pi}{32}(120)^4 = 20.4 \times 10^6 \text{mm}^4$$

and relation for the length of the shaft, $\dfrac{T}{J} = \dfrac{G\theta}{l}$

$$\text{or} \quad \frac{190 \times 10^6}{20.4 \times 10^6} = \frac{\left(90 \times 10^3\right)(2\pi / 180)}{l}$$

$$\text{or} \quad 9.31 = (3.14 \times 10^3)/l$$

$$\therefore \quad l = (3.14 \times 10^3)/9.31 = 0.337 \times 10^3 \text{ mm}$$

$$\therefore \quad l = 0.337 \text{ m} \quad \textbf{Ans.}$$

EXAMPLE 12.10. Find the maximum torque, that can be safely applied to a shaft of 80 mm diameter. The permissible angle of twist is 1.5 degree in a length of 5 m and shear stress not to exceed 42 MPa. Take G = 84 GPa.

SOLUTION. Given: Diameter of shaft (D) = 80 mm; Angle of twist (θ) = 1.5° = (1.5π)/ 180 rad; Length of shaft (l) = 5 m = 5 × 10^3 mm; Maximum shear stress (τ) = 42 MPa = 42 N/mm^2 and modulus of rigidity (G) = 84 GPa = 84 × 10^3 N/mm^2.

First of all, let us find out the values of torques based on shear stress and angle of twist.

1. **TORQUE BASED ON SHEAR STRESS:** We know that the torque (T_1) which can be applied to the shaft,

$$T_1 = \frac{\pi}{16}\tau D^3 = \frac{\pi}{16} \times 42(80)^3$$

$$= 4.22 \times 10^6 \text{ N-mm} \qquad \text{...(1)}$$

2. **TORQUE BASED ON ANGLE OF TWIST:** We know that polar moment of inertia for a solid circular shaft,

$$J = \frac{\pi}{32} D^4 = \frac{\pi}{32}(80)^4$$

$$= 4.02 \times 10^6 \text{ mm}^4$$

and relation for torque that can be applied, $T_2/J = (G\theta)/l$

$$\text{or} \qquad \frac{T_2}{4.02 \times 10^6} = \frac{(84 \times 10^3)(1.5\pi/180)}{5 \times 10^3}$$

$$= 0.44$$

$$\therefore \qquad T_2 = 0.44 \times (4.02 \times 10^6)$$

$$= 1.77 \times 10^6 \text{ N-mm} \qquad ...(2)$$

We shall apply a torque of 1.77×10^6 N-mm I(i.e., lesser of the two values). **Ans.**

EXAMPLE 12.11. A solid shaft is subjected to a torque of 1.6 kN-m. Find the necessary diameter of the shaft, if the allowable shear stress is 60 MPa. The allowable twist is 1° for every 20 diameters length of the shaft. Take G = 80 GPa.

SOLUTION. Given:

Torque (T) = 1.6 kN-m = 1.6×10^6 N-mm;

Allowable shear stress (τ) = 60 GPa = 60 N/mm^2;

Angle of twist (θ) = 1°= $\pi/180$ rad; Length of shaft (l) = 20 D, and

Modulus of rigidity (G) = 80 GPa = 80×10^3 N/mm^2.

First of all, let us find out the value of diameter of the shaft for its STRENGTH and STIFFNESS.

1. DIAMETER BASED ON STRENGTH: We know that TORQUE transmitted by the shaft,

$$T = \frac{\pi}{16} \tau D^3$$

$$\therefore \qquad 1.6 \times 10^6 = \frac{\pi}{16} \times 60 \times D_1^3 = 11.78 \, D_1^3$$

$$\text{and} \qquad D_1^3 = \frac{1.6 \times 10^6}{11.78} = 0.136 \times 10^6$$

$$\therefore \qquad D_1 = (0.136 \times 10^6)^{\frac{1}{3}}$$

$$= 51.4 \text{ mm} \qquad ...(1)$$

2. DIAMETER BASED ON STIFFNESS: We know that polar moment of inertia for a solid circular shaft, $J = \frac{\pi}{32} D_2^4 = 0.098 \, D_2^4$ and relation for the diameter is, $T/J = (G\theta)/l$

$$\text{or} \qquad \frac{1.6 \times 10^6}{0.098 \, D_2^4} = \frac{(80 \times 10^3) \times (\pi/180)}{20 \, D_2}$$

$$\therefore \qquad D_2^3 = \frac{(1.6 \times 10^6) \, 20}{0.098 (80 \times 10^3)(\pi/180)} = 234 \times 10^3$$

$$\therefore \quad D_2 = (234 \times 10^3)^{1/3}$$

$$= 61.6 \text{ mm}$$

For safe working we should provide a shaft of 61.6 mm diameter (i.e., greater of the two values) **Ans.**

EXAMPLE 12.12. Derive the STIFFNESS EQUATION FOR A SHIFT: Consider a solid circular shaft of length l, radius r fixed at one end and free at other subjected to a torque T (Twisting moment) as shown in Fig. 12.1. The fixed end will have a balancing of the same magnitude but of opposite direction.

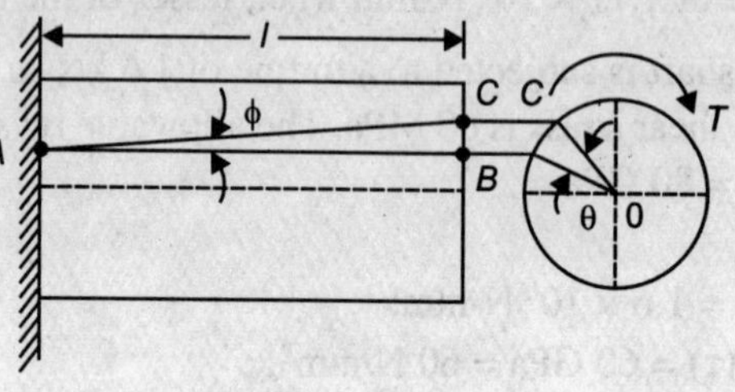

Fig, 12.1

The torque T causes the free end to rotate through an angle θ, i.e., the radial line OB is rotated to the new position OC.

Also the line AB on the surface of the shaft makes an angle ϕ with the new position AC.

Now shear strain = $\tan \phi = \phi$ = Deformation/original length

$$= BC/l = (r\,\theta)/l$$

But Shear stress/shear strain = Modulus of Rigidity

$$\therefore \quad \tau/\phi = G$$

or

$$\tau = \phi G = \frac{r\,\theta}{l} G$$

$$\therefore \quad \frac{\tau}{r} = \frac{G\,\theta}{l}$$

POWER TRANSMITTED BY A SHAFT (SOLID AND HOLLOW): Consider a rotating shaft, which transmits power from one of its end to another. Let, N = No. of revolutions per minute, and T = Average Torque in kN-m.

We know that work done per minute = Force × Distance

$$= T \times 2\pi N = 2\pi NT$$

$\therefore$ Work done per second = $(2\pi NT)/60$ kN-m, and

Power transmitted = Work done in kN-m per second

$$= (2\pi NT)/60 \text{ kW}$$

EXERCISE-12

1. A circular shaft of 80 mm diameter is required to transmit torque in a factory. Find the torque, which the shaft can transmit, if the allowable shear stress is 50 MPa.
2. A solid shaft is required to transmit a torque of 6.5 kN-m. What should be the minimum diameter of the shaft, if the maximum shear stress if 40 MPa?
3. A solid shaft of 40 mm diameter is subjected to a torque of 0.8 kN-m. Find the maximum shear stress induced in the shaft.
4. A circular shaft of 80 mm diameter is required to transmit power at 120 r.p.m. If the shear stress is not to exceed 40 MPa, find the power transmitted by the shaft.
5. A hollow shaft of external and internal diameters of 60 mm and 40 mm is transmitting torque. Find the torque it can transmit, if the shear stress is not to exceed 40 MPa.
6. A solid circular shaft of 100 mm diameter is transmitting 120 kW at 150 r.p.m. Find the intensity of shear stress in the shaft.
7. A hollow shaft is to transmit 200 kW at 80 r.p.m. If the shear stress is not to exceed 60 MPa and internal diameter is 0.6 of the external diameter, find the diameters of the shaft.
8. A hollow shaft of external and internal diameters as 80 mm and 50 mm respectively is transmitting power at 150 r.p.m. Determine the power, which the shaft can transmit, if the shearing stress is not to exceed 40 MPa.
9. A hollow shaft has to transmit 53 kW at 160 r.p.m. If maximum shear stress is 50 MPa and internal diameter is half of the external diameter, find the diameters of the shaft.
10. Find the torque a solid shaft of 100 mm diameter can transmit, if the maximum angle of twist is 1.5° in a length of 2 m. Take $G = 70$ GPa.
11. A shaft is transmitting 100 kW at 180 r.p.m. If the allowable shear stress in the shaft material is 60 MPa, determine the suitable diameter for the shaft. The shaft is not to twist more than 1° in a length of 3 meters. Take $G = 80$ GPa.
12. A hollow shaft of external and internal diameters as 80mm and 40mm is required to transmit torque from one pulley to another. What is the value of torque transmitted, if angle of twist is not to exceed 1° in a length of a 2m. Take $G = 80$ GPa.
13. A solid shaft of 150 mm diameter is to be replaced by a hollow shaft of the same material with internal diameter equal to 60% of the external diameter. Find the saving in material, if maximum allowable shear stress is the same for both the shafts.
14. A solid shaft and a hollow circular shaft, whose inside diameter is 3/4 of the outside diameter are of equal lengths and are required to transmit a given torque. Compare the weights of these two shafts, if maximum shear stress developed in both the shafts is also equal .
15. A solid shaft of 200 mm diameter has the same cross-sectional area as a hollow shaft of the same material with inside diameter of 150 mm. Find the ratio of:

    (i) Power tranmitted by both the shafts at the same angular velocity, and

    (ii) Angles of twist in equal lengths of these shafts, when stressed to the same intensity.
16. A solid steel shaft of 60 mm diameter is to be replaced by a hollow steel shaft of the same material with internal diameter equal to half of the external diameter. Find the diameters of the hollow shaft and saving in material, if the maximum allowable shear stress is same for both shafts.

17. A solid shaft of 80 mm diameter is to be replaced by a hollow shaft of external diameter 100 mm. Determine the internal diameter of the hollow shaft if the same power is to be transmitted by both the shafts at the same angular velocity and shear stress.
18. A solid aluminium shaft 1 m long and 50 mm diameter is to be replaced by a hollow shaft of the same length and same outside diameter, so that the hollow shaft could carry the same torque and has the same angle of twist. What must be the inner diameter of the hollow shaft? Take modulus of rigidity for aluminium as 28 GPa and that for steel as 85 GPa.
19. A hollow steel shaft of 300 mm external diameter and 2000 mm internal diameter has to be replaced by a solid alloy shaft. Assuming the same values of polar modulus for both, calculate the diameter of the latter and workout the ratio of their torsional rigidities. Take G for steel as 2.4 G for alloy.
20. A hollow shaft of 3 m length is subjected to torque such that the shaft experiences a maximum shear stress of 75 MN/m^2. Find the angle of twist if G = 75m GN/m^2 and external and internal diameters of shaft are 150 mm and 100 mm respectively. Also find the shear stress at the inner surface of the shaft and show the distribution of the shear stress on the section.
21. A hollow shaft transmits power at 60. r.p.m. Its maximum permissible shear stress is 70 MN/m^2 and external and internal diameters are 250 mm and 160 mm respectively. If maximum torque is 40 percent more than the mean or average torque, Calculate
    (i) The power transmitted by the shaft, and
    (ii) Maximum angle of twist if length of the shaft is 5 m. Assume G = 80 GN/m^2.

ANSWERS

1. 5.03 kN-mm
3. 63.7 MPa
4. 50.5 kW
5. 1.36 kN-m
6. τ = 39/mm^2 = 39 MPa
7. D = 132 mm, and d = 79.2 mm
8. 53.6 kW
9. D = 70mm, d = 35 mm
10. 9.0 kN-m
11. D = 103.8 mm
12. T = 2.63 kN-m
13. 30.9%
14. 1.76
15. 1.7 and 0.8
16. D_1 = 61.30 mm, d = 30.65 mm and 21.7%
17. d = 83.6 mm
18. d = 45. 25 mm
19. D_1 = 278.8 mm and Ratio = 2.58
20. θ = 2.29°, and τ = 50MN/m^2
21. 802 kW

CHAPTER 13

Practicals

EXPERIMENT NO. 1

OBJECT

To conduct tensile test

APPARATUS

Universal Testing Machine (U.T.M.), test specimen, extensometer, graph paper and pencil.

INTRODUCTION

The tensile test of a metal is generally performed to determine:

1. Proportional and elastic limit,
2. Yield point,
3. Ultimate tensile strength, and
4. Percentage elongation.

The tensile test for a ductile materials is generally carried out by pulling out the test piece at a constant rate by gradually increasing the axial pull, till the rupture takes place. The test is carried out on a specimen having uniform cross-section through out the gauge length as shown in Fig. 13.1. Bureau of Indian Standards (B.I.S.) has recommended to use a specimen of 50 mm gauge length and 10 mm diameter. The ends of the test specimen to be gripped should suit the holders of a U.T.M. For ductile material plain ends and for brittle materials threaded ends may be used.

The test piece is loaded axially, which responds to a applied axial load in the form of axial elongation with simultaneous lateral reduction.

Upto certain value of load the stress induced in the test specimen is directly proportional to the strain. Upto this point (*A*) stress strain curve is a straight line (*OA*). Beyond point *A*, the strain increases slightly more than stress, but the materials is elastic. Hence point *B* indicates elastic limit.

If the mateials is stressed beyond point *B*, the deformation will take place. Point *C* and *D* are upper and lower yield points respectively. Between points *B* and *C*, the strain increases more rapidly than the stress. At this point (*C*) the dial, which gives the reading of the load, suddenly becomes stationary for few seconds to point *D*. Beyond point *D*, the load again starts increasing but the elongation now increases at faster rate than load upto point *E*. Hence *E* indicates maximum or ultimate stress point. The bar of specimen begins to form a local neck. Point *F* is the breaking point. The extension remains continuous even with lesser load and fracture occurs at point *F*.

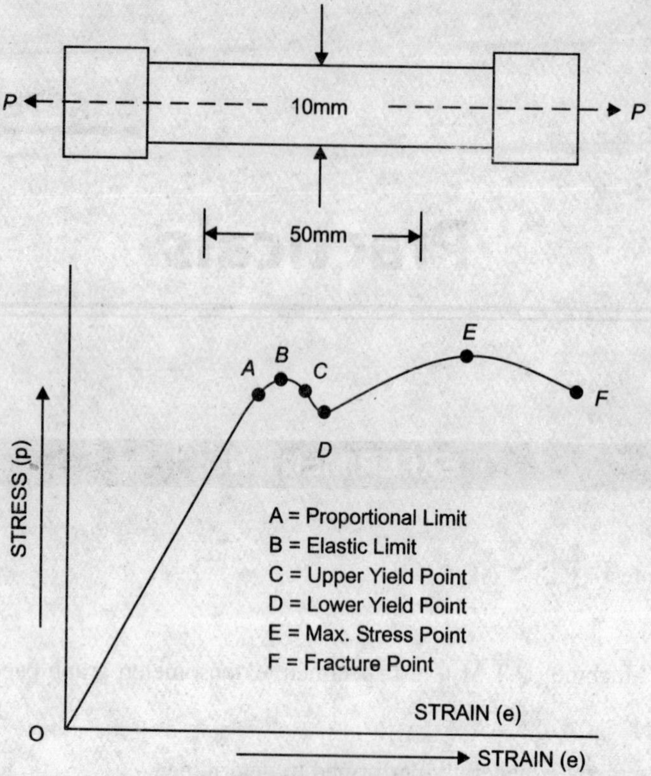

ELASTICITY CURVE

Fig. 13.1

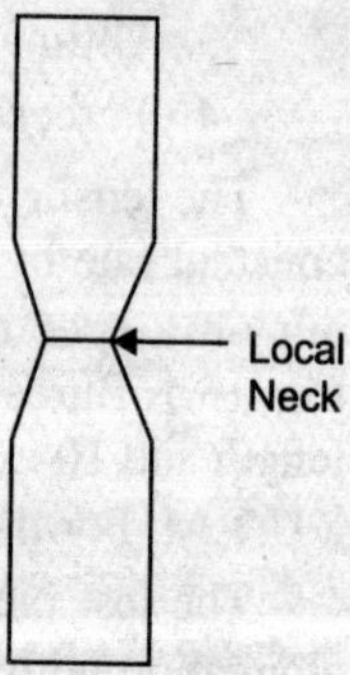

Fig. 13.2

The stress corresponding to the peak load is called ultimate tensile stress or ultimate tensile strength or tensile strength. The stress coresponding to the load when the specimen ruptures is called rupture strength.

ULTIMATE STRESS: The ratio of maximum load to the original cross-sectional area of a bar is called ultimate stress.

$$\therefore \quad \text{Ultimate stress} = \frac{\text{Maximum load}}{\text{Original cross-sectional area}}$$

PERCENTAGE ELONGATION: The ratio of percentage increase in gauge length to the original gauge length is called the percentage elongation.

$$\therefore \quad \text{Percentage Elongation} = \frac{L_1 - L_0}{L_0} \times 100$$

Where,

L_0 = original gauge length

L_1 = Final gauge length after fracture

PROCEDURE

1. Measure the gauge length and diameter of the test specimen.
2. Insert suitable jaws in the grips and select a suitable load scale on the universal testing machine.
3. Insert the test specimen in the grips by adjusing the cross head of the machine.
4. Fix the extensometer on the test specimen and set its dial indicator to zero position. Also set the vernier scale on the vertical column of the machine to zero position.
5. Set graph paper and pencil on automatic graph recording system to have a load elongation curve followed by the test specimen.
6. Start the machine and record the extensiometer readings for different values of loads.
7. Continue applying load and recording the extension values corresponding to the load till the test specimen ruptures.

OBSERVATIONS

1. Original diameter of the test specimen, d_0 =
2. Dia. of the test specimen after fracture, d_f =
3. Original gauge length (L_0) =
4. Final gauge length at fracture, L_1 =
5. Original cross-section area, A_0 =
6. Final cross-sectional area, A_1 =

S.No.	Load (P) Newton	Stress (p) N/mm^2	Extension δl mm	Strain $e = \delta l/l$	$E = p/e$

CALCULATIONS

(i) Ultimate stress $= \dfrac{\text{Maximum load}}{\text{Original cross-sectional area}}$

(ii) Percentage elongation $= \dfrac{L_1 - L_0}{L_0} \times 100$

RESULT

(i) Ultimate tensile strength

(ii) % elongation

PRECAUTIONS

1. There should not be any scratch mark in the gauge length portion of the specimen.
2. While fixing the test specimen axial load must be ensured. If loading is not perfectly axial, load value shown will be on higher side.
3. Rate of loading should not be high.
4. Readings of load and extension must be recorded very carefully.

EXPERIMENT NO. 2

FATIGUE TEST

The failure of material, under repeatedly applied stresses, is called fatigue. It has been observed that some of the machine parts such as axles, shafts, crank shafts, connecting rods, springs, pinion teeth etc., are subjected to varying stresses. It includes the variations of intensity of same type of stress as well as the different types of stress. The most common test is conducted on a rotating beam fatigue testing machine as shown in Fig. 13.3.

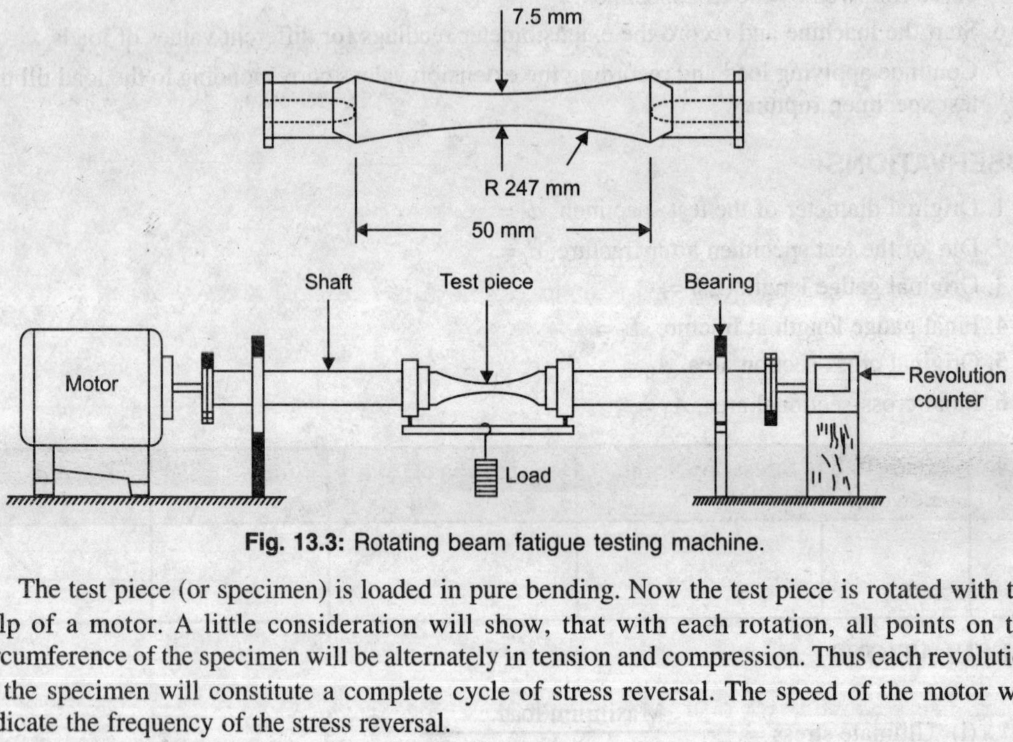

Fig. 13.3: Rotating beam fatigue testing machine.

The test piece (or specimen) is loaded in pure bending. Now the test piece is rotated with the help of a motor. A little consideration will show, that with each rotation, all points on the circumference of the specimen will be alternately in tension and compression. Thus each revolution of the specimen will constitute a complete cycle of stress reversal. The speed of the motor will indicate the frequency of the stress reversal.

In this test, a number of identical test pieces of specimens (say 8 to 10) are made from the same material The first test piece is fixed in the machine, and is loaded as shown in figure. Generally, this load is not less than that which can produce a stress equal to 3/4 of the tensile strength of the material upto its elastic limit. The speed of the motor shaft is kept constant. It has been found that after a sufficient number of stress reversals (or rotations) a crack is formed, on the outer surface, in the form of a ring. This crack goes on extending towards the centre of the test piece, till it breaks away. It has also been observed that the speed of the motor (or frequency of stress reversal) has no effect on the result. But it is the load or intensity of the stress, which controls the result.

After the first test piece breaks away, the second piece is tested with a decreased load. Similarly third, fourth ... etc., test piecs are then tested with still decreased loads. It will be interesting to know that the number of stress reversals will go on increasing each time with the decrease in load. After some tests, a limit is reached, when the stress is not sufficient to break the test piece even after 10×10^6 stress reversals (in some countries this limit is 20×10^6). This safe stress, which after reversing for 10×10^6 times does not cause the test piece to break is called endurance limit or fatigue limit.

Now the fatigue test results are plotted on diagrams known S-N diagrams. In this diagram, the stress is plotted against vertical axis and log of N (i.e., number of cycles) is plotted against horizontal axis as shown in Fig. 13.4.

The given figure shows the test results for steel, grey cast iron and aluminium alloy

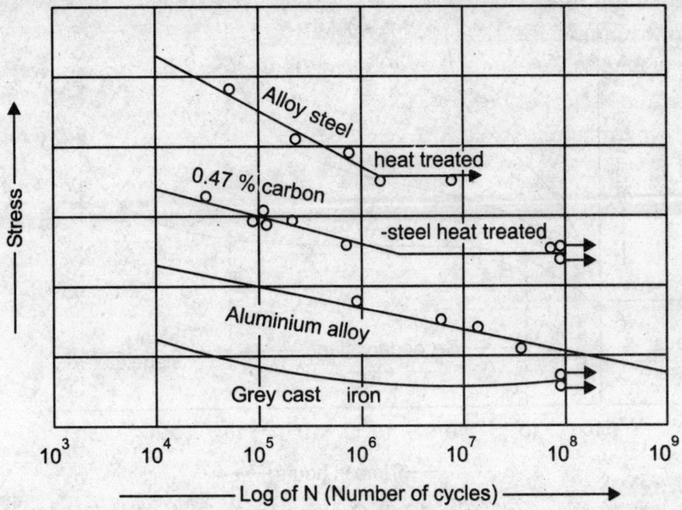

Fig. 13.4: Fatigue test curve.

EXPERIMENT NO. 3

CREEP TEST

The continuous deformation of a metal, under a steady load, is known as creep. This test is very essential to predict the working life of some members or machine components which are subjected to creep. It is always exhibited in metals like iron, nickel, copper and their alloys at increased temperatures. But some metals like zinc, tin, lead and their alloys also creep at room temperatures. It has been observed that some organic metals such as plastics and rubber are very sensitive to creep.

The creep in metals is caused by the deformation of grain boundary. Most of the deformation in case of metals, in non-recoverable. However, a small fraction of this plastic deformation is recovered with the time after the load is removed.

The creep test is generally performed by applying a static load to one end of the lever system. The other end is attached to the specimen, under test in the furnace, and held at constant temperature as shown in Fig. 13.5.

The axial deformation is read, periodically, throughout the test, a curve is plotted between extension (i.e., strain) along the vertical axis and time along the

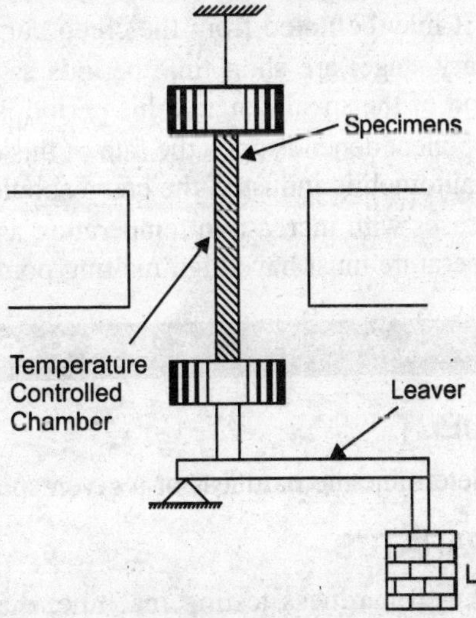

Fig. 13.5: Creep test

horizontal axis. This procedure is repeated for different loads at the same temperatures. The maximum permissible strain and working life can be estimated from these curves.

Fig. 13.6 shows typical creep curves representing the extension or strain along the vertical axis and the time along the horizontal axis under the application of load. The creep curve indicates the following three different stages of creep:

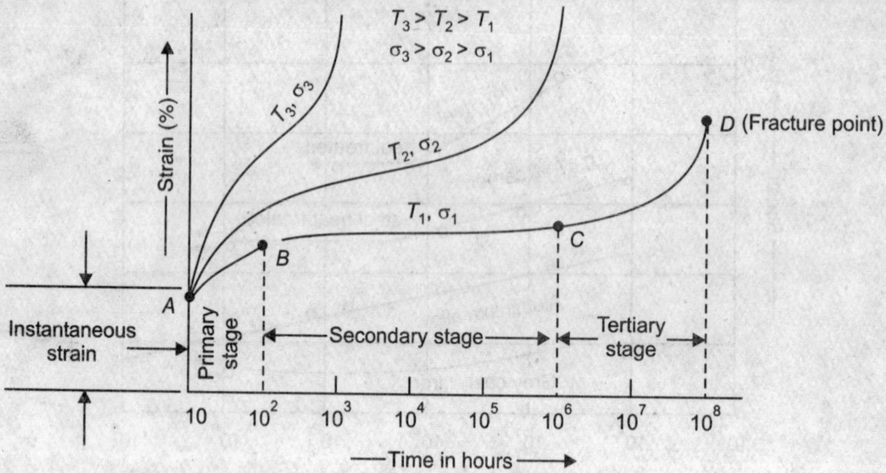

Fig. 13.6: Creep curves.

1. **PRIMARY STAGE:** This is the initial part of the curve. In this part, the curve indicates rapid extension of the specimen. This part of the curve helps us in providing proper clearance in the various components of machines.

2. **SECONDARY STAGE:** This the most important stage, which (indicates that the creep occurs at more or less constant rate, known as minimum creep rate. It will be interesting to know that it is the secondary stage of the creep, which has maximum practical utility.

3. **TERTIARY STAGE:** This is the part of the curve, which indicates rapid extension of the specimen, which finally lead to rupture.

It may be noted from the creep curve that the portions *AB* and *CD* (i.e., primary stage and tertiary stage) are short time periods as compared to portion *BC* which represents the entire life period of the specimen and this period is of great importance, because the life time of a machine component depends upon the rate of this extension. In the design of moving parts in steam turbines and automobile industry, the creep should not exceed 1 percent in 1000 hours. The value of creep increases with increase in temperature as well as stress. Hence, the materials to be used at a high temperature must have high melting point.

EXPERIMENT NO. 4

OBJECT

To determine the hardness of a given specimen.

APPARATUS

Rockwell hardness testing machine, diamond cone penetrator, steel ball penetrator and given specimen.

INTRODUCTION

Hardness is defined as the property of material by virtue of which it is able to resist the wear, scratching, identation (penetration), deformation, machinability, and cutting. Various parts of machines and structures, such as gears, axles and rails are subjected to service requirements where high resistance to identation or abrasion is required. The hardness values of engineering materials are obtained by penetration method.

In this method, the materials is subjected to a known magnitude of load mechanically applied through a very hard and specifically chosen indenting tool called as a penetrator. This penetrator, under the influence of impressed load, penetrates into the surface of material thereby bearing a permanent impression clearly visible to the naked eye. The dimensional measurements of such an impression are put to valuable consideration for deciding the hardness value of a material.

This method of determining the hardness value has been widely used in engineering practice for all metals hard or soft and also for non-metallic materials such as timber, plastic etc. The types of tests included in the category of penetration hardness are (a) Brinell Hardness Test; (b) Rockwell Hardness Test; (c) Vicker's Hardness Test, and (d) Micro-hardness Test.

METHOD: BRINELL HARNESS TEST: It involves making a prism type test block of metal being tested, placing the test sample on the table and raising the table to such a position that the top surface of the specimen will just touch the ball. The ball is made of hardened steel, usually of 10 ± 0.01 mm diameter. Once that position is reached the ball is pressed into the surface of the specimen by gradually applying the load. The load is maintained there for about 10 to 15 seconds and then withdrawn. In the mean while the spherical ball has made an impression or identation on the piece. The Brinell Harness Number (BHN), which is indicative of the relative hardness of the test piece, is read from the scale available on the machine. The approximate B.H.N. for steel is above 200, for brass and copper alloys 30 - 200. Alumnium alloys 15 - 100 and for lead, tin and their alloys it is 3 - 20.

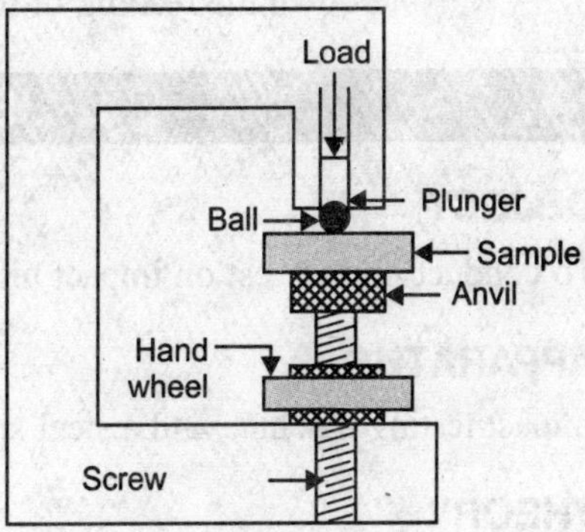

Fig. 13.7: Hardness Testing Machine.

ROCKWELL HARDNESS TEST: This test uses a direct reading instrument based on the principle of differential depth measurement (Fig. 13.8). The test is performed by slowly raising the specimen against the indenter until a fixed minor load of 10 kg has been applied. This is indicated on the dial guage. Then major load (60,100 and 150 kg) is applied through a loaded lever system. After the dial pointer comes to rest the major load is removed and, with minor load still acting, the rockwell hardness number is read on the dial gauge. A variety of indenters and levels may be used and each combination determines a particular rockwell scale. Indenters include hard steel balls of 1/16, 1/8, 1/4, and 1/2 inch diameter and a 120° conical diamond (brale) point.

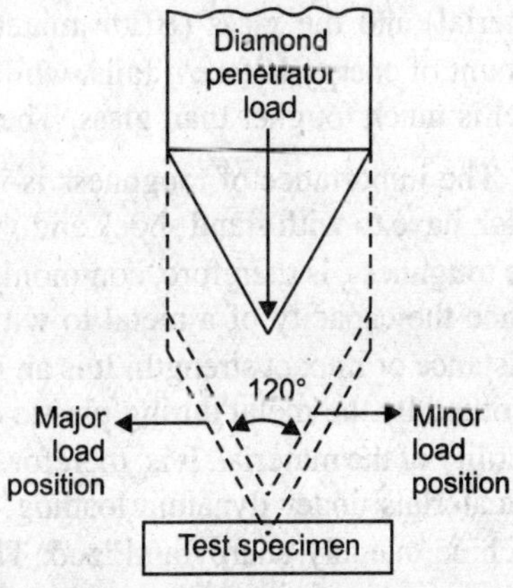

Fig. 13.8 Principle of Rockwell testing.

The Rockwell Hardnes Tester usually consists of a hand operated vertical hydraulic press designed to force a conical diamond point or steel ball indenter into the specimen. The equipment is designed to facilitate slow and progressive loading at right angles to the test surface. A gauge is provided to display the quantity of force at an instant. In this machine there are two scales on the dial, *B* marked into red and *A* is black. Zero of *A* scale is opposite to number 30 on the scale *B*, so that there is a difference of thirty hardness numbers between the two scales at any point.

PROCEDURE

1. Place the specimen on anvil.
2. Fix the penetrator into the penetrator holder.
3. Rotate the hand wheel to raise the anvil so that the testing specimen touches the penetrator.
4. Press the specimen against penetrator until the small needle on the dial comes to set. In this position, there is minor load of 10 kg on the specimen.
5. Turn the diamond cone penetrator until the indicator comes to zero on black scale and 30 on red scale.
6. Release the major load lever to apply major load.
7. Note down the reading of the scale for hardness number.

EXPERIMENT NO. 5

OBJECT

To conduct impact test on impact testing machine.

APPARATUS

Impact testing machine and a steel specimen of 55 × 10 × 10 mm size.

THEORY

Toughness is defined as the property of a material by virtue of which it can absorb maximum energy before fracture takes place. When a sudden load is applied on a piece of mild steel (tough material) and the glass (Britte material), we see that the mild steel piece absorbs a substantial amount of energy before it fails, while the glass piece breaks suddenly. Thus it is said that the mild steel is much tougher than glass. The value of toughness decreases when the material is heated.

The importance of toughness is in the selection of a material for structural and machine parts which have to with stand shock and vibrations such as power press punch and pneumatic hammers. The toughness, is therefore, commonly associated with shock or impact loading i.e. impact strength. Hence the capacity of a metal to with stand sharp blows without fracture is known as an impact resistance or impact strength. It is an indicative of the toughness of metal i.e., the amount of energy absorbed by the metal during plastic deformation. Toughness takes into account both strength and ductility of the material. It is, therefore, impact test becomes essential in order to study the behaviour of materials under dynamic loading. There are two types of specimen used in an impact testing machine, namely charpy and izod. The charpy specimen is placed just as simply supported beam whereas izod specimen is placed in a vice such that it acts as a centilever.

Charry impact test is performed on a square cross-section specimen having a notch on one edge in the central cross-section (Fig. 13.9), For conducting the test the specimen is held in the supports

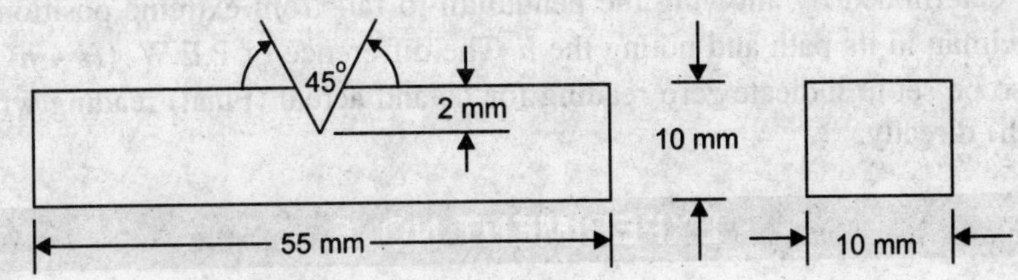

Fig. 13.9: Standard specimen for charpy impact test.

of the impact testing machine as a simply, supported beam (Fig. 13.10) such that swinging pendulum hammer strikes the specimen at central cross-section but at the opposite face of the V-notch is made in the centre having included angle, 45° and depth 2 mm.

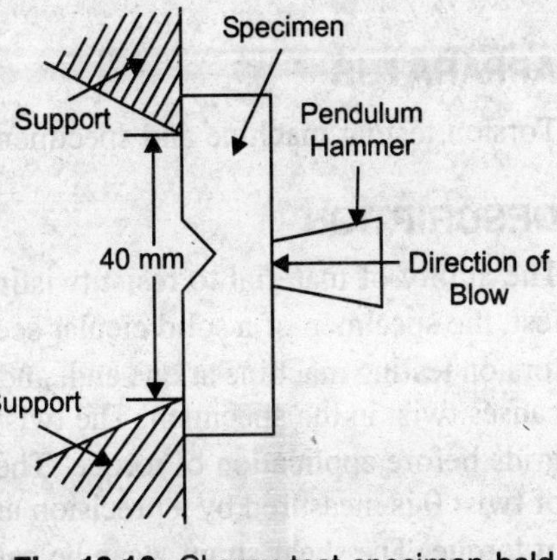

Fig. 13.10: Charpy test specimen held in supports in proper position for test.

The pendulum is locked at a proper height (H) in starting position, the specimen is placed in supports in proper position and the pendulum is unlocked to swing and strike the specimen at its centre to break the specimen. As usual, the pendulum swings to the other side after breaking the specimen and its final height (h) at the end of the swing is noted.

The principle for both the tests is shown schematically in Fig. 13.11 and the impact strength may be found by using the expression.

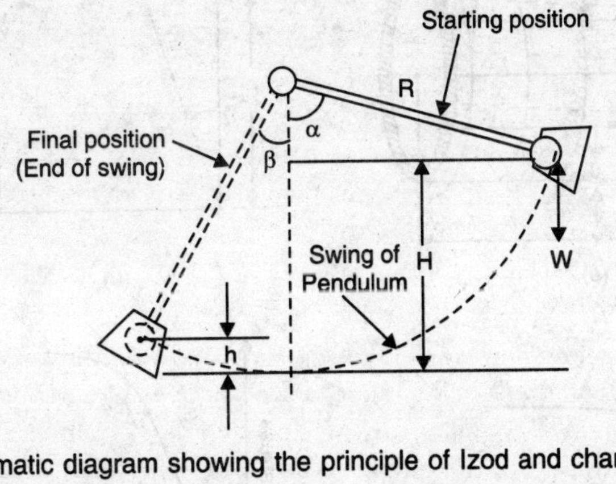

Fig. 13.11: Schematic diagram showing the principle of Izod and charpy impact tessts.

$U_i = W(H - h) - U_f$, where

W = Weight of the pendulum

H = Extreme (raised) position of the pendulum from specimen.

h = Maximum height of the pendulum after fracturing the specimen.

U_f = Energy loss (may be due to bearings of the pendulum and resistance of air offered to the swinging pendulum)

U_i = Impact strength of the specimen.

U_f may be determined by allowing the pendulum to fall from extreme position (H) without placing the speciman in its path and noting the h. The difference of P.E.W. ($H - h$) will give U_f. Needle may also be set to indicate zero reading for U_f and actual (Final) reading will indicate U_i (Impact strength) directly.

EXPERIMENT NO. 6

OBJECT

To conduct torsion Test

APPARATUS

Torsion testing machine and specimen.

DESCRIPTION

The ability of material to resist twisting moment (Torque) is determined by a torsion test. In this test, the specimen of a solid cicular section or a hollow tube (Torsion Tube) is taken. It is held in a torsion testing machine at one end, and the other end is given the torque T (Fig. 13.12). This torque causes twist in the specimen. The twist is shown by deformed dotted lines which were rectangular grids before application of torque. The torque is increased gradually and the corresponding angle of twist θ is measured by a precision angular instrument or by a graduated dial for different values of torque. The shear strain γ can be calculated by $\gamma = s/l_u = r\,\theta$.

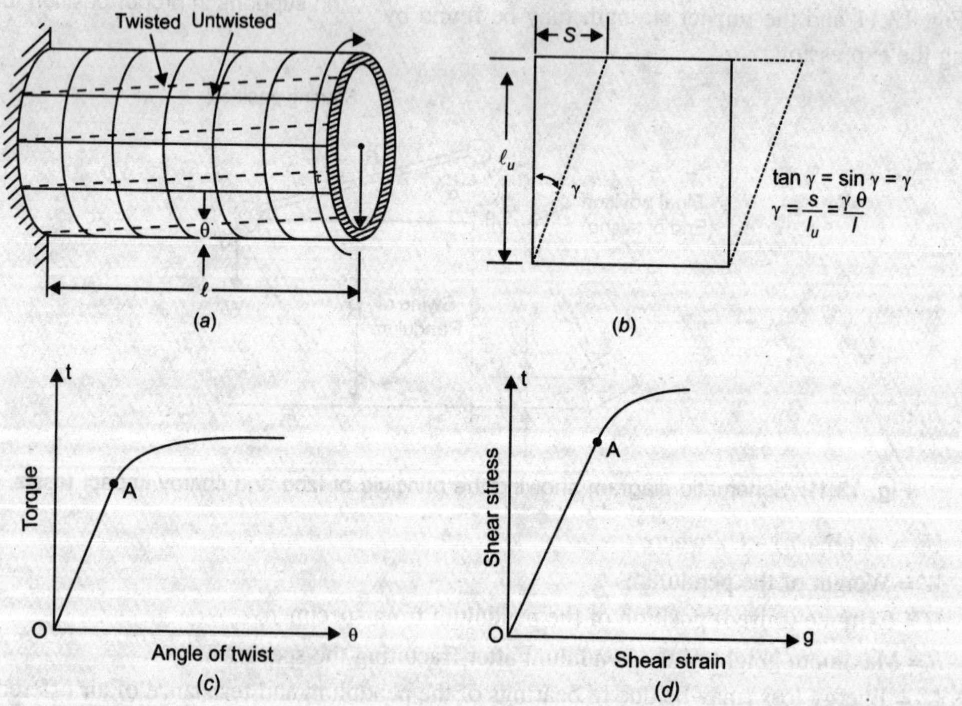

Fig. 13.12: Torsion test showing (a) deformation in shaft, (b) shearing strain in a grid , (c) torque versus angle of twist diagram obtained from torsion test, and (d) t = f curve.

Where s is the unit shearing displacement in unit length l_u of the rectangular grid (Fig. 13.12 *b*). Here r is the mean radius of thin hollow tube or outer radius of a solid shaft and θ the angle of twist per unit length. The torque is read on the dial of the machine. From the observed data, the torque versus twist diagram is plotted whose likely shape is shown in Fig. 13.12(*c*). Its variation is linear upto A which implies that the elastic limit is from O to A. The elastic limit is upto A and mateiral obeys HOOKE's law in OA range. Slope of this curve yields $\tau\gamma = G$, the shear modulus

The effect of torque is to create shear stress in the specimen. The torsional shear strength τ at the outer periphery of the solid circular specimen of diameter d is obtained from, $\tau = \dfrac{(16T)}{\pi d^3}$ and for hollow circular specimen by $\tau = \dfrac{16TD_0}{\pi(D_0^4 - D_i^4)}$ where D_0 and D_i are outer and inner diameters.

CHAPTER 14

Solved Examples

EXAMPLE 14.1. A car is moving with a velocity of 72 km. p.h. After seeing a child on the road the brakes are applied and the vehicle is stopped in a distance of 15 m. If the retardation produced is proportional to the distance from the point where the brakes were applied, find the expression of retardation.

SOLUTION : Let the expression for retardation be $a = -Ks$, where s = Distance travelled, and k = constant

$$\therefore \quad v \cdot \frac{dv}{ds} = -ks$$

$$vdv = -ks\, ds$$

$$\therefore \quad \frac{v^2}{2} = -\frac{Ks^2}{2} + C_1 \qquad \text{...(i)}$$

After the time the brakes are applied,

$$s = 0,$$

and

$$v = 72\ kmph$$

$$= \frac{72 \times 1000}{60 \times 60} = 20 \text{ m/sec}$$

From expression (i), we have

$$\frac{20 \times 20}{2} = -0 + C_1$$

or

$$C_1 = 200 \qquad \text{...(ii)}$$

$$\therefore \quad \frac{v^2}{2} = -\frac{ks^2}{2} + 200 \qquad \text{...(iii)}$$

When the vehicle stops, $v = 0$ and $s = 15$ m

$$\therefore \quad 0 = -K\frac{(15)^2}{2} + 200$$

$$\therefore \quad K = \frac{400}{225} = 1.778$$

Hence the expression for retardations is $a = -1.778\ s$ **Ans.**

EXAMPLE 14.2. State and explain the theorem of (i) Pappus and (ii) Guldinus

SOLUTION : When a plane curve rotates about a fixed axis, it generates a surface called the surface of revolution.

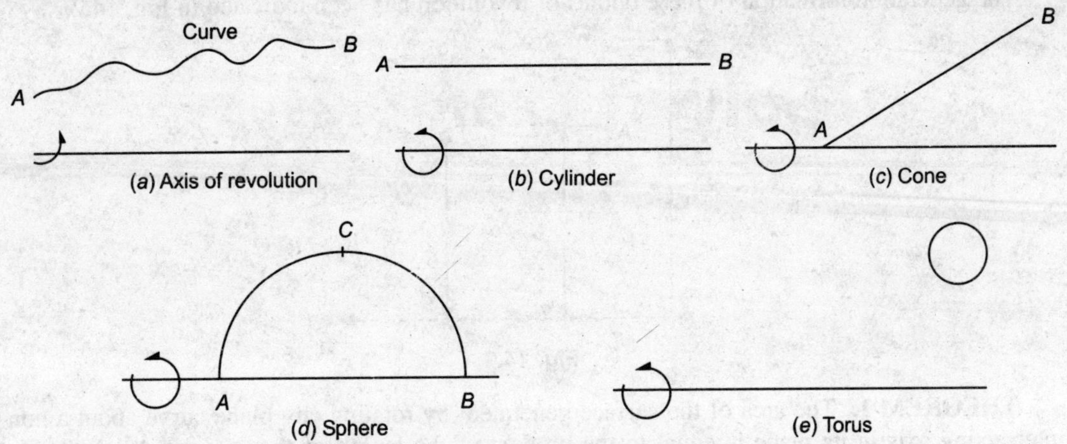

Fig. 14.1: Generation of surface of revolution

Examples:

(i) The surface of a sphere is obtained when a semi-circular arc ABC is rotated about the diameter AC.

(ii) The surface of a cone gets generated when a straight line AB is rotated about an axis AC.

(iii) The surface of a ring or torus gets formed when the circumference of a circle is rotated about a non-intersecting axis.

(iv) The surface of a cylinder is generated when straight line AB is rotated about an axis.

The generation/formation of these surfaces of revolution has been indicated in Fig. 14.2.

When a plane area is rotated about a fixed axis, it generates a body called the body of revolution.

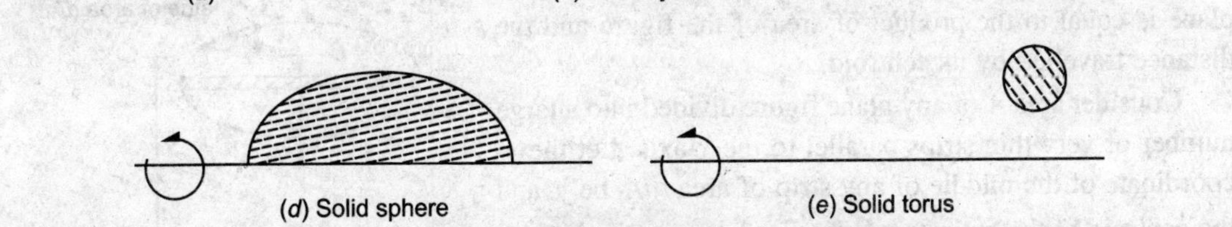

Fig. 14.2

Example: A solid cylinder may be generated by rotating a rectangular area, a cone by rotating a triangular area, a solid sphere by rotating a semi-circular area, and a solid torus by rotating a full circular area.

The generation/formation of these bodies of revolution has been indicated in Fig. 14.2.

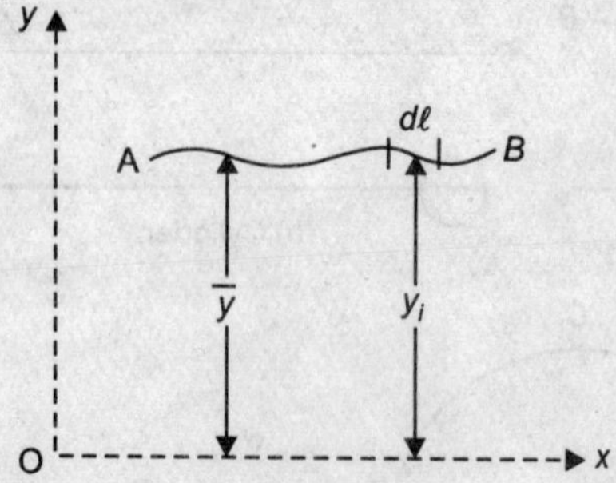

Fig. 14.3

THEOREM 1. The area of the surface generated by rotating any plane curve about a non-intersecting axis in its plane is equal to the product of the length of the curve and the distance travelled by its centroid.

Let *AB* be any plane curve of length *l* that lies in the *x-y* plane and does not intersect the *x*-axis. Consider an elemental length *dl*, so short that it may be thought to be a minute portion of a straight line. Let *y*-coordinate of its mid point be y_i, and that of the centroid of the entire curve be $\bar{y}$.

When this curve is rotated about the *x*-axis, then

area generated by the elementary length = $2\pi y_i dl_i$

area generated by the entire line = $\int 2\pi y_i\, dl_i$

Thus integral $\int y_i dl_i$ is equal to $\bar{y}l$ and therfore

area generated $= l \times 2\pi\bar{y}$

where $2\pi\bar{y}$ is the distance travelled by the centroid of the curve

area generated = (length of the generating curve) × (distance travelled by centroid of the curve).

It is to be noted that the generating curve does not cross the axis about which it is rotated. If it does so, then the two sections on either side of the axis would generate areas of opposite signs and the theorem would not apply.

THEOREM II. The volume of the solid generated by rotating any plane figure about a non-intersecting axis in its plane is equal to the product of area of the figure and the distance travelled by its centroid.

Consider area *A* of any plane figure divided into a large number of very thin strips parallel to the *x*-axis. Let the *y*-coordinate of the middle of any strip of area dA_i be y_i and the centroid of the entire curve by $\bar{y}$.

When the plane of the figure is rotated about the *x*-axis, then

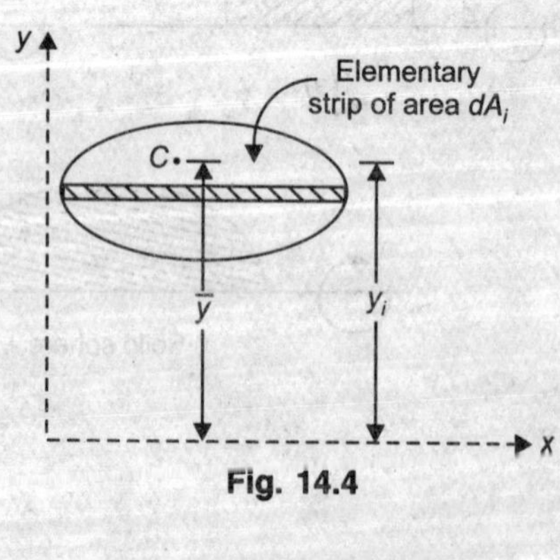

Fig. 14.4

Volume generated by the elementary area = $2\pi y_i \, dA_i$

volume generated by the entire area = $\int 2\pi y_i dA_i$

The integral $\int y_i dA_i$ is equal to $\bar{y}A$ and therefore

volume generated $V = A \times 2\pi\bar{y}$

The parameter $(2\pi\bar{y})$ is the distance travelled by the centroid of the area being rotated.

∴ Volume generated = (area of the figure) × (distance travelled by the centroid)

UTILITY : The theorem of Pappus - Guldinus offer a simple way to compute the areas of surfaces of revolution and the volumes of bodies of revolutinon.

Conversely their application lies in determining the centroid of a plane curve when the area of the surface generated by the curve is known or to determine the centroid of a plane area when the volume of the body generated by the area is known.

EXAMPLE 14.2(a). Using pappus – guldinus theorems, calculate the

(i) Area of a surface of revolution obtained by revolving a quarter circular arc of radius r about o - y (Fig. 14.5a)

(ii) Volume generated by revolving a quarter ellipse about o - x (Fig. 14.5b)

(iii) Volume of a sphere of radius r.

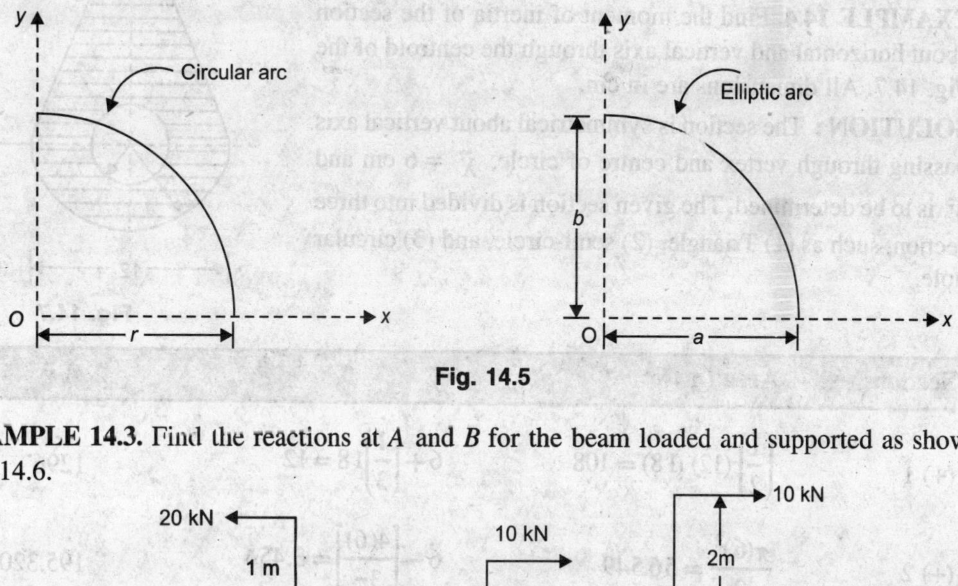

Fig. 14.5

EXAMPLE 14.3. Find the reactions at A and B for the beam loaded and supported as shown in Fig. 14.6.

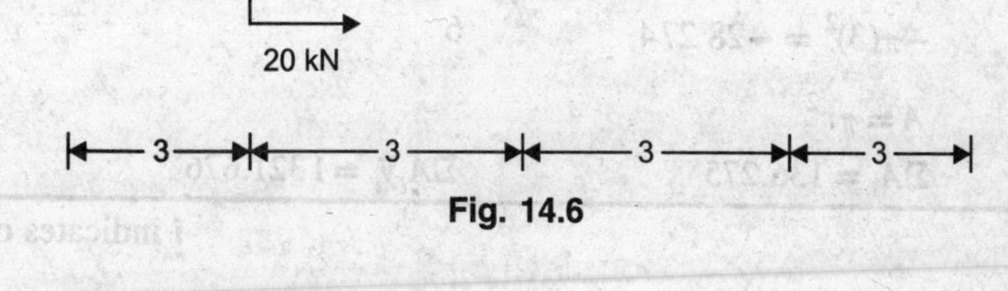

Fig. 14.6

SOLUTION : For $\Sigma MA = 0$

$$V_A \times 0 + 20 \times 2 - 10 \times 1 - 10 \times 2 + 12\, V_B = 0$$

or
$$40 - 10 - 20 + 12\, V_B = 0$$

or
$$V_B = -\frac{10}{12}$$

$$= -0.833 \text{ kN} \downarrow \textbf{ Ans.}$$

$\because$ $\quad V_A + V_B = 0$ (No vertical load)

$\therefore$ $\quad V_A = -V_B$

$$= 0.833 \text{ kN} \uparrow \textbf{ Ans.}$$

For $\Sigma H = 0 \ : H_A + 10 = 0$

$\therefore$ $\quad H_A = -10$ kN ($\leftarrow$) **Ans.**

The reactions at *A* and *B* are given by

$$H_A = 10 \text{ kN } (\leftarrow),$$
$$V_A = 0.833 \text{ kN } (\uparrow)$$
$$V_B = 0.833\ (\downarrow) \textbf{ Ans.}$$

EXAMPLE 14.4. Find the moment of inertia of the section about horizontal and vertical axis through the centroid of the Fig. 14.7. All dimensions are in cm.

SOLUTION : The section is symmetrical about vertical axis passing through vertex and centre of circle. $\bar{X} = 6$ cm and $\bar{Y}$ is to be determined. The given section is divided into three section, such as (1) Triangle, (2) semi-circle, and (3) circular hole.

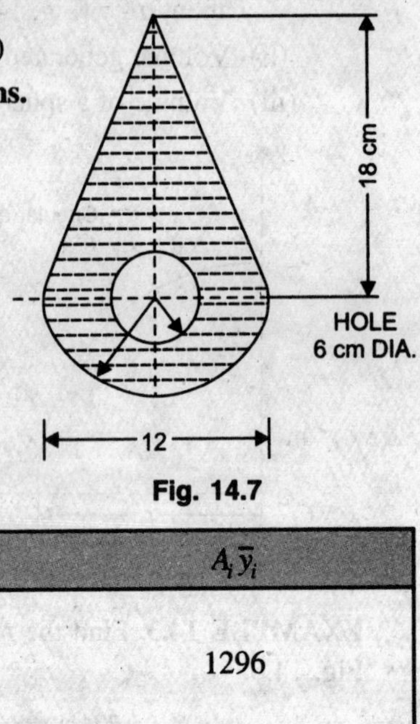

Fig. 14.7

Section	Area (A_i)	$\bar{y}_i$	$A_i\bar{y}_i$
(+) 1	$\left(\frac{1}{2}\right)(12)(18) = 108$	$6 + \left(\frac{1}{3}\right)18 = 12$	1296
(+) 2	$\frac{\pi(6)^2}{2} = 56.549$	$6 - \left[\frac{4(6)}{3\pi}\right] = 3.454$	195.320
	$A = \frac{\pi R^2}{2}$	$C.G. = \frac{4r}{3\pi}$	
(–) 3	$-\pi(3)^2 = -28.274$	6	– 169.644
	$A = \pi r^2$		
	$\Sigma A_i = 136.275$	$\Sigma A_i\bar{y}_i = 1321.676$	

i **indicates own centroidal axes**

$$\bar{y} = \frac{\Sigma A_i \bar{y}_i}{\Sigma A_i} = \frac{1321.676}{136.275} = 9.699 \text{ cm}$$

For triangle (1) $\quad I_{YY} = \frac{hb^3}{48},$

$$I_{XX} = \frac{bh^3}{36}$$

For semi-circle (2) $\quad I_{XX} = 0.11\, R^4,$

$$I_{YY} = \frac{\pi R^4}{8}$$

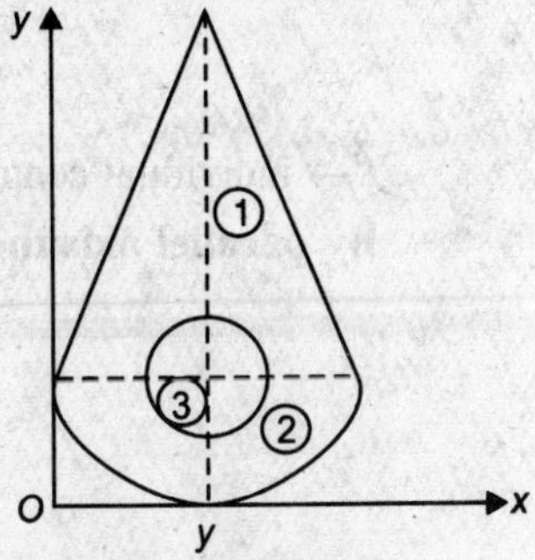

Fig. 14.8

For circle (3) $\quad I_{XX} = \frac{\pi R^4}{4},$

$$I_{YY} = \frac{\pi R^4}{4},$$

$$I_{XX} = \Sigma(I_{XX})_i + \Sigma A_i(\bar{y}_i - \bar{y})^2$$

$$I_{YY} = \Sigma(I_{YY})_i + \Sigma A_i(\bar{X}_i - \bar{X})^2$$

But $\quad \Sigma\bar{X}_i = \bar{X}$

Hence $I_{YY} = \Sigma(I_{YY})_i$

$\bar{Y}_i, \bar{X}_i$ Represent centroids of individual elemental areas $\quad \because I_{XX_i} = I_{G_1} + ah_1^2$

Section	$I_{(XX)_i}$	$I_{(YY)_i}$	$A(\bar{Y}_i - \bar{Y})^2$
(+) 1	$\frac{12(18)^3}{36} = 1944$	$\frac{18(12)^3}{48} = 648$	$108(12 - 9.699)^2 = 571.817$
	$0.11R^4$	$\frac{\pi R^4}{8}$	
(+) 2	$0.11(6)^4 = 142.56$	$\frac{\pi(6)^4}{8} = 508.938$	$56.549(3.454 - 9.699)^2$ $= 2205.412$
	$\frac{\pi R^4}{4}$	$\frac{\pi R^4}{4}$	
(–) 3	$\frac{\pi(3)^4}{4} = -63.617$	$-\frac{\pi(3)^4}{4} = -63.617$	$-28.274\ (6\text{-}9.699)^2$ $= -386.862$
	$\Sigma I_{(XX)_i} = 2022.943$	$\Sigma I_{(YY)_i} = 1093.321$	$\Sigma A(\bar{y}_i - \bar{y})^2 = 2390.367$

$$\therefore \quad I_{XX} = 2022.943 + 2390.367$$
$$= 4413.31 \text{ cm}^4 \textbf{ Ans.}$$
$$I_{YY} = 1093.321 \text{ cm}^4 \textbf{ Ans.}$$
$$\bar{X} = 6 \text{ cm}$$
$$\bar{Y} = 9{,}699$$
$$A = \mathbf{136.275 \text{ cm}^2}$$

$i \rightarrow$ individual centroidal axes

By parallel axis theorem

$$I_{XX} = I_{xx} + A(\bar{Y})^2$$
$$= \Sigma(I_{xx})_i + \Sigma A_i(\bar{Y}_i - \bar{Y})^2$$
$$I_{AA} = I_{xx} + A\,(h_A)^2$$
$$I_{BB} = I_{xx} + A\,(h_B)^2$$
$$I_{YY} = \Sigma(I_{YY})_i + \Sigma A_i(\bar{X}_i - X)^2$$

EXAMPLE 14.5. Find the moment of inertia of the shaded area shown in Fig.14.9 about the axis *AB*.

SOLUTION : The section is divided into a triangle *PQR*, a semi-circle *PQS* having base on its axis *AB* and a circle having its centre on axis *AB*. Now moment of inertia of the shaded section about axis *AB* = moment of inertia of *PQR* about *AB* + Moment of inertia of semi-circle *PQS* about *AB* - moment of inertia of circle about

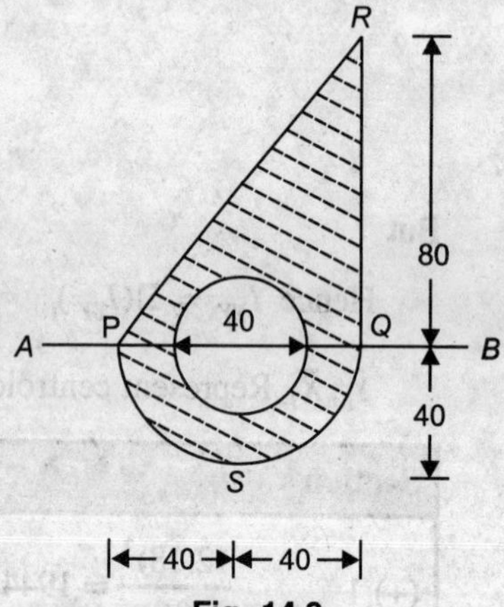

Fig. 14.9

$$AB = \frac{bh^3}{12} + \frac{\pi R^4}{8} - \frac{\pi R^4}{4}$$

$$= \frac{80 \times 80^3}{12} + \frac{\pi(40)^4}{80} = \frac{\pi(20)^4}{4}$$

$$= 3413333.3 + 1005309.6 - 125663.70$$
$$= 42929791.19 \text{ mm}^4$$

$$\therefore \quad I_{AB} = 42{,}92{,}979.19 \text{ mm}^4 \textbf{ Ans.}$$

EXAMPLE 14.6. A body of mass 10 kg is suspended by a string of length 1 m. It is struck by a bullet travelling horizontally with a velocity of 450 m/sec. The bullet weighs 30 gms and gets embedded into the body after striking it. Determine the maximum angle through which the body swings.

SOLUTION : Refer Fig. 14.10, which shows the given system with the various parameters inserted.

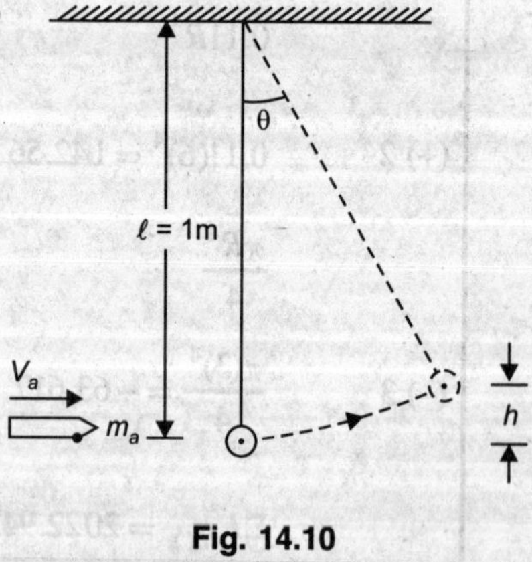

Fig. 14.10

Applying the principle of conservation of momentum

Momentum before impact = Momentum after impact

$$m_a V_a + m_b V_b = (m_a + m_b)V$$

Where V is the common velocity with which the body and the bullet together move after impact.

$$\therefore \quad \frac{30}{1000} \times 450 + 10 \times 0 = \left(\frac{30}{1000} + 10\right) V$$

or $$13.50 = 10.03\ V$$

$\therefore$ $$V = 1.346 \text{ m/sec}$$

Now applying principle of conservation of energy

Loss of kinetic energy = Gain of potential energy

$$\frac{1}{2}(m_a + m_b)V^2 = (m_a + m_b)gh,$$

Where h is the height to which the body rises.

or $$h = \frac{V^2}{2g} = \frac{(1.346)^2}{2 \times 9.81} = 0.0923m$$

From Fig. 14.10,

$$\cos\theta = \frac{\text{base}}{\text{diagonal}} = \frac{\ell - h}{\ell} = \frac{1 - h}{1}$$

or $$\cos\theta = 1 - 0.0923 = 0.9077$$

$\therefore$ $$\theta = \cos^{-1}(0.9077) = 24.81° \textbf{ Ans.}$$

EXAMPLE 14.7. A wooden block of weight 40 N rests on a rough horizontal plane having friction coeffiient $\mu = 0.35$. The block is struck by a bullet travelling horizontally with a velocity of 750 m/sec and weighing 0.25 N. Workout the distance by which the block is displaced from its initial position.

It may be presumed that the bullet after striking the block gets embedded in it.

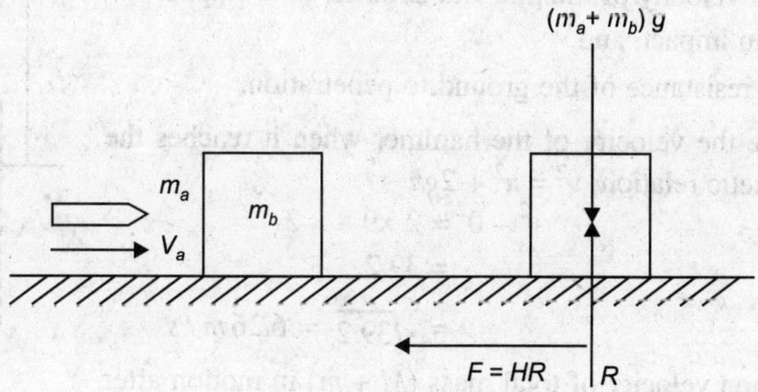

Fig. 14.11

SOLUTION : Refer Fig. 14.11, which shows the block with various parameters inserted.

Applying the principle of conservation of momentum

Momentum before impact = Momentum after impact

or $$m_aV_a + m_bV_b = (m_a + m_b)V$$

or $$\frac{0.25}{9.81}\times 750 + \frac{40}{9.81}\times 0 = \left(\frac{0.25+40}{9.81}\right)V$$

or $$19.11 = 4.103V$$

$\therefore$ $$V = 4.656 \text{ m/sec}$$

Normal reaction,

$$R = (m_a + m_b)g$$
$$= 0.25 + 40 = 40.25 \text{ N}$$

Force of friction,

$$F = \mu R = 0.35\times 40.25$$
$$= 14.088N$$

To find the distance travelled by the block, apply the principle of work and energy.

Work done to over come the frictional force = Kinetic energy lost by the block with bullet embedded.

$$F.s. = \frac{1}{2}(m_a + m_b)V^2$$

or $$18.088s = 0.5\left(\frac{0.25+40}{9.81}\right)(4.658)^2$$

or $$14.088s = 44.556$$

$\therefore$ $$s = 3.163\ m \textbf{ Ans.}$$

EXAMPLE 14.8. A hammer of mass 200 kg is made to fall freely from 2m height on a head of a pile 1500 kg mass. The pile is drawn 5 cm into the ground in one blow. Determine (Refer Fig. 14.12)

(a) The common velocity of the pile and hammer after impact

(b) Energy lost in impact, and

(c) The average resistance of the ground to penetration.

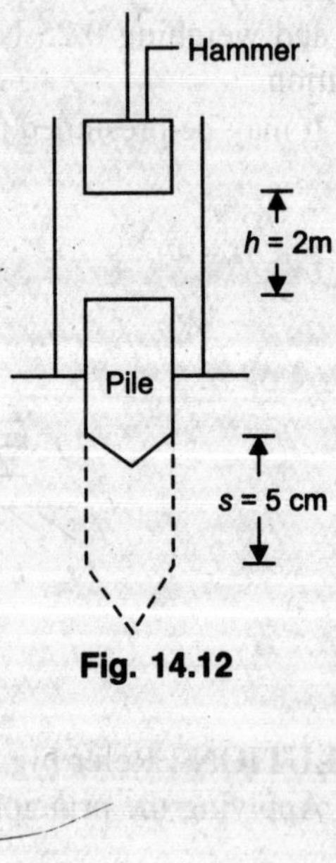

Fig. 14.12

SOLUTION : Let v be the velocity of the hammer when it reaches the pile. Now using the kinetic relation, $v^2 = u^2 + 2gh$

$$v^2 - 0^2 = 2\times 9.8\times 2$$
$$= 39.2$$

$\therefore$ $$v = \sqrt{39.2} = 6.26\ m/s$$

Let V be the common velocity of total mass $(M + m)$ in motion after the impact. Then from the principle of conservation of momentum.

Momentum before impact = Momentum after impact

$$mv = (M + m)V$$

or $$200 \times 6.26 = (1500 + 200)V = 1700\,V$$

$\therefore$ $$V = \frac{200(6.26)}{1700} = 0.736\ m/\text{sec}\ \textbf{Ans.}$$

(b) $$\text{Kinetic energy before impact} = \frac{1}{2}mv^2 = \frac{1}{2}(200\,(6.26)^2$$

$$= 3918.76\ Nm$$

$$\text{Kinetic energy after impact} = \frac{1}{2}(M + m)V^2$$

$$= \frac{1}{2}(1500 + 200)\,(0.736)^2$$

$$= 460.44\ N - m$$

$\therefore$ $$\text{Loss in kinetic energy at impact} = 3918.76 - 460.44$$
$$= 3458.32\ N - m.\ \textbf{Ans.}$$

(c) After penetration in the ground the velocity of the system (Pipe + hammer) becomes zero. Hence using the kinematic relation, $v^2 = u^2 + 2as$, we have

$$0^2 - (0.736)^2 = 2a\,(0.05)$$

$\therefore$ $$a = 5.417\ \text{m/sec}^2\ \text{(Retardation)}$$

Let F_R be the average resistance exerted by the ground. Then net force acting on the system in upward direction $F_n = F_R - W$, where, W = weight of hammer and Pile.

Applying Newton's second law of motion, $F = ma$

$$F_R - (1500 + 200)\,9.8 = (1500 + 200)\,(5.417)$$

or $$F_R - 1700\,(9.8) = 1700\,(5.417)$$

$\therefore$ $$F_R = 9208.9 + 16{,}660$$
$$= 25868.9\ \text{N}\ \textbf{Ans.}$$

EXAMPLE 14.9. A square hole is punched out of a circular lamina, the diagonal of the square being radius of the circle. Find the C.G. of the remainder, if R is the radius of the circle.

SOLUTION : Let the C.G. of the circular lamina be at G, from which a square $EFGH$, whose one end is at the centre G of the circle and diagonal of the square $EG = R$ = Radius of the circle, has been punched (Refer Fig. 14.13).

Let the C.G. of the circle, square and remainder be at points G, G_1 and G_2 respectively. These three will be on a straight line i.e. axis of symmetry.

$\because$ Area of big circle $= \pi R^2$

$\therefore$ Area of punched portion $= R \times \frac{R}{2} \times \frac{1}{2} + R \times \frac{R}{2} \times \frac{1}{2}$

$$= \frac{R^2}{2} = 0.5R^2 \quad \text{...(i)}$$

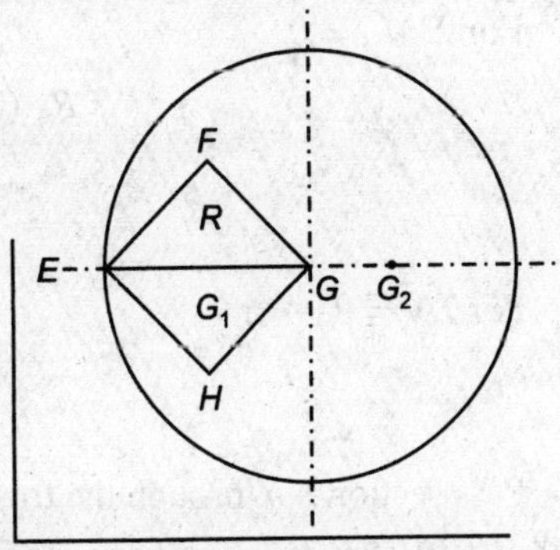

Fig. 14.13

Area of remainder portion

$$\pi R^2 - 0.5R^2 = 2.615R^2 \quad \text{...(ii)}$$

Now C.G. of square *EFGH*, whose area is $0.5R^2$, is at G_1 and the *C.G.* of the remainder having an area of 2.6415 R^2 be at G_2.

$\therefore$ $$0.5 R^2 (GG_1) = 2.6415R^2 (GG_2)$$

or $$0.5R^2 (0.5R) = 2.6415R^2 (GG_2)$$

or $$0.25R = 2.6415 (GG_2)$$

$\therefore$ $$GG_2 = \frac{0.25R}{2.6415}$$

$$= 0.095R$$

Hence, the *C.G.* of the remainder lamina is at a distance of 0.095*R* from the centre of the circle.

EXAMPLE 14.10. A plane truss is supported and loaded as shown in Fig. 14.14. Find the axial forces in members *CD*, *EF* and *CF* by method of sections.

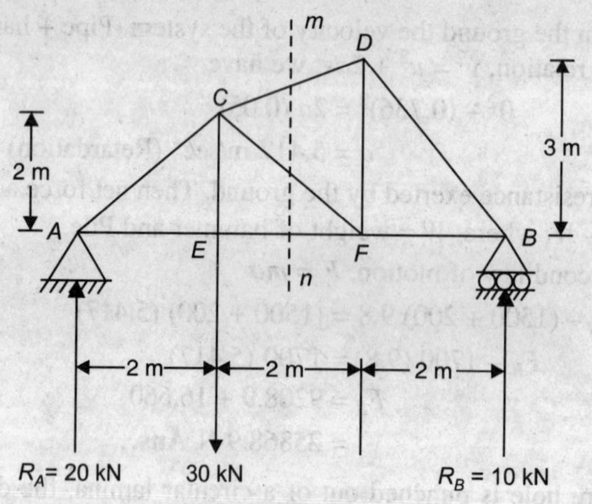

Fig. 14.14

SOLUTION : Support Reactions : Consider the equilibrium of the entire truss shown in Fig. 14.14

For $\Sigma M_A = 0$

$$R_A (0) + 30 \times 2 = 6R_B$$

$\therefore$ $$R_B = \frac{60}{6} = 10 \text{ kN} \quad \text{...(i)}$$

For $\Sigma V = 0$,

$$R_A + R_B = 30$$

or $$R_A = 30 - R_B = 30 - 10 = 20 \text{ kN} \quad \text{...(ii)}$$

Pass section *mn* through the truss. Consider the equilibrium of the left hand portion of the truss (Fig. 14.15)

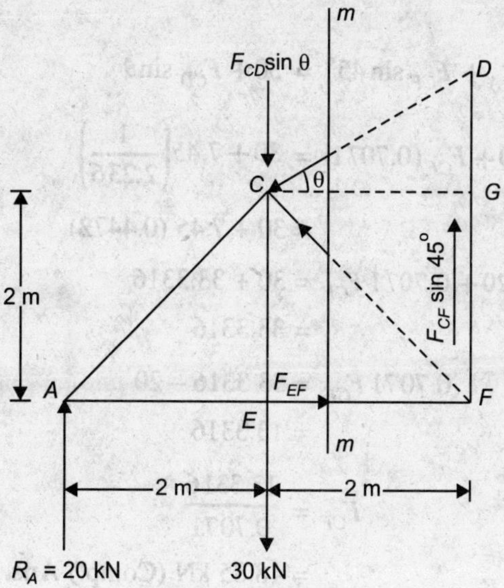

Fig. 14.15

For $\Sigma M_C = 0$

$$2R_A = F_{EF}(CE)$$

or $$2 \times 20 = 2F_{EF}$$

$\therefore$ $$F_{EF} = \frac{40}{2} = 20 \text{ kN (Tension) } \textbf{Ans.}$$

For $\Sigma M_F = 0$

$$4R_A - 30 \times 2 - F_{CD}\cos\theta(3) = 0$$

or $$4 \times 20 - 30 \times 2 - 3F_{CD}\cos\theta = 0$$

or $$80 - 60 - 3F_{CD}(0.894) = 0$$

or $$80 - 60 = 2.682F_{CD}$$

or $$F_{CD} = \frac{20}{2.682} = 7.45 \text{ kN (Comp.)}$$

$\therefore$ $$F_{CD} = 7.45 \text{ kN (Comp.) } \textbf{Ans.}$$

In right angle ΔCGD:

$$\cos\theta = \frac{\text{Base}}{\text{Diag.}} = \frac{CG}{CD}$$

$$= \frac{2}{2.236} = 0.894$$

$$(CD)^2 = (2)^2 + (1)^2$$

$\therefore$ $$CD = 2.236 \text{ m}$$

For $\Sigma V = 0$

$$R_A + F_{CF} \sin 45^\circ = 30 + F_{CD} \sin\theta$$

or
$$20 + F_{CF}(0.7071) = 30 + 7.45\left(\frac{1}{2.236}\right)$$
$$= 30 + 7.45\ (0.4472)$$

or
$$20 + 0.7071\ F_{CF} = 30 + 33.3316$$
$$= 33.3316$$

or
$$0.7071\ F_{CF} = 33.3316 - 20$$
$$= 13.3316$$

$\therefore$
$$F_{CF} = \frac{13.3316}{0.7071}$$
$$= 18.85 \text{ kN (Comp.)} \textbf{ Ans.}$$

EXAMPLE 14.11. Neglecting friction and inertia of pulleys, find the acceleration of the block Q if the mass of block P equals mass of block Q (Fig. 14.16).

SOLUTION : It is evident from the Fig. 14.16 given arrangement that when mass Q moves a unit distance downwards the mass P travels half the distance upwards. Acceleration is proportional to the distance travelled and therefore if a is acceleration of mass Q (Fig. 14.16), the mass P will have acceleration equal to $a/2$ (Fig. 14.16). P moves upwards and mass Q moves downwards.

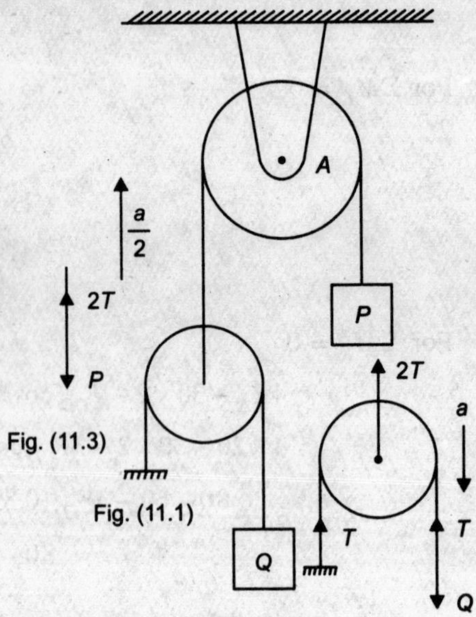

Fig. 14.16

With reference to free body diagrams (14.16, 14.17), the equations of motions are as follows :

$$m_q g - T = mg \,.\, a \qquad \text{...(i)}$$

$$2T - m_q g = m_p \cdot \frac{a}{2} \qquad \text{...(ii)}$$

Adding (i) and (ii) we get

$$T = a\left(m_q + \frac{1}{2} m_p\right)$$

$$= a\left(\frac{3}{2} m\right) \qquad \text{...(iii)}$$

Substituting the value of T in equation (i)

$$m_q \cdot g - a\left(\frac{3}{2} m\right) = m_q \cdot a \qquad (\because P = Q, \therefore m_q = m_p = m)$$

or $$g - \frac{3}{2}a = a$$

or $$g - \frac{3}{2}a - a = 0$$

or $$g - \frac{5}{2}a = 0$$

$\therefore$ $$a = \frac{2g}{5} = 3.924\ m/\sec^2 \textbf{ Ans.}$$

EXAMPLE 14.12. In a system of connected bodies (Fig. 14.17) the pulleys are frictionless and of negligible weight. Determine the value of weight A required to give $0.6g$ acceleration to weight B

(i) In downward, and

(ii) In upward, directions

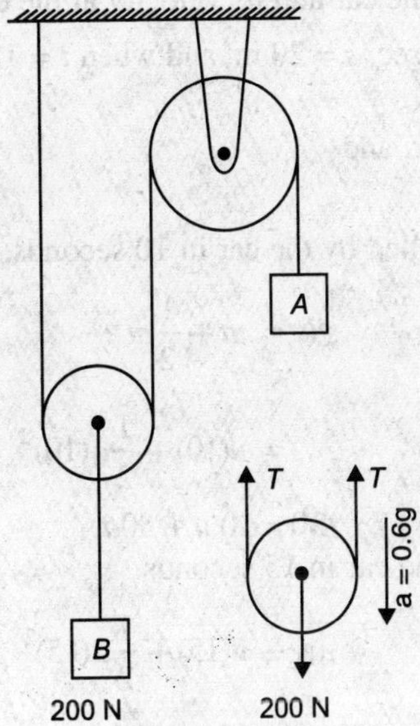

Fig. 14.17

SOLUTION : Considering downward motion of weight B (Free body diagram Fig. 14.17)

$$200 - 2T = 200\ (0.6) \quad ...(i)$$

$$T - m_a g = m_a\ (2 \times 0.6g) \quad ...(ii)$$

or $$2T - 2W_a = 2\ (1.2\ W_a) \quad ...(iii)$$

$$200 - 2W_a = 200\ (0.6) + 2.4\ W_a \quad \text{Adding (i) and (iii)}$$

or $$200 - 120 = 2.4\ W_a + 2W_a$$

$$= 4.4W_a$$

$\therefore$ $$W_a = \frac{8}{4.4} = 18.18 \text{ N } \textbf{Ans.}$$

(ii) Upward motion of block B : The equations of motion are :

$$2T - 200 = \frac{200}{g}(0.6g) \quad \text{...(i)}$$

$$m_a g - T = m_a(1.2g) \quad \text{...(ii)}$$

$$2m_a g - 2T = 2.4\, m_a \cdot g \quad \text{...(iii)}$$

$$-200 + 2m_a g = 120 + 2.4\, m_a g \quad \text{Adding (i) and (ii)}$$

or
$$2W_a - 2.4W_a = 120 + 200$$

or
$$-0.4\, W_a = 320$$

$\therefore$
$$W_a = -\frac{320}{0.4}$$

$$= -800 \text{ N (not possible)} \textbf{ Ans.}$$

EXAMPLE 14.13. A motorist takes 10 seconds to cover a distance of 20 m and 15 seconds for 40 m. Find the uniform acceleration of the car and its velocity at the end of 15 seconds.

SOLUTION : Given : When t = 10 sec, s = 20 m, and when t = 15 sec, s = 40 m

UNIFORM ACCELERATION

Let, u = Initial velocity of the car, and

a = Uniform acceleration

We know, that the distance travelled by the car in 10 seconds,

$$20 = ut + \frac{1}{2}at^2$$

$$= u(10) + \frac{1}{2}a(10)^2 = 10u + 50a$$

$\therefore$
$$20 = 10\,u + 50a \quad \text{...(i)}$$

Similarly distance travelled by the car in 15 seconds.

$$40 = u(15) + \frac{1}{2}a(15)^2$$

$$= 15u + 112.5a$$

$\therefore$
$$30u + 225a = 80 \quad \text{...(ii)}$$

Multiplying equation (i) by 3, we get,

$$60 = 30u + 150a \quad \text{...(iii)}$$

Substracting equation (iii) from (ii)

$$75a = 20$$

$\therefore$
$$a = \frac{20}{75} = 0.267 \text{ m/sec}^2 \textbf{ Ans.}$$

VELOCITY AT THE END OF 15 SECONDS.

Substituting the value of a in equation (ii), we get

$$80 = 30u + 225\,(0.267)$$

$$= 30u + 60.075$$

or $$80 - 60.075 = 30\,u$$

$\therefore$ $$u = \frac{19.925}{30} = 0.664 \text{ m/sec}$$

Hence velocity of the car after 15 seconds,

$$v = u + at$$
$$= 0.664 + 0.267\,(15)$$
$$= 4.672 \text{ m/sec } \textbf{Ans.}$$

EXAMPLE 14.14. A stone is dropped into a well and the sound of splash is heard after 4 seconds. Assuming the velocity of sound to be 350 m/sec, find the depth of the well.

SOLUTION : First of all, consider the downward motion of the stone. Here, $u = 0$

Let,

t = Time taken by the stone to reach the bottom of the well.

We know that the depth of the well.

$$s = ut + \frac{1}{2}gt^2 = 0(t) + \frac{1}{2} \times 9.8(t)^2 = 4.9t^2 \qquad \text{...(i)}$$

and time taken by the sound to reach the top

$$= \text{(Depth of the well)/Speed}$$

$$= \frac{s}{350} = \frac{4.9t^2}{350} \qquad \text{...(ii)}$$

Since the total time taken (i.e. stone to reach the bottom of the well and the sound to reach the top of the well) is 4 seconds. Therefore,

$$t + \frac{4.9t^2}{350} = 4$$

or $$4.9t^2 + 350 = 1400$$

or $$4.9t^2 + 350t - 1400 = 0$$

or $$t = \frac{350 \pm \sqrt{(350)^2 - 4(4.9)(-1400)}}{2 \times 4.9}$$

$\therefore$ $$t = 3.798 \text{ secs}$$

If

$$ax^2 + bx + c = 0,$$

then $$x = \frac{-b \pm \sqrt{b^2 \pm 4ac}}{2a}$$

Now substituting the value of t in equation (i), i.e.

$$s = 4.9(t^2)$$
$$= 4.9\,(3.798)^2 = 70.70\ m\ \textbf{Ans.}$$

EXAMPLE 14.15. Two cylinders, A of the weight 4000 N and B of weight 2000 N rest on a smooth inclines as shown in Fig. 14.18. They are connected by a bar of negligible weight hinged to each cylinder at its geometric centre by smooth pins. Find the force P to be applied as shown in figure such that it will hold the system in the given position.

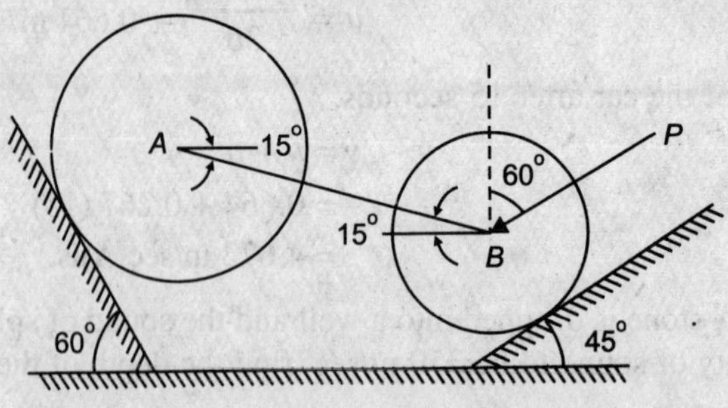

Fig. 14.18

SOLUTION : Fig. 14.19, and 14.20 show the free body diagram of the two cylinders. Applying Lami's theorem to the system of forces on cylinder A, we get

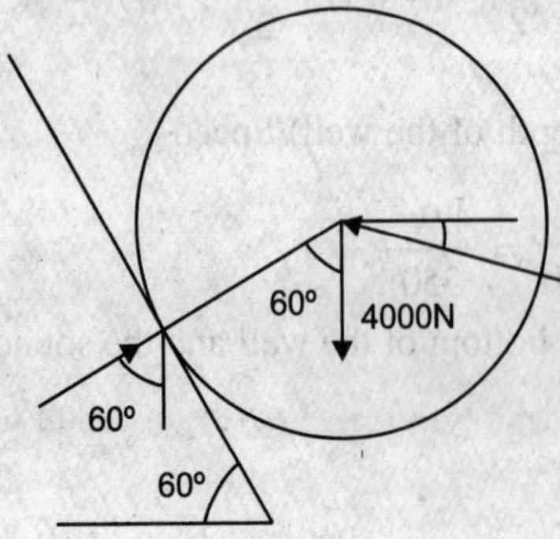

Fig. 14.19

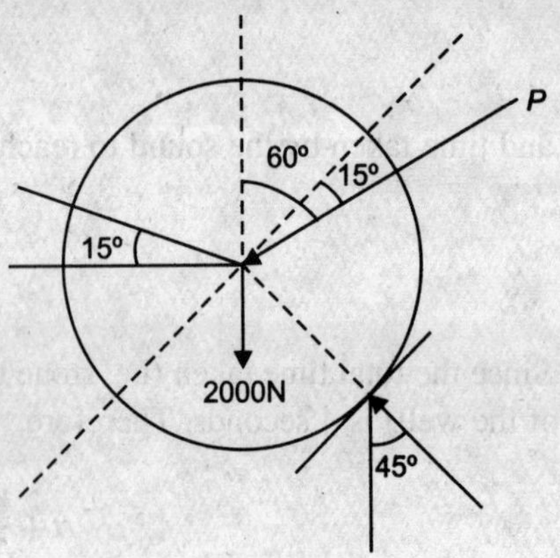

Fig. 14.20

$$\frac{C}{\sin 60^0} = \frac{4000}{\sin(60+90-15)} = \frac{4000}{\sin 135^0}$$

or
$$\frac{C}{0.866} = \frac{4000}{0.7071}$$

$\therefore$
$$C = 4898.98 \text{ N}$$

CONSIDERING CYLINDER – B : Summation of the forces parallel to the inclined plane (45° to horizontal) = 0, gives,

$$P \cos 15° + 2000 \cos 45° - C \cos 60° = 0$$

$\therefore$
$$P = \frac{4898.98 \cos 60^0 - 2000 \cos 45^0}{\cos 15^0}$$

$\therefore$
$$P = 1071.8\text{N} \textbf{ Ans.}$$

EXAMPLE 14.16. Direct central impact occurs between a 300N body moving to the right with a velocity of 6 m/sec and 150 N body moving to the left with a velocity of 10 m/sec. Find the velocity of each body after impact if the coefficient of restitution is 0.8.

SOLUTION : Referring Fig. 14.21. Initial velocity of 300 N body,

$$\mu_1 = 6 \text{ m/sec}$$

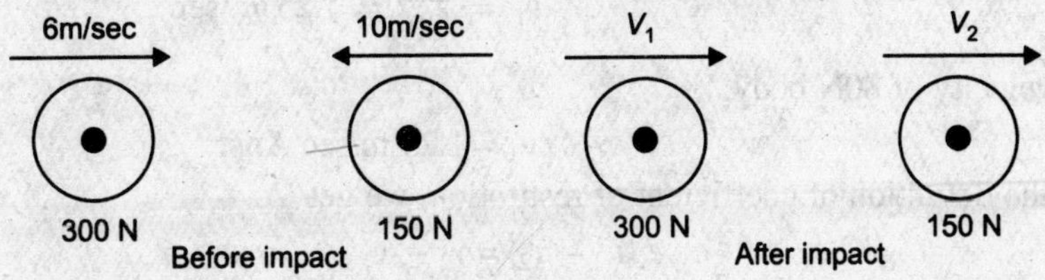

Fig. 14.21

Initial (before impact) velocity of 150 *N* body, $u_2 = 10$ m/sec

Let final (after Impact) velocity of :

(i) 300 N body = v_1 m/sec, and

(ii) 150 N body = v_2 m/sec

Now from the principle of conservation of momentum,

$$\because \quad W_1u_1 + W_2u_2 = W_1v_1 + W_2v_2$$

$$\therefore \quad 300 \times 6 + 150\,(-10) = 300\, v_1 + 150\, v_2$$

or $$1800 - 1500 = 300\, v_1 + 150\, v_2 = 300$$

$$\therefore \quad 2v_1 + v_2 = 2 \qquad \text{...(i)}$$

From the definition of coefficient of restitution, we have $e\,(u_1 - u_2) = v_2 - v_1$

$$\therefore \quad 0.8\,(6 + 10) = v_2 - v_1$$

$$\therefore \quad v_2 - v_1 = 0.8\,(16)$$

$$= 12.8 \qquad \text{...(ii)}$$

From (i) and (ii), we get,

$$3v_1 = -10.8$$

$$\therefore \quad v_1 = -3.6 \text{ m/sec } \textbf{Ans.}$$

But $$v_2 = 12.8 + v$$

$$= 12.8 + (-3.6)$$

$$= 9.2 \text{ m/sec } \textbf{Ans.}$$

EXAMPLE 14.17. An 80N body moving to the right at a speed of 3 m/sec strikes a 10 N body that is moving to the left at a speed of 10 m/sec. The final velocity of 10 N body is 4 m/sec to the right. Calculate the coefficient of restitution and the final velocity of the 80 N body.

SOLUTION : Given : $W_1 = 80$N, $W_2 = 10$ N

$u_1 = 3$ m/sec, $u_2 = -10$ m/sec, $v_1 = ?$, $v_2 = 4$ m/sec

Applying the principles of conservation of momentum to the colliding bodies, we get

$$\frac{W_1}{g}u_1 + \frac{W_2u_2}{g} = \frac{W_1v_1}{g} + \frac{W_2v_2}{g}$$

or $$W_1u_1 + W_2u_2 = W_1u_1 + W_2u_2$$

$\therefore$ $$80 \times 3 + 10\,(-10) = 80\ v_1 + 10 \times 4$$

or $$240 - 100 = 80v_1 + 40$$

or $$100 = 80\ v_1$$

$\therefore$ $$v_1 = \frac{100}{80} = 1.25\,m/\text{sec}$$

Final velocity of 80N body,

$$v_1 = 1.25 \text{ m/sec } \textbf{Ans.}$$

From the definition of coefficient of restitution, we get

$$e\,(u_1 - u_2) = v_2 - v_1$$

or $$e\,(3 + 10) = 4 - 1.25$$

$$= 2.75$$

$\therefore$ $$e = \frac{2.75}{13} = 0.212 \textbf{ Ans.}$$

EXAMPLE 14.18. A ball $M_1$of mass 1kg traverses a frictionless tube falling through a height of 1.5 m. It then strikes a ball (M_2 of mass 2 kg hanging from a cord 1.5 m long. Determine the height to which this ball M_2 will rise assuming the impact to be perfect elastic.

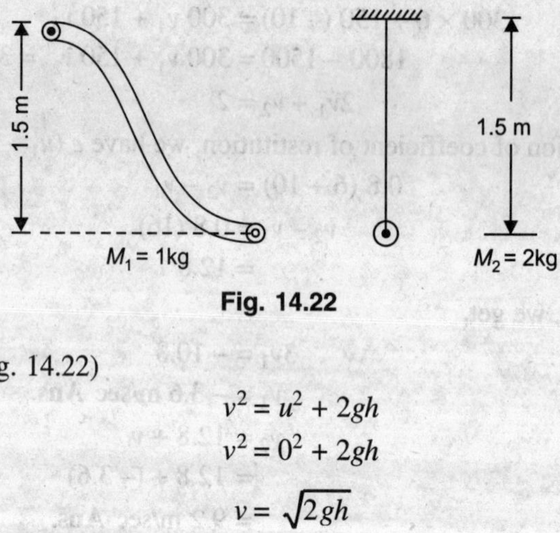

Fig. 14.22

SOLUTION : (Refer Fig. 14.22)

$\because$ $$v^2 = u^2 + 2gh$$

or $$v^2 = 0^2 + 2gh$$

$\therefore$ $$v = \sqrt{2gh} \qquad \text{(when } u = 0)$$

$\therefore$ Velocity of 1 kg mass ball falling through 1.5 m height,

$$u_1 = \sqrt{2gh}$$

$$= \sqrt{2 \times 9.81 \times 1.5}$$

$$= \sqrt{29.43}$$

$$= 5.4249 \text{ m/s}$$

Velocity of 2 kg mass ball before impact, $u_2 = 0$

Let the velocities of 1 kg and 2 kg balls after impact be v_1 and v_2 respectively.

By the principle of momentum,

$$m_1u_1 + m_2u_2 = m_1v_1 + m_2v_2$$

or $$1(5.4249) + 2(0) = 1\,(v_1) + 2\,(v_2)$$

$\therefore$ $$v_1 + 2v_2 = 5.4249 \qquad ...(i)$$

From the principle of coefficient of restitution, we have

$$e\,(u_1 - u_2) = v_2 - v_1$$

But $e = 1$ (As the impact is perfectly elastic)

$\therefore$ $$u_1 - u_2 = v_2 - v_1$$

i.e.. $$v_2 - v_1 = u_1 - u_2$$

$$= 5.4249 \qquad ...(ii)$$

From equations, (i) and (ii), we have

$$v_1 + 2v_2 = 5.4249 \qquad ...(i)$$

$$v_2 - v_1 = 5.4249 \qquad ...(ii)$$

$$3v_2 = 10.8498$$

$\therefore$ $$v_2 = \frac{10.8498}{3}$$

$$= 3.617 \text{ } m/\text{sec}$$

Let h be the height to which hanging ball will rise after impact. Applying work energy equation.

Change in kinetic energy = work done

$$0 - \frac{1}{2} \times 2v_2^2 = -2(9.81)\,h$$

or $$-\frac{1}{2}(2)\,(3.6166)^2 = -19.62\,h$$

or $$-13.07979 = -19.62\,h$$

$\therefore$ $$h = 0.666 \text{ m } \textbf{Ans.}$$

EXAMPLE 14.19. The masses of two balls are in ratio of 2 : 1 and their respective velocities are in the ratio of 1 : 2, but in the opposite direction before impact. If the coefficient of restitution be 5/6, prove that after the impact, each ball will move back with 5/6th of its original velocity.

SOLUTION : Given : $m_1 = 2M$, $m_2 = M$, $u_1 = 1U$, $u_2 = -2U$, $e = 5/6$

Let,

v_1 = Final velocity of the first ball, and

v_2 = Final velocity of the second ball

We know that,

$$m_1u_1 + m_2u_2 = m_1v_1 + m_2v_2$$

$\therefore$ $$2M(U) + M\,(-2U) = 2M(v_1) + M(v_2)$$

or $$0 = 2Mv_1 + Mv_2$$

$\therefore$ $$v_2 = -2v_1 \qquad ...(i)$$

We know that,

$$v_2 - v_1 = e\,(u_1 - u_2)$$

Hence, $$v_2 - v_1 = \frac{5}{6}[U - (-2U)] = \frac{5}{2}U \qquad \text{...(ii)}$$

Substituting the value of v_2 from equations (i)

$$-2v_1 - v_1 = \frac{5}{2}U$$

or $$-3v_1 = \frac{5}{2}U$$

$\therefore$ $$v_1 = -\frac{5}{6}U$$

Minus sign indicates that the direction of v_1 is opposite to that of U. Hence the first ball will move back with 5/6th of its original velocity **Ans.**

Now substituting the value of v_1 in equation (i)

$$v_2 = -2v_1 = -2\left(-\frac{5}{6}U\right) = +\frac{5}{6}(2U)$$

Plus sign indicates that the direction of v_1 is opposite to that of U. Hence the second ball will also move back with 5/6th of its original velocity. **Ans.**

EXAMPLE 14.20. A sphere of a mass 2 kg is released from rest and strikes a block of mass 2.5 kg resting on a horizontal surface. How far the block will move after the impact? Assume $e = 0.75$ and coefficient of friction between the block and the floor is 0.25 (Fig. 14.23).

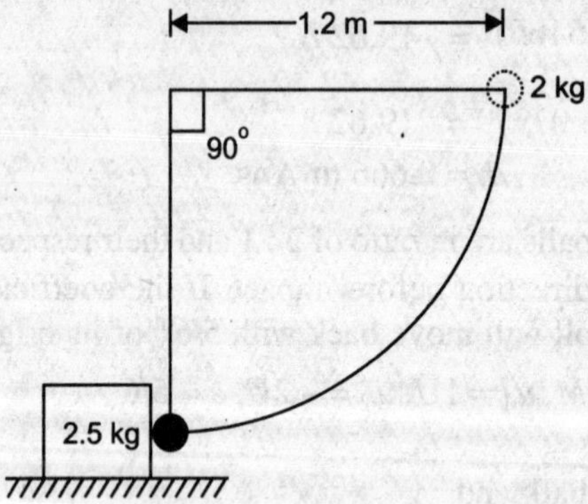

Fig. 14.23

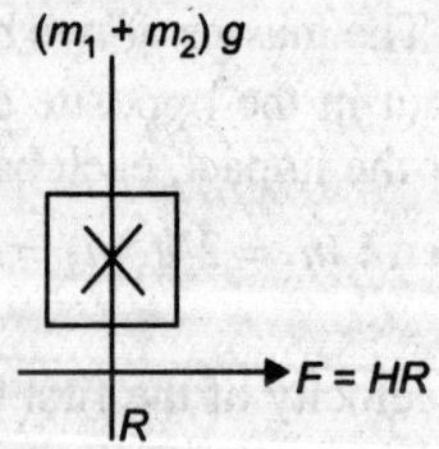

Fig. 14.24

SOLUTION : Given : $m_1 = 2$ kg, $m_2 = 2.5$ kg, $e = 0.75$, $u = -.25$, $h = 1.2$ m, $s = ?$

Velocity of 2 kg mass sphere falling through 1.2 m height,

$$u_1 = \sqrt{2gh} = \sqrt{2 \times 9.81 \times 1.2}$$

$$= 4.8522\, m/\text{sec} \qquad \text{...(i)}$$

Velocity of 2.5 kg mass block before impact, $u_2 = 0$

Let the velocities of 2 kg and 2.5 kg masses after impact be v_1 and v_2 respectively.

By the principle of momentum,

$$m_1u_1 + m_2u_2 = m_1v_1 + m_2v_2$$

$\therefore$ $$2(4.8522) + 2.5(0) = 2(v_1) + 2.5\,(v_2)$$

or $$9.70443 = 2v_1 + 2.5v_2 \quad \text{...(ii)}$$

From the principle of coefficient of restitution, we have,

$$e\,(u_1 - u_2) = v_2 - v_1$$

or $$0.75\,(u_1 - u_2) = v_2 - v_1$$

or $$1.50\,(u_1 - u_2) = 2v_2 - 2v_1$$

or $$1.50\,(4.8522) = 2v_2 - 2v_1$$

$\therefore$ $$7.2783 = 2v_2 - 2v_1 \quad \text{...(ii)}$$

$$9.7044 = 2v_1 + 2.5v_2 \quad \text{...(i)}$$

Adding (i) and (ii), we have $$16.9827 = 4.5v_2$$

$\therefore$ $$v_2 = \frac{16.9827}{4.5} = 3.774\ m/\text{sec}$$

$\because$ Normal reaction,

$$R = (m_1 + m_2)g \quad \text{...(Fig. 19.2)}$$

$\therefore$ Force of friction,

$$F = \mu R = \mu(m_1 + m_2)g$$

$$= 0.25\,(4.5)\,9.81 = 11.036\text{N}$$

Now work done to overcome the frictional force =

Kinetic energy lost by the block with sphere

$$F.S. = \frac{1}{2}(m_1 + m_2)v_2^2$$

or $$11.036 \times s = \frac{1}{2}(2 + 2.5)\,(3.774)^2$$

or $$11.036(s) = 32.047$$

$\therefore$ $$S = 2.90 \text{ m } \textbf{Ans.}$$

EXAMPLE 14.21 (a). Define the terms (i) Toughness, (ii) Brittleness, and (iii) Fatigue.

(b) A flywheel, which accelerates at a uniform velocity is observed to have made 100 revolutions to increase its velocity from 120 r.p.m. to 160 r.p.m. If the wheel originally started from rest, determined :

(i) The value of acceleration,

(ii) Time taken to increase the velocity from 120 r.p.m. to 160 r.p.m, and

(iii) Revolutions made in reaching the velocity of 160 r.p.m. starting from rest.

SOLUTION : θ = 100 revolutions = 200π radians

$$\omega_0 = 120 \text{ r.p.m.}$$

$$= \left(\frac{120 \times 2\pi}{60}\right) = 4\pi \; rad/sec$$

$$\omega = 160 \text{ r.p.m}$$

$$= \left(\frac{160 \times 2\pi}{60}\right) = 16.755 \; rad/sec$$

Using the kinematic relation, $\omega^2 = \omega^2 + 2\alpha\theta$, we get

$$(16.755)^2 = (4\pi)^2 + 2\alpha\,(200\pi)$$

$$\therefore \quad \alpha = 0.0977 \text{ rad/sec}^2 \textbf{ Ans.}$$

From the kinematic relation, $\omega = \omega_0 + \alpha t$, we get,

$$16.755 = 4\pi + 0.0977t$$

$$\therefore \quad t = 42.86 \text{ sec. } \textbf{Ans.}$$

Let θ' be the total angular displacement in reaching the velocity of 160 r.p.m., then

$$(16.755)^2 = (0)^2 + 2\,(0.0977)\theta'$$

or

$$\theta' = 1436.1 \text{ rad}$$

$$\therefore \quad \theta' = \frac{1436.1}{2\pi} = 228.57 \text{ revolutions } \textbf{Ans.}$$

EXAMPLE 14.22. A train starting from rest is uniformly acclerated. The acceleration at any instant is $\frac{10}{v+1} m/\sec^2$, where, v is the velocity of the train in m/sec at the instant. Find the distance, in which the train will attain a velocity of 36 km. p.h.

SOLUTION : Given : $a = \frac{10}{v+1}$

Rewriting the given equation,

$$v \cdot \frac{dv}{ds} = \frac{10}{v+1} \qquad \left(\because a = v \cdot \frac{dv}{ds}\right)$$

$$\therefore \quad v\,(v+1)\,dv = 10ds \qquad \text{...(i)}$$

or

$$(v^2 + v)\,dv = 10ds$$

Integrating both sides of equation (i)

$$\frac{v^3}{3} + \frac{v^2}{2} = 10s + C_1 \qquad \text{...(ii)}$$

Where C_1 is the first constant of integration

Substituting the values of $s = 0$ and $v = 0$ in equation (ii)

$C_1 = 0$. Now substituting the value of $C_1 = 0$ in equation (ii)

$$\frac{v^3}{3} + \frac{v^2}{2} = 10s$$

$$\therefore \quad 2v^3 + 3v^2 = 60\,s \qquad \text{...(iii)}$$

Now for the distance travelled by the train,

Substituting $v = 36$ km. p.h. = 10 m/sec in equation (ii)

$$2(10)^3 + 3(10)^2 = 60s$$

or
$$2000 + 300 = 60s$$

$\therefore$
$$s = 38.33 \text{ m } \textbf{Ans.}$$

EXAMPLE 14.23. A screw jack has a square threads of mean diameter 10 cm and a pitch of 1.25 cm. Determine the force that must be applied to the end of 50 cm lever

(i) To, raise, and

(ii) To lower the weight of 50 kN.

Find the efficiency of the jack. Is it self tocking? Assume, $\mu = 0.20$.

SOLUTION – Given : Pitch, $p = 1.25$ cm, $d = 10$ cm, $r = 5$ cm

Length of lever, $l = 50$ cm, $W = 50$ KN, $\mu = 0.2$

$\because$ Helix Angle,
$$\tan\theta = \frac{p}{2\pi r} = \frac{1.25}{2\pi(5)} = 0.039$$

$\therefore$
$$\theta = \tan^{-1}(0.039)$$
$$= 2.28° \qquad \text{...(i)}$$

Angle of friction, $\phi = \tan^{-1}\mu = \tan^{-1}(0.2) = 11.31°$

(i) TO RAISE THE LOAD

Effort required, $P_1 = W\tan(\theta + \phi)$

Since P_1 is related to the force F_1 applied to the handle by the relation $F_1 l = P_1 r$

i.e.,
$$F_1 = P_1\frac{r}{l}$$

$\therefore$
$$F_1 = \frac{W\tan(\theta+\phi)\,r}{l}$$

Hence,
$$F_1 = \frac{50{,}000\tan(2.28°+11.31°)\,0.05}{0.05}$$
$$= 1205N = 1.205 \text{ kN } \textbf{Ans.}$$

(ii) TO LOWER THE LOAD

$$F_2 = \frac{W\tan(\theta-\phi)\,r}{l}$$
$$= \frac{50{,}000\tan(2.28°-11.31°)\,0.05}{0.05}$$
$$= -794.5N = -0.794 \text{ kN } \textbf{Ans.}$$

(Force required in opposite sense)

Efficiency of the jack,

$$\eta = \frac{\tan\theta}{\tan(\theta+\phi)}$$

$$\eta = \frac{\tan 2.28^\circ}{\tan(2.28^\circ + 11.31^\circ)}$$

$$= \frac{0.0398}{0.241} = 0.1646$$

$$= 16.46\% \text{ Ans.}$$

As $\theta = 2.28°$, $\phi = 11.31°$, so $\phi > \theta$ is satisfying the condition or a self lucking machine.

The efficiency of the jack is 16.46% which is less than 50% verifying further that it is self locking machine **Ans.**

EXAMPLE 14.24. The end of a vertical shaft of 30 cm diameter and weighing 20 kN rests on a flat surface. If coefficient of friction between the surfaces is 0.12, find the frictional torque assuming constant pressure.

SOLUTION : We know that in case of thrust bearing, the frictional torque (T) i.e. moment required to overcome frictional resistance.

$$T = M = \frac{2}{3}\mu PR$$

$$\therefore \qquad M = \frac{2}{3}\frac{(20 \times 1000)(15)(0.120)}{100}$$

$$= 240 \; Nm \text{ Ans.}$$

EXAMPLE 14.25. In a reciprocating engine mechanism (Fig. 14.25) the length of crank OB and connecting rod AB are 30 cm and 1 m respectively. If the crank rotates at a constant angular velocity of 200 rev/min, determine

(i) Angular velocity of connecting rod, and

(ii) The velocity of piston when the Crank makes an angle of $\theta = 45°$ with the horizontal.

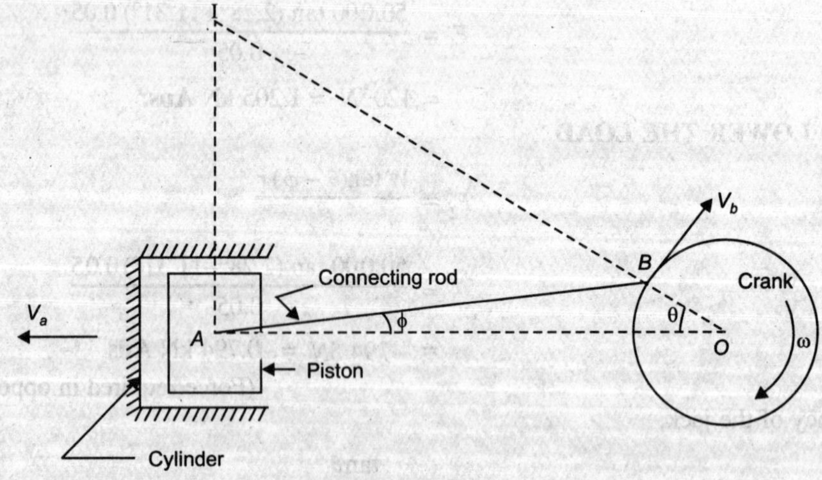

Fig. 14.25

SOLUTION : Angular velocity of the crank

$$= \frac{(2\pi N)}{60} = \frac{(2\pi \times 200)}{60}$$

$$= 20.93 \text{rad/sec.}$$

$$V_b = \omega r = 20.93 \times 0.3$$

$$= 6.279 \text{ m/sec.}$$

The point B moves in a circle whose centre is O, and the direction of V_a is perpendicular to OB. The velocity V_a of the piston, at any instant must be horizontal. The instantaneous centre I of the connecting rod AB is the point of intersection of perpendiculars to V_a and V_b through A and B respectively. Then angular velocity ω_{ab} of the connecting rod about I is,

$$\omega_{ab} = \frac{V_a}{I_A} = \frac{V_b}{I_B} = \frac{Wr}{I_B} \quad \text{...(i)}$$

Let ϕ be the angle between the connecting rod AB and the line AO. Then applying sine rule to ΔOAB.

$$\frac{OB}{\sin\phi} = \frac{AB}{\sin\theta}$$

$$\sin\phi = \frac{OB}{AB}\sin\theta$$

Hence,

$$\sin\phi = \frac{0.3}{1}\sin 45° = 0.2121$$

$\therefore$

$$\phi = 12.25° \quad \text{...(ii)}$$

The distance I_A and I_B are worked out from the relations :

$$I_A = l\cos\phi\tan\theta + r\sin\theta$$

$$= (1 \times \cos 12.25° \times \tan 45°) + 0.3 \sin 45°$$

$$= 0.9772 + 0.2121 = 1.1843 \text{ m}$$

amd

$$I_B = \frac{l\cos\phi}{\cos\theta} = 1 \times \frac{\cos 12.25}{\cos 45°}$$

$$= 1.382 \text{ m}$$

Then from expression (i)

Angular velocity of connecting rod,

$$\omega_{ab} = \frac{6.279}{1.382} = 4.543 \text{ rad/s } \textbf{Ans.}$$

Velocity of piston

$$V_a = \omega_{ab} \times I_A$$

$$= 4.543 \times 1.1843$$

$$= 5.38 \text{ m/sec } \textbf{Ans.}$$

EXAMPLE 14.26. A cylinder of diameter 3m rolls without slipping along a horizontal surface *PQ* as shown in Fig. 14.26. If its centre has a uniform velocity of 30 m/sec, determine the velocities of the points *B* and *D* lying on the rim of the cylinder.

SOLUTION : When the cylinder rolls without slipping, its point of contact with the horizontal surface at any instant has zero velocity. Thus the point *A* is instantaneously at rest and every other point on the cylinder has angular velocity about *A*. Hence *A* is instantaneous centre of the cylinder. Then,

$$V_C = \omega \times AC;$$

$$V_B = \omega \times AB;$$

$$V_d = \omega \times AD$$

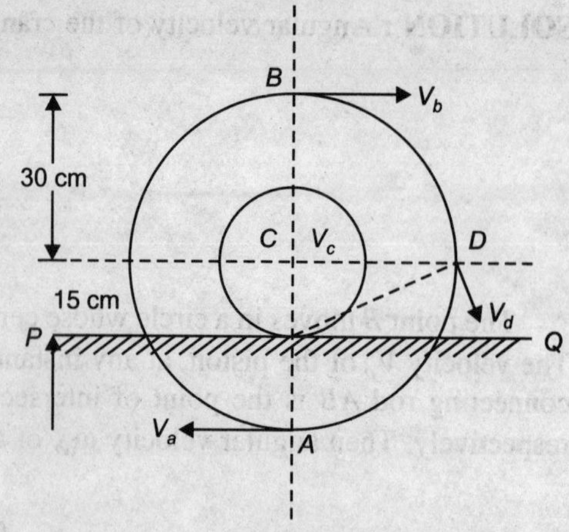

Fig. 14.26

Angular velocity of the cylinder,

$$\omega = \frac{V_C}{AC} = \frac{30}{3/2} = 20 \text{ rad/sec}$$

Distance

$$AD = \sqrt{(DC)^2 + (AC)^2}$$

$$= \sqrt{(1.5)^2 + (1.5)^2} = 1.121 \text{ m}$$

∴ Velocity of point B : $V_b = \omega\,(AB) = 20(3)$

$= 60$ m/sec **Ans.**

Velocity of point D : $V_d = \omega\,(AD) = 20\,(2.121)$

$= 42.42$ m/sec **Ans.**

EXAMPLE 14.27. A flywheel 0.5 m in diameter accelerates uniformly from rest to 360 r.p.m. in 12 seconds. Determine,

(i) The velocity, and

(ii) Acceleration of a point on the rim of the wheel 1 second after it has started from rest.

SOLUTION : $\omega_0 = 0, \quad \omega = \dfrac{2\pi N}{60} = \dfrac{2\pi(360)}{60} = 37.699$ rad/sec

From the kinematic relation, $\omega = \omega_0 + \alpha t$, we have,

Angular acceleration,

$$\alpha = \frac{\omega - \omega_0}{t} = \frac{37.699}{12}$$

$$= 3.14 \text{ rad/sec}^2$$

Angular velocity of the wheel 1 second after starting

$$\omega = \omega_0 + \alpha t$$

$$= 0 + 3.14\,(1) = 3.14 \text{ rad/sec}$$

The linear velocity and angular velocity are connected by the relation, $v = \omega r$.

Hence linear speed,

$$v = \omega r = 3.14 \times \frac{0.5}{2}$$

$$= 0.785 \text{ m/sec } \textbf{Ans.}$$

The linear velocity will be tangential to the rim

The components of acceleration are :

Tangenetial acceleration,

$$\alpha_t = \alpha r = 3.14 \times \frac{0.5}{2}$$

$$= 0.785 \text{ m/sec}^2 \textbf{ Ans.}$$

Normal acceleration,

$$\alpha_n = \omega^2 r = (3.14)^2 \times \frac{0.5}{2}$$

$$= 2.46 \text{ m/sec}^2$$

Magnitude of total acceleration,

$$\alpha = \sqrt{\alpha_t^2 + \alpha_n^2}$$

$$= \sqrt{(0.785)^2 + (2.46)^2}$$

$$= 2.5822 \text{ m/sec}^2$$

Let ϕ be the angle between the total acceleration vector and the radius, then

$$\phi = \tan^{-1}\left(\frac{\alpha_t}{\alpha_n}\right) = \tan^{-1}\left(\frac{0.785}{2.46}\right)$$

$$= 17.72° \textbf{ Ans.}$$

EXAMPLE 14.28. A cantilever truss is loaded and supported as shown in Fig. 14.27. Find the value of load P which would produce an axial force of magnitude 3 kN in the member AC.

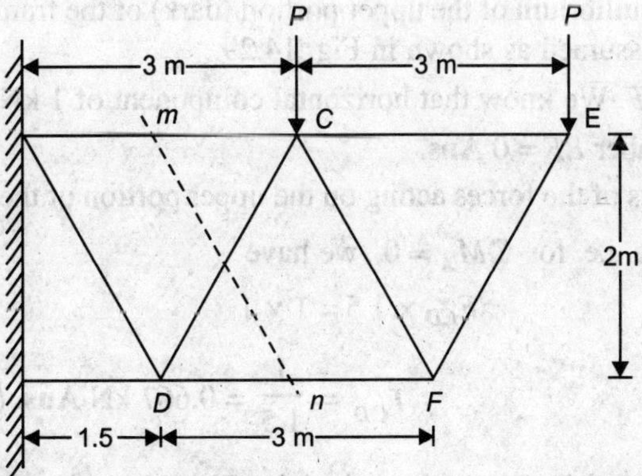

Fig. 14.27

SOLUTION : In this case we need not to determine the support reactions.

The force in the member AC can be determined using the method of sections.

Pass a section mn cutting the members AC, CD and DF.

Consider the equilibrium of the right hand portion of the truss.

Now taking moment about D i.e., for $\Sigma M_D = 0$,, we have,

$$P \times 1.5 + P \times 4.5 = F_{AC} \times 2$$

or $$6P = 2F_{AC}$$

$\therefore$ $$3P = F_{AC}$$

But as per condition give in the questions

$$F_{AC} = 3 \text{ kN}$$

$\therefore$ $$3P = 3 \text{ kN}$$

Hence $P = 1$ kN **Ans.**

EXAMPLE 14.29. A truss is loaded and supported as shown in Fig. 14.28. Find the axial forces in the members AB, EF, and CD.

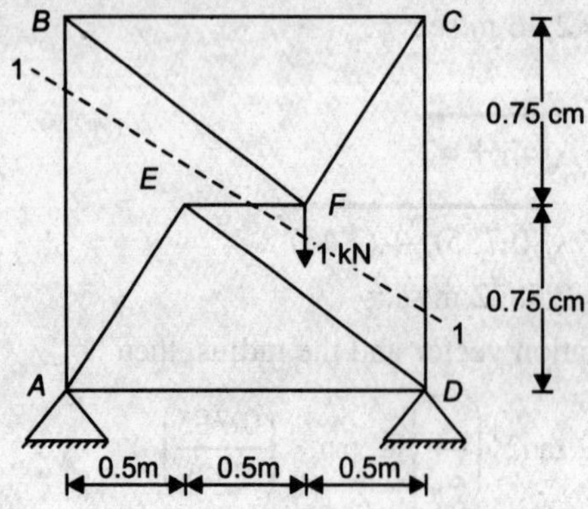

Fig. 14.28

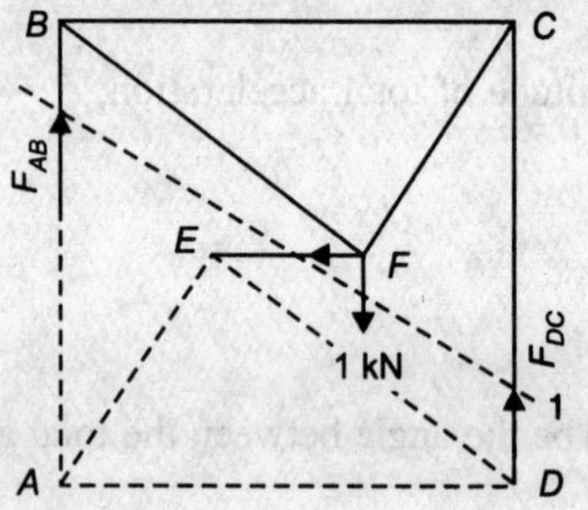

Fig. 14.29

SOLUTION : Pass a section 1 –1 cutting the truss through the members AB, EF, and CD as shown in Fig. 14.29.

Now consider the equilibrium of the upper portion (dark) of the frame. Let the directions of the forces F_{AB}, and F_{DC} be assumed as shown in Fig. 14.29.

Now consider joint F. We know that horizontal component of 1 kN load is zero.

Hence force in member $EF = 0$ **Ans.**

Now taking moments of the forces acting on the upper portion of the frame only about the joint A, and equating the same, i.e. for $\Sigma M_A = 0$, we have

$$F_{CD} \times 1.5 = 1 \times 1$$

$\therefore$ $$F_{CD} = \frac{1}{1.5} = 0.667 \text{ kN } \textbf{Ans.} \text{ (comp.)}$$

Now taking moments of the forces about the joint D and equating the same, i.e. for $\Sigma M_D = 0$, we have

$$F_{AB} \times 1.5 = 1 \times 0.5$$

$$\therefore \qquad F_{AB} = \frac{0.5}{1.5} = 0.333 \text{ kN } \textbf{Ans.} \text{ (Comp.)}$$

EXAMPLE 14.30. Find the moment of inertia of the cross-section of an iron beam (Fig. 14.30) with respect to centroidal axis.

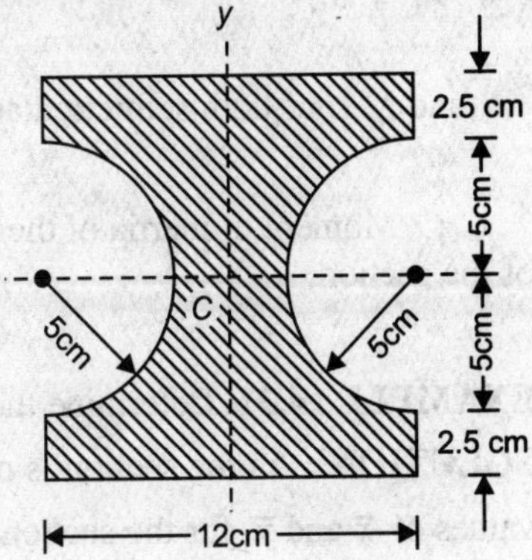

Fig. 14.30

SOLUTION : MOMENT OF INERTIA OF THE SECTION ABOUT HORIZONTAL AXIS PASSING THROUGH THE CENTROID OF THE SECTION

As the section is symmetrical about its horizontal and vertical axes, therefore, C.G. of the section will lie at the centre of the rectangle. It is clear that when the two semi-circles are placed together, it will form a circular hole with 5 cm radius or 10 cm daimeter. We know that moment of inertia of a rectangular section about its horizontal axis passing through its C.G.

$$= \frac{bd^3}{12} = \frac{12(15)^3}{12} = 3375 \text{ cm}^4,$$

and moment of inertia of the circular section about a horizontal axis passing through its C.G.

$$= \frac{\pi}{4}(r)^4 = \frac{\pi}{4}(5)^4 = 491 \text{ cm}^4$$

$\therefore$ Moment of inertia of the whole section about horizontal axis passing through the centroid of the section

$$I_{XX} = 3375 - 491 = 2884 \text{ cm}^4 \textbf{ Ans.}$$

MOMENT OF INERTIA OF THE SECTION ABOUT VERTICAL AXIS PASSING THROUGH THE CENTROID OF THE SECTION :

We know that M.I. of the rectangular section about the vertical axis passing through its C.G.

$$I_{G_1} = \frac{db^3}{12} = \frac{15(12)^3}{12} = 2160 \text{ cm}^4$$

and area of semi-circular section with 5 cm radius,

$$a = \frac{(\pi r^2)}{2} = \frac{\pi(5)^2}{2} = 39.27 \text{ cm}^2$$

We also know that moment of inertia of a semi-circular section about a vertical axis passing through its C.G.

$$I_{G_2} = 0.11r^4 = 0.11(5)^4 = 68.75 \text{ cm}^4$$

and distance between C.G. of the semi-circular section and its base

$$= \frac{4r}{3\pi} = \frac{4 \times 5}{3\pi} = 2.12 \text{ cm}$$

∴ Distance between C.G. of the semi-circular section and C.G. of the whole section,

$$h_2 = 6 - 2.12 = 3.88 \text{ cm}$$

∴ M.I. of one semi-circular section about C.G. of the whole section

$$I_{G_2} + a \cdot h_2^2 = 68.75 + [(39.27)(3.88)^2$$
$$= 659.9 \text{ cm}^4$$

and M.I. of both semicircular sections about C.G. of the whole section

$$= 2 \times 659.9 = 1319.8 \text{ cm}^4$$

∴ Moment of inertia of the whole section about the vertical axis passing through the centroid of the section,

$$I_{YY} = 2160 - 1319.8 = 840.2 \text{ cm}^4 \textbf{ Ans.}$$

EXAMPLE 14.31. Determine the co-ordinates of the centroid of a section as shown in Fig. 14.31

SOLUTION : As the section is not symmetrical about any axis, therefore we have to find out the values of $\bar{x}$ and $\bar{y}$ for the section. Split up the section into two rectangles (Fig. 14.31).

Let left face (*OY*) of the vertical section and bottom face of the horizontal section (*OX*) be the axis of reference.

(i) **RECTANGLE – I :**

$$a_1 = 10 \times 1.5 = 15 \text{ cm}^2,$$

$$x_1 = \frac{1.5}{2} = 0.75 \text{ cm}$$

$$y_1 = \frac{10}{2} = 5 \text{ cm}$$

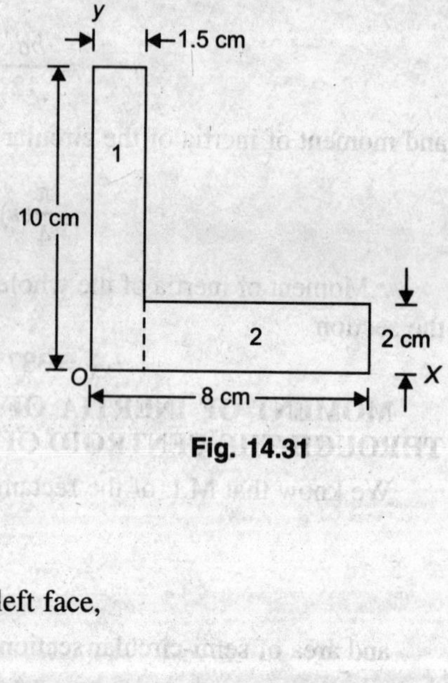

Fig. 14.31

(ii) **RECTANGLE – II :**

$$a_2 = 6.5 \times 2 = 13 \text{ cm}^2,$$

$$x_2 = 1.5 + \frac{6.5}{2} = 4.75 \text{ cm}$$

$$y_2 = \frac{2}{2} = 1 \text{ cm}$$

We know that distance between C.G. of the section and left face,

$$\bar{x} = \frac{a_1 x_1 + a_2 x_2}{a_1 + a_2}$$

$$= \frac{15(0.75) + 13(4.75)}{15 + 13} = 2.61 \text{ cm } \textbf{Ans.}$$

Similarly distance between C.G. of the section and bottom face,

$$\bar{y} = \frac{a_1 y_1 + a_2 y_2}{a_1 + a_2} = \frac{15(5) + 13(1)}{15 + 13} = 3.14 \text{ cm } \textbf{Ans.}$$

EXAMPLE 14.32. Find the centroid of a channel section as shown in Fig. 14.32

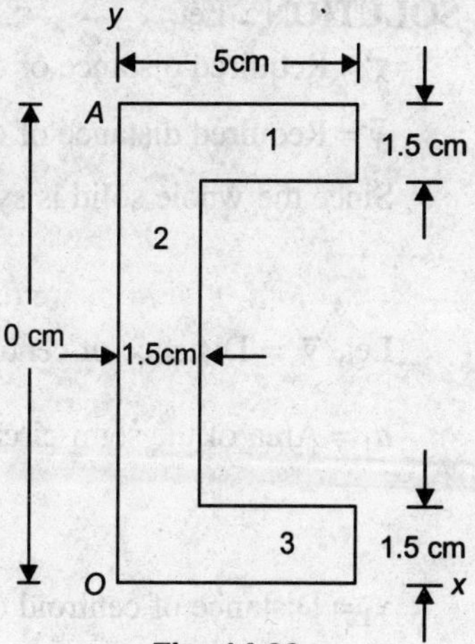

Fig. 14.32

SOLUTION : As the section is symmetrical about x-x axis, therefore the C.G. of the section will lie on this axis. Now split up the whole section into three parts (1), (2) and (3). Let OY be the axis of reference.

(i) RECTANGLE – I :

$$a_1 = 5 \times 1.5 = 7.50 \text{ cm}^2,$$

$$x_1 = \frac{5}{2} = 2.5 \text{ cm}$$

(ii) RECTANGLE – II :

$$a_2 = 7 \times 1.5 = 10.50 \text{ cm}^2$$

$$x_2 = \frac{1.5}{2} = 0.75 \text{ cm}$$

(iii) RECTANGLE – III :

$$a_3 = 5 \times 1.5 = 7.50 \text{ cm}^2,$$

$$x_3 = \frac{5}{2} = 2.5 \text{ cm}$$

We know that the ditance between C.G. of the section and face OA,

$$\bar{x} = \frac{a_1 x_1 + a_2 x_2 + a_3 x_3}{a_1 + a_2 + a_3}$$

$$= \frac{7.50(2.5) + 10.50(0.75) + 7.50(2.5)}{7.50 + 10.50 + (5 \times 1.5)}$$

$$= \frac{45.375}{25.50} = 1.78 \text{ cm } \textbf{Ans.}$$

$$\bar{y} = \frac{10}{2} = 5 \text{ cm } \textbf{Ans.}$$

EXAMPLE 14. 33. Find the co-ordinates of the centroid of a semicircular area as shown in Fig. 14.33

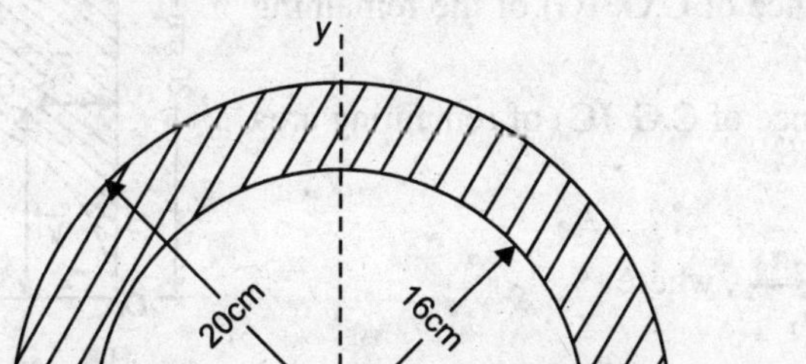

Fig. 14.33

SOLUTION : Let,

$\bar{x}$ = Required distance of centroid (G) from y-axis, and

$\bar{y}$ = Required distance of centroid (G) from x-axis

Since the whole solid is symmetrical about y-axis, its centroid (G) will lie on y-axis.

$\therefore \qquad \bar{x} = 0$ **Ans.**

Let, $\bar{y}$ = Distance of centroid from x-axis, then, $\bar{y} = \dfrac{a_1 y_1 - a_2 y_2}{a_1 - a_2}$, where

a_1 = Area of the semi-circle of 20 cm radius

$$= \frac{\pi}{2} r^2 = \frac{\pi (20)^2}{2} = 628.3185 \text{ cm}^2 \qquad \text{...(i)}$$

y_1 = Distance of centroid of outer semi-circle from x-axis

$$= \frac{4r}{3\pi} = \frac{4 \times 20}{3\pi} = \frac{80}{9.425} = 8.488 \text{ cm} \qquad \text{...(ii)}$$

a_2 = Area of the semi-circle of 16 cm radius

$$= \frac{\pi}{2} r^2 = \frac{\pi (16)^2}{2} = 402.124 \text{ cm}^2 \qquad \text{...(iii)}$$

y_2 = Distance of centroid of inner semi-circle from x-axis.

$$= \frac{4r}{3\pi} = \frac{4 \times 16}{3\pi} = \frac{64}{3\pi} = 6.790 \text{ cm} \qquad \text{...(iv)}$$

$$\therefore \qquad \bar{y} = \frac{a_1 y_1 - a_2 y_2}{a_1 - a_2}$$

$$= \frac{628.319(8.488) - 402.1241(6.790)}{628.319 - 402.124}$$

$$= \frac{5333.17 - 2730.42}{226.194} = \frac{2602.75}{226.195} = 11.50 \text{ cm } \textbf{Ans.}$$

EXAMPLE 14.34. Find the coordinates of the centroid of the area obtained after removing a semicircle of radius 10 cm. from a quadrant of a circle of radius 20 cm.

SOLUTION : Let,

$\bar{x}$ = Required distance of C.G. (G) of the remaining area from y-axis, and

$\bar{y}$ = Required distance of C.G. (G) of remaining area from the x-axis.

Now, $\bar{x} = \dfrac{a_1 x_1 - a_2 x_2}{a_1 - a_2}$, where

a_1 = Area of quadrant of the circle $OAB = \dfrac{\pi r^4}{4}$

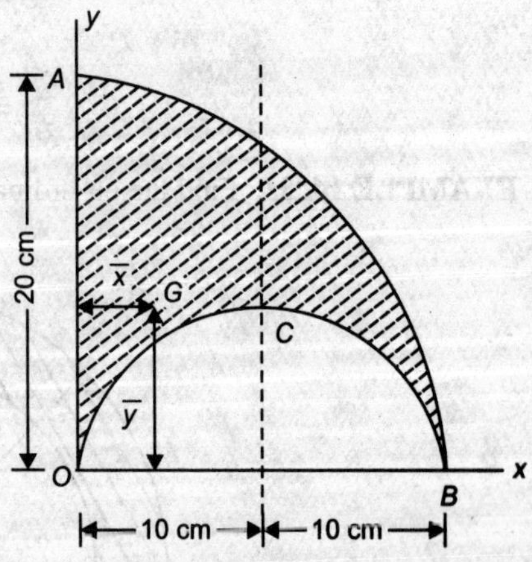

Fig. 14.34

$$= \frac{\pi(20)^2}{4} = \frac{400\pi}{4} = 100\pi = 314.159 \text{ cm}^2 \quad ...(i)$$

a_2 = Area of the cut out semi-circle $OCB = \dfrac{\pi r^4}{2}$

$$\frac{\pi(10)^2}{2} = \frac{100\pi}{2} = 50\pi = 157.0796 \text{ cm}^2 \quad ...(ii)$$

x_1 = Distance of C.G. of the quadrant OAB from y-axis

$$= \frac{4R}{3\pi} = \frac{4(20)}{3\pi}$$

$$= \frac{80}{3\pi} = \frac{80}{9.425} = 8.488 \text{ cm} \quad ...(iii)$$

x_2 = Distance of C.G. of the semi-circle OCB from y-axis

$$= r = 10 \text{ cm} \quad ...(iv)$$

$$\therefore \quad \bar{x} = \frac{a_1 x_1 - a_2 x_2}{a_1 - a_2}$$

$$= \frac{314.159(8.488) - 157.0796(10)}{314.159 - 157.0796} = 6.98 \text{ cm } \textbf{Ans.}$$

Now, $\bar{y} = \dfrac{a_1 y_1 - a_2 y_2}{a_1 - a_2}$, where

y_1 = Distance of C.G. of the quadrant OAB from x-axis

$$= \frac{4R}{3\pi} = \frac{4(20)}{3\pi}$$

$$= \frac{80}{3\pi} = 8.488 \ cm \quad ...(iv)$$

y_2 = Distance of C.G. of the semi-circle OCB from x-axis

$$= \frac{4R}{3\pi} = \frac{4(10)}{3\pi}$$

$$= \frac{40}{9.425} = 4.244 \text{ cm} \quad ...(v)$$

$$\therefore \quad \bar{y} = \frac{a_1 y_1 - a_2 y_2}{a_1 - a_2}$$

$$= \frac{314.159\,(8.488) - 157.0796(4.244)}{314.159 - 157.0796}$$

$= 12.73$ cm **Ans.**

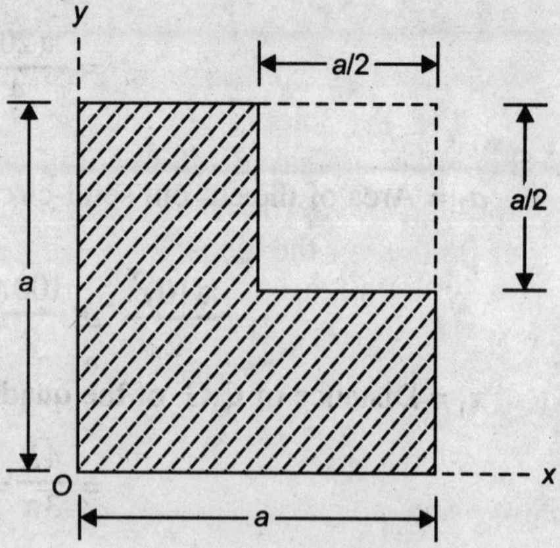

Fig. 14.35

EXAMPLE 14.35. Find the co-ordinates of the centroid of the area left after removing a square area from a square plate as shown in Fig. 14.35.

SOLUTION : Let,

$\bar{x}$ = Required distance of C.G. (G) of the remaining area from y-axis.

$\bar{y}$ = Required distance of C.G. (G) of the remaining area from x-axis.

a = Length of each side of original square

$a/2$ = Length of each side of cut out square

Now,

Area of original square,

$$a_1 = a \times a = a^2 \quad \text{...(i)}$$

Area of cut out square,

$$a_2 = \frac{a}{2} \times \frac{a}{2} = \frac{a^2}{4} \quad \text{...(ii)}$$

x_1 = Distance of C.G. of the area of original square from y-axis

$$= \frac{a}{2} \quad \text{...(iii)}$$

x_2 = Distance of C.G. of the cut out section from y-axis

$$= \frac{a}{2} + \frac{a}{4} = \frac{3a}{4} \quad \text{...(iv)}$$

$$\bar{x} = \frac{a_1 x_1 - a_2 x_2}{a_1 - a_2}$$

$$= \frac{a^2\left(\frac{a}{2}\right) - \frac{a^2}{4}\left(\frac{3a}{4}\right)}{a^2 - \frac{a^2}{4}} = \frac{\left(\frac{5a^3}{16}\right)}{\frac{3a^2}{4}} = \frac{5a}{12} \textbf{ Ans.}$$

Now, y_1 = Distance of C.G. of whole area from x-axis $= \frac{a}{2}$ ...(i)

y_2 = Distance of C.G. of cut out square from x-axis $= \frac{a}{2} + \frac{a}{4} = \frac{3a}{4}$ ...(ii)

$$\bar{y} = \frac{a_1 y_1 - a_2 y_2}{a_1 - a_2} = \frac{a^2\left(\frac{a}{2}\right) - \frac{a^2}{4}\left(\frac{3a}{4}\right)}{a^2 - \frac{a^2}{4}}$$

$$= \frac{(8a^3 - 3a^3)4}{16(3a^2)} = \frac{5a}{12} \textbf{ Ans.}$$

EXAMPLE 14.36. (a) Derive an expression for the frictional torque required to overcome friction in the case of a thrust bearing assuming the pressure to be uniform.

(b) Two blocks are connected by a horizontal link AB and rest on two planes as shown in Fig. 14.36. What is the smallest weight W_A of the block A for which the equilibrium can exist? Assume the coefficient of friction for the block A and the horizontal surface to be 0.4 and the angle of friction for the block B on inclined plane is $\phi = 20°$.

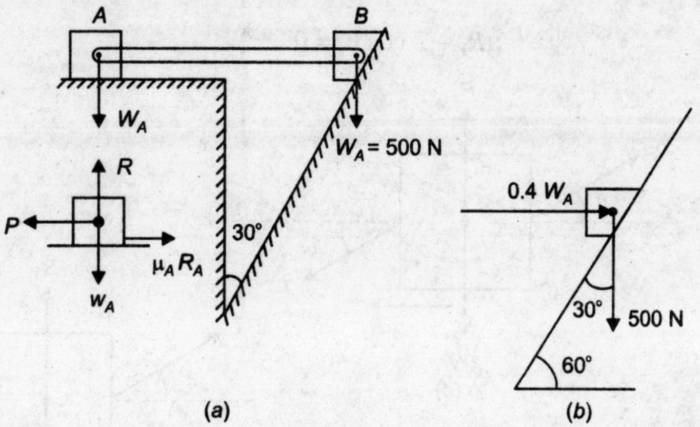

Fig. 14.36

SOLUTION : Given : $\mu_A = 0.4$, $W_B = 500$ N

Let W_A = Smallest weight of block A

Considering the equilibrium of block A

Let P be the force of friction of block A, which is acting horizontally on the block B.

$$\therefore \quad P = \mu_A R_A = 0.4\,(W_A) = 0.4 W_A \quad \text{...(i)}$$

This force ($P = .4W_A$) will be transmitted to block B through rod AB.

We also known that the smallest force, which will hold the system in equilibrium or will prevent the block B from sliding downwards.

$$\therefore \quad P = W_B \tan(\alpha - \phi) \qquad (\because \tan\phi = \mu_B \text{ and } P = \mu_B . R_B = \tan\phi . W_B)$$

$$\therefore \quad 0.4\ W_A = W_B \tan(60° - 20°)$$

$$\text{or} \quad 0.4 \times W_A = 500 \tan 40°$$

$$\text{or} \quad 0.4\ W_A = 500 \times 0.8391$$

$$\therefore \quad W_A = \frac{500 \times 0.8391}{0.4} = 1049\ N \textbf{ Ans.}$$

EXAMPLE 14.37. Two blocks of weight W_1 and W_2 are connected by a string and rest on a horizontal plane as shown in Fig. 14.37. Find the magnitude and direction of the least force P that should be applied to the upper block to induce sliding. The coefficient of friction for each block is to be taken as μ.

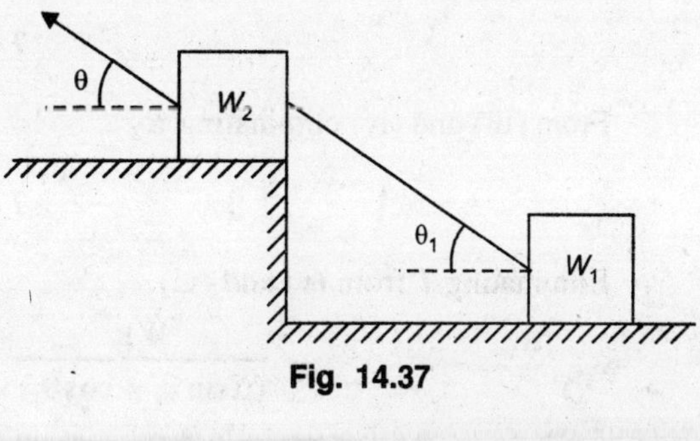

Fig. 14.37

SOLUTION : Let the force P makes an angle θ with the horizontal. Note that the angles θ_1 and θ are not known.

Free body diagram of each block is shown separately in Fig. 14.38. Let T be the tension in the string.

Writing the equations of equilibrium of block W_1 (Fig. b)

For $\Sigma H = 0$,

$$\mu R_1 - T\cos\theta_1 = 0 \qquad \text{...(i)}$$

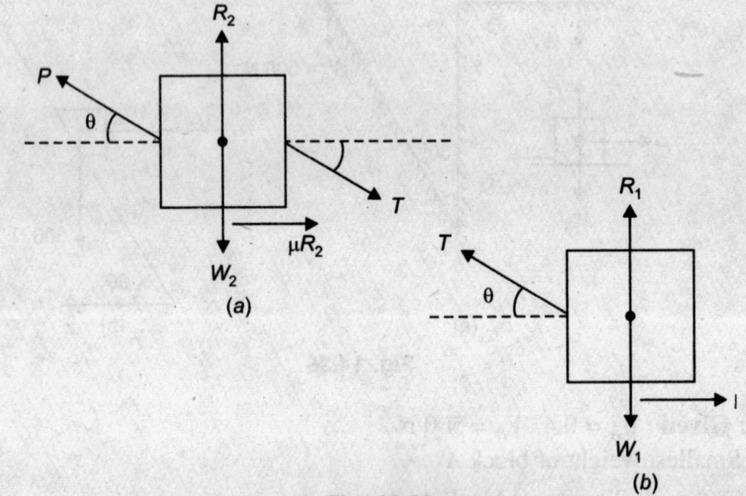

Fig. 14.38

For $\Sigma V = 0$,

$$T\sin\theta_1 + R_1 - W_1 = 0 \qquad \text{...(ii)}$$

Now writing the equations of equilibrium of block W_2

For $\Sigma H = 0$,

$$\mu R_2 + T\cos\theta_1 - P\cos\theta = 0 \qquad \text{...(iii)}$$

For $\Sigma V = 0$,

$$R_2 + P\sin\theta - T\sin\theta_1 = 0 \qquad \text{...(iv)}$$

There are four equations and six unknowns ($R_1, R_2, T, P, \theta_1, \theta$)

Let us eliminate T, R_1, R_2 and θ_1

From (i) and (ii) eliminating R_1

$$T = \frac{W_1\mu}{(\mu\sin\theta_1 + \cos\theta_1)} \qquad \text{...(v)}$$

From (iii) and (iv) eliminating R_2

$$T = \frac{P(\cos\theta + \mu\sin\theta) - \mu W_2}{(\mu\sin\theta_1 + \cos\theta_1)} \qquad \text{...(vi)}$$

Eliminating T from (v) and (vi)

$$\frac{W_1\mu}{(\mu\sin\theta_1 + \cos\theta_1)} = \frac{P(\cos\theta + \mu\sin\theta) - \mu W_2}{(\mu\sin\theta_1 + \cos\theta_1)}$$

$$\therefore \qquad P = \frac{\mu(W_1 + W_2)}{(\cos\theta + \mu \sin\theta)}$$

But
$$\mu = \tan\phi = \frac{\sin\phi}{\cos\phi}$$

$$\therefore \qquad P = \left\{\left(\frac{\sin\phi}{\cos\phi}\right)(W_1 + W_2)\right\} \Big/ \left(\cos\theta + \frac{\sin\phi}{\cos\phi}\cdot\sin\theta\right)$$

$$= \frac{(W_1 + W_2)\sin\phi}{\cos(\theta - \phi)}$$

For P to be minimum $\cos(\theta - \phi)$ should be maximum, i.e.,

$$\cos(\theta - \phi) = 1,$$

$$\theta - \phi = 0, \text{ and } \theta = \phi$$

$\therefore$ $P_{min} = (W_1 + W_2) \sin\theta$ and acts at an angle $\theta = \phi$ with the horizontal **Ans.**

EXAMPLE 14.38. Determine the relation $\dfrac{T_1}{T_2} = e^{\mu\theta}$ for belt drive.

SOLUTION : The transmission of power in factories from one rotating shaft to another that lies at a considerable distance is achieved through bells and ropes.

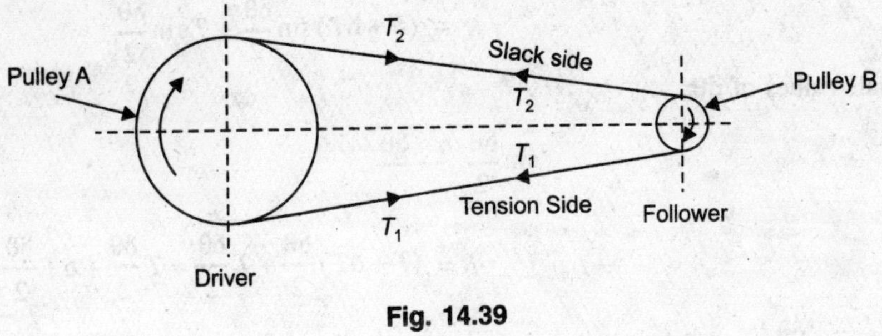

Fig. 14.39

With reference to Fig. 14.39 the pulley A which is keyed to the rotating shaft is called the driver. The pulley that needs to be driven is kown as follower. When the driver rotates, it carries the belt because of friction that exists between the pulley and the belt. The frictional resistance develops all along the contact surfaces. That makes the belt carry the follower which too starts rotating. The driving pulley pulls the belt from one side (called tension side) and delivers it to the other side (called slack side). The tension T_1 in the belt on the tension side is more than tension T_2 on the slack side.

RATIO OF TENSIONS : Fig. 14.40, shows a flexible belt resting on a stationary drum. The tensions T_1 and T_2 are such that motion is impending between the belt and the drum. Considering impending motion of belt to be counter clockwise relative to the drum, tension T_1 in more than T_2.

Let attention be focussed on small segment RS of the belt which subtends an angle $\delta\theta$ at the center. This segment RS is acted upon the following set of forces.

1. Tension T in the belt as S,

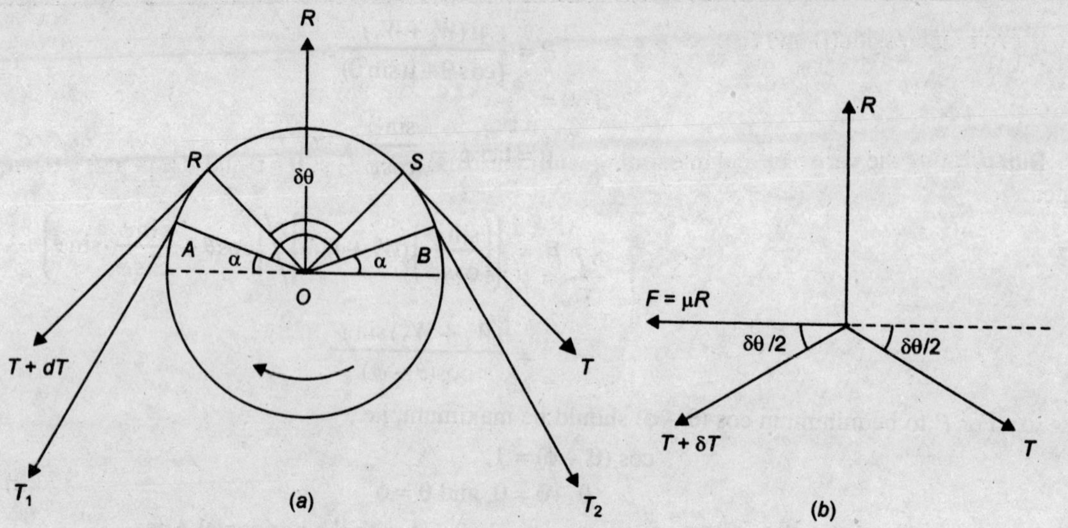

Fig. 14.40

2. Tension $T + \delta t$ in the belt at R,
3. Normal reaction R and
4. Frictional force $T = \mu R$

Considering equilibrium of forces in the radial direction

$$R = (T + \delta T)\sin\frac{\delta\theta}{2} + T\sin\frac{\delta\theta}{2}$$

For small values of $\delta\theta$;

$$\sin\frac{\delta\theta}{2} \to \frac{\delta\theta}{2}$$

$$R = (T + \delta T)\frac{\delta\theta}{2} + T\frac{\delta\theta}{2} = T\frac{\delta\theta}{2} + \delta T\frac{\delta\theta}{2} + T\frac{\delta\theta}{2}$$

The term $\delta T\frac{\delta\theta}{2}$ is small in magnitude and can be neglected

$$\therefore \quad R = T\,\delta\theta \qquad \text{...(i)}$$

Considering equilibrium of forces in the tangential direction,

$$\mu R = (T + \delta T)\cos\frac{\delta\theta}{2} - \cos\frac{\delta\theta}{2}$$

For small values of $\delta\theta$; $\cos\frac{\delta\theta}{2} \to 1$

$$\mu R = (T + \delta T) - T = \delta T$$

$$\therefore \quad R = \frac{\delta T}{\mu} \qquad \text{...(ii)}$$

From expression(i) and (ii),

$$T\delta\theta = \frac{\delta T}{\mu}$$

Separating the variables and integrating within the limits $T = T_2$ at $\theta = 0$ and $T = T_1$ at $\theta = \theta$, we get

$$\int_{T_2}^{T_1} \frac{\delta T}{T} = \mu \int_0^{\theta} \delta\theta\,;$$

$$\log \frac{T_1}{T_2} = \mu\theta$$

$$\therefore \qquad \frac{T_1}{T_2} = e^{\mu\theta} \qquad ...(7.22)$$

The value of $e = 2.718$ can be used for numerical calculations.

EXAMPLE 14.39. Calculate the force required to hold a weight of 10 kN suspended on a rope wrapped twice around a post. Take coefficient of friction $\mu = 0.2$.

SOLUTION : $\mu = 0.2$ and $\theta = 2 \times 2\pi \times 4\pi$ radian

Invoking the relation $\frac{T_1}{T_2} = e^{\mu\theta}$, we have

$$\frac{10}{T_2} = e^{0.2\times4\pi} = (2.718)^{2.512} = 12.326 \qquad (\pi = 3.142)$$

$$\therefore \qquad T_2 = \frac{10}{12.326} = 0.811 \text{ kN} = 811 \text{ N } \textbf{Ans.}$$

EXAMPLE 14.40. Two blocks of weight $W_1 = 50$ N and $W_2 = 50$ N rest on a rough inclined plane and are connected by a string as shown in Fig. 14.41a. The coefficients of friction between the inclined plane and W_1 and W_2 are $\mu_1 = 0.3$ and $\mu_2 = 0.2$ respectively. Find the inclination of plane for which slipping will impend.

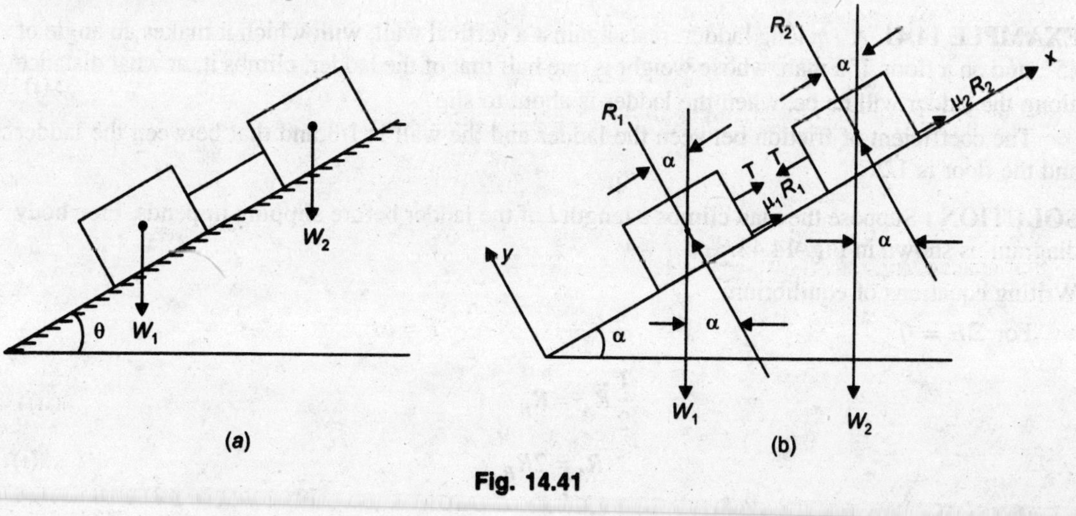

Fig. 14.41

SOLUTION : Free body diagrams of the two blocks are shown in Fig. 14.41(b) where T is the tension in the string.

Consider the equilibrium of W_2.

For $\Sigma X = 0$ (i.e. along the plane)

$$\mu_2 R_2 = T + W_2 \sin \alpha \qquad \text{...(i)}$$

For $\Sigma Y = 0$ (i.e. along the plane)

$$R_2 = W_2 \sin \alpha \qquad \text{...(ii)}$$

Consider the equilibrium of W_1

For $\Sigma X = 0$

$$\mu_1 R_1 + T = W_1 \sin \alpha \qquad \text{...(iii)}$$

For $\Sigma Y = 0$

$$R_1 = W_1 \cos \alpha \qquad \text{...(iv)}$$

Add (i) and (ii)

$$\mu_1 R_1 + \mu_2 R_2 = W_1 \sin \alpha + W_2 \sin \alpha + T - T$$

or $$\mu_1 R_1 + \mu_2 R_2 = \sin \alpha \, (W_1 + W_2)$$

or $$\mu_1 (W_1 \cos \alpha) + \mu_2 \, (W_2 \cos \alpha) = \sin \alpha \, (W_1 + W_2)$$

Putting the values of R_1 and R_2

or $$\cos \alpha \, (\mu_1 W_1) + \cos \alpha \, (\mu_2 W_2) = \sin \alpha \, (W_1 + W_2)$$

or $$\cos \alpha \, (\mu_1 W_1 + \mu_2 W_2) = \sin \alpha \, (W_1 + W_2)$$

or $$\frac{\mu_1 W_1 + \mu_2 W_2}{W_1 + W_2} = \frac{\sin \alpha}{\cos \alpha} = \tan \alpha$$

Putting $\mu_1 = 0.3$, $\mu_2 = 0.2$, $W_1 = 50$ N, $W_2 = 50$ N

$$\tan \alpha = \frac{0.3 \times 50 + 0.2 \times 50}{50 + 50}$$

or $$\tan \alpha = 0.25$$

$\therefore$ $$\alpha = \tan^{-1} (0.25) = 14° \textbf{ Ans.}$$

EXAMPLE 14.41. A 7 *m* long ladder, rests against a vertical wall, with which it makes an angle of 45°, and on a floor. If a man, whose weight is one half that of the ladder, climbs it, at what distance along the ladder will he be, when the ladder is about to slip?

The coefficient of friction between the ladder and the wall is 1/3 and that between the ladder and the floor is 1/2.

SOLUTION : Suppose the man climbs a length l of the ladder before slipping impends. Free body diagram is shown in Fig. 14.42.

Writing equations of equilibrium.

For $\Sigma H = 0$

$$\frac{1}{2} R_A = R_B$$

$\therefore$ $$R_A = 2R_B \qquad \text{...(i)}$$

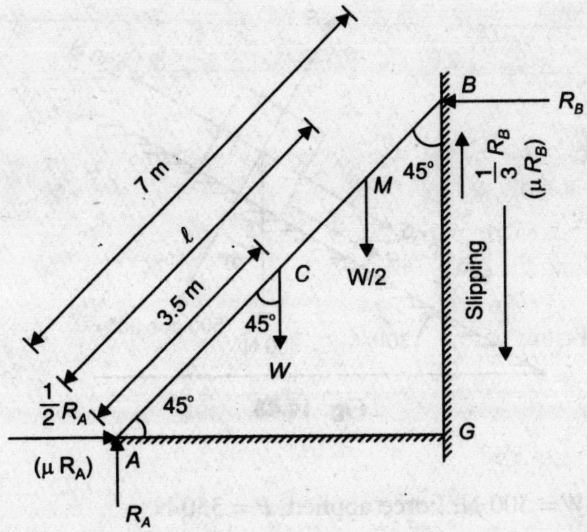

Fig. 14.42

For $\Sigma V = 0$

$$R_A + \frac{R_B}{3} = W + \frac{W}{2} \quad \text{...(ii)}$$

or
$$2R_B + \frac{R_B}{3} = 1.5\,W$$

or
$$R_B = 0.6429W \quad \text{...(iii)}$$

$$R_A = 2R_B$$

$$= 1.2857W \quad \text{...(iv)}$$

$$R_B(7\sin 45°) + \frac{1}{3}R_B(7\cos 45°) = W(3.5\cos 45°) + \frac{W}{2}(l\cos 45°)$$

or
$$0.6429W(4.9497) + \frac{1}{3}(0.6429W)(4.9497) = W(2.4749) + \frac{W}{2}(l)(0.7071)$$

$$3.1822W + 1.0607W = 2.4749W + \frac{W}{2} \times 0.7071\,l$$

$$4.2929W - 2.4749W = 0.3536Wl$$

or
$$1.768W = 0.3536\,Wl$$

$\therefore$
$$l = \frac{1.768}{0.3536} = 5 \text{ m } \textbf{Ans.}$$

EXAMPLE 14.42. A body of weight 500 N is pulled up on inclined plane, by a force of 350N. The inclination of the plane is 30° to the horizontal and the force is applied parallel to the plane. Determine the coefficient of friction.

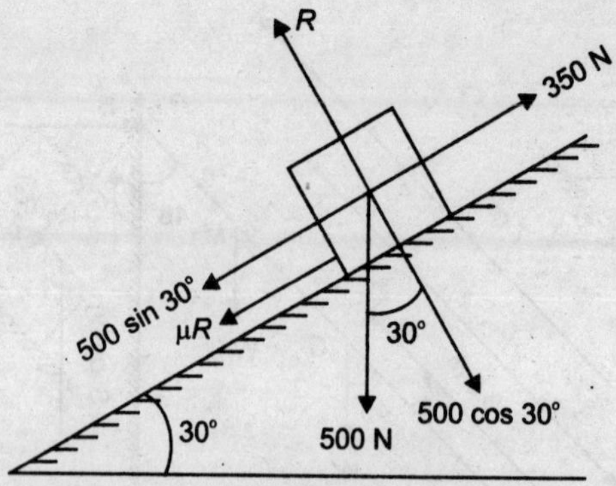

Fig. 14.43

SOLUTION :Given :

Weight of the body, $W = 500$ N, Force applied, $P = 350$ N

Inclination, $\alpha = 30°$

Let,

μ = Coefficient of friction,

R = Normal reaction

F = μR = Force of friction.

The body is in equilibrium under the action of the forces shown in Fig. 14.43.

Resolving the forces along the plane

$$500 \sin 30° + \mu R = 350 \qquad \text{...(i)}$$

Resolving the forces normal to the plane

$$R = 500 \cos 30° = 500 \times 0.866 = 433 \text{ N}$$

Substituing the value of R in equation (i), we get

$$500 \sin 30° + \mu \times 433 = 350$$

or $$500 \times 0.5 + 433\,\mu = 350$$

or $$433\,\mu = 350 - 250 = 100$$

$\therefore$ $$\mu = \frac{100}{433} = 0.23 \textbf{ Ans.}$$

EXAMPLE 14.43. (a) Define co-efficient of friction and limiting friction.

(b) Block A weighing 15N is a rectangular prism resting on a rough inclined plane as shown in Fig. 14.44(a). The block is tied up by a horizontal string which has a tension of 5N. Find :

(i) Frictional force on block

(ii) Normal reaction of inclined plane

(iii) Coefficient of friction between the surfaces of contact.

SOLUTION : Given :

(i) Weight of block, $W = 15$ N

(ii) Horizontal tension in the string, $T = 5$ N

(iii) Inclination of plane, $\alpha = 45°$

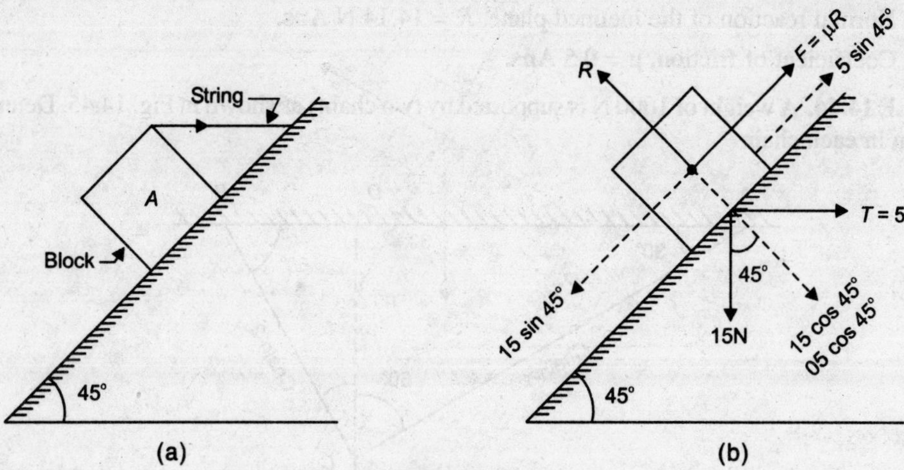

Fig. 14.44

Let,

F = Frictional force,

R = Normal reaction and

μ = Coefficient of friction

Since there is tension in the string which mean if the string is removed, the block will slide down the plane. Hence force of friction ($F = \mu R$) will be acting in the upward direction.

The block A is in equilibrium under the action of force shown in Fig. 14.44(b). These forces are:

1. The weight of the block, $W = 15$ N
2. Horizontal tension in the string, $T = 5$N
3. Normal reaction, R
4. Force of friction, $F = \mu R$, acting upwards.

Resolving the forces along the inclined plane,

$$15 \sin 45° = F + 5 \cos 45°$$

or
$$F = 15 \sin 45° - 5 \sin 45°$$

∴
$$F = 15 \times 0.707 - 5 \times 0.707$$
$$= 10 \times 0.707 = 7.07 \text{ N} \quad ...(i)$$

Resolving the forces normal to inclined plane,

$$R = 15 \cos 45° + T \cos 45°$$
$$= 15 \cos 45° + 5 \cos 45°$$

∴
$$R = 15 \times 0.707 + 5 \times 0.707$$
$$= 20 \times 0.707 = 14.14 \text{ N}$$

∴
$$F = \mu R$$

∴
$$\mu = \frac{F}{R} = \frac{7.07}{14.14} = 0.5 \text{ Ans.}$$

Hence,

(i) Frictional force on the block, F = 7.07 N **Ans.**

(ii) Normal reaction of the inclined plane, $R = 14.14$ N **Ans.**

(iii) Coefficient of friction, $\mu = 0.5$ **Ans.**

EXAMPLE 14.44. A weight of 1000 N is supported by two chains as shown in Fig. 14.45. Determine the tension in each chain.

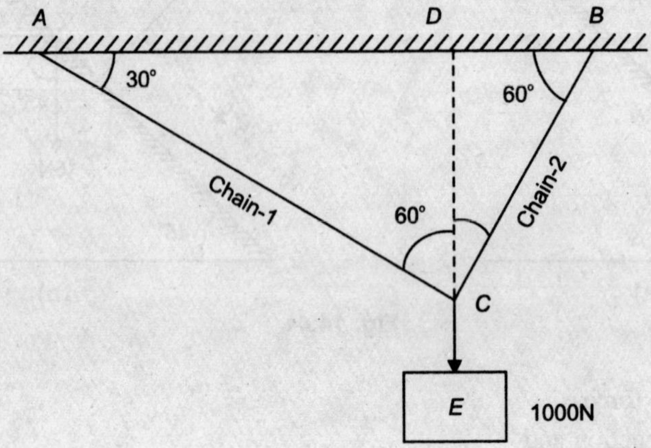

Fig. 14.45

SOLUTION : Given : $\angle CAB = 30°$, $\angle CBA = 60°$, $\angle ACB = 90°$

In right angled triangle ADC,

$$\angle ACD = 90° - 30° = 60°$$

In right angled $\angle BDG$,

$$\angle BCD = 90° - 60° = 30°$$

$\therefore$ $$\angle ACE = 180° - 60° = 120°$$

$$\angle BCE = 180° - 30° = 150°$$

Let,

T_1 = Tension in chain – 1

T_2 = Tension in chain – 2

Applying Lami's theorem at point C (Fig. 14.46)

$$\frac{T_1}{\sin 150} = \frac{T_2}{\sin 120} = \frac{1000}{\sin 90}$$

or $$\frac{T_1}{0.50} = \frac{T_2}{0.866} = 1000$$

$\therefore$ $$T_1 = 0.50 \times 1000$$

$$= 500 \text{ N } \textbf{Ans.}$$

$$T_2 = 0.866 \times 1000$$

$$= 866 \text{ N } \textbf{Ans.}$$

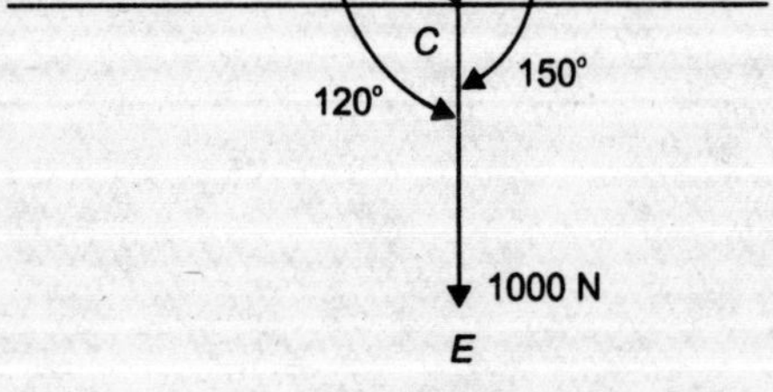

Fig. 11.46

EXAMAPLE 14.45. Two bars AC and BC are hinged together at C. Their other ends are hinged to a vertical wall at A and B as shown. Find the axial force in the bar.

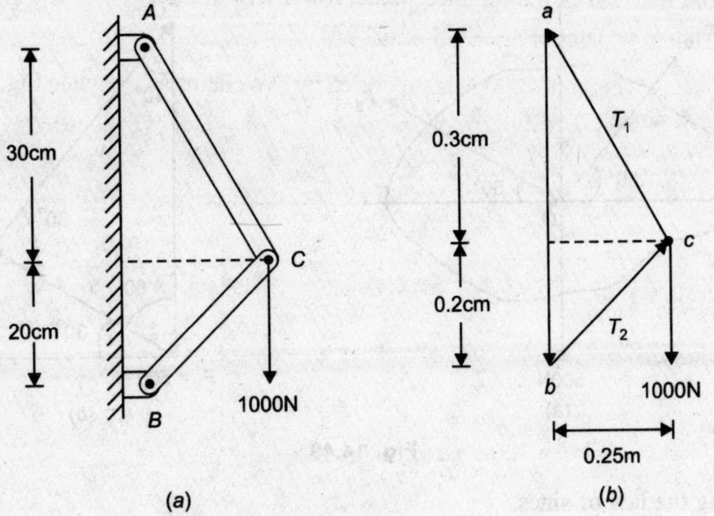

Fig. 14.47

SOLUTION : Axial forces induced in the bars *AC* and *BC* are internal forces. But when we consider the free body diagram of point *C* these become the external forces acting at a point *C*. Let these be T_1 and T_2. Here each bar is acted uon by only two forces at its ends. One of these forces is the component of 1000 N and the other is the reaction at the hinge. So each bar is a force member.

Free body diagram of the point *C* is shown in Fig. 14.47.

As the point *C* is in equilibrium under the action of three forces, they must be concurrent and should form a closed triangle of force *abc* similar to the triangle *ABC*.

$$\frac{T_1}{BC} = \frac{T_2}{AC} = \frac{1000}{AB}$$

Where,

$$AC = \sqrt{(0.3)^2 + (0.25)^2} = 0.3905 \text{ m}$$

$$BC = \sqrt{(0.2)^2 + (0.25)^2} = 0.3206 \text{ m}$$

Hence,

$$\frac{T_1}{0.3206} = \frac{T_2}{0.3905} = \frac{1000}{0.50}$$

$\therefore$

$$T_1 = \frac{1000 \times 0.3206}{0.50} = 651.20 \text{ N}$$

$$T_2 = \frac{(1000 \times 0.3905)}{0.50} = 781 \text{ N}$$

EXAMPLE 14.46. A body acted upon by three forces F_1 and F_2. and 500 N is in equilibrium. Find the forces F_1 and F_2.

SOLUTION : Since the three forces are non-parallel and are in equilibrium they must intersect at a common point *O* and must form a closed triangle of force as shown in Fig. 14.48(b).

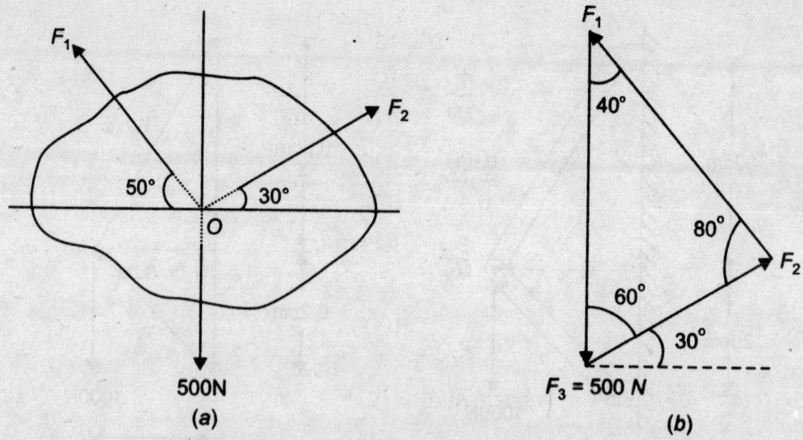

Fig. 14.48

Now applying the law of sines,

$$\frac{500}{\sin 80^0} = \frac{F_2}{\sin 40^0} = \frac{F_1}{\sin 60^0}$$

or
$$507.713 = \frac{F_2}{0.6428} = \frac{F_1}{0.866}$$

∴
$$F_1 = 507.713 \times 0.866$$
$$= 439.68 \text{ N}$$
$$F_2 = 507.713 \times 0.6428$$
$$= 326.35 \text{ N } \textbf{Ans.}$$

EXAMPLE 14.47. A corner plate *ABC* is hinged to a fixed support at *A* and rests on a roller at *C*. If a force $W = 1000$ N is acting as shown find the reactions at the support.

SOLUTION : Consider the free body daigram of the plate. The forces acting on the plate are:

1. Force $W = 1000$ N, acting vertical donward
2. Reaction R_C acting normal to the surface of contact, i.e. acting horizontally.
3. Reaction at the hinge R_A.

As the plate is in equilibrium under the action of three forces, the forces must pass through a point *O* as shown in Fig. 14.49.

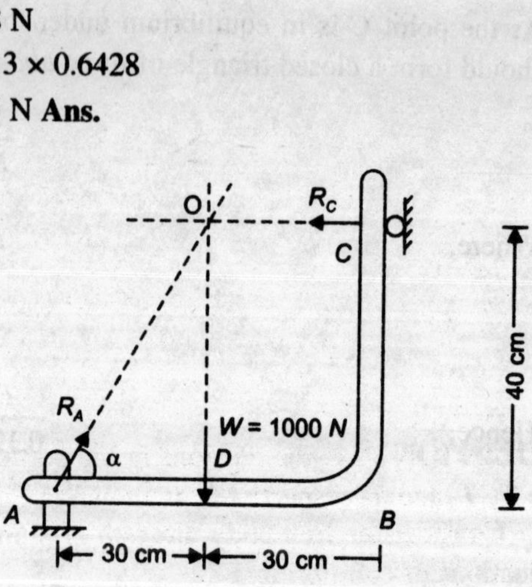

Fig. 14.49

Forces *W* and R_C intersect at point *O* therefore, the reaction R_A at the hinge must also pass through *O*.

The three forces must form a closed triange which is similar to triange *AOD*.

$$AO = \sqrt{(.4)^2 + (.3)^2} = 0.5 \text{ m}$$

Therefore,

$$\frac{W}{OD} = \frac{R_C}{AD} = \frac{R_A}{AO}$$

or $$\frac{1000}{0.4} = \frac{R_C}{0.3} = \frac{R_A}{0.5} \qquad (\because AO = 0.5 \text{ m})$$

or $$R_A = \frac{1000 \times 0.5}{0.4} = 12.50 \text{ N } \textbf{Ans.}$$

$$R_C = \frac{1000 \times 0.3}{0.4} = 750 \text{ N } \textbf{Ans.}$$

Now angle α that R_C makes with horiozntal is

$$\tan \alpha = \frac{\text{perpendicular}}{\text{base}} = \frac{0.4}{0.3} = 1.333$$

$\therefore$ $$\alpha = \tan^{-1} (1.333) = 53.13° \textbf{ Ans.}$$

EXAMPLE 14.48. Two equal loads of 2500 N are supported by a flexible string *ABCD* at points *B* and *C*. Find the tensions in the portions *AB*, *BC* and *CD* of the string.

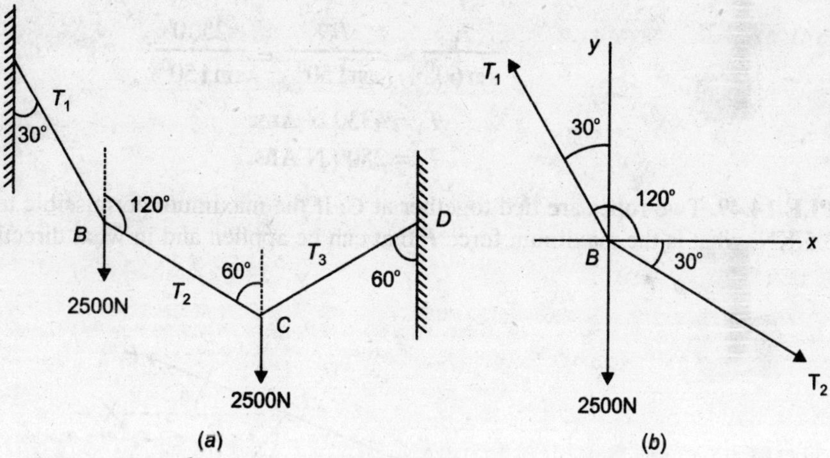

Fig. 14.50

SOLUTION : Let the tensions in the portions *AB, BC* and *CD* be T_1, T_2 and T_3 respectively as shown in Fig. 14.50(a).

Consider the free body diagram of point *B* and writing the equations of equilibrium.

For $\Sigma H = 0$

$$T_1 \cos 120° + 2500 \cos 270° + T_2 \cos 330° = 0$$

or $$-0.5T_1 + 2500 \times 0 + 0.866\, T_2 = 0$$

$\therefore$ $$1.732T_2 = T_1 \qquad ...(i)$$

For $\Sigma V = 0$

$$T_1 \sin 120° + 2500 \sin 270° + T_2 \sin 330° = 0$$

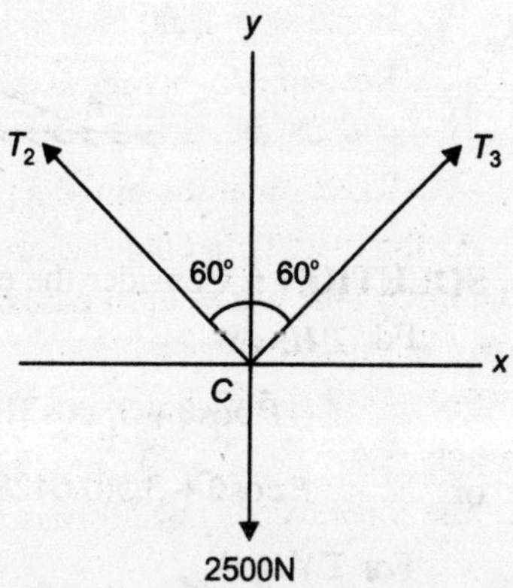

Fig. 14.50(c)

or $0.866\ T_1 - 2500 \times 1 - 0.50\ T_2 = 0$

or $1.732\ T_1 - T_2 = 2500 \times 2$ ...(ii)

or $1.732\ (1.732)\ T_2 - T_2 = 5000$

or $2.999824 T_2 - T_2 = 5000$

$\therefore$ $$T_2 = \frac{5000}{1.999824} = 2500 \text{ N } \textbf{Ans.}$$

$\therefore$ $$T_1 = 1.732\ (2500) = 4330 \text{ N } \textbf{Ans.}$$

Consider the free body diagram for point *C*.

For $\Sigma H = 0$

$$T_3 \cos 30° + T_2 \cos 150° + 2500 \cos 270 = 0$$

or $0.866 T_3 - 0.866025 \times 2500 - 2500 \times 0 = 0$

or $0.866 T_3 - 2165.0625 = 0$

$\therefore$ $$T_3 - \frac{2165.0625}{0.866} = 2500 \text{ N } \textbf{Ans.}$$

Alternate Method: Applying Lami's theorem at point B.

$$\frac{T_1}{\sin 60^0} = \frac{T_2}{\sin 150^0} = \frac{2500}{\sin 150^0}$$

$\therefore$ $$T_1 = 4330 \text{ N } \textbf{Ans.}$$

and $$T_2 = 2500 \text{ N } \textbf{Ans.}$$

EXAMPLE 14.49. Two ropes are tied together at *C*. If the maximum permissible tension in each rope is 3.5 KN, what is the maximum force *P* that can be applied and in what direction?

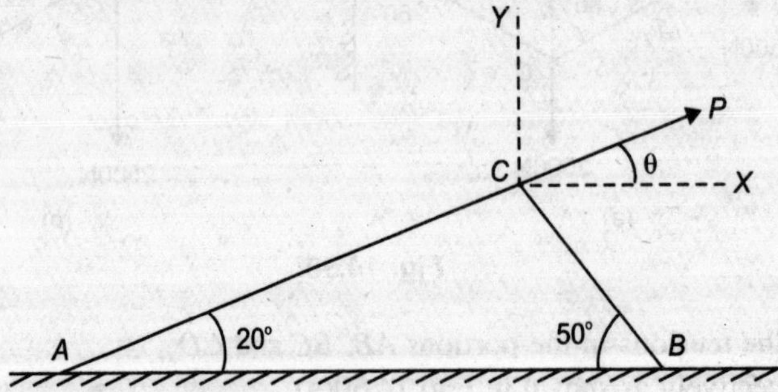

Fig. 14.51

SOLUTION : Consider the equilibrium of point *C*.

For $\Sigma H = 0$

$$P\cos\theta + T_1 \cos 310° + T_2 \cos 200° = 0$$

or $P\cos\theta + 3.5(0.6428) - 3.5\ (0.9397) = 0$ ...(i)

For $\Sigma V = 0$

$$P\sin\theta + T_1 \sin 310° + T_2 \sin 200° = 0$$

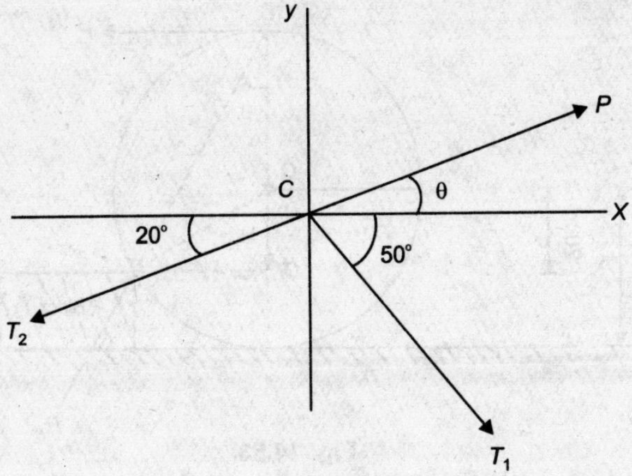

Fig. 14.52

$$P\sin\theta - 3.5\,(0.7660) - 3.5\,(0.3420) = 0 \qquad \text{...(ii)}$$

$$\therefore \qquad \frac{P\sin\theta}{P\cos\theta} = \tan\theta$$

$$= \frac{0.7660 + 0.3420}{0.9396 - 0.6428} = \frac{1.108}{0.2968}$$

$$\therefore \qquad \theta = \tan^{-1}(3.733)$$

$$= 75° \textbf{ Ans.}$$

Substituting $\theta = 75°$ in equation (i), we have,

$$P\cos 75^0 + 3.5\,(0.6428) = 3.5\,(.9397)$$

or $$P(0.2588) + 2.2498 = 3.28895$$

or $$.2588\,P = 3.28895 - 2.2498$$

$$\therefore \qquad P = \frac{1.03915}{0.2588} = 4 \text{ kN } \textbf{Ans.}$$

EXAMPLE 14.50. A roller of radius 40 cm, weighing 3000 N is to be pulled over a rectangular block of 20 cm height as shown in Fig. 14.53, by a horizontal force applied at the end of a string wound round the circumference of the roller. Find the magnitude of horizontal force which will just turn the roller over the corner of the rectangular block. Also determine the magnitude and direction of the reactions at *A* and *B*. All surfaces may be taken as smooth.

SOLUTION : Given :

Radius of roller = 40 cm, Weight, W = 3000 N

Height of the block = 20 cm

Let,

The horizontal force = P and reactions R_A and R_B at points A and B when the roller just turns over the block.

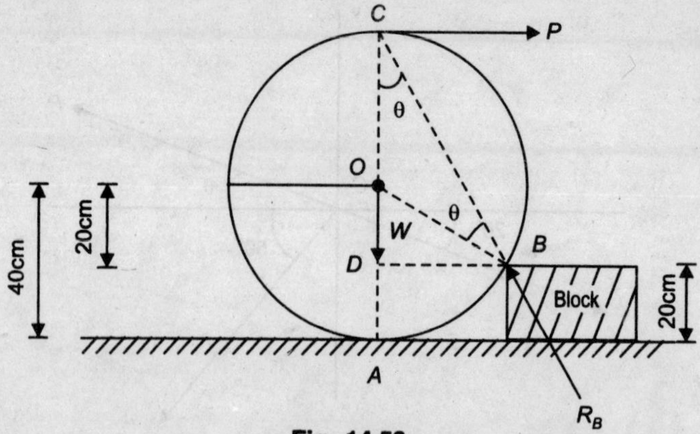

Fig. 14.53

When the roller is about the turn over the corner of the rectangular block, the roller lifts at point A and then there will be no contact between the roller and the point A. Hence reaction R_A at point A will become zero.

Now the roller will be in equilibrium under the action of the following three forces :

(i) Its weight W acting vertically donward

(ii) Horizontal force P.

(iii) Reaction R_B at point B. The direction of R_B is unknown.

In $\angle BOD$, BO = Radius = 40 cm, $OD = OA - AD = 40 - 20 = 20$ cm

$$\therefore \quad BD = \sqrt{BO^2 - OD^2}$$

$$= \sqrt{40^2 - 20^2} \; 34.64 \text{ cm}$$

For the equilibrium, the above three forces should pass through a common point. As the force P and weight W is passing through point C, hence the reaction R_B must also pass through the point C. Hence the line BC gives the direction of the reaction R_B.

Now in ΔBCD,

$$\tan\theta = \frac{\text{Base}}{\text{Perp.}} = \frac{BD}{CD}$$

Hence,
$$\tan\theta = \frac{34.64}{40+20} = 0.5773$$

$$\therefore \quad \theta = \tan^{-1}(0.57773) = 29.999° = 30°$$

Now taking moments of all the three forces about the point B (i.e. corner of the rectangular block)

$$P \times CD = W \times BD$$

or
$$P \times 60 = 3000 \times 34.64$$

$$\therefore \quad P = \frac{3000 \times 34.64}{60}$$

$$\therefore \quad P = 1732 \text{ N } \textbf{Ans.}$$

EXAMPLE 14.51. A circular roller of weight 100 N and radius 10 cm hangs by a tie rod AB = 20 cm and rests against a smooth vertical wall at C as shown in Fig. 14.54(a).

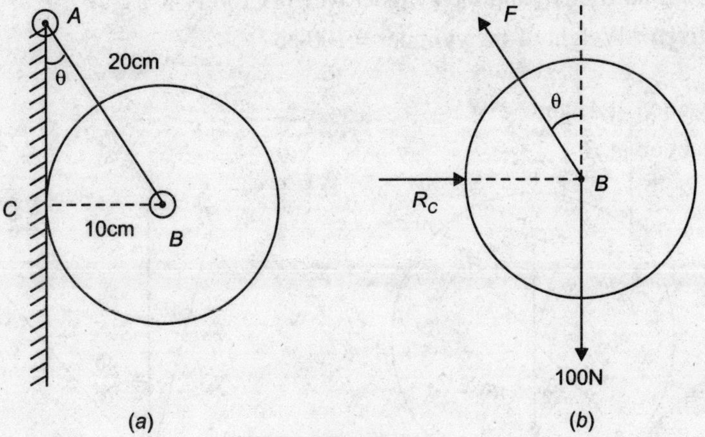

Fig. 14.54

Determine force F in the tie rod and (ii) The reaction R_C at point C.

SOLUTION : Given : Weight of the roller, W = 100 N

Radius of roller BC = 10 cm, Length of tie rod, AB = 20 cm

From ΔABC, we get,

$$\sin\theta = \frac{\text{Perp.}}{\text{Diag.}}$$

$$= \frac{10}{2} = 0.5$$

∴ $$\theta = \sin^{-1} = (0.50) = 30°$$

The free body diagram of the roller is shown in Fig. 14.54 (b) in which R_C = Reaction at C.

F = Force in the tie rod AB

Free body diagram shows the equilibrium of the roller. Hence the resultant force in x-direction and y-dirction should bc zcro.

For $\Sigma H = 0$,

$$F \sin 30° - R_C \sin 90° + 100 \sin 180° = 0$$

or $$0.5F = R_C \quad \text{...(i)}$$

For $\Sigma V = 0$,

$$F \cos 30° - R_C \cos 90° + 100 \cos 180° = 0$$

or $$0.866\ F - R_C \times 0 + 100\ (-1) = 0$$

or $$0.866\ F = 100$$

∴ $$F = \frac{100}{0.866} = 115.47\text{N}\ \textbf{Ans.}$$

But $$R_C = 0.5F = 115.47\ (0.5) = 57.73\text{N}\ \textbf{Ans.}$$

EXAMPLE 14.52. Smooth circular cylinder of radius 1.5 meter is lying in a triangular groove, one side of which makes 15° and other 40° angle with the horizontal. Find the reactions at the surfaces of contact, if there is no friction and the cylinder weights 100 N.

SOLUTION : Given : Weight of the cylinder = 100 N

Let,

R_A = Reaction at A, and

R_B = Reaction at B

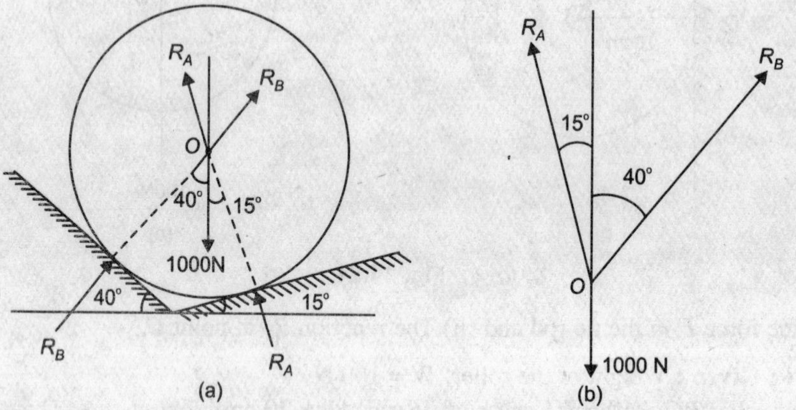

Fig. 14.55

The smooth cylinder is lying in the groove as shown in Fig. 14.55 (a). In order to keep the system in equilibrium; three forces i.e. R_A, R_B and weight of the cylinder (100 N) must pass through the centre of the cylinder. As there is no friction, hence the reactions R_A and R_B must be normal to the surfaces (Fig. 14.55a). The system of forces is shown in Fig. 14.55(b)

Applying Lami's theorem, at point O,

$$\frac{R_A}{\sin(180° - 40°)} = \frac{R_B}{\sin(180° - 15°)} = \frac{100}{\sin(15° + 40°)}$$

or $$\frac{R_A}{\sin 140°} = \frac{R_B}{\sin 165°} = \frac{100}{\sin 55°}$$

or $$\frac{R_A}{0.64278} = \frac{R_B}{0.2588} = 122.077$$

∴ $$R_A = 122.077 \times 0.64278 = 78.47 \text{ N } \textbf{Ans.}$$

$$R_B = 122.077 \times 0.2588 = 31.59 \text{ N } \textbf{Ans.}$$

EXAMPLE 14.53. Two equal heavy spheres of 50 mm radius are in equilibrium within a smooth cup of 150 mm radius. Show that the reaction between the cup of one sphere is double than that between the two spheres.

SOLUTION : Given : Radius of spheres = 50 mm

Radius of cup = 150 mm

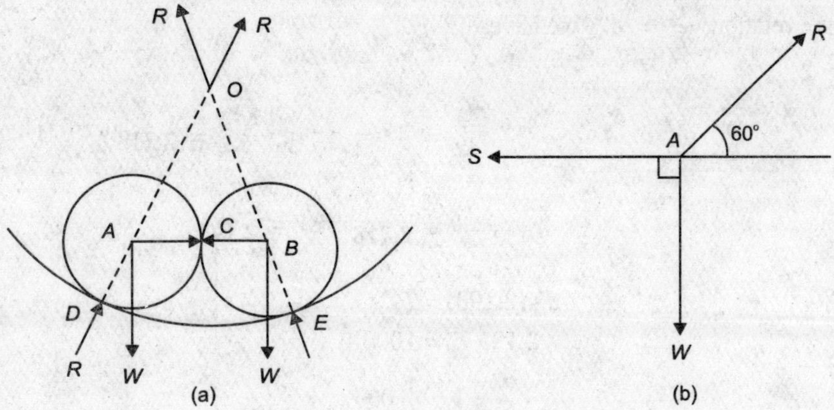

Fig. 14.56

The two spheres with centres A and B, lying in equilibrium, in the cup with O as centre are shown in Fig. 14.56(a). Let the two spheres touch each other at C and touch the cup at D and E respectively.

Let,

R = Reaction between sphere and cup

S = Reaction between two spheres at C

From the geometry of the figure, we find that $OD = 150$ mm and $AD = 50$ mm.

$$\therefore \quad OA = 100 \text{ mm}$$

Similarly, $OB = 100$ mm. We also find that $AB = 100$ mm

$\therefore$ OAB is an equilateral triangle. Hence the system of froces (FBD) is shown in Fig. 14.56(b).

Applying Lami's theorem

$$\frac{R}{\sin 90} = \frac{W}{\sin 120^0} = \frac{S}{\sin 150^0}$$

or
$$\frac{R}{1} = \frac{W}{0.866} = \frac{S}{0.5}$$

$$\therefore \quad 0.5\,R = S$$

and
$$R = 2S$$

Hence the reaction between the cup and the sphere is double than that between the two spheres. **Ans.**

EXAMPLE 14.54. A belt supports two loads W_1 and W_2 over a pulley as shown in Fig. 14.57 If $W_1 = 1000$ N, find the maximum Weight W_2 to keep W_1 in equilibrium. Assume that the pulley is locked and $\mu = 0.25$.

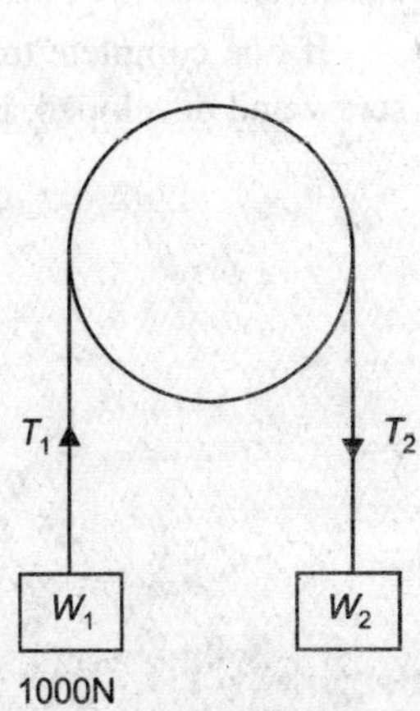

Fig. 14.57

SOLUTION : Let the tensions in the belt be T_1 and T_2 as shown in Fig. 14.57

Since the weight W_2 just checks the tendency of weight W_1 to move down, the tension on the side of W_1 is larger, i.e., $T_1 > T_2$, $\mu = 0.25$, $\theta = \pi$ and $W_1 = 1000$ N, then W_2 = ?

Using the relation, $\frac{T_1}{T_2} = e^{\mu\theta}$ we have,

$$\frac{T_1}{T_2} = e^{\mu\theta} = 2.718^{(0.25)\pi} = 2.718^{(0.25)(3.1416)}$$

or $$\frac{T_1}{T_2} = 2.718^{0.7854} = 2.193$$

$\therefore$ $$T_2\,(2.193) = T_1$$

or $$2.193\,T_2 = 1000$$

$\therefore$ $$T_2 = \frac{1000}{2.193} = 456 \text{ N}$$

But, $W_2 = T_2 = 456$ N **Ans.**

FRICTION IN SQUARE THREADED SCREW : Consider a screw jack consisting of square threaded screw and a base. The screw carries a load W which can be raised by turning a handle of length l with a force F.

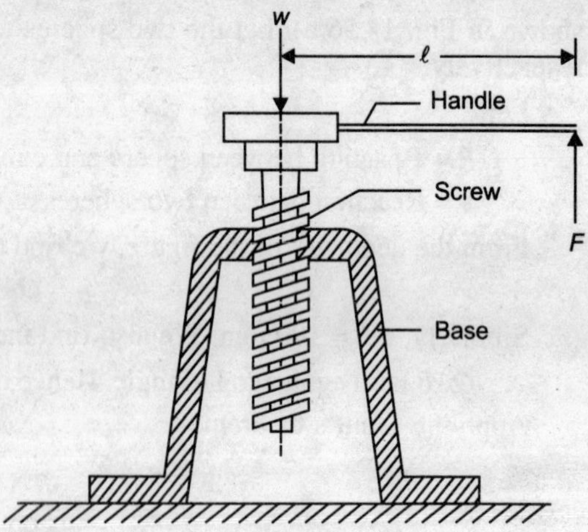

Screw Jack

Fig. 14.58

Let,

α = Helix Angle

r = Mean radius of the thread, and

p = Pitch of the thread

PITCH : It is the axial distance measured between two consecutive threads.

LEAD : It is the axial distance through which the screw advances in one turn.

For single threaded screw lead and pitch are equal (lead = N × Pitch)

If one complete turn of the screw thread be imagined, to be unwound, from the body of the screw and developed, it will form an inclined plane (Fig. 14.59).

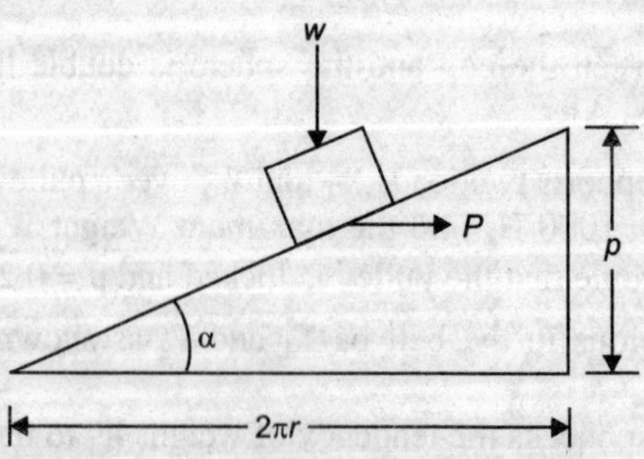

Fig. 14.59

From the geometry of the Fig. 14.59, we find

$$\tan\alpha = \frac{p}{2\pi r} \qquad ...(1)$$

Now let,

P = Effort applied at the mean radius of the screw to lift the load.

W = Weight to be lifted

μ = Coefficient of friction, between screw and nut

ϕ = Angle of friction = $\tan^{-1}(\mu)$

$\therefore \quad \mu = \tan\phi$

As the screw works on the principle of an inclined plane hence the horizontal force required to (1) Lift a load on an inclined rough plane,

$$P = W\tan(\alpha + \phi) \qquad ...(2)$$

and horizontal force required to (ii) lower a load on an incline rough plane,

$$P = W\tan(\alpha - \phi) \qquad ...(3)$$

Force P is related to the force F applied on the handle by the relation,

$$Fl = Pr$$

$$\therefore \quad P = \frac{Fl}{r} \qquad ...(4)$$

$$\eta = \frac{\tan\alpha}{\tan(\alpha + \theta)} \qquad ...(5)$$

$$\eta_{max.} = \frac{1 - \sin\phi}{1 + \sin\phi} \qquad ...(6)$$

SELF LOCKING : When the load W on the head of the screw remains in place after the effort is removed (when the effort is zero). it is called self locking machine. For a screw to be self locking,

$$\phi > \alpha \qquad ...(7)$$

and efficiency less than 50%

EXAMPLE 14.55. A screw jack has square threads of mean diameter of 10 cm and a pitch of 1.25 cm. Determine the force that must be applied to the end of 50 cm lever, (i) To raise, and (ii) To lower a weight of 50 KN. Find the efficiency of the jack. Is it self locking? Assume $\mu = 0.20$.

SOLUTION : Given :

$p = 1.25$ cm, $d = 10$ cm, $r = 5$ cm $= .05$ m

$l = 50$ cm, $W = 50$ kN and $\mu = 0.20$

Helix angle,

$$\tan\alpha = \frac{p}{2\pi r} = \frac{1.25}{2\pi(5)} = \frac{1.25}{31.416} = 0.0398$$

$$\therefore \quad \alpha = \tan^{-1}(0.0398) = 2.28°$$

Angle of friction,

$$\phi = \tan^{-1}(\mu) = \tan^{-1}(.2) = 11.31°$$

(i) TO RAISE THE LOAD :

$\because$ Effort required, $P = W \tan(\alpha + \phi)$ and $F_1 l = Pr$

$$\therefore \quad F_1 = \frac{Pr}{l}$$

$$F_1 = \frac{W\tan(\alpha+\phi)r}{l}$$

$$= 50\times1000\tan(2.28°+11.31°)\times\frac{0.05}{0.5}$$

$$= 50{,}000\tan(13.59°)\times0.1$$

$$= 5{,}000\tan(13.59°) = 1208.70 \text{ N}$$ **Ans.**

(ii) TO LOWER THE LOAD :

$$F_1 = \frac{Pr}{l}$$

$$= W\tan(\alpha-\phi)\times\frac{r}{l}$$

$$= 50\tan(2.28°-11.31°)\times\frac{0.05}{0.5}\times1000$$

$$= 50{,}000\tan(-9.03)\times0.1$$

$$= -794.61 \text{ N}$$ **Ans.**

FORCE REQUIRED IN OPPOSITE SENSE

$$\eta = \frac{\tan\alpha}{\tan(\alpha+\phi)}$$

$$= \frac{\tan 2.28°}{\tan(2.28°+11.31°)}$$

$$= \frac{0.0398}{\tan(13.59°)} = \frac{0.0398}{0.2417}$$

$$\therefore \quad \eta = 0.1647 = 16.47\%$$

As $\eta < 50\%$ and $\phi > \alpha$, Hence screw is self locking **Ans.**

EFFICIENCY OF SCREW :

$$\because \quad P = W\tan(\alpha+\phi)$$

$$\therefore \quad P_{ideal} = W\tan\alpha \qquad (\text{As } \mu = 0)$$

$$\therefore \quad P_{actual} = W\tan(\alpha+\phi)$$

$$\eta = \frac{\text{Ideal effort (when friction is zero)}}{\text{Actual effort}}$$

$$= \frac{W\tan\alpha}{W\tan(\alpha+\theta)} = \frac{\tan\alpha}{\tan(\alpha+\theta)}$$

EXAMPLE 14.56. Determine the centroid of the cross-sectional area of an unequal I-section shown in Fig. 14.60.

SOLUTION : The figure is symmetrical about *y*–*y* axis. *x*-*x* axis may be chosen to coincide with the bottom edge *AB*.

The figure may be considered to be made up of three rectangles *ABCD*, *EFGH* and *IJKL*.

Due to symmetry, centroid of the total figure lies on *y*-*y* axis. Let $\bar{y}$ be the distance of centroid along *y*-*y* from the base line *AB*.

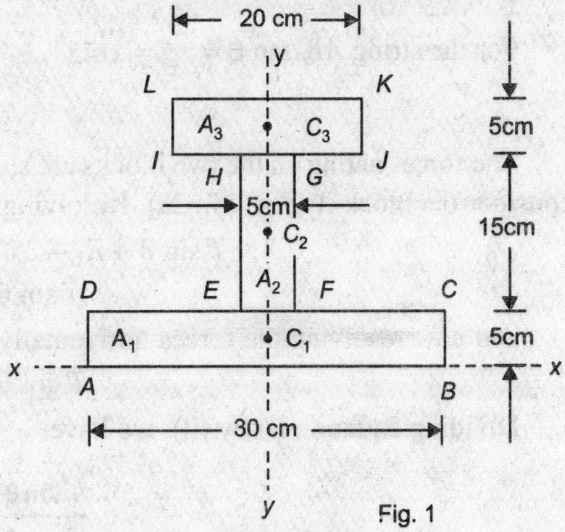

Fig. 14.60

S.No.	Area in cm^2	Y-co-ordinate of the centroid in cm
1	$A_1 = 5 \times 30 = 1500$	$Y_1 = \frac{5}{2} = 2.5$
2	$A_2 = 5 \times 15 = 75$	$Y_2 = 5 + \frac{15}{2} = 12.5$
3	$A_3 = 5 \times 20 = 100$	$Y_3 = 5 + 15 + \frac{5}{2} = 22.5$

$$\bar{y} = \frac{A_1Y_1 + A_2Y_2 + A_3Y_3}{A_1 + A_2 + A_3}$$

$$= \frac{150 \times 2.5 + 75 \times 12.5 + 100 \times 22.5}{150 + 75 + 100}$$

$$= \frac{3562.50}{325} = 10.96 \ cm \ \textbf{Ans.}$$

EXAMPLE 14.57. A block of weight W_1 = 1000 N rests on horizontal surface and supports on its top another block of weight W_2 = 250 N. The weight W_2 is attached by an string *AB* to the vertical wall (its indication shown in Fig. 14.61). Find the magnitude of the horizontal force *P* applied to the lower block to cause slipping to impend. The coefficient of friction for all contacting surfaces may be assumed to be μ = 0.3.

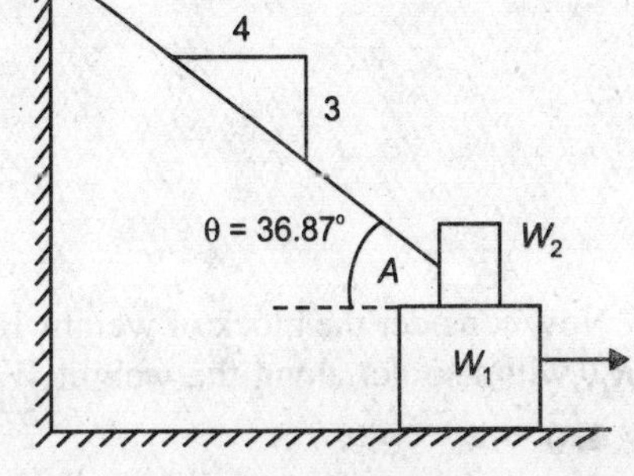

Fig. 14.61

SOLUTION : Given :

$$W_1 = 1000 \text{ N}, \ W_2 = 250 \text{ N}, \ \mu = 0.3$$

For the string *AB*, $\tan\theta = \frac{3}{4} = 0.75$

$$\therefore \qquad \theta = \tan^{-1}(0.75) = 36.87°$$

The forces acting on the two blocks are shown in Fig. 14.62(a), and (b) respectively. First of all consider the block *A* (Fig. 14.62a). Resolving the forces vertically. We have

$$T\sin\theta + R_1 - 250 = 0$$

$$\therefore \qquad T\sin\theta = 250 - R_1 \qquad \text{...(i)}$$

and now resolving the forces horizontally, we have,

$$T\cos\theta = F_1 = \mu R_1 = 0.3\,R_1 \qquad \text{...(ii)}$$

Dividing equation (i) by (ii), we have,

$$\frac{T\sin\theta}{T\cos\theta} = \frac{(250 - R_1)}{0.3R_1}$$

$$\text{or} \qquad \tan\theta = \frac{(250 - R_1)}{0.3R_1} = 0.75$$

$$\text{or} \qquad 0.75\,(0.3R_1) = 250 - R_1$$

$$\text{or} \qquad 0.225\,R_1 + R_1 = 250$$

$$\text{or} \qquad 1.225\,R_1 = 250$$

$$\therefore \qquad R_1 = \frac{250}{1.225} = 204.08 \text{ N}$$

$$\text{and} \qquad F_1 = \mu R_1 = 0.3\,(204.08) = 61.22 \text{ N}$$

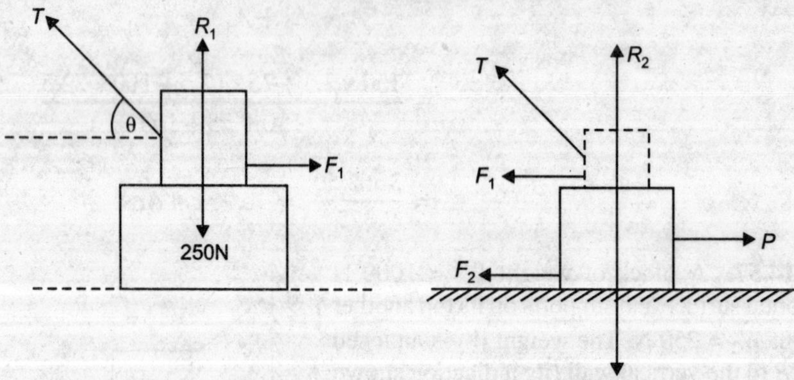

Fig. 14.62

Now consider the block of weight 1000 N (W_1). The downward force of block W_2 weight equal to R_1, will also act along the weight W_1 (1 kN). Resolving the forces vertically we have, i.e. for $\Sigma V = 0$

$$R_2 = 1000 + R_1 = 1204.08 \text{ N}$$

For $\Sigma H = 0$

$$P = F_1 + F_2 = 61.22 + \mu R_2$$
$$= 61.22 + 0.3\,(1204.08)$$
$$\therefore \quad P = 61.22 + 361.2$$
$$= 422.42 \text{ N } \textbf{Ans.}$$

EXAMPLE 14.58. Determine the location of co-ordiantes x and y of the centre of a 100 mm diameter circular hole cut in the thin plate such that this point will be the centroid of the remaining shaded area as shown in Fig. 14.63. All dimensions are in mm.

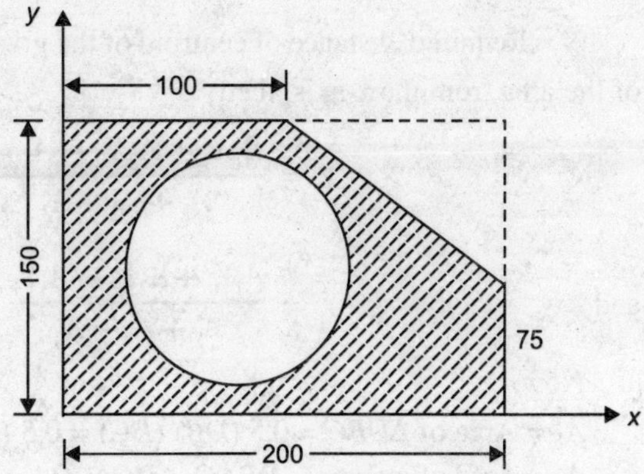

Fig. 14.63

SOLUTION : If x_3 and y_3 are the co-ordinates of the centre of the circle, centroid also must have the co-ordinates x_3 and y_3 as per condition given in the problem. The shaded area may be considered as a rectangle of size 200 mm × 150 mm minus *a* Δ of sides 100 mm × 75 mm and a circle of diameter 100 mm.

∴ Area of shaded portion (ΣA) = Area of rectangle – Area of Δ – Area of circle

$$= 200 \times 150 - 100 \times 75\,(0.5) - \frac{\pi}{4}\,(100)^2$$
$$= 18,396 \text{ mm}^2$$

$$\bar{x} = x_3 = \frac{A_1X_1 - A_2X_2 - A_3X_3}{A_1 - A_2 - A_3}$$

$$= \frac{200\times150\times100 - 100\times75(0.5)\times\left[200 - \frac{100}{3}\right] - \frac{\pi}{4}\times100^2\times(X_3)}{18,396}$$

$$X_3\,(18,396) = 200\times150\times100 - 100\times75\times166.67 - \frac{\pi}{4}\times100^2\,(X_3)$$

$$\therefore \quad X_3 = \frac{23,75000}{26,250} = 90.48 \text{ mm } \textbf{Ans.}$$

Similarly,

$$18,396\,(Y_3) = 200\times150(75) - 100\times75(150-25)\,(0.5) - \frac{\pi}{4}\times100^2\,(Y_3)$$

$$\therefore \quad Y_3 = \frac{17,81250}{26,250} = 67.86 \text{ mm } \textbf{Ans.}$$

Hence the centre of the circle should be located at 90.48 mm and 67.86 mm so that the point will be the centroid of the remaining shaded area of the Fig. 14.63.

EXAMPLE 14.59. Locate the centroid of the shaded area as shown Fig.14.64.

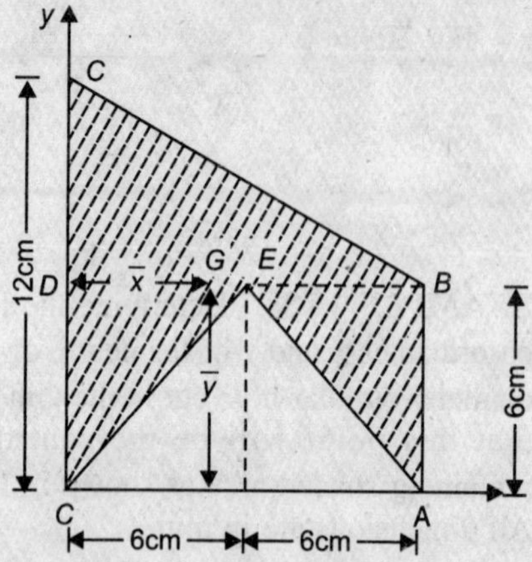

Fig. 14.64

SOLUTION :

Let,

$\bar{x}$ = Required distance of centroid of the given portion of the area from *y*-axis, and

$\bar{y}$ = Required distance of centroid of the given portion of the area from the *x*-axis, then

$$\bar{x} = \frac{A_1X_1 + A_2X_2 - A_3X_3}{A_1 + A_2 - A_3}$$

and
$$\bar{y} = \frac{A_1Y_1 + A_2Y_2 - A_3Y_3}{A_1 + A_2 - A_3}$$

Now,

A_1 = Area of ΔDBC = 0.5 (*DB*) (*DC*) = 0.5 (12) (6) = 36 cm^2

A_2 = Area of rectangle *DBAO* = *DO* × *OA* = 12 × 6 = 72 cm^2

A_3 = Area of Δ *OEA* = 0.5 (*OA*) (*AB*) = 0.5 (12) (6) = 36 cm^2

X_1 = Distance of C.G. of the area *DBC* from *y*-axis

$$= \frac{1}{3}(DB) = \frac{1}{3}(12) \;\; 4 \text{ cm}$$

X_2 = Distance of C.G. of the area *DBAO* from *y*-axis

$$= \frac{12}{2} = 6 \text{ cm, and}$$

X_3 = Distance of C.G. of the area *OEA* from *y*-axis = 6 cm

Now,

$$\bar{x} = \frac{A_1X_1 + A_2X_2 - A_3X_3}{A_2 + A_2 - A_3}$$

$$= \frac{36(4) + 72(6) - 36(6)}{36 + 72 - 36} = 5 \text{ cm } \textbf{Ans.}$$

Y_1 = Distance of C.G. of the area *CBD* from *x*-axis

$$= 6 + \frac{1}{3}(6) = 8 \text{ cm}$$

Y_2 = Distance of C.G. of the area *DBAO* from *x*-axis

$$\frac{6}{2} = 3 \text{ cm}$$

Y_3 = Distance of C.G. of the area *OEA* from *x*-axis

$$= \frac{6}{3} = 2 \text{ cm}$$

$$\bar{y} = \frac{A_1Y_1 + A_2Y_2 - A_3Y_3}{A_1 + A_2 - A_3}$$

$$= \frac{36(8) + 72(3) - 36(2)}{36 + 72 - 36} = 6 \text{ cm } \textbf{Ans.}$$

Hence, $\bar{x}$ = 5 cm, and $\bar{y}$ = 6 cm **Ans.**

EXAMPLE 14.60. A truss of 12 m span is loaded as shown in Fig. 14.65. Determine forces in the members *DG*, *DF* and *EF*, using method of section (2004).

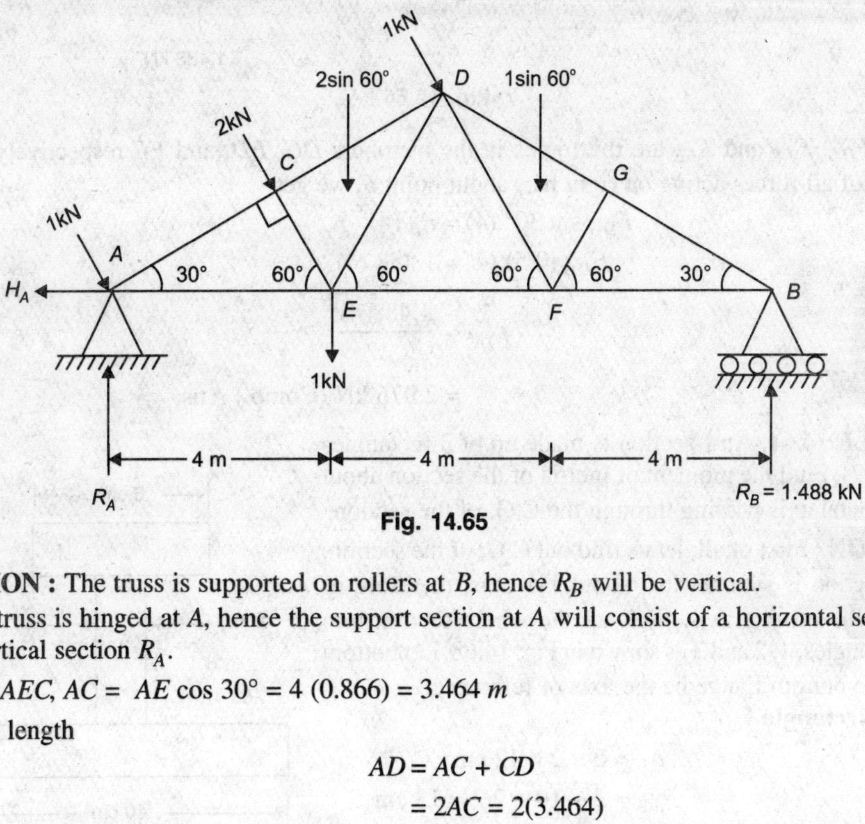

Fig. 14.65

SOLUTION : The truss is supported on rollers at *B*, hence R_B will be vertical.

The truss is hinged at *A*, hence the support section at *A* will consist of a horizontal section H_A and a vertical section R_A.

In Δ *AEC*, *AC* = *AE* cos 30° = 4 (0.866) = 3.464 *m*

Now length

$$AD = AC + CD$$
$$= 2AC = 2(3.464)$$
$$= 6.928 \; m$$

For $\Sigma M_A = 0$, we have

$$2(AC) + 1\,(AD) + 1\,(AE) - 12\,(R_B) = 0$$

or $$2(3.464) + 1(6.928) + 1\,(4) = 12\,R_B$$

∴ $$R_B = \frac{17.856}{12} = 1.488 \text{ kN}$$

Now draw a section line (1 – 1), passing through the members *DG*, *DF* and *EF* in which the forces are to be determined. Consider the equilibrium of right part of the truss (Fig. 14.66).

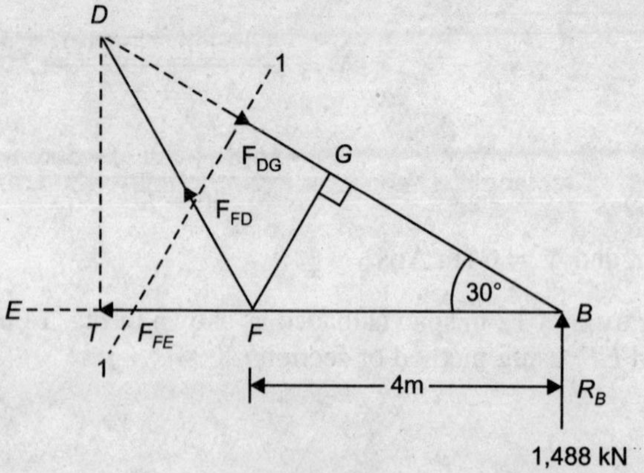

Fig. 14.66

Let, F_{DG}, F_{FD} and F_{FE} are the forces in the members *DG*, *FD*, and *FE* respectively. Taking moments of all forces acting on right part about point *F*, we get

$$F_{DG} \sin 30° (4) = R_B (4)$$

or

$$F_{DG} (0.5) (4) = 1.488 (4)$$

∴

$$F_{DG} = \frac{1.488(4)}{2}$$

$$= 2.976 \text{ kN (Comp.) } \textbf{Ans.}$$

EXAMPLE 14.61. An I-section is made up of 3 rectangles (Fig. 14.67). Find the moment of inertia of the section about the horizontal axis passing through the C.G. of the section.

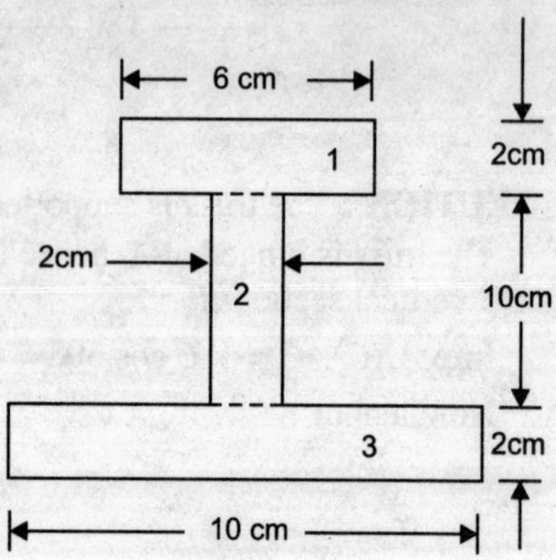

Fig. 14.67

SOLUTION : First of all, let us find out C.G. of the section. As the section is symmetrical about *Y-Y* axis, therefore its C.G. will be on this axis. Split up the whole section into three rectangles, 1, 2 and 3 as shown in Fig. 14.68. Let bottom face of the bottom flange be the axis of refernece.

(i) Rectangle I

$$a_1 = 6 \times 2 = 12 \text{ cm}^2$$

$$y_1 = 2 + 10 + 2/2 = 13 \text{ cm}$$

(ii) Rectangle II

$$a_2 = 10 \times 2 = 20 \text{ cm}^2$$

$$y_2 = 2 + 10/2 = 7 \text{ cm}$$

(iii) Rectangle III

$$a_3 = 10 \times 2 = 20 \text{ cm}^2$$

$$y_3 = 2/2 = 1 \text{ cm}$$

We know that the distance between C.G. of the section and botom face,

$$\bar{y} = \frac{a_1 y_1 + a_2 y_2 + a_3 y_3}{a_1 + a_2 + a_3}$$

$$\bar{y} = \frac{(12\times13)+(20\times7)+(20\times1)}{12+20+20}$$

$$= 6.08 \text{ cm}$$

We know that M.I. of rectangle (I) about an axis through its C.G. and parallel to *X-X* axis,

$$I_{G_1} = \frac{6(2)^3}{12} = 4 \text{ cm}^4$$

and distance between rectangle (1) and *X-X* axis,

$$h_1 = 13 - 6.08 = 6.92 \text{ cm}$$

∴ M.I. of rectangle (2), about *X-X* axis,

$$= I_{G_1} + ah_1^2 = 4 + [12(6.92)^3]$$

$$= 578.6 \text{ cm}^4 \quad \text{...(i)}$$

Similarly, M.I. of rectangle (2) about an axis through its C.G. and parallel to *X-X* axis.

$$I_{G_2} = \frac{2(10)^3}{12} = 166.67 \text{ cm}^4$$

and distance between of rectangle (2) and *X-X* axis.

$$h_2 = 7 - 6.08 = 0.92 \text{ cm}$$

∴ M.I. of rectangle (2), about *X-X* axis,

$$= I_{G_2} + ah_2^2 = 166.67 + [12(0.92)^3] \text{ cm}^4$$

$$= 183.8 \text{ cm}^4 \quad \text{...(ii)}$$

Now M.I. of rectangle (3) about maxima through the C.G. and parallel to *X-X* axis.

$$I_{G_3} = \frac{10(2)^3}{12} = 6.67 \text{ cm}^4$$

and distance between of C.G. of rectangle (3) and *X-X* axis.

$$h_3 = 6.08 - 1.0$$

$$= 5.08 \text{ cm}$$

∴ M.I. of rectangle (3) about *X-X* axis.

$$= I_{G_3} + a\cdot h_3^2$$

$$= 6.67 + [20(5.08)^2] \text{ cm}^4$$

$$= 522.8 \text{ cm}^4 \quad \text{...(iii)}$$

Now M.I. of the whole section about *X-X* axis.

$$I_{XX} = 578.6 + 183.6 + 522.8$$

$$= 1285.0 \text{ cm}^4 \textbf{ Ans.}$$

EXAMPLE 14.62. Find the moment of inertia about the centroidal *X-X* and *Y-Y* axis of an inverted L-section 15 cm × 10 cm × 2.5 cm.

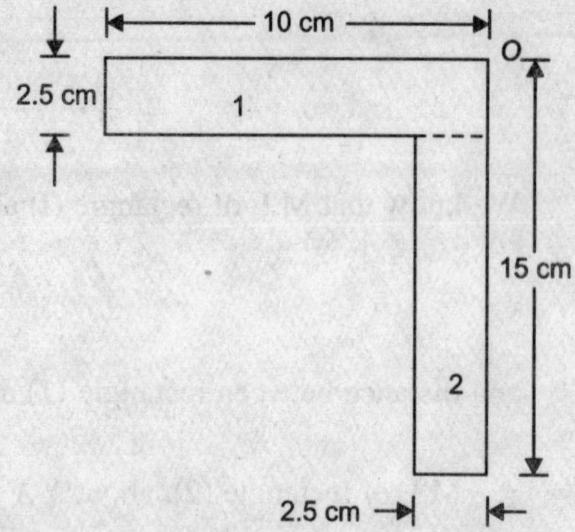

Fig. 14.68

SOLUTION : First of all, let us find out the C.G. of the section. As the section is not symmetrical about any section, therefore we have to find out the values of both $\bar{x}$ and $\bar{y}$ for the angle section. Split up the section into two rectangles 1 and 2 as shown in Fig. 14.68. Let left face of the horizontal section and bottom of the vertical section be the axes of reference.

(i) Rectangle 1

$$a_1 = 10 \times 2.5 = 25 \text{ cm}^2$$

$$x_1 = \frac{10}{2} = 5 \text{ cm}$$

$$y_1 = 15 - \frac{2.5}{2} = 13.75 \text{ cm}$$

(ii) Rectangle 2

$$a_2 = (15 - 2.5)2.5 = 31.25 \text{ cm}^2$$

$$x_2 = 10 - \frac{2.5}{2} = 8.75 \text{ cm}$$

$$y_2 = \frac{12.5}{2} = 6.25 \text{ cm}$$

We know that distance between C.G. of the section and left face,

$$\bar{x} = \frac{a_1 x_1 + a_2 x_2}{a_1 + a_2}$$

$$= \frac{(25 \times 5) + (31.25 \times 8.75)}{25 + 31.25} \text{ cm} = 7.08 \text{ cm}$$

Similarly, distance between C.G. of the section and bottom face,

$$\bar{y} = \frac{a_1 y_1 + a_2 y_2}{a_1 + a_2}$$

$$= \frac{(25 \times 13.75) + (31.25 \times 6.25)}{26 + 31.25} \text{ cm} = 9.58 \text{ cm}$$

From the right angled triangle *BTD* :

$$\tan 30° = \frac{\text{Perp.}}{\text{Base}} = \frac{DT}{BT} = \frac{DT}{6}$$

$$\therefore \quad DT = 6 \tan 30° = 3.464 \text{ m}$$

For $M_D = 0$, we have,

$$F_{EF}(DT) = R_B(6)$$

or $$F_{EF}\ (3.464) = 1.488\ (6)$$

$\therefore$ $$F_{EF} = \frac{(1.488)(6)}{3.464}$$

$$= 2.577 \text{ kN (Tensile) } \textbf{Ans.}$$

For $M_B = 0$, we have,

$$F_{FD}\ (\sin 60°) = R_B\ (0)$$

$\therefore$ $$F_{FD} = 0 \textbf{ Ans.}$$

EXAMPLE 14.63. A beam *AB* of 6m span is loaded as shown in Fig. 14.69 Determine the reaction at *A* and *B*.

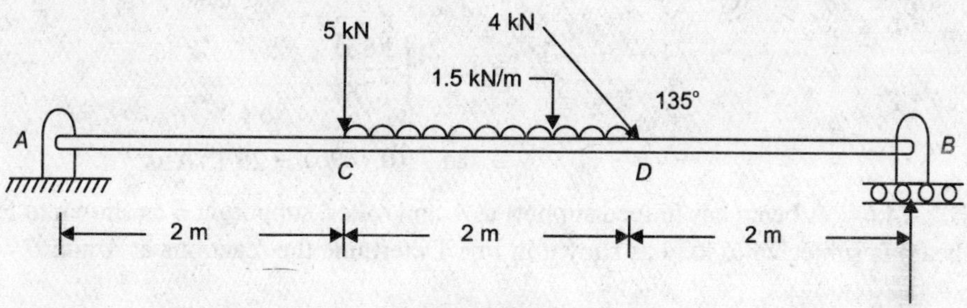

Fig. 14.69

SOLUTION : Given : span = 6m

Let,

R_A = Reaction at *A*, and

R_B = Reaction at *B*

As the beam is supported on rollers at the right hand support (*B*), hence the reaction R_B will be vertical (because of horizontal support). As the beam is hinged at the left support (*A*) and it is also carrying inclined load, hence the reaction at this end will be resultant of horizontal and vertical forces, and thus will be inclined with the vertical.

For $\Sigma M_A = 0$, we have

$$R_A \times 0 + 5(2) + 1.5 \times 2\ (3) + 4 \sin 135°\ (4) - R_B\ (6)$$

or $$0 + 10 + 9 + 11.314 - 6\ R_B = 0$$

or $$6R_B = 30.32$$

$\therefore$ $$R_B = 5.05 \text{ kN } \textbf{Ans.}$$

For $\Sigma H = 0$,

$$R_H = 4 \cos 135° = 2.83 \text{ kN}$$

For $\Sigma V = 0$, We have

$$R_A + R_B = 5 + 1.5\ (2) + 4 \sin 135°$$

$$= 10.83$$

$\therefore$ $$R_A = 10.83 - R_B = 10.83 - 5.05$$

$$= 5.78 \text{ kN} \uparrow \text{ (Vertical Component)}$$

Now reaction, R at A,

$$R = \sqrt{(\Sigma H)^2 + (\Sigma V)^2}$$

$$= \sqrt{(5.78)^2 + (2.83)^2} = 6.44 \text{ kN}$$

$\therefore$ $R = 6.44$ kN **Ans.**

Let, θ = Angle, which the reaction R at A makes with the vertical,

Then,

$$\theta = \tan^{-1}\left(\frac{\Sigma H}{\Sigma V}\right)$$

$$= \tan^{-1}\left(\frac{2.83}{5.78}\right)$$

$$= \tan^{-1}(0.4896) = 26.1° \textbf{ Ans.}$$

EXAMPLE 14.64. A beam has hinged support at A and roller, support at B as shown in Fig. 14.70 The beam is subjected to load as shown in Fig. Determine the reactions at A and B.

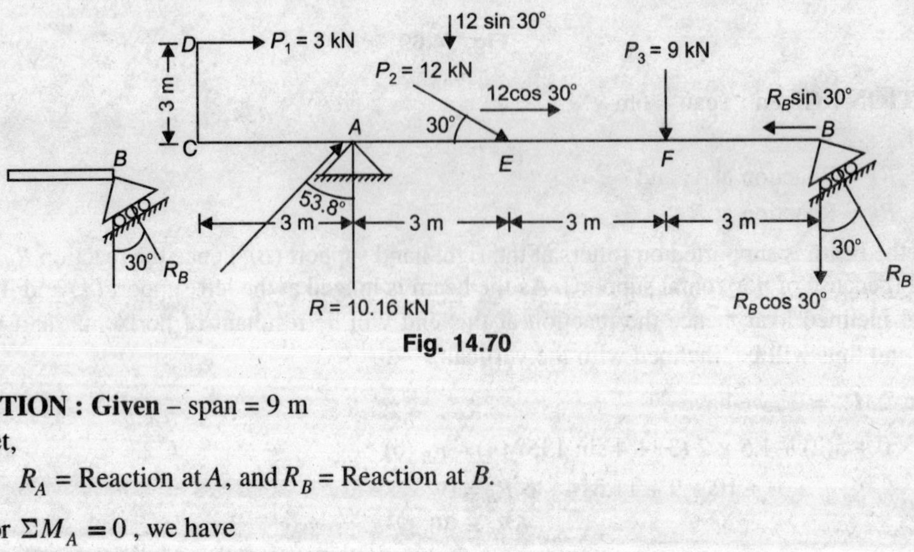

Fig. 14.70

SOLUTION : Given – span = 9 m

Let,

R_A = Reaction at A, and R_B = Reaction at B.

For $\Sigma M_A = 0$, we have

$$3(3) - R_B\,(0) + 12 \sin 30°\,(3) + 9(6) - R_B \cos 30°\,(9) = 0$$

or $$9 - 0 + 6(3) + 54 - 7.79\,R_B = 0$$

or $$9 + 18 + 54 - 7.79\,R_B = 0$$

or $$7.79\,R_B = 81$$

$\therefore$ $$R_B = 10.4 \text{ kN } \textbf{Ans.}$$

For $\Sigma M_B = 0$, we have

$$3(3) + R_B\,(9) - 12 \sin 30°\,(6) - 9(3) - R_B \cos 30°\,(0) = 0$$

or $$9 + 9R_A - 36 - 27 = 0$$

or $$9R_A = 54$$

∴ $$R_A = 6 \text{ kN } (\uparrow)$$

or Vertical component of reaction

$$R_B = R_B \cos 30°$$
$$= 10.4\,(.86) = 9 \text{ kN}$$

∴ For $\Sigma V = 0$, we have

$$R_A\,(V) + R_B\,(V) = 12 \sin 30° + 9 = 6 + 9$$

∴ $$R_A\,(V) = 6 + 9 - R_B\,(V)$$
$$= 6 + 9 - 9 = 6 \text{ kN}$$

Horizontal component of reaction

$$R_B = R_B \sin 30°$$
$$= 10.4(0.5) = 5.2 \text{ KN}$$

∴ Horizontal component of reaction R_A

$$= (3 + 12 \cos 30°) - 5.2\,(\leftarrow) = 8.2 \text{ kN}$$

∴ $$R = \sqrt{(\Sigma H)^2 + (\Sigma V)^2}$$
$$= \sqrt{(8.2)^2 + (6)^2} = 10.16 \text{ kN } \textbf{Ans.}$$

Let θ = Angle, which the reaction at *A* makes with the vertical.

∴ $$\tan\theta = \frac{\Sigma H}{\Sigma V} = \frac{8.2}{6} = 1.3667$$

∴ $$\theta = \tan^{-1}(1.3667) = 53.8° \textbf{ Ans.}$$

EXAMPLE 14.65. A simply supported beam *AB* of 6 m span is subjected to loading as shown in Fig. 14.71. Find support reactions.

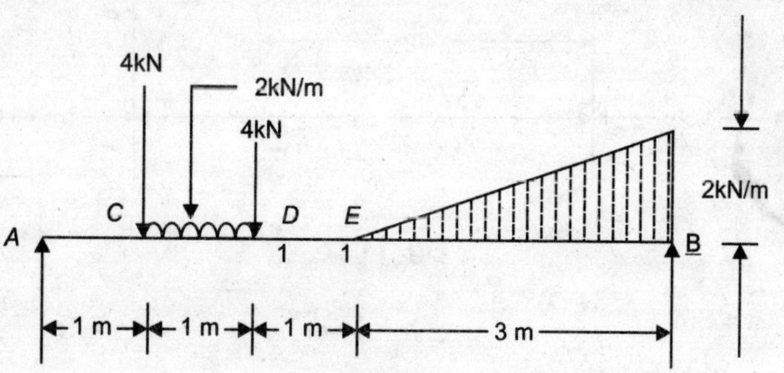

Fig. 14.71

SOLUTION : Given : span = 6m

Let,

R_A = Reaction at *A*, and

R_B = Reaction at *B*

For $\Sigma M_A = 0$, we have

$$R_A(0) + 4(1) + 2\times 1\left(1+\frac{1}{2}\right) + 4(2) + \frac{0+2}{2}(3)\left(3+\frac{2\times 3}{3}\right) - 6R_B = 0$$

or $\quad 0 + 4 + 2\,(1.5) + 8 + 1(3)\,(5) - 6\,R_B = 0$

or $\quad 4 + 3 + 8 + 15 - 6\,R_B = 0$

or $\quad 30 - 6\,R_B = 0$

$\therefore \quad R_B = \frac{30}{6} = 5$ kN **Ans.**

For $\Sigma V = 0$, we have

$$R_A + R_B = 4 + 2(1) + 4 + \left(\frac{0+2}{2}\right)3$$

$$= 4 + 2 + 4 + 3 = 13 \text{ kN}$$

$\therefore \quad R_A = 13 - R_B = 13 - 5 = 8$ kN **Ans.**

OVER HANGING BEAMS: A beam having its end portion (or portions) extended in the form of a cantilever, beyond its support, as shown in Fig. 14.72, is known as an overhanging beam. It may be noted that the beam over hanging on one of its sides or both the sides. In such cases, the reactions at both the supports will be vertical as shown in Fig.

EXAMPLE 14.66. A beam of span 3m, over-hanging on both sides is loaded a shown in Fig. 14.72. Determine the reactions at the supports *A* and *B*.

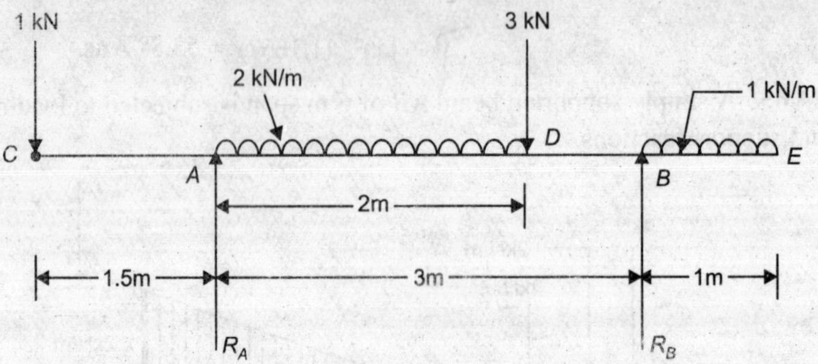

Fig. 14.72

SOLUTION : span = 3m

Let,

R_A = Reaction at *A*, and

R_B = Reaction at *B*

For $\Sigma M_A = 0$, we have

$- 1\,(1.5) + R_A\,(0) + 2\times 2\,(1) + 3(2) - R_B\,(3) + 1\times 1\,(3.5) = 0$

or $\qquad -1.5 + 4 + 6 - 3R_B + 3.5 = 0$

or $\qquad 3R_B = 12$

$\therefore \qquad R_B = 4$ kN **Ans.**

For $\Sigma V = 0$, we have

$$R_A + R_B = 1 + 2 \times 2 + 3 + 1 \times 1$$
$$= 1 + 4 + 3 + 1 = 9 \text{ kN}$$

$\therefore$
$$R_A = 9 - R_B$$
$$= 9 - 4 = 5 \text{ kN } \textbf{Ans.}$$

ROLLER SUPPORTED BEAMS : In such a case, the end of the beam is supported on rollers, and the reaction on such an end is always normal to the support as shown in Fig. 14.73. All the steel trusses of the bridges, have one of their ends as supported on rollers.

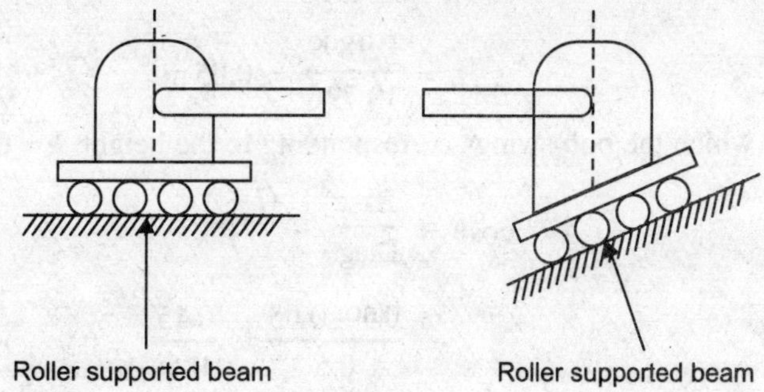

Fig. 14.73

The main advantage, of such a support is that the beam can move easily towards left or right, on account of expansion or contraction, due to change in temperature.

EXAMPLE 14.67. A bullet of mass 20 gm moving with a velocity of 100 m/sec hits a 2 kg bob of a simple pendulum horizontally as shown in Fig. 14.74. Determine the maximum angle through which the pendulum string 0.5 m long may swing if :

(a) The bullet gets embedded in the bob,

(b) The bullet escapes from the other end at 20 m/sec;

(c) The bullet is rebounded from the surface of the bob at 20 m/sec.

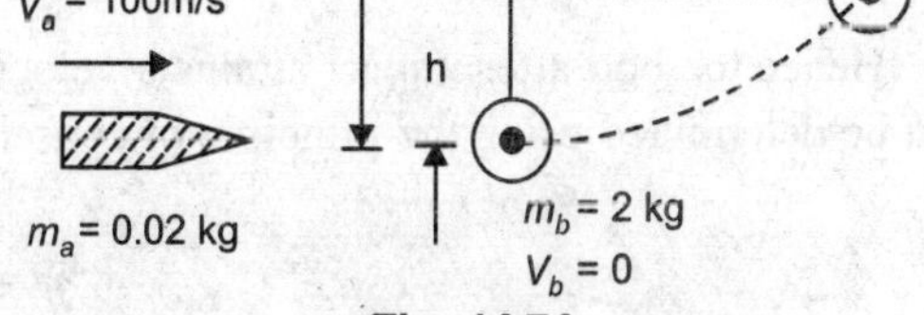

Fig. 14.74

SOLUTION : Given : $m_a = 20$ gm $= 0.02$ kg

$V_a = 100$ m/sec, $m_b = 2$ kg, $V_b = 0$, $V = ?$

(a) The bullet gets embedded in the bob.

Applying the principle of conservation of momentum , i.e.,

Momentum before impact = Momentum after impact

$$m_a V_a + m_b V_b \; (m_a + m_b)V$$
$$0.02\,(100) + 2(0) = (0.02 + 2)V$$

or
$$2 = 2.02\,V$$

$$\therefore \quad V = \frac{2.00}{2.02} = 0.99 \text{ m/sec} \qquad \text{...(i)}$$

Now applying the principle of conservation of energy, i.e. loss of kinetic energy = gain in potential energy.

$$0.5\,(m_a + m_b)\,V^2 = (m_a + m_b)\,gh \qquad \left[h = \frac{0.5(.99)^2}{9.8} = 0.05\,m\right]$$

or
$$0.5\,(0.02 + 2)\,(0.99)^2 = (2.02)\,(9.8)h = 0.5\,(2.02)\,(0.99)^2$$

or
$$19.796\,h = 0.9899$$

$$\therefore \quad h = \frac{0.9899}{19.796} = 0.05 \text{ m} \qquad \text{...(ii)}$$

For the angle θ by which the bob swings corresponding to the height, $h = 0.05$ m

$$\cos\theta = \frac{\text{Base}}{\text{Diag.}} = \frac{(l-h)}{l}$$

$$= \frac{0.5 - 0.05}{0.5} = \frac{0.45}{0.5} = 0.9$$

$$\therefore \quad \theta = \cos^{-1}(0.9) = 25.84° \textbf{ Ans.}$$

(b) When the bullet pierces and escapes with a velocity $V_a' = 20 \text{ m/sec}$, From the principle of conservation of momentum.

Momentum before impact = Momentum after impact

$$m_a V_a + m_b V_b = m_a(V_a') + m_b(V_b')$$
$$0.02(100) + 2(0) = 0.02(20) + 2(V_b')$$

$$\therefore \quad V_b' = 0.8 \text{ m/sec} \qquad \text{...(iii)}$$

Hence the bob after impact attains a velocity $V_b' = 0.8$ m/sec and will rise to a height h' that can be determined using the principle of conservation of energy i.e.

$$h' = \frac{(V_b')^2}{2g} = \frac{(0.8)^2}{2 \times 9.8}$$

$$= \frac{0.64}{19.6} = 0.033 \text{ m} \qquad \text{...(iv)}$$

Hence the angle of swing corresponding to height

$$h' = 0.033 \text{ m};$$

$$= \cos^{-1}\left(\frac{0.5 - 0.033}{0.5}\right) = 20.93° \textbf{ Ans.}$$

(c) When the bullet is rebounded with a velocity $V_b' = -20$ m/sec

$\because$ Momentum before impact = Momentum after impact

$$\therefore \quad m_a V_a + m_b V_b = m_a V_a'' + m_a V_b''$$

or
$$0.02(100) + 2(0) = 0.02(-20) + 2(V_b'')$$

or
$$2 + 0 = -0.4 + 2V_b''$$

$$\therefore \quad V_b'' + \frac{2.4}{2} = 1.2 \text{ m/sec} \qquad \text{...(v)}$$

The bob after the impact attains a velocity $V_b'' = 1.2$ m/sec and will rise to a height h'' that can be determined using the principle of conservation of energy.

$$h'' = \left(\frac{(V_b'')^2}{2g}\right)$$

$$= \frac{(1.2)^2}{2 \times 9.8} = 0.073 \text{ m} \qquad \text{...(vi)}$$

The corresponding angle of swing.

$$\theta = \cos^{-1}\left(\frac{0.5 - 0.073}{0.5}\right) = 31.35° \textbf{ Ans.}$$

EXAMPLE 14.68. A bullet of mass 10 gm is fired into a body of mass 1 kg which is suspended by a string 1 m long. The bullet gets embedded in the body and due to impact, the body swings through an angle of 18.2°. Find the velocity of the bullet.

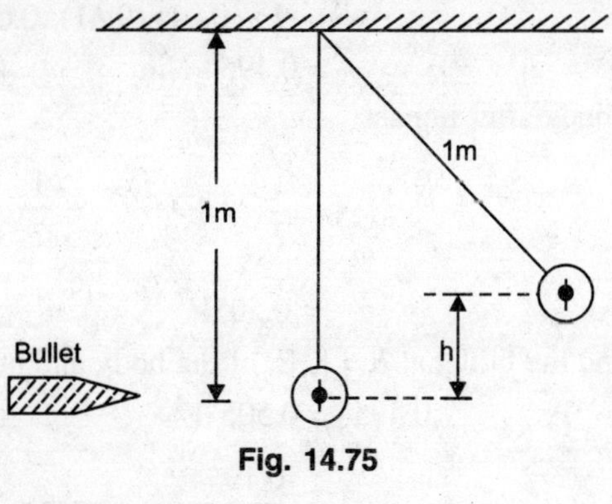

Fig. 14.75

SOLUTION : Given : Mass of bullet 10 gm = 0.01 kg

Mass of body, M = 1 kg, length of string, L = 1 m, Angle of swing, θ = 18.2°.

Let,

u = Velocity of bullet

V = Common velocity of bullet and body.

Initial velocity of body = 0

The moment of the bullet and body before impact = $m \times u + M \times$ Initial velocity of the body

$$= 0.01\, u + 1(0)$$

$$= 0.01\, u \text{ kg m/sec} \quad ...(i)$$

Bullet gets embedded in the body and both of them move together with common velocity.

The momentum of bullet and body after impact

$$(M + m)V = (1 + 0.01)V$$

$$= 1.01V \text{ kg m/sec} \quad ...(ii)$$

Equating (i) and (ii), we get,

$$0.01u = 1.01\, V \quad ...(iii)$$

Now let us apply the law of conservation of energy.

The potential energy of the body and bullet at B = K.E. of the body and bullet after impact.

Let us first find the height 'h' to which the body with bullet rises after impact.

$$\therefore \quad \cos\theta = \frac{\text{base}}{\text{diagonal}} = \frac{1-h}{1}$$

or $$1 - h = 1 \cos\theta$$

or $$-h = 1 \cos\theta - 1$$

$$\therefore \quad h = 1 - 1 \cos\theta$$

$$= 1 - 1\,(\cos 18.2°)$$

$$\therefore \quad h = 1 - .94997 = 0.05 \text{ m}$$

The potential energy of the body and bullet at B

= Total weight of the bullet and body $\times h$

$$= [(M + m)g]h$$

$$= (1 + 0.01)\,(9.81)\,(0.05)]$$

$$= 0.4954 \text{ Nm} \quad ...(iv)$$

K.E. of the bullet and body after impact

$$= \frac{1}{2}(M+m)V^2 = \frac{1}{2}(1+0.01)V^2$$

$$= 0.505V^2 \quad ...(v)$$

But P.E. of the body and the bullet at B = K.E. of the body and bullet after impact.

or $$0.4954 = 0.505\, V^2$$

or $$V^2 = \frac{0.4954}{0.505} = 0.98099$$

$$\therefore \quad V = \sqrt{0.98099} = 0.990449 \text{ m/sec}$$

Substituting this value in equation (iii), we get

$$0.01\, u = 1.01\, V$$

or $$0.01u = 1.01\,(0.98099) = 1.00035$$

$$\therefore \qquad u = \frac{1.00035}{0.01} = 100 \text{ m/sec } \textbf{Ans.}$$

EXAMPLE 14.69. Ball *A* of mass 1 kg moving with a velocity of 2 m/sec, strikes directly on a ball *B* of mass 2 kg at rest. The ball *A*, after striking, comes to rest. Find the velocity of ball *B* after striking and coefficient of restitution.

SOLUTION : Given : Mass of ball *A*, $m_1 = 1$ kg,

Initial velocity of ball *A*, $u_1 = 2$ m/sec

Mass of ball *B*, $m_2 = 2$ kg

Initial velocity of ball *B*, $u_2 = 0$

Final velocity of ball *A*, $v_1 = 0$

Hence it is a case of direct impact

Let,

v_2 = Velocity of ball *B* after impact, and

e = Coefficient of restitution.

Total initial momentum $= m_1u_1 + m_2u_2 = 1 \times 2 + 2 \times 0 = 2$ kg m/s

Total final momentum $= m_1v_1 + m_2v_2 = 1 \times 0 + 2 \times v_2 = 2\,v_2$ kg m/s

According to the law of conservation of momentum

Total initial momentum = Total final momentum.

or
$$2 = 2v_2$$

$$\therefore \qquad v_2 = \frac{2}{2} = 1 \text{ m/sec } \textbf{Ans.}$$

Coefficient of restitution,

$$e = \frac{v_2 - v_1}{u_1 - u_2} = \frac{1-0}{2-0} = 0.5 \textbf{ Ans.}$$

EXAMPLE 14.70. Direct central impact occurs between a 300 N body moving to the right with a velocity of 6m/sec and 150N body moving to the left with a velocity of 10 m/sec. Find the velocity of each body after impact if the coefficient of restitution is 0.8.

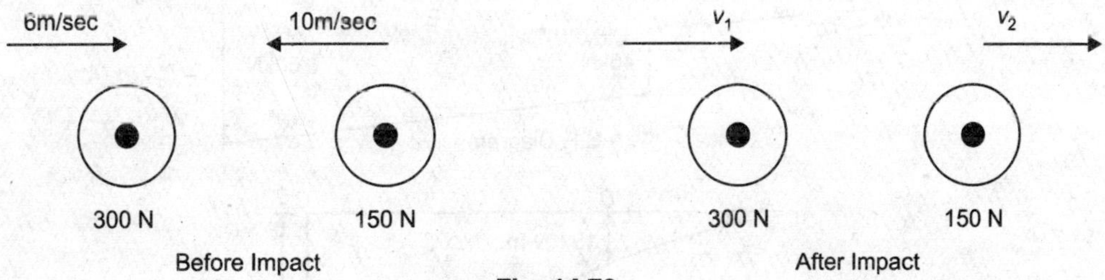

Fig. 14.76

SOLUTION : Referring Fig. 14.76

Initial velocity of 300 N body

$$u_1 = 6 \text{ m/sec}$$

Initial (Before impact) velocity of 150 N body,

$$u_2 = -10 \text{ m/sec}$$

Let final (after impact) velocity of :

(i) 300 N body = v_1 m/sec, and

(ii) 150 N body = v_2 m/sec

Now from the principle of conservation of momentum,

$$W_1u_1 + W_2u_2 = W_1v_1 + W_2v_2$$

or $$300\,(6) + 150(-10) = 300v_1 + 150\,v_2$$

or $$1800 - 1500 = 300\,v_1 + 150\,v_2$$

or $$300 = 300\,v_1 + 150\,v_2$$

$\therefore$ $$2v_1 + v_2 = 0 \qquad \text{...(i)}$$

From the definition of coefficient of restitution, we have

$$e\,(u_1 - u_2) = v_2 - v_1$$

or $$0.8\,(6 + 10) = v_2 - v_1$$

$\therefore$ $$v_2 - v_1 = 0.8\,(16) = 12.8 \qquad \text{...(ii)}$$

From (i) and (ii) expression, we get $3v_1 = -10.8$

$\therefore$ $v_1 = -3.6$ m/sec **Ans.**

But $v_2 = 12.8 + v_1$

$= 12.8 + (-3.6) = 9.2$ m/sec **Ans.**

EXAMPLE 14.71. Construct the S.F. and B.M. diagrams for the cantilever beam loaded as shown in Fig. 14.78.

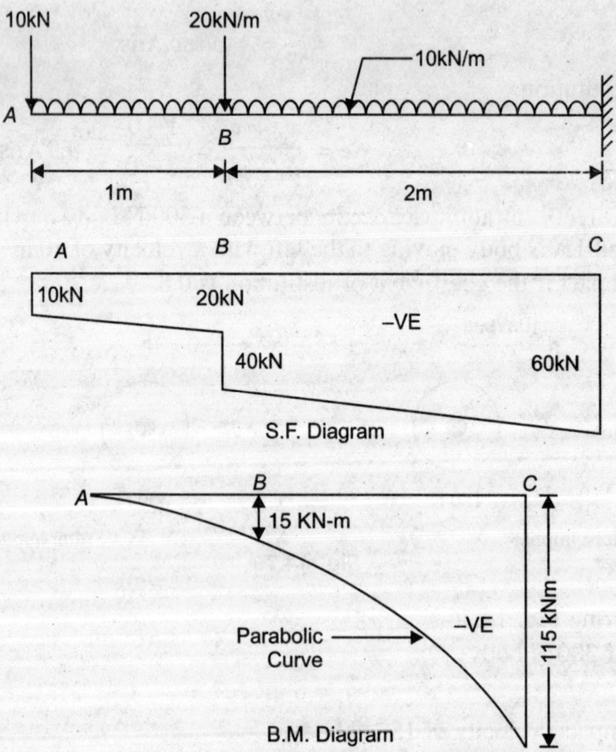

Fig. 14.78

SOLUTION : For S.F. Diagram :

$$F_A = -\ 10 \text{ kN}$$
$$F_B = -\ (10 + 10 \times 1 + 20) = -\ 40 \text{ kN}$$
$$F_C = -\ (10 + 20 + 10 \times 3) = -\ 60 \text{ kN}$$

For B.M. Diagram:

$$M_A = 0,$$
$$M_B = -(10 \times 1 + 10 \times 1 \times 0.5) = -\ 15 \text{ kN-m}$$
$$M_C = -(10 \times 3 + 20 \times 2 + 10 \times 3 \times 1.5)$$
$$= -\ (30 + 40 + 45) = -115 \text{ kN-m}$$

Index